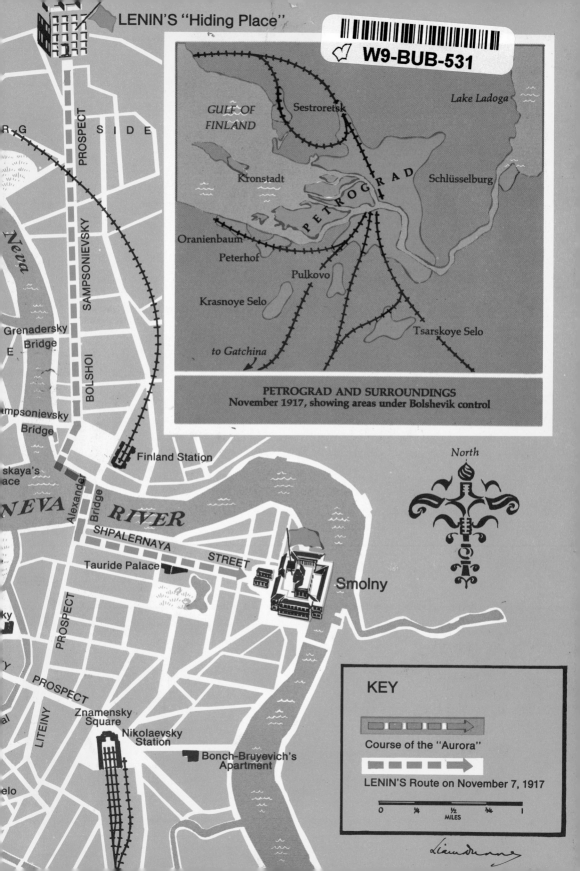

LENIN'S "Hiding Place"

W9-BUB-531

GULF OF FINLAND

Lake Ladoga

Sestroretsk

Kronstadt

Schlüsselburg

PETROGRAD

Oranienbaum

Peterhof

Pulkovo

Krasnoye Selo

Tsarskoye Selo

to Gatchina

PETROGRAD AND SURROUNDINGS
November 1917, showing areas under Bolshevik control

Neva

PROSPECT

SIDE

R G

SAMPSONIEVSKY

BOLSHOI

Grenadersky Bridge

E

ampsonievsky Bridge

skaya's ace

Finland Station

Alexander Bridge

NEVA RIVER

SHPALERNAYA STREET

Tauride Palace

Smolny

North

PROSPECT

ky

PROSPECT

LITEINY

Znamensky Square

Nikolaevsky Station

Bonch-Bruyevich's Apartment

elo

al

KEY

Course of the "Aurora"

LENIN'S Route on November 7, 1917

0   ¼   ½   ¾   1
MILES

THE LIFE AND DEATH OF

LENIN

BY ROBERT PAYNE

SIMON AND SCHUSTER, NEW YORK

LIBRARY OF CONGRESS CATALOG CARD NUMBER: 64-11190
MANUFACTURED IN THE UNITED STATES OF AMERICA
PRINTED BY THE MURRAY PRINTING CO., FORGE VILLAGE, MASS.
BOUND BY H. WOLFF BOOK MFG. CO. INC., NEW YORK, N. Y.

To the Martyrs

Do not believe we have forgotten Marx, Engels and Lenin. They will not be forgotten until shrimp learn to sing.

—Nikita Khrushchev

В. Ульянов (Ленин)

CONTENTS

Introduction   13

THE FORERUNNER   17

THE EDUCATION OF A REVOLUTIONARY   35

    FAMILY TREE   37
    A NEST OF GENTLE FOLK   47
    DEATH OF A HERO   63
    THE YOUNG LAWYER   75
    THE CONSPIRATOR   93
    SHUSHENSKOYE   111
    THE ENCHANTED KINGDOM   124

THE YEARS OF THE WILDERNESS   137

    WHAT IS TO BE DONE?   139
    THE LONDON YEAR   155
    THE BANGING OF THE DOOR   168
    THE YEAR NINETEEN FIVE   183
    ELIZABETH DE K.   201
    THE LONDON CONFERENCE   212
    PARIS   223
    WANDERINGS   238
    Illustrations   *following page* 252

THE STORM GATHERS   269

    LETTERS FROM AFAR   271
    THE SEALED TRAIN   285
    THE FINLAND STATION   301

THE CONQUEST OF POWER   315

    THE APRIL THESES   317
    EXILE IN FINLAND   338
    ON THE EVE   358
    THE CONQUEST OF PETROGRAD   373
    THE FIRST DAY OF THE REVOLUTION   395
    THE EXALTATIONS OF REVOLUTION   411

THE ICE IS BROKEN   423

    THE DESTRUCTION OF THE CONSTITUENT
       ASSEMBLY   425
    PEACE WITH GERMANY   442
    THE CORRUPTIONS OF POWER   455
    A ROOM IN THE KREMLIN   471
    LENIN WOUNDED   485
    THE THIRD INTERNATIONAL   501
    THE MAN OF SORROWS   516
    THE MACHINE BREAKS DOWN   530

THE LONG DEATH   543

    THE BITTEREST BLOW   545
    LAST TESTAMENT   561
    THE LIVING DEATH   581
    THE MURDER OF LENIN   593
    THE APOTHEOSIS OF A GOD   608
    THE APE AND THE SKULL   626

APPENDIXES: 635

1. Lenin's Autopsy   637
2. Bibliography   641
3. Chapter Notes   645
4. Chronological Table   652
Acknowledgments   656
Index   657
Maps: 1. Petrograd, 1917   *front endpapers*

        2. Russia   *back endpapers*

INTRODUCTION

A SPECTER HAUNTS THE WORLD—the specter of Lenin.

No man ever did more to change the face of Russia or the world. More than anyone else—more than Alexander the Great or Tamerlane or Napoleon—he has changed the course of the world's history. What is now known as Communism was his invention, the child of his resourceful brain, shaped during long years of exile. His fanatical will was like a lever which attempted to throw the whole globe into an orbit more to his liking; and because he pressed so hard on the lever, the earth still shudders.

To understand Communism, it is necessary to confront the man who spun the theory and its attendant dogmas out of his own entrails. There could have been no Russian Revolution without him. He called himself a Marxist, but in fact he hammered and bent Marx to his own will, using Marx whenever it was necessary and jettisoning him whenever it served his purpose. He was closer to the medieval autocrats than to Marx.

Because he reached a position of towering eminence in world history, it was inevitable that legends should grow about him. In its simplest form the legend describes the son of a poor schoolmaster who proclaimed himself a revolutionary at a very early age and was thrown into jail and sentenced to the living death of hard labor in Siberia. Then he escaped from Russia and led the life of an impoverished exile in Europe until in 1917 he returned to Petrograd and led the workers in an armed uprising against the Tsar. Thereafter, living calmly and modestly, a detached scholar with no vices, he ruled over

Russia as the acknowledged dictator until his death of a cerebral hemorrhage in 1924. He was the epitome of the Russian genius, a man of pure Russian ancestry, with gifts which were typically Russian.

As we shall see, the legend has no relation to the man. He was the son not of a poor schoolmaster, but of the superintendent of education over an entire province, a landowner and hereditary nobleman who was addressed as "Your Excellency." Arrested and sent to Siberia, Lenin lived there comfortably, quietly, in the seclusion necessary for his work; he was never physically assaulted, and he was permitted to carry a gun. In Europe, too, he lived comfortably in middle-class comfort: at least three immense fortunes passed at various times through his hands. Like other men, he had mistresses, and he was not always the detached scholar. When he returned to Petrograd he conquered the city with the help of Trotsky and the armed forces, the sailors of the Baltic fleet and the local garrisons. The Tsar had been dethroned long before. There was no drop of Russian blood in him, and he died of poison administered at the orders of Stalin.

He was a man of astonishing energy and directness, but also of great inner turmoil, constantly suffering from nervous prostration, at the mercy of dark impulses of destruction. There were things he could see with blinding clarity, and others which he saw only dimly. He could see, for example, that many of the institutions built by man serve to increase rather than to diminish human misery, and he knew what institutions were corrupt and could easily be destroyed; but the institutions he built in their place were equally corrupt and equally dangerous to human society. He was a man who genuinely believed that he was born to make life happier for the people, but at the end of his life he, like Shigalov in Dostoyevsky's *The Possessed*, could say, "I am perplexed by my own data; my conclusion is in direct contradiction of the original idea with which I start. Starting with unlimited freedom, I end with unlimited despotism." The greatest moment of Lenin's life was when, already dying, he apologized to the Russian workers for his crime.

In the following pages I have attempted to divorce Lenin from his legend and to see him whole, alive and breathing. I wanted to know how he walked through life, and how he laughed, and what he said in those moments when he was not holding a tight rein on himself, and how he came to those exclusive fanatical dogmas which once threatened to destroy the world. I wanted to see him as he braced himself for his most dangerous exploits, and see whether he was afraid.

I wanted to know, too, how he dealt with the women who entered his life, and whether he had enduring friendships with men. I was especially interested in his notebooks, which enable us to catch his thought on the wing. I have quoted him at length, because his living voice sometimes comes through even the most labored translation. I have relied chiefly on his collected works and the reminiscences of the people who knew him; and since Stalin played such a small role in his life, there seemed no necessity to introduce him at any length, and so he appears as an occasional footnote in the story.

It is not always easy to dissociate a man from his legend, for the legend is sometimes inextricably woven into his life; and Lenin himself was perfectly aware that he possessed legendary qualities. He was a man of vast potentialities for good and evil, and of such furious energy that even when he was dead, his power continued to reach out from the grave. For the rest, this is a study of an embattled, tormented, and variously gifted man who is perhaps the only indisputable political genius to emerge in our time.

ROBERT PAYNE

THE
FORERUNNER

Our task is total, terrible, universal
and merciless destruction . . .

THE FORERUNNER

HE PRISONER who stood in the dock in the Moscow
District Court on January 20, 1873 did not resemble the ordinary picture of a revolutionary. He was short, stocky and rather commonplace.
He had a long dark face, a flat nose, thick chestnut-colored hair, and
piercing blue eyes. He was frail, and he lived on his nervous energy.
Stories were told of his extraordinary adventures; he had invented
most of them, but those that really happened were unbelievable. In
the court he wore a black jacket and a dirty waistcoat, and he held
himself with an air of contemptuous disdain, rarely paying any attention to the judges, biting his fingernails. A bemused reporter at the
trial wrote that the most extraordinary thing about him was that he
was not in the least extraordinary. He was twenty-four, and the court
was in awe of him.

The prisoner's name was Sergey Genadievich Nechayev, and he is
almost forgotten today. Few people read his writings, and only a handful of students of nineteenth-century Russia have been concerned with
his existence. Yet singlehandedly he hammered out a code of revolutionary conduct which was to have a convulsive effect on the world.
He was one of those whom the Russian philosopher Chernyshevsky
described as "the movers of the movers." He was the shout that let
loose the avalanche.

In his upbringing there was nothing to suggest there would ever
come a time when even the Tsar would be afraid of him. He was born
on September 20, 1847 at Ivanovo, near Vladimir, a hundred miles
to the northeast of Moscow. In those days Ivanovo was a small textile

town, hardly more than an overgrown village: it had not yet blossomed into the great manufacturing city of Ivanovo Voznesensk. His father was an innkeeper, sometime small merchant, artisan and factotum, who married the daughter of a house painter from Kostroma. After the marriage he followed his father-in-law's trade. He was on good terms with the local gentry, attending weddings and putting up the decorations. He was a good worker and much sought after.

The boy spent some of his early years with his maternal grandparents in Kostroma, which even in the Fifties of the nineteenth century was a city of medieval splendor. In Kostroma, loyalty to the Tsar was as instinctive as breathing. No one needed to be reminded that the "little father" ruled sternly and kindly over all the reaches of his empire. In Ivanovo however loyalty to the Tsar was gradually succumbing to the disloyalties that came in the wake of the industrial revolution. Kostroma was like a city painted on a backdrop, all towers and battlemented walls and onion-shaped domes. Ivanovo, with its clicking shuttles and underpaid workers, was real and urgent. In his childhood the boy moved between the two towns.

From house painting Nechayev's father went on to scene painting for the local theater attended by the gentry. Sometimes the boy would be given a role to play; and it was remembered that he acted well. He had a rasping voice, but he had a keen sense of drama. Years later he wrote in an outline on revolutionary techniques: "This is the prologue. Let us act, my friends, in such a way that the play will soon begin."

The first act of the play had come to an end when Nechayev stood in the dock in the Moscow District Court. Although in the entire course of his life he had committed only one purposeless murder, he knew that he could expect no mercy. In theory he was being tried for the murder of a young student called Ivan Ivanov, but both Nechayev and the court knew that this was not the real crime which was being debated in the courtroom. His real crime was that he had discovered the key to the box containing the forces of dissolution which destroy the state.

He knew this, and the court was perfectly aware that he knew it. Every day the minutes of the trial were laid before the Tsar, who studied them carefully, together with a report written by the major in charge of the security guards who watched over the prisoner. From time to time Nechayev would stir a little, thrust his hands deeper in his pockets, and with the attitude of a man who must do something to relieve his boredom, he would shout in his rasping voice, "I do not recognize the court! I do not recognize the Tsar! I do not recognize the laws!" The president of the court would then order him to be silent, and Nechayev would be quiet for a while, leaning up and gazing at the gallery as though searching for someone he knew, or drumming on the ledge. He had some knowledge of music, and it is recorded that he played the flute well. Once, while he was being questioned by the president of the court, he lost all interest and pretended to play the piano on the ledge, using both hands.

There was method in Nechayev's madness. He was deliberately provoking the court, and he was also acting out his role as the dedicated revolutionary, contemptuous of all laws, all judges and all courtrooms. Prisoners on trial for murder rarely show icy disdain toward their accusers. Nechayev had iron nerves. He was determined to use all the weapons available to a defenseless man confronted with the power of the state; his principal weapon was contempt.

The crime for which he was accused was a peculiarly unpleasant one. Claiming to be the leader of a revolutionary movement with four million members throughout Russia, Nechayev was in fact the leader of three or four small groups, of which the largest was composed of students from St. Petersburg. There were groups in Moscow and Tula, where the Imperial Armaments Factory was situated. Altogether his adherents probably numbered no more than three or four hundred. Working in secrecy and under many names—at various times he called himself Ivan Petrov, Ivan Pavlov, Dmitry Fyodorov, Captain Panin and Special Agent Number 2664—he was continually moving about between the various groups, collecting dues, drawing up proclamations to be issued at some future time, compiling lists of important officials to be assassinated, and writing short pamphlets which the students were ordered to post up on the college bulletin boards, where as often as not they were torn down either by other students or by the police. Whenever Nechayev appeared at one of these groups, he would explain that he would shortly have to hurry away to an important meeting of the Central Executive Committee which was being held in some remote place.

Ivan Ivanov was among a small group of Nechayev's followers at the Petrovsky Agricultural College in Moscow. One day in November 1869 Nechayev ordered him to post an inflammatory pamphlet entitled "From Those Who Are United to Those Who Are Scattered" on the walls of the students' dining hall. Ivanov refused.

"I tell you," Nechayev said, "the Society has ordered it. Are you disobeying the Society?"

"I refuse to listen to the Society when it tells me to do completely senseless things."

"Then you refuse to submit to the Society?"

"Yes, when it behaves stupidly."

Nechayev brooded over the refusal, but did nothing to punish Ivanov at the time. He vanished from Moscow and is believed to have spent the following two weeks in Tula, where serious preparations were being made for an attack on the Imperial Armaments Factory. When he returned to Moscow he decided to kill Ivanov for defying the Society and being a traitor to its cause. A conference was held; Ivanov was solemnly condemned to death. It was arranged that Ivanov should be invited to enter one of the caves in the park near the Petrovsky College on the pretext that a printing press had been hidden there and that he was needed to examine it. A student, Nikolayev, was ordered to accompany him to the cave.

Nechayev was waiting inside the cave. He had a revolver and a length of rope. With Nechayev in the cave were two students, Kuznetsov and Uspensky, and a middle-aged author, Ivan Prizhov, who only the year before had published his *History of Russian Taverns*. Prizhov was a destitute author whose ambition was to write a history of destitution in Russia. Ivanov and Nikolayev walked into the cave, where it was pitch dark. Nechayev was unable to distinguish between them, and hurled himself on Nikolayev, attempting to strangle him. Then, realizing his mistake, he turned his attentions to Ivanov, who struggled free and ran screaming out of the cave. Nechayev caught up with him, threw him to the ground and struggled with him. In the struggle Ivanov succeeded in biting Nechayev's thumb, leaving a mark which remained to the end of his life. Finally Nechayev killed him with a shot in the back of the neck. The body was then dragged to a neighboring pond. Nechayev searched the dead man's pockets, but found nothing incriminating. Ivanov seemed to stir—it was perhaps only the sudden sharp reflex action of the dead—and Nechayev fired another shot in his head. By this time the three other conspirators had lost their nerve. They were all running around aimlessly, and at least two were screaming. Nechayev and Nikolayev tied heavy stones to the neck and feet, and then threw the body into the pond, where it sank to the bottom. Nechayev had not quite finished, for he suddenly hurled Nikolayev into the lake; but whether this was a conscious and deliberate act or simply the meaningless act of an overwrought man, Nikolayev did not trouble to ask when he emerged. The murder accomplished, all the conspirators made their way to Kuznetsov's apartment, where Nikolayev dried his clothes and Nechayev bandaged his bleeding thumb. The following day Nechayev left for St. Petersburg, and three days later the body rose to the surface.

When the police found the body, they did not at first suspect that it was anything more than a common murder. They made inquiries among the friends of the dead student. Little by little they learned about the existence of a secret society with its mysterious agents who were constantly on the move. In a Moscow bookshop they uncovered documents which seemed to relate to a vast conspiratorial movement extending over the length and breadth of Russia. The trail led to St. Petersburg and then to Tula, and the discovery of a plan to seize the Imperial Armaments Factory was perhaps more disturbing to the police than anything else. How far the conspirators had progressed in Tula was never made clear, but there was some evidence that they had made contact with men inside the factory and were only awaiting the signal of the revolutionary leader. The tone of the documents found in the bookshop was menacing and urgent, suggesting that the revolution would break out at any moment. Gradually, as they examined the documents and interrogated the arrested students, the police came to the conclusion that all the mysterious agents creating revolutionary cells, giving orders, and collecting dues were one agent with many aliases and many disguises. Within a few days he was identified as Nechayev, and orders were given to arrest him, but he had vanished without a trace. He had returned from St. Petersburg and was in fact living quietly in Moscow under the noses of the police. A small circle of friends rallied round him, and in January he slipped across the frontier disguised as a woman.

Altogether 152 people were arrested in connection with the murder of Ivanov and the mysterious society over which Nechayev ruled with a mixture of bluff and sheer personal domination. Of these, seventy-nine were put on trial on the charge of conspiracy to overthrow the government. They were mostly young students, boys and girls in their late teens or early twenties, with a sprinkling of older men like Prizhov, men with time on their hands, radicals by instinct but with no sense of discipline. Except for Nikolayev, Uspensky, Kuznetsov and Prizhov, all of whom had a share in the murder of Ivanov, there was scarcely one of the accused who could be regarded as a dedicated revolutionary. It was known as the trial of the *Nechayevtsi*. In fact Nechayev was on trial, though absent.

The Tsarist police were perfectly aware that the murder of Ivanov was one of those vulgar and commonplace murders which sometimes occur among quarreling students. Nor were they ever able to establish exactly what happened, for each of the four gave his own version and each was concerned to show that he had little part in it. Far more important than the murder were the documents found in the bookshop. They could only have been written by a man with an extraordinary knowledge of the weaknesses which reside in governments, all governments—a man who had pondered coldly and passionately on the subject of how governments could be overthrown by small groups of determined and dedicated revolutionaries.

The most significant and far-reaching of these documents was written in Russian, but in Latin letters and in code. It was called *The Revolutionary Catechism;* and it should be quoted in full, because it represents the supreme achievement of Nechayev as the expounder of revolutionary doctrine:

THE REVOLUTIONARY CATECHISM
The Duties of the Revolutionary toward Himself

1. The revolutionary is a doomed man. He has no personal interests, no business affairs, no emotions, no attachments, no property and no name. Everything in him is wholly absorbed in the single thought and the single passion for revolution.

2. The revolutionary knows that in the very depths of his being, not only in words but also in deeds, he has broken all the bonds which tie him to the social order and the civilized world with all its laws, moralities and customs and with all its generally accepted conventions. He is their implacable enemy, and if he continues to live with them it is only in order to destroy them more speedily.

3. The revolutionary despises all doctrines and refuses to accept the mundane sciences, leaving them for future generations. He knows only one science: the science of destruction. For this reason, but only for this reason, he will study mechanics, physics, chemistry, and perhaps medicine. But all day and all night he studies the vital science of human beings, their characteristics and circumstances, and all the phenomena of the present social order. The object is perpetually the same: the surest and quickest way of destroying the whole filthy order.

4. The revolutionary despises public opinion. He despises and hates the existing social morality in all its manifestations. For him, morality is everything which contributes to the triumph of the revolution. Immoral and criminal is everything that stands in its way.

5. The revolutionary is a dedicated man, merciless toward the State and toward the educated classes; and he can expect no mercy from them. Between him and them there exists, declared or concealed, a relentless and irreconcilable war to the death. He must accustom himself to torture.

6. Tyrannical toward himself, he must be tyrannical toward others. All the gentle and enervating sentiments of kinship, love, friendship, gratitude and even honor must be suppressed in him and give place to the cold and single-minded passion for revolution. For him there exists only one pleasure, one consolation, one reward, one satisfaction—the success of the revolution. Night and day he must have but one thought, one aim—merciless destruction. Striving coldbloodedly and indefatigably toward this end, he must be prepared to destroy himself and to destroy with his own hands everything that stands in the path of the revolution.

7. The nature of the true revolutionary excludes all sentimentality, romanticism, infatuation and exaltation. All private hatred and revenge must also be excluded. Revolutionary passion, practiced at every moment of the day until it becomes a habit, is to be employed with cold calculation. At all times and in all places the revolutionary must obey, not his personal impulses, but only those which serve the cause of the revolution.

The Relations of the Revolutionary toward his Comrades

8. The revolutionary can have no friendship or attachment except for those who have proved by their actions that they, like him, are dedicated to revolution. The degree of friendship, devotion and obligation toward such a comrade is determined solely by the degree of his usefulness to the cause of total revolutionary destruction.

9. It is superfluous to speak of solidarity among revolutionaries. The whole strength of revolutionary work lies in this. Comrades who possess the same revolutionary passion and understanding should, as much as possible, deliberate all important matters together and come to unanimous conclusions. When the plan is finally decided upon, then the revolutionary must rely solely on himself. In carrying out acts of destruction each one should act alone, never running

to another for advice and assistance except when these are necessary for the furtherance of the plan.

10. All revolutionaries should have under them second- or third-degree revolutionaries—i.e., comrades who are not completely initiated. These should be regarded as part of the common revolutionary capital placed at his disposal. This capital should, of course, be spent as economically as possible in order to derive from it the greatest possible profit. The real revolutionary should regard himself as capital consecrated to the triumph of the revolution; however, he may not personally and alone dispose of that capital without the unanimous consent of the fully initiated comrades.

11. When a comrade is in danger and the question arises whether he should be saved or not saved, the decision must not be arrived at on the basis of sentiment, but solely in the interests of the revolutionary cause. Therefore it is necessary to weigh carefully the usefulness of the comrade against the expenditure of revolutionary forces necessary to save him, and the decision must be made accordingly.

The Relations of the Revolutionary toward Society

12. The new member, having given proof of his loyalty not by words but by deeds can be received into the society only by the unanimous agreement of all the members.

13. The revolutionary enters the world of the state, of the privileged classes, of the so-called civilization, and he lives in this world only for the purpose of bringing about its speedy and total destruction. He is not a revolutionary if he has any sympathy for this world. *He should not hesitate to destroy any position, any place, or any man in this world.** He must hate everyone and everything in it with an equal hatred. All the worse for him if he has any relations with parents, friends or lovers; *he is no longer a revolutionary if he is swayed by these relationships.*

14. Aiming at implacable revolution, the revolutionary may and frequently must live within society while pretending to be completely different from what he really is, for he must penetrate everywhere, into all the higher and middle classes, into the houses of commerce, the churches and the palaces of the aristocracy, and into the worlds of the bureaucracy and literature and the military, and also into the Third Division and the Winter Palace of the Tsar.

* The italics are in the original.

15. This filthy social order can be split up into several categories. The first category comprises those who must be condemned to death without delay. Comrades should compile a list of those to be condemned according to the relative gravity of their crimes; and the executions should be carried out according to the prepared order.

16. When a list of those who are condemned is made and the order of execution is prepared, no private sense of outrage should be considered, nor is it necessary to pay attention to the hatred provoked by these people among the comrades or the people. Hatred and the sense of outrage may even be useful in so far as they incite the masses to revolt. It is necessary to be guided only by the relative usefulness of these executions for the sake of the revolution. Above all, those who are especially inimical to the revolutionary organization must be destroyed; their violent and sudden deaths will produce the utmost panic in the government, depriving it of its will to action by removing the cleverest and most energetic supporters.

17. The second group comprises those who will be spared for the time being in order that, by a series of monstrous acts, they may drive the people into inevitable revolt.

18. The third category consists of a great many brutes in high positions distinguished neither by their cleverness nor their energy, while enjoying riches, influence, power and high positions by virtue of their rank. These must be exploited in every possible way; they must be implicated and embroiled in our affairs, their dirty secrets must be ferreted out, and they must be transformed into slaves. Their power, influence and connections, their wealth and their energy will form an inexhaustible treasure and a precious help in all our undertakings.

19. The fourth category comprises ambitious officeholders and liberals of various shades of opinion. The revolutionary must pretend to collaborate with them, blindly following them, while at the same time prying out their secrets until they are completely in his power. They must be so compromised that there is no way out for them, and then they can be used to create disorder in the state.

20. The fifth category consists of those doctrinaires, conspirators and revolutionists who cut a great figure on paper or in their cliques. They must be constantly driven on to make compromising declarations: as a result the majority of them will be destroyed, while a minority will become genuine revolutionaries.

21. The sixth category is especially important: women. They can be divided into three main groups. First, those frivolous, thoughtless and vapid women, whom we shall use as we use the third and fourth category of men. Second, women who are ardent, capable and devoted, but who do not belong to us because they have not yet achieved a passionless and austere revolutionary understanding; these must be used like the men of the fifth category. Finally, there are the women who are completely on our side—i.e., those who are wholly dedicated and who have accepted our program in its entirety. We should regard these women as the most valuable of our treasures; without their help we would never succeed.

The Attitude of the Society toward the People

22. The Society has no aim other than the complete liberation and happiness of the masses—i.e., of the people who live by manual labor. Convinced that their emancipation and the achievement of this happiness can only come about as a result of an all-destroying popular revolt, the Society will use all its resources and energy toward increasing and intensifying the evils and miseries of the people until at last their patience is exhausted and they are driven to a general uprising.

23. By a revolution the Society does not mean an orderly revolt according to the classic western model—a revolt which always stops short of attacking the rights of property and the traditional social systems of so-called civilization and morality. Until now such a revolution has always limited itself to the overthrow of one political form in order to replace it by another, thereby attempting to bring about a so-called revolutionary state. The only form of revolution beneficial to the people is one which destroys the entire state to the roots and exterminates all the state traditions, institutions and classes in Russia.

24. With this end in view, the Society therefore refuses to impose any new organization from above. Any future organization will doubtless work its way through the movement and life of the people; but this is a matter for future generations to decide. Our task is terrible, total, universal and merciless destruction.

25. Therefore, in drawing closer to the people, we must above all make common cause with those elements of the masses which, since the foundation of the state of Muscovy, have never ceased to protest, not only in words but in deeds, against everything directly or indirectly connected with the state: against the nobility, the bureauc-

racy, the clergy, the traders, and the parasitic kulaks. We must unite with the adventurous tribes of brigands, who are the only genuine revolutionaries of Russia.

26. To weld the people into one single unconquerable and all-destructive force—this is our aim, our conspiracy and our task.

Such is *The Revolutionary Catechism,* which was to have important consequences for the world, since it was read by Lenin and profoundly influenced him. Like Nechayev, Lenin was concerned more with destruction—terrible, total, universal and merciless destruction —than with the creation of a new world; and like Nechayev, too, he was determined that all the powers of the state should fall to the industrial workers led by a handful of dedicated revolutionaries, and that all the other classes should be abolished. *The Revolutionary Cathechism* would be restated in the arid terms of Marxist philosophy, but in all its essentials it would remain the guiding principle of Lenin's political activity. One of the characters of Dostoyevsky's novel *The Possessed* is made to say, "To level the hills is a good idea." Nechayev showed succinctly, clearly, and almost without emotion how the leveling process could be carried out. Lenin carried it out.

Nechayev was not, of course, the first revolutionary to urge the destruction of an entire civilization: the ancient prophets had called for fire to descend from heaven, and more recently the leaders of the eighteenth-century peasant rebellions had called for the destruction of whole cities "until not one stone lies on another." Michelet, the nineteenth-century French historian, prayed that the cities would become forests and that men would once more be forest dwellers "until, after many centuries have elapsed, their wickedness and perversity will have disappeared beneath the rust of barbarism, and they will be ready once more to become civilized." The romantic vision of the destruction of civilization persisted throughout the nineteenth century; even Robert Louis Stevenson prayed for the day when he would hear the sound of cities crackling in the flames after the long boredom of the Victorian era. But these were dreams and visions. Nechayev was saying, "It can be done."

Though he was able to show with remarkable penetration how a small conspiratorial group could corrupt the government and take over power, Nechayev was not always a very convincing revolutionary. He mingled extraordinary cunning and ruthlessness with conjuring tricks and sleight of hand. In 1869, after a brief foray of revolutionary activity among the St. Petersburg students, he decided that his life was in danger and the time had come to leave the country. He would not escape in any ordinary way, but in a blaze of glory, leaving behind the legend that he had been arrested and had escaped from prison. He employed a very simple ruse. He simply sent two letters to a young girl-student who was one of his ardent admirers, knowing that she would broadcast the letters to all her friends. The letters were unsigned and were enclosed in a single envelope. The first read:

> I was walking on Vasilyevsky Island this morning, and I passed the prison coach. As it went by, a hand appeared at the window and I heard the voice of a dear friend: "If you are a student, send this to the address given." I feel it is my duty to fulfill what is demanded of me. Destroy this note in case the handwriting is recognized.

The other letter, scribbled in pencil in Nechayev's well-known handwriting, read:

> They are taking me to the fortress. Do not lose heart, beloved comrades. Continue to have faith in me, and let us hope we meet again.

Vera Zasulich was not an overly credulous person, but she believed the letters were genuine. There was nothing improbable in them, except perhaps the reference to the fortress, by which he could only mean the Peter and Paul Fortress overlooking the Winter Palace on the north bank of the Neva. It was the grimmest prison in all Russia, where only the most dangerous state prisoners were held.

Vera Zasulich spread the story of Nechayev's arrest through the St. Petersburg colleges. The story swept through Moscow, where it encountered another story—that Nechayev had made a breath-taking escape from the Peter and Paul Fortress and had been seen in Kiev. The legend of Nechayev's invincibility was only beginning. Vera Zasulich, too, became a figure of legend among Russian students. On July 25, 1877, she attempted to assassinate General Trepov, the St. Petersburg chief of police. She found him in the House of Preliminary Detention, fired at him point-blank, and seriously wounded him. She was arrested, placed on trial, and to the surprise of everyone, including herself, she was acquitted. Then she fled the country, and later joined forces with the young Lenin when he was editing *Iskra* (The Spark). She was the direct link between Nechayev and Lenin, but there were many other links.

After the murder of Ivanov, Nechayev fled Russia for the second time. In Switzerland, France and England he lived the life of an exile, on terms of familiarity with the old anarchist Mikhail Bakunin, whom he blackmailed. He described himself as the leader of a widespread revolutionary organization that was on the verge of acquiring great wealth from a Russian nobleman. He edited revolutionary newssheets, stole Bakunin's secret journals, and acquired such power over the daughter of Alexander Herzen that he was soon making her design banknotes—she was a gifted artist, and he had a scheme of flooding Russia with false 100-ruble notes. Nothing came of the scheme. Reduced to poverty, he went into hiding in obscure villages in Switzerland, making an occasional living as a sign painter. The Tsar's secret police were after him. Finally, on August 14, 1872, they caught up with him in a Zurich restaurant. The Swiss government, informed that he was wanted for murder, permitted him to be extradited. Brought to trial, he was sentenced to twenty years' imprisonment in Siberia.

The Tsar however had no intention of letting him off so lightly. He had long ago decided that this small and unimpressive revolutionary possessed a relentless, destructive purpose—he was an explosive force which must be kept tightly boxed. He therefore ordered that Nechayev should be kept for the rest of his days in the sinister Alexis Ravelin of the Peter and Paul Fortress. It was in this wing of the prison that Peter the Great murdered his son Alexis.

Henceforth Nechayev had no name; he was "the prisoner in Cell No. 5." He was permitted to read and to walk each day in the grass-grown courtyard, but once he was returned to his cell he was shackled to the iron bed. Weekly reports on his behavior were sent to the Tsar. On February 23, 1873, the report read:

> The prisoner in Cell No. 5 of the Alexis Ravelin has from February 16 to February 23 behaved quietly. He is now reading the *War Gazette* of the year 1871 and is generally cheerful. Exception is made under the date of February 19, the first day of Lent. Given Lenten food, he remarked: "I have no belief in God and none in Lent. So give me a plateful of meat and a bowl of soup, and I'll be satisfied." On February 21 he walked about continually, often lifted his hands to his head, was thoughtful and went to sleep only at 1:30 in the morning.

So the days passed in a narrow, thick-walled cell: reading, pacing the floor, quietly testing himself against his adversaries. He announced that he intended to write a history of the Tsardom, he asked for more and more books, and on each book he read he made the scarcely perceptible prisoners' signs by which messages were conveyed to the next reader. His plan was simple. He would defy the Tsar to the end. He would widen every crack, unloosen every bar. Bakunin, when he heard of his arrest, said of him: "An inner voice tells me that Nechayev, who is irretrievably lost and who certainly knows it, will this time from the depths of his innermost being, which is chaotic, tainted, but never base, summon up all his inherent courage and steadfastness—he will perish like a hero."

Nechayev did exactly as Bakunin had prophesied. There seems to have been never a moment when he gave in or faltered. He wrote a letter to the Tsar in his own blood. He carried on curious negotiations with the prison governor, explaining how he was prepared to show the government methods of ruling Russia which would make a revolution unnecessary. Once a general came into his cell. He slapped the general across the face and received no punishment. Gradually, hour by hour, day by day, month by month, he was able to suborn the guards, and he worked so well on them that eventually he was able to send messages out to the Narodnaya Volya (People's Freedom), the close-knit and expertly organized terrorist group which was planning to assassinate the Tsar. There came a time when the Narodnaya Volya was seriously discussing whether instead of killing the Tsar they should not bend all their energies to releasing Nechayev from prison. And when the plans had been discussed in secret messages transferred by the guards, Nechayev just as seriously declared that he would prefer that they killed the Tsar rather than release him. He suggested that immediately after the assassination of the Tsar there should be issued a secret order, ostensibly from the Holy Synod, informing all the priests of the land that the new Tsar was suffering from "a confusion of the mind" and it was therefore necessary to say special prayers for him in secret. So that the order should be communicated to the entire people, Nechayev suggested that it should conclude with the warning, "May this secret be confided to no one."

Wit, cunning, dæmonic energy and endurance—Nechayev had all these in abundance. He pronounced himself a member of the Succession Party, spoke meaningfully of his princely origins, and almost convinced the guards that he would be the successor to the throne, as Prince Alexis would have been the successor to the throne of Peter the Great. He was a young lion shaking the bars of his cage, terrifying everyone who set eyes on him, strangely powerful, though weak.

The Narodnaya Volya assassinated Tsar Alexander II as he was riding through the snowbound streets of St. Petersburg on March 13, 1881.

For Nechayev it was the beginning of the end. Alexander II had been a comparatively mild Tsar; his successor, who soon learned of Nechayev's connection with the Narodnaya Volya, was implacable. The guards who had taken his messages were arrested and punished; all privileges were removed from him; no one spoke to him; he lived in the silence of the grave. He was moved to cell No. 1 and completely isolated. Plagued with tuberculosis, dropsy and scurvy, half-mad and suffering from hallucinations, fed on bread, water and a little soup, with a half bottle of milk and a lemon each day, he was allowed only to vanish into a final obscurity. His punishment was "total, terrible and merciless destruction."

On December 3, 1882 the prison doctor, having been summoned by an astonished warder, stepped into the quiet cell. Nechayev was lying dead in a corner. The doctor wrote a brief report to the prison governor:

> I have the honor to inform you that the prisoner in Cell No. 1 of the Alexis Ravelin died on the morning of November 21 around 2 o'clock. His death was caused by dropsy complicated by scurvy.

The news of Nechayev's death was kept secret, but among the surviving revolutionaries of the Narodnaya Volya his memory remained alive. They remembered the *Revolutionary Catechism* and the singular audacity and courage of the man who was so dangerous that he became the Tsar's special prisoner. They forgot the stupid and gratuitous murder of Ivanov, which took place thirteen years to the day before his own death. For them, he was a revolutionary hero, utterly uncompromising, superbly in command of himself, wise and understanding. He became a legend. He had been a blackmailer, a liar, a seducer, a murderer, but all these sins were forgiven him for the power of his audacity.

In *The Possessed* Dostoyevsky drew a haunting portrait of that revolutionary adventurer. Again and again in his notebooks Dostoyevsky returns to contemplate the figure of the "Nechayev monster," satisfied with nothing less than destruction on a universal scale.

How deeply Lenin was influenced by Nechayev we know from his actions, his way of thinking, his turns of phrase. He had made over the years a profound study of Nechayev, until in the end he could almost put himself in Nechayev's skin. To his close friends and associates he made no secret of his debt to Nechayev. To his lifelong friend Vladimir Bonch-Bruyevich, the secretary of the Council of People's Commissars, he spoke often about this "titanic revolutionary" who gave his thoughts "such startling formulations that they were forever printed on the memory." Here is Bonch-Bruyevich remembering Lenin as he talked shortly after he came to power:

> Vladimir Ilyich often mentioned the cunning trick the reactionaries play with Nechayev through the light-fingered hands of Dostoyevsky. He thought *The Possessed* a work of genius, but sickening, for as a consequence people in revolutionary circles have started to treat Nechayev negatively, completely forgetting that this titanic revolutionary possessed such strength of will and enthusiasm that even when he was in the Peter and Paul Fortress, submitting to terrible conditions, even then he was able to influence the soldiers around him in such a way that they came wholly under his influence.
>
> People completely forget that Nechayev possessed a talent for organization, an ability to establish the special technique of conspiratorial work everywhere, and an ability to give thoughts such startling formulations that they were forever printed on the memory. It is enough to recall his words in one of his pamphlets, where he replies to the question "Which member of the reigning house must be destroyed?" He gives the neat answer: "The whole responsory." And this is so simply and clearly formulated that it could be understood by everyone living in Russia at a time when the Orthodox Church was a powerful force and the majority of the people, in one way or another, went to church, and everyone knew that "the responsory" meant all the members of the Romanov dynasty. "Which of them are to be destroyed?" the most simple reader would ask himself, and there at a glance is the answer: "The whole Romanov dynasty." It is simple to the point of genius. All of Nechayev should be published. It is necessary to learn and seek out everything he wrote, and where he wrote, and we must decipher all his pseudonyms, and collect and print everything he wrote.
>
> And Vladimir Ilyich said these words many times.

THE
EDUCATION
OF A
REVOLUTIONARY

"Permit me to observe," said Nikolay Petrovich, *"that if you deny everything, or to put it more precisely, if you destroy everything, then you must also construct, you know."*

"That is not our business," Bazarov replied. *"Our first task is to clear the ground."*

—Turgenev, *Fathers and Sons*

FAMILY TREE

WHEN TOWARD THE END of his life Lenin was presented with one of those questionnaires which were continually being sent around the Kremlin offices, he noted against the words: *Name of grandfather*—"I do not know." Lenin's impact on the world, however, was so great that the biographer cannot afford to be equally disinterested in his origins. The ancestry of a man is a living part of a man, for his ancestors remain alive in him; sometimes they explain him. As we shall see, the ancestry of Lenin does go a little way to explain the formidable person he became.

Among the archives of Astrakhan are two documents relating to the Ulyanov family. One dated May 14, 1825 is an order issued by the Astrakhan provincial government permitting a certain Alexey Smirnov to take possession of "the healthy girl Alexandra Ulyanova, who has been released from serfdom and who is hereby ordered to surrender herself to thee." The formula was a common one, and there is no reason to believe that Alexey Smirnov took Alexandra Ulyanova as a concubine. It was simply that Alexey Smirnov had some interest in the girl and was prepared to pay the head tax and take her under his roof.

Little is known about Alexey Smirnov, who is described in the official document as a *starosta*, a village elder. He was evidently a man of some means and influence. As for Alexandra Ulyanova, who is described as a "healthy girl," we can guess that she was of an age between fifteen and twenty. We know that she was released from serfdom on March 10 of the same year, and except for one other important fact this is all we know about her. The important fact is that the Smirnovs and Ulyanovs were related by marriage, for about the year 1821 Nikolay Vasilyevich Ulyanov had married Anna, the daughter of Alexey Smirnov. A census record, also found in the Astrakhan archives, records that on January 29, 1835, Nikolay Vasilyevich Ulyanov, aged seventy, living with his wife, Anna Alexeyevna Ulyanova, aged forty-five, had four children: Vasily, thirteen, Maria, twelve, Fedosiya, ten, and Ilya, three. They lived in a two-story wooden frame house at No. 9 Stenka Razin Street. The house, which was still standing in 1935, was a large one. From other records we learn that Nikolay earned a living as a tailor and that he died in poverty. The name Ulyanov (from *ulei* = beehive) was not yet fixed, and at various times he was known as Ulyaninov and Ulyanin. So we find in the church records that a son, Ilya, was born on July 14, 1831, to Nikolay Vasilyevich Ulyanin. The son was the father of Vladimir Ilyich Ulyanov, who chose to be known as Lenin.

There has been some mystery about the origin of the name Lenin. It was probably nothing more than a pleasant variation on the family name Ulyanin.

Now the names Smirnov and Ulyanov were common among the Chuvash tribes who had been wandering along the banks of the Volga since time immemorial. They were peaceful nomadic tribesmen speaking a language related to Finno-Ugrian. A short, stocky people, with red hair, yellowish skins, high cheekbones and oblique eyes with puckered eyelids, they had no history and only the most rudimentary laws and social organization; they lived quietly in the backwaters, far from the main currents of civilization. They survived the Tartars by fleeing to the woods, but when Catherine the Great opened up the Volga and distributed the lands to her favorites, the peaceful Chuvash became the serfs of Russian masters. They were farmers, woodcutters, shepherds, beekeepers, hunters; they were rarely fighters. They became family servants, peasants working the estates; the old, free tribal life came to an end in serfdom, and their old shamanistic gods were taken away from them by the priests; and their language perished. Their names, too, were taken from them. They were given new Russian names, like Ulyanov, based on their occupations, or like Smirnov (from *smirenniy* = humble) based on their characters, or what the Russians thought to be their characters. They were not humble, and they ached for revenge.

Even before the time of Catherine the Great the Chuvash and

Mordvin tribesmen, who lived on the banks of the Volga in the region
of Kazan and Simbirsk had felt the weight of Russian imperialism
driving toward the east. Kazan, the capital of the Tartar kingdom, was
conquered in 1552 by Ivan the Terrible. A hundred years later Simbirsk was founded by the Russians as a fortress against Tartar invasions. But neither under the Tartars nor under the Russians did the
tribesmen take easily to foreign domination, and in the great Pugachev
rebellion the Chuvash were especially active. "Burn, pillage, destroy,"
said Pugachev. "Seize the gentry who have enslaved you, and hang
them, and let there be none left." And when the rebellion was broken,
the plight of the peasants was greater than before.

Serfdom was hereditary, and there was no escape from it except
by flight and on rare occasions by purchase. Alexandra Ulyanova
therefore belonged to a long line of serfs. Serfdom involved entire
families with all their descendants; and if Alexandra was a serf, then
at one time Nikolay Ulyanov must have been a serf. The obscure tailor
of Astrakhan, who married late in life, had known slavery, and inevitably this knowledge was passed on to his descendants. It was not a
conscious knowledge perhaps, but it was nevertheless deeply rooted.

The Ulyanovs came to Astrakhan because it was a large and thriving port where skilled men, whatever their origins, could climb up in
the world. Though the city belonged by right of conquest to the Russians, it had in those early years of the nineteenth century the appearance of being outside Russia altogether. With its bazaars, its mosques
and Buddhist temples, the winding streets ankle-deep in dust during
the long, hot summers, it might have been in Afghanistan or even in
China, so fiercely did it cling to its Oriental heritage. Tamerlane had
rebuilt it, a Tartar khan had ruled over it, Stenka Razin had taken it
by storm, and Peter the Great had used it for a stepping-off place in
his campaign against Persia. Only the green cupolas of the churches
and a handful of government buildings suggested the presence of the
Russian masters. On this seething Oriental frontier, which commanded the trade of the Caspian into the Volga, there was only a thin
veneer of Russian influence.

Though we know little about Nikolay Ulyanov, we know a good
deal more about his elder son Vasily, who became the head of the
family on his father's death in 1838. Vasily was then sixteen, and Ilya
was seven. The tailor had left no money, and the family would have
been reduced to destitution but for Vasily's determination to assume
the role of his dead father. He took a job in an office and singlehand-

edly provided for the whole family. He was one of those completely self-denying men who derive their satisfactions from helping others. He had wanted to become a teacher and planned to go to a university, but when he saw that it was impossible he simply accepted his fate and channeled his own ambitions into achieving an education for his young brother. Ilya lived up to his expectations. He did well at school. He was intelligent, kind and thoughtful, and he was especially gifted in mathematics. He was thirteen or fourteen when he helped to eke out the family fortunes by giving lessons. While Vasily was the model family-provider, Ilya was the model student. In later years Ilya was to say quite simply, "My brother was a father to me."

Still, even with Vasily's total self-abnegation, it would have been impossible to put Ilya through college without the help of scholarship funds. Ilya wanted to go to Kazan University to study mathematics and physics under Professor Nikolay Lobachevsky, the inventor of non-Euclidean geometry. By a statute of limitations introduced in 1848, only 540 students were permitted to study at the university, and competition for the Crown scholarships was keen. Ilya however had an impressive school record. The principal of the *gymnasium* wrote a long letter to the rector of the university, urging the acceptance of young Ilya Ulyanov. "Without a scholarship," he wrote, "this extremely talented boy will be unable to complete his education, for he is an orphan and completely devoid of financial resources."

From 1850 to 1854 Ilya attended the courses of the faculty of science at Kazan University. He wore the blue uniform with the glittering gilt buttons, the cocked hat, and the short sword on the left hip. University rules were harsh and exacting, as the young Count Leo Tolstoy discovered when he attended courses in jurisprudence only a few years before at the same university, which he thoroughly disliked and soon abandoned. Ilya Ulyanov, being a Crown scholar, had to observe the rules with especial promptitude. He was the butt of the richer students, for he had no taste for gambling or wenching, and no fortune to squander. He lived in the university like a monk, obeying the absurd regulations as though born to a life of obedience, and caring nothing at all for the outward manifestations of university life so long as he could study and obtain the degree which was the passport to a career of teaching.

In those days universities in Russia were scarcely to be distinguished from military institutions. The rector of the university was usually a well-known scholar, but he was outranked by the curator, who was appointed by the Tsar and whose purpose it was to see that education was administered with parade-ground efficiency and that total loyalty was inculcated. Punishments were severe. Woe betide the student who forgot to salute a passing general in the manner due to his rank. The salute to a general was as follows: The cloak to be removed off the left shoulder as far as the sword-hilt, the left hand to be placed upon the seam of the trousers, and the hat touched with two fingers of the right hand. Such inanities left Ilya Ulyanov unscathed. He was utterly loyal to the Tsar and punctiliously obedient to the laws of saluting. He received no bad marks during the whole course of his life at the university, and he left with the highest honors. On May 7, 1855, he received his first appointment. He became the teacher of mathematics at the school for girls of the nobility at Penza, some three hundred miles southwest of Kazan. On the recommendation of Professor Lobachevsky he was also given the post of director of the local meteorological station.

He might have spent his whole life as an obscure mathematics teacher in a provincial city, had it not been for his friends the Veretennikovs, who encouraged him to marry. Professor Veretennikov was one of the teachers at the school, and his wife Anna was a woman of considerable culture who read German, French and Russian with equal ease. Her sister Maria was still unmarried. Introductions were arranged, and so it came about that the thirty-two-year-old Ilya Ulyanov married the twenty-six-year-old Maria Blank, who had spent most of her life on the family estate near Kazan.

On a wedding photograph which has survived, Maria Ulyanova appears as a woman of considerable presence, plump, high-waisted, wearing a long embroidered dress of the style of the Second Empire. She was not beautiful—she was one of those women whose beauty matures late in life—but the round face suggests stubbornness, intelligence and good humor. It is a strong face, and one feels that she would defend herself passionately and even ruthlessly. Ilya Ulyanov, on the contrary, suggests only kindness and an innate sweetness of character. Already bald, clean-shaven, with a curiously flat face, deep-set eyes, broad nose and generous mouth, he gazes at the world with an expression of amused affection and tolerance. Responsible, understanding, given to no sudden alterations of mood, he might be taken for a young priest or a dedicated schoolmaster who would remain all his life the servant of his pupils. Only two other photographs of him survive; in them he is heavily bearded and his hair is combed in such a way that his forehead seems unnaturally narrow and oddly misshapen, while the grizzled beard gives him a look of untamed ferocity which was wholly foreign to his nature.

The marriage arranged by the Veretennikovs was a happy one. Ilya Nikolayevich followed the fashionable habit of giving an English intonation to his wife's Christian name: she was Mary or Merry, rather than Maria. Until the day of his death she loved him with an unyielding love mingled with a kind of reverence. In his gentleness, tolerance and generosity, there was something almost superhuman about him.

The marriage coincided with his new appointment at a school in Nizhni Novgorod, a larger and more colorful city than Penza. They lived in one of the buildings attached to the school. Their lives were quietly comfortable in the bourgeois manner of the time. In the evenings they sang round the piano, played cards, attended the theater, visited with the other professors. Between looking after her husband, singing, gardening, and taking part in the social life of the community, her life was full. Her only complaint was that she never saw enough of her husband, who would sometimes spend the long weekends tutoring a pupil who was having difficulty with his lessons. It was a calm and rather sedate life; in St. Petersburg or Moscow it would have been regarded as hopelessly provincial. So it was, but in Russia more than in most countries the provinces were the reservoirs of intellectual strength. Novelists might brood on the intolerable boredom of provincial life, but in fact all these provincial capitals seethed with a rich intellectual life of their own. As a teacher, Ilya Nikolayevich was perfectly aware of his responsibility to sustain and encourage the cultural activities of the city. He was developing a marked talent for administration, and soon the educational authorities were discussing how best they could use his talents. He was in danger of becoming a pillar of society.

Six children were born of the marriage. Anna was born in 1864, Alexander followed two years later, and then there was an interval of four years before Vladimir was born. Then in quick succession came Olga, born in 1872, and Dmitry, born in 1874. Then again there was an interval of four years before the birth of Maria. Nikolay, born in 1873, died after only a few weeks. Ilya Nikolayevich, the loyal servant of the Tsar, would have been dumfounded if he had known that all his surviving children would become revolutionaries.

Until recently very little was known about the family of Maria Blank. The Soviet authorities threw a veil of silence over Lenin's maternal ancestry, for reasons which at last have become clear. In time Ilya Nikolayevich was to obtain the rank of hereditary nobleman, enjoying the honors and appointments reserved for the special favorites of the monarchy, but all this could be excused by the fact that he had risen from poverty by his own unaided efforts and spent his entire life as an educator. He was a worthy father of a famous son. His mother's family, by Communist standards, was considerably less worthy. They were landed proprietors, kept serfs on their estate, and lived in quiet luxury.

There are still some mysteries about the Blank family, but there is no mystery about Alexander Dmitrievich Blank, the young medical student who attended the Medical-Chirurgical Academy in St. Petersburg in 1818 and after graduating six years later went to work as a doctor in Smolensk *guberniya*, then in Perm, and then in the armaments factories at Zlatoust, in the Urals. He was descended from one of the German families who were invited by Catherine the Great in 1762 to settle on the lower Volga, so providing a barrier against Tartar invasions. These families usually intermarried, and Alexander Blank accordingly married a German girl, Anna Ivanovna Groshopf. The Groshopfs were solid middle-class citizens, cultured, sensible, with good business heads. Anna's brother Karl became the vice-president of an export trading company, and another brother Gustav became a customs inspector in Riga. Everyone in the family spoke three languages: Russian, German and Swedish. They spoke Swedish because their mother was a Swede, born Anna Karlovna Ostedt.

In 1847 Alexander Blank, still in his early middle age, decided to give up doctoring and live the life of a country gentleman. He was a tempestuous, determined man who liked to have his own way, and he may have felt hampered by the strict regimen of a practicing doctor. He had six children: a son Dmitry, and the five girls Anna, Liubov, Ekaterina, Maria and Sophia. With his wife and children he settled down on a thousand-acre estate at Kokushkino on the banks of the Ushna river, some thirty miles from Kazan. He belonged to the Volga, and there he remained until he died.

Although he was a doctor, he seems to have had very little faith in medicine. He believed most of all in the sovereign powers of water internally and externally applied; he even wrote a book on the subject with the odd title *As thou livest, so heal thyself* in which he described the benefits to be derived from baths, douches, and colonic irrigation. He was something of a crank, but these ideas were by no means original with him, for he lived at a time when the medicinal virtues of water were being eagerly discussed. What was original with him was his capacity to carry his theories to extremes, as when he ordered his daughters to wrap themselves in damp sheets when they went to bed "in order to strengthen their nerves." Winter and summer he made them wear short-sleeved and open-necked calico dresses, and he absolutely refused to let them drink tea or coffee, which he regarded as poisons.

The dangerous expedient of wrapping them in wet sheets seems to have had no ill effects. His daughters did not die of pneumonia, but grew up into personable and handsome young women. Anna, as we have seen, married Professor Veretennikov, the teacher at the Penza school for daughters of the nobility. Liubov married a certain Ardashev, who had connections with the nobility, and Sophia married a certain Lavrov, a landowner with a large property near Stavropol on the Volga. Ekaterina married a teacher called Zalezhsky. Maria was the second from youngest of his daughters and his favorite. His wife had died, and he may have hoped to keep his remaining daughter by his side a little while longer.

For landowners all over Russia these were difficult times. The emancipation of the serfs in 1861 proved disappointing to landowners and peasants alike. Both felt they were cheated. According to the Act of Emancipation the peasants were endowed with the land they tilled, but had to pay the landowner for it. Alexander Blank's property was reduced in size and value; he lost his mill and perhaps two hundred acres. Yet even with these losses he was the owner of a substantial property, with servants to do his bidding and carriages to take him where he pleased. Sometimes he would remember that he was a doctor, and he would look over his peasants in their sicknesses. He died at last in 1873, having spent more than a third of his life as lord of the manor of Kokushkino.

No one could be more bourgeois than the half-German, half-Swedish Alexander Blank, the doctor who settled down into baronial obscurity. By the standards of his time the property was a small one —we hear of estates as large as a quarter of a million acres in the Volga region—but it was large enough to support him and his family in ease and contentment. In time Vasily Ulyanov became moderately rich as a senior clerk in an export-import firm in Astrakhan, so that whenever

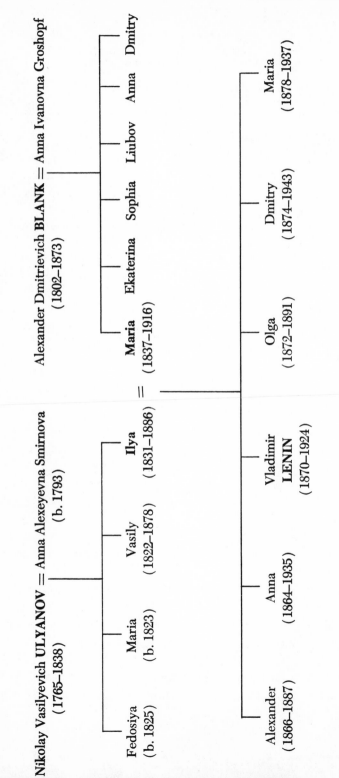

LENIN'S FAMILY TREE

Nikolay Vasilyevich ULYANOV = Anna Alexeyevna Smirnova
(1765–1838)   (b. 1793)

Alexander Dmitrievich BLANK = Anna Ivanovna Groshopf
(1802–1873)

Fedosiya (b. 1825)
Maria (b. 1823)
Vasily (1822–1878)
Ilya (1831–1886)

Maria (1837–1916)
Ekaterina
Sophia
Liubov
Anna
Dmitry

=

Alexander (1866–1887)
Anna (1864–1935)
Vladimir LENIN (1870–1924)
Olga (1872–1891)
Dmitry (1874–1943)
Maria (1878–1937)

his brother Ilya was in need of money, he had only to ask for a loan and the money was forthcoming. A photograph of Vasily Ulyanov has survived. Dressed in casual elegance, he sits negligently in a chair with a mysterious half-smile on his lips; but what is especially notable is his extraordinary resemblance to his nephew, Lenin.

One side of Lenin's family descended from German and Swedish merchants, staid and businesslike, possessors of all the bourgeois virtues, landowners who employed serfs on their estates; the other side descended from Chuvash tribesmen who became serfs under Catherine the Great. From his Teutonic and Scandinavian ancestry came his iron will and his relentless sense of method; from his Chuvash ancestry came his lawlessness, and his slanting eyes.

He was German, Swedish and Chuvash, and there was not a drop of Russian blood in him.

A NEST OF GENTLE FOLK

IN THE YEAR 1870 Simbirsk was a drowsy river town of 50,000 people living on the margins of history. There was no railway, and the steamers could navigate only during part of the year. Though it was the capital of the province, it had all the appearance of an overgrown village climbing up and down the steep slopes. The rich and the nobility lived in the district known as the Venets, meaning "the crown," high above the rest of the population, the merchants gathering on the slopes and the poor at the bottom of the cliffs. On the Venets the air was purer, and there were magnificent views of the surrounding plains and the Volga. In winter you could look down over the thick ice of the endless frozen river, and in the spring the hills were white with blossom, and there were orchards to the water's edge.

Those who lived in Simbirsk claimed that it was one of the most beautiful towns in Russia, and so it was, though the thick dust whirled in the summer winds and the autumn rains turned the streets to mud. There were no industries to poison the air. In summer the surrounding fields were like an endless sea, filled with the songs of peasants who mowed the rich, fragrant grass and built it into hayricks. But if the country enveloped the town, the town itself was very much aware of its provincial fame as the birthplace of Karamzin, the historian and essayist, whose vast library was given to the people and housed in an imposing building on the Venets. Goncharov, the creator of Oblomov, the aristocrat who was so exquisitely lazy that he spent his days in bed, was the son of a Simbirsk merchant and served briefly as the secretary of the governor. Other notables included Protopopov, the

Tsar's last minister of the interior, who was born in the town and always gave it the benefit of his dangerous protection. But the chief glory of Simbirsk was its annual horse fair, when the peasants gathered for miles around and everyone took a week's vacation. It was a town where a man could spend his days pleasurably.

When Ilya Nikolayevich came to Simbirsk in September 1869 he was an inspector of schools, with two children, Anna and Alexander. At first they settled down in a large house on Strelitskaya Street, where Vladimir was born on April 22, 1870, and where he spent the first five years of his life. A new and larger house on Moskovskaya Street was purchased in 1875, a year after Ilya Nikolayevich had been appointed director of the entire school system of the province.

The house on Moskovskaya Street still stands, converted now into a memorial museum with the rooms and furniture restored to make them exactly as they were in Vladimir's boyhood. It is a large wooden house, not unlike the houses of New England, designed by men with an instinctive knowledge of wood. Ten windows look out on the wide street; there is a porte-cochere and a driveway for the family carriage. Everything about the house suggests a quiet upper-middle-class opulence. The downstairs rooms are spacious. The living room has an old-fashioned grand piano with the score of Bellini's *I Puritani* on the music rest, with crystal mirrors, candelabras, an immense Turkish rug, mahogany furniture carved delicately, without heaviness. Potted palms and aspidistras stood against the wall, for Maria Alexandrovna had a passion for plants as well as for flowers. The living room opened on the father's book-lined study, with the desk facing the window, and the black leather couch, where he sometimes slept, against the wall. Both living room and study were wallpapered in pastel-yellow tones. Off a corridor lay the parents' bedroom, and this too was spacious. These downstairs rooms were large, comfortable and flooded with light.

Upstairs were the children's bedrooms. Alexander, Anna and Vladimir had bedrooms of their own; the other children shared the remaining room. These rooms were low-ceilinged, with bright wallpaper. Vladimir's room was covered with maps, while the younger children decorated the walls with cut-outs. The nurse, Varvara Grigorievna, who came to the house when Vladimir was born, occupied a small room in a kind of annex. From the low windows the children could look out on balconies filled with morning-glory vines.

The orchard was planted with apple and cherry trees, and heaped flowerbeds. Maria Alexandrovna's chief passion was gardening. The orchard was her special province; she liked to do most of the work herself with the help of the children and the house servants, never employing a gardener except to dig round the apple trees and do other heavy work in spring and autumn. On long summer evenings the children were commanded to carry water from the garden well to the flower beds. Everything that could hold water was put into service, while the children scampered about the garden and their mother super-intended the operations like a commander organizing the battle to safeguard her parched flowers.

There were so many apple and cherry trees and berry bushes of all kinds that they had as much fruit as they could eat. There were strict laws against picking the unripe apples; they were allowed to gather and eat only the windfalls; and similar laws applied to the cherry trees, the raspberry bushes, and the strawberry rows. She announced which fruit might be "grazed upon," and which must be left severely alone. Ilya Nikolayevich had a passion for cherries, and the three graceful cherry trees near the arbor where they regularly took their evening tea in summer were always left untouched until his birthday on July 20, when there was a kind of ceremonial gathering of the cherries.

The orchard led off to a fairly large garden with a croquet court and a giant swing. Croquet was another of Ilya Nikolayevich's passions, and he liked to organize matches between the children. There was a wicket in the garden fence, and through this the children would slip out to a skating rink in winter and the bathing places on the Sviaga river in summer. It was a family where everyone was quietly con-tented.

Alexander was quiet and reserved, with a peculiarly studious ex-pression even as a child, so that he always seemed to be trying to solve some problem. There was no malice in him. He was good-looking, with regular features, high cheekbones, a well-shaped mouth, and fine eyes. He had a passion for the fret saw and could make intricately carved pieces of furniture, which he liked to give away. He was eight or nine when he learned to play chess, and he showed remarkable pro-ficiency at it, sometimes winning a game from his father, who was some-thing of a dedicated chess player. He walked, even when young, with a princely stride. Refinement shone on his features. He was one of those children of whom it is possible to prophesy that they will achieve almost any ambition they desire, and all their accomplishments will be marked by kindness and intelligence.

Vladimir, on the other hand, was an unruly, noisy child, given to tantrums. He learned to walk late, and in the first months of walking he was always falling down and screaming at the top of his lungs. One fall, when he was three or four, was more serious than the others, and he may have sustained some brain damage. His tantrums were sometimes violent, and they were sometimes accompanied by acts of cruelty. His sister Anna remembered that he was always breaking his toys. One day on his birthday his nurse gave him a papier-mâché troika. He ran off with it, and when they saw him again he had hidden himself behind a door and with quiet concentration was twisting off one by one all the legs of the three horses. When he was five, Anna gave him a ruler. He immediately ran off and broke it across his knee, and then went to his sister to show her the pieces. "How did it happen?" she asked. "I broke it," he said, and raised his knee to show how he had done it. Given a linnet in a cage, he let it die. There was something very set and determined in his occasional destructive frenzies, and more than any of the other children he was punished by being made to sit still in the black armchair in his father's study. It was a punishment he took lightly, for he simply curled up and went to sleep.

But if he was unruly and destructive, there were some discernible reasons for his behavior. He was so plump that they called him the "little barrel." His habit of falling down was explained by the fact that "his head was too big for his body." He had none of the easy grace of Anna or Alexander, who were four and six years older, and therefore in a position to exercise their domination over him. He both resented and adored them. He especially adored Alexander, and when in doubt about a course of behavior he would watch his brother and say, "I'll do what Sasha does." He followed Alexander's habits down to the smallest things. Asked what game he wanted to play, or whether he would prefer milk or butter on his porridge, he would invariably look at Alexander before answering. And because Alexander knew his younger brother liked to imitate him, he would deliberately take his time and look at his brother with a faintly amused expression before deciding whether he preferred milk or butter on his porridge, or whether he wanted to play. Vladimir was Alexander's slave.

Unlike Alexander, who was scrupulously truthful, Vladimir could tell lies cheerfully. He was eight years old when his father took him and the elder children to Kazan for the first time to visit one of their aunts in Kokushkino. He was playing a game with his cousins, his brothers and sisters, when he accidentally pushed a table and a decanter smashed to the floor. The aunt came into the room and asked the children who had done it. They all said they were innocent, including Vladimir, who some months later when his mother was putting him to bed suddenly burst into a fit of weeping and when he had calmed down confessed what he had done.

He could be a plague to the other children when they were doing their homework, for he had a quick mind and usually finished before them. Then, in his malicious way, he would fool around the room, talk in a loud voice, tease and bother them, until they cried out to their mother for help, and she would sweep in and remove them to the comparative quiet of the drawing room. He especially liked to tease Dmitry, who was four years younger. Dmitry was quiet and sensitive and easily frightened. There was a song called "The Little Goat," about a helpless kid eaten by wolves until nothing was left except the little hoofs and horns. Dmitry would fight against his tears while gallantly continuing to sing the sad verse. Then Vladimir would make a fierce face and bellow at him, "And then the big, bad wolves ate him up." And there was an even fiercer face and a still more triumphant bellowing when they came to the last verse, "And there was nothing left for Granny except the little hoofs and the horns."

But if Vladimir was continually up to mischief, and his mother and Anna were continually scolding him, he was often gay and sweet-tempered. He was especially fond of his sister Olga, a year and a half his junior, the prettiest member of the family. They spent hours sitting together, quietly reading children's books or playing the piano together. Olga had a passion for the piano and practiced her scales with a perseverance he envied; and he would say, "There's endurance for you!" His mischief was often lighthearted. He was on the river boat going to Kazan when he started bawling at the top of his lungs.

"You mustn't shout like that on the steamer," his mother said.

"Why not?" he replied. "The steamer is shouting, too."

Such stories about his childhood were remembered and written down by his surviving brother and sisters long after he was dead, and they ring true. They describe a plump, round-faced, red-haired boy with a quick mind and a gift for impertinence, nearly always lively and carefree, but sometimes sullen and resentful, with a curious habit of breaking things. There was nothing to distinguish him from thousands of other boys, except his early difficulty in walking and the terrible falls he took. In every large family there is usually one eager-eyed mischief-maker who plagues the rest and suffers from tantrums;

such boys sometimes grow up to become mischief-makers in adult life.

But increasingly as the years passed he came under the sway of Alexander, who was calm and even-tempered and incapable of mischief. The father was often away, making his tours of inspection, which sometimes lasted for two or three months, and at such times Alexander became the acting head of the family. "We loved him dearly for his tact and tenderness, for his sense of fair play and firmness," Anna wrote. "Vladimir was quick-tempered, but Alexander's even temper and great self-control influenced all of us, especially Vladimir, who started to imitate his brother and finally came to overcome his shortcomings by a conscious effort."

Alexander's influence was especially to be observed in his attitude toward other people. He believed firmly, as an act of faith, that people should be kind to one another and that even gentle mockery was to be avoided. He had a deep respect for people, all people. At a very early age he had worked out a philosophy of life which involved the need for an exquisite generosity, since life was a very precious gift which could be maintained only if everyone acted generously to one another. On the question of study he was equally learned: study opened the doors of the world, and everyone was duty-bound to push those doors open a little wider. To study was therefore a task to be embraced with single-minded devotion, at whatever cost and whatever risk. This attitude toward study was not original with him, for it was derived from his father, who was continually establishing new schools and making speeches on the need for education to lift the backward province out of its lethargy. At the age of twelve or thirteen, Alexander had decided to become a zoologist, and Vladimir very nearly followed in the same path. He would watch his brother carrying out his experiments in nature study, and he would read the same books that Alexander was reading. Alexander's room was crowded with books on natural history, philosophy, science, and foreign languages, but there were also butterfly nets, test tubes, glass pipes, albums of pressed leaves, and jars containing specimens found in the river Sviaga. When any of their noisy cousins came to invade their privacy, they would say peremptorily, "Oblige us by your absence."

They were not, of course, wholly devoted to study. They went on long walks together in the countryside. Vladimir was especially fond of fishing. Once he heard there were carp in a water-filled ditch near the Sviaga, and he went with a friend to investigate, and when he reached the ditch he leaned over and fell in, headfirst. The bottom was silty, and he was sucked under. He would have drowned if a workman from a nearby factory on the riverbank had not come up just in time. Thereafter he was never allowed to play near the river except in winter, when it was covered with ice. Anna remembered the two brothers going out on skating jaunts. They were daredevil affairs, over the Sviaga's steep slopes, which were so terrifying that children thought twice before going down them on toboggans. She remembered them sweeping down from the top of the steepest slope, bending almost double, then straightening up gradually as they gained speed, until at last they came out on the smooth surface of a skating rink. Alexander was tall and sinewy, Vladimir short and sturdy, and he was the better skater. There was nothing timid about either of them.

Vladimir was nine and a half when he first went to school, in the autumn of 1879. There was nothing unusual in going to school so late; he was given lessons by his parents, and tutors came regularly to the house from the local schools, or else the children went to visit the tutors. During the last year before he went to school he took lessons regularly every morning from a local schoolmistress, to prepare himself for the entrance examination. He enjoyed these lessons, and it was remembered that he was always an affectionate and obedient pupil. When he entered the *gymnasium*, he wore the blue uniform prescribed for all schoolboys. He found schoolwork easy, and he had a capacity for attention and concentration which enabled him to grasp the lessons so well that he had little need for homework. Usually he was at the head of the class, and he was notably conscious of being the intellectual superior of the other students. When Ilya Nikolayevich was at home, it was the custom of the children to go to his study and report briefly on the marks they had attained. Vladimir would simply run past the door and shout out, "Greek, excellent; German, excellent; Algebra, excellent," and then vanish upstairs to his study. Ilya Nikolayevich would exchange a pleased smile with his wife at the appearance of the sturdy boy with a tuft of chestnut hair showing from under his school cap as he flashed by the door and recited the daily record of marks; but sometimes he would wonder whether everything did not come too easily to his son. There was a touch of pride in him. There was something a little alarming in his facility. Ilya wondered whether he would ever settle down to a real job of work.

From his mother came his sense of method; from his father came the burning determination to excel.

His intellectual habits were already formed in his schooldays.

Dmitry, his younger brother, was a gentle soul who grew up to be a doctor. He could never quite get used to the relentless, rather mechanical ways in which Vladimir wrote his themes and term papers. It was always the same way. First, he would take half a sheet of paper and sketch out the plan of the theme, being careful to fill in the beginning and the conclusion. Then he would take a full sheet, fold it neatly down the middle and on the left side he would jot down the outline blocking it out, and carefully introducing by numbers or bracketed Greek letters the stages of development of the argument. The right side would be left blank, to be filled in later with new arguments as they occurred to him and with references to books and with any necessary changes. The left side provided the skeleton, the right a covering of flesh. He would ponder both skeleton and flesh until the time came for writing a first draft in pencil, and this would be followed by a final version written down neatly in ink in an exercise book. It was always the same logical order, the same five steps leading to the completion of the theme. In later life he wrote his books in the same way.

Dmitry remembered, too, that he always wrote his rough drafts in pencil. The pencil was always sharpened to a fine point "with a sort of special tenderness, so that the letters came out like delicate threads." He could not abide pencils which did not have stilettolike points, and as soon as the pencil became blunt, or if it was becoming blunt, he was busily sharpening it again. He was a great sharpener of pencils. This habit too continued with him for the rest of his life.

He had none of Alexander's interest in the sciences: what chiefly delighted and fascinated him were languages. He studied Russian, Slavonic, Latin, Greek, French and German at school. It was book learning—when he eventually went to live in France and Germany he discovered to his surprise that he had no facility in speaking the languages—and it would seem that his mother rarely, if ever, spoke German at home. Latin excited him. He liked the weight of the language, and its hard muscular strength; but at the most dazzling moment of his life he burst out in Greek. He had something like reverence for the shapes and subtleties of languages, but he had little patience with the methods by which they were taught in Russian schools. He told his sister Anna, "The eight-year course is stupid! If he should set his mind to it, anybody could learn a language in two years!"

Even at school there was something of the pedagogue in him. He liked coaching students, and he would cheerfully write their compo-

sitions for them. During the school break he would go out of his way
to help students with their difficulties, translating difficult passages
in Greek or Latin for their benefit, or explaining some complicated
theorem to them. And he was especially pleased when a student got
a good mark with his help.

Looking back on his schooldays, Anna was inclined to paint them
in rosy colors. "The entire class depended on Vladimir," she wrote.
"In going ahead he drew others with him." He was the popular one,
the acknowledged leader in games and scholarship. But there is some
evidence to suggest that Anna paints too rosy a picture. Schoolboys
will respect those who are more gifted than themselves, but they do
not love them. Vladimir was brash, forward, contemptuous; there was
always a sharp edge to his tongue. He was acutely aware of his intellectual attainments, and no one was ever left in any doubt of his
intellectual superiority. But he did not make friends easily. "He has
a somewhat excessive tendency toward isolation and reserve, a tendency to avoid contact with acquaintances and even with the best of
his schoolfellows outside school hours." So wrote the director of the
gymnasium in a letter to the authorities of Kazan University, after
Vladimir graduated from school. The letter, which was otherwise full
of praise for the boy, hints at an alarming lack of ordinary humanity
and a chilling remoteness.

How chilling he could be we know from his conduct toward his
French teacher, Monsieur Port, who had married into the local squire-
archy and whose chief fault seems to have been the nervousness of a
Frenchman lost in the Godforsaken desert of Russian provincial society. Monsieur Port dressed elegantly, and no doubt his manners were
expansive. He was an ingratiating teacher, and he spoke Russian with
an execrable accent. Vladimir openly ridiculed him—his manners, his
voice, his way of running to the director of the *gymnasium* on the
slightest provocation. Safe in the knowledge that his father was Inspector of Schools, and that he was himself the special favorite of the
director of the *gymnasium*, Vladimir declared war on the wretched
Frenchman. It was a shocking performance, because all the advantages lay with the pupil, who bullied and goaded the teacher unmercifully. Finally Monsieur Port took his courage in his hands and said it
was absurd that the boy should be given the highest marks for good
conduct when he was continually demonstrating his unbounded insolence, and he demanded that his good conduct marks be reduced.
It is sufficient testimony to Vladimir's position as the son of the In-

spector of Schools that his marks were not reduced. The director of the *gymnasium* however had no alternative but to tell Ilya Nikolayevich what had happened. Vladimir was summoned to his father's library; there followed the inevitable tongue-lashing; and the boy promised that he would never again show the slightest disrespect to Monsieur Port. It was a grim moment in the boy's life. Ilya Nikolayevich made no effort to conceal his dissatisfaction, and when Anna returned from St. Petersburg, where she was studying to become a schoolteacher, he went out of his way to tell her about the incident. He was not always proud of his second son, who never brought friends home from school and who possessed a fund of insolence which might in the end prove to be damaging.

Perhaps it was as a result of this incident that Vladimir showed in the same year the more pleasant side of his character. A Chuvash tribesman, who had been given the Russian name Okhotnikov, meaning "hunter," had been teaching Chuvash boys, but he wanted to go on to the university. He knew little Greek and Latin, both obligatory subjects for entering the university, and even his Russian was poor. The inspector of the Chuvash schools, a man called Yakovlev, suggested that Vladimir might like to teach the tribesman. Yakovlev was a close friend of the family, and his suggestion therefore carried a good deal of weight. Vladimir was in his senior year at school, working harder than ever, but his pedagogic instincts were aroused and Okhotnikov became his pupil. He was a born teacher like his father and unlike Alexander, who was more interested in studying than in teaching.

There were times when Vladimir seemed to live for study, when his sharp brain knew only the satisfactions that derive from books. During the nine-month school year, broken only by a week at Christmas and ten days at Easter, he became a kind of scholastic machine, but during the summer vacation he became another person altogether. Then, for three long months, he enjoyed the life of a young aristocrat on a country estate.

Every summer the Ulyanovs left Simbirsk to stay on the Blank estate at Kokushkino. They would close up the house and take the river steamer up the Volga to Kazan, where they would stay overnight with the Veretennikovs. In the morning they would drive out to the estate in carriages crammed with children and wicker hampers, laughing and shouting, all the arduous work of the year forgotten. In front of them lay golden days of quiet ease and contentment, the days so bright that they faded into one another, so that afterward there remained only the image of a single endless day.

Those summers were like paradise. Everything that could possibly enchant the children was theirs for the asking. The large white house with the columns and the two verandas looked down on the river Ushna. There were woods and coppices near the riverbank and the wheat fields stretched into the distance. They could go hunting or swimming or sailing in the river. There were bears in the woods, hares scampered through the undergrowth, and sometimes they heard the howling of wolves. Sometimes, too, they would come upon elk grazing calmly. There was a boathouse with three boats. Stables, carriage house, farmyard, a long avenue of lime trees, another of birches, and a small village for the peasants who worked on the estate. Such were the commonplaces of the manors of those days, and all were present at Kokushkino.

Not that Kokushkino was a large estate by the standards of the time. About a thousand acres were attached to the manor, and there were rich merchants nearby who had ten times as many acres. Grandfather Blank had bought the land when it was cheap, and he had installed himself comfortably. He had even added to the house by building what he called a wing, which was in fact another house, separate from the main house. Altogether, if we include the stables, the carriage house and the peasant village, there were some forty or fifty houses on the estate.

Life during the summer vacation centered on the two white houses overlooking the river, and there was a constant coming and going between them. The smaller house was especially notable for a large billiard room. Here the children gathered and made plans for their daily forays, or played billiards, or huddled together during the summer thunderstorms. Most of them slept in the large house, and the bedrooms of the smaller one were reserved for visitors. Usually Ilya Nikolayevich occupied his father-in-law's book-lined study, while Maria Alexandrovna and her sister Anna, the mother of the Veretennikov children, occupied the corner room. Vladimir and his cousin Nikolay Veretennikov shared the room next to the study. All these were large rooms overlooking the flower beds which surrounded the house. Maria Alexandrovna threw all her energies into gardening, with the result that her flower beds were famous for miles around.

Vladimir learned to swim in the river Ushna. At first he splashed about in the shallows, but at the age of ten or eleven he could swim across to the other bank. He became an expert boatman, and no one was ever perturbed if he took out one of the boats and sailed away for a whole day. There were two small boats and a larger one which resembled a pinnace. But though he excelled as a boatman and a swimmer, he was remembered chiefly for his talents as a gatherer of mushrooms. There were many varieties of mushrooms, and they were all colors: bronze, pink, snow-white, green and yellow. There were butter mushrooms beloved by black beetles, and birch mushrooms covered with chocolate-colored caps. He knew them all and was regarded as something of an authority on their provenance and cultivation. During the last year of his life when he was living in retirement at Gorki, a prematurely old man struck down by a disease of the brain, gathering mushrooms became almost his chief preoccupation.

In those days he was superlatively content. Everything about those long summer vacations pleased him. Picking berries, sailing on the river, examining the books in his grandfather's library, hunting in the thick junglelike woods, talking with old Efim, the coachman, or the houseboy Roman—all these he remembered vividly in the years to come. One day glided effortlessly into another, and the only danger was boredom. "The Russian country gentleman," wrote Turgenev, "revels in his boredom like a mushroom frying in sour cream." So he did, and those long summer days on Russian country estates in the last century were like extensions of paradise. It was only when the winter came in that boredom became menacing.

There were firework displays on their father's name day, July 20. On that day visitors and relatives would come from miles around to pay tribute to Ilya Nikolayevich. Ilya, of course, is Elijah, and on that day the Russian peasants believed his chariot could be seen striding across the heavens. They also believed that Ilya had inherited all the powers and attributes of the old Slavic god Perun, the lord of thunder, war and violence. On his name day they all vied with one another to make him happy. Years later, when he was a confirmed revolutionary dedicated to atheism and the destruction of the state which Ilya Nikolayevich regarded with extreme devotion, Vladimir would always remember to celebrate Saint Ilya's day and to send his mother a specially heartening letter for the occasion.

Sometimes however brief shadows fell over the leisurely life on the estate. Relations between the peasants and the landed proprietors continued to be strained. The memory of Pugachev, who had raised the Volga peasants against the landlords and the Crown, was still very keen, and landlords who for some reason had incurred the enmity of the peasants were likely to find their houses burned down. Landlords were well advised to be especially careful in their dealings with the peasants in July. This was the time when the harvest was reaped, and the peasants worked eighteen hours a day. They had a name for these days, calling them the *strada,* which means "suffering."

Yet there was very little trouble with the peasants at Kokushkino. To the end Vladimir was to remember those orderly summer days with acute affection. "There is nothing more beautiful than Kokushkino," he wrote; and when he traveled to Italy, he would say that even Capri was not so lovely. The estate haunted him. A fifth share belonged to each of the five daughters of Alexander Blank, and it remained in the possession of the family until the October Revolution.

During the school year Vladimir kept close to his schoolbooks. At Kokushkino he gave himself up to desultory reading over a wide range of classics. He enjoyed Pushkin especially and developed an affection for the novels of Turgenev, liking most of all *A Nest of Gentlefolk,* which described a kind of life very similar to his own. He read Turgenev first when he was thirteen, and he continued to read Turgenev all through his adolescence.

In *A Nest of Gentlefolk* Turgenev contented himself with describing the rich and untroubled lives of the country gentry. Nothing very much happens except that Lavretsky falls hopelessly in love with the beautiful and deeply religious Liza Kalitina, although his faithless wife is still alive. Turgenev describes the calm sunlit world of the gentry in glowing colors. The novel has no social significance, and in fact Turgenev showed almost no interest in social movements in Russia. Even in *Fathers and Sons,* his masterpiece, and the first of his novels to appear after the emancipation of the serfs, the portrait of the merciless nihilist Bazarov is subservient to a love story, and here too there is a loving depiction of country estates and the pleasures of country life. Bazarov himself, with his green eyes and yellow side whiskers, continually submits to the temptations which afflict the gentry, and for the greater part of the novel he wanders from one country estate to another, discussing nihilism as another man might discuss the rotation of crops. Like Nechayev's dedicated revolutionary, he is concerned with destruction, but he is concerned more with theory than with practice.

There are passages in *Fathers and Sons* which could disturb any sensitive schoolboy. "What is a nihilist?" asks Arkady, Bazarov's faithful disciple; and he answers, "A nihilist is one who refuses to bow to authority and accepts no principles on faith, however much those principles may be revered." From time to time in the course of the novel there are discussions on the nature of nihilism:

> "We act by virtue of what we recognize as useful," Bazarov was saying. "At present the most useful thing is denial, so we deny—"
> "Everything?"
> "Yes, everything."
> "You mean not only art and poetry . . . ? It is a terrifying thought!"
> "I mean everything," Bazarov repeated with indescribable composure.
> Pavel Petrovich stared at him. He had not expected this, and Arkady even blushed with satisfaction.
> "Permit me to observe," said Nikolay Petrovich, "that if you deny everything, or to put it more precisely, if you destroy everything, then you must also construct, you know."
> "That is not our business," Bazarov replied. "Our first task is to clear the ground!"

Nechayev was to write in very similar terms a few years later, and Vladimir Ulyanov would say the same thing shortly before he came to power. The romantic temptations of nihilism were not new—Goethe's Mephistopheles had enlarged upon them with considerable power and authority—but in the Eighties of the last century they were being conveyed with remarkable force and subtlety. A schoolboy, the son of a hereditary nobleman living on his ancestral estate, would read about Bazarov with pleasant excitement and weep over the closing pages in the book before running off to swim in the river or to help his mother plant dahlias, nasturtiums and mignonettes in the carefully cultivated flower beds.

Vladimir's taste in literature was already formed in his school days. Pushkin, Tolstoy and Turgenev always delighted him, and he reread their works many times. Many years later, his sister Anna claimed that their father encouraged them to read the revolutionary works of Dobrolyubov and that he would sing revolutionary songs while taking walks with his children, but this was only a legend invented to explain the revolutionary bent of the children. Ilya Nikolayevich was a liberal, deeply aware of the social welfare of the pupils under his charge, but he had not the slightest interest in social revolution. He was proud of the honors he had received under the monarchy; he attended church regularly and went to some trouble to see that the catechism was taught in the schools, and he was incapable of any subversive thoughts.

As long as he lived, his children shared his beliefs and his political principles by force of his example.

The summer of 1885 was the last summer of his life. He was aging rapidly. In the spring of the year he had been feted on the completion of the twenty-fifth year of his service as an official of the Ministry of Education. School directors were sometimes retired after twenty-five years of service, but with his excellent record he could look forward to being retained on full salary for an extra five years. Suddenly he learned to his horror that he would be retained for only one more year. Shocked, he wrote off to the Ministry of Education, only to learn that the decision was irrevocable. Today no one knows why this decision was taken. Probably someone with highly placed connections wanted his job. When he returned from Kokushkino at the end of the summer vacation he knew he was about to begin his last school year.

He was a man of great strength of character, but easily hurt. He felt that he had lost the confidence of the Minister, and to some extent the confidence of all the teachers who worked under him. He was the prey to anxieties and uncertainties. The Christmas holidays came. All his children except Alexander were with him. Alexander, who was studying in St. Petersburg, had been invited to return to Simbirsk for the Christmas holidays, but characteristically he explained that he had no intention of wasting their money with a long and expensive journey. The cost of putting Alexander through college was forty rubles a month, and this money was sent to him regularly. By careful budgeting Alexander had discovered he could live on thirty rubles, and so at the beginning of the summer vacation in 1885 he silently handed his father the eighty dollars he had saved. Ilya Nikolayevich remonstrated with him. It was absurd for the son of an Actual State Councilor to live like a poor student and to starve himself when the money was available. Alexander said nothing. He lived by his principles, and he refused to take more money.

One evening, when Anna was reading the newspaper aloud to her father in the study, she heard him muttering to himself. She looked up, and suddenly realized that he was talking nonsense. He was delirious. He was like someone talking in another world, in another language, terribly remote from her. But the spell passed. Later in the evening he seemed to have recovered completely.

The next day, January 12, he remained all morning in his study. He had spent the night there, as he often did, lying on the black leather sofa. He had slept little, and he looked worn and haggard.

He was well enough to work in his study and to have two brief conversations with his inspectors Strizhalkovsky and Yakovlev, the man who had suggested that Vladimir should tutor the Chuvash tribesman. Once during the morning he suddenly appeared at the door of the dining room with a curiously fixed gaze, a long lingering look—he seemed to be searching for something in the room—and then silently closed the door. His wife said later that he had the expression of a man bidding farewell.

He died at five o'clock in the afternoon, lying on the black leather sofa which stood against the wall. His wife was with him. Just before he died, Vladimir and Anna were summoned to see him for the last time and to receive his blessing. But there was no blessing, and they reached his side only in time to hear the death rattle.

Vladimir saw his father die. He was sixteen years old. He told one of his friends twenty years later, "I was sixteen when I gave up religion."

In his whole life he saw only three people die: his father, his sister Olga, and his mother-in-law.

The funeral of Ilya Nikolayevich Ulyanov was attended by teachers and educators from the whole province. The impressive ceremonies of the Russian Orthodox Church accompanied him at his baptism in Astrakhan, and they now accompanied him at his death. Tributes were paid in the newspapers, and in the funeral oration he was described as a public servant who thought only of the welfare of the people and possessed exemplary zeal: he was a man of deep humanity and did not deserve these empty encomiums, nor did he deserve the words which Vladimir wrote later about officials "who justify 'their general usefulness' by their political apathy, their obsequiousness before the government of the knout."

Ilya Nikolayevich Ulyanov, Actual State Councilor, holder of the Order of St. Vladimir, hereditary nobleman, founder of nearly five hundred schools was dead; and as far away as Moscow and St. Petersburg there were announcements of his death in the newspapers.

To his widow went a pension of 2,200 rubles a year, corresponding to perhaps $8,800 in today's money. It was the same pension which was offered to the widows of major generals.

DEATH OF A HERO

WHEN A MAN SUFFERS a death in the family, it sometimes happens that he spends the rest of his life at the mercy of his grief. He goes through the motions of living, he marries, brings up children, pursues his ambitions, gives every appearance of leading a normal life, while some part of him remains stunned and nerveless. The recurrent shock waves do not always diminish with time; sometimes they grow stronger. The death of a father can have the effect of an explosion of shrapnel, leaving a gaping hole in the family and everyone wounded.

The death of Ilya Nikolayevich came without warning, and at a time when the children had most need of him. Alexander was in St. Petersburg, studying biology at the university. One might have expected him to take the news calmly and sensibly, but instead it drove him close to madness. His sister Anna, in her memoirs, recounts that he took the news so hard that for many days he abandoned his work and did nothing at all except to pace from one corner of the room to the other, like a caged animal. Afterward his character changed. He became harder, sterner, more determined, and from being the most gentle of men he became demanding and silently tyrannical.

There was also a change in the character of Vladimir, who now had to assume the role in the family previously occupied by his father. When Anna left for St. Petersburg the day after the funeral, Vladimir, now fifteen, became the head of the family at Simbirsk. He was confronted with problems he had never had to face before. He had to make decisions about the running of the house, prepare official documents about his father's pension, and see to the education of the younger children; and all this had to be done in the intervals of tutoring Okhotnikov and doing his own lessons so well that he could maintain his position at the top of the class. It was a time of almost unbearable strain. Characteristically he deadened his brief by throwing himself more fiercely into his work.

In that year he was especially close to his sister Olga, who was growing up into a charming and slightly wayward young woman. Anna was inclined to be severe, Olga laughed easily. She sang well, played the piano well, and could sometimes beat her brothers at chess. Of all the children, she had the best ear for music and for languages— she spoke German, French, English and Swedish, which she had learned from her mother, by the time she was eighteen. She was also the handsomest of the children, having the regular German features of her mother and a sweet and gentle expression. Vladimir especially liked the quality of her mind, which was quick and intricate. They said of her that her mind rested only when she was asleep.

That summer, the first after the death of their father, the children did not go to Kokushkino. Instead they stayed in the house on Moskovskaya Street. Half the house was rented to paying guests, but the better half—the half that looked out on the Sviaga river—remained in their hands. The family was not poor, for Maria Alexandrovna had her pension, and there was always money coming in from the Kokushkino estate; but there were four children to feed in Simbirsk and two more to put through college in St. Petersburg. The money was spread thin.

During the previous summer Alexander had demonstrated his talent for playing chess while carrying on a game of billiards. He would simply shout the moves while manipulating the billiard cue. Vladimir was quite properly awed by this feat, and in time he too would learn to play chess without looking at the board. Meanwhile, the two brothers resumed their chess games, and long afterward Dmitry remembered how they played every evening after dinner with deadly seriousness, never arguing or even speaking to one another, as they hunched over the chessboard. They usually played in a small room on the ground floor overlooking the courtyard. One day the twelve-year-old daughter of a neighbor wandered into the courtyard and behind the barred window she saw two people, immobile as statues, with their heads bowed. "Why, they are like prisoners behind bars," she exclaimed, and she went running away. Alexander and Vladimir exchanged glances, looked out of the window for a moment to watch the girl vanishing into the distance, and then they resumed playing.

On one occasion Maria Alexandrovna called out to tell Vladimir there were some chores he had to do. "I'm too busy," Vladimir retorted, his old habits of insolence returning to plague him. He scarcely had uttered the words when Alexander sprang up and said, "Either you'll do what your mother tells you to do, or I'll never play chess with you again." Without a word Vladimir rose and did what his mother told him to do. It was not the only occasion when Vladimir showed the extent of his insolence. It was a brooding, harsh and resentful insolence, with no gaiety in it. There were quarrels among the children, and Alexander was especially disturbed by the way Vladimir was growing up. Vladimir was in desperate need of parental control, and he was too quick, too intelligent, and too conscious of his power to be argued with. When Alexander returned to St. Petersburg with Anna at the end of the summer vacation, he said sadly, "Vladimir is certainly talented, but we don't understand each other any more."

"Why is he like that?" Anna asked, but there was no answer.

Quite certainly, Vladimir had reached one of those stages of adolescence when profound changes take place in the human spirit. Grief, loneliness, the conscious realization of his own intellectual brilliance, the continuing rivalry with Alexander—all these things had worked on him and subtly changed him. There was a war in his soul between the nomadic ancestors of his father, primitive tribesmen of the plains, and the disciplined and civilized ancestors of his mother with their strict German and Scandinavian heritage; and for the rest of his life there were to be these clearly marked alternations between wild, brooding insolence and civilized behavior.

Alexander too was going through profound changes of character. Normally cautious and calm, with a brilliant mind severely disciplined, spending his time patiently examining living forms under a microscope, he was the dedicated scholar who might have gone on to hold an important chair at St. Petersburg University. Instead, in a period of a few months, he became the dedicated revolutionary determined to kill the Tsar and overthrow the social order.

How this came about, by what roads he convinced himself that it was his appointed task to kill the Tsar even at the sacrifice of his own life, is not clear. He went about his revolutionary purposes with considerable secrecy; there are no letters, no diary entries to indicate the stages of his conversion from scholar to revolutionary. We know that he was depressed when he returned to St. Petersburg after the first visit to his family since his father's death, and was therefore in a mood to be easily influenced. He felt deeply for others, and was capable of acts of astonishing self-abnegation. Even when he was a child, it was remarked that whenever he worked on anything, he would throw himself wholly into the task, holding nothing back. Unlike Vladimir, who was often calculating, Alexander possessed a quality of innocence which was completely disarming; and in this he resembled Dostoyevsky's saintly Alyosha Karamazov, who lived only to serve others and to shed on them the light of his holiness. But even Alyosha could become a terrorist, for in the last months of his life Dostoyevsky told his publisher Alexey Suvorin that he intended to write a novel in which Alyosha would appear as a regicide. "You seem to think there is a good deal of clairvoyance in my latest novel *The Brothers Karamazov*," Dostoyevsky declared, "but wait till you read the sequel. I am working on it now. I am taking Alyosha Karamazov out of his holy retreat in the monastery and I am making him join the Nihilists. My pure Alyosha shall kill the Tsar!"

Alexander had no contact with terrorist groups until he returned to St. Petersburg in September 1886, and in fact no well-organized terrorist groups existed. The Narodnaya Volya had collapsed after the arrest of all the participants in the assassination of Alexander II in 1881. The few who had escaped the police net were people who had played no direct role in the assassination and were incapable of organizing a successor group. The Narodnaya Volya lived on in its legends. Already Mikhailov, Zhelyabov, Sophie Perovskaya, Grinevitsky, and the others who had taken part in the assassination of the Tsar were being regarded as the legendary heroes of an age that had passed away.

In St. Petersburg their memory burned brightest, and there were always some students at the university who toyed with thoughts of following in the path of their heroes. Among them was a twenty-three-year-old fanatic, dying of consumption, who imagined himself to be the inheritor of the revolutionary tradition of the Narodnaya Volya. He had no talent for organization and succeeded in converting only a few students to his cause. His name was Pyotr Shevyrev. He had a high forehead, deep-set eyes, and a small chin; his skin was marble-white, and he resembled a skull. About twenty students took part in the conspiracy, some of them, like the student Andreyushkin, in a spirit of wild romantic excitement far removed from the quiet deliberations of Zhelyabov and his companions. Andreyushkin wrote to a student friend in Kharkov a letter which amounted to a hymn in praise of terrorism. "If you should ask me to describe the advantages and the significance of the Red Terror," he wrote, "it would take me centuries to do so, considering it is my *dada*, and it is what keeps me hating the Social Democrats." The long letter was intercepted by the police early in February 1887, but it was not until February 27 that they succeeded in identifying the sender. Pyotr Shevyrev, Alexander Ulyanov, and a few others intended to kill the Tsar on March 1.

They were revolutionaries without training or discipline. They had no money, no organization, no carefully thought-out plan, and no reliable weapons. The conspiracy was financed by the sale for a hundred rubles of the gold medal which Alexander had been awarded by the university for a paper on the structure of fresh-water Annelida. Between them the conspirators succeeded in accumulating no more than three bombs and two Browning pistols. The bombs were designed and largely fabricated by Alexander, whose entire knowledge of bomb making came from reading up the subject in the university library. They were of an unusual kind, for around the metal container holding the dynamite were packed hollowed-out leaden pellets filled with strychnine. Strychnine was easily obtainable through a pharmacist friend of one of the conspirators, and they seem to have had no trouble in getting dynamite. They did, however, have considerable trouble in obtaining the nitric acid which would trigger the explosion, and it was finally obtained in Vilna. Among those who were involved in the purchase of the nitric acid were Bronislav and Joseph Pilsudski, students at the university. They had no leading part in the conspiracy, and it is possible that neither of them knew exactly what was afoot. Joseph Pilsudski was to become the dictator of Poland, as Alexander's brother Vladimir was to become the dictator of Russia.

The conspirators had planned to kill the Tsar on the anniversary of the death of Alexander II. As it happened, the Tsar was staying in the Winter Palace and making his customary tours of inspection in the city. On most of these journeys he would have to drive along the Nevsky Prospect, the broad street which, beginning in Admiralty Square, cuts through the heart of St. Petersburg. The bombing squad consisted of Andreyushkin and two other students. On Feburary 27 they began to reconnoiter the Nevsky Prospect. The police were on the trail of Andreyushkin, recognized him, and kept him under observation. The three students were obviously up to mischief, but no arrests were made that day. The police report noted that they were behaving oddly and had been followed from midday to five o'clock in the afternoon. The Tsar did not leave his palace that day, nor did he leave it the next day, when the conspirators were again patrolling the street. On March 1 they appeared again. This time Andreyushkin was observed to be holding a very large book, while the others had bulky objects under their overcoats. The police arrested them, and immediately examined the book, which proved to be a dictionary of medicine hollowed out and enclosing a cardboard box. Inside the box was the bomb.

One of the students, Osipanov, drew his pistol and fired at the police. The pistol proved to be completely unserviceable, and dangerous only to the person holding it. For some reason the police failed to search Osipanov; they led him off to the police station after wresting his weapon from him. At the police station Osipanov removed a cardboard box from his pocket and hurled it to the floor. It failed to explode. It was obvious that a terrorist group of unparalleled inefficiency had been discovered.

Though the police congratulated themselves on the capture of three potential regicides, they had very little reason for complacency. The letter written by Andreyushkin had been intercepted many weeks before. Without that letter there would have been nothing to indicate that Andreyushkin was a man to be watched, and it was only by the merest accident that one of the bureaucrats in the Okhrana had found the letter in the archives and suggested that something should be done about it. A report, highly creditable to the police, was sent to the Tsar, who wrote on the margin, "This time God has saved Us, but for how long? We congratulate the officials and the policemen who have been on guard and acted so effectively."

Two of the students became communicative, and soon the police were rounding up all their associates. They went straight to Alexander's room in a lodginghouse on the Alexandrovsky Prospect. Anna was sitting in the room, and they immediately put her under arrest. Alexander was discovered in a student's lodging a few hours later. Within a few days some seventy-four friends of the conspirators were under arrest, but fifty of them were shortly released for lack of evidence. Shevyrev succeeded in escaping through the police net. He made his way to Yalta, where he was picked up on March 7.

News of Alexander's arrest reached Simbirsk two days later in a

letter addressed to Vera Kashkadamova, a school-teacher. She was a
middle-aged lady, a close friend of the family, a woman of impeccable
tact, and one who could be counted upon to soften the blow. Vladimir
was in his last few weeks at school, preparing for his final examinations. She summoned him, showed him the letter and watched him
closely. The boy was in complete control of himself. He said slowly,
"It's a serious matter and may turn out badly for Sasha." For a long
time he was silent, knitting his brow. He went home to tell his mother
the news; half an hour later Maria Alexandrovna sought out Vera
Kashkadamova and said, "Give me the letter." She read it and immediately made up her mind that her duty was to go to St. Petersburg
and try to save her son. "I will leave for St. Petersburg today," she
said. "Please keep an eye on the children while I am away."

She left that day, after sending Vladimir to find someone to accompany her on the coach to Syzran, the nearest railroad station.
Syzran was about 120 miles away, and people making the journey by
coach usually arranged to have companions to share the expenses.
Many years later Krupskaya told a strange story of how Vladimir went
in vain to all their "liberal" friends to find someone who would accompany his mother, but by this time everyone in the town knew she was
the mother of two arrested terrorists and they were all afraid of being
associated with her. He never forgave them. In his rage against the
"liberals," Krupskaya relates, he "began to think hard, and Chernyshevsky's writings took on new meaning for him, and he looked to
Marx for the answers to his questions, finding among Alexander's
books a copy of *Das Kapital*, which had proved difficult reading in
the past, though now he attacked it with new zest."

The story is not very convincing. Except for this passage in Krupskaya's memoirs there is no indication that Vladimir showed the slightest interest in revolutionary works while he was at school. This interest came afterward, when he was living in Kazan and felt the full
weight of his brother's actions. In Simbirsk he was too busy running
the house, looking after the other children, tutoring Okhotnikov, and
preparing for the final examinations, which took place ten weeks later.

In St. Petersburg Maria Alexandrovna went about saving her son's
life with absolute dedication. There were Blank relatives in high
positions, and she could count on being received in the ministries
without delay, since she belonged to the hereditary nobility as the
widow of an Actual State Councilor. From morning until night she
held conferences with lawyers and ministers. She petitioned the Tsar

to be permitted to see her son, and Alexander III wrote on the margin of the petition, "I think it would be advisable to allow her to see her son so that she can see for herself what kind of person this precious son of hers is." She was taken to his cell. Alexander wept, but showed no remorse, for he felt none. He seemed strangely indifferent to his fate, exalted, and very calm. Except for the fit of weeping when he first caught sight of his mother, he was completely unemotional. He seemed to be saying, "I attempted to kill the Tsar, the attempt failed, and that is all there is to it."

Originally the police had arrested seventy-four people, but only a very few seem to have had any connection with the conspiracy. Fifteen were brought to trial. They included nine students from St. Petersburg University, a seminarian, a pharmacist, and a man described as "a petty bourgeois" by occupation. Two of the three women on trial were described as midwives, the third was Anna, who was described as a primary-school teacher.

The trial was held behind closed doors, before a court of senators hand-picked by the Tsar. As a special favor Maria Alexandrovna was allowed to attend. An artillery general, summoned as a witness for the prosecution, gave his professional opinion on the five weapons found on the prisoners: the Brownings were incapable of firing, and the dynamite bombs could not have been exploded with the elementary mechanism inside them. The defense made no use of the appalling inefficiency of the conspirators, but sought to show that they were misguided youths who scarcely knew what they were doing, but when at the end of the trial the principal offenders were called upon to make their own speeches before sentence was passed on them, they indicated that they knew only too well what they were doing. Only Shevyrev sought to minimize his guilt. This was not surprising, since he was the most guilty. Alexander wanted to assume the whole burden of guilt. To Lukashevich, one of the minor conspirators, he whispered, "If you need to, put all the blame on me!" Anna said later that he would have rejoiced at being hanged twenty times over if it would have helped the others.

Bronislav Pilsudski proved to be the most difficult witness in his own defense. He was so evasive and cunning in his replies that both the court and the prisoners came to despise him. It was established that Alexander had prepared the bombs in his room. Joseph Pilsudski admitted that he had sent the telegram about the nitric acid to Vilna, but he claimed, perhaps truthfully, that he did not know what the telegram was really about.

Alexander made a long speech in self-justification. He was interrupted several times by the president of the court, who reminded him that he should not speak in theoretical terms, but he proceeded to lecture his judges on the theory of terrorism and the inevitability of socialism. He spoke of the vague discontent with the existing social order which he had known in his youth, and how at last he had found the equation between this discontent and scientific socialism which alone showed the path to the future. "Then it was," he declared, "that these ill-defined dreams of freedom, equality and brotherhood took possession of me in their truly scientific and social aspects, and I learned that it was not only possible to change society, but that change was inevitable." He was like a lecturer patiently leading his judges through an elementary course in socialist theory, explaining how each country "develops according to clearly defined laws, passes through clearly defined phases, and finally achieves a social organization" which cannot be anything but socialist. "For such are the inevitable products of the existing social order and the contradictions contained within it."

He claimed that terror was the only method left to the intelligentsia, since all other methods had proved abortive. Only by terror could men achieve the right to think freely in a world where nothing was published until it had received the imprimatur of the government, and no one dared think at all without first acquiring governmental approval. He said:

> Our intelligentsia is physically so weak and disorganized at the present time that it cannot embark on open war. Only the terrorist is in a position to defend the right to think freely and the right to participate intellectually in the life of society. Terror, as a form of warfare, originated in the nineteenth century; it is the sole defensive weapon which a minority can resort to in order to demonstrate its physical strength and the consciousness that it is fighting for justice. Russian society is so constituted that we can defend our rights only in these duels with the state power.

As he spoke about terror he was still the lecturer patiently expounding a thesis. What he had to say had been said before by Nechayev, Zhelyabov, and perhaps twenty others, but Alexander said it more clearly and with more intellectual authority than they had ever possessed. His speech, covering three closely printed pages, was logical, orderly, without the least appeal to sentiment, and it was perhaps the coldness of the speech which terrified Maria Alexandrovna, who hastily left the courtroom while her son was speaking. He took full blame for the attempt to kill the Tsar and asked for no mercy. "Among the Russian people," he said, "you will always find ten men so devoted to their ideals and with such a burning sympathy for the sufferings of their country that they will not consider it a sacrifice to lay down their lives for the cause. Such people cannot be intimidated."

If the prisoners had thrown themselves on the mercy of the court, they might have received short prison terms. But it was clearly not Alexander's intention to go to prison. Even the prosecutor was touched by his evident desire to assume all the blame. "I have the greatest faith in the declarations of the accused Ulyanov," he declared. "If he errs, it is in taking on his shoulders more than he actually performed."

The five ringleaders were sentenced to death, while most of the others received long prison terms. Bronislav Pilsudski was sentenced to fifteen years of hard labor in Siberia, while his brother Joseph was merely sent into exile for five years. Anna was clearly guiltless; she was freed a few days later with orders to remain under police surveillance.

In prison Alexander behaved as everyone expected him to behave. He did not break down. His only request was for a volume of Heine's poems. Someone who saw him at the time spoke of his "dark pallor, high forehead, furrowed brows, and lips pressed firmly together." It is a ghostly portrait of a man, but a curiously effective one.

On May 20 Alexander was hanged in the courtyard of the Schlüsselburg fortress. Shevyrev, Andreyushkin, Genyeralov, and Osipanov were hanged at the same time. When Vladimir received his mother's telegram announcing the death of his brother, he rubbed his forehead and said quietly, "We must find another way."

Maria Alexandrovna returned to Simbirsk. She too was strangely calm. The old nurse who had been with the household as long as the children could remember spoke of her homecoming: "She did not ring or knock, but came in quietly by the back door. The younger children crowded round her and clung to their mother. I noticed that her hair had gone quite gray." For a few more weeks she was to stay in Simbirsk. Then, very sensibly, in an effort to erase all the evil memories that crowded in on her—the death of her husband and of her favorite son—she sold the house and the furniture, and left the town for ever.

Vladimir showed no signs of emotion. He did not weep and did not permit himself the least alteration in his plans. He would work just as assiduously as before; he would continue to tutor Okhotnikov, and he would continue to supervise the education of the younger children. On April 18, while his brother was in prison, he had written officially to the director of the *gymnasium*, "most humbly requesting Your Excellency to permit me to sit for the school-leaving certificate," which would enable him to enter the university; and His Excellency Fyodor Kerensky, who had worshiped the boy's father and was now entrusted by the courts with the management of Vladimir's affairs, immediately assented. Vladimir sat for the examination and passed with honors. He received 5, the highest mark, in Scripture, Latin, Greek, French, German, Russian and Slavonic, mathematics, history, physics, and geography. Only on one subject, logic, did he receive less than the highest marks; and against the word "logic" on his report there was the ominous figure 4.

Fyodor Kerensky was a man of great gentleness and charm, and to protect those he loved he was capable of any number of white lies. Vladimir had been an unruly and often impudent pupil, brilliant and self-assertive to the highest degree, and curiously friendless. In spite of the boy's failings, the director possessed a genuine affection for him and wrote a glowing testimonial for him, which has been preserved. He wrote:

Very gifted, always neat and assiduous, Ulyanov was first in all subjects, and upon completing his studies received a gold medal as the most deserving pupil with regard to his ability, progress and behavior. Neither in the school, nor outside, has a single instance been observed when he has given cause for dissatisfaction, by word or by deed, to the school authorities and teachers. His mental and moral instruction has always been thoroughly looked after, first by both his parents, and upon the death of his father in 1886 by his mother alone, who concentrated all her care and attention on the upbringing of her children. Religion and discipline were the basis of this upbringing, the fruits of which are apparent in Ulyanov's behavior.

Looking more closely at Ulyanov's character and private life, I have had occasion to note a somewhat excessive tendency toward isolation and reserve, a tendency to avoid contact with acquaintances, and even with the very best of his schoolfellows outside school hours.

Ulyanov's mother intends to be with him throughout his university career.

Armed with this testimonial, his school-leaving certificate, a statement of the services rendered to the country by his father, his birth certificate and certificate of baptism, and two photographs, he wrote to the rector of Kazan University asking for permission to enter the faculty of law as a student. According to Fyodor Kerensky it was an unwise choice. The boy, he thought, would have done better if he had entered the faculty of letters and studied literature and history. In fact, Vladimir never learned very much history and he was deficient in logic to the end of his life.

The photographs sent to the rector showed him in his *gymnasium* uniform, plump, handsome, with an appealing boyishness. The hair is brushed smoothly back, the trim uniform gives an impression of neatness. There is no hint of grief in the young, fully fleshed face or in the unfurrowed brows. He has the full lips of a woman. Only the rather flat nose and the eyes, which are long and slanting, suggest his Finno-Ugrian and Chuvash ancestry. He gazes out of the photograph with a look of eagerness and intelligence, aware of his gifts but not unduly aware of them.

He does not look like a man who will set the world on fire.

THE YOUNG LAWYER

WHEN VLADIMIR ULYANOV became a law
student at Kazan University, his intention was to become a lawyer.
He had not the slightest intention of pursuing a revolutionary career,
knew no revolutionaries, and had read no books with revolutionary
tendencies. To his sister and others he declared that Alexander had
followed "the wrong path," and if Russia was to be changed it would
have to be in the legal way. The lawyers, not the revolutionaries, held
the destiny of the country in their hands.

Now that the house on Moskovskaya Street in Simbirsk was sold,
the whole family except for Anna, who was living under police surveillance on the estate at Kokushkino, decided to follow Vladimir to
Kazan. Ilya Nikolayevich had studied there, and to this extent the
small thriving city was familiar to them. It was the capital of the
guberniya, the seat of the archbishop, and the headquarters of the
16th Army Corps; on the left bank of the Volga stood the crumbling
mosques of the ancient Tartar city, and on the right bank there was
a park with the surprising name of Russian Switzerland. They took an
apartment in the Pervaya Gora, a fashionable street near the university.

Among the books Vladimir read that summer was Chernyshevsky's
What Is To Be Done?, written when the author was a political prisoner
in the Peter and Paul Fortress in St. Petersburg. This novel, which had
an extraordinary effect on three generations of revolutionaries, is almost unreadable today because it is disorganized and disoriented,
moving by fits and starts, rarely keeping to its main purpose, which

is to extol the "new men" who would build a new society in which everyone is completely free. To one of the characters there is granted a dream of a future in which the workers live in palaces of metal and glass, with indirect lighting and steam tables which render the presence of waiters unnecessary. Scientific agriculture had produced the age of abundance. In this anarchist paradise, "no one need work unless he desires to, and the cheerful peasant may spend the long afternoon beside his table heaped with huge cups of wine." Chernyshevsky describes the people who are working to bring this paradise about. One of them is a certain Rakhmetev, descended from Tartar ancestors, rich and aristocratic, the inheritor of four hundred serfs and seven thousand acres of land, who lived the pure ascetic life and subjected himself to intense privations in order to prepare himself for—he was not sure what he was preparing himself for, but it is clear that it was in some way connected with the vision of a socialist or anarchist paradise.

We are given only a few tantalizing glimpses of Rakhmetev, yet his powerful and convincing presence is vividly rendered by brief anecdotes about him. Once, for example, he read for eighty-two hours consecutively, remaining awake on the first two nights by sheer will power and fortifying himself on the third night with eight cups of strong coffee. At another time, to harden himself he slept on nails. He lived by the clock: so much time for reading, so much time for helping others. He made rules for the strict government of his physical, moral and intellectual life, but sometimes he would break the rules in order to study people. He was "the pure rigorist," with no nonsense in him. For a while he became a farm laborer, and later a carpenter. When he was traveling along the Volga, he fell in with some boat haulers and joined their ranks. He lived chiefly on raw beefsteak and was powerfully built, with the result that the Volga boat haulers were in awe of him and christened him "Nikitushka Lomov," in memory of a legendary boat hauler of that name. Then he vanished, and strange rumors were heard of his wanderings in Europe. They said that he suddenly appeared at the house of one of the greatest European thinkers of the century with the words, "I have thirty thousand thalers; I need but five thousand; the remainder I beg you to accept." Though the philosopher was living in great poverty, he was startled by the offer and asked why it was made. Rakhmetev answered, "For the publication of your works." Of his further adventures, according to Chernyshevsky, little was known except that he had planned to settle down in the United States, "the country I must study more than any other."

Rakhmetev is sketched out in a few pages in the middle of a long and tiresome novel, but for thousands of Russian students that solitary chapter, entitled "An Unusual Man," was like a draught of intoxicating wine. Rakhmetev was continually saying, "I must"; he was driven by the categorical imperative to know everything and suffer everything. Some powerful ingredient, absent in most men, was present in him. He made an art of living strenuously and rigorously. "No luxury, no caprices; nothing but the necessary," he declared. "Such men are the best among the best," wrote Chernyshevsky. "They are the movers of the movers, the salt of the salt of the earth."

There is not the least doubt that Rakhmetev made an extraordinary impression on Vladimir, who spent weeks poring over the novel and consciously modeled himself on that half-Tartar landowner whose only failing was an addiction to cigars. Vladimir too decided to smoke. He enjoyed smoking. He was not unduly impressed when his mother pointed out that he was endangering his health, for like Rakhmetev he could answer that smoking was a powerful aid to clear thinking. He was more impressed by her argument that he was not yet earning any money and he had no right to depend on her for his smoking allowance. The argument proved conclusive. He gave up smoking and never resumed it. In nearly all other respects he trained himself to be like Rakhmetev, and in the small book of pasted-up photographs of his heroes which he carried about with him everywhere Chernyshevsky was placed first.

He was perfectly aware of the impact of the book on his mind. Years later he told his friend Celia Bobrovskaya-Zelikson, "It is great literature, because it teaches, guides and inspires you. I read the novel five times altogether in a single summer, and each time I found new and potent ideas in it."

Because he bore a name which Alexander had made famous, Vladimir behaved cautiously at the university. He knew he was being watched closely, and he was determined to be a model student. He had promised his mother he would do nothing to draw the attention of the university inspectors upon himself. He had not, however, counted on the actions of the Minister of Education, who regarded all universities as hotbeds of sedition, dismissed all professors with liberal tendencies, and ordered all the fraternities of students coming from the same *guberniyas* to disband. Unrest swept through all the Russian universities. On December 4 the students of Kazan University held a mass meeting to protest the actions of the Minister of Education and they drew up a respectful petition addressed to the chief of the local inspectorate. Detectives were present at the mass meeting. They took down the names of students. Included among the names was that of Vladimir Ulyanov, who was observed to be standing in the front row with his fists clenched. He had not spoken during the meeting, but his mere presence was regarded as an incitement to revolt. That night he was arrested at home, and with thirty-nine other students he was taken off to the police station. There is a story, perhaps apocryphal, that on the way to the station the police officer said, "What's the use of rebelling, young man? Don't you see you are up against a stone wall?"

"Yes, there's a wall," Vladimir is supposed to have replied, "but it is a thoroughly rotten one, and given a good push, it will topple over."

He remained in prison for a few days and was then formally expelled from the university. After three months his university career had come to an end. Because he was the brother of Alexander Ulyanov, he was regarded with especial suspicion and was ordered out of Kazan. On his mother's pleading he was permitted to stay on the Kokushkino estate, where his sister was still living under police surveillance.

In fact he was perfectly innocent of the charge. He had been scrupulously careful to avoid the attention of the authorities, and he had attended the mass meeting only because all the other students were present. The detectives had picked on him at random. Some months later, when he was applying for readmission, a report on his criminal activities was laid before the rector. It is a completely unconvincing report and suggests that the detectives were put to some trouble to find excuses for arresting him. The report read:

> During his short stay in the university he was conspicuous for his reticence, lack of attention and even rudeness. Only a day or two before the students meeting he gave grounds for suspicion that he was fomenting trouble. He spent a great deal of the time in the smoking room conversing with the most suspect of the students, went home and returned bringing something which the others had requested, and generally behaved in a strange manner. On December 4 he ran into the main hall to the front seats and, together with Polyansky, he was the first to run down the corridor shouting and waving his arms as if inciting the others, and on leaving the meeting he gave up his registration card.
>
> In view of the exceptional circumstances surrounding the Ulyanov

family, the behavior of Ulyanov at the meeting gave the inspectors ground for believing that he was quite capable of various kinds of legal and criminal demonstrations.

The truth was that Vladimir was guilty by association—with his dead brother. He seems to have taken his arrest philosophically, and he spent the winter in Kokushkino as he had spent the summer in Kazan, reading voluminously and borrowing books from all the libraries within reach. Boxes of books came to him regularly from Kazan University, and there were the books and magazines which had belonged to grandfather Blank, gathering dust in the library. So many books arrived that the postman piled them into a basket, and in the same basket books would be sent back to the post office and so to the libraries which supplied them. Newspapers came with every post. Soon Maria Alexandrovna arrived, to keep house for them, a saddened gray-haired woman obviously distressed by the change in the family fortunes, but never by word or gesture complaining. The arrest of Vladimir and his dismissal from the university was only one more staggering blow added to the others she had received during the past two years. "Her courage," Vladimir was to say later, "was a thing to wonder at."

That winter the days passed slowly in the snowbound house. Except for the police inspector who came regularly to see that Anna and Vladimir were up to no harm, and their cousin Nikolay Veretennikov who drove out from Kazan, there were few visitors. Sometimes Vladimir would go out hunting in the woods—or rather he would saunter out with a gun under his arm; Anna remembered that in the entire course of the winter "he never brought home a single thing." The family sometimes teased him about his lack of success as a hunter. One day in the following summer, returning from a walk with Nikolay, he announced that they had seen a hare. "I suppose," said Anna, "it is the same hare you were after all winter."

According to Anna he had none of the instincts of a hunter, unlike his brothers, who were both excellent shots. "He was never a hunter at heart," Anna said. Many years later, when Vladimir was in exile in Siberia, his wife would wonder at his habit of walking out into the woods with a gun and returning empty-handed. Once when a fox appeared within a few yards of him, he refused to kill it. "Why?" he was asked; and he answered, "Because it was so beautiful."

When Anna remembered that winter of exile, it seemed to her that the house was uncomfortably chilly and curiously empty. There was the feeling of being cooped up in a nightmare. They had never stayed in the house in winter before. They had known it in the luxuriant summers, when the grain was ripening and the sunlight poured through dappled leaves. Now they were haunted by the ghosts of a dead father and a dead brother.

Vladimir kept busy. He read from morning till night, helped Dmitry and Maria in their studies, played chess with Olga, talked about Alexander with Anna, and went skiing. He had not the least intention of giving way to despair; he expected to be allowed to enter the university the following year. He had no social consciousness, had read no Marx, and was so completely devoid of conspiratorial instincts that, although he must have known that his mail would be censored, he wrote a long, excited letter to a school friend about the events leading up to his expulsion full of calculated insults directed against the university inspectors and professors. He wrote the letter with intense concentration, obviously relishing every moment of it. Since he scarcely ever wrote letters, Anna was puzzled and watched him closely. The basket came. Books and letters were poured into it, and Vladimir contentedly added his letter. It was evening, the children would soon be going to bed, and the basket would go off the next morning.

Anna knew—she could scarcely not have known—that an adolescent letter written by a student in St. Petersburg to a friend in Kharkov had led to the arrest and execution of her brother. There was no harm in asking what he had written with such an expression of concentrated excitement. He told her, and she argued with him, pointing out that he was placing his friend in grave danger. As innumerable revolutionary leaders were to learn later, Vladimir was not a man who changed his mind lightly. He had written the letter; it was final; he refused to change a word. Pacing up and down the room, he quoted long passages of it, relishing each brutal epithet, each abrupt turn of phrase. It was the first of a long series of harsh, implacable, ruthless letters written in cold fury, and having discovered a gift for calculated invective, he was not prepared to surrender this first fruit of his creation without a fight. He argued with her pitilessly. She argued back. Finally, looking thoughtful, he admitted the force of her arguments and with obvious reluctance removed the wretched letter from the basket. Even then he refused to part with it. For months it remained on his desk, to be reread and savored at intervals. When spring came, he finally destroyed it.

In spring the house lost its sequestered, lonely appearance. The birds sang, the earth shone black, the first green shoots appeared, and only a few small pockets of snow lingered in the gullies. The estate came to life again. Vladimir would fill a basket with books every morning and sit on a bench in the shade of a lime tree, reading in the open air all day. In the afternoon there would be dinner followed by a walk in the woods with Olga or Anna, and perhaps some desultory hunting, or swimming, or sailing in one of the boats, and then he would be at his books again until bedtime. Sometimes the Veretennikov cousins came to join them. They were older than Vladimir, and not so quick as the Ulyanov children. Anna remembered that "they were no match for his well-aimed barbs and his sly grin."

On May 9 Vladimir wrote a formal request to the Minister of Public Instruction begging for permission to return to the university. He gave his address as the Veretennikov apartment on Professorsky Street in Kazan, and presumably he was no longer under continual police surveillance at Kokushkino, but could go to Kazan whenever he pleased. The Minister called for a report on the boy's conduct, and without reading to the end he wrote on the margin: "Isn't this the brother of that other Ulyanov? He too came from the Simbirsk *gymnasium*, didn't he? So I see at the end of the page. Under no conditions should his request be granted."

So the summer passed, while Maria Alexandrovna wrote endless letters to influential friends in St. Petersburg in the hope of mitigating the punishment which had descended on her children, but to no avail. In September Vladimir sent a formal request to the Minister of the Interior, explaining that "to support his family and acquire a higher education" it was necessary for him to seek permission to study in a foreign university, since it was no longer permitted to him to study in a Russian one. This request also was refused, but one small mitigation was permitted to him. He no longer had to live in Kokushkino, but could settle down in Kazan.

The family returned to Kazan. Once more they took an apartment in the Pervaya Gora, which wandered along the side of a hill. There was a balcony looking down over a steep garden, and for some reason the entire ground floor was given over to two kitchens. One of the kitchens was not being used, and Vladimir made it into his study, filling it with books. Here for the greater part of the day he studied, leaving the kitchen only to run errands for his mother or to raid the university library.

That autumn was a particularly momentous one, for among the books that fell into his hands was Marx's *Das Kapital*.

Day after day he remained in the kitchen, absorbed in the study of that immensely long and argumentative work where capital is excoriated as an invention of the devil, though the bourgeois civilization based on capital is praised to the skies for all the benefits it has conferred on human society.

Vladimir was exactly of an age when Marx's curious mingling of Germanic logic and Messianic fervor were likely to excite him beyond measure. Though himself a capitalist, living on the rents from Kokushkino and his mother's pension, and with no knowledge whatsoever of the industrial proletariat, he could recognize the validity of Marx's theorem that the proletariat were the rightful inheritors of the surplus value which had hitherto fallen into the hands of the capitalists. It never occurred to him that the simplicity of the theorem was in direct contradiction to the complexities of the forces which move industrial society; and to the end of his life he believed he had found in Marx a world savior, the prophet of an unalterable truth. He had lost his faith in religion the previous year, when Alexander was executed. Within eighteen months he had discovered a new faith.

The discovery of Marx filled him with elation. His sister Anna describes how she would come down to the kitchen in the evening to listen to him expounding his new-found philosophy with extraordinary fervor and enthusiasm. "I can see him as if it were yesterday," she wrote, "sitting on a kitchen stove covered with newspapers and making violent gestures, as he spoke of the new horizons which opened out to anyone who followed Marx's theories. There emanated from him a cheerful confidence that was very winning. Even in those early days he had the gift of persuasion, of carrying others with him. Even then he never kept his knowledge to himself, but sought to share it with his friends and win them over to his side."

Vladimir was not, of course, alone in discovering Marx. All over Russia there were students who were falling under his spell and eagerly forming small study groups. There was even a small study group organized by a brilliant student called Fedoseyev in Kazan itself, but he was completely unaware of the existence of the group, and even if he had been aware of it he would not have dared to become associated with it. Few visitors except the Veretennikov relatives came to the apartment. In all the days they spent at Kazan, Anna could remember only two obscure former revolutionaries whom Vladimir met secretly: one was a middle-aged woman who had once been a member of the Narodnaya Volya; the other was a student. She hints at other meetings, and no doubt Vladimir, in his enthusiasm for Marx, did have some peripheral contacts with groups of students studying social questions on Marxist lines. Later he met Fedoseyev, whose study group came to an end in July 1889, when all its members were arrested. If Vladimir had been in Kazan, he too might have been arrested. He was not in Kazan because two months earlier Maria Alexandrovna had bought an estate near Samara, a hundred and fifty miles to the south, with the intention of setting up Vladimir as a landed proprietor and gentleman farmer.

Above everything else, Maria Alexandrovna feared that Vladimir would become a revolutionary like his elder brother. She wanted to live in peace and security, without the nagging thought that at any moment the police would descend on her house, arrest him, and sentence him to prison or worse. She knew of his leanings toward Marxism, and she feared for him. With Vladimir's grudging approval she therefore bought a large farm some thirty miles east of Samara and proposed to settle the family on the estate. Vladimir and Mark Elizarov, Anna's fiancé, would work the land. Samara had no university. It was a place where they could all settle down quietly and forget the past.

The property consisted of 225 acres of farmland, steppe and woodland, with a mill, stables, a lake, and a not very imposing manor house, near the hamlet of Alakayevka. For this Maria Alexandrovna paid 7,500 rubles, the sum she had received for the sale of her house in Simbirsk. The purchase was arranged by Mark Elizarov, who had been brought up in one of the neighboring villages until he became a student at St. Petersburg University, where he met Anna. He had been a friend, though not a particularly close one, of Alexander, and he had an engaging sweetness of character. Maria Alexandrovna was fond of him, trusted him, and looked forward to the marriage which would take place later in the year. What particularly attracted her to Mark Elizarov was that he gave no sign of any interest in social affairs; and it was her misfortune that he too became a revolutionary.

As for the estate, it formed part of a large complex of villages which had passed into the possession of a certain Sibiryakov, who after making a fortune from gold mining in Siberia in the Seventies had taken up large-scale farming with modern methods. He imported steam plows from abroad, erected barns and cattle sheds of clay brick, and attempted to teach the peasants how to work the land profitably. He was a kindly, intelligent man, liberal in his political views, and sympathetic to political exiles. Gleb Uspensky, the famous publicist, who spent a lifetime describing the arduous lives of village laborers, had lived on the estate, and these were the villages which filled his stories. Sibiryakov built schools, engaged teachers, and saw that the peasant children did their lessons. He spent money lavishly—too lavishly. The huge agricultural establishment proved to be uneconomical, and gradually he was forced to retrench, selling off parcels of land one by one, until in the end nothing was left. Long before the last parcel was sold, he had retired to St. Petersburg.

The Alakayevka estate was almost the last piece of property left in his hands. Elizarov knew his way around law offices, and he was able to arrange the purchase at a bargain rate. It was good land. There were eighty-four families living in the village, perhaps three hundred peasants altogether. Most of them had their own horses and cows, and owned their own houses. Vladimir set to work to become a farmer superintending his estate, but it was soon evident that he had no heart for it, and the work of the farm was put in the hands of an agent. "The moment I started," he said later, "I knew it wouldn't work out. My relations with the peasants became abnormal."

Though Vladimir's tenure as landlord superintending his property proved to be short, there was no question of the family's affection for the estate, which reminded them of Kokushkino. The air of the steppes came rolling over the fields. There were woods and coppices, a long rambling manor house, a wild garden which ended in a small wandering brook. Raspberries grew wild in the woods. At Kokushkino the river flowed just below the house, but here it was a good ten minutes' walk to the lake, where they swam on the long summer days. After months of wandering they had found paradise again.

The children divided the empire among themselves: each had his favorite corner, his own unassailable property. Olga had her tall old maple tree, Anna her avenue of birches, Vladimir his garden shaded by lime trees, where he set up a bench and a table. There he worked most of the day, taking notes in his neat, rather cramped handwriting, interrupted only by the occasional visits of his brothers and sisters who came to have their lessons corrected. He had his own room in the house, but rarely entered it except to sleep; the windows were covered with navy-blue curtains to keep out the swarms of flies and mosquitoes and gnats. At night they lit a lamp on the porch to attract the insects, hoping in this way to keep them out of the house.

Vladimir would be drowned in his books until three in the afternoon, when they regularly took their dinner. Afterward he would go for a walk or swim, or he would chin himself on the horizontal bars he set up not far from his lime-tree bower. He taught his younger brother Dmitry to play chess, never permitting him to take back a move once he had touched a piece. What Vladimir enjoyed, according to Dmitry, was the pleasure of extricating himself from an apparently hopeless situation; the winning or losing of the game presented very little interest to him. Yet he was an expert on end games, and when Mark Elizarov arranged a correspondence game between Vladimir and Andrey Khardin, a famous chess master of the time, the battle was waged strenuously. Vladimir lost the first game, but he continued to play against Khardin, who was a lawyer in Samara, during all the years he remained in Samara *guberniya*. "You must understand that chess is nothing more than a game, it mustn't be taken too seriously," he said when Dmitry suggested that chess should be taught at school instead of dead languages as a means of memory training. For Vladimir, the really serious matter was Marx. Directly or indirectly, all his studies were concerned with the application of Marx's theories to the problems of Russia.

During the day the family was dispersed, everyone going about his separate business. In the evening, however, they came together for companionship at the long table set up on the porch. A pail of cool milk would be brought up from the cellar; gray wheaten loaves would be distributed. Sometimes they read quietly; sometimes they sang, with Vladimir ridiculing the verses if they proved too sentimental. It was a habit that never left him. There was a song addressed to a pair of beautiful eyes, with the line, "Your eyes will be the death of me!" Invariably Vladimir would burst out in mocking laughter, wave his hands and shout, "They're the death of me already!"

They were evenings of quiet contentment: the family together and the world lost in the surrounding darkness. Anna was so moved that she once wrote a poem about the family on the porch:

> Night falls, the earth lies sleeping.
> Quietness all around.
> Dark shadows flow over the fields,

The village sleeps.
The moon lies hidden in a somber cloud,
And there are no stars save one,
Glowing with sudden brightness.
There is a small lamp on the porch,
And now the whole family has come together,
All of us very serious, plunged in our books,
In an austere silence; only the eyelids
Of our beloved Maria are heavy with sleep,
While the unceasing swarm
Of gnats and moon-moths
Coming out of the dark
Play around the lamp.
Warmed by the lamplight,
They believe they have returned
To the heat of summer.

Such poems, of course, were written by young women all over
Russia, and Anna never had the makings of a poet. Yet these verses
tell us some things we want to know. For example, they tell us of the
influence of the German poet Heine, whom Anna is consciously imitating, and how much they hated the coming of winter on the estate.
Seen through her eyes, those deadly serious children and adolescents
take on a German look, their austerity and quietness interrupted only
by a rustling sound as they turn the pages of their books. No Russian
children would behave with quite that solemnity. Consciously or unconsciously Maria Alexandrovna, German to the core, was subtly in-
fluencing her children.

When they were living in Simbirsk the children had always spent
the summer at Kokushkino, returning to the town when the leaves
were falling. The familiar pattern was now repeated. They had decided to stay on the estate during the summer and to spend their
winters in Samara. In much the same way, the princely owners of
great estates would spend the summer in the country, returning to
Moscow or St. Petersburg for the winter season.

A large apartment on Voskresenskaya Street was found for them,
and the entire family trooped into the town, leaving Alakayevka to a
steward. Elizarov had friends in Samara, a surprisingly large number
of them possessing a clandestine interest in social revolution. They
were watched by the police, but they were not under strict surveillance. In Samara, for the first time, Vladimir took an active part in
revolutionary circles.

There remained the question of his livelihood, a question never very far from his mother's thoughts. He had proved to be incompetent as the manager of an estate. He had set his heart on becoming a lawyer, and he knew that in special cases students were permitted to sit for the examination without attending classes at the university. In October he wrote to the Minister of Public Instruction, pleading to be allowed to sit for the examination "at any institute of higher learning." He said that without a university degree it was impossible for him to follow any profession and thereby support his family "consisting of an aged mother and a brother and sister of tender years." His mother was scarcely "aged"; she was fifty-two, and she had nearly thirty years more to live. Nor was the humble petition any more successful than the others. He seemed to be destined to spend his years among his books, a perpetual student lost in some backwater of the provinces, with no regular income and no hope of advancement. There were hundreds of these perpetual students in Russia. Vladimir was determined not to become one of them.

The following May, Maria Alexandrovna took the matter into her own hands by appealing "as a widow and a mother" to the Minister himself. She listed the services rendered to his country by her late husband and spoke of "how painful it was to see my son wasting the best years of his life without being able to make use of them." This time the Minister relented, and permission was granted for him to take the examination at any university of his choice. Vladimir wrote to thank the Minister, asked to be examined at the University of St. Petersburg, and signed the letter: Dvoryanin Vladimir Ulyanov. *Dvoryanin* means "nobleman." He was perfectly within his rights in employing his title. In his letter to the Minister he used the title twice, once at the top, and then at the bottom. Similarly his letters to his mother always bore the address *To Her Excellency M. A. Ulyanova.* He was a member of the nobility by hereditary descent from his father, and for this reason his appeals and requests were placed directly in the hands of the Minister.

At once he threw himself into work. Nothing mattered except to pass the examination with honors. Olga, too, was in the throes of preparing for her entrance examination at the University of Helsingfors, where she hoped to enter the faculty of medicine. She was a brilliant student. Like Alexander and Vladimir she received the coveted gold medal when she left the *gymnasium*. She tempered her book learning with gaiety, and tempered her gaiety with a deep sense of social purpose: she had decided to be a doctor in order to serve the poor. When she discovered that she would have to learn Finnish to enter the University of Helsingfors, she abandoned the attempt. Women were not yet permitted to take courses in medicine in Russia. She decided to be a teacher instead of a doctor, and registered at the Bestuzhev School in St. Petersburg for courses in physics and mathematics. She was already ill from overwork when she reached St. Petersburg, and in the spring of 1891 she caught typhoid fever. At the time, Vladimir was in St. Petersburg, attending to his examinations. He took her to a hospital, complaining bitterly that the hospital was so filthy that it was unlikely she would be cured there. Typhoid was complicated by a streptococcus infection. She was already dying when Vladimir sent the telegram to his mother announcing her illness; and Maria Alexandrovna reached St. Petersburg just in time to see her daughter die. Olga died on May 8, exactly four years to the day after the execution of Alexander.

Of the seven children of Maria Alexandrovna three were now dead. In her lifetime no more were to die.

The death of Olga was a blow from which she never completely recovered. It often happens in large families that there is one superbly gifted and handsome child, who is quietly adored and worshiped by the rest. They feel quite naturally, without envy, that this child has received superior gifts and that they must live out their lives in his shade. The Ulyanov family was remarkable in having two such children. The calm and dedicated Alexander, the quick and eager Olga were made of some rare metal which seemed to have been denied to the others. Anna, Maria and Dmitry possessed commonplace minds; and it was said of Vladimir that he would pass unnoticed through the bazaars of Astrakhan or any town along the Volga, so much did he resemble all the other youths who lived on the river bank. But more than any one else in the family, he possessed a relentless and undeviating will.

By sheer will power he forced himself to study law to such effect that when he took his final examination in November 1891, he passed first among a hundred and twenty-four. Except for the ten weeks he had spent at the University of Kazan, he was completely self-taught. Learning law through books, he was deprived of the benefits of discussion with professors. He knew the facts; he did not always know the reason behind the facts, and like many self-taught men he thought he knew more than he knew. When he returned to Samara to take up the practice of law, he proved to be a remarkably poor advocate.

All the court cases in which Vladimir took part only proved that he had no flair as a defense attorney. He defended eight or nine peasants and workers, and all were found guilty. He was more successful as a prosecuting attorney.

Somewhere among the dusty files of the Syzran law court there may still be the documents relating to the case *Ulyanov v. Arefyev*. These documents have never been published, but Vladimir's brother Dmitry has described the affair at some length in his memoirs. It seems that in the summer of 1882 Vladimir and his brother-in-law Mark Elizarov were paying a short visit to Mark's rich brother, a peasant proprietor living in the village of Bestuzhevka, not far from Syzran. To reach the village, it was necessary to cross the Volga. The right to ferry passengers belonged to the merchant Arefyev, who owned a small steamer and a barge for ferrying horse carts and cattle. Vladimir refused to take the steamer and persuaded a boatman to ferry them over. Arefyev himself was sitting on the pier beside his samovar, and recognizing Mark Elizarov, he shouted cheerfully, "You had better stop all this, Mark Timofeyich. I'm paying rent for running the ferry and won't allow boatmen to take passengers across. So come up and have tea with me instead, and bring your friend with you. You will have to cross in my steamer anyway, because I am sending orders to have your boat turned back."

Arefyev had paid good money to the local government for the right to ferry passengers across the river, but there was a law making it illegal to obstruct passengers as they went about their lawful affairs; and Vladimir knew his law. He urged the boatman to continue rowing them across the river. When they were in midstream, the steamer overtook them and threw down grappling hooks. Vladimir made a list of the names of all the members of the crew and warned them that they were all guilty of obstructing his lawful passage across the river and if brought to trial they would receive sentences of imprisonment without the option of a fine. There followed a long and exhausting lawsuit, which Vladimir prosecuted relentlessly, periodically making the seventy-mile journey from Samara to Syzran to attend the *zemstvo* court, while Arefyev's counsel employed all the delaying tactics possible, and even Maria Alexandrovna grew weary of her son's stubbornness, asking what there was to gain in this strange lawsuit which was ruining his health and temper. Vladimir made it clear that he was prepared to make any sacrifices to secure his rights. About a year later he had the satisfaction of seeing Arefyev sentenced to one month's imprisonment.

His weakness as a defense attorney and his successful and relentless attack on Arefyev were characteristic of the man. So, too, was his attitude toward the famine which swept through the Volga region in the lean years 1891–92. All over Russia relief committees were set up, soup kitchens were opened, special trains were run to bring food to the starving peasants. The example of Tolstoy and Chekhov, who threw themselves wholeheartedly into bringing relief to the distressed areas, was followed by thousands of others. In Samara everyone who could possibly afford it contributed to the relief measures. Only Vladimir and one other political exile in Samara refused to have anything to do with the soup kitchens or the relief committees. His view—with which Nechayev would have sympathized—was that every calamity which fell on Russia should be regarded as a blessing because it hastened the day of the revolution. It was a peculiarly bleak and cold philosophy, and he held to it with astonishing tenacity.

The famine passed, the grain ripened again, and he was still a fledgling assistant to an established lawyer in a provincial town where boredom grew like clusters of weeds in stony soil. To stay in Samara for the rest of his life was simply to submit to slow suffocation. Month after month he stayed on because his mother needed him, because his younger brother and sister were still in school and wanted a substitute father, and because he still hoped to make a name for himself as a lawyer. More and more he became immersed in revolutionary literature. Fedoseyev's revolutionary essays were being surreptitiously circulated in manuscript, and copies of *The Communist Manifesto* and *Das Kapital* were being eagerly read by political exiles. But Samara was not a place where revolutionaries could put down roots. Vladimir decided to take his chances in St. Petersburg.

In November 1892 there appeared in the magazine *Russkaya Mysl* a short story by Chekhov called "Ward No. 6." It is one of the most somber and powerful of Chekhov's stories, and Vladimir read it shortly after it appeared. The story describes a hospital in a remote town in Russia, a hundred and fifty miles from the nearest railroad station. The local postmaster lives on his memories, dreaming of the days when he was a cavalry officer in the Caucasus. The doctor dreams of the day when he will once more be able to find someone he can talk to on his own intellectual level. Every night until three o'clock in the morning he sits up reading, and every half hour he pours out a shot of vodka and chews on a cucumber. He is a patient, kindly, incompetent man; he knows he is running the hospital badly, but there is little he can do about it. One day he falls into a conversation with one of the patients in the ward reserved for lunatics. This patient, Ivan Gromov, was well-born and well-educated, a former court usher and provincial secretary. His brother had died, and this death was the forerunner of a series of catastrophes affecting the family. His father, a completely upright man with his own house on the principal street of the town, was brought to trial on a trumped-up charge of misappropriating funds and died shortly after, leaving Ivan the sole support of his mother. Now he was in Ward No. 6, suffering from persecution mania, completely mad, making continual convulsive movements, and hiding from the world. Sometimes he is heard saying, "I am afraid of going mad. I want terribly to live!"

To Ivan Gromov comes the shabby old doctor, whose only interest is to discover someone with whom he can discuss higher things. So they talk together, the doctor and the madman, discussing the nature of man's pilgrimage through the world, and reducing all things to cosmic significance. "You see a peasant beating his wife," says the madman. "Why interfere? They will both die sooner or later." He celebrates the Stoics who advocate indifference to wealth and a contempt for suffering and death. Together they celebrate the infinite vanity of all things, and slowly the doctor loses his reason, sucked into the vortex of madness until at last he becomes a permanent resident of Ward No. 6. When he shakes the bars, the guard kicks him into insensibility. He dies in agony after dreaming of a herd of graceful deer, which he had read about in a book the day before.

Vladimir read the story late at night, when everyone had gone to bed. He felt the story had been written for him. It terrified him, and he wanted to share his terror with someone, but he dared not wake anyone. His dead brother, his dead father, the hospital where Olga died, the appalling bleakness of life in the provinces, the sense of the nothingness of existence and the ultimate valuelessness of human life —all these things weighed heavily on him. "I was absolutely terrified when I read the story," he said the next morning. "I couldn't remain in my room any longer. I simply had to get up and go out. I had the feeling that I myself was shut up in Ward No. 6!"

This same feeling would recur at intervals in his life. That core of nihilism sometimes sustained him, giving him the courage to pursue the most audacious and senseless experiments, but it also sapped at his vitality, creating within him a vacuum in which all values were equated with zero, in the classic equation: $0 = 0$. His nihilism did not derive from Chekhov's story. It was in the air he breathed, in the slow corruptions of provincial life, in Nechayev's *Revolutionary Catechism*, and in his own failure as an advocate. To the end of his life he was a man tormented by the nothingness of existence.

For another eight or nine months he remained in Samara because his mother wanted it. Then at last, at the age of twenty-three, he broke the umbilical cord and set out for St. Petersburg, where his real life as a revolutionary began.

THE CONSPIRATOR

ST. PETERSBURG in the early Nineties of the last century was a city groping its way back into sanity. The Eighties, which opened with the assassination of Alexander II, were a period of bleak reaction when life seemed to move at a snail's pace and nothing was accomplished. "When I look back at the Eighties," the historian Pokrovsky remarked, "it seems to me that there was nothing but a yawning chasm." Now once again the reaction was being tamed, and the lifeblood was flowing through the city. Industry was booming. The peasants were streaming into the towns to take up work in the shops and factories. The national income was soaring. It was not perhaps a very good time for starting a revolution.

Vladimir arrived in St. Petersburg with a handful of books, his father's top hat and frock coat, and his mother's promise of moderate support from the income arising from the Alakayevka estate. A friend in Samara had arranged for him to work in the office of a St. Petersburg lawyer called Volkenstein, but such work was not likely to be very remunerative. He found a lodginghouse where he could live for fifteen rubles a month. He worked in the law office by day, but every night was devoted to revolutionary affairs.

The charming adolescent who appears on the photograph taken when he was entering Kazan University had in the space of six years given place to a man who appeared twice as old. He was almost completely bald, there were deep lines on his narrow face, and he wore a carefully trimmed beard and mustache. In revolutionary circles in St. Petersburg he was known by the name of Nikolay Petrovich; more

93

commonly he was addressed as *Starik,* meaning "the old man." Already he had the gravity of a middle-aged person, and he spoke with the authority of one who had spent a lifetime in revolutionary affairs. He was twenty-three years old.

Marxist study groups were already in existence in St. Petersburg. They were to be found especially among young lawyers, and long articles of an impressive subtlety and scholarship were being written on Marxism in the *Yuridichesky Vestnik* (The Legal Herald), but there was no concerted effort to attract the workers. Here and there a few workmen gathered together to take instruction from a student of Marxism. In those early days Vladimir's chief contribution was to insist that no advance could be made until the workers themselves were thoroughly saturated with revolutionary ideas and the theoreticians were thoroughly saturated with the habits and tastes and modes of thought of the working classes. The dialogue between theory and practice must be maintained.

In the first months he made little progress. He was feeling his way, establishing contacts, studying and writing. As he confessed to Nadezhda Krupskaya a few months later, he was spending most of his free time pounding the streets in search of Marxists, and rarely finding them. For a young intellectual to be seen in the company of workmen was to court danger, for police spies were everywhere. He would throw on a workman's cap and a shabby overcoat, and wander through the desolate working class districts of the Petersburg Side and Vasilyevsky Island, interrogating anyone who would permit himself to be interrogated, asking all manner of questions about the cost of living and labor contracts and under what conditions the workmen would strike; and all this information would be carefully entered into his notebooks. He may have known that he was already being watched by the police.

At this time Maria Alexandrovna was living in Moscow with the younger children, having abandoned Samara and the life of the provinces so that Maria and Dmitry should have a better education. Vladimir spent the winter holidays with them, and one evening in January he attended a student meeting which was being addressed by Vasily Vorontsov, a medical doctor who had some claim to fame as the author of a book called *The Destiny of Capitalism in Russia.* He belonged to that remnant of the Narodnaya Volya party which was called "Land and Freedom," and he was all for the overthrow of capitalism before it struck deep roots in Russia. Like Chernyshevsky, he envisioned a kind of peasant paradise in which all large-scale industries were abolished. It was his constant complaint that the peasants coming to Moscow and St. Petersburg were being melted down in the Satanic mills. Like Marx, but for different reasons, he wanted to overthrow the existing order and bring about the ideal state.

Vladimir had been given a ticket for the meeting at the last moment by a girl who had known him in Samara. The meeting took place in a three-room apartment on Bronnaya Street and was deliberately designed to bring together the different revolutionary groups opposing the government. Victor Chernov, later to become a leading member of the Socialist Revolutionary Party, was among the guests, and years later he remembered someone whispering to him, "Look at that young bald fellow over there; he's a very remarkable person, and something of a big wheel among Marxists in Petersburg." The young bald fellow was Vladimir, who had taken up a position just outside the main room where the speakers of the evening were gathered.

Vorontsov, the chief speaker, known affectionately as "V.V.," was regarded with deep respect by the students, who had read his book and were inclined to regard him as a prophet. He was middle-aged, thickset and corpulent; he, too, was bald and like Vladimir sported a red beard. Vladimir had studied his books and had written in Samara a pamphlet attacking them.

When Vorontsov rose to speak, the audience was hushed; they regarded him with the deference due to a man who was not merely the speaker of the evening, but a legend, a man who incarnated the revolutionary tradition of Russia. For some reason, perhaps because he was partly deaf, Vladimir failed to catch the name of the speaker. He listened attentively, took notes, and when the speaker had finished, he launched into a withering attack on the Narodnaya Volya and all the arguments advanced in its defense. Victor Chernov remembered that it was an unusually vehement and destructive onslaught, delivered with conscious superiority, well argued and without malice, and the gutter words which Vladimir later incorporated in his speeches were notably absent. When he sat down there were murmurs of approval from the audience.

Vorontsov listened to the speech with mounting fury. He realized that his authority as a revolutionary was being questioned and he must fight back.

"You have offered no proof to any of your arguments," he declared. "Your statements are quite gratuitous. Show us, if you can, your basis for making these baseless statements. Submit an analysis of your facts and figures. I have the authority to demand these proofs from you. My authority rests on my published works, and may I ask what published works have come from your pen?"

Vorontsov was no longer arguing. He was simply giving way to injured innocence. Vladimir replied, more self-assured than ever now that he knew the older man was at his mercy, cutting across Vorontsov's arguments with the sharp edge of his mockery. The battle royal kept the students on the edge of their seats until at last it degenerated into name calling; then it was abruptly terminated.

Some moments later Vladimir turned to the girl who had accompanied him and said, "What is the name of the fellow I have been arguing with?"

"Vorontsov, of course. He's mad at you!"

"Vorontsov? Why didn't you tell me earlier? If I had known, I would never have debated with him!"

Such was the story told by Maria Golubeva, his friend from Samara, and it is not entirely necessary to believe that Vladimir did not know the name of the speaker. It was his first appearance in a public debate outside the small debating society he attended in Samara, and he was perfectly aware of the impact he had created. The secret police were also aware of it, for a report dated January 20, 1894, was found forty years later in the official archives testifying that "a certain Ulyanov (almost certainly the brother of the Ulyanov who was hanged) made a spirited attack against the writer V.V."

Vladimir returned to St. Petersburg, wearing the laurels of his victory over Vorontsov. He was now a marked man, one to be sought after and invited to all the gatherings of Marxist revolutionaries. So it happened that on Shrove Tuesday he found himself at a party attended by most of the leading Petersburg Marxists, who had been invited to meet him. Once again his sharp tongue was in evidence. They were talking about the important tasks facing Marxists in Russia, and someone suggested that the Committee of Literacy was especially worthy of support. Vladimir replied scornfully, "If anyone wants to save the country by working for that committee, let him go ahead!"

Among those who were present at the party was a short, delicate-featured young woman called Nadezhda Konstantinovna Krupskaya. She had a marble-white skin, a broad forehead, full lips, a smoothly rounded chin. It was a face which might have belonged to one of Chekhov's heroines, with its look of youthful daring, responsibility and gentleness. She dressed in somber black and wore her hair brushed sternly back from her forehead, but though she tried to imitate the other women of her time who devoted themselves to revolutionary work and lost their femininity in their driving determination to sacrifice themselves for the revolution, she remained wholly feminine. In time she was to become fat and ungainly, but in those early years she possessed a quiet beauty.

Like Vladimir, she came from the gentry. Both her parents belonged to the nobility; neither had inherited an estate. Her father may have been descended from Prince Andrey Kurbsky, the famous boyar who courageously attacked Ivan the Terrible, for the coats of arms of the Krupsky and Kurbsky families are notably similar. As a very young officer her father had been sent to put down the Polish insurrection of 1863. Unlike the majority of Russians who took part in that savage punitive expedition, he developed a lifelong fondness for the Poles, and he eagerly accepted the post of military governor of a district in Poland when it was offered to him. He was a liberal who detested cruelty in any form; as military governor he shielded the population from the ruthless policy of Russification then being enforced by Alexander II. He forbade the hounding of Jews and the infliction of arbitrary punishment on the Poles. He built a hospital and a school. The population worshiped him; but a general, visiting the district on a tour of inspection, found him too sympathetic to the Poles and ordered his arrest. He was brought to trial on the charges of speaking Polish and of not attending church. There were appeals and counter-appeals. The trumped-up charges were debated in the courts for ten years, while the family sank deeper and deeper into poverty. Nadezhda's father became an insurance agent, a clerk, a factory inspector, always wandering from city to city. He died when she was thirteen or fourteen. He had been vindicated by the courts before his death, but he left his family in debt and poverty.

At fourteen Nadezhda was already helping to support the family by giving lessons to the neighboring children. She took evening courses at the *gymnasium* and spent the rest of the day teaching, or helping her mother with the boarders, or writing out envelopes for business firms. (Nearly a quarter of a century after her meeting with Vladimir she was still writing addresses on envelopes, in Switzerland, to make ends meet.) Her mother's small widow's pension was not enough to keep them alive.

During the years of her adolescence she was oppressed by the sense of society's failure to help the poor. She was twenty-one when she first realized that men and women had been questioning the bases of society for centuries; and she studied textbooks on the social sciences. It occurred to her that if the workers could read these books, they would soon improve their working conditions, and she therefore regarded the Committee of Literacy, which had been brought into existence by a group of philanthropists, with especial favor. For two years she had been a member of a Marxist study circle. When she met Vladimir and heard him scornfully attacking the committee, she was shocked and at the same time strangely moved; perhaps, after all, there were sharper weapons which could be used to change the existing social system.

In the course of the following months she saw more of him. Once while they were walking along the banks of the Neva he told her about his dead brother Alexander, and about the last summer they spent together, and how Alexander would rise with the first light to peer at worms under a microscope. "I never thought he would become a revolutionary," he told her. "A revolutionary doesn't give himself up to the study of worms!" Vladimir took to spending more and more time with her. He valued her knowledge of the working class, her understanding and sympathy for the oppressed, and she in turn valued his incisive judgments and soaring ambition. Over him she threw the mantle of her maternal protection; and since she was never capable of disputing with him on doctrinal matters, but simply served him faithfully and obediently, endlessly performing chores for him, writing his letters and coding and decoding secret messages, the relationship remained quietly affectionate to the end.

Meanwhile the organization of the study circles continued. It was difficult work, and sometimes dangerous. Vladimir lived in an apartment on Kazachy Street not far from the Fontanka Canal and fifteen minutes' walk from the heart of the city. To reach a worker's apartment he would usually take a roundabout route to shake off any police spies. A dockworker, Vladimir Kniazev, remembered how Vladimir attended these study meetings in appropriate disguise, wearing a cap drawn over his eyes and his coat collar turned up to hide the lower part of his face. He remembered, too, that Vladimir, whom he knew as Nikolay Petrovich, wore an autumn coat even in the heat of summer. The first time they met the following conversation took place:

"Are you Kniazev?"

"Yes."

"I'm Nikolay Petrovich. I'm late. I had to go a long way round. Well, is everyone ready?"

But the visitor resembled a headmaster rather than a conspirator; he asked precise questions and expected precise replies; he encouraged those who were backward and castigated those whose answers came too easily. He seemed to know everything, and there was something even intimidating in his calm self-assurance. Kniazev describes one of those meetings:

> When he bade good evening to the workers, he took his place and explained the reason which had brought us together, and the program to be followed. He spoke seriously, precisely, carefully reflecting on each word; he spoke as though he admitted no counterarguments. The workers listened attentively and answered his questions about their work, the factories, labor conditions, their comrades, what interested them most and what they read and whether they were capable of understanding and assimilating socialist ideas, and so on.
>
> The principal idea of Nikolay Petrovich, as we understood it, was that the working class was not sufficiently conscious of its own interests and did not yet know how to make profitable use of its potentialities. Workmen failed to realize that once they were united, they could break through all the obstacles placed in their path. By continually developing their knowledge, they could improve their situation and ultimately free themselves from slavery.
>
> Nikolay Petrovich spoke for more than two hours. He was easy to listen to, for he explained everything precisely and simply. Comparing his talk with those of other intellectuals we knew, we came to the conclusion that he was altogether different because more convincing; and when he left us after arranging the date of the next meeting, the comrades turned to one another and said, "Well, there's a fellow who knows what he is talking about."

So Nikolay Petrovich went about his secret journeys, establishing cells of six workers, addressing them, saturating himself in their problems—as mysterious a figure as Nechayev, who also used the name Petrovich—and Kniazev might never have known his name except for the fact that his mother died and left him a small legacy, and when he asked for the name of a lawyer who would help him to collect the legacy, he was told of a certain V. Ulyanov who for some reason wanted his address to be kept secret. The address was Apartment 13, at 7 Kazachy Street. Kniazev was told to commit the address to memory. He set out to find the lawyer, rang the bell, and was told that Mr. Ulyanov had not yet returned, though he was expected shortly;

meanwhile why not wait for him in his apartment? It was a small apartment: an iron bed, a bureau, a chest of drawers, three or four chairs, nothing more. He had not long to wait. Soon the lawyer came in and threw off his overcoat, saying, "Ah, so you've been waiting. Wait a moment while I change." He vanished into another room, and the dockworker suddenly realized that Nikolay Petrovich and V. Ulyanov were the same person. Kniazev gives a characteristic portrait of the young Petersburg lawyer:

> While I was still collecting my wits Nikolay Petrovich reappeared, wearing another suit of clothes. He led me to a chair and said, "Tell me everything, but in the proper order!" I sat down and told him about the affair as well as I could. From time to time he interrupted me, asked for more precise details, drew out of me significant facts which I would otherwise not have mentioned. When he heard that my grandmother died in the service of a general, and that the general was in a position to lay claim to her effects even though he possessed a two-story brick house of his own, Nikolay Petrovich rubbed his hands together and said, stressing each word, "Excellent! If we win, we'll take possession of the house. There is only one difficulty, and that is that it is going to be hard to get hold of a list of all the members of your family, inasmuch as your late grandmother was born to serfs."
>
> Then he reached for a sheet of paper and drew up an official request to permit me to see the census reports, and explained where I should go and to whom I should make application, and asked me to return as soon as I had found the information.
>
> "And now," he said, "let us pass to other matters. What's happening in the study circles? What's happening in the factories?"

Vladimir Kniazev was a workman who never played a great revolutionary role. Ivan Babushkin was a revolutionary in his own right, a man of extraordinary resourcefulness who spent many years transporting illegal documents across the frontier, and was finally shot by order of General Rennenkampf when he was discovered rushing a trainload of arms to Chita, in Siberia, where a Soviet of Workers and Soldiers Deputies had been created following the Moscow insurrection of December 1905. Babushkin was working at the Kronstadt Naval Base when he joined a study circle. He too came in contact with Nikolay Petrovich. "He never consulted any notes," Babushkin said, "and he was continually pausing to provoke us to speak or start an argument, and if we answered he would always make us justify our positions. These conversations were always lively and interesting, and of course they accustomed us to speaking in public. We were always amazed by the learning of the lecturer. We used to say among ourselves that he had such big brains that they had pushed his hair out." Babushkin complained that Nikolay Petrovich set him so many tasks to do that he had almost no time to do his own work, and his toolbox was full of little notes about wages and working conditions to be reported to the lecturer.

Vladimir was, in fact, making a survey in depth of industrial conditions in St. Petersburg; and all the facts garnered from the workers were grist to his mill. He was compiling vast statistical systems to be used later when he wrote his first full-length work, *The Development of Capitalism in Russia*. Meanwhile he wrote pamphlets, the most important of them being a hundred-page essay written in reply to an attack on Marxism in the magazine *Russkoye Bogatstvo* (Russian Wealth). This first pamphlet, like his last, followed a form which was to become familiar. He begins by accusing the adversary of misunderstanding Marx and deliberately distorting Marxist doctrine; he then examines selected passages from the offending work and, after worrying them like a dog chewing on a rag, he shows how implausible and ridiculous are their pretensions. Finally, he makes his own selection of passages from Marx's writings and describes what he conceives to be the pure doctrine of Marxism. The destruction of the adversary is accompanied by a heavy Germanic ill humor, special pleading, and considerable distortion of the evidence. Sarcasm is one of the principal weapons. It is not a weapon which commends itself often to Russians; nor, in his hands, is it always effective. Too often we are made aware of the lion licking his chops as he is about to tear an inoffensive animal apart. The title of the pamphlet, directed against men like Vorontsov, was *What the "Friends of the People" Are and How They Fight against the Social Democrats*.

"Scratch a 'Friend of the People' and you will find a bourgeois," he writes; and the pamphlet may be regarded as a prolonged attack upon the bourgeois and upon the peasants, who are, according to the author, merely bourgeois in disguise. Those who think otherwise "are throwing out the meat from the egg and playing with the shell." Their arguments are "filthy," and their opinions "childish." They are so despicable that it is scarcely worth arguing with them. So he writes, while arguing with them bitterly, coming to the conclusion that the argument is worthwhile only because it offers useful lessons to Russian socialists. As for the bourgeois, they are double-faced, progressive and reactionary at once, demanding an end to all the medieval tyrannies which continued to plague Russia, while seeking to preserve their own position of domination; and while attacking the bourgeois, he reserves his most bitter denunciations for the bureaucracy, which is roundly described as "a pack of little Judases" who conceal their vast designs "behind the fig leaves of little phrases about loving the people." He writes:

> The workers must know that unless these pillars of reaction are overthrown, it will be completely impossible for them to wage a successful struggle against the bourgeoisie, because so long as they exist, the Russian rural proletariat, whose support is an essential condition for the victory of the working class, will never cease to be downtrodden and cowed, capable only of sullen desperation and not of intelligent and persistent protest and struggle.

By the "rural proletariat" he means the landless peasants, and the dream of an alliance between the workers and these disfranchised peasants was to pursue him for many years.

What the "Friends of the People" Are and How They Fight against the Social Democrats is an extremely important document in the development of Russian Communism, but the attacks on the "Friends of the People" are the least satisfactory part of it. The document is most powerful when argument is abandoned for statements delivered ex cathedra, with a passionate conviction in their truth and certainty. At such moments the twenty-four-year-old author takes on the role of a prophet, seeing far beyond the confines of Russia to a world where there will be no nobility, no bureaucracy and no bourgeois, and all the unnumbered millions on the earth will follow the Russian proletariat to bring about a world-wide revolution. In the final passage of the pamphlet, to which he attached great importance, he devised different arrangements of type to underline the significance of his message. The peroration reads:

> Accordingly, it is on the working class that the
> Social Democrats concentrate all their attention and all
> their energy. When its advanced representatives have
> appropriated and mastered the ideas of scientific social-
> ism, the idea of the historic mission of the Russian workers,
> and when these ideas have become widespread, and when
> enduring organizations have been established among the
> workers, transforming the present sporadic economic
> struggle for the workers into conscious class warfare,—

then the Russian WORKER, having placed himself at the
head of all the democratic elements, will overthrow
absolutism and lead THE RUSSIAN PROLETARIAT (side by
side with the proletariat OF ALL COUNTRIES) a l o n g
t h e   s t r a i g h t   r o a d   o f   o p e n
p o l i t i c a l   s t r u g g l e   t o   t h e   VICTORIOUS
COMMUNIST REVOLUTION

ванную борьбу. На классъ рабочихъ и обращаютъ соціалъ-демокра-
ты все свое вниманіе и всю свою дѣятельность. Когда передо-
вые представители его усвоятъ идеи научнаго соціализма, идею
объ исторической роли русскаго рабочаго, когда эти идеи полу-
чатъ широкое распространеніе и среди рабочихъ создадутся проч-
ныя организаціи, преобразующія теперешнюю разрозненную экономичес-
кую войну рабочихъ въ сознательную классовую борьбу, - тогда
русскій Р А Б О Ч І Й, поднявшись во главѣ всѣхъ демократичес-
кихъ элементовъ, свалитъ абсолютизмъ и поведетъ Р У С С К І Й
П Р О Л Е Т А Р І А Т Ъ (рядомъ съ Пролетаріатомъ В С Ѣ Х Ъ
С Т Р А Н Ъ) п р я м о й д о р о г о й о т к р ы т о й п о -
л и т и ч е с к о й б о р ь б ы к ъ П О Б Ѣ Д О Н О С Н О Й

К О М М У Н И С Т И Ч Е С К О Й Р Е В О Л Ю Ц І И.

Once written, the pamphlet was regarded as having sufficient importance to deserve printing, and a young engineer, Alexey Ganchin,
was instructed to set up a printing press. He knew a printer who lived
in Yuryev-Polski a hundred miles to the northwest of Moscow, and
went off hopefully to help set the type, but after protracted negotiations nothing came of the venture. Finally he bought a typewriter and
a lithographic stone, and with the help of friends he succeeded very
slowly in producing a few copies. He began work in June. It was November before the final copies on yellow paper were distributed secretly in Moscow.

Winter was the time for agitation, the time when the study circles
gathered momentum and more and more workers were caught in the
secret web. Previously Vladimir had been something of an amateur
revolutionary; now he became a professional, living only for the work
of winning disciples to his cause. He was continually building up contacts, devising secret codes, inventing new stratagems to outwit the
police spies. He knew all the short cuts in the workers' districts, and
the shadowy roads where the police dared not enter. The groups of

six members, each group forming a study circle and a close-knit committee for agitating among the workers, were kept separate from one another; only Vladimir knew them all. If he was arrested, the secret organization of workers' groups would fall apart. It was decided therefore to appoint a "successor": the choice fell on Krupskaya who, though an active revolutionary, was never followed by the police.

The organization of the St. Petersburg study circles followed closely on the lines laid down by the old Narodnaya Volya. Vladimir deliberately modeled himself on Alexander Mikhailov, the close friend of Zhelyabov, who was constantly inventing new techniques of secrecy. Vladimir ordered that all messages, of whatever kind, should be sent in code, or in invisible ink, or in books where words or letters were marked with penciled dots. Once Krupskaya and others undertook to translate a whole book into code, with unfortunate results. They had translated half the book when they decided to see whether they could translate it back again into ordinary Russian; they failed.

For printing or hectographing revolutionary pamphlets, for building up libraries of books, and for occasional bribes to the police, large sums of money had to be found. During his two years in St. Petersburg, Vladimir relied largely on the financial support of Alexandra Kalmykova, a woman of wealth married to a high official in the government, who despised her own class and threw herself into the revolutionary struggle. She opened a bookshop on the Liteiny, one of the principal streets of St. Petersburg, and built up a small publishing empire distributing cheap books for the masses. Like Krupskaya, who was her close friend, she gave lectures to the workers. On all matters connected with printing illegal literature Alexandra Kalmykova could be relied upon for help. The first struggle—the struggle for printing presses and the means to provide an unending stream of illegal literature—seemed to be over in the early spring of 1895. The time had come to strengthen the foundations of the party.

In the spring Vladimir could look back on an exhausting year and a half spent in building up a tenuous web of secret study circles. He had tramped through countless streets, met countless workers, slipped out of the nets of countless police spies, and he knew as much as any intellectual knew about the mood of industrial St. Petersburg. Suddenly in March he fell ill. The illness was sufficiently serious to bring his mother up from Moscow to his bedside. It was pneumonia. He rallied quickly, but he was too weak to take an active part in conspiratorial affairs. He had been planning a trip abroad to confer with

Plekhanov and Axelrod, the two exiled leaders of the Social Democratic Party who were living in Switzerland. A passport, dated March 15, was already in his possession, but he did not leave Russia until April 25. Thin, pale, suffering from some undiagnosed stomach trouble and not completely recovered from the effects of pneumonia, he took the train to Berlin, and so by way of Salzburg to Switzerland.

At Salzburg, where he changed trains, he wrote a letter to his mother complaining with a kind of amused tolerance that whenever he tried to speak German on the train no one could understand him, and he understood the Germans "with the greatest difficulty, or rather I don't understand them one little bit." He had trouble understanding the simplest words. He tried to say something to the conductor, but the conductor obviously understood nothing at all and began shouting, growing more and more angry with the strange red-bearded passenger who seemed to be talking some incomprehensible foreign language. Then he was gone, and Vladimir was left to reflect that the important thing was not to lose courage but to go on trying to talk German even though it meant assiduously distorting the language.

In Geneva he met Plekhanov, who twelve years before had founded with Axelrod and Vera Zasulich the "Group for the Emancipation of Labor," which aimed through the publication of books and pamphlets to arouse a conscious working-class movement in Russia. Plekhanov himself belonged to the nobility, but as a very young man he had thrown himself into the struggle on behalf of the workingmen in St. Petersburg. He was completely fearless. He made fiery speeches against the Tsar's government. He led demonstrations. He was always in the forefront, but for some reason the police were never able to get their hands on him. In 1880, at the age of twenty-three, he was forced to leave Russia, having already led a full revolutionary life. Tall and elegant, always impeccably dressed, with a pointed black beard and sweeping mustaches, he spent his time writing books on the nature of socialism in a villa overlooking the lake.

Though Plekhanov was the high priest of Russian Marxism, and all the young Marxist revolutionaries looked up to him, he had long ago lost any effective control of the revolutionary movement. The Group for the Emancipation of Labor existed in a kind of limbo, with Plekhanov speaking and writing as though he were drawing up the preliminary blueprints for a revolution to take place in a hundred years. Vladimir found him cold and distant, though courteous and well-disposed. Plekhanov read some of the articles Vladimir had written, uncomfortably aware of their violence. Reading one of these articles he said, "You show the bourgeois your behind!" and then he added, "We, on the contrary, look them in the face." It was a just rebuke. For the rest of his life Plekhanov was to be troubled by the raw violence and venomous passion which filled so many of Vladimir's articles.

Axelrod was made of coarser material than Plekhanov. This was at once apparent in their appearance: Plekhanov carrying about with him an air of refinement, Axelrod resembling a shaggy bear. Plekhanov was reserved, Axelrod quivered with excitement. On intellectual matters they were in agreement, but in all other matters they were at poles apart. When Vladimir reached Zurich the day after his meeting with Plekhanov, Axelrod greeted him like a long-lost brother. They talked late into the night, resumed their conversation the next morning, and went on talking for three or four days. As usual there were Russian police spies in Zurich. Axelrod suggested they should go into the country and continue their discussions unmolested by the attentions of the spies. For a week they wandered among the hills, endlessly debating the coming revolution in Russia, which seemed to grow closer and more desirable the more they debated it. On one subject Axelrod was firm. In all his articles Vladimir poured scorn on the liberals. Axelrod, whose roots were deep in the Narodnaya Volya, insisted that there must be a common front of all revolutionary parties, in the common need to overthrow the autocracy. Nothing was to be gained by relentlessly reviling the other parties who were also aiming to make Russia a socialist state. Vladimir professed to be convinced by the force of the argument, though with secret reservations. He had no reservations however in agreeing with Axelrod's suggestion that the study circles should be organized into an active political party. It was also agreed to publish a political magazine to include articles written inside Russia and smuggled out. Finally Vladimir agreed to try to seek funds to support the exiled revolutionaries. They parted on the best of terms. Axelrod was particularly impressed by Vladimir's courtesy and fair-mindedness.

From Zurich, Vladimir went on to Paris. He was amazed by the size of the city, the wide, well-lighted streets, the boulevards, the Frenchmen's lack of restraint, "so different from the respectability and severity of St. Petersburg." Living was cheap—he could obtain a furnished room for six to ten francs a week. He thought of settling down for a month or two of study. The Paris Commune had taken place a quarter of a century before, but there were men still living who could describe it as though it had happened a week ago. Among them was Paul Lafargue, the son-in-law of Marx, who was living quietly with his wife Laura in Passy. Vladimir could scarcely contain his excitement. He brought flowers to them and talked at length about the coming revolution, describing how the workmen of St. Petersburg spent their evenings poring over the works of Karl Marx.

"You mean the workers are reading Marx?" Lafargue asked incredulously.

"Yes, they are reading him."

"But do they understand him?"

"Yes, they understand him."

"I am afraid you are mistaken," Lafargue said gently. "No, they don't understand anything. Here in France, after twenty years of socialist propaganda, nobody understands Marx!"

Vladimir spent about a month in Paris, going everywhere. It was summer, and he no longer felt an overmastering desire to work. He sauntered along the boulevards, examined the shops, visited the Mur des Fédérés at Père Lachaise, where the Communards were shot, and sought out French socialists. Though he had been learning French from childhood, he had the usual trouble making himself understood. His stomach still troubled him. A friend told him about a Swiss watering place where he might effect a cure, and he was off again to Switzerland, his money low, his spirits high, and there was apparently no thought in his head about study circles and illegal printing presses and the grim tasks of the future. He spent a few days at the watering place, and wrote off a letter to his mother, "I have exceeded my budget, and cannot hope to manage on my resources. Please send me another hundred rubles." Evidently his mother had already been providing him with funds.

From Switzerland during the first days of August he went on to Germany. In Berlin he took a small apartment near the Tiergarten. The doctors had told him to bathe as frequently as possible, and so he bathed every morning in the Spree and spent the rest of the day in the Royal Library; and sometimes, weary of study, he would spend whole days sauntering through the streets, picking up the sounds of German which he still found difficult to understand, or buying books. He bought so many books that he was soon out of funds again and more money had to be sent to him. In the evening he sometimes attended the theater. Before a performance of Hauptmann's *The*

Weavers he read the play through in the hope that he would understand everything being said on the stage; but the sounds of German proved too much for him. Maria Alexandrovna hinted that he would be well advised not to return home too soon—she may have heard that the police had been following him and knew all about his movements. "It's nice to be invited out, but home is best," he answered, and early in September he was on his way to St. Petersburg. When he crossed the frontier, the police officials examined his luggage minutely. They failed to find the polygraph machine and the illegal literature concealed in the false bottom of his trunk.

In St. Petersburg he was restless. He had difficulty picking up the threads of his existence. There were revolutionary matters to attend to, but there was also the pressing problem of earning a living. He had trouble finding a suitable apartment, and he was continually having to ask for more money from his mother. His cousins, the Ardashevs, thought of employing him on a lawsuit over an inheritance, but nothing came of it. To make matters worse, a wave of strikes was spreading over St. Petersburg and he wanted to spend every moment of the day in writing propaganda leaflets and in seeing that they fell into the right hands. He was in continual correspondence with Plekhanov and Axelrod, sending them reports about the strikes in the bindings of books, receiving in exchange books which had to be torn apart in order to find the letter hidden somewhere in the spine; he complained that Axelrod was using too strong a glue and said that ordinary potato flour was sufficient. He planned a newspaper for workers to be printed on the illegal press of the Narodnaya Volya. It was to be called *Rabocheye Dyelo* (The Workers' Cause). The police were shadowing him. They were becoming more expert; he would leave his apartment only to discover a police spy in the street and, after shaking him off and taking a streetcar and then wandering down some deserted street, he would find another waiting for him at a turn in the road. They were like ghosts, and they sprang up everywhere.

The first issue of *Rabocheye Dyelo* was ready to go to the printer by December 20, 1895. On that evening there was a meeting in Krupskaya's apartment to discuss last-minute changes in the copy; one set of proofs was given to a young revolutionary called Vaneyev, the other remained in Krupskaya's hands. It was arranged that Vaneyev should make the final revisions, and Krupskaya would call for them in the morning. There was no sign of Vaneyev in his lodgings the next morning. The night before, the police had spread their net wide and caught nearly all the leading members of the revolutionary organization. Interrogated, Vladimir answered calmly, denied that he was a Social Democrat, and when asked to explain why illegal literature had been found on him, he shrugged his shoulders and said he must have picked it up merely as reading matter in the house of someone whose name he had forgotten.

Thrown into a small narrow cell in the House of Preliminary Detention on Shpalernaya Street, he became a model prisoner. Outwardly he was obedient, helpful, disciplined. Inwardly he was a seething volcano of activity, working as hard as ever to bring about the revolution. The workers' study groups were still in existence, and lectures and pamphlets were secretly smuggled out. He learned a little to his surprise that he was permitted to borrow books from outside libraries, and he borrowed hundreds: some of them contained secret messages indicated by microscopic dots on the letters. He planned a vast work on the development of capitalism in Russia and set about writing it. Communication with the outside world depended on the supply of milk. Between the lines of perfectly innocuous letters there would be words written in milk; and when they were held over a candle flame the messages in milk would appear in yellowish brown. In his cell he kneaded bread to form hollow pellets for the milk; when he heard the peephole being opened, he popped the pellets into his mouth. Once he wrote, "Today I have eaten six inkpots." Since he could not use a candle flame in his cell to decipher the messages sent to him, he immersed them in boiling tea. Every waking moment was spent in agitation. An angry proclamation entitled "To the Tsar's Government," first written in milk, was produced in hundreds of hectographed copies, while the police went in search of the author. "I'm in a far better position than most of the citizens of Russia," he wrote in one of his milk letters to his mother. "They can never find me."

He spent a little more than a year in prison. Prison life agreed with him. He gained weight and rejoiced in exercising his revolutionary authority while hoodwinking the guards. To keep fit, he did Swedish exercises in his cell. He was luckier than some of the other prisoners who were arrested with him. Vaneyev contracted tuberculosis, from which he never recovered, and another went insane. The prison was bitterly cold in winter, and most prisoners found it difficult to sleep on their iron beds with their rough straw mattresses and thin gray sheets which smelled of disinfectant. Vladimir attacked the problem of sleep with the same careful planning which went into his reading and his messages written in milk. He decided that just before going to bed he would perform fifty genuflections. Fifty times every evening he prostrated himself in his cell, to the amusement of the guard who sometimes watched through the peephole, wondering at the religious devotions of this man who refused to attend services in the prison chapel. These exercises sent a warm glow through his body, and he was able to sleep in the coldest weather as soon as he lay down on the bed. He did not waste his strength in nightlong quarrels with himself, like most of the other prisoners.

Like Nechayev, he was already powerful, though behind bars. The small man in Cell 193, with his books and his bread pellets, was already exerting an influence out of all proportion to his means. Among the study groups he was still Nikolay Petrovich or K. Tulin, or any of the other psuedonyms which he gathered about him as though these changing names provided him with a cloak of invisibility. In a few years another and more memorable name would arise. It would be a soft and caressing name like a girl's—a strange name for a man so hard and so determined to destroy the world from which he sprang.

Vladimir Ulyanov vanishes, and instead there is Lenin.

SHUSHENSKOYE

THE LIFE OF A POLITICAL EXILE in the Nineties of the last century was usually quiet and peaceful. Savage floggings and arbitrary killings such as Dostoyevsky had witnessed during his Siberian exile in the Fifties were things of the past. Here and there in Siberia were to be found prisons where tyrannical warders ruled, but these were for "hard" cases; a man who had murdered or attempted to murder a minister could expect short shrift, but a revolutionary who called for the destruction of the social order could expect to be treated as an intellectual and provided with all the necessities of life. If he had money, he could live exactly as he had lived in European Russia. He could have a house of his own, receive mail, write books, travel among the surrounding towns, and go hunting. His punishment was that he was separated from the great cities, and for many revolutionaries in need of rest and leisure to think out their revolutionary programs, exile was more a blessing than a punishment.

When Dostoyevsky wrote *The House of the Dead*, describing his long imprisonment in Siberia, he said that in spite of the harsh regimen he had undergone, he would always be grateful for those years; in them he had come face to face with the Russian people and recovered his mental health. Lenin would later say the same of his own period of exile. He suffered no harsh injustices and spent the three years of his exile in the quiet backwater of a pleasant Siberian village, free to go about his own affairs as he pleased. They were among the happiest years of his life.

On February 10, 1897, the tsarist government made the final disposition of his case by ordering him to a three-year term of exile under police surveillance in eastern Siberia. They were in no hurry to inform him of their decisions, and two more weeks passed before he was summoned from his cell to the prosecutor's office and told about his punishment. He sighed with relief. He could have been sentenced to hard labor or a long prison term, but in fact he was given a very light sentence, which became progressively lighter during the following days, for his mother was able to use her influence to see that he was sent to a place in southern Siberia where he would not suffer from the cold, and she was also able to arrange that he should be permitted to travel there in comfort at his own expense, instead of in a convoy of prisoners under armed guard. Her impulse was to accompany him, but he was able to convince her that she was too old and too frail for the journey.

The prison system under the tsars was remarkably permissive. Given three days to make all the necessary arrangements for the long journey to Siberia, he simply took the train for Moscow and stayed with his family. He visited the famous Rumyantsev library in search of material for his book on the development of capitalism in Russia, and he was even able to attend a secret meeting of the younger members of the party who had remained at liberty. It was not an altogether pleasant meeting, for after a year and a half of solitary confinement he had lost contact with them, and to his horror he discovered that the purity of Marxism was being diluted by the gentler theories of Eduard Bernstein, who believed that the labor movement would gain more by increasing its economic strength through the trade unions than by revolution. In his view these young revolutionaries were already tainted with Philistinism.

When he set out from Moscow, he might have been any young traveler making his way to the east. He did not travel alone; his mother and his two sisters accompanied him as far as Tula. There was no armed guard, and he was treated like any other passenger. He had about a hundred books, a trunkful of clothes, and a thousand rubles in cash. His instructions were to proceed to Krasnoyarsk and there to await further orders. In the past, long railroad journeys had usually exhausted him, and he had confessed to being "completely played out" by the three days' journey from Samara to St. Petersburg. But, for some reason, he found the journey to the east exhilarating, perhaps because he slept soundly each night, enjoyed the passing scenery, and was no longer under any compulsion to write. His letters to his family glow with unobtrusive affection. He was in high spirits.

On the train he met the young revolutionary Krutovsky, who was also on his way to exile. Lenin asked him what would happen when they reached Krasnoyarsk, and he was told they would almost certainly have a few days in the town, to enjoy the amenities of civilization before being sent to some remote village. There was a famous library nearby, and this was an added attraction. He was overjoyed by the presence of another revolutionary, and only the thought that he might have to pass rapidly through the town gave him a faint feeling of uneasiness. He wrote to his mother:

> Thanks to this talk with the doctor [Krutovsky], I am much clearer in my mind—though only approximately clear—about many matters, and that is why I feel so calm. I have left my nervousness behind me in Moscow. The only reason for nervousness was the uncertainty of my position, nothing else. Now there is less uncertainty, and I feel well.

He need not have worried. At Krasnoyarsk he learned that no one had the least idea what to do with him, and he was left to his own resources. Krutovsky had told him of a certain Claudia Popova, a woman who was kind to the revolutionaries passing through the town, and for two months he stayed in her house. He found the famous library belonging to the merchant Yudin just outside the town. There were some 80,000 volumes together with files of newspapers and magazines going back to the eighteenth century—this library was later bought by the Library of Congress in Washington and forms the nucleus of the Library's Slavic section. The millionaire merchant greeted Lenin warmly, offered him every inducement to work in the library, and was a little surprised when, after a few days, Lenin stopped coming to work there. In his letters to his mother he said he was afraid of putting the merchant to trouble; but in fact he was in no mood for study. He was enjoying his freedom. He went for long walks. Sometimes he would drop in at the municipal library to read the newspapers, eleven days late from Moscow, and sometimes, but very infrequently, he would return to the sumptuous five-story house full of books, though far too few of them were concerned with economics and statistics, and there were none at all concerned with the working-class movement.

Spring had come, the wild, torrential Russian spring, which made him feel languid with excitement, so that an hour's walk would leave him pleasantly drowsy. No letters came from home, Krutovsky was sent off to Irkutsk, and soon he felt lonely and a little frightened—there might be some ominous meaning behind all this web of silence.

At last on April 16 the train bearing the rest of the prisoners—those unable to travel at their own expense—steamed into the railroad station. Lenin had heard about their coming, and he was waiting for them. There was a military escort on the train with orders to prevent the prisoners from speaking to anyone or even from standing near the window, but Martov describes how they were able to escape the vigilance of the guards and all spoke to Lenin briefly and shook his hand. A day or two later Lenin met them again, disguised as a baggage agent—the guards paid no attention to the plump, bearded man wearing a fur hat and a fur coat who resembled a merchant. To his great satisfaction he was able to have a long conversation with Fedoseyev, who had been deputed to act as baggagemaster. Then the prisoners went on to their places of detention and once more Lenin was a free man, wandering the streets of Krasnoyarsk and wondering what the authorities intended to do with him.

At last on April 17, a whole month after arriving in Krasnoyarsk, he heard he would be sent to Minusinsk. Rather oddly, the information did not come from the police authorities but from his friend Krutovsky, who had reached Irkutsk and had there received word from the chief of police of the destinations of all the prisoners. Lenin was overjoyed. He calculated that he still had a few more days in Krasnoyarsk, for the roads had been washed away by the spring floods and the river steamers were not yet running upriver. Both Krasnoyarsk and Minusinsk were on the Yenisey river, and it seemed likely enough that they would send him by river. Another week passed before he was able to pinpoint the exact place where he would have to spend the years of exile. It turned out to be the village of Shushenskoye some forty miles to the south of Minusinsk, and there was not the least doubt that strings had been pulled in St. Petersburg to give him the most privileged treatment, for the lands south of Minusinsk had long been known as "the Siberian Italy," and no other prisoners among those who were arrested with him were sent there. Martov and Vaneyev were sent to Turukhansk in the north, Starkov, Krzhizhanovsky and Lepechinsky went to Minusinsk. The truth was that Lenin, who was growing fat and luxuriating in his new-found health, was being described in official reports and in the pleas sent to the government by his mother as a man suffering from tuberculosis and therefore in need of a temperate climate, and in all Siberia there was hardly another place so well favored.

As soon as Lenin learned that he was being sent to Shushenskoye, he burst into song. He intended to write a long ode, but completed only the first verse; of this verse there has survived only the first line, which he quoted in a letter to his mother:

In Shushu, at the feet of the Sayan Mountains . . .

This line of verse has some small importance, as being the only example of Lenin's poetry which has come down to us.

He had good reason to burst into song. Everything he read or heard about Shushenskoye made it seem charming and desirable. The village was not on the Yenisey, but on one of its tributaries, a mile or two from the forest, the Sayan Mountains lying on the horizon. It was good hunting country, with game to be found on the banks of the river and in the pine woods, with bears, reindeer, wild goats, squirrels and sable in the taiga. There was the further advantage that living was cheap. Here a man could live quite comfortably on eight or nine rubles a month.

The police took their time. Lenin was still wandering about the streets of Krasnoyarsk and dreaming about the beautiful village which awaited him like a mirage hovering over the future. He was in no mood to work. "I have some books on statistics, and I think I told you about this," he wrote to his mother and his sister Anna, "but I do little studying. I spend most of my time idling." It was a confession he made only once or twice in his lifetime.

What pleased him more than anything else was the fact that at Shushenskoye he would be out of reach of the other prisoners. He detested the continual bickering and quarreling of the exiles; and he had the aristocrat's contempt for the mob. He wanted to immerse himself in study, and he arranged that books should come with every post. He wanted to give himself up to contemplation and writing, and he looked forward to a life of cultivated loneliness. When his mother or Anna begged to be allowed to join him, he rebuked them sternly, saying that they would suffer greatly from the rigors of a Siberian winter and that they should think themselves blessed because they were living in civilization. His sister said he was being "inhospitable"—which was true. But when he learned that his brother Dmitry, a medical student at Moscow University, was threatening to leave Moscow to work in the plague-stricken areas of the south, he had a sudden change of heart. Why, instead of becoming contaminated by the plague, didn't Dmitry come to Siberia, where doctors were needed even more urgently than in European Russia? "He would be very welcome," Lenin went on. "We could go hunting together, if only Siberia succeeds in turning me into a hunter, and so long as Dmitry works and hunts not too far away." He was hurt and a little bemused by the thought of Dmitry's deliberate self-sacrifice. Such acts always puzzled him, and sometimes he would inveigh against them passionately, as though they were no more than the product of wanton self-deception.

So the days passed, while he complained good-humoredly because the books he had ordered had not arrived, or because his money was running out. He wanted books, innumerable books, and begged Anna to make arrangements that the articles he wrote should be paid for in the only currency he recognized—books. He offered to translate books or to be the chief co-ordinator of a vast translation bureau which would embrace all the other political exiles, "and of course I will be responsible for the supervision of the translations and for their satisfactory execution." And after books came magazines. He thought he would have enough money to subscribe to five, and since he was still writing and revising his history of capitalism in Russia, he was particularly anxious to obtain *Vestnik Finansov,* the official organ of the Ministry of Finance, and *Russkoye Bogatstvo,* which usually had a section dealing with economics. His passion—a passion that never left him—was for statistics. He enjoyed their nakedness and clean-cut brevity, and he bequeathed to the Communist Party a reverence for statistics which, while often beguiling, sometimes assumed the form of numerical gigantomania. On the whole he found the libraries in Krasnoyarsk surprisingly dull: there were few books on statistics in them.

But while Lenin was lazing in a comfortable rooming house at Krasnoyarsk, he was also gathering strength for the arduous work ahead. He had no intention of wasting his time: exile must be put to use. There were countless books and articles to be written, countless broadsheets to be smuggled out of Siberia, countless books to be read. The party network must be maintained, and illegal literature must be printed and distributed. The comrades left in St. Petersburg must be sustained and, whenever necessary, corrected. Plekhanov and Axelrod were abroad, and continual contact must be made with them.

On May 12, 1897, the long holiday came to an end. Two gendarmes called for him at the rooming house and ordered him to embark on the river steamer. It was a slow steamer: there were constant stops and delays. He arrived in Minusinsk nearly a week later, and then traveled by carriage to Shushenskoye in the company of the two gendarmes,

who proceeded to hand him over to the village constable. There were
no formalities. The constable simply noted his arrival and let him loose
to make whatever arrangements he pleased. In theory, he had to report to the constable whenever he strayed outside the village, but in
fact the constable let him wander away whenever he liked.

He decided to stay with a moderately rich peasant called Apollon
Zyrianov, who had a large wooden house with five windows overlooking the street. For his room, his meals and his laundry he paid eight
rubles a month, and since his monthly income amounted to 150 rubles
a month he was probably the wealthiest person in the village. Zyrianov
built shelves for the books, which soon reached to the ceiling. There
was a wooden bed, a table, four chairs, a Siberian carpet, books everywhere. Books came with every mail: they were his real food, and there
was never enough of them. But though he had planned an extensive
program of writing, he was still under the spell of the enforced leisure
he had enjoyed at Krasnoyarsk, and there were whole days when he
abandoned his books and writing altogether. Zyrianov would go hunting with him, and sometimes they wandered along the marshy banks
of the Shusha river for five days at a stretch, spending the nights
stretched out on the sweet-smelling hay in one of the shelters in the
forest. They were days of quiet, dreamlike contentment.

Summer came with its relentless heat—the only way to avoid the
heat was to go bathing. Sometimes he would bathe twice a day. At
night he would unfurl a mosquito net around his bed and listen to the
droning of the mosquitoes in the darkness, comforting himself with
the thought that they were worse in the north. He usually took his
meals with the Zyrianovs, and many years later they remembered him
sitting at the head of the table, a small, deeply sunburned man, tend-
ing to fat, laughing uproariously, and seemingly without a care in the
world. He did not in the least resemble a dangerous revolutionary.

Friends came to call on him. He was especially fond of a young
revolutionary called Raichin, who was among his first visitors. Krzhizhanovsky came later. "Gleb is coming for some hunting and fishing, so
I shall not be bored," he wrote to his mother in the tones of an owner
of a small estate who finds time lying heavy on his hands. He talked
of "my" Shushenskoye. Sometimes with his old fowling piece under
his arm he would wander away from the other hunters and sit down on
a tree stump and gaze at the flowing waters.

Except for a short pamphlet on the recently promulgated labor
laws, he did little work that summer. The pamphlet was smuggled out

of the country—apparently with great difficulty, for it was not printed until two years later in Geneva. The new laws restricted working time in factories to 11½ hours a day, and 10 hours on Saturdays; until then, the average working day was 12½ hours. Lenin's attack on the law, therefore, was somewhat blunted by the recognition that it was a victory of the workers over the employers and the government. His pamphlet was designed to show how small and meaningless were the gains promised to the workers, and how large and meaningful were the gains acquired by the employers, who could always interpret the law in their favor, but he acknowledged that substantial concessions had been wrung from the employers. Meanwhile it was the duty of the advanced workers to bring the unskilled workers into the struggle for the eight-hour day, "for which the workers are now striving all over the world." It is a diffuse pamphlet, much of it urbane and legalistic, with little fire in it. Here and there we recognize the note of trenchant mockery, as when he discusses the "etceteras" concealed in all Russian laws:

> In general, we may divide Russian laws into two categories: there are the laws which grant some rights to the workers and the common people generally, and others which prohibit something, or permit officials to prohibit it. In the first category of laws, even the most trivial rights of the workers are *enumerated with complete precision* (even, for example, the worker's right not to go to work if he has good cause), and *not the least* departure is permitted on pain of very severe penalties. In these laws you will never come upon a single "etcetera" or "and so on." In the laws of the second category we *always* find the prohibitions taking a general form *without any precise enumeration,* so that the management can prohibit anything it pleases; and in these laws you will always find those small yet very important addenda: "etcetera" and "and so on." These little words strikingly demonstrate the infinite power of Russian officials, and the utter powerlessness of the people before them, and the senselessness and savagery of the foul bureaucracy and red-tapery which permeates every institution of the Imperial Russian Government.*

It is possible that Lenin was reminded of this passage when he in turn came to promulgate the laws of Russia, where "not the least departure is permitted on pain of very severe penalties," and "the management prohibited anything it pleased." Except for this passage there

---

* I have followed Lenin's use of italics throughout. He evidently attached considerable importance to them, but it should be noted that they are not always used for emphasis, and often have ironical effect.

is very little in the pamphlet worth remembering.

A more important pamphlet was written later in the year under the title *The Tasks of the Russian Social Democrats*. This was nothing less than an attempt to map out the program of an insurrectionary movement led by the Social Democrats among the factory workers, "who are the most susceptible to our ideas, the most intellectually and physically advanced, and the most important by virtue of their numbers and concentration in the nation's political centers." The pamphlet was at once an appeal to the workers and a closely reasoned argument intended to show that they alone have the power to overthrow the government, for the peasants were weak and disorganized, the bourgeoisie and petty bourgeoisie were "two-faced," and the intelligentsia, bound to the autocracy and the bourgeoisie, were compelled to compromise and sell their revolutionary ardor for "an official salary or a share of the profits." "The proletariat alone," he wrote," can be the *front-line fighters* for political liberty and democratic institutions." And then again: "The proletariat alone is unreservedly hostile to the autocracy and the Russian bureaucracy; the proletariat alone has no *ties* with those aristocratic-bourgeois members of society; and the proletariat alone is capable of irreconcilable hostility toward them and of waging a determined struggle against them."

There are moments when the pamphlet reads like a hymn to the proletariat, in whom all virtues are gathered, as compared with the tzarist government—"the omnipotent, irresponsible, corrupt, savage, ignorant and parasitic Russian bureaucracy." Those chains of adjectives hint at a curious respect for the government he claimed to despise. He thunders about "the complete lack of rights of the people," and in the next breath he claims that the recently promulgated labor laws were wrested from the government by the growing political power of the workers. He points to England as a country to be imitated, for "in England powerful political control is exercised over the administration, even though it is *far from being complete* and the bureaucracy retains not a few of its privileges."

What Lenin wanted and called for, without naming it, was the dictatorship of the proletariat, and of the proletariat alone. He inveighed against those who wanted to merge the "democratic" activity of the proletariat with the "democratic" activities of other parties: on the contrary any alliance with other parties and classes will only weaken the class-conscious proletariat in its struggle for freedom and democracy. There must be no compromises.

Lenin never deviated from the principles outlined in *The Tasks of the Russian Social Democrats*. Exactly twenty years later they were to become the basic principles of the Communist state, but by that time many definitions had changed and there was rarely any talk about political freedom or of England as an example to be followed.

Following Nechayev, Lenin insisted that nothing was to be gained by discussing the form of the state after the autocracy has been destroyed. The core of his program is announced near the beginning of the pamphlet, where he explains that the most urgent task of the proletariat under the guidance of the Social Democrats was quite simply to torment the autocracy to death:

> By leading the class struggle of the proletariat, by developing organization and discipline among the workers, by helping them to fight for their economic needs and to win position after position from capital, by politically educating the workers and systematically and unswervingly attacking the autocracy and making life a torment for every tsarist *bashibuzuk* who makes the proletariat feel the heavy paw of the police government—such an organization would be at one and the same time a workers' party organization adapted to our conditions, and a powerful revolutionary party directed against the autocracy.
>
> To discuss in advance the methods this organization will resort to in order to inflict a decisive blow on the autocracy, whether, for example, it would choose insurrection, or a mass political strike, or some other form of attack—to discuss such matters in advance and to decide the question at the present time would be merely empty doctrinairism. It would be like generals calling a council of war before they had mustered their troops, mobilized them, and undertaken a campaign against the enemy. But when the army of the proletariat fights unswervingly and under the leadership of a strong Social Democratic organization for its economic and political emancipation, this army will itself indicate the methods and means of action to the generals.

Such pronouncements suggest that Lenin had not thought out the problem and was simply evading the issue. He would speak in the most general terms about the seizure of power by the Social Democrats, insisting that they were not to be compared with the Blanquists, "who can only conceive of political struggle in the form of political conspiracy," while reserving to himself the right to be as conspiratorial as he pleased. "The Social Democrats," he warns, "do not believe in conspiracies, for they believe that the age of conspiracies has long since passed away." Yet there was no doubt about the conspiratorial nature of his program, which derived as much from Nechayev as from Marx.

When Lenin wrote *The Tasks of the Russian Social Democrats*, there were no more than three or four hundred men in Russia who professed to belong to the party. But the pamphlet itself did much to increase the party's strength. Smuggled out of Russia, it was printed anonymously in Geneva the following year. Thereafter the tsarist secret police continually mentioned it in their reports, as they found printed or hectographed copies among the possessions of arrested revolutionaries. During the years 1898–1905 copies were discovered in St. Petersburg, Moscow, Smolensk, Kazan, Orel, Kiev, Vilna, Irkutsk, Arkhangelsk, Kovno, and other towns. It was not surprising that the pamphlet should be disseminated so widely, for by pitting the factory workers against the rest it possessed a romantic appeal to the proletariat all over Russia. There is a sense in which all Lenin's later writings were no more than footnotes to *The Tasks of the Russian Social Democrats*, with its vision of the armed proletariat riding roughshod over the rest.

But writing was almost the least of his occupations that year. Hunting, fishing, talking to the peasants, setting up an unofficial law office, where the villagers for miles around consulted him on Sundays, and endless reading—these were his main occupations. The writing of his book *The Development of Capitalism in Russia*, which he had once intended as the Russian equivalent of Marx's *Das Kapital*, went on slowly, haphazardly, having something of the appearance of a series of magazine articles welded together without too much sense of order and with no discernible pattern. It was a book to be added to at intervals, growing by fits and starts. His real life was in the open air. It was as though he knew that for the rest of his life he would live in smoke-laden towns, and here, in Siberia, for the last time he would enjoy the sensation of being a human animal, no longer compelled to move at the mercy of his theories.

In late September Lenin visited Tesinskoye, where Starkov and Krzhizhanovsky lived in comfortable exile in a large two-storey house; there were long discussions, sometimes lasting all night, and they went hunting. Krzhizhanovsky was suffering from the disease of exiles—nervous prostration and sudden bouts of intense melancholy. Lenin, who was made of sterner metal, seemed surprised, but in November, when Shushenskoye seemed to be cut off from the rest of the world by solid curtains of snow and ice, he too suffered from the disease and went off secretly to Minusinsk to see his young friend Raichin and the other exiles, content to be in the company of friends, dreading the return to the lost village, and careless of the inevitable punishment if he was found out.

Even in southern Siberia winters can be hard, with the villages cut off from one another for months on end, but this winter proved to be particularly pleasant, with warm sunny days interrupted by occasional snowstorms. Krzhizhanovsky came to stay with him for ten days. It was another happy interlude for Lenin, who, in spite of his frequently expressed denials, had no particular affection for a life of prolonged seclusion. Then Krzhizhanovsky was gone, and there was only the interminable silence of the long Siberian winter and the mail arriving irregularly. Needing more companionship than the village could offer, he wrote to his mother asking whether a hunting dog could be found and sent to him. In the summer, when Mark Elizarov had first suggested sending a dog, Lenin had been less than co-operative. Now he yearned for it. Perhaps, after all, a small puppy could be sent in a basket. Loneliness was beginning to torment him.

In Shushenskoye there were not many people he could talk to on his own level. There was only one other Social Democrat in the village. He was a Pole, called Prominsky, who had been exiled in 1895. By profession he was a hatmaker, and he was one of those revolutionaries who suffer for the rest of their lives for a single act of protest. He was a calm, pleasant, ineffective man with a wife and six children; he read little, had almost no education, but was full of revolutionary fervor, which he expressed by singing revolutionary songs in Polish with the children joining in the choruses. Lenin liked him, sang with him, went out hunting with him, but never grew intimate with him. Long after the October Revolution Prominsky was still living in Shushenskoye, making felt hats, singing his revolutionary songs and ineffectually beating his revolutionary wings. At last, in 1923, he wrote to Lenin for permission to return to his native Poland, and died of typhus on the train.

There was one other exile at Shushenskoye. He was a young workman from the Putilov factory in St. Petersburg, arrested as a strike leader. His name was Oscar Engberg, and he was of Finnish descent. He was, if possible, even more ignorant than Prominsky, though it was known that he had read several books. Lenin was genuinely fond of these two exiles, but there was a vast barrier stretching between him and them. He made some effort to form an acquaintance with the local schoolteacher and the local priest, but without result. They preferred playing cards and drinking, and perhaps they were wary of the young red-bearded revolutionary in their midst.

There remained the peasants, with whom he liked to go on his hunting and fishing expeditions, but he was not altogether at ease with them. They had no interest in revolution, and very little interest in the affairs of the world. His favorite among them was the simple-minded Sosipatych, who was continually bringing him presents—a live crane, cedar cones, anything which he thought would please the cultivated stranger from the west. Sosipatych knew all the local lore, and sometimes he would tell long, pointless stories which sent Lenin to sleep, but he possessed a fund of knowledge about the lives of peasants in eastern Siberia, and he was probably closer to Lenin than anyone else in that long winter.

Then for a few weeks winter set in in earnest, and there was only a small, cramped room overflowing with books, and the landlord, Apollon Zyrianov, singing noisily and drunkenly in the next room, while the wind whistled and the snow fell and from somewhere far off there came the honking of the wild geese. The snow piled up against the double windows, while Lenin wrote at the book-covered table his regular Sunday morning letter to his mother, thanking her for books and newspapers which arrived so late that he had long ago forgotten whether he had asked for them, and then he would go on to give her the small news of his obscure village—how Engberg had fallen ill and been sent to the hospital at Minusinsk, and how for some mysterious reason the allowance of Prominsky, the Polish hatmaker, had been reduced from thirty-one to twenty-one rubles a month, and heaven knows how he would be able to feed and clothe his wife and six children on such a paltry sum, and nobody was buying his hats. "The weather is still very, very cold," he wrote. "Truly the Siberian winter means to make itself felt."

THE ENCHANTED KINGDOM

ALL OVER RUSSIA spring comes like a thunderclap. One day there is a cold and deadly stillness, and then overnight the air is full of murmuring sounds, as the snow melts and the sap rises and the empty sky is loud with bird song. The smell of the earth pours through the snow. Spring, for the Russians, is always an intoxication.

So it was in Shushenskoye, as the ice melted on the river and the larches and birches put forth their leaves. In the forests small patches of snow would remain for many weeks, and the Sayan Mountains would have their covering of snow until the late summer. Lenin did not write about the coming of spring—he wrote about the weather only when it was unbearable—but the excitement comes through in his letters. Suddenly the pace is quicker, more and more books are wanted, more and more plans are being made. Then, too, there was encouraging news about Nadezhda Krupskaya, whose sentence of exile to Ufa *guberniya* in the north had been commuted to exile in Shushenskoye at her request, the official rescript reading that she had applied for the transfer on the grounds of her intention to marry Vladimir Ulyanov and it was expected that the marriage would take place *immediately*. Lenin was overjoyed at the thought of Krupskaya's coming. His sister Anna, who had met Krupskaya in Moscow, was less overjoyed. She was a jealous woman and wrote to her brother, "Nadya is staying here. She looks like a herring."

Herring or no herring, Lenin awaited her coming impatiently. In those early days he had no overwhelming affection for her. She was

124

simply a loyal party worker, obedient, trustworthy, cool in emergencies, an adept at sending messages in chemical ink, who was pretty when she was young, but was now rather plain and looked older than her years. Yet, when he looked back, he could remember many other women he had been attracted to, but he could remember none so selfless or so determined to yield to his wishes. There was still another reason for awaiting her arrival impatiently. She was bringing a whole library of books.

Her coming was attended with interminable delays, and she did not reach Shushenskoye until one evening in May. There was no one to meet her, for Lenin had gone out hunting. Apollon Zyrianov, however, had been warned that she might arrive and showed her into his room, which was in a fearful state of disorder, for Oscar Engberg had entered it and thrown all the books about in a fit of drunkenness. Her mother was with her. She was a tall, imperious woman who liked to have her own way and stood no nonsense from anyone; and she was appalled by the state of the room. When at last Lenin returned from his hunting expedition, she snapped, "You've grown awfully fat!"

That night everyone talked at once. The Zyrianovs gathered around, and half the village came to inspect the young woman who resembled a herring, and her stately, aristocratic mother. Toasts were drunk, and it was a long time before they were left alone. Then the books were sorted out, and the messages written on the backs of photographs were read, and it was nearly dawn before they went to bed.

From the beginning Krupskaya took a distaste to the Zyrianovs. They drank too much, they were too inquisitive and too talkative. What she wanted and insisted upon having was a house to herself, or at least half a house, rather than the two rooms set aside for them at the Zyrianovs. Lenin made cautious inquiries, and soon he found he could lease half of a larger house for four rubles a month. He was considered a good tenant, being chosen above the village priest who had long coveted the property.

From being a man alone, contentedly going about his studies and leaving them for a casual walk along the river or in the woods whenever he desired, Lenin found himself at the mercy of two women who sought to regulate his life. His future mother-in-law, Elizaveta Vasilyevna, had a tart tongue; in addition she was deeply religious, and her daughter had forgotten to inform her that Lenin was intolerant of all religions. So there were quarrels which usually ended with Lenin's mocking *mea culpa* as he bowed himself out of her presence. He would raise an eyebrow and pull at his beard with an expression of comic indignation which would reduce both mother and daughter to hilarious laughter. The "fat one" knew how to deal with women.

Krupskaya settled down in the new house as though she had been born a Siberian, complaining only that it was impossible to find a maidservant. There was a small vegetable garden, and she immediately set about planting cucumbers, beets, carrots and pumpkins; she was very proud of them. She was less proud of her cooking, for she was always thinking about other things, with the result that the dumpling soup was sometimes spoiled. Help came later in the year with the arrival of a thirteen-year-old Siberian girl with skinny elbows, who knew her way about a kitchen better than Krupskaya. She was called Pasha. Krupskaya took her in hand, taught her to read and write, and felt rewarded when she discovered that the girl kept a diary. Her diary, however, was not very informative, for she wrote only about the things that interested her. Years later Krupskaya could remember only one entry: "Oscar Engberg and Prominsky came to visit. They sang, and so did I."

Except for the bad cooking of Krupskaya and the occasional flurries of angry words from Elizaveta Vasilyevna, life had few hardships. More and more Lenin came to be regarded as the seigneur of the village, the portly owner of the largest library and the chief consumer of writing paper, which he bought from the village store. When he traveled, he borrowed a horse and cart, and he was a memorable figure as he sat in the driving seat, flicking the whip over the horse's head. The police troubled him hardly at all, and he traveled as he pleased.

One day during the summer he drove off to Tesinskoye to spend a few days with the exiles. Alexander Chapovalov, a metallurgist who had been arrested in 1896 for taking part in strikes, remembered him driving into the small town early one morning with Krupskaya beside him. Chapovalov did not know who they were, but he knew by their costumes that they were not Siberians, and when he heard they had driven through the night from Shushenskoye he was properly amazed, for the village was sixty miles away and there were bandits on the road. Lenin had given no advance warning of his coming, and the revolutionaries he wanted to meet were out hunting. Chapovalov invited them to make use of his room, gave them water, soap and a towel, commanded the peasant proprietor of the house to prepare a meal for them, and as a good host he led the horse to the trough and set about finding some hay. Then he went through the town, leaving messages at the houses of the revolutionaries telling them that Lenin had arrived and where they could find him when they returned from hunting.

Lenin and Krupskaya had finished their meal when Chapovalov came back to the house, and he was a little surprised to discover that his visitors had gone through all his books and papers. Chapovalov knew German. He had made his own translation of *The Communist Manifesto* into Russian, and he had translated a number of sentimental poems. He had also compiled a small anthology of revolutionary verses, chiefly those in which the revolutionary dies gloriously only to be buried in an unmarked grave, for he saw himself as a heroic and dedicated revolutionary doomed to an early death. Lenin professed to be pleased with the examination of the young revolutionary's books and documents, making no apologies for this invasion of privacy. Chapovalov had the feeling that he was in the presence of a learned and demanding schoolmaster, and he had passed his examinations creditably. Suddenly Lenin darted a question at him: "Do you often use a dictionary?"

Chapovalov shrugged his shoulders. "Yes, but not very often," he answered carelessly.

"I, on the contrary, consult the dictionary very, very often," Lenin replied; and then Chapovalov knew he had been rebuked and had perhaps failed in his examinations.

In fact Lenin's attitude toward a good dictionary had much in common with his attitude toward the writings of Karl Marx, and in the course of a lifetime he accumulated a vast number of them. He spent a good deal of his time at Shushenskoye translating Sidney and Beatrice Webb's *Theory and Practice of English Trade Unionism* with the help of a German translation. He would get Krupskaya sometimes to read out the English text, and then he would shake his head sadly. "The teacher at school did not make it sound like that," he said. Every night, sitting at his desk in the light of a kerosene lamp with a green shade, he would wrestle with the English language, consult the dictionaries and put the English, the German, and the Russian texts side by side. It was slow work carried on with dogged persistence, and when he had finished—there were about a thousand pages of his Russion version—he sighed with relief.

The Webbs' book and his own work on the development of Russian capitalism occupied only a small part of his time. With the coming of Krupskaya and Elizaveta Vasilyevna, he had promised to discipline himself severely, and to work seven or eight hours every day, but in fact he worked only when he felt like it. There were always too many distractions. As soon as he woke up in the morning, a little boy called Minka would come from his house across the way and demand to be played with. Minka was the son of a Lettish settler, a felt-boot maker by trade. He was six years old, with a wan little face and bright eyes, and very grave of speech; he was the apple of Elizaveta Vasilyevna's eye. "It's me!" Minka would say morning after morning. It was like cockcrow, and there came a time when the whole family would be shaken with fear if he was so much as five minutes late. Minka's mother had given birth to fourteen children, but Minka was the sole survivor.

Prominsky and Oscar Engberg continued to be distractions: they would tramp unannounced into the house with their guns under their arms, determined to go hunting and to drag Lenin with them. Work would be abandoned, Lenin would put on a pair of leather britches, and they would be off to the woods or the marshes. It was not only that Lenin did very little work; he was finding innumerable excuses for avoiding work altogether.

Krupskaya was overwhelmed when she saw her first Siberian winter. The world turned white before the first snow fell; the hares turned white, and the sky was white and glowing. They would walk over the frozen river and see the fish and the pebbles gleaming distinctly below, and sometimes when it was very cold the river was frozen solid. In the woods the bare larch trees seemed to throw white shadows. "It was like living," she said, "in an enchanted kingdom."

On those frozen days Lenin would go ice skating. He had become proficient in the art, and much to Krupskaya's admiration he would sail over the ice in a professional manner, with his hands in his front pockets. Krupskaya rarely accompanied him, and Elizaveta Vasilyevna went out skating only once. She fell flat on her back.

This idyllic life continued through the whole period of their exile. From time to time there were minor revolutionary crises, as when Lenin's friend Raichin suddenly escaped from his place of exile and the question of whether to encourage other escapes was seriously discussed by the revolutionaries in secret conference. Lenin's view was that nothing was to be gained by escaping, because the police only made life more difficult for the rest. A few weeks later there came news that Fedoseyev had shot himself. Apparently another political exile called Yukhotsky had picked a quarrel with him, accusing him of stealing common funds, and this had so preyed on Fedoseyev's mind that he had refused help from anyone and suffered terrible hardship. Ill and weak, he lost the ability or desire for work, suffered from persecution mania and delusions, and shot himself in a moment of extreme depression. A few hours later, as soon as she heard the news, his closest friend, a woman who was also in exile, shot herself. The two deaths came like a shock on the exposed nerves of the exiles living in the north, but the exiled revolutionaries in the south remained relatively unscathed. "There is nothing worse in exile than these exile scandals," Lenin wrote, and though he tried to find out exactly what had happened, and opened a fund for buying a tombstone for the dead revolutionary, he felt confirmed in his resolution to live apart from the personal quarrels of the exiles. There was always an element of remoteness in him.

Outwardly, the revolution itself seemed to be frozen in those long winters, where every day was like every other day. Krupskaya, writing one of her long postscripts to Lenin's letters to his mother, confessed that she could remember neither the day nor the month nor the year, for time seemed to be standing still. She was still lost in her enchanted kingdom.

But in fact, deep below the surface, the revolution was gathering strength. The moles were burrowing deep. They would emerge to the surface and then vanish again on their mysterious errands; and there would come voices telling them in which direction they should explore. They were not blind moles, and some of them knew what they were doing.

In the first winter of Lenin's exile, in March 1898, a meeting of the revolutionaries had been held in Minsk, with the purpose of establishing a Russian Social Democratic Workers' Party. Only ten delegates attended, representing organizations in St. Petersburg, Moscow, Kiev and Ekaterinoslav, and from the Jewish General Workers' Union, commonly known as "the Bund," of which Martov was one of the more important members before his arrest and exile. This obscure meeting of a handful of revolutionaries, whose names are nearly forgotten, has some claim to historic significance. It was, in fact, the first congress of the Russian Communist Party, and all subsequent congresses are numbered from it.*

* The names of the delegates were: Peter Struve, S. Radchenko (Moscow League for the Liberation of the Working Class), A. Vannovsky (Ekaterinoslav League), K. Petruse-

The congress lasted three days and resulted in a considerable body of decisions and pronouncements, out of all proportion to the pathetically small number of participants. The party was given a name and a form, a central committee was appointed, a program and a manifesto were written, and the decision was taken to launch a party organ. The manifesto was drafted by Peter Struve, then a twenty-seven-year-old economist and revolutionary, later to become a member of the Duma and a defender of the constitutional monarchy. One paragraph of his manifesto has remained deservedly famous:

> The farther east we go in Europe, the weaker, more abject and cowardly does the bourgeoisie become politically, and the greater the cultural and political tasks which devolve upon the proletariat. On its strong shoulders the Russian working class must and will carry the work of conquering political liberty. This is an essential step, but only the first step, to a realization of the great historic mission of the proletariat, to the foundation of a social order in which there will be no place for the exploitation of man by man.

This document was a clarion call to the workers to take power into their own hands and to destroy the rule of the bourgeoisie, which had proved to be incapable in Struve's view of making the major changes necessary to bring political liberty to the Russian Empire. Significantly, when giving a name to the party, Struve had insisted upon using the word *Rossiiskaya* rather than *Russkaya*. *Rossiiskaya* denoted not Russia alone, but all the territories under Russian domination from Siberia to Poland, Finland, Latvia, Esthonia and Lithuania. This was to be a party embracing nearly fifty ethnic groups.

The Minsk congress was no more than a small ripple on the surface. At least one of the delegates seems to have been in the pay of the secret police, for eight of them were immediately arrested, and a lengthy summary of the debates was later found in the secret police archives. The police could congratulate themselves on having strangled the party at its birth.

The party however lived on, thriving on imprisonment and persecution. For twenty years it was to grow slowly, biding its time, strengthened rather than weakened by the quarrels that broke out in

---

vich (Kiev League), P. Tuchapsky, Boris Eidelman and I. Vigdorchik (the last two representing the Kiev *Workers' Gazette*), and three delegates from the Bund—A. Kramer, A. Mutnik and S. Katz. Only Struve and Eidelman achieved later fame—Struve as a prominent economist and Eidelman as the head of the Cheka in the Ukraine in 1919–21. These delegates were the founding fathers of the Bolshevik party.

its ranks. Congress would follow congress. Leaders would emerge and then sink into obscurity. But the determination to build a revolutionary party around the armed proletariat remained.

Lenin was aware of the significance of the congress. Through Krupskaya, who had been in frequent contact with Struve, he was also aware that there was no strong guiding hand among the revolutionaries who attended the congress. What was needed was a hardening of the revolutionary impulse, firm guidelines, a far more deliberate policy. For a little while longer he would speak of political liberty, imagining that in some way the armed revolution would lead to truly democratic institutions, but soon enough he would be seduced by the vision of an armed dictatorship.

What disturbed him more than anything else in his Siberian exile was any weakening of the original Marxist fiber. When Engels died, his friend Eduard Bernstein became his literary executor and the claimant to the throne left vacant by Marx. He immediately set to work to redefine the tenets of Marxism, strengthening them here, weakening them there, elaborating them in terms of the industrial and social development in Germany, where great concessions had been wrung by the workers from Bismarck, who was the first to introduce social insurance. The publication of Bernstein's work *Die Voraussetzungen des Sozialismus und die Aufgaben der Sozialdemokratie* ("The Bases of Socialism and the Tasks of Social Democracy") was a landmark in the development of Marxist theory and was bound to enrage the extremists. Lenin heard about the book, read attacks upon it, and pestered his sister to send him a copy. Months passed. It arrived at last in September 1899, wrapped up in old newspapers, and he exploded long before he finished reading it. He wrote to his mother:

Nadya and I both sat down to read Bernstein's book as soon as it arrived, and we have now read more than half of it. We are completely astounded by what we found. Theoretically it is incredibly weak, nothing more than a repetition of other people's ideas. He merely plays with ideas; there is no attempt at serious and independent criticism. I would say it is opportunism (or rather, Fabianism, for the immediate source of a number of his ideas and contentions is to be found in the later works written by the Webbs). It is indifferent opportunism and "perhapsism," and cowardly opportunism at that, for Bernstein simply has no desire to avail himself of a real program. There can be no doubt that it will be a failure. The insinuation that many Russians agree with him absolutely infuriated us.

Infuriated or not, Lenin was forced to take the book seriously, and he went about attacking it at every opportunity. With growing astonishment he saw that the basic ideas of Bernstein were taking root, and that in Western Europe and even in Russia there were serious-minded socialists who had little faith in seizure of power by the armed proletariat. Bernstein looked forward to a political alliance between the proletariat and the bourgeoisie; he saw neither reason nor excuse for bloody revolutions and the extermination of entire classes. Against Bernstein and all that he represented Lenin was to wage implacable war.

About a month before he received Bernstein's book Anna had sent him another alarming document, *Credo of the Young*. The pamphlet seems to have had no title, and this was the name she gave to it. Written by a former member of the Social Democratic Party, Ekaterina Kuskova, then living abroad, it was a closely reasoned attack against the extreme revolutionary wing of the party in favor of the struggle to increase the wages and security of the workers by political action rather than by revolution. She insisted that the problem was essentially an economic problem, which could be solved by strikes and by strengthening the power of the trade unions. Marxist revolutionary ideas were described as negative, primitive and intolerant. Instead of making war on society, the working class should be integrated into society. It was too weak, too disorganized and backward to fight on its own. According to this document, Russian Marxists were introducing wholly alien concepts into Russia and demonstrating their incapacity to understand the Russian workmen by denouncing every liberal reform; they were political innocents and it was time they helped the workers to enjoy a better standard of living.

Credo of the Young admittedly derived from a study of Bernstein's book and paid tribute to *The Communist Manifesto*. It was written by a young woman who could argue persuasively and knew her social history. She did not despise the revolutionary wing, but treated them as romantic children who had forgotten the elementary facts of life —that workmen were living on starvation wages and their organizations were still so weak that they were unable to protest effectively. Strengthen their organizations, give them certain clearly defined aims, teach them and inspire them to act within the framework of society, and they will eventually receive satisfaction from the government. Teach them to rise up against the government, and they will lose all they have gained.

Lenin read *Credo of the Young* in cold fury. He saw it, as he was to see all attacks on his own position, as a deliberate act of treachery. Ekaterina Kuskova had used his own weapons: irony, ridicule, the casual transition from attack to defense and then to a still stronger attack. Her program involved completely basic revisions of policy, for she demanded that priority be given to "a more energetic prosecution of the economic struggle and consolidation of the economic organizations, but also, and most importantly, there must be a change in the party's attitude to other opposition parties." She was demanding that the Social Democrats work hand in hand with the liberals.

Lenin's first reaction came in a brief comment to his sister. "The *Credo*," he said, "is interesting and infuriating." It was also, as he recognized, extremely dangerous to the fortunes of the Social Democratic Party, and he began to think about methods of combating it. He decided to call a secret conference of exiles and present them with his rebuttal; if they agreed, his rebuttal could be published as a protest delivered at a special meeting of the Social Democratic Party. The meeting was held in the small village of Yermakovskoye, and seventeen party members attended. Vaneyev, dying of consumption, was carried into the room on his bed; he was to die a few days later. Lenin read his denunciation of the *Credo*, and as he had expected, there were no dissenting votes. His speech was smuggled out of the country and under the title "A Protest by the Russian Social Democrats" it was printed by Plekhanov in *Rabocheye Dyelo* later in the year.

Lenin's "Protest" evades most of the issues raised by Ekaterina Kuskova. He was less concerned with argument than with restating his own categorical position. He quoted approvingly the manifesto of the Minsk congress, especially the words, "On its strong shoulders the Russian working class must and will carry the work of conquering political liberty." He admitted that the secret police had brought the work of the party to a virtual standstill and that its official organ had ceased publication. Ekaterina Kuskova had praised the Narodnaya Volya. Lenin embroidered on the theme and praised it still more fervently, saying, "While the Narodnaya Volya succeeded in playing an enormous role in Russian history without possessing a revolutionary theory, Social Democracy, armed with the class struggle of the proletariat, will render itself invincible." Previously he had demanded that the Social Democratic Party should wage incessant war against all other parties; now, perhaps because he was aware of the force of

Ekaterina Kuskova's argument, he claimed that the Social Democrats would never refuse to co-operate with other parties. "On the contrary," he wrote, "the Social Democrats must take part in all political and social life, they must support the progressive classes and parties against the reactionary classes and parties, they must support every revolutionary movement against the existing system and champion the interests of every oppressed nationality and race and every persecuted religion." But what he gave with one hand he took away with the other, for he added immediately: "The *Credo* merely reveals a desire to obscure the class character of the struggle of the proletariat, to weaken the struggle by a meaningless 'recognition of society,' and to reduce revolutionary Marxism to trivial reformism." On the subject of the economic struggle demanded by the *Credo* he had very little to say, merely observing that "the conviction that the class struggle must necessarily combine the political and economic struggle into one integral whole has entered into the flesh and blood of international Social Democracy."

It was, on the whole, a lame attack on the *Credo*. He was bruised and angry, and uncertain of his aim. He knew even at this distance that the *Credo* would fall on fertile soil and that he would have to continue fighting it. Ekaterina Kuskova had spoken about the amoeba-like lack of organization among the Russian working class. Henceforward, *organization* was to become his watchword.

Bernstein's book and the *Credo* shattered whatever complacency Lenin may have had. In the last months of his exile his character seemed to change. Gone was the sunburned man with the gift of laughter. He became dour and relentless, given to sudden explosions of ill temper, sleeping badly, losing his covering of fat. Unable to sleep, he would sit up all night, making plans for a revolutionary future, thinking out more and more arguments to destroy the "Economists," who failed to realize, or perhaps realized too well, that they were sabotaging the holy principles of Marx. The party had been destroyed, but he would build it. He would edit its newspaper from abroad and smuggle it into Russia through hundreds of trusted agents, and this newspaper would serve a party obedient to his commands, for he could see himself only as the sole ruler and he had no intention of co-operating with other members or other parties except in so far as they served his will.

Gaunt and haggard, he was a man consumed by an idea, endlessly pacing his room, endlessly wandering through the forests. His term

of exile would expire in January 1900, and Krupskaya's a year later—
she would have to complete her exile in Ufa unless he remained with
her. Impatient for action, it never occurred to him to stay a further
year in Shushenskoye to be by her side.

At last, when official authorization had been received for his return to European Russia, there came the time for leave-taking. To
the boy Minka and the girl Pasha went most of their small possessions.
Oscar Engberg presented Krupskaya with a small handmade brooch
in the shape of a book bearing the name of Marx. Elizaveta Vasilyevna
put herself in charge of packing the household implements, and Lenin
tied up the books. The villagers came. There were speeches and toasts,
and then the small party drove to Minusinsk to say more farewells to
the revolutionaries there and to take on Krzhizhanovsky and his wife,
who were also returning to Europe. The first stop was to be Ufa,
where Krupskaya and her mother would be left to spend the last year
of exile.

There were no speeches in Minusinsk—the revolutionaries had no
use for sentiment. The sleigh was piled high with books. Huddled in
long fur coats against the cold, and wearing high felt boots, the
women took their places. For some reason Lenin wore no fur coat, but
he buried his hands in a muff borrowed from Elizaveta Vasilyevna.
Then by day and by night, stopping only at the stagehouses to change
the horses, they drove for two hundred miles along the ice-covered
Yenisey river. At night there was a full moon. The journey over the
white river was a prolonged excursion into an enchanted kingdom.

For Lenin the years of exile had passed like a dream interrupted
with occasional nightmares. There would come a time when he would
forget completely that he had ever been at Shushenskoye. In 1921 he
was asked to fill a questionnaire where there was the question: Where
have you lived in Russia? He answered: "Only on the Volga and in
the capital cities." It was as though Shushenskoye and the journey in
the covered sleigh had never been.

THE YEARS
OF THE
WILDERNESS

*Let go of our hands, don't clutch at
us, and don't dirty the great word of
freedom, because we too are "free" to go
wherever we wish, free to fight not only
against the marshes, but also against
those who are turning toward the marshes . . .*

WHAT IS TO BE DONE?

Now that he was free, Lenin threw himself into conspiratorial work like a man who has been starved of everything that made life worth living. In the past he had been an agitator, addressing small groups of workers, traveling at night from one worker's house to another with the police dogging his heels; but these days were over. Now the task was to publish a secret revolutionary newspaper and to capture the imagination of the workers through the press.

By police orders he could stay anywhere he liked, except in St. Petersburg. He chose to stay in Pskov—a town he had never visited before—because it was close to St. Petersburg. In this way he thought he would be able to move in and out of the capital as he pleased, hoodwinking the police by wearing different disguises and making the journey in unconventional ways. His friends were in St. Petersburg; here, if anywhere, the revolution would break out; here, too, were the most trusted agents of the Social Democratic Party who would be responsible for distributing most of the revolutionary leaflets, pamphlets and newspapers which would be printed by the party press, probably in Switzerland. In Pskov he was under police surveillance, and journeys to the capital proved more difficult than he had thought. In February or the beginning of March he slipped out of Pskov and had a secret rendezvous in St. Petersburg with Vera Zasulich, who had been sent by Plekhanov to discuss the illegal newspaper. It was already assumed that Plekhanov would be editor in chief, with Axelrod, Vera Zasulich, Lenin and Martov as active participants.

In those days Vera Zasulich was no longer the handsome young

139

woman who had befriended Nechayev. She was about twenty-five when she shot at General Trepov and her name resounded in headlines round the world. Since then she had grown fat, dowdy and very deaf. She was nearly fifty, but looked older, and there was about her appearance something that suggested an old washerwoman from Mongolia, for age had only increased the Mongoloid cast of her features.

Lenin seems to have spent three or four days in her company, discussing the plan for the newspaper. Vera Zasulich was particularly concerned with its financial aspects, and she emphasized the need for raising large sums of money in Russia. They also discussed which local organizations would be allowed to participate. Through her, Lenin was close to Plekhanov, the fountainhead of Russian Marxism, and to Nechayev, the fountainhead of the philosophy of destruction which was to haunt him for the rest of his life.

Returning to Pskov, Lenin made out that he was intent on pursuing a legal career and had done with politics. Prince Obolensky, the most influential person in the town, took a liking to him and arranged a meeting of the town's lawyers, suggesting that "Mr. Ulyanov might like to look them over before finally deciding which one he would work with." At first everything went well, but Lenin was completely incapable of discussing anything except politics and soon he was launched into a long tirade against the government, and the meeting broke up. Prince Obolensky was not particularly alarmed; other meetings were arranged with the leading people of the town, where Lenin was regarded as a man who would eventually settle down and become an exemplary citizen.

Lenin had not the slightest intention of settling down. With his friend Martov, and with several suitcases full of illegal literature, he set out for St. Petersburg at the beginning of June. The plan was to go by a roundabout route through Gatchina and Tsarskoye Selo, changing trains at each place. Everything went well. They were able to dispose of the illegal literature when they reached St. Petersburg, and they spent the night quietly in a house on Kazachy Street, congratulating themselves on having outwitted the police. Such journeys augured well for future visits to the capital.

The next morning when Lenin and Martov left the house, the police pounced on them. Their arms were pinioned to their sides, to prevent them from throwing anything away or from swallowing incriminating documents, and they were carried off to the police station in separate cabs. Lenin was particularly disturbed because there was a letter to Plekhanov outlining the whole scheme of the secret revolutionary newspaper in his pocket; the letter was a receipt, with all the writing in invisible ink, but he knew that the police were sometimes able to develop these writings, and body heat would sometimes cause them to develop of their own accord. At the police station they were both searched; the police found the receipt, but paid no attention to it. They were thrown into a cell and then brought out for interrogation.

"We want to know what you are doing here," the police inspector said. "You know perfectly well that you are forbidden to come to the capital."

Apparently through the good offices of Prince Obolensky, Lenin had acquired a passport permitting him to travel abroad. It was his most precious possession, and he saw now that it would probably be taken away from him, and in addition he might have to serve another term of exile in Siberia.

The police inspector was laughing.

"What an extraordinary person you are!" he exclaimed. "We trailed you, of course, and you had the impudence to change trains at Tsarskoye Selo, where we have one of our agents standing behind every blade of grass. Did you really think we wouldn't notice you?"

The Tsar and the royal family lived at Tsarskoye Selo—Lenin might have known that it would be heavily guarded.

He was not brought up for trial, but simply kept in prison. It was the height of summer: gnats, fleas, and mosquitoes made life unbearable. He complained that the police played cards in a room opposite his cell all night, and this too kept him from sleeping. Suddenly, two weeks after his arrest, he was ordered to leave the prison and make his way under guard to Podolsk, where his mother was living. She had used her not inconsiderable influence to have him set free.

At Podolsk he was first taken to the police station. An officious chief inspector asked for his passport, examined it, and then tossed it into a drawer. Lenin was outraged, demanded it back, and was told that it might be returned to him at some future time.

"Then I shall bring the case to the attention of the Police Department," Lenin said. "I shall file a complaint—"

He turned and was walking out of the police station when the inspector shouted after him, "Come back, Mr. Ulyanov. You can have your passport if you want it!"

Such at any rate was the story Lenin told with glee when he reached his mother's house. It was a small victory, and there were to be many similar victories.

He was a former exile who had been arrested and had spent two weeks in prison; he was still under police surveillance; and already there were voluminous records on his activity in the police files. He could expect to be treated harshly. In fact he was treated with great leniency, and when he asked for permission to visit Nadezhda Konstantinovna in her place of exile in Ufa, a thousand miles to the east, his mother once more used her influence, and permission was granted on condition that she accompanied her son. They decided to make most of the journey by river. Anna went with them, and she has left an idyllic account of the long days spent on the open deck as they steamed down the Volga, and then took a much smaller river boat up the Kama and the Belaya rivers to Ufa. Maria Alexandrovna was then sixty-three, a small, white-haired, birdlike woman in failing health, but still vigorous. The last years had exhausted her, for while Lenin was in exile in Siberia, her son Dmitry was arrested in Tula and her daughter Maria in Nizhni Novgorod, and so she was continually running between these towns and St. Petersburg to obtain their release or to see that they were well treated. When Lenin was arrested with Martov, she rushed again to St. Petersburg where, according to Anna, "she camped on the steps of the police station." Now, on the river boat, she could forget her harassed life as the mother of revolutionaries and admire the flooded river and the forests crowding the banks. Anna remembered that in the evenings she tired quickly and went early to bed.

They spent a week at Ufa. Lenin had already worked out the secret code to be used by revolutionaries corresponding with him abroad, and he took the opportunity to distribute the code among the exiles he found there. He had not come simply to say good-bye to his wife. On the train returning from Ufa, he saw the Volga for the last time. He spent a week in Podolsk, and then he was on the train again —this time for Switzerland.

He had expected miracles to happen in Switzerland, but instead there were outbursts of temper, bitter conflicts within the party, interminable debates. Maxim Gorky once described Plekhanov as an unbending patrician who was in love with his frock coat and especially with one of its buttons, which he would stroke caressingly until the moment came when he felt the need to press it as though it were an electric bell, and at that moment there would be a pause in his speech, a painful confrontation with an invisible destiny, until the words flowed again. Plekhanov always spoke like a commander calmly ordering his troops into battle.

Lenin was in no mood to be ordered into battle and took the offensive. He seems to have disliked Plekhanov from the beginning; and though he worshiped Vera Zasulich—he described her as "true all the way through," meaning that every drop of her blood was fired with revolutionary ardor—he was dismayed to discover that she regarded Plekhanov with veneration, echoed his words, and was likely to consider anyone who disagreed with him as an enemy. The battle was fought largely between Lenin and Plekhanov, with Axelrod and Vera Zasulich acting as the older man's shield-bearers; it was fought, predictably, over the question of who would have control of the newspaper and the theoretical magazine which would be printed at the same time.

Lenin won the battle, but as with all his battles until he assumed power, there was no clear-cut victory. He won by default and by provoking the enemy to overplay his hand. The quarrel which flared up during a hot August evening only to be resumed the following morning was described in an extraordinary document, which covers seventeen closely printed pages of the standard edition of Lenin's works. It is called "How *The Spark* Was Nearly Extinguished" and was written in anger when the impressions were still fresh, in a hand that races imperiously across the page; the whole narrative seems to have been written in one long, angry breath.

There is not the least doubt from Lenin's account of the quarrel that he was offended by Plekhanov's Olympian manner and deliberately goaded him. Lenin wanted vigorous polemics; Plekhanov wanted none of them, saying that he had never taken any part in personal attacks on people. Lenin relished the reply, for Plekhanov had actually published some private letters, including one from Ekaterina Kuskova, in a booklet designed to demonstrate his own political principles. Was this not polemics? And how could one fight a war without weapons? Plekhanov was stubborn; Lenin found himself playing the role of the prosecuting counsel. "Plekhanov," wrote Lenin, "displayed complete intolerance, an inability or an unwillingness to understand other people's arguments, and what can only be called insincerity."

What had happened was that Lenin had written a very dull and prolix "Draft of a Declaration of the Editorial Board of *Iskra* and *Zarya*." *Iskra* (Spark) was the newspaper; *Zarya* (Dawn) was the magazine. Plekhanov had returned the draft to Lenin with a note saying that it should be rewritten "in a more elevated style." Lenin was infuriated. He rewrote it, presented it a second time to Plekhanov, and was thunderstruck when Plekhanov simply passed it on to Vera Zasulich, suggesting that she might find time to do some rewriting. They quarreled on the voting strength of the editorial board; it was finally agreed that there should be six members—Plekhanov, Axelrod, Vera Zasulich, Lenin, Martov, and Potresov; but Plekhanov should have two votes. Lenin resented this, but it is clear from his long diatribe that he was wounded more by Plekhanov's manner than by anything he said or by any proposals made by his shield-bearers. He was stung by Plekhanov's unspoken contempt, the implied suggestion that he was a "Johnny-come-lately." He wrote:

My "infatuation" for Plekhanov disappeared as if by magic, and I felt offended and embittered to an unbelievable degree. Never, never in my life had I regarded any other man with such sincere consideration and respect, such *vénération*, never had I stood so "humbly" before any man, and never had I received such a brutal "kick in the backside." And that is exactly what happened: we got "kicks." We were frightened out of our wits like little children, frightened because our elders threatened to leave us alone, and when we panicked (the shame of it!) we were swept aside with incredible unceremoniousness. We now realized very clearly that Plekhanov had quietly been laying a trap for us that very morning when he declined to be co-editor; it was a calculated chess move, a snare for simple "pigeons." . . . And since this man, with whom we desired to co-operate closely and establish the most intimate relations, was resorting to chess moves in dealing with his comrades—there can be no doubt at all that this man was bad, yes, a bad man, inspired by petty motives of personal vanity and conceit—an insincere man. This discovery—and it was indeed a discovery—hit us like a thunderbolt; for up to that moment we had unfeigningly admired him, and as with those we love, we had forgiven him everything; we had closed our eyes to all his shortcomings, trying hard to persuade ourselves that they did not exist, that they were small things that bothered only people who had no proper regard for principles.

So he goes on to lambaste Plekhanov at extraordinary length, relating all their meetings and discussions, remembering the exact tone of his voice, the exact quality of his icy disdain; and it seems never to have occurred to Lenin that there was no disdain, only impatience. "We decided to throw everything up and return to Russia," Lenin says. But he thought better of it and arranged a final meeting with "this dictator." He confessed he did not look forward to the meeting; it was like going to a funeral. Bluntly, Lenin accused him of being "bad." Plekhanov replied that no doubt Lenin was attaching importance to impressions which were not important, and in any event he was not dependent upon Lenin's help; he had his own work to do; he would not sit back and fold his arms simply because there were disagreements between them. He even suggested that, if necessary, he was prepared to abandon political work altogether, a statement which incensed Lenin so much that he abandoned the conversation, only to return the next day to argue once more whether they should permit polemics (Plekhanov refused) and how they should vote (Plekhanov said there could be no voting on fundamental questions). Lenin had met his match, and he was still quivering with fury when he set off for Nuremberg to begin the work of issuing the paper.

"How *The Spark* Was Nearly Extinguished" is of quite exceptional importance to an understanding of Lenin. It is the only sustained example of his narrative prose that has survived, and perhaps the only narrative he ever wrote. He tells of the separate meetings with Plekhanov, what was said, his own and Plekhanov's attitudes, and though there is bitterness there is also a basic honesty; the portrait of Plekhanov, cultured, evasive, and uncompromising, comes through, and so does the portrait of Lenin, uncompromising, never evasive, uncultured, and inclined to self-pity. There are long maudlin passages in which he weeps over his thwarted ambitions, but there is a hardness in the narrative that suggests that they have been thwarted only for a little while. Indeed, he says as much toward the end of the narrative:

> As the affair became more and more remote, we began to think of it more calmly and came to believe that it was altogether unreasonable, and there was simply no reason to be afraid of assuming the editorship at this time, even if it was only a collection of *articles,* and indeed it was necessary for us to undertake it, for there was absolutely no other way to make the machine work properly and of preventing it from being ruined by the disruptive "qualities" of Plekhanov.

Lenin's style flows freely in "How *The Spark* Was Nearly Extinguished"; but in general it was never a free-flowing style. He wrote with some difficulty, at the mercy of those columns of preliminary notes in which the basic ideas are expressed on the left side and the additional ideas arising out of them are added on the right side. Each paragraph rounds the thought, leaving nothing left to be said on the subject; it is a heavy, rather mechanical documentary style. From time to time, usually at the end of an article, he will permit himself the luxury of vehement invective, denouncing his enemies with ferocious arrogance and threats, imitating or enlarging on the great passages of invective which already appeared in Russian and Socialist literature, of which the classic examples occur in Marx's *Das Kapital* and Pisarev's *On the Shedo-Ferrotti Pamphlet.* Here is Pisarev's denunciation of the autocracy, written in 1862:

> On the side of the government there are only scoundrels, bought with the money squeezed by fraud and violence from the poor. On the side of the people there is all that is fresh and youthful, all that is capable of thinking and doing. What is dead and rotten must of itself fall into the grave. All we have to do is to give it a final push, and cover the stinking corpse with dirt.

Here is Karl Marx inveighing against capital:

> If money, as Augier says, "came into the world with a congenital bloodstain on one cheek," then capital comes dripping from head to foot, from every pore, with blood and dirt.

Lenin knew these passages by heart, and paid them the tribute of countless imitations. Plekhanov disliked them, claiming that they derived from a literary trick and that angry vehemence was unsuited to socialists. But it was Lenin who prevailed.

In Germany Lenin set up the machinery for the publication of *Iskra* and *Zarya*, keeping the leading strings in his hands. When Krupskaya at last finished her term of exile and joined him in Munich, he appointed her chairman of the editorial board, thus further strengthening his control. They lived in a typical German working-class home for a month, and then moved to an apartment of their own in Schwabing. Martov, Vera Zasulich, and Blumenfeld, who set up the type, lived nearby, while Plekhanov remained in Switzerland, a remote and brooding figure who would sometimes attempt to call a halt to Lenin's more outrageous theories, though his remoteness permitted Lenin nearly as much latitude as he wanted. When Lenin left Germany for England, it was chiefly to increase the distance between himself and Plekhanov.

The theoretical magazine *Zarya* had a short life, and only three numbers were published. The second number, which appeared in December 1901, has some claim to be remembered, for it included an article on "The Agrarian Question and the 'Critics of Marx,'" signed *N. Lenin*. It was the first time that signature had ever appeared.

Lenin had a bewildering number of pseudonyms. A list of more than seventy-five of his pseudonyms has been published, many of them consisting of initials apparently chosen at random. At various times he used the names Petrov, Tulin, Ilin, Ivanov, Frey, Piryuchev, Karpov, Jacob Richter, Meyer; but his articles would often be signed I, L, S.T.A., F.P., T.P., T.Ch., or with variations of his own initials— V, V.I., V.U., V.Ul., V.Il. There is no discernible pattern in his use of pseudonyms.

From the moment he met Plekhanov, Lenin seems to have realized that he suffered from the disadvantage of never having written a volume of theoretical writings which could stand up against Plekhanov's shelf of theoretical works. In the autumn and winter of 1901, borrowing the title of Chernyshevsky's famous novel, he wrote a book of some two hundred pages in which he sketched out the revolutionary principles which he employed sixteen years later.

With *What Is To Be Done?* Lenin finally hammered his revolutionary philosophy into shape. Not surprisingly, this philosophy has very little to do with Marx and derives straight from Nechayev and Pisarev. Marx is scarcely mentioned, and the Marxist thesis that "the emancipation of the working class is the work of the working class itself" is conveniently ignored, while the concept of the small, highly trained group of intellectuals acting as "the vanguard of the revolution" is maintained stubbornly and excitedly against all opposition. "By their own efforts," says Lenin, "the working class can only arrive at a trade union mentality"—meaning that they can only bargain with their employers, strike and protest on a limited scale. In order that the dictatorship of the proletariat should come into existence, there must be a hard core of professional revolutionaries leading the way and keeping the workers under tutelage. Around this hard core gather the socially conscious workers wrapped in revolutionary flames. The war to the death against the bourgeoisie is fought by the professional revolutionaries in alliance with a small and militant group of workers.

What Is To Be Done? is an extraordinary work. Krupskaya described it as "an ardent appeal for organization": but that is to describe it in its simplest possible terms, for in his usual fashion Lenin combines furious invective, stark prophecy, special pleading, and bitter attacks against his enemies with a temper so authoritarian that it can chill the blood. He alone has found the key to unlock the door, and woe betide anyone who dares to dispute with him! "Freedom is a great word," he says with heavy sarcasm. "Under the banner of industrial freedom the most predatory wars have been waged, and under the banner of freedom to work, the workers have been plundered." Freedom of criticism, the common Russian pastime, is outlawed, since the laws governing society have now been discovered and there is nothing to be gained by disputing with scientific laws. The entire first chapter is devoted to a violent diatribe against freedom. He pictures the revolutionaries as men making their way along dangerous roads, concentrating on the task ahead—and what would happen if the ignorant were permitted to shout out directions to these intrepid wanderers? In a passage of sustained irony he describes the plight of the revolutionaries and the even greater plight of those who dare to offer them advice:

> We are marching in a close-knit group along a difficult and precipitous road, gripping each other firmly by the hands. On all sides we are surrounded by enemies, and nearly all the time we have to advance under their fire. We have combined together after freely deciding to fight the enemy, and not to retreat into the nearby marshes, where from the very beginning the inhabitants have reproached us for having formed exclusive groups and for having chosen the path of struggle rather than the path of conciliation. And when some of us begin to shout, "Let us go into the marshes!"—why, then we begin to shame them,

and they exclaim, "What backward people you are! Why aren't you ashamed to deny us the freedom to show you a better road?" Yes, gentlemen, you are free to show us the better road and to go wherever you like, even to the marshes. We even believe that the marshes are the proper place for you, and we will give you *every* assistance to get there. Only let go of our hands, don't clutch at us, and don't dirty the great word of freedom, because we too are "free" to go wherever we wish, free to fight not only against the marshes, but also against those who are turning toward the marshes.

Lenin rarely uses sustained imagery; this passage is one of the very few in which he works out an image to a conclusion. He is the master of the contemptuous phrase, and with this picture of the dedicated revolutionaries shaking off their pursuers and abandoning them in the swamps and marshlands, he sets the scene for the drama which follows.

What Is To Be Done? is high drama in the same way that Nechayev's *Revolutionary Catechism*, from which it is very largely derived, is high drama; but where Nechayev is content to set his villains and heroes on Russian soil, describing the inevitable punishments of the villains within a frame of reference which is wholly Russian, Lenin goes further: the whole world is his stage. The villains are the bourgeoisie everywhere, not only in Russia, but the heroes are still Russians, for they alone have been given the task of leading the world-wide revolution by virtue of the sacrifices of the Seventies, by which he can only mean Nechayev and the Narodnaya Volya. In a breathtaking passage, speaking like a new Moses, Lenin declares his allegiance to the revolutionary past and points the way to the revolutionary future:

> History has set before us a task to be accomplished in the near future which is *far more revolutionary* than all the *immediate* tasks of the proletariat of any other country. The fulfillment of this task, the destruction of the most powerful bulwark of European and (we may even say) of Asiatic reaction, would surely make the Russian proletariat the vanguard of the international proletarian revolution. And we rightly count on acquiring this honorable title, already earned by our predecessors, the revolutionaries of the Seventies, if we succeed in inspiring our movement—a movement which is a thousand times broader and deeper —with the same limitless steadfastness and energy.

With these words Lenin abandons the role of revolutionary agitator and assumes the robes of a prophet. Henceforward these words were to inspire him to more and more audacious interpretations of revolution, but the core of his theory of revolution never departed from this basic conception. His sister Maria said of him that he was a man of one idea, and the idea was a very simple one. It was that the proletariat of Russia would take power, and they would be followed by the proletariat of the whole world.

There was nothing in the works of Marx to substantiate this prophecy, and it is noteworthy that Lenin makes no attempt to find support in Marx. Instead, he looks back to the revolutionary battles of the Seventies in Russia, fought by small dedicated groups of students who believed in the virtues of terrorism. As Lenin elaborates his theory of revolution in *What Is To Be Done?* it becomes increasingly clear that he is merely adapting Nechayev. Like Nechayev he demands a terrorist elite acting in complete secrecy, infiltrating "in the postal services, on the railways, in the customs, among the nobility, the clergy and *every* other walk of life, including the police and the Court." This powerful and secret organization would be centralized, concentrating in its hands the threads of all its secret activities, and in its own time it would rise up and destroy the autocracy. There was the danger that it might order an uprising at the wrong time, and Lenin answers that this is a danger that has to be faced, because "every battle bears within itself the abstract possibility of defeat." Nevertheless he sees no alternative. There *must* be a revolutionary elite. There *cannot* be a democracy of revolutionaries. Discussion among the rank and file *must not* be permitted. One man, or a very small number of men, *must* make the ultimate decisions.

Lenin does not deny that the revolutionary movement is a conspiratorial one. On the contrary, he glories in it and pours some of his most bitter scorn on the armchair theorists who speak of "spontaneous revolutions" arising out of the needs of the people. The revolution he envisages is coldly calculated and manipulated, led by archrevolutionaries with their staffs, their specialists, and well-disciplined military or paramilitary organizations capable of exquisite maneuvers, sudden thrusts, circuitous retreats.

As Lenin goes on to describe his revolutionary elite at length, it begins to wear an oddly Germanic coloring, as though Nechayev were transplanted among the Stormtroopers. Lenin admits that he has been deeply impressed by the iron leadership of the German socialists; in page after page he celebrates the German discovery that "no class in modern society can wage a determined struggle without the 'dozen' tried and talented leaders, professionally trained, schooled by long experience and working in complete harmony." What is needed is German organization imposed upon Russian enthusiasm: the German sense of order and obedience, the Russian fire. In all this he was perhaps doing no more than expressing the split in his own soul.

Nechayev believed in the revolutionary elite, but he was far from having any understanding or sympathy with the German mind. *The Revolutionary Catechism* describes a purely Russian conspiratorial activity: menaces, threats, sudden raids into the heart of enemy territory, mines and countermines, a war of shadows. The revolutionary elite are like the medieval princes of Russia evolving stratagems to bring about the downfall of the Tsar: they are doomed men, and they will perish in the flames. Lenin removes the doom by giving them Germanic method.

Not that Lenin is ever very far from Nechayev. Throughout *What Is To Be Done?* there are echoes of Nechayev's peculiar revolutionary *tone*. Here, for example, is Lenin describing how young intellectuals would be used in the revolution:

> We would husband them very carefully and even train people especially for special functions, remembering that many students could be of much greater use to the party as "special assistants" holding official posts than as "part-time" revolutionaries.

It is the authentic voice of Nechayev, the pupil imitating the master so accurately that one has the feeling that Nechayev must somewhere have spoken these same words. Lenin speaks equally enthusiastically of Tkachev, the friend of Nechayev, who spoke of invoking a "terrifying" terror which really terrified and so frightened the autocracy that it gave up the ghost; of this triple terror, a terror so overwhelming that no power on earth could resist it, Lenin spoke approvingly, saying that it was "majestic." But what if this terror was exerted by "ordinary people"? Lenin's consciousness of his own revolutionary superiority was nowhere more manifest than when he spoke of the "ordinary people," who had neither the daring nor the professional ability of the scholar of revolution who had trained himself by arduous study to become a member of the elite.

In *What Is To Be Done?* Lenin never moves very far from contemplation of the elite. The prophet who proclaims that "the time is near" must be followed by the chosen ones, the professional knights of the faith, the gaudy professionals. And while Nechayev is evidently

responsible for the conception of the tightly knit group of archrevolutionaries, Lenin's feeling for the professionals was reinforced by his
own experience within the League for the Emancipation of Labor,
where he was confronted with rank amateurs, himself among them. He
describes his feelings in one of the few autobiographical passages in
the book:

> I used to work in a circle that set itself very wide, all-embracing tasks,
> and all of us who were members of the circle suffered to the point of
> actual torture from the consciousness that we were proving ourselves to
> be such amateurs at such a historic moment when, paraphrasing a well-
> known saying, we might have been able to say, "Give us an organization
> of revolutionaries, and we shall turn Russia upside down!" And since
> then, whenever I have remembered the burning sense of shame I ex-
> perienced, my bitterness toward the pseudo–Social Democrats was in-
> creased, because their teachings "disgrace the calling of a revolutionary"
> and because they fail to understand that our task is not to effect the
> degrading of the revolutionary to the level of the amateur, but to *raise*
> the amateur to the level of the revolutionary.

According to Lenin there must be professional expertise and a code
of professional behavior; the "dozen" must have the place of honor; as
for the "broad democracy" in the party organization, this is nothing
more than a useless and harmful toy. This implication is clear: up to
this time the revolutionaries have been children, but the time has
come for grown men to step in. "In former times," he declared, "our
revolutionaries relied on a theory which in substance was not a revolutionary theory at all, because they did not know how to combine
their movement with the class struggle within developing capitalist
society, or else they were unable to bring it about." Lenin provides
the theory—the proletariat must take the place of the Tsar. It is not a
theory which he pursues at any very great depth, because to him it is
self-evident, but it permits him to elaborate on his favorite theme
of the revolutionary elite acting as the vanguard of the proletariat;
and it never occurred to him until too late that the vanguard would
inevitably destroy the initiative of the proletariat and act as an unlimited autocracy. Since from the beginning he assumes that liberty
to criticize is intolerable, and democracy is unworthy, and the triple
terror is alone majestic, there is no escaping the authoritarian nature
of the regime which he discussed abstractly in 1901 and brought into
existence sixteen years later.

Already in *What Is To Be Done?* Lenin has hammered out those definitions which seem so strange to western readers because he uses words in a way which crudely distorts their accepted meanings. For him, democracy has nothing whatsoever to do with the kind of government which Cleisthenes brought to Athens and which Aristotle defined as "to govern and to be governed." He has a very simple definition of democracy: "the abolition of class domination." He has an equally simple and startling definition of liberty: "bourgeois tyranny." These definitions need to be remembered, because he is continually talking of his love for democracy and his hatred of liberty.

When Lenin announced that history had given the Russian working class a role of supreme importance, he was perfectly aware of the prophetic and visionary character of the statement. He knew that in 1901, when the Russian proletariat was far less advanced than the German, British or American proletariat, and therefore far less capable of carrying out a successful revolution, he was stretching credulity to the utmost. He admitted it was a dream, almost beyond thinking about, and quoted Pisarev in defense of dreaming:

My dream may run ahead of the natural march of events or may fly off at a tangent in a direction where no natural march of events will ever follow it. In the first case my dream will not have done any harm; it may even help and add fuel to the energy of the working classes. . . . If a man were completely deprived of the ability to dream in this way, if he could never run ahead and mentally conceive in an entire and completed picture the results of the work which his hands are only just beginning to shape, then I cannot imagine what stimulus there would be to induce men to undertake extensive and exhausting work in the sphere of art, science and practical endeavor. . . . The rift between dreams and reality causes no harm if the dreamer believes seriously in his dream, if he attentively observes life, compares his observations with his castles in the air, and if, in general, he works conscientiously toward achieving his fantasies. If there is some connection between dreams and life then all is well.

To Pisarev's observations on dreams Lenin adds his own comment:

But of this kind of dreaming there is unfortunately too little in our movement. And those who are most responsible are the ones who boast of their sobriety, their "closeness" to "reality."

Lenin seems to have been aware that he was walking on dangerous ground, that ground which had been so carefully explored by Chekhov in his story "Ward No. 6." But there was nothing he could do about it. For the rest of his life he was to remain the prisoner of the ideas expounded in *What Is To Be Done?* They possessed, for him, a fatal finality. He would continue to dream to the limits of his dream, and there would come a point when the dream would have to be replaced by another dream. He foresaw that Russian Social Democracy, which had already gone through two phases, would in its third phase acquire maturity and power. And what then? In the last chilling words of the book he says:

> To the question What is to be done? we may give the following brief reply:
>
> Liquidate the Third Phase.

It was perhaps the clearest statement of his essential nihilism that he ever made.

The book, however, is a work of cardinal importance in the history of the Russian Revolution. All of Lenin is there: the boldness of his conceptions intermingled with long diatribes against those who disagree with him, bursts of sarcasm, page after page of garrulous invective, which suddenly give way to clear, visionary statement. Within its pages are to be found his best writing—indeed, his only good writing. It is the work of a man discovering himself as he goes along, sustained by intellectual excitement, before he began to utter interminable, monotonous parodies of himself.

The book which covers 180 closely printed pages in the current edition of his complete works had been his constant companion for a period of about six months. Finally, it was printed with a chocolate-covered jacket by a press in Stuttgart in March 1902. It was scarcely off the press when the printers of *Iskra* decided that printing a revolutionary newspaper was too risky a venture, and they categorically refused to go on printing it. A hurried meeting was called. There was a stormy debate. Plekhanov and Axelrod insisted that they should move to Switzerland; but Lenin, with one eye on the British Museum library, insisted that it could be printed more safely on a socialist press in England. In this way London became the temporary headquarters of the revolution.

THE LONDON YEAR

WHEN LENIN AND KRUPSKAYA ARRIVED in London, a dense fog hung over the city. It was one of those days when you can scarcely see a street lamp five paces away. The dark, cavernous railroad station, the smoke, and the thundering roar of the trains terrified Krupskaya, but Lenin was excited by everything he saw. He knew English well, or rather he thought he knew English well; and he thought he knew London well, for he had spent many hours poring over a map, working out in advance all the possible roads which led to the British Museum. And yet, like many travelers before him, within an hour of being in London, he realized that his English was lamentable, and his knowledge of the city was for practical purposes valueless.

What staggered him, as it had staggered Dostoyevsky forty years before, was the sheer immensity of the place, the continual traffic, the uproar. He was accustomed to living in small provincial towns; now he was confronted with a great metropolis, a place so vast that men can be lost in it and never find their way out again. At first he was uneasy in London. Then gradually, as he became accustomed to the noise and as he settled down into an orderly routine, he came to have a genuine liking for it, and visitors from abroad would be treated to conducted tours through the city, with Lenin acting as a knowledgeable guide.

At that time, a considerable group of Russian revolutionary exiles were living in London. Prince Peter Kropotkin and Nikolay Tchaikovsky, veterans of an earlier revolutionary age, were living quietly

155

in London, and there were a hundred others of lesser importance. Among these was Nikolay Alexeyev, who had been a member of the League for the Liberation of the Working Classes, had been arrested and sent to Siberia, and somehow had escaped and made his way to London, where he arrived in December 1899. He was under thirty, with a quick and resourceful mind, and he took Lenin and Krupskaya under his wing, putting them up first in a furnished room in Sidmouth Street, off Gray's Inn Road, and then in an unfurnished two-room apartment at 30 Holford Square, kept by a Mrs. Yeo, who charged them thirty shillings a week. It was Alexeyev, always in high good humor, who led Lenin through the intricate mazes of the revolutionary exiles, telling him which group was worth seeing and which to be avoided, and making contacts wherever necessary with English socialists, like Harry Quelch, the editor of *Justice*, and Isaac Mitchell, the secretary of the General Federation of Trade Unions.

Lenin had no sooner settled down in the apartment in Holford Square than he wrote off for a ticket of admission to the reading room of the British Museum, enclosing a letter of recommendation from Isaac Mitchell. Lenin had hoped to begin work in the reading room immediately, but there was some delay. Mitchell had written from a house in a new street which did not appear in the London Directory, and the British Museum officials, always cautious, were not disposed to issue a ticket unless they were convinced of the *bona fides* of the recommender. But in fact Mitchell's *bona fides* was unassailable, as the British Museum recognized when he wrote another letter of recommendation on the stationery of the General Federation of Trade Unions, and at last on April 29 a ticket for three months was issued to Lenin under the name of Jacob Richter, LL.D., who declared that he was not under twenty-one years of age and had read the directions respecting the reading room:

29/2

A72453

3m   4332

I have read the " DIRECTIONS respecting the Reading Room,"
And I declare that I am not under twenty-one years of age.

Jacob Richter LLD.
30. Holford Square. Pentonville. N.

30. Holford Square.
Pentonville. W.C.

Sir,

I beg to apply for a ticket of admission to the Reading Room of the British Museum. I came from Russia in order to study the land question. I enclose the reference letter of Mr. Mitchell.

Believe me, Sir, to be Yours faithfully

Jacob Richter.

April 21. 1902

To the Director of the British Museum.

Thereafter, as regularly as clockwork, Lenin would walk every day to the British Museum, arriving shortly after opening time, and work steadily through the morning; then at one o'clock he would put his books away in the reserve section and walk out into Great Russell Street and sit down in one of four or five restaurants. The afternoon was usually given to meetings with revolutionaries, and the evenings were usually spent alone in the apartment in Holford Square with Krupskaya. He was a creature of habit, and every day was like every other day.

He spent his days in London exactly as he would spend all the remaining years of his life: quietly, modestly, working during the morning in a library, seeing revolutionaries in the afternoon, studying at night. It was a life without incident, brightened only by occasional trips round London on the top of a bus and by Sunday visits to the socialist churches, where the officiating clergyman was often a workman in a surplice, breathing fire and brimstone on the rich while reserving his benedictions for the downtrodden poor. There were also occasional visits to Hyde Park to hear the open-air speakers, traditionally permitted the fullest liberty of expression. Here the atheists thundered against God, the Salvation Army offered to baptize everyone in the blood of the Lamb, and the socialists held forth on the subject of sweated labor. Lenin would plant himself very close to the speakers, not because he had the slightest interest in what they were saying, but because he wanted to follow their lip movements closely. It was one of his ways of learning English.

He was determined to speak English well, and not long after he reached London he inserted an advertisement in the *Athenæum*, announcing that a doctor of laws of St. Petersburg University was prepared to give Russian lessons in exchange for English lessons. There were three applicants. There was a workman called Young and an office worker called Williams, and of these two nothing is known. The third, a portly gentleman with a white beard, was called Raymond: he worked in the publishing house of George Bell and Sons. Raymond had traveled widely in Europe, he had been to Australia, and he was a sensible, knowledgeable man. He was a convinced socialist, and he shocked Lenin by saying that he had been given to making socialist speeches until his employer sent for him and told him he would have to choose between his job and making public declarations in favor of socialism. Because he had a wife and children to support, he abandoned speechmaking. Though Lenin was friendly enough, he seemed to think that Raymond suffered from the characteristic Philistinism of the English: a better socialist would have abandoned his job rather than abandon the sacred task of making converts to socialism. One day he took Raymond to a socialist meeting in Whitechapel, where Russian Jews wearing their long kaftans and fur hats lived in a closed community amid the slums. Raymond confessed he had never visited Whitechapel before, and Lenin was puzzled that a man who had traveled as far as Australia should know so little about his own city.

The habits of the English continued to puzzle him. Mrs. Yeo, his landlady, was extremely worried because Krupskaya did not hang curtains up in her living room, those dust-catching curtains of thick lace which at that time ornamented every English room, even the kitchen and the servants' attic. All her other tenants had bought lace curtains. Why should Mrs. Richter try to be different from anyone else? Then, too, there was the matter of Mrs. Richter's wedding ring— or rather, the absence of a wedding ring. Mrs. Yeo went so far as to mention the missing ring, hinting at the impropriety of a man and woman living together outside the sacramental bonds of marriage. Krupskaya realized that this was a serious matter, and it would be necessary to put an end to Mrs. Yeo's doubts in the shortest possible time. Accordingly, she went to her friend Apollinaria Takhtareva, another Siberian exile living in London, married to the former editor of *Rabochaya Mysl*, and it was Apollinaria's husband who bearded Mrs. Yeo in her den and threatened her with a lawsuit unless she put an end to these aspersions upon a couple who had been properly married according to Russian law. Mrs. Yeo had no desire to face a lawsuit, or to lose her tenants who paid their rent promptly, and she never mentioned the matter again. She never guessed that the meek and quiet Krupskaya, who had a passion for the Yeo cat, teaching it to shake hands and miaow good morning, was a superb conspirator who spent her days deciphering cryptograms or warming letters over a candle flame until the invisible ink became legible, and that when she went out in the morning her shopping bag concealed letters which would ultimately make their way to revolutionary centers all over Russia.

The main purpose of Lenin's stay in London was the printing of *Iskra* on an English printing press. Though Lenin wrote a good deal of the material, he could not write all of it, and he could not take charge of all the physical details of printing and distributing the paper. For this purpose helpers were needed, and soon Martov and Vera Zasulich came over from Munich, staying in a house on Sidmouth Street where

Alexeyev had rented five rooms on two floors, so providing a communal settlement for Russian revolutionaries passing through London. This house was only a stone's throw away from Lenin's apartment on Holford Square, and there was a continual coming and going between the two places.

In Alexeyev's "commune" the revolutionaries lived in happy squalor. They cooked their food on a gas jet, and sometimes forgot to cook. Vera Zasulich seemed to have stepped out of a nineteenth-century Bohemian novel. She spent her days writing articles which she rarely finished, suffering all the torments of literary creation, as she paced up and down her small room, her slippers flapping. She smoked endlessly, and there were always cigarette butts on the tables and the window sills, and she would spray the ashes all over her blouse, her arms, her skirt, and even her face; and there were more ashes on her manuscripts and in her teacup. Anyone who spoke with her for more than half a minute would find himself covered in a shower of ashes. The samovar was kept boiling, and she lived on cigarettes and tea.

Martov, in his own way, was equally capricious. He was wildly talkative—so much so that Lenin went to some trouble to avoid meeting him, except when it was absolutely necessary. He arranged that Martov should come over to Holford Square in the morning to go over the correspondence with Krupskaya; by this time he had already left for the British Museum. Generous and sensitive, descended from a long line of Hebrew scholars, with a style which could sometimes lose itself in oblique refinements and passionate subtleties, Martov found it increasingly difficult to work with Lenin, who showed not the slightest interest in subtleties and whose verdicts, when any problems were put to him, were invariably harsh and uncompromising. Of Plekhanov, Vera Zasulich liked to say, "He is like a greyhound, who bites and lets go!" Of Lenin, she said, "He is like a bulldog, who bites and doesn't let go!" Martov shared her affection for Plekhanov and was ill at ease in Lenin's company. Some weeks later, saying he was going over to Paris for a few days, he left London and never returned.

As the summer came on, Lenin was becoming increasingly worried by the problems presented by *Iskra*, and he was only too well aware that he disagreed with everyone else on the editorial board. His article "The Agrarian Program of Russian Social Democracy" had been discussed by the editorial board, and various comments had been made on the style and contents. Exasperated by the tone and still more by the implications of Plekhanov's letter, Lenin wrote a slashing reply, terminating all personal relations:

> I received the article with your comments. You have a fine conception of tact with regard to your colleagues on the editorial board! You do not restrain yourself in the least in choosing the most contemptuous expressions, not to mention the "voting" on the suggestions, which you did not even take the trouble to formulate, and even the "voting" about style. I would like to know what you would say if I answered your article on the program in the same way? If you are aiming to make our mutual work impossible—then the way you have chosen will very speedily accomplish your aim. As for our personal, apart from our working relations, you have finally spoiled them—or, more exactly, you have brought about their complete cessation.

Lenin's ferocious outburst probably came about as a result of overwork and a tubercular infection from which he had never fully recovered, but there was a long history of literary and political disagreements between them. They were always hacking each other's writings to pieces. Plekhanov wrote with charm and dignity, Lenin crudely with sudden passages of revolutionary lyricism: their writings clearly mirror their character. So Lenin would write on the margins of Plekhanov's manuscripts: *"Not clear, crude, simplify, repetition, your style needs brushing up."* Plekhanov would return the compliment in the same coin and with more devastating force, for his manners like his bearing were aristocratic. They fought like scorpions in a bottle.

But Lenin had scarcely written his letter breaking off personal relations with Plekhanov when he was writing another letter in a tone of cordiality. Plekhanov may have hoped that Lenin would vanish into obscurity, but Lenin realized that he had need of Plekhanov. They continued to claw at each other's manuscripts, while their personal relations continued outwardly unimpaired.

In the middle of June, in need of a rest, Lenin left for a vacation in France, visited Paris, and then settled down at a small French watering place on the coast of Brittany to await the coming of his mother and his sister Anna. Why they should have chosen to meet in the obscure town of Loguivy is something of a puzzle: there are a thousand other places in France which are more attractive. He went alone, leaving Krupskaya in London to deal with correspondence. In France he wrote an article declaring war on the Socialist Revolutionaries, the inheritors of the Narodnaya Volya tradition, for while in *What Is To Be Done?* he had acknowledged that the Social Democrats stemmed from the same tradition, he felt that his own party had now acquired professional status. "The Socialist Revolutionaries are simply advocating *single combat*," he declared, "a method which has been wholly condemned by the experience of history." It was a taunt he repeated in many later articles. What was needed, he wrote in a letter to the Moscow Committee, was "bolder, more widespread, more *unified* and more centralized work." At the same time—as he indicated in a famous "Letter to a Comrade on Our Organizational Tasks," written later in the year—there were dangers in centralization, and he offered a new formula: "*The greatest possible centralization* in the ideological and practical *leadership* of the movement, and *the greatest possible decentralization* in keeping the party *informed* about the movement." The discovery that centralization had its dangers was a brutal one and he wrestled with it continually for the rest of his life, continually offering new permutations and combinations of centralization and decentralization, adapting one to the other, equating them and spinning webs of theory around them. Lenin liked to speak of the inner contradictions of capitalism; but the inner contradictions of communism were even more dangerous, exhausting and insoluble.

But he was not continually wrestling with insoluble problems: there were friendships to be cultivated, visitors to be seen, stratagems to be invented, and there was always London to be explored. His nerves were better after the trip to France; and when one early morning in the autumn there arrived in the apartment in Holford Square a fugitive from Irkutsk who went by the name of "the Pen," a young man with wavy hair, brilliant eyes and a melodious voice, with a manner designed to please and a brain of remarkable agility, Lenin was delighted. The young man—he was only twenty-two, but already a veteran of revolution—had no money, and so Krupskaya was sent out to pay the cab, while he stormed into Lenin's bedroom and talked as though he were merely resuming a conversation interrupted a few days before, though in fact they had never met.

Lev Davydovich Bronstein, who took the name Trotsky and was known in the secret communications of the Social Democratic Party as "the Pen," was exactly the kind of revolutionary Lenin had discussed in *What Is To Be Done?* He was steel-hard, dedicated and determined. He had no moral conscience, very little sympathy or understanding of people, and he was incapable of playing a minor role; he belonged, as though by right of birth, to a revolutionary elite. There was about him, as about Lenin, a sense of unfolding drama, but while Lenin saw himself as a Promethean figure from a contemporary tragedy, Trotsky, who had no tragic sense, saw himself as a mysterious robed and garlanded figure from grand opera. Both were ruthless egoists determined to play outstanding roles in history, and very early in their careers they had assumed the postures appropriate to their talents.

Trotsky's talents were obvious, perhaps too obvious. He relates that at their first meeting the expression on Lenin's face "was tinged with a justifiable amazement." He continued to amaze Lenin by his charm, his stubbornness and his astonishing capacity to rise to the surface in every critical revolutionary situation in which he found himself. Lenin spoke; Trotsky orated. Lenin bludgeoned his opponents; Trotsky wielded a rapier. Lenin was the abstract theoretician; Trotsky was the practical politician, the specialist in insurrection. They were at poles apart, and from the beginning they seem to have recognized their differences and their separate powers.

Trotsky's first task was to report on the political situation in Siberia, where he had been exiled, and the impressions he had gathered in brief visits to the party centers at Kiev, Kharkov and Poltava. There had been breakdowns of communication, with innumerable copies of *Iskra* lost or captured or sent to the wrong address for redistribution, and all this he reported to Lenin in the tone of a man who sees failure everywhere around him, but is buoyed up by a vast hope for the future. He had a small list of secret addresses to give to Krupskaya, and he told stories about his own exploits. Then it was time to find a lodging for him, and inevitably it was decided that he could live with Vera Zasulich and Martov in that extraordinary house nearby, which had already acquired the appearance of a Russian outpost in England.

Lenin was amazed by Trotsky; he was also puzzled. He had never before come across anyone who possessed that particular kind of fervor and brilliance. Accordingly, Trotsky was compelled to submit to a prolonged examination, which took place during a long walk around London, while from time to time Lenin would indicate the sights, saying, "This is their Westminster" or "This is their Tower of London." Trotsky knew enough about Lenin's way of looking at the world to know that "their" did not refer to the people of England, but to the hated ruling classes, whose shadowy presence Lenin saw everywhere even on the days of brightest sunlight.

Trotsky showed very little interest in the architecture of London, but Lenin was not taking him for a walk to educate him in architecture. His purpose was to fathom Trotsky's mind—to ask questions and to ponder over the responses. Trotsky, by an adroit mixture of flattery and intelligence, seems to have passed the examination with flying colors. He knew how to flatter.

"When we were in prison in Moscow," Trotsky said, "we often spoke with astonishment about your colossal work *The Development of Capitalism in Russia.*"

Lenin accepted the compliment as his due. "Yes, indeed, it was not done all at once," he answered, pleased because the young party members were following in his path.

But what he chiefly wanted to know about Trotsky was whether he possessed the intellectual equipment to be a member of the revolutionary elite. What books did he read? What was his interpretation of history? Whose philosophical works did he study? Trotsky confessed to an admiration of Bogdanov and an intense dislike for Bernstein. It was the right answer. What about *Das Kapital?* Trotsky had read the first volume, but had not yet had time to get down to the second. What about Kautsky? Yes, Trotsky had read Kautsky and was in substantial agreement with his ideas. And Plekhanov? Trotsky was disturbed by Plekhanov; there was no doubt of his brilliance, but he seemed to be remote from the struggle, uninformed and altogether too philosophic. Lenin commented modestly, "I am not a philosopher." The implication seemed to be that philosophy could be safely left to Plekhanov—and ignored.

After the first examination Trotsky saw Lenin rarely; they lived in separate worlds. Occasionally they would meet for brief discussions. Trotsky wrote an article for *Iskra* on the two hundredth anniversary of the capture of Schlüsselburg by Peter the Great, taking care to display his erudition with a quotation from Homer. Lenin, who had no fondness for Homeric quotations, took him to task, and the article appeared without any reference to Homer.

Sometimes Trotsky would be permitted to accompany Lenin to socialist meetings in London. It was the time when socialism in England was being advanced with religious fervor and enthusiasm; at Sunday services in the East End of London sermons on socialist brotherhood would alternate with hymns. The hymns sometimes wore a republican character, and Trotsky says he heard them singing, "Lord Almighty, let there be no more kings or rich men!" Lenin was puzzled by the English propensity for mixing the most diverse elements in their culture. When they left the church he said, "There are many revolutionary and socialist elements among the English proletariat, but they are all mixed up with conservatism, religion and prejudice, and somehow the socialist and revolutionary elements never break through the surface and unite."

To the end of his life Lenin was puzzled by the English, and contemptuous of them: what particularly disturbed him was their lack of socialist unity. He preferred the Germans, who obeyed rules and regulations and liked to see themselves as a unified mass. As Trotsky said, "British Marxism was not interesting." It lacked drama, tension, war between powerful personalities. It was in fact essentially parochial, and the Russians were incapable of thinking in parochial terms. For them the revolution was always meaningless unless it embraced the whole world, and if possible the entire universe.

While Lenin saw himself as a prophet, another Isaiah prophesying the downfall of kingdoms, Trotsky saw himself as a young David making war on the Philistines. Even at the age of twenty-two he walked about the earth with a kingly air. Vera Zasulich worshiped him and gave him her blessing. When Plekhanov arrived in London for a short visit, she took him aside and expounded on the brilliance and promise of her young protégé. "The boy is undoubtedly a genius," Plekhanov said. An apocryphal variant of the story says that he added, "I shall never forgive him for it."

Plekhanov was having enough trouble with geniuses and prima donnas. He had the timidity of men who are conscious of their intellectual superiority, but he was not so timid that he did not enjoy a fight. Sometimes he fought Lenin to a standstill. Krupskaya tells the story of Lenin returning from an editorial meeting in a terrible rage. "A damned fine state of affairs," he said. "Nobody had the courage to stand up to Plekhanov. Look at Vera Zasulich! Plekhanov attacks Trotsky, and all Vera can say is: 'Just like our George! All he does is shout!'" And then Lenin, beside himself with frustration and despair, burst out: "I can't go on like this!"

It is a revealing story, for when Lenin said that nobody had the courage to stand up to Plekhanov he was obviously including himself.

Fighting for power, Lenin saw Plekhanov standing in his way; and since Plekhanov was not a fortress which could be taken by assault, there would inevitably come a time when Lenin would have to make a detour round him and establish his own independent headquarters.

The possibility that he might be able to destroy Plekhanov by setting up his own organization seems to have come to him about the time he was writing *What Is To Be Done?* He knew the risk, and he went about it carefully. He had two advantages over Plekhanov: first, his secret contacts with Russia were more widespread; secondly, he had hammered out a simple authoritarian formula for victory which, if not particularly Marxist, was calculated to cut across the wordy arguments of the other professional revolutionaries. At all costs he must maintain his contacts and defend his philosophy; and in his mind these two ideas were inseparable.

Whenever his contacts with Russia broke down and whenever his philosophy of revolution was questioned and assailed, Lenin suffered acute physical anguish. He needed a constant flow of comunications from Russia to sustain him. He was continually writing urgent letters to the party agents, begging them to write more punctually. "We beg you again most urgently and insistently to write more often and more fully," he wrote. "Answer us without fail immediately you receive our letter, or at least drop us a line that you have received it." *Urgently, insistently, without fail, immediately*—these words were not yet the commonplaces of his mind. He slept badly when the letters failed to come, and he did not sleep at all when there came messages saying, "Sonya is silent as the grave"; or "We have had no contact with the Old Woman"—meaning that his correspondents had been arrested or killed or, as sometimes happened, they had abandoned party work because it was too exhausting and too dangerous. When he slept badly, his health and his temper suffered; he became a ghost of himself. Unlike Plekhanov, he was never able to develop an inner calm.

And when his authoritarian philosophy was assailed, the physical suffering was even worse. When the editorial committee finally decided in the spring of 1903 that *Iskra* should be printed in Switzerland, because it was nonsensical to have half the committee in England and the other half in Switzerland, he collapsed completely; the transfer to Switzerland meant that he would have to surrender his hard-won independence. The physical symptoms of the collapse took the form of an inflammation of the nerve endings of his back and chest. He was writhing in physical and mental pain. The upper part of his body had turned bright red. Krupskaya looked up a medical handbook and decided to undertake the treatment herself, and being completely ignorant of medicine she chose exactly the wrong treatment: she painted him with iodine, which caused excruciating suffering. Wearing a robe of fire, Lenin set off for Geneva in April 1903.

He had spent a year in London—a year of frustrations and illness, of many sorrows and resounding defeats. In Switzerland he would dig in his heels and fight back, spinning the web which would eventually lead him to dominate the party.

THE BANGING OF THE DOOR

IN HIS MORE TRANQUIL MOODS Lenin would sometimes explain to his followers that the art of being a revolutionary lay in complete identification with the cause of the working class: one must be able to think like a workman, behave like a workman, be like a workman. It was not enough to possess a specialized revolutionary instinct. What was needed was a total absorption in the cause of the proletariat.

But though Lenin often spoke in this way, he remained curiously remote from the working class. To the end his temperament was bourgeois and even aristocratic. The huggermugger ways of the proletariat, cheerfully taking on each others' burdens, were not for him. He enjoyed his privacy, he demanded silence when he worked, and he was happier among books than among people. He had a horror of landladies, and he was especially pleased when he found in the working-class district of Secheron in the suburbs of Geneva a small house at a rent he could afford. Now, for the first time since he left Samara, he was master of his own household.

It was a poor house, with a stone-floored kitchen downstairs and three modest rooms upstairs. There was almost no furniture, but Lenin had brought a great number of books with him and the packing cases served as chairs and tables. The kitchen became the living room where all business was conducted. Especially secret business would be discussed in the nearby park or on the shores of the lake. Secheron was almost in open country, and Lenin had the countryman's delight in having green grass around him. He was also delighted by the

Société de Lecture in Geneva, a private library where the reader was charged a small fee. Here Lenin could take down books from the shelves and write at a table which from long usage came to be known as "Mr. Ulyanov's table."

In those days he bore very little resemblance to the familiar portrait of the revolutionary posters. He was thin and frail, his enormous bald head accentuating both the pallor and the narrowness of his face. He wore a long silky red beard and the long, drooping mustaches fashionable at the time. Panteleimon Lepechinsky, who had known him in Siberia, visited him a little later in the year and was surprised to discover how much he had changed in the intervening years. "He no longer wore the look of a conqueror which had illuminated his face when he left Siberia," Lepechinsky wrote. "He sat there on the sofa, thin and pale, and there was an uncertain smile lingering behind his long mustaches, which he had not yet shaved off."

Reclining on the sofa, very weak, the prey to lassitude and exhaustion, Lenin looked like a character who had stepped out of one of Proust's novels. Lepechinsky saw him shortly after the Second Congress of the Social Democratic Party, which was convened in a large Brussels warehouse in the summer. At the Congress he had won everything he hoped to win except the most important thing—he was not yet the acknowledged leader of the party. He had fought off all his enemies, surmounted one crisis after another, and in the process destroyed or reduced to impotence many of his former friends. With tenacious rigidity he had fought for a centralized party machine with himself occupying the central role. The result was to split the party wide open; from that summer the party consisted of two contending factions—Bolsheviks (the majority) and Mensheviks (the minority).

The First Congress, held in Minsk in 1898, resulted in nothing more inflammatory than a forgotten manifesto by Peter Struve. It was a ghostly congress, remembered by the revolutionaries who convened in Brussels, but remote from their present preoccupations. Much had happened in the interval: pogroms, peasant uprisings, strikes. The government was increasingly out of touch with the people. No one doubted that Russia was on the eve of radical changes and that the purpose of the Brussels Congress was to establish a program to overthrow the autocracy.

At the Congress no one was so autocratic as Lenin, who ruled on the podium and behind the scenes with a savage intolerance. A surprisingly large number of the delegates were his hand-picked nominees; he had himself arranged the order of business; and he acted throughout as though the Congress had merely assembled to do his bidding.

The Jewish Socialist Bund had played a large role in disseminating Marxist ideas in Poland, Lithuania and White Russia. It included among its members the most politically conscious workers in Russia; and it was in no mood to take orders from Lenin. The Bundists demanded their own autonomy within the party, or at least a partial cultural autonomy, since they largely represented the unassimilated Jews and saw no reason to sacrifice the existence of the Bund to the group which had gathered around *Iskra*. Plekhanov and Lenin were determined to bring about a centralized party which would cut across all nationalist separatism, and if possible destroy it. Their aim was to bring about the supranational socialist state in which the Jews would merge with the rest of the population. The Bundist claim for autonomy was therefore regarded as heresy, and it was overwhelmingly defeated. Between them Plekhanov and Lenin, acting in an uneasy alliance, could muster enough votes to defeat any combination of forces; and their first triumph was won over the Bundists. As Krupskaya said, employing a phrase that sounds as though it had been borrowed from Lenin, "they were brought to their knees."

There followed a debate on the nature of the dictatorship of the proletariat. Why substitute one dictatorship for another? Why talk about freedom of speech, assembly, press, the workers' and peasants' right to move about the country freely and take whatever job they please when all these rights and freedoms are canceled by the mere existence of the revolutionary dictatorship? What is the constitution of the dictatorship of the proletariat? How can there be a Constituent Assembly within a dictatorship? And what part do the peasants play?

All these were important questions, and they pointed at the irreconcilable contradictions within the party program, which proclaimed freedom and tyranny in the same breath.

Lenin's attitude was firm—he wanted power at all costs, and he was prepared to offer everything to everybody on condition that power was surrendered to him. To those who wanted a parliament he offered a parliament, to the proletariat he offered a dictatorship, to the peasants he offered the abolition of all taxes and freedom to work as they pleased, to the religious he offered freedom of worship, to parents he offered the free education of their children. This dazzling display of gifts, all put forward with the utmost seriousness, had the effect of sugar-coating the pill of dictatorship. "Yes, indeed, there will be an iron dictatorship," Lenin seemed to be saying, "but look how free everyone will be under it!"

The Belgian police, exercising their right to dictate to Russian revolutionaries on Belgian soil, banned the Congress. The delegates then made their way to London, where it was resumed.

With the Bund discredited as an independent force, and the dictatorship of the proletariat affirmed, it remained to hammer out a basic program and to provide a compendium of definitions. There was, for example, the question of defining a party member. Lenin's draft definition described a party member as "anyone who accepts the program of the Party, supports it with material means, and personally participates in one of its organizations." Martov suggested an amendment that a party member could be any worker who co-operated "personally and regularly under the guidance of one of the organizations." This was not hairsplitting. What was at stake was the whole existence of the party. Under Martov's definition, it would be a party of friendly associates, including those who merely assisted in the underground work from time to time. Under Lenin's definition, the party would consist only of active participants taking direction from the Central Committee. According to Lenin, the party was to be limited to small, close-knit and disciplined groups. Since it was perfectly clear that Lenin envisaged a revolutionary elite with himself standing in the place of authority, he was inevitably taunted for his unbridled lust for power. Trotsky had sensed that lust for power shortly after their meeting in London, when he accused Lenin of putting too many *I*'s in his articles and received the reply that his authority permitted him to employ as many *I*'s as he pleased. At the Second Congress Lenin's lust for power was not a pleasant spectacle; it was too naked, too close to the surface. He must dominate everyone and everything, reduce all opponents to a state of "negative extension"—meaning that they were cast out and possessed no independent existence—and sabotage every incipient revolt at its source. He openly admitted that he wanted the complete dictatorship of the Central Committee. When Trotsky jibed at such a concentration of power in so few men, Lenin answered, "What is bad about that? In the present situation it cannot be otherwise." Axelrod and many others were alarmed by Lenin's pride and bitterness. Axelrod, ousted from the editorial committee of *Iskra* by some sharp in-fighting, complained: "What kind of fly has stung him?"

We learn something of Lenin's mood during the Congress from

four pages of doodles and brief summary notes which have survived. Two of the pages are illustrated here. On the upper part of the left-hand page he has written the word BEREZA (birch tree) seven times. Four times the word is printed in bold capitals, three times in cursive letters which scramble and melt into one another, as though he could no longer contemplate them with any happiness, but must change them until they are unrecognizable. It was three years since he had been in Russia, and in these doodles he seems to be invoking and then destroying a vision of birch trees, which form a ring around words that seem to represent his most profound convictions. The words are:

> No. 1 (*inflexibly*)
> narrowing of circle and breadth
> hardness and purity
> ideological grouping
> our party organization must be an
> "organization of professional revolutionaries"

Below these words, heavily underlined, appears the word VRED (harm), with a long arrow pointed to something scratched out on the right-hand page. In purple pencil there are heavy oblongs and sharp corners which seem to testify to the "hardness and purity" he had already mentioned.

On the right-hand page he writes notes on what he has heard, but more revealing are those in which he simply writes down what he is thinking. He writes:

> either the "organized utopia" of Lenin
>   or 99/100 outside the party
> truth does not lie in any of the party members
> responsibility

This last word, like "harm," is underlined three times.

On another page of doodles written at the same time Lenin wrote an accurate summary of Trotsky. The note reads: "Trotsky—strictly conspiratorial comprehension of the party."

And again: "He who enters danger, that man will be the professional revolutionary."

These pages with their angry arrows and sudden insights are among the most revealing that Lenin ever wrote. They show him nakedly: he is in the shape of the harpoonlike arrow, the purple hatchings and the strident underscorings. Almost these pages provide an abstract portrait of a man determined to tighten his grip on the party.

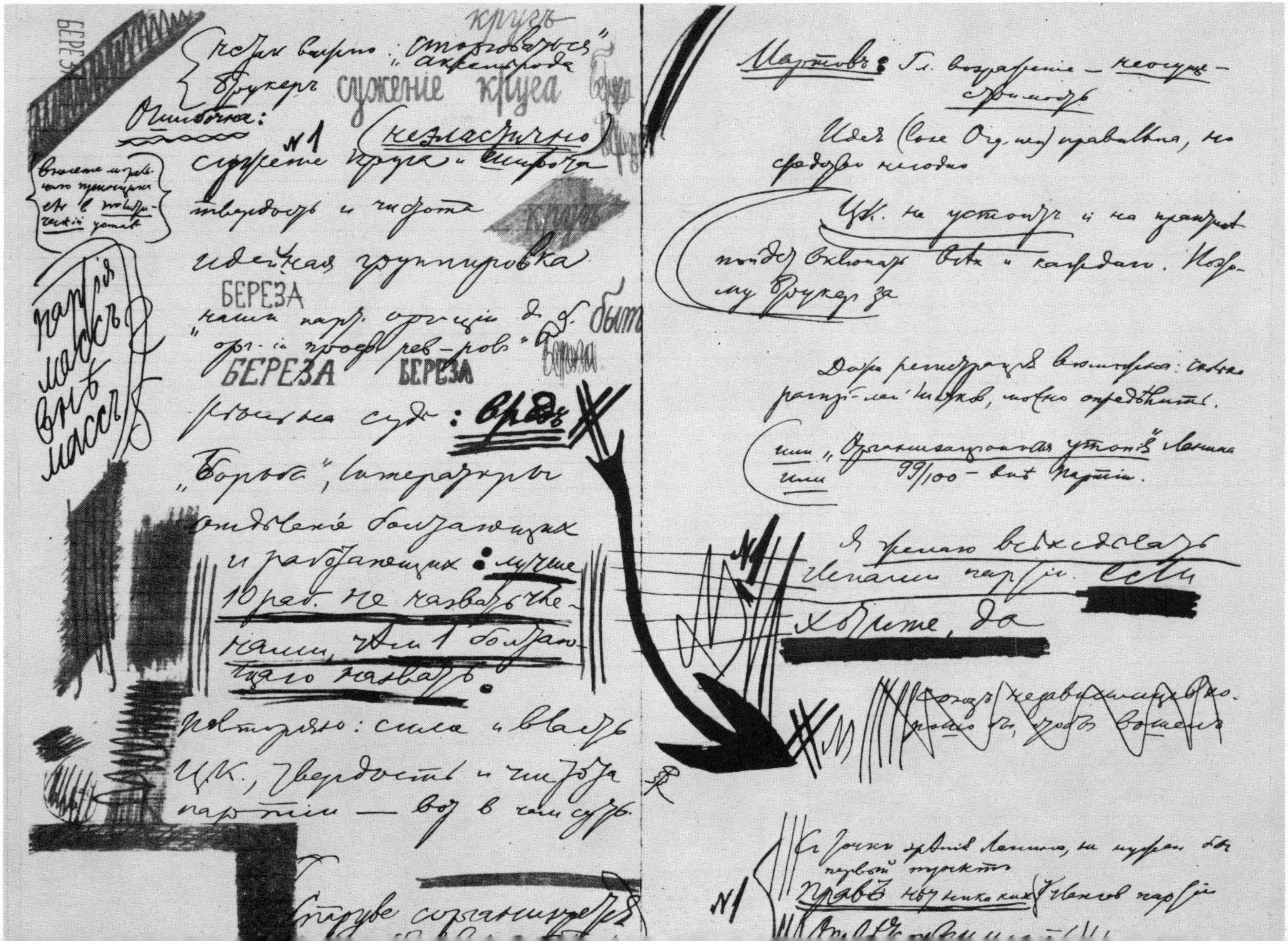

БЕРЕЗА

БЕРЕЗА КРЕПА

Look, for example, at the top of the left-hand page where he writes the word KRUG, meaning "circle," and immediately underneath, in letters which are harder and sterner, the words SUZHENIYE KRUGA, meaning "narrowing the circle." Here we see the naked will at work. As Trotsky says, he was a man who took pleasure in bending the bow to the uttermost. "Out of such dough," said Plekhanov, "Robespierres are made."

At the Second Congress Lenin destroyed two of his closest associates—Martov, the gentle and cultured Jew who had worked with him in terms of the closest intimacy he would have with any man except perhaps Trotsky, and Vera Zasulich, the link with Nechayev, the woman who had placed the inheritance in his hands. Neither Martov nor Vera Zasulich recovered from the blow. Ousted from *Iskra*, they felt they were ousted from the party which gave them a reason for existence; and Krupskaya was saying no more than the truth when in her memoirs she described how Vera Zasulich felt that she had received a mortal blow. "Leaving *Iskra* meant that she was once more isolated from Russia, faced with the prospect of sinking deeper and deeper into the morass of Russian *émigré* life abroad. Her pride was not involved; it was a matter of life and death." Henceforth *Iskra* was to be edited by Plekhanov, Axelrod and Lenin.

The Lenin who clawed his way to a position of power and authority at the Second Congress was a desperately sick and neurotic man. Krupskaya says he never slept during the days the Congress met in London, and while it was sitting in Brussels he could scarcely bring himself to eat. His pallor, his nervousness, his brusque interruptions, the sharp cutting edge to his voice, which many observers remarked on—all suggest a man in the process of subordinating everything to his will. He was perfectly aware that he had behaved abominably, but it never occurred to him to surrender the gains he had achieved by his abominable behavior.

During the months following the close of the Congress, Lenin had ample opportunity to consult the stenographic records and to consider his behavior. He composed a diary of the Congress and a dozen articles concerned with different facets of the Congress; then he wrote an entire book which he called *One Step Forward, Two Steps Back*, dealing with his own interventions, defending himself against "the chicaneries and idiocies" of his opponents. In the text he is always right. In the long footnotes there are guarded apologies which quickly transform themselves into denunciations of those who had opposed him;

yet it is evident that to some greater or lesser degree his conscience was troubling him.

Martov had complained bitterly against the vehemence of Lenin's personal attacks on him during discussions on the organization of *Iskra*, and Lenin makes his footnote-reply with a curious mingling of apology and brutality:

> Lenin behaved—according to his own expression—like a madman. True. He banged the door. True. His conduct aroused the indignation of the members who remained at the meeting. So it did! But what follows? Only that my arguments on the substance of the questions in dispute were convincing and were borne out during the course of the Congress. In the end 9 of the 16 members of the *Iskra* organization agreed with me, and this must have come about *notwithstanding* and *in spite of* my reprehensible vehemence. And had it not been for my "vehemence," perhaps more than nine would have sided with me. This means that the more my arguments and facts were convincing, the more "indignation" had to be overcome.

Lenin's explanation leaves a good deal to be desired, for he seems to have been perfectly aware that his vehemence was a form of shock treatment, a small private reign of terror among his friends, and that he used it with skill and self-assurance: in the same way neurotic people often terrorize their friends by an instinctive knowledge of their weaknesses.

Inevitably Martov fought back, accusing Lenin of "Bonapartism of the worst type." Lenin answered by defining Bonapartism as "acquiring power by *formally* legal means, but actually in defiance of the will of the people," and then pointing to his own demonstrable triumph at the Congress as proof that he had not defied the will of the party, but on the contrary merely followed its wishes. Bonapartism was only one of the charges leveled against him. "The shells rained down on my head," he wrote. "Autocrat, bureaucrat, formalist, lopsided, stiff-necked, obstinate, narrow-minded, suspicious, quarrelsome . . . Well, my friends, have you finished? Have you nothing more in reserve? Poor ammunition, I must say. . . ."

But if it was poor ammunition, he would not have returned so frequently to the charges. He was wounded to the quick, for he recognized their truth, or at least he was aware that something had gone wrong. In another footnote to *One Step Forward, Two Steps Back*, he

described a conversation with one of the delegates and his own belli-
cose reply:

> I cannot help recalling a conversation I happened to have at the Con-
> gress with one of the Center delegates.
>
> "What a depressing atmosphere there is in the Congress," he com-
> plained. "All this bitter fighting, this agitation one against another, these
> sharp polemics, this uncomradely attitude!"
>
> And I replied, "What a splendid Congress we are having! A free and
> open struggle. Opinions expressed. Tendencies revealed. Groups acquir-
> ing shape. Hands raised. A decision taken. A stage passed through. For-
> ward! That's something I understand. So different from the endless,
> wearying word-choppings of intellectuals, which come to an end not
> because they have solved the problems but because they are tired of
> talking.
>
> The Center delegate looked at me with a perplexed expression and
> shrugged his shoulders. We were speaking in different languages.

Krupskaya, who quotes the passage, says that it contains "the
whole of Lenin," but there was more to him than that easy triumph.
He was the master of "narrowing the circle," of the ruthless centralized organization, of the process by which men are cast out into "negative extension," perhaps the most terrifying of all his verbal inventions, but he was also a man who, on occasion, could be uncommonly
sensitive in human relations. He would insult and degrade a man to
his face and then wonder why the man disliked him. Half of *One
Step Forward, Two Steps Back* consists of a brutal attack on Martov,
and he was genuinely surprised that Martov took offense. The cold
Germanic and Scandinavian part of him was at war with the warm
Chuvash part of him, and most of his life he was torn between ice-cold
disdain of his fellow men and a fierce love for them.

From time to time he would send out peace-feelers to Martov and
Trotsky, who had also elected to join the Mensheviks. Writing to
Potresov in a letter clearly intended to be read by Martov, he wrote:
"I admit I often acted with fearful irritation and rage, and *I am prepared to acknowledge my fault to any comrade whatsoever.*" But
Martov and Trotsky knew his character too well to be induced to fall
into the spider's web again, at least for some time. The division between them was clear. Lenin wanted his revolutionary elite which
would, in Trotsky's words, form "a dictatorship over the proletariat."
The Mensheviks wanted a revolution that sprang out of the people,
and if they used the words "the dictatorship of the proletariat," they

meant that the workers, not the intellectuals, should rule. Of the delegates who attended the Congress perhaps four were workers.

Though Lenin won the battle of the Congress, he lost the peace. Through him, the party was split wide open, and the Bund broke all connections with it. Lenin's entire program had been carried through by the Bolsheviks, and he had shown himself to be a man of extraordinary political talents; but he was hated for his intolerance and despised for his overweening ambitions. And now once more, as so often in the past when things went against him, he suffered a nervous collapse. Quite suddenly he abandoned *Iskra,* so consigning himself to "negative extension." On November 18, 1903, he sent a brief note to the editorial board asking them to announce in the forthcoming issue that "N. Lenin is no longer a member of the board." He wrote to his old friend Alexandra Kalmykova, "Leaving *Iskra* has brought me to a dead end."

He was almost at the end of his strength, so bitter and despondent that he seemed out of his mind. Plekhanov, too, had gone over to the Mensheviks, and it amused Lenin to tell Celia Zelikson, who came from Russia to visit him in the winter, that in letters to Plekhanov he no longer signed "Yours truly," but instead, with a slight change of the Russian words, "Whom you betrayed." When he met the Mensheviks on the street, he would ostentatiously cross the street to avoid saluting them.

Celia Zelikson was an intelligent woman, and she has left a perceptive account of Lenin in the days when he was consumed by bitterness and at odds with the world. Though thin and obviously exhausted, he could still laugh pleasantly. Homesick, he would listen for hours to anyone who had just come from Russia. The house at Secheron was no more than a cottage; wooden stairs led to the upper floor; the bedrooms were pathetically bleak with their small beds and rows of bookshelves and tables littered with magazines. The kitchen was a friendly place, wide and spacious, with a large enameled kettle permanently boiling on the stove. Here Krupskaya's mother, Elizaveta Vasilyevna, presided over the comforts of visitors and complained about her daughter and son-in-law. "All they do is pore over their books and notebooks," she said. "Vladimir Ilyich worries himself to death with his work, and Nadya is always tired out. As for getting them down to eat . . ." It happened that Elizaveta Vasilyevna had pondered deeply on the split within the party, and she had come to certain conclusions about mending it. She had a high opinion of Vera

Zasulich. "So you see," she would say, "the important thing is to knock some sense into the heads of Martov and Lenin, and Vera Zasulich is exactly the person to do it. One day I'm going to have a chat with Vera, and you'll see—after she has been at work on them—they won't quarrel any more. And the best thing is that Nadya won't be worrying so much. . . ."

But Elizaveta Vasilyevna's dream of a reconciliation between the Bolsheviks and Mensheviks was not destined to be realized. The label of Bonaparte-Robespierre still clung to Lenin, however much he might dispute it, or refuse to dispute it as beneath his dignity. He wrote some notes for an appeal to the party which began, "Reply to tittle-tattle about Bonapartism. Rubbish. Beneath dignity to reply. Freedom of agitation for the Congress . . ." But without a party he had little freedom to agitate, and the Mensheviks in disgust were concerned to remind one another that they had seen Bonaparte in the flesh, while the Bolsheviks, whom he had led to a dubious victory, were in no mood to submit to his will. He could not live a life of "negative extension," and therefore he did what everyone expected he would do: he founded a new newspaper and a new party. "We have no party," he wrote in July 1904, "but we have a new party coming into being, and no subterfuges and delays, no senile malicious vituperation from *Iskra* can hold back the final and decisive victory of this party."

Once again he had powerful advantages: they were the familiar ones—a clear authoritarian philosophy, and the web of secret contacts he had maintained with Russia. To his faithful supporters he wrote withering attacks on *Iskra*, the Mensheviks, and everyone else who opposed him; and since, very often, they knew nothing about the real issues at stake, he was in a position to convince them that the enemy had behaved with unparalleled malice and stupidity.

In Geneva, too, he still had a small following, which met in one of the back rooms of the Café Landolt looking out on one of the squares in the center of Geneva. His enemies would meet in another back room, and sometimes it would happen that the meetings took place on the same evening. Celia Zelikson recounts how Lenin and Krupskaya would wait for their guests, a handful from Geneva and another handful from Russia still dressed in the clothes they wore when they escaped over the frontier, while down the passageway they could see Plekhanov and Martov and a small crowd of Mensheviks disappearing into the other back room. "Our numbers," says Celia Zelikson, "were

very modest." About ten or twelve people would sit there and listen
to Lenin making speeches in which the enemy was no longer the
autocracy but "the so-called ambassadors of the working class, Plekhanov, Martov and the rest." Within six months of his triumph at the
Second Congress, Lenin's fortunes had reached their lowest ebb.

In the summer of 1904 he abandoned revolutionary work to wander among the Swiss mountains with Krupskaya. At first they were
accompanied by a woman comrade who went by the party name Zver
(Wild Animal). Her real name was Maria Moïsseyevna Essen, and
she was one of those revolutionaries, always being arrested and always
escaping from prison, who belonged to the Narodnaya Volya tradition. She knew all the Ulyanovs and was particularly fond of Lenin's
mother, and when she was in Geneva she stayed in the cottage at
Secheron. She was thirty-two, but looked much younger, and Krupskaya described her as a woman who was "full of joyous energy, which
she communicated to all those around her."

In her memoirs Krupskaya is very gentle toward her husband's
female friends; she evidently enjoyed their company. She says that
Zver set out with them but soon gave up, complaining, "You like to go
in places where there isn't a living cat, but I must have human society." Zver herself remembered it differently. She spent a good deal
of time with them, with a rucksack on her back. She describes how
they took the boat to Montreux, visited the Castle of Chillon, and
then, enchanted by the beauty of the mountains after the darkness
of the castle, she and Lenin decided to climb one of them, leaving
Krupskaya in a nearby hotel. Before leaving Geneva they had extracted from Lenin the promise that there would be no talk of politics,
and especially that there would be no talk about the Mensheviks and
Bundists. Zver tells the story of the mountain climb:

> To reach the summit more quickly, we decided not to follow the road
> but to take a short cut. At every step the climb became more arduous.
> Vladimir Ilyich strode briskly up the mountain, very self-assured, throw-
> ing jibes at me for all my efforts to keep up with him. There came a time
> when I was climbing on all fours, clinging to the snow, which melted in
> my hands, but I refused to let him outdistance me.
>
> Then we came to the top of the mountain, and there was the land-
> scape stretching in all directions in marvelous colors. We saw below us,
> as in the hollow of a hand, all the climates of the world. Below the
> blinding snow were the pines, and below this lay the rich Alpine pas-
> tures and the luxuriance of southern climes. I was preparing to declaim

the verses of Shakespeare and Byron, when I caught sight of Lenin sitting down, absorbed in his thoughts. Suddenly he shouted, "All the same, those Mensheviks—they're all wrong!"

Lenin had a very close feeling for Zver. He was continually mentioning her in his letters, and he sometimes used her as an emissary in important negotiations. Once he sent her to Paris to discuss the founding of a new paper with Lunacharsky, Bogdanov and Olminsky. She asked him what she should look out for during her visit to Paris, and he answered characteristically that she should go first to the Mur des Fédérés in the Père Lachaise cemetery, then to the Museum of the French Revolution, and then to the waxworks at the Musée Grévin. At the Mur des Fédérés the Communards had been executed, and he would always visit the wall when he came to Paris. He wrote once, "The banner of the Commune is the banner of the world republic." It was one of those revealing phrases thrown off when he was drawing up notes for a speech, and it conveyed his deep feeling for the Communards.

But Zver was disappointed with the list of things to see in Paris, and she asked whether there was anything else worth seeing.

"You can always go to the Jardin des Plantes," Lenin answered carelessly. "You'll have the feeling you have seen all the countries on earth."

"Isn't there anything else to see?"

"If you want to see the museums and exhibitions, you'd better ask Plekhanov," Lenin replied in tones of disgust. "He knows all about such things!"

Zver accompanied them for about a week and then returned to Geneva, while Krupskaya and Lenin continued their journey alone. "We always chose the loneliest trails that led into the wilds, away from people," Krupskaya relates. "We spent a month of wandering, not knowing today where we would be tomorrow, and after each weary day we would throw ourselves on our beds dead-tired and fall asleep instantly."

Occasionally Lenin would remind himself that he was still the head of a political party, even though probably fewer than a hundred people belonged to it, and from obscure villages in Switzerland he would write letters to his supporters in Russia about "the new, growing, young Party," which was still no more than a gleam in his eye. He began to translate J. A. Hobson's *Imperialism*, a savage and rancorous study, which must have been greatly to his taste. "Imperial-ism," wrote Hobson, "is the besetting sin of all successful states, and its penalty is unalterable in the order of nature." Hobson's work reads as though it had been translated from Russian, and Lenin could have no difficulty in translating it; but the manuscript of his translation is lost, and the translation that finally appeared in Russia is not by his hand. Krupskaya was also translating, and Lenin carried her heavy French-Russian dictionary uncomplainingly in his rucksack.

But though they loaded themselves with books, they rarely had time to read them. Their aim was a very simple one—to restore Lenin to health and sanity. He had been sleeping badly, he suffered from hives, and he had sudden fits of melancholia; there were days when he could not work and other days when he worked for twenty-four hours without stopping. His resignation from *Iskra* had almost cost him his life. Distrusting doctors, he regarded a long spell of wander-ing in the countryside as a cure for all diseases of the flesh and mind. By August he was well again. "I walk, I bathe and do nothing in par-ticular," he wrote to his mother. "I have been having a splendid rest this summer."

In their wanderings they lived on cheese and eggs, washed down with wine or water from a well. They preferred to sleep in farmhouses, partly because they had little money and partly because Krupskaya had an unreasoning dislike of hotels and their clients. Once they found a small inn patronized by Social Democrats and spent the night there, taking the advice of a worker who advised them not to eat with the tourists, but with the coachmen and inn servants. "It's twice as cheap, and more filling," the worker said. "We took our meals with the serv-ants," Krupskaya wrote, adding sententiously that "in Europe they talk a good deal about democracy, but it is more than these bourgeois can stomach to sit down at a table with a hotel servant."

They returned to Geneva in September, bronzed and rested, to pick up the threads of their existence. Lenin began to work on his plans for a new newspaper to be called *Vperyod* (Forward), and he made small sums of money by lecturing. The small house at Secheron was abandoned, and he took an apartment closer to the heart of the city. Bogdanov, Olminsky, Lunacharsky and Vorovsky had fallen under his spell and offered to work with him on the paper. The "new, growing, young Party" was beginning to take shape. Lenin calculated that he would need 2,000 rubles a month to keep *Vperyod* going, and urgent letters were dispatched all over Europe and Russia for funds.

"I insistently request . . ." he would write, but the requests usually fell on deaf ears; and when at last the first number of *Vperyod* appeared, they were in desperate financial straits and had to borrow money to pay the printer's bill.

Yet he could scarcely have chosen a better time for beginning a clandestine revolutionary newspaper to be distributed in Russia. The Russo-Japanese War was still going on, and Russians of all classes were complaining against a government which seemed to be incapable of ruling the country or of fighting the Japanese. Terrorist activity was growing more daring. In June a terrorist assassinated the Governor General of Finland; in July, as he was riding in his carriage in broad daylight in St. Petersburg, the Minister of the Interior, Vyacheslav Plehve, was assassinated by Yegor Sazonov, a revolutionary of quite unusual nobility of purpose. The new Minister of the Interior, Prince Svyatopolk-Mirsky, was a liberal, well-meaning and genuinely determined to improve the relations between the autocracy and the people, but without any clear idea of how it could be done. A national convention of representatives of all the zemstvos was called for November; it was forbidden by the government, but the organizers ignored the order. The police watched, took notes, made detailed reports, and arrested none of the delegates, even though they called for an end to the autocracy and demanded freedoms which no previous Tsar would ever have thought of granting. The vat was seething. The second six months of 1904 were called "the spring," and they were to be followed by a riotous "summer."

On the first page of the first number of *Vperyod*, which appeared on January 4, 1905, Lenin wrote:

> A military collapse is now inevitable, and together with it there will come inevitably a tenfold increase of unrest, discontent and rebellion. For that moment we must prepare with all energy. At that moment one of those outbreaks which are recurring, now here, now there, with such growing frequency, will develop into a tremendous popular movement. At that moment the proletariat will rise to take its place at the head of the insurrection to win freedom for the entire people and to secure for the working classes the possibility of waging an open and broad struggle for socialism, a struggle enriched by the whole experience of Europe.

Eighteen days later the streets of St. Petersburg were flowing with blood.

THE YEAR NINETEEN FIVE

I<small>T SOMETIMES HAPPENS</small> that a nation will live through an entire year of disaster, when everything that could possibly go wrong goes wrong, and the very air seems to be impregnated with fatality. So it was in Russia in 1905.

On January 22, "Bloody Sunday," Father Gapon, a former prison chaplain, led a vast procession numbering some two hundred thousand men, women and children through the streets of St. Petersburg to present a petition to the Tsar in the Winter Palace. It was a bitterly cold day, with snow and piercing winds, but the procession was calm and orderly. They carried ikons and banners painted with portraits of the Tsar, and they sang "God Save the Tsar." There was about that solemn procession, marching so quietly, something that suggested an irresistible force of nature. An observer who watched it gathering in the great square in front of the Winter Palace said that "it could have moved through houses and palaces and even over the river." Yet the crowds were patient, humble and good-tempered. They expected that the Tsar would appear at one of the windows of the Winter Palace, address them, and give them his blessing.

The petition which Father Gapon intended to present to the Tsar had been written skillfully, with mingled stubbornness and devotion, by a master of political polemic. This long document, which covered five closely printed pages, demanded seventeen changes of government practice and several long-overdue reforms; it had been discussed widely in workingmen's meetings, and its contents were already known to the Tsar's ministers. Among the demands were universal and compulsory elementary education, a progressive income tax, habeas corpus, an eight-hour working day, and an end to the Russo-Japanese War. The tone of the petition was obscurely medieval, but the medieval wrappings concealed none of the fire below; on the contrary, they gave dignity to the flames:

> Sire! We, the workers and people of St. Petersburg, of various classes, our wives, our children and aged and helpless parents, are come to Thee, Sire, to seek for truth and protection. We are become beggars, bowing under oppression and burdened by toil beyond our powers, scorned, no longer regarded as human beings, treated as slaves who must suffer their bitter lot in silence. And having suffered, we are driven deeper and deeper into the abyss of poverty, lawlessness, and ignorance. We have been strangled by despotism and arbitrary rule, and we have lost our breath. We have no more strength, Sire. The limit of our patience has been reached. There has come for us the grave moment when death is preferable to a continuation of our intolerable torture. We have abandoned our work and declared to our masters that we shall not begin to work again until they comply with our demands. We ask but little: we demand only that without which life is not life, but hard labor and eternal torture. The first request we made to our masters was that they should discuss our needs with us, but they refused this request, saying we had no right to bring to them an appeal not recognized by the law. They also declared that our requests to diminish the working day to eight hours was illegal, and it was illegal to make agreements about wages or to consider our disagreements concerning the inferior management of the mills or to accept our demand that the minimum daily wage should be one ruble per day and that overtime should be abolished and medical aid should be given to us without insulting us and that the factories should be built in such a way that it is possible to work in them without suffering from terrible draughts and from rain and snow. . . .

. . . .

> Sire! These are the great needs which have brought us to Thee. Let Thy decree be known, order and take an oath to comply with these requests, and Thou shalt make Russia happy and famous, and Thy name shall be impressed upon our hearts and in the hearts of our descendants for all eternity. If, however, Thou wilt not order and wilt not answer our prayer, we shall die here in this place before Thy palace . . .

Die they did, for the Cossacks opened fire with volley after volley, leaving some three hundred dead and perhaps fifteen hundred wounded on the palace square. No accurate figures were ever com-

piled, but it is certain that an act of pure butchery had been committed. The Grand Duke Vladimir, uncle of the Tsar, had given the
order to fire. With that order he sealed the fate of the dynasty.

The news of the butchery reached Geneva the following morning.
Lenin and Krupskaya were on their way to the library when they met
the Lunacharskys, Anatoly and his wife Anna, who had read the morning newspaper and were beside themselves with excitement. They
could scarcely speak, and Krupskaya remembered afterward only
Anna Lunacharskaya's muff making strange signals in the air. Then
they went to a restaurant kept by Russian exiles and sang a revolutionary funeral march in honor of the fallen.

For two or three days news of what actually had happened on the
palace square remained scanty. On that Monday, before any full accounts had been received, Lenin wrote a brief and delirious editorial
for *Vperyod,* which had already gone to press. He wrote:

> The prestige of the Tsarist name has been ruined forever. The uprising
> has begun. Force against force. Street fighting has begun, barricades
> have been thrown up, rifle fire is crackling, guns are cannonading. Blood
> flows in rivers, and a civil war for freedom is blazing. Moscow and the
> South, the Caucasus and Poland are ready to join forces with the Peters-
> burg proletariat. The slogan of the workers is: Death or freedom!

In actual fact there had been no uprising; there had been only the
massacre of an unarmed procession. But his excitement was excus-
able, for it took very little knowledge of the situation to know that
the massacre was the beginning of a war to the death against the
autocracy. At first Lenin was inclined to believe that Father Gapon
was an *agent provocateur,* and indeed the role played by this priest
who had extensive connections with the police department has never
been fully explained. He escaped from St. Petersburg and wrote—
or someone wrote for him—a manifesto addressed to the Tsar and an
open letter to the socialist parties of Russia. The first denounced the
Tsar in terms of a prophet seeking vengeance from an unworthy emperor, the second was a stern admonition to the workers to dethrone
the emperor, and both the manifesto and the open letter contained an
appeal to use "bombs and dynamite, terror by individuals and by the
masses," to bring about the downfall of the dynasty. In their context
these seven Russian words—*"bombi i dinamit, terror edinichniy i
massoviy"*—are as chilling as any that can be imagined.

Not many days later Father Gapon himself arrived in Geneva, a small, pale, black-bearded man still wearing his vestments and with the smoke of gunpowder still on him. A Socialist Revolutionary woman told Lenin that the priest wanted to see him, and arrangements were made for their meeting on "neutral ground," a café not frequented by any of the revolutionary parties. Lenin was impressed by the priest's fervor and honesty, and by his failure to evolve a clear revolutionary philosophy. "He has a lot to learn," Lenin reported to Krupskaya. "I said to him, 'Don't listen to flattery, little father. If you don't study, this is where you will be—' and I pointed under the table."

Father Gapon took Lenin's advice, studied the works of Plekhanov, and prepared himself for the role of revolutionary leader by learning how to ride a horse and to shoot with a pistol. His understanding of revolution was emotional, uncritical and unscholarly; he could make nothing of Plekhanov's works, and he seems to have been one of those speakers who have nothing of their own to say, but who possess an astonishing gift for reproducing the unspoken thoughts of his audience. The revolutionaries, knowing his past connections with the police, distrusted him. Once he had left Russia, everything he touched seemed to disintegrate like Dead Sea fruit. Large sums of money were placed at his disposal, he bought weapons in England and arranged for them to be shipped to Russia in the *John Grafton,* but the ship ran aground and blew up off the Finnish coast. Lenin encouraged the shipment of arms, supplied him with secret addresses in St. Petersburg and a false passport, and looked forward to an uprising the moment the arms fell into the hands of the workers. All that summer his hopes dwelt on the success of the gun-running expedition, and when the *John Grafton* blew up early in September he was brokenhearted.

Father Gapon's subsequent career has never been adequately studied. There are many loose ends, and the report that he was sentenced to death and hanged in April 1906 by revolutionaries who learned that he was once again working for the police is not completely convincing. All that is certain is that he rose high on the revolutionary wave on Bloody Sunday, and then step by step walked into a land of treachery and obscurity.

Lenin took the advice he had offered to Father Gapon. In the past he had studied the theory of revolution; now he studied the practical aspects of civil war. He read Clausewitz, translated an article on street fighting by Gustave-Paul Cluseret—a remarkable Frenchman who fought in the American Civil War and in the Paris Commune—and revised and edited a Russian translation of Marx's *Civil War in France*. His mind, which had moved among abstractions, now moved more happily among armaments and battle plans. And every morning he came to the Société de Lecture with the punctuality of clockwork, a small, slight man who wore his trousers rolled in the Swiss fashion, always patting his bald head before he sat down at his table beside the window, a creature of habit, methodical, accurate, orderly in all his movements, the papers arranged neatly on the table, his chair at exactly the right angle to the window, as he plunged into a course of nightmarish reading on murder and assassination and all the tumultuous details of armed revolt.

In that quiet library in Geneva he was living in a state of extraordinary exaltation. A vast and dangerous excitement breathes through all his writing during this time. According to his theory, first announced in *What Is To Be Done?* the revolution in Russia was to be followed by a conflagration in Europe. So in August we find him writing, almost carelessly in an outline for an article called "The Working Class and Revolution," two words as spine-chilling as the famous seven words of Father Gapon. The words were *"Zazhech Evropu"*; they mean "Put Europe to the flames." It was as though the old Germanic dream of the flaming *Götterdämmerung* had him by the throat.

He was dreaming vast dreams, seeing the revolution taking place before his eyes, though as yet there was no revolution. In June or July —the manuscript, which was first published two years after his death, is undated—he described in prophetic terms the stages of the revolutionary war. The manuscript should be quoted at some length because the war he envisaged in the summer of 1905 did, in fact, take place twelve years later, very much as he described it:

> The setting. Tsarism smashed in Saint Petersburg. The autocratic government overthrown—smashed, but not completely destroyed, not killed, *not annihilated,* not dug up by the roots.
>
> The provisional revolutionary government—appeals to the people. *Spontaneous activity* of workers and peasants. Complete freedom. The people themselves organize their lives. *The government program =* full republican liberties, peasant committees for the *complete* reform of agrarian relations. The program of the Social Democratic Party *standing by itself.* Social Democrats in the Provisional Government = delegates summoned by the Social Democratic *Party.*
>
> Then—the Constituent Assembly. *If* the people have reason, they

. . .* (even though not immediately) *may* find themselves in the majority (peasants and workers). *Ergo,* the revolutionary *dictatorship* of the proletariat and the peasantry.

Frantic resistance of dark forces. Civil war *in full swing,—annihilation* of Tsarism.

Organization of the proletariat grows, propaganda and agitation of the Social Democrats increases ten thousandfold: all government printing presses etc. etc. "*Mit der Grundlichkeit des geschichtlichen Aktion wird auch der Umfang der Masse zunehmen, deren Aktion sie ist.*"†

The peasantry itself takes *all* agrarian questions in its hands, and *all* the land. *In this way nationalization* comes into existence.

Tremendous growth of productive forces—all the rural intelligentsia, all technical knowledge is placed at the service of agricultural production, clearing out of the way (kulturniks, narodniks etc. etc.) Gigantic development of *c a p i t a l i s t* progress . . .

War: *the fortress* keeps changing hands. Either the bourgeoisie overthrows the revolutionary dictatorship of the proletariat and the peasantry, or the dictatorship sets Europe in flames, and then . . . ?

Lenin did not answer the question; it was enough, perhaps, to have seen the entrancing vision. In the original the scenario is orchestrated with compulsive hammer beats: in the opening paragraph the effect of the words "not completely destroyed, not killed, *not annihilated,* not dug up by the roots" suggests a formidable pawing of the ground before hurling himself into the nightmare landscape. Kautsky had foreseen in 1902 that the next revolutionary war would not be fought against the government, but between opposing classes. Lenin saw the classes in mortal struggle, with all the attendant "flames and dark forces," those symbols of his romantic excitement.

But what is chiefly astonishing in this visionary fragment is Lenin's ambivalent attitude toward the forthcoming revolution. At one and the same time he sees immense productive forces released by the revolution and a gigantic development of capitalist progress—presumably he means state capitalism—while simultaneously he is confronted with the appalling prospect of the fortress continually changing hands. The land is given to the peasants, but it is immediately taken back from them by an edict of nationalization. There is no longer the dictatorship of the proletariat, but another dictatorship, vaster and more

---

* Word illegible.

† "As the thoroughness of the historic action increases, so too does the magnitude of the mass, whose action it is." This was Lenin's favorite quotation from *The Holy Family,* by Marx and Engels.

significant, called the "dictatorship of the proletariat and the peasantry." And once again, as so often before, we see him writing of
"complete freedom," and immediately we are confronted with the
party "standing by itself" and acquiring all those powers which will
ensure an end to all freedom. Of one thing he is certain: if the dictatorship wins the battle, then all Europe will go up in flames.

Lenin ardently believed in these flames. He was not playing with
fire. In that quiet library in Geneva he was already warming his hands.

Yet in the serious matter of bringing the revolution about, there
was, for the moment, very little he could do. In April he had summoned a meeting of his followers to decide on a new program. The
meeting took place in London and resulted in a rather perfunctory
call for an armed uprising. Thereafter he was continually urging the
peasants and workers to rise against the government, which had survived Bloody Sunday, peasant uprisings, strikes, innumerable clashes
between workmen and the police. "To arms, peasants and workers!"
he wrote in early April. "Hold secret meetings, form fighting units, get
weapons wherever you can, and send trustworthy representatives to
consult with the Social Democratic Labor Party." In October he was
still crying out "To arms!" and like Nechayev, who once amused himself with a similar list, he suggests the weapons which might reason-
ably be used—rifles, revolvers, bombs, knives, brass knuckles, sticks,
rags soaked in kerosene for starting fires, ropes, rope ladders, spades
for digging barricades, pyroxylin cartridges, barbed wire, nails—the
nails were to be used against cavalry. He suggests that these instruments be used for killing spies, policemen, gendarmes, blowing up
police stations, liberating prisoners and robbing banks. He was perfectly serious in demanding an uprising by workmen and peasants
armed only with homemade weapons. He wrote to the military section of the St. Petersburg Committee of the Social Democratic Party:

> In affairs of this kind the very last thing we need are debates and dis-
> cussions and talk about the functions of the military section and its
> rights. What we need is furious *energy* and *more* energy. I am appalled,
> absolutely appalled, to know that *for more than half a year* you have
> been talking about bombs—and not a single bomb has yet been made.
> And those who do the talking are very learned people. . . . Go to the
> youth, gentlemen! Organize at once and everywhere fighting brigades
> among students, and particularly among workers. Let them arm them-
> selves immediately with whatever weapons they can put their hands on
> —knives, revolvers, kerosene-soaked rags for setting fires . . . Let the

units begin to train for immediate operations. Some can undertake to assassinate a spy or blow up a police station. Others can attack a bank to expropriate funds for an insurrection. Let every unit learn to fight, if only by beating up policemen. These dozens of sacrifices will be repaid with interest by producing hundreds of battle-hardened veterans who will lead hundreds of thousands tomorrow.

It is doubtful whether any workmen in Russia listened to these appeals, for all through the summer and autumn the revolution was moving at its own momentum with no perceptible influence from Lenin's wing of the Social Democratic Party. Nevertheless Lenin worked relentlessly to affect the course of events. When the battle cruiser *Prince Potemkin* mutinied on June 16 while at target practice in the Black Sea and then anchored off Odessa flying the red flag at her masthead, the censors were able to keep the news from reaching Europe for four or five days. When Lenin heard of the mutiny he immediately summoned one of his followers, Mikhail Vasilyev, recently arrived from Russia, and said, "Comrade, by a decision of the Central Committee, you will leave at the earliest possible moment for Odessa—tomorrow will be best."

"I am ready to leave today," Vasilyev said. "What do I have to do?"

"It's a very important mission. You know the battle cruiser *Prince Potemkin* is now in Odessa. We are afraid the comrades in Odessa will not be able to take advantage of the mutiny. Whatever the cost, I want you to board the ship. Persuade the sailors they must act quickly and resolutely. See that they send a landing party on shore and that they don't hesitate to bombard government buildings. We must capture the city, and then immediately we must set about arming the workmen, and we must agitate energetically among the peasants. Mobilize the greatest possible number of comrades in the Odessa organization. Appeal to the peasants, by word of mouth and by leaflets, to take the land from the landowners and join in a common struggle with the workers. You must attach a great, an enormous importance, to the alliance of workers and peasants."

According to Vasilyev, who relates his conversation with Lenin in his memoirs, Lenin was in an extraordinary state of excitement as he outlined the plans by which, almost singlehanded, the twenty-nine-year-old Vasilyev was to bring about the revolution. Lenin, however, had not yet done with his plans.

"Afterward," he went on, "it is essential that we get the rest of the fleet in our hands. I am certain the majority of ships will rally to the

Prince Potemkin. But you must act boldly and decisively. Then you must send me a torpedo boat immediately. I shall be going to Rumania."

"Do you really think all this is possible?" Vasilyev asked, surprised by his own temerity.

"Of course it is possible," Lenin said. "All that is necessary is to act boldly and decisively."

The conversation was written down many years after the event, but it has the ring of authenticity. It shows Lenin clutching at straws and pretending they are daggers, his mind running furiously among improbabilities, yet with breath-taking audacity. One man, Vasilyev, would capture one ship, and then the entire fleet would fall into his hands, and then it would be the turn of Odessa and all of southern Russia, and then St. Petersburg would be captured and the Tsar would fall, and even the fall of the Tsar would be only an incident along the way until finally—*diktatura zazhigaet Evropu,* the dictatorship sets fire to Europe.

There are men who possess the gift of audacity raised to a pitch of genius, and Lenin was one of them. He failed to take possession of the Imperial battle fleet in 1905; but with a very similar technique, and with the same unwearying audacity, he captured Petrograd in 1917.

Vasilyev obeyed his instructions. After promising Lenin he would send a battleship rather than a torpedo boat to pick him up in Rumania, he set out for Russia with a false passport and high hopes of being the vehicle of the coming revolution. But when at last he reached Odessa, the *Prince Potemkin* had already fled in the direction of Rumania and the Social Democrats in Odessa were in no mood for revolt. The mutiny was over.

Increasingly, as he wandered through the streets of Geneva, Lenin became aware that all his attempts to intervene in the revolution were ending in failure. At all costs he must return to St. Petersburg, where Trotsky and a host of other revolutionaries were already fanning the flames of revolt. Trotsky had been in the capital since February, and he was already playing an active role, while Lenin's influence had been progressively declining. And when he set out for Russia in October, at a time when the country was in the grip of a general strike and the opportunities for agitation were greater than they had ever been, he was accompanied during the whole journey by frustrations which seemed to be designed to drive him to the limits of his patience.

He reached Stockholm safely, only to discover that the comrade supposed to meet him with a false passport did not turn up. Then storms delayed his steamer, and he spent two nervous weeks pulling strings and buttonholing whoever would listen to him in an effort to reach St. Petersburg quickly. He had an absolute horror of those moments when history passed him by.

When he finally reached St. Petersburg, it was to discover that the revolution was taking place without his assistance and in a way which was not to his liking. In St. Petersburg and Moscow there had arisen Councils of Workers' Delegates which, speaking in the name of the workers, were demanding the reforms described in Father Gapon's petition to the Tsar, and they had power behind them. They had the power to strike, the power to bring the country to an economic standstill; and on October 30, when the strike had been in existence a week, the Tsar bowed to the inevitable. Habeas corpus, a new constitution, freedom of speech and assembly—all these were granted. "I crossed myself and gave them everything they wanted," the Tsar wrote in a letter to his mother; and he seems to have thought that with these gifts he could bring peace to the people.

The Soviets of Workers' Delegates—the Russian word *soviet* simply means "council" or "committee"—came about spontaneously; they were not so much organs of revolutionary protest as instruments for bringing about the general strike. The president of the St. Petersburg Soviet of Workers' Delegates was a young lawyer, Georgy Khrustalyov-Nosar, a Menshevik, with a gift for oratory and very little gift for practical work. Trotsky soon supplanted him, and as the star of Khrustalyov-Nosar fell, so Trotsky's rose to dizzy heights. In his memoirs Lunacharsky speaks of how someone brought up the subject of Trotsky's new-found eminence in Lenin's presence. "For a moment Lenin's face seemed to darken," relates Lunacharsky, "and then he said, 'Well, Trotsky has won it by his tireless and striking work.'" It was grudging approval, and it seemed to be forced out of him.

Lenin's attitude toward the Soviets was one of bewilderment. He never participated in their sittings, and at first he had considerable difficulty relating them to his own plan of revolution. The man who was to make the word "Soviets" famous throughout the world began by distrusting them.

Legends have inevitably accumulated around Lenin's arrival in Russia at the end of 1905, and Soviet historians have gone to some pains to show that he played a leading role in the Moscow uprising which broke out at the end of the year. Maria Essen mentions a speech he made to a meeting of the executive committee of the St. Petersburg Soviet on November 26, in which he trounced Trotsky and Martov, and gave a clear, forthright description of the proper conduct of revolutionaries at this time, but the speech and his appearance at the Soviet is otherwise unrecorded. The Moscow uprising, which the Bolsheviks claim to have instigated, seems to have been a spontaneous one. It began on December 20 and was mercilessly put down by the Semyonovsky Regiment before the year was over, with artillery shells fired into the working-class quarter of Presnaya. The Tsar had had second thoughts; he was not prepared to give everything to a rebellious people.

Almost from the moment Lenin reached Russia he was shadowed by the secret police. So dangerous and famous a revolutionary deserved to be watched. He would shake off the spies, spend a night in a friend's house, attend a secret meeting, and while he was walking to still another friend's house, the secret police would appear again. It was uncanny. His sister arranged for him to live on the fashionable Grechesky Prospect, but he had no sooner registered than the house was surrounded by a swarm of secret agents, with the result that the friend who owned the apartment took to carrying a pistol and pacing about the apartment all day and all night, until Lenin, exasperated, fled, saying, "This man is going to bring a lot of trouble on our heads." He became a specialist in forged passports, acquiring a new one every two or three weeks, while Krupskaya contented herself with a passport made out in the name of Praskovia Onyegina. Lenin enjoyed wearing disguises, but they were usually rudimentary and offered no obstacle to the secret agents who continued to trail him wherever he went. Only when he slipped over the frontier to Finland did they lose track of him. He was in Finland between December 24 and December 31, and therefore missed the Moscow uprising.

Maria Andreyeva, the mistress of Gorky, had founded a newspaper called *Novaya Zhizn* (New Life) for the benefit of her literary and political friends. The poet Nikolay Vilenkin, known as Nikolay Minsky, was the editor, and the Bolsheviks were represented by nearly all the contributors of Lenin's *Vperyod*. Maria Andreyeva wanted a newspaper which would print the best poems, the best short stories of the time and the most spirited political articles; she succeeded in her literary efforts and was less successful in her politics. *Novaya Zhizn* published stories by Gorky, Leonid Andreyev, and Chirikov, and there were political essays by Lenin, Bogdanov, and Lunacharsky. Characteristically Lenin immediately attempted to take over full control of the newspaper. "It goes without saying," wrote Krupskaya, "that the presence of such men as Minsky and Balmont in the newspaper was intolerable, and finally the newspaper passed completely into the hands of the Bolsheviks." It was a process which had happened before and would happen again. But Lenin's victory was short-lived, for *Novaya Zhizn* was banned by the censor after only twenty-eight issues, and a few weeks later Gorky and Maria Andreyeva slipped over the frontier to Finland and abandoned all active participation in the revolution.

In his memoirs Nikolay Vilenkin describes the impression Lenin produced on him while they were working on *Novaya Zhizn.* He felt no bitterness toward Lenin for ousting him as editor in chief. He remembered Lenin as a man dedicated to his work, with a bitter tongue and an innocently sly smile. "We are down-to-earth Marxists," he said, and instead of demolishing arguments he was more likely to attack them with derision.

> When you met him for the first time [Vilenkin wrote] you would take him for a small bureaucrat. He was always ungainly, ill-dressed, rather stoop-shouldered, and you would never believe that this bald man with the impenetrable Mongoloid features and slow, deliberate movements was one of the most completely fearless, skillful and determined men of our time. It was only when you looked carefully at his sharp, narrow eyes and unforgettable smile that you perceived the extraordinary will power concealed behind the very ordinary mask of his face. But those who knew him well twenty years ago never doubted that sooner or later he would play the chief role in the history of his country. There was a legendary, heroic halo about him.

Meanwhile the interminable conferences went on, and Lenin continued to write pamphlets and speeches marked by increasing frustration. The Soviets were largely in the hands of the Mensheviks, but the liberal Cadets and the Socialist Revolutionaries were in the ascendant. The Bolsheviks, far from being a majority, formed the small extreme left wing of the Social Democratic Party; and they played an ineffective and undistinguished role in that revolutionary winter, when the barricades went up in Moscow and Trotsky emerged as president of the St. Petersburg Soviet at the age of twenty-six.

But although Lenin had broken with the Mensheviks, he continued to fight them from within. At party conferences, which were usually held in Finland, he would appear with his chosen delegates and attempt to win the entire party over to his views. He was the battering ram ceaselessly hammering at the fortress walls, and if he could not break through in one place he would attempt to break through in another. The technique was exhausting, but it was essentially a simple one. One day he explained it to Lunacharsky:

> "If we have the majority in the Central Committee or in the central organization, then of course we shall demand the most rigorous discipline. We shall insist on the most absolute submission of the Mensheviks to the unity of the party. So much the worse for them if their petty bourgeois mentality prevents them from marching with us. Then they will take upon themselves the shame of having caused a split in a party formerly united at great expense of time and thought. And if they go, it is certain that they will take away from the 'united' party fewer workmen than they brought into it."
>
> "And what happens," I asked him, "if we are in the minority?"
>
> "That depends on circumstances," he replied with an enigmatic smile. "Whatever happens, we shall never permit them to put a running noose round our necks or lead us by a chain!"

Such tactics were essentially piratical; they could sometimes be made to work within the confines of the party; outside the party they were nearly always useless. Lenin's "we" was the imperial "We": he had so identified himself with the party that it was unthinkable to him that anyone in the party could disagree with him, even though there was continual disagreement with him. To the Mensheviks he was saying, "If we have any advantage over you, we shall exact stern obedience. If you have any advantage over us, we shall employ all the permissible freedoms and refuse to obey you. I shall never permit you to put a running noose round my neck."

The Russians were in no mood to exchange the autocracy of the Tsar for the autocracy of dogmatic socialists, and when the elections were held in April the Cadets (Constitutional Democrats), who followed the western liberal tradition, obtained a clear majority. The Tsar and his close advisers regarded the Cadets with undisguised horror; so, for a different reason, did Lenin, who immediately set about writing a long pamphlet in which he demonstrated a talent for unrestrained invective. The pamphlet, called *The Victory of the Cadets*, is among the most powerful of his works, the vehemence of his anger acquiring at times an almost formal elegance. He denounces them with all the fury of a prophet denouncing the heretics and the worshipers of the golden calf:

> The Cadets are the worms in the grave of the revolution. The revolution lies buried. The worms gnaw at it. But the revolution has the power of coming quickly to life again and of blossoming forth magnificently on the well-turned soil. Splendidly and marvelously has the soil been turned during the October days of freedom and the December uprising. And we are far from denying that the worms perform a useful work in this age when the revolution lies buried. Look how well these greasy worms are preparing the soil . . .

The Victory of the Cadets takes the form of a long threnody. Hatred and anguish are mingled with bitterness and wit, and the author is so beside himself with fury that he no longer sounds like himself. It is another voice, sharper, shriller, almost voluptuous in its passion for denunciation. "No, comrades," he says, "you must not believe that the workers should support the Cadets: that would be like saying that the function of steam is not to drive the ship's engine but to blow the ship's siren." So he goes on, hymning the death of the victors with incomparable malice. But the victors were not dead, and he was defeated.

He lived in the murky depths of conspiracy, rarely coming to the surface. Secret stores of ammunition were being collected, secret meetings were being held, he moved like a shadow through the streets of St. Petersburg, and nearly always there was another shadow following him. Only once, during all this period in Russia, did he rise to the surface and speak at a public meeting.

It happened at the palace of Countess Panina, which she had transformed into a "House of the People," where political meetings were held. On May 22, 1906, a crowded meeting was being addressed by one of the leaders of the Cadet party; there were workmen in the audience, and the police for some reason were notably absent. Lenin had slipped into the hall. The Cadet leader was speaking well, defending the recent negotiations between the Duma and the government, explaining that these negotiations did not involve capitulating to the Tsar. From time to time he looked down at his notes, and there would be a ripple of applause, while Lenin smiled his slow malicious smile, waiting his turn. He had come to denounce the negotiations, and one of his supporters had whispered to the chairman of the meeting that a certain Karpov, a distinguished Bolshevik, wished to take the floor.

The chairman had never heard of Karpov, and when the Cadet came to the end of his speech, Lenin was left in doubt whether he would be permitted to address the crowd. The thought of failure always brought on a crisis, and he was visibly trembling. Finally the chairman said, "Mr. Karpov has the floor," and Lenin mounted the rostrum. Krupskaya was in the hall. "Ilyich was terribly agitated," she said. "He stood silent for about a minute, very pale. All the blood had flowed to his heart. You could sense immediately that the speaker's agitation was being communicated to the audience. And this was followed by a sudden burst of handclapping, which swept through the hall, as the party comrades recognized him."

He made a vigorous speech, denouncing the Cadets, accusing them of being a party without roots in the present, conniving with the past, and therefore deserving to be discredited; only the Russian Social Democratic Party possessed the key to the future. According to a brief report which appeared in *Volna* (The Wave), one of the semilegal newspapers run by the Bolsheviks after *Novaya Zhizn* was banned, he declared that "our present task is to do everything in our power to enable the organized proletariat to become the leaders of the victorious revolutionary army during the present upsurge and during the inevitable decisive struggle that lies ahead." According to Krupskaya, Lenin was greeted with an ovation, red shirts were torn up and waved, and for a long time after the speech workers remained in the palace and in the streets outside, eagerly discussing it. Then Lenin went into hiding again.

Some years later, when he was asked whether any of the events of 1906–07 had given him any pleasure, he answered, "Yes, the meeting in Countess Panina's palace."

Yet it is difficult to understand why he took pleasure in it. His speech was not exceptional, and there was little to be gained by attacking the Cadets at this moment; they, too, were powerless, for the autocracy refused to permit them to form a government. Nicholas II had bowed to the will of the people by permitting elections; he then bowed to the will of his advisers by refusing to permit the Cadets, who were voted into power, to rule. Once again the war between the Tsar and the people had reached a state of stalemate.

Frustrated, powerless, always in hiding and always being shadowed, Lenin took refuge in Finland. A large, rambling country house near the railroad station at Kuokkala became the Bolshevik headquarters, and here Lenin wrote the articles which were printed in

Volna, Vperyod and *Echo,* those newspapers which were always being banned: only *Echo* survived for more than a month. A special messenger would come from St. Petersburg every day with newspapers and letters. and Lenin would then glance through the newspapers and immediately write off the article for the day. "It was strange to watch him," said one of the messengers. "He would write straight off, without a pause, as though he were merely copying something." And in effect, that is exactly what he was doing, for the well-worn arguments are constantly repeated. One can read a hundred of these articles without coming upon a new idea.

The old ideas remained dominant to the end of his life: the dictatorship of the proletariat, mass terror, the destruction of all opposition parties—especially the Mensheviks, who belonged to his own party but were nevertheless more to be hated than the Cadets and Socialist Revolutionaries; he hated them because he loved them and they had rejected his advances. Against the Mensheviks he continued to speak with undisguised bitterness and hostility. In January 1907 he wrote an article called "The St. Petersburg Elections and the Hypocrisy of the Thirty-one Mensheviks," in which he accused them of crawling on their bellies to make peace with the Cadets. There is none of the ferocious invective of his article against the Cadets. This time he is merely vituperative and repetitive. "The Mensheviks have betrayed the workers and gone over to the Cadets," he says, ringing the changes but always coming to the same conclusion. The Mensheviks had had enough. They summoned him to stand trial before a party court, accusing him of conduct "impermissible in a party member."

The trial of Lenin took place before nine judges—three selected by the Mensheviks, one each by the Lettish and Polish Social Democrats and the Bundists, and three by Lenin. Rafael Abramovich was the presiding judge. The court held two brief sessions, examined three witnesses, and listened to Lenin's defiant speech, in which he took the offensive and announced that all means were permissible in a disunited party, *because a disunited party has ceased to exist as a party.* There were no rules which had to be obeyed when a party had split and thereby lost its soul. To all accusations that he was using poisoned weapons, he answered mockingly that all weapons were poisonous, and he did not care what weapons he used as long as he produced the desired result. He reminded the "comrade judges" that struggle is a serious matter and must be carried to its proper conclusion, which is the annihilation of the enemy. Four times in the course of a short speech he insisted that he would always act in this way, and it was inconceivable to him that anyone should expect him to act in any other way. For him, there had been no morality in his dealings with the autocracy; now he announced publicly that morality was equally meaningless in his dealings with any party members who disagreed with him.

Lenin's speech at the trial is a shattering one. It is a lawyer's brief for any kind of treachery, double-dealing, and immorality. He celebrates and glories in the absolute nihilism of Nechayev. He said:

> It was necessary to break up the ranks of the Mensheviks, who were leading the proletariat into the arms of the Cadets; it was necessary to carry confusion into their ranks; it was necessary to arouse in the masses hatred, contempt and detestation for these people who had ceased to be members of a united party, who had become political enemies, who were trying to put a spoke in our Social Democratic organization in its election campaign. In my relations with political enemies of this kind I then conducted—and in the event of a repetition and development of a split I shall always conduct—a war of extermination. . . .
>
> .   .   .   .
>
> They say, "Fight, but not with poisoned weapons." This is a very charming and impressive idea, it goes without saying. Either it is charming and empty verbiage, or it expresses in a vague and nebulous fashion the very same idea of struggle, of spreading among the masses hatred, contempt and detestation of their opponents—of a struggle which is impermissible in a united party when a split has occurred, by the very nature of the split—an idea which I have already expounded earlier. However much you twist this phrase, or this metaphor, you will not squeeze out of it a single grain of real sense unless it is this difference between the loyal and correct method of fighting by means of argument within the organization and the method of fighting by means of a split—that is, by destroying the enemy organization, by rousing among the masses hatred, contempt and detestation for this organization. The poisoned weapons are dishonest splits, and not the war of extermination which results when a split has already taken place.

So, ruthlessly and deviously, he threw the blame on his opponents and gave himself the utmost freedom to wage a war of extermination whenever he pleased. Henceforward, he would give himself absolution for every war he fought and every poisoned weapon he used. Since by his own definition a split meant that the party ceased to exist, "then it follows that the limits of the struggle are not party limits, but general political limits, or rather, general civil limits, the limits set by criminal law and by nothing else." The argument is a dizzy one, and ultimately meaningless, for Lenin had no more respect for criminal laws than he had for political laws. At all costs there must be submission to his will.

Believing in his own absolute rightness, he used the Mensheviks for his own purposes. Though they distrusted him, they were never able to expel him; and though from time to time he abandoned the struggle in despair, he always returned to it. Over a period of fourteen years he fought them to a standstill.

He was a dogmatic nihilist fighting against socialists, Nechayev against Marx. He fought with weapons which never appeared in any Marxist handbook, and with a total disregard for the opinions of others. He never argued; he merely laid down the law.

There are indications that he was oppressed by a sense of loneliness, and that the break with Martov was especially painful to him. Years later, after his second stroke, he whispered to Krupskaya, "They say Martov is dying, too." It was as though at that moment, when it was too late, he realized that all their quarrels had ended in disaster.

ELIZABETH DE K.

Fʀᴏᴍ ᴛʜᴇ ᴛɪᴍᴇ ʜᴇ ʟᴇꜰᴛ sᴀᴍᴀʀᴀ Lenin devoted his life to the revolution. There was almost no moment of the day when he was not wholly immersed in his revolutionary work. He was like Nechayev's doomed revolutionary who had subordinated all his interests, all his talents and capabilities in a single cause which he served with priestly devotion. He had no interest in or understanding of the arts, no knowledge of painting or music or sculpture, no feeling for literature. He lived in a world of statistics and arid dialectics, those harsh and elementary tools with which he hoped to break open the closely guarded mysteries of government. He was not without humor, but it was a dry, sardonic humor. He had no wit and no small talk. Many who knew him found something frightening in his relentless single-mindedness. Trotsky, who in those days disliked him, spoke of him as a man who always looked at other men as though he wanted to give them orders. In his own eyes he had become the "incorruptible Robespierre" of the revolutionary movement.

There were however rare moments when he forgot to see himself as a historical figure, when he unbent sufficiently to set aside for a few hours his obsessive determination to bring about a revolution. Three times in his life he fell in love. Of the first love affair very little is known, and it seems to have been short-lived. Apollinaria Yakubova came from the same social background as Krupskaya. They were close friends, working together in the illegal organization in St. Petersburg as messengers and propagandists. Krupskaya describes how they would go out together with shawls over their heads, disguised as millworkers, and in this way they would mingle with the women workers at the Thornton Mills; afterward they would draw up reports, which Lenin used for writing the leaflets that were thrust into the hands of the millworkers as they came through the factory gates when the work shift was over. Together the two young women performed a hundred similar escapades. Lenin was very fond of Apollinaria. She was prettier and more intelligent than Krupskaya, who was gentle and plodding, and never very proficient in Marxian dialectics. A friend described her as "broad-shouldered, with vivid brown eyes, blond hair and a fine color, the epitome of health." Quick-witted, adventurous, popular, she had already carved out a niche for herself among the young revolutionaries in St. Petersburg.

Lenin proposed marriage to her just before he was arrested, and from his prison cell he wrote a letter asking Apollinaria and Krupskaya to stand in Shpalernaya Street outside the prison gate so that he would see them when he was being led down the corridor to exercise in the yard. There was a window in the corridor which looked out on the street, and he hoped to catch a brief glimpse of them. Krupskaya, who relates the incident in her memoirs written more than twenty-five years later, says that "for some reason" Apollinaria was unable to come, and therefore she went alone to take up a long vigil in the street. It was generally believed that Apollinaria's absence meant that she had considered his proposal and rejected it. She went on working for the party, was arrested and sentenced to exile in Siberia. She had served only a few months of her sentence when she was rescued by a young professor of law named Takhterev. They fled the country and settled in London, where Lenin encountered them during his exile. The two families remained on friendly terms. It was Takhterev who silenced the gossiping Mrs. Yeo, and who made all the arrangements for the London Congress, hiring the hall and finding accommodation for the delegates. After Lenin left London, Apollinaria played no more part in his life. She died of tuberculosis in May 1913.

The second love affair was longer, more turbulent, and more demanding. It began promisingly in St. Petersburg and ended disastrously in Galicia nine years later.

Like Apollinaria Yakubova, Elizabeth de K. was pretty, quick-witted and adventurous. She was independently wealthy and had a taste for fine clothes, traveling and the arts. She was well-read. She knew a great many writers. She was at home in the aristocratic society of St. Petersburg. She had married and divorced her husband, and she was at loose ends when she met Lenin for the first time in a Tartar restaurant one evening in November 1905.

Lenin was working in the editorial office of *Novaya Zhizn*. For the Bolsheviks it was a time of extraordinary excitement; they were printing 80,000 copies each day, and they were not overly disappointed when, as often happened, the police raided the printing press and confiscated an entire edition. They were attracting attention.

Under the name "N. Lenin," there appeared a series of inflammatory articles which were being spoken about all over St. Petersburg. They were among his more impressive journalist works, clear and forthright, written in the tone of a man exulting in his precarious freedom to denounce the government and to incite the populace to rebellion. That these articles could be published at all testified to the astonishing liberalism of the government.

Writing under one alias, Lenin was living under another. His passport was made out in the name of William Frey, an Englishman. He was in hiding, sleeping in different places each night, planning insurrection, holding clandestine meetings in the working-class districts. Occasionally, very occasionally, like a man who had been living underground too long, he would emerge from his hiding place and take a meal in a fashionable restaurant.

That evening he was dining with his friend Mikhail Rumyantsev, who also worked on *Novaya Zhizn*. Elizabeth de K. was sitting alone in the restaurant. Rumyantsev knew her well, and seeing that Lenin was showing unusual interest in the young woman, he walked over to her and suggested that she come to their table.

"You'll meet a very interesting man," he said. "He is very famous, but you mustn't ask too many details."

Amused and delighted by the air of mystery, she walked over to the table and was introduced to "William Frey." She asked him whether he was English.

"No, I'm not exactly English," he said, and she detected an ironic smile.

They had a pleasant conversation lasting about an hour. Lenin's sharp tongue was held in check. He seemed to be well informed and he spoke with an undertone of raillery which she found curiously exciting. She could not guess what he was famous for or why there was such an air of mystery about him. It never occurred to her to connect him with the "N. Lenin" who signed the inflammatory articles in *Novaya Zhizn*.

A week later she was visiting the offices of *Novaya Zhizn* to see one of the contributors when she encountered the mysterious stranger again.

"I am happy to see you," he said. "What has happened that you don't patronize the Tartar restaurant any more?"

He gave her a faintly mocking smile. She understood that he was inviting her to dinner, but they had known each other for too short a time to make any arrangements on the spot. She sought out Rumyantsev. He laughed.

"You don't understand," he said. "My friend Frey is certainly interested in women, but chiefly from a collective, social, and political point of view. I doubt very much whether he has any interest in women as individuals. Allow me to add that after our dinner the other evening he asked me whether I can vouch for you, because he is suspicious of new acquaintances, fearing informers. I had to tell him who you are. I also told him that your apartment is wonderfully suited for secret meetings."

From this, Elizabeth de K. learned that he was a revolutionary. The temptation to meet him for a third time could hardly be resisted. Three days later Rumyantsev arranged a small dinner party. In the course of the friendly conversation the question of the secret meetings was raised. Her apartment was in a fashionable district, on the street level, and visitors could slip in and out without being observed, and the police were unlikely to suspect that revolutionaries would be gathering there. She liked and admired Rumyantsev; she was intrigued by William Frey; and she was perfectly willing to let them use the apartment twice a week.

The pattern of these meetings was quickly established. Elizabeth de K. would send her maid away, carry the samovar into the dining room, prepare sandwiches, and act as doorkeeper. William Frey always came first. He would tell her the password of the day, and she would admit any visitors who answered to the password. While the meeting was being held, she scrupulously retired to her bedroom.

On several occasions there was no secret meeting. William Frey came alone and they spent the evening together, dining tête-à-tête and talking late into the night. She remembered that he was especially fond of washing up the dishes and liked to keep watch on the samovar. She was an excellent pianist and sometimes played for him. On a famous occasion she was playing the third movement of Beethoven's *Sonata Pathétique* when he asked her to play it again from the beginning, and then again. She wondered what attracted him so much to the opening bars, and she was a little put out when he answered that they reminded him of a revolutionary song sung by the Jewish Bund.

Sooner or later he would talk to her about the coming revolution. The world without revolution oppressed him. Sometimes he would fall into fits of profound dejection, slumped in her armchair, with such a look of misery and worry on his face that she feared for his sanity. There were times, too, when he seemed to talk mechanically, almost meaninglessly, using words like counters which fell with a hollow ring. "There were days," she wrote, "when I could not tell whether he was a man or a machine."

The love affair followed its inevitable course. When he went to live in Stockholm, she followed him. Even in Sweden he was living the conspiratorial life: secret signs, passwords, meetings in obscure places. Over the telephone he instructed her to meet him at an automat, but if other Russians were present she must pretend not to recognize him. When she arrived at the automat, she saw two Georgians ferociously hammering away at a vending machine. When they caught sight of Lenin, they shouted, "Comrade Ilyich, please help us with this damnable bourgeois machine. We asked for ham sandwiches and all we get is pastry!" He succeeded in getting them ham sandwiches. She pretended not to see him, and he was pleased with her. "Do you know who those Georgians were?" he said. "They are our delegates from the Caucasus. Splendid boys, but absolute savages!"

Lenin was attending a Congress and had little time to spare for her except on Sundays. One Sunday he hired a rowboat and took her out on the lake. He had broad, heavy shoulders, and rowed well.

"I don't see you as a professional revolutionary," she said.

"How do you see me?" he asked.

"As a farmer, or a fisherman, or a sailor, or a metalsmith, but not as a professional revolutionary."

When they came to the open stretches of the lake with its vast expanse under the northern sky, she said it reminded her of Knut Hamsun's novels. Predictably Lenin launched into a discussion of the novel *Hunger* "which, as you know, demonstrates the physical and physiological symptoms of those who starve under the inexorable capitalist regime." But she was not thinking of *Hunger*: she was thinking of his quieter, more pastoral novels. She knew them all. She discovered that Lenin had read only *Hunger* and had no intention of reading the others.

"It's quite obvious," he said, "that you will never make a Social Democrat."

She shook her head sadly. "And you— You will never be anything but a Social Democrat."

She returned to St. Petersburg. Some weeks later she received an urgent letter demanding an immediate response: "Write to me at once and tell me precisely where and how we can meet, otherwise there will be delays and misunderstandings." The peremptory tone did not please her. She decided to put an end to the affair, which had long since become a burden to her.

But two years later, when she was in Geneva, she read in a newspaper that he was giving a speech in Paris. She took the train, without exactly knowing what induced her to renew an affair which was doomed from the beginning. Probably it was the fact that he had once placed himself under her protection, and women do not easily surrender the role of protectress. This had happened in June 1906, when with Rumyantsev she attended a secret meeting which took place in a field outside St. Petersburg. Wearing a peasant kerchief around her head and a borrowed peasant skirt, she took the horse-drawn bus to the outskirts of the city and followed interminable country roads until at last a man sitting in a ditch pointed in the direction of the field where the meeting was being held. There was wild enthusiasm when Lenin appeared. He spoke in his usual inflammatory manner, calling for an immediate revolt, and so working on the emotions of the audience that, with a red banner fluttering from a branch, they formed a long procession and marched jubilantly on St. Petersburg. They were making their way down the long Pulostrovsky Prospect when the Cossacks drove into them, slashing them with their whips. In the confusion Rumyantsev disappeared under the hoofs of the horses and Lenin flung himself into a ditch. It was obvious that Lenin was in danger of arrest for inciting rebellion. She asked him whether he was prepared to place himself under her protection and obey her implicitly, and when he agreed she took him across fields and byways to Lesnoy and so by streetcar back to the heart of St. Petersburg. He was in an exalted mood and spoke of a *boevaya druzhina,* a detachment of armed workers, which would take care of the Cossacks.

"Do you know," she asked bitterly, "what would have happened if you had had your *boevaya druzhina*? There would be dead Cossacks and workers lying in the streets. As it is now, we have suffered a few cuts and bruises, but everyone is alive."

It was an argument which seemed to carry very little weight with him.

There was another incident which profoundly affected her. One evening when they were alone in her apartment a blazing cinder from the samovar fell on her dress and set fire to it. He threw himself on her, smothered the flame, and then released her. It had been a very small flame and no harm had been done, but Lenin was in a state of shock, trembling, pale as ice. For some reason he turned away and ran out of the house. At that moment she had the feeling that he was in love with her and could not forgive himself for having harmed her.

She attended the lecture in Paris. What he said made no impression on her, but she remembered his nervous pacing up and down the platform as he delivered the lecture. During the intermission she went to see him in a small room behind the platform, only to find him surrounded by his admirers, unapproachable. At last he caught sight of her. He was startled, his eyes opened wide, but he checked himself quickly and said, "What on earth brought you here?"

"I came to hear you," she answered, "and then, too, I have a commission to you from a certain person." She gave him an envelope with her name and address and telephone number. Then she left.

The next morning the expected telephone call failed to materialize. Instead Lenin himself appeared, looking bewildered and at the same time jaunty. He had never hoped to see her again. He threw out his arms to embrace her, but she said, "It is all over now, my friend."

"Yes, it is all over," he laughed. "But you must admit you are a very interesting woman."

So they talked and resumed a friendship which was no longer a love affair. They were older and more experienced, and wanted less from each other. A few days later she returned to Geneva. During the following years they met at long intervals and kept up an occasional correspondence. Her letters have not survived, but a good dozen of his letters remained in her possession.

The letters are remarkable because they show him in a mood of acquiescence, accepting her as she was. Occasionally, of course, he would make the inevitable halfhearted attempt to instill some Marxist discipline in her mind. He wrote to her shortly after her return to Geneva:

> I truly believe it would be a good thing if you stopped living like one of those birds of heaven. The truth is that you resemble one of those heavenly birds who neither sorrow nor labor. And as everyone knows

these divine birds neither sow, nor reap, nor are they harvested. It is my profound conviction that you are exactly like one of those birds. You should study more profoundly and conduct your personal life in a healthy and comfortable atmosphere, without of course being caught up in a mean and bourgeois monotony in the manner of Chirikov.* No, you should live in such a way which is natural to you, and with all your necessities provided for, on condition that you make continual intellectual progress, so that you can leave some traces of yourself for those who come after you.

She replied good-humoredly that she had every intention of progressing intellectually, so long as her intellectual progress did not involve reading *Das Kapital* or becoming a member of the party. She reminded him that she detested intolerance, especially the kind of intolerance which was evident in the editorial office of *Novaya Zhizn* when the Bolsheviks rid themselves of journalists who did not hew to the party line. He replied with a sermon on the necessity of rigid controls —it was the inevitable reply, and she was not particularly surprised by the dogmatic tone. She had observed that there was a curious disparity between the announced program of the Bolsheviks and their tactics. He answered with another sermon, in which he made a careful distinction between French opportunism and British compromise—opportunism being "a series of accommodations to the facts, traffic with one's conscience, concessions at the expense of the basic program, submitting to outside influence, taking a step backward when necessary." Compromise, on the other hand, was a process which "worked within the existing forces" and did not involve any backward steps. The important thing was to go forward, at whatever the cost. "The program remains, the tactics change."

These sermons were perhaps intended to convince her of the error of her ways: the tone is sardonic, the manner professorial. She remained unconvinced. He was more convincing when he wrote about subjects remote from his preoccupations. After the death of Tolstoy she asked for his opinion on that strange and adventurous death. He wrote back:

> In the first place I have always followed the rule of avoiding depressing thoughts, if necessary by an act of will, even when those thoughts are relevant and even when they are intimately connected with my personal affairs. It is perfectly possible to live in this way. Now about Tolstoy—it seems to me that his flight remarkably ennobled and completed

* Evgeniy Chirikov (1864–1932) was a famous author of sentimental novels and plays.

his life. It was like the last stroke which a painter puts on the canvas, and the most brilliant—inasmuch as one can reproach him for only one thing, and that is that he lived in a manner absolutely contrary to his preachings. But "the little Countess" took care to remove his body to her own house, and she never permitted it to lie *beneath the branches of poverty*. She was indeed an extremely tenacious woman! I feel that no one should ever try to imitate the life of Tolstoy. That was his fate, and all of us have our own fates. I am continually quoting that poem by Zhukovsky in which he speaks of how men are always trying on different crosses, some heavy, some light, some dear, some cheap, and none of them fit his shoulder. The only proper cross is the one we already bear. And though Tolstoy must have been saddened by the thought that his life was ending, nevertheless his time had come. We should admire the perfect art with which he completed his life.

But if he approved of Tolstoy's death, he raged against the death of Paul Lafargue, who committed suicide with his wife, Laura, who was Karl Marx's daughter. "No, I cannot approve of it," he wrote. "They could still write, they could still accomplish things, and even if they could no longer work efficiently they could still observe and give good advice." He was shaken by the deaths of the Lafargues, and at different times in his life he would return briefly to the problem of suicide, saying sometimes that it was good and at other times that it was morally reprehensible, depending upon his mood at the moment. To Krupskaya he said in a moment of depression, "If you can no longer work, then you should face the truth and die like the Lafargues."

When August Bebel, the great German socialist leader, died in 1913, he asked Elizabeth to send him some edelweiss to be placed on the grave. He wrote:

DEAREST,

Since you are leaving for Switzerland, there is something I would like you to do for me. I am sure you remember that we have often spoken about that famous flower: the edelweiss. I have just been reading about edelweiss in connection with the wreaths which were placed on the coffin of Bebel. If you can't climb up to the places where the edelweiss grows, please buy some flowers for me and dry them, and if it is at all possible bring back some living ones.

And may I remind you that I have already written to you a hundred times about *Kompleto Lernolibro Esperantistoy*, published in Zurich at 1 franc 25. You asked me to give you the title of the pamphlet, which I did twice, and there has been simply no further news about it. No doubt you thought I had forgotten, but I shall go on reminding you until you send me the book.

Enjoy yourself, get fat, and never stop laughing. And be good.

The reference to the book on Esperanto was a very serious one. Troubled by the difficulties encountered among delegates at the various congresses over which he presided, he had come to the conclusion that Esperanto provided an intelligent solution. This invented language was already in current use in international congresses, and he liked its "pleasant and agreeable" sound. For a short while he appeared among Esperantist groups in Zurich, but his interest in the language quickly subsided.

Most of the surviving letters deal with political and social problems. They read like speeches. Though precise, peremptory, almost deliberately dull, they have a curious air of improvisation, as though he had long ago lost hope of convincing her and was only going through the motions of answering her questions. Her world was foreign to him. Once he told her that he had never known a woman who had read *Das Kapital* right through, or who could understand a railroad timetable, or who could play chess. He gave her a chess set in the hope that she might prove the exception to the rule. Of him, she might have said that she had never known a man who was so remote from the ordinary preoccupations of humanity, or who was so determined to change a world he understood so little, or who was so insensitive to the arts. When she sent him a postcard with a reproduction of the *Mona Lisa,* requesting him to study it and tell her about his reactions, he answered:

> I can make nothing of your *Mona Lisa.* Neither the face nor the dress tell me anything at all. I believe there is an opera of this name, and a book by d'Annunzio. I simply don't understand anything about this thing you have sent me.

She thought he was teasing her, assuming an attitude which was not in fact his own. But he meant exactly what he said, for some time later she received a postcard from him: "Have you forgotten your *Mona Lisa?* You said you would explain her to me, but in spite of repeated requests you have not done so. Write, and don't forget."

During the nine years of their friendship it was the only time he wrote to her about a work of art.

They met for the last time in Galicia just before the outbreak of World War I. She had written to him to say she would like to see him;

he suggested she should come to Poronino, where one of his agents would meet her. The air of secrecy surrounding the meeting disturbed her, and she was even more disturbed when she met the agent, who proved to be Ganetsky, smooth-faced, self-important, menacing. In later years Ganetsky was to play an important role in the arrangements for bringing Lenin across Germany in the sealed train. She hated his cultivated air of mystery, and his obsequiousness, his elaborate manners. She thought he resembled a well-trained hotel servant. And when, at last after many delays, she met Lenin, she was surprised by the change in him. He seemed more abrupt, more desperate than ever, at the mercy of uncontrollable passions. Greatly daring, she asked whether he had grown more tolerant with the passage of time. Surely he no longer believed in the iron-hard Marxist dialectics. Surely there must be a place for ordinary liberty.

"The people have no need for liberty," he told her. "Liberty is one of the forms of the bourgeois dictatorship. In a state worthy of the name there is no liberty. The people want to exercise power, but what on earth would they do if it were given to them? There are three things that have to be done: You must give the earth to the peasants, peace to the soldiers, power to the working class; and every action which does not directly aim to bring about these three things is non-Marxist and therefore false."

It was an unhappy meeting, and she left after a short while. Just before leaving, she remembered the poem by Zhukovsky which he had often mentioned in his letters. She reminded him of the poem and said, "Sometimes I think you have chosen a cross which is not your own." She never saw him again.

One other woman entered Lenin's life. This was Inessa Armand, to whom he also addressed letters in Russian with the familiar "thou." This love affair was more lasting, ending only with her death.

THE LONDON CONFERENCE

O
F ALL THE CONFERENCES in which Lenin took part before he came to power, the London conference held in the spring of 1907 was the stormiest, the most exhausting, and the most critical. Other conferences followed, so many that they are almost beyond counting—he had a talent for conferences, and he would bring them about on the slightest provocation. But this London conference had an air of finality about it. He stamped his own image on it, shaped it, molded it, driving roughshod over all his opponents. No one who attended it ever forgot how he dominated it by the force and brutality of his arguments and by the sheer weight of his personality.

Originally it was planned to hold the conference in Copenhagen; at the last moment the Danish government refused its permission, and the delegates, numbering more than three hundred, wearily made their way to Malmö in Sweden. They had hardly settled in the town when they were told they would have to leave—the Swedish authorities did not relish the presence of so many Russian revolutionaries on their soil. With the help of the English socialists H. N. Brailsford and George Lansbury, arrangements were made to transfer the conference to London. The meeting place was the Reverend F. R. Swan's Brotherhood Church in Southgate Road, Whitechapel, one of those wretchedly bleak churches with no denominational character which were once to be found all over England. Gorky, who attended the conference as an observer, remembered the horror of it twenty years later. "I can still see vividly before me," he wrote, "those bare wooden walls unadorned to the point of absurdity, the lancet windows looking down on a small, narrow hall which might have been a classroom in a poor school." The church no longer exists, having been mercifully obliterated by a German bomb during the last war.

The conference opened on Monday, April 30, 1907, at seven o'clock in the evening. Five organized groups attended: Bolsheviks, Mensheviks, Bundists, Latvian and Polish Social Democrats. They were arranged along wooden benches, with the Mensheviks on the left, the Bolsheviks on the right, and the other groups in between. Most of them were prima donnas of revolution, and there was scarcely one of them who had not been arrested and sentenced to at least one long term of imprisonment. Their names were little known at the time. Few would have guessed that among them were future conquerors, labor leaders, and philosophers whose names would become household words over a large part of the world.

Stalin was there, looking thin and sickly, speaking with a Georgian accent which could scarcely be understood; so were Kamenev, Zinoviev and Trotsky, who were to be murdered at his orders. The indestructible Voroshilov, the stubborn Bubnov who was to become Commissar of Education, and Rykov, who was to become Vice-Chairman of the Council of Commissars, second only to Lenin, took minor parts in the conference, rarely raising their voices. Pokrovsky and Lyadov, the Soviet historians, were present, neither having yet written any history. Litvinov sat as an observer in the gallery. Nogin, who was to command the Moscow insurrection in November 1917, sat close to Lenin. Shaumyan, who was to become Extraordinary Commissar of the Caucasus, a dictator over vast regions of southern Russia until he was shot by the British, represented the Georgian Bolsheviks, together with Mikha Tskhakaya, who was later to travel with Lenin in the sealed train. Few came under their own names; nearly all were provided with false passports. Stalin, for some reason, chose to be known as Ivanovich. He had no voice in the proceedings and was permitted to attend on sufferance, because he had no credentials from any recognized Caucasian organization.

Many of the Bolsheviks were to become famous later, but in 1907 the Mensheviks were already well known. Plekhanov, Axelrod, Deutsch, Martov, and Dan were already figures to be reckoned with, with reputations extending far beyond the frontiers of Russia. Plekhanov was still regarded as the outstanding socialist theoretician, and he was therefore called upon to open the proceedings. Appropriately, he wore a morning coat, a high white collar, and a silk tie; he was one of the very few who were well dressed. But it was the gentle, irascible Martov who defended the Menshevik cause, pitting his humanitarian concepts against the pitiless stratagems of Lenin, so that this long conference, which lasted for nearly three weeks and comprised some thirty-five separate sessions, ultimately resolved itself into a duel between Lenin and Martov. Altogether 105 Bolsheviks and 97 Mensheviks attended, and there were some 134 delegates representing the other parties.

The Polish Social Democrats formed a powerful close-knit group of 44 members, of whom the most impressive were Rosa Luxemburg and Jan Tyszka-Yogiches, her constant companion. Rosa Luxemburg was small, dark and fiery, and suffered from a hip ailment which cruelly deformed her frail body; she had a quick-witted intelligence and came in the end to despise the authoritarian temper of the Bolsheviks. Like Jan Tyszka-Yogiches, she had emerged from prison only a few weeks before. Felix Dzerzhinsky was another delegate of the Polish Social Democrats, but he had been arrested in Russia and therefore could not appear. Dzerzhinsky was to become the head of the Cheka, Lenin's secret police, a far more effective machine for destroying the opposition than the tsarist Okhrana. Of the Latvian Social Democrats the most impressive was probably Hermann Danishevsky, who was to become a powerful force in the Cheka and the Red Army.

The Bundists numbered 57, deriving their strength from the young Jewish intellectuals; their sympathies were with the Mensheviks. Among them were the brilliant and gentle Vladimir Medem, who was appointed chairman because he alone had the gift of bringing peace to the warring factions, and the courageous Rafael Abramovich, who was always rising on a point of order to denounce the importunities of the Bolsheviks.

The conference opened in an atmosphere of good will; there was a general feeling that momentous decisions would be made, and there was cause for celebration that the five factions had at last been brought together. Plekhanov had been speaking for perhaps twenty minutes when it was observed that the Bolsheviks were restless and in no mood to accept the liberal socialism he was proclaiming from the platform. Gorky, writing many years later, remembered the curiously unpleasant effect produced by Lenin's fidgeting. "One moment he would hunch himself up as though shivering with cold, and then he would sprawl out as though overcome by the heat. He poked his fingers in his armpits, rubbed his chin, shook his head, and whispered something to Tomsky. When Plekhanov declared there were no revisionists in the party, Lenin bent down, the bald spot on his head grew red, and his shoulders shook with silent laughter." From the beginning, Lenin was introducing diversionary tactics. The insolence was contrived and deliberate; and this insolence directed at Plekhanov was very like the insolence which he had shown to the unhappy Monsieur Port in the *gymnasium* at Simbirsk, and which he was to show again during the meeting of the Constituent Assembly in 1918.

After Plekhanov had spoken, Rafael Abramovich took the floor to propose the election of a presidium of five members corresponding to the five organized groups. There was unanimous agreement that a presidium should be chosen, and each group selected its own representative. The Mensheviks chose Dan, the Bundists chose Medem, the Latvians chose Azis-Rozin, the Poles chose Tyszka-Yogiches, and the Bolsheviks chose Lenin. At once the Mensheviks protested vigorously. Lenin had openly disobeyed the orders of the party in the matter of the "expropriations." He had defended the robberies and holdups which had brought vast sums of money into the coffers of the Bolsheviks, and he was in no mood to apologize. His attitude was the simple one that money had to be obtained, and if it was obtained by acts of terrorism so much the better. The Mensheviks were inclined to regard the Bolsheviks as half-educated, ill-mannered children. The party, they said, could not tolerate such highhanded actions, and they seriously discussed Lenin's competence as a delegate. Suddenly the whole building seemed to be full of people screaming at one another and waving their fists; and there would have been bloodshed if Medem had not brought them to order. Lenin took his place on the presidium.

Lenin's attitude throughout the conference was one of uncompromising attack against all those who refused to support what he called "revolutionary democracy." He had lost all hope of being able to co-operate with the Mensheviks; it remained to use them, and if necessary to destroy them. He accused them, with some justice, of being in league with the bourgeoisie, and therefore against a revolutionary victory by the proletariat. Plekhanov was demanding an alliance with the bourgeoisie; Lenin replied scornfully that one does not align oneself with one's enemy except in extreme emergencies, and the extreme emergency had not arisen. The Mensheviks complained against "the one-sided hostility of the proletariat toward liberalism," and Lenin answered that it was precisely the liberals who had become counterrevolutionaries; and instead of aiding the revolu-

tion they were in fact doing all in their power to smother it. Again and
again he insisted that revolutionary action must be based solidly on
the proletariat. As for the peasants, they could not be depended upon.
They were a vacillating force, at the mercy of their inborn sense of
property—what could be done with them? He said:

> In the peasant lives the instinct of the proprietor—if not of today,
> then of tomorrow. The proprietor's, the owner's instinct repels the peas-
> ant from the proletariat, engendering in him dreams and aspirations of
> climbing up in the world, of becoming a bourgeois, and so walling him-
> self off from the rest of society on his own plot of land, on his own dung
> heap.

Lenin raged against the Mensheviks, the peasants, the Duma, the
Cadets, the liberal bourgeoisie, the landowners and the aristocracy;
so many were his enemies that he seemed to be deliberately cutting
himself off from all aspects of Russian life. Only the proletariat received his benediction, while he poured anathemas upon the rest of
society. Trotsky was trying to build up a small group which might, he
thought, form a bridge between the Mensheviks and Bolsheviks. Lenin
turned on him roundly, accusing him of being a Menshevik in disguise
and of organizing a splinter group, which in the very nature of things
was doomed to perish. Trotsky was enraged and called Lenin a hypocrite, and even Angelica Balabanoff, who was fond of him, spoke of
Lenin's dishonesty during the proceedings. It was not only that he
played to the gallery and insisted that attention should be riveted on
himself, but he was equally unscrupulous behind the scenes, bar-
gaining with members of the Bund and with every splinter group in
the hope of gaining a few votes. Though Lenin was the most powerful force at the conference, Martov still held his own. A complete
transcript published in Russia in 1933 shows that Martov spoke 126
times, Lenin 120 times, Trotsky, Lieber, Dan, Martynov, Zhordania,
Tseretelli, Tyszka-Yogiches and Abramovich all spoke fifty or sixty
times. The transcript covers 748 pages of closely printed type.

To attempt to read those pages today is to grow dizzy over speeches
which seem to have no relevance to our time, or to any time. The jargon of these revolutionary parties has long ago been supplanted. All
the voices are uniformly angry, petulant, hoarse with frustrated emotion. They exhausted each other with their complaints. They were
five parties pretending to be one party, and though they would an-

nounce and agree upon resolutions, there was no solid agreement between them.

Gorky was amazed by the fury of the disputes. He had never met Lenin, and like so many others he was surprised by his appearance of ordinariness. There was simply nothing about the man at first sight which suggested the leader. He had a strong handshake and unusually bright eyes, but he was otherwise unimpressive until he spoke, and then quite suddenly the brutal strength of the man became apparent. Gorky had been listening to Rosa Luxemburg—in his view the best speaker at the conference, because she combined passionate intensity with a gift for irony—and suddenly he saw Lenin making his way to the podium:

"Comrades!" Lenin said in a guttural voice, and at first I thought he was speaking badly, but after a minute I and everyone else were "devoured" by his speech. For the first time I heard complicated political questions discussed simply. He made no effort to produce eloquent phrases, but every word was uttered distinctly, and the exact thought was made amazingly clear. It is very difficult to explain the unusual effect he had on us.

His arm was stretched forward with a slight raising of the palm, weighing each word, sifting out the remarks of his opponents, exchanging them for weighty arguments in favor of the right and duty of the working classes to go their own way, not marching with the liberal bourgeoisie and not following behind them—all this was unusual, and Lenin seemed to be speaking not of his own accord, but according to the will of history. The unity, completeness, directness and strength of his speech, his whole appearance on the podium—all this had the effect of classic art: for everything was there, nothing was superfluous, and if it was ornamented in any way, the ornaments remained invisible, being as natural and inevitable as the two eyes in a face or the five fingers of a hand.

He gave a shorter speech than the orators who preceded him, but he made a vastly greater impression. I was not alone in thinking in this way. Behind me people were whispering excitedly, "He's really pouring it on!" So he was, and every argument advanced of itself, with its conclusion contained within it.

The Mensheviks made no effort to hide their displeasure with the speech and their even greater displeasure with Lenin himself. The more convincingly he displayed the necessity for the party to develop revolutionary theory to the utmost extent, in order that practice should be thoroughly tested, the more exasperatedly did they interrupt his speech.

"The Congress isn't the proper place for philosophical discourses!"

"Don't teach us—we're not schoolboys!"

One tall, bearded man with the face of a shopkeeper was especially aggressive. He jumped up from the bench and shouted in a stuttering voice:

"C-c-conspirators! All you do is p-p-play at c-c-conspiracy! B-b-blan-quists!"

Gorky had an ambiguous attitude toward Lenin. He genuinely liked the man and feared the politician, admired his daring and feared the consequences. Some time after Lenin's death he wrote down what he could remember of his occasional meetings with Lenin, but he seems to have written against the grain. When he wrote similar accounts of Chekhov and Tolstoy, his characters are vividly alive. Lenin was too remote, too classical, too abstract, to be brought to life. One cannot imagine Gorky speaking of "the unity, completeness, directness and strength" of Tolstoy's speeches or Chekhov's conversations.

Occasionally however he was able to break through the classical reserve which Lenin usually showed to people he could not completely understand. Once when Lenin came to visit him at his hotel, Gorky was rather surprised to discover him feeling the bedding with a preoccupied air.

"What are you doing?" Gorky asked.

"I'm looking to see whether the sheets are damp or not," Lenin replied.

And then, seeing Gorky's perplexity, Lenin said, "You really must take care of your health."

On one occasion a small group of revolutionaries spent an evening at the music hall. Lenin enjoyed the clowns and remarked about a certain kind of eccentric pantomime: "It expresses a satirical or skeptical attitude toward the conventional, attempts to turn conventions inside out, to distort them, and to show the illogicality of all our usual accepted practices. Complicated, but very interesting!"

He had evidently been watching Dan Leno or the young Charlie Chaplin, and there may have come to him a dawning awareness that the white-faced clown and the revolutionary leader had much in common. Both, in their different ways, were attempting "to turn conventions inside out, to distort them, and to show the illogicality of all our usually accepted practices."

But there were not many evenings when Lenin attended the music hall. As usual, the work of the Congress exhausted him, and he was already a sick man before it was over. "He was pale, his eyes had gone dead, and his hands trembled," said one visitor to the Congress. When at last he returned to Finland, with no beard, his mustache clipped short, and wearing a straw hat, he was almost unrecognizable. He had lost weight, he was unable to eat, and there were signs of a nervous breakdown. He was sent off to a remote country district, where it was hoped he would recover. At first he kept falling asleep at all hours of the day. Krupskaya says he would be sitting under a pine tree, and then quite suddenly he would fall asleep for no apparent reason. Gradually his health returned. He began to eat again and to go bicycling with Krupskaya. "We used old galoshes for patches," she said, "and we spent more time repairing than bicycling." The country air did him good, and deer steaks and omelettes filled out his cheeks again.

The pattern, of course, had been established long before: every Congress was a crisis, and after nearly every Congress there was a period of nervous exhaustion and debility, when he could no longer grapple with the ordinary problems of living. People spoke of his strong constitution, but it was never strong.

When he recovered he lived for a while with two maiden sisters in a village near Helsingfors. It was an ideal hideout for a revolutionary who was being hunted by the police: a small house, lace curtains, the piano playing all day in the next room, and the spinsters always giggling. In this spotless bourgeois house he continued to write his articles, pacing up and down on tiptoe so as not to disturb his hosts. Every day the articles were collected by messenger and taken to Vyborg or St. Petersburg, to be printed on the party's secret press.

The autocracy was in the saddle and the strength had gone out of the revolutionaries. Lenin had been hunted ever since he reached Russia toward the end of 1905; now at last the police were on his track. He decided to leave Finland and make his way to Switzerland. But how? There was no easy way. The police were watching all the steamers and had already achieved a considerable reputation for arresting revolutionaries as they walked up the gangplank. Lenin took the calculated risk of walking across three miles of thin ice at night in order to reach an island where a steamer would put in. Two peasants offered to lead him over the ice. They were drunk; the ice gave way under them, and they jumped to safety only just in time. He related afterward that when the ice cracked, he felt no fear—only an overwhelming sense of the stupidity of dying in this way. It was the dead of winter when he reached Geneva, the city empty, the lake frozen over, the clouds hanging low. "I feel," he said, "that I have come here to be buried."

For nine years he led the life of an exile, eating the bread of strangers, at war with his party, happy only when he was confronting his enemies, his consuming interest being the publication of an illegal newspaper and its distribution in Russia. Congress followed congress; bitter dispute followed bitter dispute; wars of extermination were being continually declared. Yet the overwhelming impression created by Lenin during the early months of exile was one of inexpressible boredom. He would spend his days in the library, and these hours were tolerable; but the nights were unbearable. He had lost his band of faithful followers, and he was almost alone. "In the evenings," says Krupskaya, "we simply did not know what to do with ourselves. We did not want to sit in the cold, cheerless room we had rented, and we longed to be among people. Every evening we went to the cinema or the theater, seldom staying to the end, usually leaving in the middle to wander around the streets." A man can go mad wandering night after night through the empty streets of Geneva.

He still wrote tirelessly, and his articles appeared in *Proletary* with the same regularity with which they had appeared in *Iskra, Novaya Zhizn, Volna, Echo,* and all the other newspapers he had edited. There were no longer any financial difficulties, for the textile millionaire Savva Morozov and his nephew Nikolay Schmidt, both of whom committed suicide or were murdered in 1905, left substantial sums of money which found their way to the party, and in addition comrades in the Caucasus were proving adept at robbing banks "so that the Tsar can pay for the revolution," and Bonch-Bruyevich obtained large sums of money in the United States. The confused and intricate stories of how the Morozov and Schmidt legacies came into Lenin's hands have been told many times, but with the omission of all the relevant documents. The wills have never been published, and the exact details of the transmission are unknown to this day. The figures of the redoubtable Kamo, who robbed the bank in Tiflis, and the no less redoubtable Taratuta, who was married to Nikolay Schmidt's younger sister, emerge briefly from obscurity and then vanish. Though the London conference placed a ban on expropriations, Lenin was not likely to obey the ban. Publicly he declared that they were permissible only under certain circumstances, which he described in an article called "Guerrilla Warfare," published in 1906—no expropriations of private property; expropriations of government property could take place only when recommended by the party; and terrorist acts were permitted only when "the conditions of the working class were taken into account." In fact, he approved of expropriations and regarded them with considerable benevolence.

It was this ruthlessness which set him apart from the Mensheviks, but it was not only the Mensheviks who were wary of him. Gorky, too, found him intolerant and inflexible. Invited to Capri, where Gorky had established a kind of university for exiles, Lenin argued so bitterly against all the other Russians on the island that his presence became unwelcome; he stayed only two days, and Krupskaya says he ever afterward refused to discuss what had happened there. Yet it is not difficult to discover what happened there. We have the letters exchanged between Lenin and Gorky, and Gorky himself has written a brief account of the visit:

> Vladimir Ilyich Lenin stood before me even more firm and more inflexible than he had been at the London Congress. In those days he had been very agitated, and there were moments when it was obvious that the party split had given him a difficult time. Now he was in a quiet, rather cold and mocking mood, sternly rejecting all philosophical conversations and altogether on the alert.
>
> And at the same time there was in Capri another Lenin—a wonderful companion and lighthearted person with a lively and inexhaustible interest in the world around him, and very gentle in his relations with people.

Gorky could make nothing of those two irreconcilable elements; and when he looked back at the hours he and Lenin had spent together in Capri, he had, he said, "a very strange feeling that he must have come twice to Capri and in two sharply differing moods."

There was the Lenin who cursed the exiles for not helping him with his newspaper and cursed them still more for believing in religion and liberalism; and there was the Lenin who enjoyed fishing and liked the company of the peasants and laughed good-naturedly. There was the Lenin who wrote majestically to Gorky earlier in the year: "I refuse to come and talk with people who advocate combining scientific socialism with religion—the time for exercise books is over." And there was the Lenin who finally accepted the invitation and went fishing with a line hooked round his finger on the advice of a fisherman who said, *"Drin, drin. Capisce?"* *"Drin, drin"* meant the vibration on the line when the fish was biting. After he had left the island the fishermen still talked about the stranger with the infectious laughter, and they would say, "How is Drin-Drin getting on? Has the Tsar caught him yet?"

The years of tsarist reaction had set in, and the revolution was far away. Geneva was stifling. In the late autumn of 1908 he moved to Paris.

PARIS

THERE WERE TIMES when Lenin would break out in a passionate rage against Paris, but it was a city he always came back to. He loved Paris with a steadfast passion, returning again and again. He hated the bureaucrats and the police, and he never had words enough to proclaim his contempt for the bourgeoisie, but he always spoke of the Paris workmen with respect. He liked their devil-may-care faces, their happy imperturbability. They were after all the stuff out of which revolutions are made, and for him Paris was essentially the city of revolutions, the seat of the revolutionary tradition. In less than a century three great revolutions had broken out in Paris; the last of them, the Commune, was his special study, the one from which there was most to learn if revolution should break out in Russia. Pious historians have calculated that he made fifteen separate visits to Paris. This is not quite fair, for they obtained the figure fifteen by counting the number of times he crossed the frontiers of France. In fact he never stayed there for any length of time except between 1909 and 1912. There were many brief visits, but only once did he let down his roots and become a Parisian.

He arrived in Paris about December 13, 1908—the exact date is unknown—with his wife, his mother-in-law, and Zinoviev. With him came packing cases containing most of the furniture and pots and pans from the apartment in Geneva, and a small stripped-down printing press. He spent the first night or two at the Hôtel des Gobelins on the Boulevard St.-Marcel, where his sister Maria was staying while pursuing her studies, and very soon the whole family was installed in

223

an apartment at 24 Rue Beaunier near the Parc Montsouris. It was a predominantly bourgeois neighborhood, very quiet and secluded, and the apartment itself was exactly the kind that might be occupied by a shopkeeper. There were mirrors over the mantelpieces, and Krupskaya was suitably impressed by them. There was a hallway, four living rooms, a kitchen, various cupboards and closets, and a pantry; for all this, including the tax and a necessary fee to the concierge, they paid nearly a thousand francs a month, worth at that time about two hundred dollars. As Lenin admitted in a letter to his sister Anna they were living in considerable luxury. "It is expensive for Paris," he wrote, "but the place is spacious, and with any luck we should be comfortable."

As usual Lenin found himself in a nest of womenfolk, who proceeded to organize the apartment to their liking. He paid no attention to the household arrangements, for all he needed was a chair, a table, and a place to put his books. Krupskaya, feeling lost in a strange city and with only the most halting knowledge of French, complains in her memoirs about his unhelpfulness. He did not offer to go to the gas company to see that the gas was turned on, but sent her instead. The gas company was a long way away, they had difficulty understanding her, and twice they sent her away empty-handed. Only after the third visit was the gas turned on. Krupskaya understandably exploded with torrents of invective against French red tape, forgetting that it would have been just as difficult to turn on gas in Russia. To make matters worse, there was the French custom of having the landlord vouch for tenants before they were permitted to take out books from lending libraries, and when the landlord inspected their rooms furnished with the sticks they had brought from Geneva, he was of two minds about whether to vouch for them. They were like gypsies camping out in a suburban mansion. The landlord continued to eye them distrustfully until Lenin arranged through an intermediary to apprise him of the account at the Crédit Lyonnais standing in his name. The account included the greater part of the Schmidt legacy, and amounted to more than a quarter of a million francs. The landlord was shown the account and thereafter greeted all the members of the family with respect. The landlord did not know that most of the money was reserved for setting up the printing press, printing the magazine, and smuggling it into Russia.

Lenin had hardly set foot in Paris when he was confronted with a rebellion in the ranks of the Bolsheviks attending the Fifth Conference of the Social Democratic Party. Communication with Russia had broken down. There were no evident signs of revolutionary fervor in Russia, and only a handful of representatives attended the Conference; of these the majority were in opposition to Lenin, who had to employ all his resources to win them over or to reduce them to ineffectiveness. Former revolutionaries were no longer prepared to follow him along the "hard" road of insurrection and armed uprising. There was talk of liquidating the extreme left wing of the party and of abandoning the earlier dogmas, substituting a more tolerant approach to the problems of the day. Lenin was all for holding the "hard" line; he was also determined to maintain control of the Schmidt legacy and to continue to use *Proletary* as his own mouthpiece. He maintained control of the legacy, but lost *Proletary* and was compelled to accept a modified program, with the slogans of insurrection and armed uprising so muted that they lost all significance; it was the price he had to pay to remain on a new editorial board which included Lenin, Martov, Zinoviev and Kamenev. The new magazine was to be called the *Social Democrat*. Considering the differences of opinion among the editors, it was surprisingly successful, for nine issues were published during the year.

During the Fifth Conference Lenin was fighting for his political life. Only sixteen party members attended. There was no platform, no *claque* of obedient followers. They sat about in groups, debated, passed resolutions and voted on the issues. At the end of the conference Lenin, as usual, was in a state of collapse. "He looked awful," Krupskaya remembered twenty years later, "and his tongue seemed to have turned gray." He could scarcely talk, and he suffered from tremors. It was decided to send him away for a week's holiday in Nice. He went off alone, taking with him the proofs of his book *Materialism and Empirio-Criticism*, which his sister Anna had sent to him from St. Petersburg. In the evenings he read the proofs, during the day he soaked up the sun, and when he returned to Paris he was in good shape, no longer smarting from the blows he had received during the conference. He was particularly pleased by the thought of working with Martov. That little man with the goatee and the soft, melting eyes was intellectually his inferior, but there was some comfort in having on the editorial board someone he could respect.

After the upheaval, life resumed its regular course—study, visits to the printing press installed around the corner, editorial meetings, walks in the Parc Montsouris and occasional political rallies attended by Russian political exiles who were then flocking to Paris. For some period of every day he worked in a library, usually the Bibliothèque Nationale, which is in the center of the city, and therefore he had to cross half of Paris to reach it. Then, as now, the library was uncomfortable and drafty, and the catalogues seemed to have been designed deliberately to mislead and circumvent the reader. The closing hours changed according to the season of the year. From February 15 to March 31 the library closed at five in the afternoon, from April 1 to September 15 it closed at six, for the rest of the year it closed at four. These figures may not appear to be significant, but for Lenin they possessed an overwhelming importance, and he arranged his days accordingly, waking up earlier in winter than in summer because he was afraid he would never complete his work in the short time available. The librarians drove him almost insane. He raged against the catalogues, and he hated having to wait for hours before the books were delivered to him. He left his bicycle in the hallway of a neighboring apartment house—he paid a small fee to the concierge to keep an eye on it—and when it was stolen he raged as ineffectually as he raged against the Bibliothèque Nationale, for there was no redress.

Sometimes he would wonder why he came to Paris at all, so badly did he fare at the hands of the librarians. His work was with books and ideas; he needed his daily portion of books, as other people need sunlight and air. Sometimes, too, he would find himself thinking longingly of the British Museum library or the libraries of Switzerland, where the catalogues were models of perfection and he was allowed to seek out books on the shelves and when he went away for a vacation in the mountains, the books he requested would be sent to him by mail. He resolved that if a Russian revolution ever took place and if he was in any position of authority, he would introduce immediately a series of laws on the proper regulation of a library system.

It was a lonely life. Then as always he held himself a little apart from the political exiles: he was happiest when poring over his books or writing vitriolic articles. He enjoyed talking to his printers—two Russians who had followed him from Switzerland—more than he enjoyed the company of intellectuals.

The trouble about the political exiles was that they went to seed as soon as they arrived in Paris. According to Lenin, only the strongest survived transplantation. They were dogged by alcoholism, family quarrels, feuds and poverty. They spent their time in the cafés, talking endlessly for the pure pleasure of talking, with no purpose in sight, never making an attempt to reach decisions, never doing an honest day's work unless they were compelled to. Their beards and hair were unkempt, they dressed in a slovenly manner, they never took the trouble to learn more than a smattering of French. When they came to call on him—and they were always coming to call on him—they frightened the concierge out of her wits. He enjoyed seeing them when they came fresh from Russia, for then he would question them at length about what was happening in Russia until he had the feel of it and could imagine himself there; then he would lose interest in them.

It was at this time, shortly after Lenin was installed in the apartment on the Rue Beaunier, that the young student Ilya Ehrenburg went to call on him. They had met briefly in one of the cafés on the Avenue d'Orléans where a political meeting was being held in an upstairs room. Lenin spoke; Ehrenburg had the temerity to challenge him, only to have the errors of his argument convincingly pointed out to him. After the meeting, Lenin came up to him and said, "Are you from Moscow?" Ehrenburg said he had been in Moscow earlier in the year, had been arrested and released, and had settled for a while in Poltava. He evidently knew a good deal about the student movement in Russia and so he was invited to the Rue Beaunier. He remembered that Lenin wore a dark suit with a stiff white collar and looked very respectable.

When he went to call on Lenin, there was the inevitable interrogation. What was the mood among the students, what writers did they read, what plays were being performed? Ehrenburg answered as well as he could, feeling all the time like an awkward schoolboy summoned into the presence of the headmaster. He could remember some names and addresses of people who might welcome Lenin's paper, and Krupskaya took them down. Lenin's room was very neat, the desk tidy and the books arranged carefully on the shelves. Several times he turned to Krupskaya and said, "He has come straight from there, and knows what the young people are thinking." At last, having told everything he knew, Ehrenburg took his leave. He was never invited again.

For Lenin, the most important event during the spring was the publication of his book *Materialism and Empirio-Criticism,* on which he had labored for some eight months in Switzerland. A Moscow publisher had been found for it, his sister Anna had carefully read the proofs and toned down some of the more extravagant statements, and finally it appeared in a canary-yellow binding under the pseudonym of Vladimir Ilyin. It professed to be a philosophical study, and Lenin always regarded the work as his chief claim to be taken seriously as a philosopher. Unfortunately, the work only proved how little of the philosopher there was in him. It is a strident, ill-tempered and voluble attack on the opinions of his fellow Marxists; he points out the error of their ways, appealing to Engels and less frequently to Marx as his authorities, piling authority upon authority in the manner of a Christian exegete attempting to prove some point by an appeal to Holy Scripture while conveniently omitting all the texts which oppose his argument.

Far from being a serious philosophical work *Materialism and Empirio-Criticism* is an extended pamphlet addressed to members of the Social Democratic Party, demanding that they adhere to the strict Leninist interpretation of materialism. Any philosopher who deviates by an inch from his interpretation is accused of being a reactionary bourgeois and is told that his works have been consigned to the trash can. Berkeley, Hume, Kant, and twenty other philosophers are summarily dismissed, together with some twenty other philosophers who have committed the crime of refusing to believe that everything is material, knowable, objectively present, and obedient to precise and inflexible laws. Of all the philosophers who are castigated, the one who receives the most abuse is Alexander Bogdanov, who had committed the unpardonable crime of founding a school for socialism with the help of Maxim Gorky on the island of Capri and had written a book called *Empiriomonism* in which he attempted, not too successfully, to marry socialism and idealism. Lenin was determined to destroy Bogdanov—by argument, by ridicule, or simply by sheer vituperation. Here is a characteristic attack:

> "Let us set ourselves the following question," writes Bogdanov in Book I of *Empiriomonism*. "What is 'a living being'—for example, 'man'?" And he answers: " 'Man' is, before everything else, a definite complex of 'spontaneous experiences.' ". Note that he says, "*before everything else*." "*Then*," in a further development of experience, "man is shown to be both for himself and for others a physical body amid other physical bodies."
>
> So here we have an entire "complex" of nonsense, fit only for deducing the immortality of the soul, or the idea of God, and so forth. Man is, before everything else, a complex of spontaneous experiences, becoming *in the course of development* a physical body! This means there are "spontaneous experiences" *without* a physical body, *prior* to a physical body. What a pity that this superb philosophy has not yet found ac-

ceptance in our theological seminaries, where its merits would have
been fully appreciated.

In much the same way a schoolboy would point out the defects in
Descartes's *Cogito ergo sum.*

Lenin is unrelenting in his pursuit. All Bogdanov's statements are
torn out of their context and reduced to absurdity. "Idiocy," "madness," "absolute ignoramus" are some of the less unpleasant terms he
uses. Lenin's rage is such that he compels us to believe he is still unsure of himself and uncertain of his aims. The tone is arrogant, but
it is not the arrogance of a man who has reached an unassailable position and looks down from the mountaintop at the climbers far below.
Instead, he resembles a man roughly pushing his way up the steep
slopes, and whenever he finds another climber within reach he hurls
him to the bottom.

Lenin's materialism has essentially very little to do with philosophy. It is an attitude of mind derived from the early nihilists. Like
Bazarov in Turgenev's *Fathers and Sons* he will declare that "a pair of
shoes is worth all the plays of Shakespeare," forgetting that shoes and
Shakespeare do not belong to the same orders of things and cannot be
weighed in any balance known to us. The clearest statement of Lenin's
position is given in the chapter on the philosophical idealists in which
he quotes an article written by Paul Lafargue, Karl Marx's son-in-law,
which appeared in the magazine *Le Socialiste* nine years earlier:

> The worker who eats sausage and receives 5 francs a day knows very
> well that his employer is robbing him while living himself on good
> pork; he knows the employer is a thief and the sausage is pleasant to
> the taste and nourishing to the body. Nothing of the kind, says the
> bourgeois sophist, and it is all one whether he is called Pyrrho, Hume
> or Kant. The worker's opinion on this matter is entirely his own—i.e., it
> is a subjective opinion; he might with equal reason maintain that the
> employer is his benefactor and that the sausage consists of chopped
> leather, for he cannot know *things in themselves. . . .*
>
> The whole trouble lies in the fact that the question is not properly
> put. In order to know an object a man must first verify whether his
> senses deceive him or not. The chemists have gone further, they have
> penetrated into bodies, analyzed them, separated them into their ele-
> ments, and then performed the process in reverse—i.e., the synthesis—
> by which the body is recomposed out of its elements. And from the
> moment when man is able to compose things for his own use out of
> these elements, he may, as Engels says, assert that he knows the *things*

in themselves. The Christian God, if He existed and if He created the world, could do no more.

In this way Lafargue disposes of Kant, and by implication the entire history of Western philosophy from Plato onward; the problems are reduced to insignificance by deliberately misunderstanding them. And while Lafargue misunderstands in a direct and straightforward manner, Lenin's misunderstanding reflects a tortured sense of inadequacy, as he peppers the page with exclamation marks and contemptuous comments from the sidelines, interrupting for example a discussion on Mach's philosophy to shout, "We've heard that story before, honorable professor!" or to pronounce of some obscure Russian philosopher that his work lies "on the border line between philosophy and the police department."

Yet Lenin seems to have been obscurely aware of the inadequacies and contradictions inherent in his materialist attitude, and almost the last words in the book are a kind of perverted salute to idealism, "which is merely a subtle, refined form of deism, standing fully armed, commanding vast organizations and steadily continuing to exercise its influence on the masses, turning the slightest vacillation in philosophical thought to its own advantage."

Materialism and Empirio-Criticism was published in an edition of two thousand copies in May 1909. Anna had not done her work well as proofreader, and Lenin commented unhappily that "there are just as many misprints at the end of the book as at the beginning." Few people bought the book, and fewer read it, but Lenin professed to be pleased that it had come out at last. When he came to power it was reprinted in Moscow with an introduction in which once more he bitterly assailed Alexander Bogdanov. This time Bogdanov was not accused of misinterpreting philosophy so much as being one of the leaders of the Proletcult movement, celebrating a purely proletarian culture. Under Meyerhold the Proletcult theater became one of the major glories of the revolution, but Lenin was suspicious of the movement and did everything possible to thwart it. Bogdanov retired to his medical laboratory, where one day in 1928 he committed suicide by giving himself a transfusion of infected blood.

About the same time that the book first appeared the editorial board of *Social Democrat* was enlarged to prevent it from becoming wholly the mouthpiece of Lenin. Among the new members co-opted to the board was Bogdanov, who had been attacked as though he were the incarnate enemy of Marxism. Other new members included Tomsky, Rykov and Taratuta. There was also a young representative from the Moscow committee who used the pseudonym of Donat. His real name was Shulyatikov, and he suffered from hereditary alcoholism. Lenin had known him for a long time and genuinely liked him, though he caused more trouble than all the rest put together. He would vanish for weeks on end, and then he would arrive unexpectedly in a taxi outside Lenin's apartment in a state bordering on insanity, demanding to be let in. Lenin never sent him away. Screaming, he would be carried into the apartment, while Lenin and Krupskaya soothed him, held his hand, talked to him calmly in an effort to bring sense into his disordered mind. And sometimes, too, he would start up with a terrible expression on his face, saying he had just seen his sister, who had been hanged for her terrorist activities. Between Lenin and Shulyatikov there was this common bond: they both dreamed of hangings.

In those months Lenin was almost at the end of his resources. He had survived the battle in January only to face a succession of battles in the summer which left him without effective control of the editorial board. Once more he was close to nervous collapse. To make matters worse, his sister Maria had an attack of appendicitis; the operation was only just in time, and she made a slow recovery. It was decided that the whole family should go on an extended vacation in the south of France. Nice being too expensive, they settled for the small town of Bonbon in the Saône-et-Loire, halfway between Paris and the Mediterranean. The *pension* was cheap, costing no more than ten francs for Lenin, his wife, his sister, and his mother-in-law. The air was clean, the food plentiful. Lenin fussed over his sister, making her drink milk to recover her strength, and every day there was a twenty-mile bicycle ride with Krupskaya to the Clamart woods and back again. Krupskaya made a special study of the other guests in the *pension*, coming to the conclusion that they were all possessed of mediocre characters, though eminently practical in taking care of their comforts. She says rather pompously, "Of course such a large dose of mediocrity was rather boring, and it was a good thing we were able to keep aloof from them and live according to our own lights." It would be interesting to know what the other guests thought of Krupskaya, who spoke French so badly that she could not make herself understood.

They spent four or five weeks at Bonbon and returned to Paris refreshed. In the autumn they left the apartment on Rue Beaunier and took one nearby on Rue Marie-Rose. It was cheaper and less spacious, but there was an agreeable concierge, and the outward aspect of the house was imposing. Today, doctors and lawyers live in the house, which resembles thousands of other houses occupied by respectable bourgeois. Maria had returned to Russia; Lenin, Krupskaya and her mother lived in two small rooms with a kitchenette and a tiny hall. Lenin's room was the best, with the sun pouring through the two windows, which overlooked a garden. As usual, the furniture was sparse. The desk was a big table of unpolished wood covered with black oilcloth. There was a chair, a rather low, wide couch in a deep alcove, and two narrow iron beds. Gorky, who came to visit them, remarked that it looked more like a student's apartment than a family dwelling. There was something curiously bleak in the absence of any decoration except the occasional wild flowers which Lenin brought back from his bicycle trips in the countryside. Madame Rue, the concierge, was appalled by the bleakness of their lives. "Imagine," she said, "they did not have any human weaknesses. Monsieur Ulyanov neither drank nor smoked—he went out to the library or a meeting, and that was all, and he always came home promptly."

But if life on the surface seemed to be calm and equable, there were the inevitable subterranean earthquakes. The fight for control of the *Social Democrat* went on unrelentingly. Contact with Russia was improving; messengers were going back and forth across the frontier. More and more exiles were arriving, with the result that more and more visitors climbed up to the cramped apartment on the second floor of Rue Marie-Rose. If they arrived in the evening they might find Krupskaya busily coding and decoding letters, while Lenin played cards with her mother. It was the best way to prevent her complaining about the boredom of Paris life, and he would usually let her win the game. Then she would look at him and shake her head sadly, saying, "How could an intelligent man like you play so badly against a weak old woman like me?"

Only a few visitors were encouraged to take meals with them. Martov and Zinoviev were the most frequent visitors. It was remembered that Martov hated washing dishes, while Lenin thoroughly enjoyed washing them. Martov looked forward to the time when dishes would be washed by some miraculous electrical machine, and Lenin would comment, "Yes, but for the time being we must resign ourselves to the deplorable lack of progress in science and make use of the only means available to us—our hands."

Bicycling was a way of traveling about Paris; his bicycle became a hobby and a passion. Rue Marie-Rose was, and is, a small secluded street with little traffic, and he would sometimes take his bicycle out of the cellar and strip it on the sidewalk, oiling it lovingly, his sleeves rolled up, his expression that of a man wholly absorbed in the workings of a machine. Riding in the autumn near Juvisy-sur-Orge, a small hamlet on the way to Fontainebleau, he had a close escape from death when an automobile crashed into his bicycle. He jumped away just in time. The bicycle was reduced to twisted metal. The driver of the automobile was a *vicomte*, which made the destruction of the bicycle even less palatable. Lenin took him to court, won the case, and received a fine new bicycle as part of the damages. For many months he could be heard complaining about *vicomtes* recklessly driving about in high-powered cars.

In the spring of 1910 Lenin's calm bourgeois existence, now regulated like clockwork, came to an end. To the surprise of the Russian community in Paris, which had hitherto regarded him as a model of puritanism, he was seen in the company of a woman who was not his wife. Her name was Elisabeth Armand; she was the mother of five children by a rich Moscow manufacturer, and though not beautiful, she was a woman of formidable charm. Though she spoke Russian with ease and had lived many years in Russia, she was wholly French in manner and appearance, with enormous eyes, a wide sensitive mouth, and finely modeled features. Most of her high wide forehead was hidden by an unruly mass of chestnut-colored hair. She was not tall, but she gave an impression of height. She could be vivacious and playful, but she could also be unrelentingly serious when the occasion demanded. Her *nom de guerre* was Inessa, and so she was known to the members of the party who with bated breath watched her sitting with Lenin in the cafés on the Avenue d'Orléans. It was as though the cold and chaste hero of countless bitter dialectical battles had proved to be human after all.

Her story was a strange one, for there was nothing in her background to suggest that she would ever become the mistress of Lenin. She was born in Paris in 1879 and christened Élisabeth d'Herbenville. Her father was a music-hall comedian known as Stéphen when on the stage, and as Pécheux d'Herbenville in private life. Her mother was

Natalie Wild, a Scotswoman, who gave music lessons and sometimes accompanied her husband on the stage. There were three children of the marriage, and when Pécheux d'Herbenville died, Elisabeth accomplished the first of her dreams. She had always wanted to travel, and suddenly she was transported out of the music-hall atmosphere of Paris to a quiet mansion on the outskirts of Moscow. A French aunt and her Scottish grandmother had accepted positions as teachers in the household of Eugene Armand, a wealthy textile manufacturer of French extraction. The Armands lived at Pushkino. The great house was surrounded by pine woods, overlooking a small lake. They were liberal in their views, and soon Elisabeth, her aunt and her grandmother were accepted as members of the family.

Long before Elisabeth became an Armand by marriage, she had all the graces of a daughter of a rich and cultivated family. She played the piano admirably; she spoke Russian, German, French and English without an accent; she read all the advanced books. When Alexander Armand, the industrialist's second son, proposed marriage, she accepted him. She was eighteen; he was two or three years older. They settled down on a nearby estate, and in the following five years she gave her husband five children—three boys and two girls. She was happy in her husband and her children, and there seemed to be no reason why she should not have continued to live the life of a wealthy young matron. She had everything she had ever wanted—except danger, excitement, the sense of serving some cause greater than herself.

Bored with wealth and society, she suddenly abandoned her family in 1904 and settled in Stockholm to study at the feet of Ellen Key, the friend of the poet Rainer Maria Rilke and the most advanced feminist of her age. But feminism soon lost its appeal for her; she was more at ease among the young revolutionaries in the Russian colony in Stockholm, who gave her Lenin's *What Is To Be Done?* to read. This book, with its appeal for direct action, converted her to Bolshevism, and she returned to Russia with every intention of taking part in the 1905 revolution, only to be arrested a few days later. She spent nine months in prison. In the following year she continued to work as a courier for the Bolsheviks, and on April 9, 1907, she was again arrested, this time on the more serious charge of suborning the armed forces. Her husband furnished bail, but once out of prison she continued to work for the Bolsheviks and was again arrested. This time she was sentenced to exile in Arkhangelsk Province in the far north—a serious punishment, for the rigors of the northern winter took a great toll among the political prisoners. The exile was for a term of two years, but she succeeded in escaping before the term was over. With two of her children —a boy, Andrey, and a girl, Ina—she fled to Paris.

Lenin welcomed her with open arms. He had known of her exploits and regarded her as a tried and devoted revolutionary. He arranged for her to live in the apartment next door, at 2 Rue Marie-Rose. She was thirty, but she looked twenty. She was quick, intelligent, and capable of holding her own in arguments with him. She blazed with vitality, and her mere presence was calculated to inspire the exiles in Paris. Lenin spent a great deal of his life in close association with women: the slow and painstaking Krupskaya, his drab sister Maria, his querulous and demanding mother-in-law. Only his sister Olga had possessed beauty and intelligence. Inessa was another Olga, and even more radiant.

Surprisingly, Krupskaya made no objections to Lenin's attachment to Inessa. In the summer she left Paris with her mother for a vacation at Pornic, a village near St. Nazaire on the Atlantic coast, leaving Lenin and Inessa free to wander about Paris together. Inessa had no theoretical objections to free love. Just as Lenin had in his youth deliberately modeled himself on Chernyshevsky's Rakhmetev, the "man of rigor," who appears so briefly and with such dazzling effect in the novel *What Is To Be Done?*, so Inessa had modeled herself on the novel's heroine Vera Pavlovna, who abandons the rich Lopukhov for the poor law clerk Kirsanov and regards herself as an instrument designed to transform the structure of society. They had both been deeply moved by the novel at a critical period of adolescence, their characters had been subtly transformed by the fictional characters, and they were now acting out the parts which Chernyshevsky had designed for them. Soon Lenin was addressing her by the familiar *ty* (thou), which is used among educated Russians only between intimates; and when he wrote letters to her he would address her in the same way.

Krupskaya not only did not disapprove of the new attachment, but she seems to have welcomed it. She was genuinely fond of Inessa, enjoyed being with her, and was delighted with the children. Six or seven years after Inessa's death, she described how "the house grew brighter when Inessa entered it." In time Krupskaya came to realize in what direction Lenin's affections lay, and a few years later, when they were settled in Galicia, she quietly prepared to leave her husband, leaving him free to marry Inessa..Lenin would have none of it. He had come to depend on Krupskaya too much to tolerate the idea of losing her; and he depended on Inessa too much to tolerate the idea of winning her. In this quandary, like many other men, he permitted himself to drift with the tide of his affections. Krupskaya remained his wedded wife, Inessa became his occasional mistress, while both in their different ways served his revolutionary purposes.

All the years of Lenin's mature life were given over to compulsive anxieties, and this year was no different from the rest. For perhaps a year and a half he had control of the Schmidt legacy; then quite suddenly he lost it. At a meeting of the Central Committee of the Social Democratic Party it was decided to remove it outside of temptation altogether by entrusting it to the safekeeping of three German Social Democrats, Karl Kautsky, Clara Zetkin and Franz Mehring. The money was accordingly transferred from the account in the Crédit Lyonnais to a German bank. Every month the Russian group received comparatively small sums until the outbreak of the Great War, when by an order of the German Treasury all moneys belonging to enemy nationals reverted to the German government. The Schmidt legacy went to pay for the German war effort.

There were now no longer any funds available to support the crowds of political exiles who flocked to Paris. Lenin received a small regular salary. In addition he made some money by writing articles, and from time to time there came gifts from his mother. He controlled a small working fund to pay for the cost of transporting the illegal newspapers and magazines to Russia. For the political exiles a pathetically small benefit fund had been established; it could be used only in cases of extreme poverty or sickness. Poverty and sickness indeed were the commonplaces of émigré life. The émigrés died in delirium, in madness, on obscure hospital beds and in the waters of the Seine. Krupskaya tells of a man who had fought in the Moscow uprising. He fled Russia and came to live in the working-class district of a Paris suburb. He lived quietly and no one knew very much about him. One day he arrived at the apartment on Rue Marie-Rose. He was already mad, babbling incoherently about chariots piled high with corn sheaves and a beautiful girl standing on one of them. Krupskaya's mother brought him something to eat, for it was obvious that these delusions were brought about by starvation. "Ilyich was white with misery as he sat beside the man. I ran off to find a psychiatrist, who was a friend of ours, and the psychiatrist came and talked with the patient and gave it as his opinion that this was a serious case of in-

sanity brought about by starvation, which had not yet reached a ter-
minal stage; it would develop into persecution mania, and then the
patient would be likely to commit suicide." A reliable friend was sent
to accompany the man to his home, but he never reached his home.
On the way the patient gave him the slip. Later his body was found
in the Seine with stones tied to his neck and feet.

Such tragedies were happening all the time. Then, as now, the lot
of Russian exiles was to be ground between the millstones of poverty
and despair. They were rootless away from Russia, and only the most
ruthless survived. The Russian revolution was the work of exiles who
continued their habits of desperation once they were in power.

WANDERINGS

T HE FOUR YEARS before the outbreak of the
Great War were troubling times for the Social Democrats, who quarreled interminably among themselves and continually shifted their policies. New groups were formed, old groups split in several ways, and some perished by the wayside. Lenin would see a new group forming on the horizon and go out to attack it before it had acquired a consistent program; and sometimes he saw mirages and attacked them with the same total dedication with which he attacked more substantial enemies. His guiding principle was a very simple one: Divide and rule!

He was not always, or even very often, successful in his aims. Though he was recognized as a potential leader, one of the men who would inevitably come to high position if ever a successful revolution broke out in Russia, he was neither popular nor sufficiently imposing to stamp the movement with his personality. He was less the leader than a man who continually spent his time shoring up the ruins. In countless articles he laid down the path to be followed, and because these articles were written by him they have been printed in editions of millions of copies; but the equally brutal articles written against him have been forgotten. Though he called himself a Bolshevik, one who belonged to the majority, he was nearly always in the minority.

They were years of relentless struggle made more difficult by the continuing success of the tsarist police in infiltrating their ranks. The secret police possessed men of quite extraordinary ability. They had their own highly skilled agents in every revolutionary party and in

238

every faction of every party. The revolutionaries knew the dangers of using the mails, and as often as possible they sent their messages by courier. Their poverty compelled them to send thousands of messages through the mails, where they were read and copied by secret agents attached to the post offices. Krupskaya spent years of her life coding and decoding messages, little knowing that most of her codes were known to the secret police.

The gravest dangers came from the *agents provocateurs*, who were rarely unmasked. Even when Lenin's faction within the movement was at its lowest ebb there were usually police spies in trusted positions. Lenin was no judge of character; he valued men for the work they did for the party; and if they worked well he was content with them. He regarded the quality of their work as the measure of their loyalty, and he rarely sought to probe their motives. Yet couriers were continually being arrested, party agents in Russia mysteriously vanished, and the entire issues of secret newspapers sometimes fell into the hands of the police while they were being smuggled across the frontier. Lenin knew—he must have known—that the party was infiltrated by the secret police, but he maintained an attitude of curious indifference; and if someone was pointed out to him as a potential secret agent, he was likely to reply, "It is quite impossible. Look at all the good work he has done for us!"

Weary of factional quarrels, Lenin decided in the spring of 1911 to set up a school for the training of underground workers. Bogdanov had built up a school on the island of Capri the previous year with the help of Gorky and Lunacharsky and several others. Lenin deplored their methods and knew himself to be a better schoolmaster. It was decided to open the school at Longjumeau on the outskirts of Paris in two small rooms rented from a leatherworker. Lenin and Krupskaya stayed with the leatherworker, Inessa rented a house for herself and her children, and most of the students were boarded out among various families in the village. Some of the students were revolutionaries who had fought through the Moscow uprising, while others were inexperienced. The people of Longjumeau were told that the school was giving refresher courses to Russian schoolteachers. It was not perhaps a very convincing explanation, but the villagers took the invasion of Russians with good grace.

Lenin rejoiced in his new role. Never again until he came to power was he able to exercise his undoubted talents as a headmaster. He prepared his lectures punctiliously, and he saw that all the other lectures were prepared with the same care and forethought. He gave forty-five separate lectures on political economy, the agrarian question and the practice of socialism. Zinoviev and Kamenev lectured on the history of the party. Lunacharsky lectured on literature, and Charles Rappoport on the French socialist movement, while Inessa held seminars on political science and superintended the communal kitchen which was her own dining room.

Krupskaya was haunted by the poor leatherworker, who set out for his factory early in the morning and came home worn out with fatigue in the evening. There was no garden, and he would simply sit in a chair outside his house with his face buried in his hands while the darkness gathered. No friends came to visit him, and no children came to call on the leatherworker's children who spent their days in the damp, gloomy kitchen, while their mother went off to earn a pittance as a charwoman in a neighboring *château*. These people found their joy in the church on Sundays. In this thirteenth-century church nuns sang, and the splendor of their singing held them spellbound. Krupskaya wondered at their innocence. Didn't they know that the church was merely an instrument of oppression? Surely an ill-paid workman in a tanning factory has a right to protest? To all her arguments the leatherworker answered simply: "God created the rich and the poor, and all is right with the world."

For the moment all was right in Lenin's world. He loved having his students around him, and he especially enjoyed the hours he spent in Inessa's communal kitchen when he could talk to them across the table. Fields and orchards crowded round the village, and in the late afternoons when classes were over he would accompany them sometimes in their rambles along country lanes, singing melancholy Russian songs at the tops of their voices. The one with the finest voice was a youth from Kiev with a rather undistinguished appearance, who told Krupskaya how cleverly he had eluded police spies on his way to Paris. His name was Andrey Malinovsky. No one paid much attention to him at the time. Later it was learned that he was a police spy.

He was, of course, only one of many. His task, as soon as the school came to an end in August, was to report to his superiors in the Paris Bureau of the Okhrana everything that had happened and the names and addresses of everyone who took part. He would not necessarily have to report to them in person; he had only to write a letter and put it in the mails. His report would be added to the voluminous file on Lenin, and from time to time summaries from these files would be dispatched to St. Petersburg. The files of the Russian secret police in Paris have been preserved and are now in the custody of the Hoover Institution on War, Revolution and Peace at Stanford University, in California. What emerges from these files is the extraordinary competence of the police in infiltrating all the revolutionary movements. They had raised spying to a fine art. They knew everything. They knew about Lenin's love affair with Inessa Armand, and how many hours he spent in the libraries, and what books he read, and what he drank when he visited the cafés on the Avenue d'Orléans—he drank beer. They read most of his correspondence and copies of his letters were accordingly added to his files.

Some of the men closest to Lenin were police spies. There was, for example, another Malinovsky—Roman Malinovsky, a ruddy thickset man with a quick temper and a cool brain. He was born a peasant in Russian Poland; he had a peasant's craftiness and a peasant's earthy speech. Lenin came to know him well, and he admired in him exactly those qualities which he admired in himself: his craftiness, his daring, his earthiness, even his criminality. Malinovsky made no secret of his criminal youth. He had spent three years in prison. In 1905 he emerged from obscurity to play a minor role in the Moscow uprising. A gifted orator, he was soon marked out by members of the Social Democratic Party as a potential leader; and leaving Moscow for St. Petersburg he set about organizing the Metal Workers Union, while carrying out various other tasks ordered by the party. All the while he was reporting to the secret police.

There came a time when Malinovsky's usefulness to the police was such that he could demand his own price. He was in close contact with Beletsky, the chief of police. His secret messages to police headquarters were signed "Portnoy," meaning "tailor," since tailoring was one of the many trades he had practiced. To the workers of St. Petersburg he was "the great Roman," the man who would one day lead them to victory against the hated autocracy, and they quite seriously spoke of him as a man who might one day be in the government. He had boundless self-assurance and boundless ambition; and his career can only be understood on the assumption that he was perfectly prepared to betray the police, as he was always prepared to betray the workers.

Malinovsky's sympathies lay with the Mensheviks, and until 1910 he worked very largely in Menshevik circles. From time to time the police would be tipped off about a secret revolutionary meeting; they would swoop down on the meeting, arrest the revolutionaries, and if

Malinovsky was present, he too would be arrested; and while the revolutionaries were sentenced to long terms of imprisonment or exile, Malinovsky would be released quietly after a few weeks of detention. His popularity among the workers remained undiminished.

When the elections were held for the Fourth Imperial Duma in 1912 Malinovsky offered himself as a candidate. By law all candidates for election had to prove that they had no criminal record. Malinovsky's criminal record included one arrest for rape and three for burglary. It was therefore necessary for Beletsky to expunge the record, and this was done. Malinovsky was elected by a handsome majority and took his seat in the Imperial Duma as one of the thirteen Social Democratic deputies. On the advice of Beletsky he transferred from the Menshevik to the Bolshevik camp. Seven Mensheviks and six Bolsheviks were elected. Nikolay Chkheidze, a Georgian, was the chairman of the group, Malinovsky the vice-chairman. At the first session of the Duma, it was Malinovsky who was chosen to read the party program, which was carefully edited and elaborated by the secret police.

Lenin was overjoyed when the news of Malinovsky's election reached him. "*For the first time* we have an *outstanding* worker-leader representing us in the Duma," he wrote. "He is going to read the program of our party. The results may not be visible immediately, but they are bound to be *enormous*."

Malinovsky's election was to have "enormous" results: the secret police could now dictate the policy of the Bolsheviks.

Meanwhile Lenin was still the dominating force among the Bolsheviks. Earlier in the year he had called a conference of his followers in Prague. At this conference a new central committee had been elected, consisting of Lenin, Zinoviev, Ordjonikidze, Schwartzman, Goloshchekin, Spandaryan and Malinovsky. Ordjonikidze had studied under Lenin in the Longjumeau school. Schwartzman was a delegate from Kiev, and Spandaryan like Ordjonikidze was a member of the militant Baku Committee. Goloshchekin was later to become the military Commissar of the Ural region and took an active part in the murder of the Russian imperial family. Plekhanov, invited to attend the conference, refused in a letter which was a model of restraint. "The arrangement is such," he wrote, "that the delegates at the conference will vote with complete uniformity, and therefore in the interests of party unity it would be better if I had no part in it." Lenin was not alarmed by Plekhanov's absence. He had called the conference in order to achieve that "complete uniformity" against which Plekhanov complained.

From the beginning Lenin dominated the conference with an iron hand. His motions were carried unanimously. In an astonishing series of affirmations he proclaimed that the newly elected Central Committee possessed supreme power within the Social Democratic Party and that all other factions and groups who called themselves by this name were interlopers incapable of representing the Russian proletariat and with no mandate to represent them. The Central Committee alone possessed this mandate, and all communications to the Social Democratic Party must be addressed to the Central Committee through its chairman, Vladimir Ulyanov, residing at 4 Rue Marie-Rose, Paris. In this way Lenin claimed supreme power over the party.

The other affirmations and resolutions were no less surprising. The Central Committee claimed to be the rightful inheritor of the Schmidt legacy and authorized Lenin to collect the money from the German trustees. The Central Committee proclaimed that the work of the party should be carried out under three slogans: A Democratic Republic; An Eight-Hour Working Day; and Confiscation of the Large Estates and their Distribution among the Peasants. The first was aimed at the monarchy, the third at the aristocracy, while the second demonstrated the abiding affection of the party for the industrial proletariat. Lenin was well content with these slogans, and with the twelve-day conference. Malinovsky was equally content. He had charmed Lenin. He had shown that he was a man to be depended upon, and a warm and affectionate relationship had sprung up between them; and while Lenin went off to Berlin to claim the Schmidt legacy, Malinovsky went off to St. Petersburg to report on the affairs of the newly established Central Committee to Beletsky, who immediately increased his salary. Lenin was less fortunate. The German trustees resolutely refused to part with the money.

Lenin well knew that by calling the Prague conference and publishing its edicts he had given mortal offense to the men who regarded themselves as the founders of the Social Democratic Party. He had offended Plekhanov, Axelrod, Martov, Chkheidze, Trotsky, and hundreds of others by casting them into outer darkness and claiming full executive authority for himself. The conference was a *coup de théâtre*, and it was bound to have serious repercussions. If Plekhanov or any other highly placed party member had acted quickly and decisively, Lenin might have lost the gamble. In fact he won the gamble. The

Prague conference, consisting of no more than a handful of hand-picked members, dominated by Lenin, Zinoviev and Malinovsky, the new *troika*, was advertised among the Russian workmen as a resounding proof of the resurgence of the Social Democratic Party; and the very simplicity of the slogans announced at the conference appealed to the workers.

It was some time before Lenin knew how successful he had been. He wrote to his sister Anna a plaintive letter describing how he had been harassed by "more wrangling and mudslinging than there has been for a long time." A few months earlier he had told her, "I do not know whether I shall live to see the next rise of the tide." But now, although exhausted and full of the bitterness of the Prague quarrels, he began to see a future for the party. As usual, the simplest solutions were the best. At the Prague conference he had called for armed insurrection. Contact was being made with the Baltic fleet; guns and ammunition were being smuggled into Russia; it was time to get closer to Russia. He left Paris and settled in Cracow.

When Lenin looked back on the days in Cracow he sometimes wondered why he had gone to the trouble of uprooting himself from Paris. Inevitably the armed insurrection failed, and just as inevitably the advantages of living in Cracow were outweighed by the disadvantages.

"You ask me why I am in Austria," he wrote to Gorky in the summer. "The Central Committee has set up a bureau here (*entre nous*); we are close to the frontier and will take advantage of it. Also we are nearer St. Petersburg, and it is much easier to write articles for the papers in Russia, and collaboration is being arranged. There is less wrangling, and that too is an advantage. There is no good library, and that is a disadvantage. It is hard to live without books."

There were, of course, other disadvantages. The tsarist secret police, fully aware that Russian revolutionaries were in the city, had their own agents here. Then, too, the roads were bad, and this prevented Lenin from taking as much exercise on his bicycle as he would like. There were difficulties in communication, for he spoke Polish badly and had to rely almost completely on his wife, who remembered some Polish from her childhood. "We live here as we lived in Shushenskoye," Krupskaya wrote in a letter to Lenin's mother. "We live from one mail to another."

Occasionally there were visitors. Here for the first time Lenin met the thin and elegant Yakov Furstenburg, whose party name was

Ganetsky. He was a leading figure in the Polish Social Democratic
Party and became Lenin's chief adviser on the revolutionary prospects
in Poland; and in 1917 he was of some assistance in making the arrangements for the sealed train which brought the Bolshevik leaders
across Germany. On another day Lenin saw a small, jovial man called
Nikolay Bukharin coming up to the house with a heavy rucksack on
his back. Bukharin was twenty-five, but he had already spent eight
years as an active revolutionary. Like Lenin he had a high forehead,
thin hair and a slightly turned-up nose; unlike Lenin he had a disposition of quite extraordinary sweetness, which he combined with ferocious political opinions. He devoured books in five or six languages,
and he could discuss any subject under the sun with wit and passion.
Characteristically, he was carrying reproductions of German paintings
in his rucksack; the paintings were by the highly romantic painter
Böcklin.

This was Lenin's first meeting with Bukharin; there were to be
many more. Always careless of dress, always extravagant in ideas,
Bukharin was the exact opposite of Lenin, and their mutual attraction
was based on a delighted awareness of their differences. Trotsky, who
despised Bukharin, called him "a medium who simply reflects other
people's ideas and speeches," but that was to misjudge the man completely. They first met in New York, when Bukharin insisted that they
should immediately pay a visit to the New York Public Library. Trotsky, who was tired after a long journey, never forgave Bukharin for
dragging him off to the library.

"We had many visitors in Cracow," Krupskaya says in her memoirs;
but elsewhere she speaks of her boredom and loneliness, the monotony
of life under the dull Polish skies, the daily waiting for the postman,
who came at eleven in the morning and again at five in the afternoon,
and how Lenin's nerves were continually on edge because there were
no books to read. He wrote his articles and sent them to Russia by the
night train. He took short bicycle rides. Zinoviev was staying in Cracow, and Lenin liked to play with the Zinoviev baby. Most of the time
he was bored to death.

During the winter of 1913 Krupskaya's health, which had never
been good, took a turn for the worse. There were alarming symptoms
of goiter and of heart disease. She had nursed Lenin through all his
bouts of nervous prostration, and now it was her turn to be nursed.
She suffered from palpitations, trembling of the hands, and sleeplessness; and in addition to her physical infirmities, she was on the edge

of a nervous breakdown, and Lenin himself was not far from one. "We are swimming against the current," he wrote to Gorky in one of those letters demanding an article or a story for *Pravda*. "We are staying here to take advantage of the Poles' hatred for Tsarism." But there were very few good reasons for remaining in Cracow, and soon an incompetent doctor was suggesting that it would be better for Krupskaya's health if she left the low-lying plains for the high mountains. They decided to spend the summer in Poronino, a small village near Zakopane, in the Tatra Mountains. Lenin was happy. He was able to rent an enormous villa—"It is really enormous and far too big," he wrote proudly to his sister Maria—and since he had a passion for mountain scenery and liked climbing mountains he was supremely content. Krupskaya, of course, grew worse.

She became so ill that in desperation Lenin took her to Berne, to see a specialist, who operated on her goiter. She was in delirium the following day, and Lenin thought he had lost her. The doctor counseled a long rest, but Lenin was in a hurry to return to Poronino, and Krupskaya heroically accompanied him before she had fully recovered from the operation.

Still, there were advantages in Poronino, even though it rained nearly every day. In the large white house on the slope of the hill they could put up their guests and hold meetings. Inessa Armand, sent to Russia on a revolutionary mission the previous year, returned after a spell in prison. She was suffering from tuberculosis, but had lost nothing of her charm or energy. Krupskaya enjoyed their walks together, and if Inessa and Lenin went out walking alone, she thought nothing of it.

By this time the Bolshevik wing of the party had acquired a legal standing in Russia. There were six Bolshevik members of the Duma, and seven Menshevik members. Lenin raged against the Mensheviks and demanded that the "Six" be treated on terms of exact equality with the "Seven." The Mensheviks refused, with the inevitable result that Lenin continued to hold meetings, conferences and congresses in the name of the Russian Social Democratic Party without going through the formality of obtaining the permission of the Mensheviks. They were two separate organizations with their own members in the Duma and their own newspapers.

Rumors about Roman Malinovsky were now circulating throughout the party, but Lenin dismissed them out of hand. It never occurred to Krupskaya that Malinovsky was anything but a devoted party member, loyal to her husband and his principles; nevertheless, she later recalled a strange incident which occurred at Poronino after a visit to the Zinovievs, where the sinister rumors had been discussed. They were walking across a bridge when Lenin suddenly stopped with a look of horror on his face and said, "What if they are true?" Krupskaya reassured him, saying, "No, it's quite impossible!" Then they continued their journey across the bridge, while Lenin vented his rage on the Mensheviks, saying that they alone were capable of inventing the rumors.

But the rumors had not been invented, even though a secret commission set up by Lenin to investigate the accusations cleared Malinovsky completely. Lenin had known Malinovsky for years, trusted him implicitly, informed him of all the party secrets, and regarded him as one of the brightest luminaries of the party. Then, quite suddenly, on May 8, 1914, Malinovsky handed in his resignation to the Chairman of the Duma and left the country. Lenin was so shocked that he could scarcely bring himself to face the situation. He wrote to a friend, "Do you know what M-sky has gone and done? We are going out of our minds with this idiocy." He was still shuddering when the World War broke out, putting an end for a while to all further inquiries about the guilt or innocence of the former peasant who was one of the few who accepted money from both Lenin and the tsarist secret police.

The war took Lenin unawares. In the past he had joked about the possibility that the Tsar and the Kaiser between them would bring about a war which could only result in a socialist victory; and then, having made his joke, he would shrug his shoulders as though it was beyond all belief that the gods would grant him such a favor.

But the war had come—a war which was against all reason, and which owed far more to the unreasoning ambitions of a few powerful men than to the massive laws of capitalist economics—and it reached into the remote villages of Galicia, where the farm boys were rounded up and put into uniform. As a Russian living on Austrian soil, Lenin was in a precarious position. He immediately sought the assistance of Ganetsky, who was an Austrian subject, and took the precaution of sending a telegram to the chief of police in Cracow, who knew him to be a political *émigré* and who was in theory his protector. Ganetsky telegraphed to a Social Democratic member of parliament in Vienna, who was unable to act in time. The police arrived, searched the house, found a notebook full of diagrams—they were statistics which Lenin had circled and boxed, but an illiterate peasant might be excused for regarding them as battle plans—and on the next morning Lenin was ordered to take the train to Nowy Targ, the nearest military outpost, and surrender to the local gendarmery. The villagers, who had never liked Lenin's exclusiveness, and who had grown accustomed to seeing strange Russians climbing the hill to the white house, whispered about Russian spies in their midst; and the servant girl hired by Krupskaya proved to be an adept at circulating rumors. Krupskaya got rid of the girl, but the suspicions remained. Krupskaya was frantic with worry, because her seventy-two-year-old mother was in failing health and feeble-minded. She would say, "Volodya has been called up, hasn't he?" and Krupskaya would have to repeat that he had not been called up, but had voluntarily surrendered to the gendarmery.

Every day Krupskaya took the train to Nowy Targ to see her husband in jail. He was in no danger, he was treated well, and she says he was exceptionally well regarded by the other prisoners. He spent twelve days in prison and was then released, chiefly through the intervention of Victor Adler, a socialist deputy, who went directly to the Minister of the Interior. "Are you sure," asked the Minister, "that Ulyanov is an enemy of the tsarist government?" "Yes," Adler answered, "he is a more implacable enemy than Your Excellency."

But quite obviously there was nothing to be gained by remaining in Austrian Galicia, and once he was released, Lenin made plans for returning to Switzerland. From time to time his mother had supplied him with money, but this source of income was cut off. There was no market for articles on extreme left-wing socialism. The only money at their disposal consisted of a legacy of four thousand rubles left to Krupskaya by an aunt, an obscure schoolmistress from Novocherkassk. Without that money, which was carefully husbanded, they might have died of poverty and destitution in the lean years that followed.

They settled in Berne. Lenin disliked the town—"a dull, small, but cultured little place"—and chose it for no reason except that it was cheaper than Zurich. Almost at once he was agitating to transform the war between nations into a civil war between classes. Plekhanov and Kautsky, the two most famous Social Democrats in Europe, had announced their conviction that the war was just and must be fought to a conclusion. Plekhanov had even given a public address in Zurich in September, in which he said he hoped for a victory of the Cossacks and the French *poilus*, to save Europe from the despotism of the German *feldwebel;* at this meeting Lenin sprang up in disgust and denounced him as a hypocritical nationalist, a traitor to socialism, and was shouted down. He never forgave Plekhanov for this crime, but seems to have hated Kautsky more. "I hate and despise him more than anyone," he wrote. "He is nothing but a beastly, rotten, sneaking hypocrite."

Lenin was almost alone in his rage. He welcomed the war, for "it placed the bayonet on the order of the day" and marked the inevitable transition from the age when men walked "with thin and weak soles on the cultivated sidewalks of provincial cities" to the age when they climbed mountains "in thick hobnailed boots." "The slogan of peace," he declared, "is stupid and wrong." Such slogans were "fit only for priests and the petty bourgeoisie." To his friend Shlyapnikov he wrote on October 17, 1914, "We cannot *promise* a civil war, and we cannot *order* a civil war, but our duty is to conduct all our work, if necessary for a very long time, *in that direction*." He was a voice crying in the wilderness. At this time there was virtually no Social Democratic Party in Russia, and his own following outside of Russia consisted of scarcely more than twenty people. Of these perhaps only Zinoviev, who had followed him from Poland, and Inessa Armand would have willingly laid down their lives for his cause. They were living very close together in Berne—Inessa in a house opposite them, and Zinoviev five minutes' walk down the road.

It was a strangely idyllic setting in wartime, for the Berne woods lay nearby and they would all go out together to bask on the wooded slopes. "We would sit for hours there while Ilyich jotted down notes for his articles and speeches, and I studied Italian, and Inessa sewed a skirt." Inessa, a gifted pianist, would soothe his ragged nerves by playing for him on the piano. Usually she would play a Beethoven sonata— more often than not, the *Appassionata*, which Lenin never tired of hearing. Years later, talking to Gorky, he said, "I know nothing that is greater than the *Appassionata*. I'd like to listen to it every day. It is marvelous, superhuman music. I always think with pride—perhaps it is naïve of me—what marvelous things human beings can do." Then he screwed up his eyes and smiled and said sadly, "But I can't listen to music too often. It affects your nerves, makes you want to say stupid nice things and stroke the heads of people who could create such beauty while living in this vile hell. And now you mustn't stroke anyone's head—you might get your hand bitten off. You have to hit them on the head without any mercy, although our ideal is not to use force against anyone. Hm, hm, our duty is infernally hard!"

But the heavy duties of a revolutionary must have appeared wholly academic in the spring of 1915, when no one was listening to the impoverished revolutionary who believed that the war served only one purpose, and even that a dubious one; for while the war demonstrated "the filth, rottenness and beastliness" of the labor movement, it did not seem to be moving the labor movement into positions of power. On the contrary, rigid state socialism was being enforced in all the countries at war. They were practicing what Lenin preached, but in a form which was unrecognizable to him.

In the spring of 1915 Krupskaya's mother died. There is a story that one night Krupskaya left her vigil by her mother's bedside and went to bed, after asking her husband to wake her if her mother needed her. Lenin went on working. During the night his mother-in-law died. When Krupskaya awoke the next morning to find her mother dead, she turned on her husband and asked him why he failed to wake her.

"You told me to wake you if your mother needed you," Lenin answered. "She died. She didn't need you."

The story was first told by Isaac Don Levine in his excellent short biography *The Man Lenin*. It was just the kind of behavior, merciless and merciful, that we might expect from Lenin.

As the war went on, producing such intolerable hardships that men fought with a sense of growing revulsion and horror, the socialist movement gradually awoke to the pressing need of declaring a general strike against war. It was not only the extreme left wing which saw that the war was a monstrous crime. Here and there small groups of men heroically protested; some were thrown into prison, others were shot. Lenin's attitude toward the war was ambiguous: he wanted it to stop because he recognized its idiocy, and he wanted it to be prolonged until the moment when all the existing state institutions would collapse and the Communists could take power. And he also gloried in it, in the toughening of the socialist fiber which resulted as one disaster followed upon another. In the best of his wartime pamphlets, *The Collapse of the Second International*, written in May 1915, he excoriated Kautsky and set down his own views on the authentic and systematic revolution which would ultimately put an end to all wars. "The experience of war," he wrote, "like the experience of every crisis in history, of every disaster and every sudden turn in human life, stuns and shatters some, but it enlightens and hardens others." He saw himself as one of those who were hardened.

On September 5, 1915, there opened at Zimmerwald, near Berne, an international socialist conference convened by the Italian Socialist

Party. There were thirty-five delegates from Italy, Germany, France, Russia, Poland, Hungary, Holland, Switzerland, Sweden, Norway, Rumania and Bulgaria. Lenin, Safarov, Zinoviev, Martov, Axelrod and Radek were present, the last as a representative of the Polish Social Democratic Party. Robert Grimm and Fritz Platten were among the delegates from Switzerland. Trotsky represented a small group of his own. All concurred on the manifesto which said, "The warmakers lie when they assert that the war would liberate oppressed nations and serve democracy. In reality they are burying the liberty of their own nations as well as the independence of other peoples, there in the places of devastation. . . . The real struggle is the struggle for freedom, for the reconciliation among peoples, for socialism." Lenin went further. In a short manifesto signed by eight delegates, including Platten, Zinoviev and Radek, he wrote, "Civil war, not civil peace—this is the slogan." He made proposals for the inauguration of a Third International, but this proposal was defeated.

In January 1916 Lenin and Krupskaya went to live in Zurich, taking up residence in a single room in a sixteenth-century house belonging to Adolph Kammerer, a shoemaker. The room was small and inconvenient, overlooking a sausage factory, and the intolerable stench caused them to close their windows even on hot summer days. The furnishings consisted of a table, two beds, two chairs and a sewing machine. The shoemaker developed a genuine fondness for Lenin. "He was always buying bottles of hair oil to cure his baldness," the shoemaker said, "and he forgot to turn off the gas jets, but he was a good fellow." Lenin spent as little time at home as possible, usually working in the library until six o'clock in the evening, then returning to a simple dinner with Krupskaya, who had at last learned how to cook from Frau Kammerer. Poverty oppressed them. "This diabolical cost of living—it has become devilishly hard to live," Lenin wrote, though his needs were simple and the rent was low.

He was gaining converts, slowly and methodically increasing the range of his activities. He gave lectures, which were sparsely attended, and the Russian colony in Zurich looked up at him with awe and respect. He completed a work called *Imperialism, the Highest Stage of Capitalism*—it was one of his curious beliefs that imperialism arose during the years 1898 and 1900—but this hotheaded, angry book largely based on J. A. Hobson's *Imperialism* was scarcely worthy of him. *The Collapse of the Second International* was vigorous and trenchant, but this new book displayed more arrogance than anger.

His mother died in July. He was heartbroken and left Zurich for long walks in the mountains.

It was a year of defeats. He wrote to Inessa Armand in November, "There was a meeting of the Lefts here today: not everybody turned up, only 2 Swiss and 2 foreigners, Germans, and three Russian-Jewish-Poles. There was no report, just an informal talk."

Winter came. A kind of graveyard stillness descended on his hopes. In January 1917 he addressed a meeting of young Swiss workers in German at the People's House in Zurich on the 1905 revolution in Russia. He said:

> We should not be deceived by the present graveyard silence in Europe. Europe is pregnant with revolution. The monstrous horrors of the imperialist war and the suffering caused by the high cost of living engender a revolutionary spirit, and the ruling classes, the bourgeoisie and their lackeys, the governments, are moving deeper and deeper into a blind alley from which they will never be able to extricate themselves without tremendous upheavals. . . .
>
> We, the old ones, may never live to see the decisive battles of the coming revolution.

He was saying as clearly as a man can that he had almost lost hope in the revolution.

Vladimir Ulyanov, aged four, with his sister Olga, 1874.

Ilya Nikolayevich and his wife, Maria Alexandrovna.
Photographs taken in 1882–3.

The Ulyanov family, Simbirsk, 1879.
Alexander is standing in center, with Dmitry sitting below. Anna stands
at extreme right, with Vladimir sitting below. Olga is on the extreme left.
Maria is on her mother's lap.

Vladimir Ulyanov in 1887.

Nadezhda Krupskaya in 1895.

The founding members of the Petersburg League for the Liberation of the Working Class, 1897. From left to right: (sitting) V. V. Starkov, G. M. Krzhizhanovsky, V. I. Ulyanov and Yu. O. Martov; (standing) A. L. Malchenko, P. K. Zaporozhets and A. A. Vaneyev.

Lenin in Paris, 1910.

Lenin in Razliv, August 1917.

July 1920.

October 1918.

July 1921.

November 1921.

March 1919 (Sov

Lenin's study in the Kremlin

The ape and the skull. This statue stood on Lenin's desk, and can be seen just below the map, partly hidden by an electric candle.

...enin addressing crowd on Sverdlov Square, May 5, 1920, with Trotsky ...nd Kamenev beside him: a still from a newsreel.

The same scene as re-touched under Stalin, taken a few seconds later.

*Lenin,
Trotsky and
Kamenev,
May 1920.*

Second Congress of the Third International, August 1920. Gorky stands behind Lenin. Zinoviev is the second figure to the right of Lenin. Radek and Bukharin are behind railing, to the left.

Lenin with Trotsky in Red Square on second anniversary of the Revolution, November 1919.

Close-up of Lenin taken at the same time. Both photographs are taken from motion pictures.

Lenin at Gorki, August 1922.

Funeral of Lenin, January 27, 1924 (Sovfoto).

THE STORM GATHERS

To the Russian proletariat there has fallen the great honor of beginning the series of revolutions which have been caused, with objective inevitability, by the imperialist war.

LETTERS FROM AFAR

THE DAYS PASSED QUIETLY, as though in some far-off shadowy part of outer space. Great offensives were being mounted, hundreds of thousands of men were dying on the battlefields, while the Russian exiles in Switzerland looked on in grim detachment, quarreling over minor details of theory and complaining that magazines reached them slowly. Funds were low, and so were their hopes of taking an active part in public affairs.

Toward the end of February 1917 Lenin was in a hopeless mood of mingled frustration and despair. The Russian revolution, which would be the beginning of the world revolution, seemed as far off as ever. He did not share Mikha Tskhakaya's belief that it would come about in his lifetime; perhaps after all Marx was right when he said that no form of society ever comes to an end before it has exhausted all its possibilities of development. Lenin had not dreamed of a Marxian revolution. Like the terrorist Sazonov, he had hoped "to give history a push." But from his vantage point in Switzerland, that small sterilized country which seemed to exist outside of history altogether, there seemed to be no way in which he could exert even the smallest push. He had no inkling in February of how close he was to fulfilling his wildest dreams.

The mind of the conspirator in exile, cut off from news about the revolutionary movements in his own country, feeds on illusions of power. It is a desperate life, never more desperate than when all the evidence points to the disastrous defeat of his dreams. There is no middle ground for the conspirator; he must either see himself as the

271

arbiter of destinies, or he abandons the struggle, or commits suicide. The history of the Russian revolutionary movement has as many suicides as martyrs.

In his despair Lenin wrote to Mark Elizarov in Petrograd,* begging his help in producing a vast pedagogic encyclopedia to be edited by Krupskaya. Such a book was likely to be a candidate for the honor of being the least-read book in wartime Russia, but he claimed that with the vast increase in the reading public and with the special Russian predilection for encyclopedias, the time was ripe for such a publication, and he had no doubt it would go into several editions if only Elizarov could find a publisher. "I am quite sure Nadya will be able to complete the work, for she has studied pedagogy for many years, has written about it already, and has prepared herself systematically for the task. Zurich provides an ideal center for such a work, and the pedagogic museum here is the best in the world." He described the plan of the book at some length, adding that "it will be a very useful work and should bring in some money, *which is terribly important to us.*"

He begged Elizarov to go about the matter carefully, for he was afraid that if the idea became known a publisher would steal it. Probably it would be better to borrow some money from a capitalist who would underwrite the expenses; he had no high opinion of publishers. "All the publisher will do will be to take *all* the profits and keep the editor in slavery. *It does happen!*" So, perhaps, it does; but Lenin's ideas on publishing in partnership with a capitalist were oddly at variance with his principles. The truth was that he had almost no money and no prospects of making any. He was approaching his forty-seventh birthday, and there was little to show for the years of exile. Day followed day: there were long walks round the lake, long hours spent in the library, long conferences with the Swiss Social Democrats, whom he despised; and he could not imagine where it was all leading to.

At one time he had high hopes for the Social Democrats in Switzerland, but these hopes were fading. Earlier in the month Olga Ravich spoke of her feeling of hopelessness. "Quite truthfully, I may say you are not the only one to be pessimistic," he replied. "The party is riddled with opportunism; it is nothing more than a charitable institution for petty-bourgeois clerks." In these anguished letters written in February he reserved his chief contempt for Fritz Platten and Robert Grimm—

* In 1915 St. Petersburg was officially renamed Petrograd. Like most Russians, Lenin continued to use the affectionate sobriquet of 'Peters.'

Platten because he was "ineffably useless," and Grimm because he had abandoned the left and gone over to the center. Without money, without hopes, and with only a handful of friends, he felt increasingly isolated. There confronted him the prospect of living out the remainder of his life in poverty-stricken exile.

On March 8 rioting broke out in Petrograd. The workers came out on strike, demanding bread and peace. Crowds wandered aimlessly through the streets, there was some disorganized looting, and the police fired on the looters. On the Nevsky Prospect the Cossacks fired into the crowds. This was the signal for the revolt, which broke out the following day, when the people poured through the streets demanding bread, peace, the dissolution of the government and the abdication of the Tsar. It was not a planned revolt, and it had no focus. The crowds were often strangely good-tempered. People would go up to the Cossacks and say, "You won't shoot, will you?" and the Cossacks would answer, "No, we won't shoot." The revolt, such as it was, was spontaneous, arising from hatred of the Tsarist government, the great losses suffered at the front and most of all from frustration. For three days the revolt had been gradually gathering strength, searching for the focus which seemed to be always eluding it. On Sunday, March 11, it broke out in full force. The reserve troops of the Pavlovsky Regiment mutinied, killed their colonel, and went over to the people; then there was war between the regiments until one by one they went over to the people. Barracks and police stations were set on fire, and with some satisfaction the people of Petrograd heard the cries of the hated policemen as they roasted to death.

Thereafter the revolt gathered momentum and found its focus in the Duma. Huge crowds milled about the square, waiting for the installation of a provisional government and for the announcement of the abdication of the Tsar, which took place on March 15. At this stage of the revolt one of the very few who were able to give direction and purpose to the people was Alexander Kerensky, who, like Lenin, was a native of Simbirsk; unlike Lenin he was determined that there should be as little bloodshed as possible. "I shall not become the Marat of the Russian Revolution," he declared. He had been a vice-president of the Workers' and Soldiers' Soviet, organized on the model of the 1905 Soviets in the first days of the revolt, and immediately became Minister of Justice in the Provisional Government. Until October the Soviet and the Government were to be in a state of undeclared war with one another.

No news of the early riots reached the Swiss newspapers, and the first news of the setting up of the Provisional Government came in the special editions of the newspapers late in the morning of March 15. According to Krupskaya, Lenin had finished lunch and she was washing the dishes, when a Polish revolutionary friend rushed into the apartment and said, "Haven't you heard the news? There's a revolution in Russia!" He told them what he had read, and then left. Lenin and Krupskaya went down to the lake, where the newspapers were posted up as soon as they came out.

As they read the reports, they had not the least doubt that a revolution of quite extraordinary proportions had broken out, but it was still not clear in what direction it would develop, and the details were fragmentary. Yet from that moment Lenin was perfectly sure he would have some part in the revolution. That afternoon he sent off a telegram to Zinoviev in Berne, summoning him to Zurich, and a postcard went off to Mikha Tskhakaya, who had been so hopeful about the coming Russian revolution when Lenin was delivering his speech on the 1905 revolution earlier in the year. "I congratulate you on the occasion of the revolution in Russia," he wrote. "Your optimism was quickly rewarded. I am preparing to leave, and packing my bags. And you, what are you doing?" Krupskaya could hardly remember how they spent the rest of the day and night, so excited were they about the news from Russia.

Zinoviev arrived the next day. More news about the Provisional Government had arrived, including a full list of the newly appointed ministers. Lenin dashed off a long, excited letter to Alexandra Kollontay in Stockholm, saying that everything was happening as he had prophesied, and this was merely the first stage of the first revolution, which would neither be final nor be confined to Russia. The Bolsheviks must immediately carry out propaganda "for an *international* proletarian revolution and for the conquest of power by the Soviets of Workers' Deputies"—from the very beginning he was thinking in terms of world revolution. "*Never again* along the lines of the Second International! *Never again* with Kautsky! By all means a *more revolutionary* program and tactics, and by all means a combination of legal and illegal work." So he wrote, the hand racing across the page, deriding Milyukov, Guchkov and Kerensky, and all the others who had assembled around the new government which was only the "old" European pattern, revived not to bring about a revolution, but to destroy it. It never seemed to occur to him that these ministers were men of good will, determined to bring about a representative government and to build up a revolutionary state; and if it had occurred to him it would have made no difference. He had found the Archimidean point, the place where the lever could be inserted, and he was preparing to press on it with all his strength.

On the following day Alexandra Kollontay sent him a telegram asking for instructions and directives which would guide her and the party in political work. He replied at once, saying that with the pitifully scanty information available he was in no position to set down guidelines. The previous day he had thought the Provisional Government was entering into an agreement with the Tsar; now it appeared that the Tsar had fled and was preparing for a counterrevolution. "Our immediate task," he wrote, "is to broaden the scope of our work, to organize the masses, to arouse new social strata, the backward elements, the rural population, the domestic servants, to form nuclei in the army for the purpose of carrying on a systematic and detailed exposé of the government, to prepare the seizure of power by the Soviets of Workers' Deputies." Only the armed proletariat could bring peace to Russia: to this belief he held firmly. For himself he could see little hope of leaving "this accursed Switzerland" in the near future. What he hoped for in those early days was some possibility of controlling events from a distance, and he was already composing with Zinoviev a statement about the Provisional Government which might, he thought, be useful as a directive for immediate action.

These directives were found among Zinoviev's papers some years later. They show that Lenin was obsessed with the possibility of a counterrevolution led by the Tsar, "who will undoubtably offer resistance, organize a party and perhaps an army to restore the monarchy, and it is perfectly possible that, in order to deceive the people, the Tsar, if he should succeed in escaping from Russia or gaining the support of part of the army, will issue a manifesto on the subject of an immediate separate peace, which he will sign with Germany." He called the proletariat to arms. "They must offer merciless resistance to tsarist reaction and crush the tsarist monarchy completely."

Lenin's first reading of the revolutionary situation was thus largely a mistaken one. The proletariat had no need to crush the monarchy, which had abdicated and lost all control over the course of events. The last thing that would have entered the Tsar's head was the publication of a dramatic manifesto announcing a separate peace with Germany, even if he had been in any position to make any such announcement.

Characteristically Lenin saw the Tsar as a counterrevolutionary leader *doing exactly what Lenin himself was to do later*.

On March 17 the Provisional Government had announced a sweeping program of reforms, guaranteeing freedom of press and assembly, a general amnesty, the immediate convocation of a Constituent Assembly "on the basis of universal, equal, direct and secret suffrage," and the formation of a people's militia to take the place of the police, who were now disbanded. "They are only promises," Lenin wrote, but he saw at once that these freedoms gave his party considerable scope for action, and he urged members of his party to make every use of "the relative and incomplete freedoms" offered by the Provisional Government in order to agitate for a workers' government which will give "peace, bread and complete freedom" to the people. What he meant by "complete freedom" is not made clear, but he was very clear in his own mind that the government was unable to give the people peace or bread, because the members of the government belonged to "the landowning and capitalist class," who would corner the bread and sell it at their own profit, and who were in league with the foreign imperialists who profited from the continuation of the war.

As Lenin admitted in his letter to Alexandra Kollontay, this interpretation of the forces at work in Russia left much to be desired. Written hurriedly, it showed an extraordinary lack of grasp of the real situation. On one subject however he was firmly convinced: the Bolsheviks must make no entangling alliances with any other party. They must reserve to themselves complete freedom of action and embark on a program of massive agitation.

Though Lenin says that Zinoviev co-operated in the writing of these directives, there are few signs of Zinoviev's characteristic style. It reads like Lenin, and for once he seems unsure of himself, floundering in a sea of hypotheses, painfully aware that he does not know what is really happening. Remembering these days many years later, Zinoviev recounts how they spent the days aimlessly wandering through the streets of Zurich, now drenched in the spring sunshine, and ever so often they would return to the offices of the *Neue Zürcher Zeitung*, where the latest bulletins were displayed. On the small tidbits of information they raised entire edifices of theory, and with the next bulletin the theories would crumble before their eyes.

What Lenin wanted most of all was to be in Petrograd and to take charge of affairs. He could not sleep; the nights were spent in devising more and more improbable theories. He imagined that in some mysterious manner he would find an airplane which would carry him over the embattled frontiers and set him down just outside Petrograd. He thought of borrowing a passport from a neutral comrade and making his way through Germany to Sweden and so to Russia. A Swedish passport might be the most convenient: he would learn a few phrases of the language and pass himself off as a Swede. Krupskaya teased him. "Think what would happen if you fell asleep and dreamed of Mensheviks," she said. "You would start screaming, 'Scoundrels, scoundrels, scoundrels!' and you would give everything away!" He had no idea how to reach Russia, and wrote off to Ganetsky in Oslo asking if there was any way in which he could be smuggled through Germany.

The following day, March 18, was the anniversary of the outbreak of the Paris Commune. He had prepared a speech in German for the occasion to be delivered before a group of socialists in the little mountain village of La Chaux-de-Fonds, traditionally friendly to Russian revolutionaries. Here Nechayev had hidden from the Federal police and many other revolutionaries had found a safe retreat. It was a long journey to this village near the French frontier, but it was a Sunday, no postmen would bring the mail, and it was unlikely that there would be any afternoon editions of the newspapers. Also he especially liked a young Bolshevik called Abramovich who lived there. So, he went off to the village and delivered the prepared speech about the Commune and the lessons that could be learned from it and how they could be applied to the Russian revolution. The Russians in the audience were impressed, but the Swiss socialists regarded it as visionary. Lenin was highly pleased with his speech and gave the manuscript to Abramovich, who lost it. Some portions of the argument are probably incorporated in *State and Revolution*, which he wrote later in the year.

He was back in Zurich the next day, still fuming over the impossibility of reaching Russia, determined at any cost to break through the trap. The wildest and most improbable ideas occurred to him. He wrote the Ganetsky, "I cannot wait any longer. No legal means of transit available. Whatever happens, Zinoviev and I must reach Russia. The only possible plan is as follows: you must find two Swedes who resemble Zinoviev and me, but since we cannot speak Swedish they must be deaf mutes. I enclose our photographs for this purpose." As usual, Lenin gave himself away whenever he spoke of "the only possible plan." Ganetsky made no effort to find the deaf mutes, but gave the photograph of Lenin to a reporter on the newspaper *Politiken*, where it promptly appeared over the caption: "Lenin, the leader of the Russian Revolution." But at this moment he was very far from being the leader of the Russian Revolution.

On the same day an even more improbable idea occurred to him. He would assume the identity of his friend Vyacheslav Karpinsky, the capable manager of the Russian library in Geneva. Wearing a wig, he would travel to England and somehow reach Russia by way of Holland and Scandinavia. He wrote an extraordinary letter to Karpinsky outlining his plan:

> I have been considering from every possible view the best way to get out. The following is absolutely secret. I beg you to reply immediately, preferably by express (let us hope the party won't be ruined by a dozen or more express letters) so that we can be sure no one has read this letter.
>
> Please procure in your name papers for traveling to France and England, and I will make use of *these papers* while passing through England (and *Holland*) to Russia.
>
> I can wear a wig.
>
> A photograph will be taken *of me in a wig*, and I shall appear at the Consulate in Berne wearing the wig.
>
> You must then disappear from Geneva for a minimum of a few weeks (until you receive a telegram from me from Scandinavia). During this time you find an absolutely secure hiding place in the mountains, where, *it goes without saying, we shall pay* for your food and lodging.
>
> If you agree, begin *preparations immediately* with the utmost energy (and with the deepest secrecy), and in any case send me a line at once.
>
> *Your*
> LENIN
>
> Think of practical steps to be taken *in connection with this* and write in detail. I am writing to you because I am sure that everything will remain *absolutely* secret between us.

The letter to Karpinsky throws some light on Lenin's conspiratorial habits. First, the need for secrecy is continually repeated, till it almost loses all meaning. Then there is the insistence on immediate, energetic, dedicated and passionate work on the part of the man who is ordered to submit himself to Lenin's will. There is no hesitation: this must be done now, at once, without the slightest argument. A lengthy report is required, but this is no more than an afterthought. There is no attempt to examine the loopholes in the plan, which has appeared fully fledged in Lenin's brain, although only one part of the plan is seen with any imaginative understanding, and this part is the most ludicrous of all—Lenin's appearance in a wig at the French consulate in Berne. He could have had very little hope that the ruse would succeed, yet he spoke about it with complete assurance, as though nothing else at that moment was so important, so necessary, and so certain of success. It is the letter of a man huddled in despair at the bottom of a cage and improvising furiously a purely imaginary escape.

While Lenin was writing this letter, a meeting of Russian political exiles was taking place in Geneva to discuss methods of returning to Russia. Lenin took no part in the meeting, but was represented by Zinoviev. Ironically, it was Martov, Lenin's old enemy on *Iskra,* who proposed the solution which was eventually followed. He suggested that the German government be approached and asked to provide passage for the Russian exiles across Germany in exchange for an equal number of German internees in Russia. The suggestion was thrown out as one of many suggestions, all of them apparently impracticable, and it was two or three days before Lenin heard of it. He immediately seized on it, though realizing that he was in no position to enter directly into negotiations with the Germans. Karpinsky seems to have sent him the suggestion. He wrote back:

> Martov's plan is excellent: we *ought* to get busy with it, only *we* (and you) cannot go about it directly. They would suspect *us*. Except for Martov, nonparty Russians and Russian patriots should appeal to the Swiss ministers (and influential people such as lawyers etc., and that can be done also in Geneva) with the request that *negotiations be opened* with the representative of the German government in Berne. We cannot participate directly or indirectly; our participation would *ruin* everything. But the plan itself is *very* good and *very* correct.

So matters rested for a few days while "that detestable centrist" Robert Grimm made cautious inquiries at the German embassy in Berne and telegrams went out to German Imperial headquarters suggesting that since the majority of Russian exiles in Switzerland were in favor of discontinuing the war, there were advantages to be gained in letting them travel to Russia through Germany. Conferences were soon being held in Berlin. Arguments for and against the plan were eagerly debated by high government officials, by the intelligence department, and by leading generals. The novelty of the proposal appealed especially to the Germans who knew Russia well and who were aware of the defeatism spreading through the Russian army. With one bold stroke it might be possible to bring the war in the east to an end.

Meanwhile Lenin had not been idle. He was working on a series of letters intended for *Pravda,* now appearing in Petrograd. They were hard-hitting, repetitive, sometimes curiously unreal. Being a conspirator, he imagined conspiracies everywhere. In the first letter he spoke of "the conspiracy of the Anglo-French imperialists who encouraged Milyukov, Guchkov and Co. to seize power *in order to prolong the imperialist war,* and to conduct the war even more ferociously and stubbornly, and *slaughter new millions* of Russian workers and peasants, and so that Guchkov may obtain Constantinople, and the French may obtain Syria, and the English capitalists may obtain Mesopotamia." These were flights of fancy. There had been no conspiracy, in Lenin's words, "to exchange one monarch for another." There had been a sudden popular uprising in which all sections of the populace took part, and the Provisional Government represented the people and was responsible to them. Lenin believed, or pretended to believe, that in the space of eight days a revolution had been won only to have its fruits snatched away from it by Anglo-French conspirators; and having made this initial error he was compelled to believe that they were only waiting for an appropriate time to reinstate the Tsar.

But if Lenin could be, as he often was, shockingly misinformed and obtuse in his interpretation of affairs, there was one subject on which he spoke with knowledge and authority. The mere existence of the Petrograd Soviet of Workers' and Soldiers' Deputies, even though it was in the hands of people he regarded as his enemies, was a sufficient indication that a second and more powerful revolution could be made to follow hard on the heels of the first. "The Soviet of Workers' Deputies, the organization of the workers, is a workers' government *in embryo,* representing the interests of all the *poorest* masses of the population, i.e. 9/10 of the population which is striving for *peace, bread, and freedom.*" On this statement he would hold firm. From the very beginning he saw that the Provisional Government would ultimately have to bend to the will of a workers' government deriving its power from the Soviets of Workers' Deputies; and it was only a step from this new government to the dictatorship of the proletariat represented by the dictatorship of one man.

In these messages intended for publication in *Pravda* and later collected together under the title *Letters from Afar*, Lenin was deliberately attempting to incite the workers of Petrograd against the Provisional Government before it was established firmly in the saddle, and at the same time he was attempting to make clear to himself exactly what had happened. He had no illusions about the extraordinary nature of the revolution in Petrograd. It could only have happened because history was now vastly speeded up. "It was as though," he wrote, "a great, mighty, and all-powerful director had appeared upon the stage and on a vast scale accelerated the course of history and produced world-wide crises of an unprecedented intensity: economic, political, national, and international. In addition to the unusual acceleration in world history, there were also needed especially sharp changes of direction, so that in one of these swift changes the blood- and mud-stained chariot of Tsarism was overturned in a moment of time."

The first "Letter from Afar" was printed in *Pravda* a few days later; the remaining four letters remained unpublished until after his death. History, moving at an unprecedented speed, caught up with him; when he reached Petrograd the letters were already out of date.

Yet the letters are important, because they show the way his mind was working, and how he sharpened his knives. They are as remarkable for what they omit as for what they say. He never, for example, describes the kind of state which will come about when the armed workers have seized power. The armed workers will rule. They will guarantee "absolute order and a comradely discipline practiced with enthusiasm." They will see to it that every child has a bottle of good milk and that no adult in a rich family will dare to drink a drop of milk until all the children are supplied. They will ensure that the palaces of the Tsar and of the aristocracy will be converted into rest homes for the homeless and the destitute. They will assess the food requirements of all and organize the distribution of supplies; they will act as welfare officials in a welfare state. But, surprisingly, Lenin is completely silent on the form of the government which will command and organize the armed militia, and like Nechayev he is inclined to think there is no need to discuss the shape of the emerging state, because it will spring spontaneously out of the desires of the workers themselves, who are themselves the state. "It would be completely absurd to lay down a 'plan' for the proletarian militia," he wrote in his third "Letter from Afar." "When the workers and the entire population in a real mass take up this task in a practical manner, they will make a thorough job of it and establish it a hundred times better than any theoretician could propose." What, in effect, he is saying is that he had not the least idea what would happen when the armed militia smash the existing order and take power, and he was perfectly aware that he was suggesting a state no different from the kind of state proposed by the anarchists. "Unlike the anarchists," he says, "we need the state." Thereupon he defines the state as the armed militia.

Again and again in those extraordinary letters, written in a state of exhaustion, we are made aware of a mind trying to break through the bars, to resolve the contradictions inherent in the Bolshevik state. With one breath he extols the "complete freedom" which will be brought about when the armed proletariat is in control, and with the next breath he insists on the establishment of the obligatory mobilization of labor, with every man performing the duties assigned to him by the state. One moment he is pouring scorn on the weaknesses of bourgeois society, which is "rotten to the core," and the next moment, following Marx, he salutes the splendors of the bourgeois state:

> We shall not be able to overthrow the new government with one blow, nor if we bring this about (the limits of the possible in revolutionary times are increased a thousandfold) shall we be able to retain power unless we set ourselves against the magnificent organization of the entire Russian bourgeoisie and the entire bourgeois intelligentsia with the no less magnificent *organization of the proletariat,* leading the entire boundless mass of the town and village poor, the semiproletariat and the small proprietors.

This is "all" language with a vengeance, but it has the merit of showing Lenin's second thoughts about "the rotten core" of the bourgeoisie. He saw readily enough that the strength of the bourgeoisie lay in its organization, and the weakness of the proletariat lay in its lack of organization. "The slogan of the hour," he continued, "must be *proletarian organization* now, on the eve of the revolution, and on the day after the revolution." He was not talking of the revolution which had taken place, but of the new and more glorious revolution when the armed workers were in power.

In the fourth "Letter from Afar," Lenin had recourse to his undoubted talent for vitriolic denunciation against no less a person than Maxim Gorky, who had mildly suggested in a letter addressed to the Provisional Government and the Petrograd Soviets that they should sue for an honorable peace. Humanity had bled enough. It was time to put an end to the war. Not peace at any price, but a peace which would enable Russians to live honorably in the eyes of the rest of the world. Lenin regarded honor as a bourgeois prejudice, and he attacked Gorky with all the vehemence at his command, with a heavy sarcasm which suggests a steamroller bearing down upon a captive butterfly:

> One has a bitter* feeling in reading such a letter, thoroughly permeated with common Philistine prejudices. There have been occasions when the writer of these lines during meetings with Gorky on the island of Capri has had to reproach him and warn him for his political errors. Gorky parried these reproaches with his inimitably sweet smile and the candid admission: "I know I am a bad Marxist. And then, you know, we artists are a bit irresponsible." It is not easy to argue against this.
>
> There is no doubt that Gorky possesses great artistic talent, which has been and will be of great use in the proletarian movement throughout the world.
>
> But why is Gorky meddling in politics?
>
> In my view, Gorky's letter expresses prejudices which are extremely prevalent among the petty bourgeoisie and also among a section of the workers influenced by the bourgeoisie. *The entire* strength of our party, the entire strength of the politically conscious workers must be directed toward a stubborn, persistent, and all round fight against these prejudices.
>
> The Tsarist government began and waged the present war as a predatory, imperialist war for spoliation, to rob and crush the weak nations. The government of the Guchkovs and Milyukovs is a landowners' and capitalists' government, which is forced to continue and wants to continue a war *of the very same character*. To come to that government with the suggestion that it should conclude a democratic peace—that is exactly the same as approaching the proprietor of a house of ill-fame with a sermon on virtue.

Thereupon Lenin sets out his own conditions for peace. First, the Soviets of Workers' Deputies should take power, then they should immediately propose to all the warring nations that an armistice should be concluded immediately. There followed a series of demands which were not likely to be acted upon and were evidently dictated by political considerations. He went on to insist that the colonies be liberated forthwith, and that the workers of all countries should immediately overthrow their bourgeois governments, "since nothing good can be expected from them." He demanded that all secret treaties should be published and all war debts canceled.

* Gorky means "bitter." Lenin was making a pun on the name.

There is something breath-taking in the sheer range which Lenin encompasses in a few lines. It is not enough that the war should end and that there should be peace; he must go on, further and further beyond the bounds of the possible, to the immediate liberation of the colonies and the overthrow of *all* existing governments. In his feverish mind the political developments which normally take decades and even centuries to accomplish were to be brought about in the space of a few weeks.

The peculiarly nihilistic character of Lenin's mind was never more in evidence than in the fourth "Letter from Afar," where the pattern of world revolution is outlined in six or seven lines, with no effort to trace the implications of his proposals or to examine cause and effect. The orders are uttered in the harsh tones of a sergeant on a German parade ground. Nor are they orders which affect Russia alone; the whole world is implicated. First, the Soviets of Workers' Deputies shall take power; then the war will end; then the world revolution will take place. On that simple theory he was to base his hopes; and indeed the theory had not changed since he wrote fifteen years before: "History has placed before us an immediate task which is far more revolutionary than the immediate tasks of the proletariat of any other country. . . . The Russian proletariat will be the vanguard of the international proletarian revolution."

He finished the fourth "Letter from Afar" on March 25, and then sent it to Stockholm to be transmitted to Petrograd. Ten days had passed since he had heard of the outbreak of the Russian revolution, but so far nothing had happened to justify his hopes that he would bring about the world revolution. He was still an almost penniless exile eating out his heart in a workman's house in Zurich.

THE SEALED TRAIN

ON THE DAY Lenin wrote his fourth "Letter from Afar" a telegram was received at the Foreign Ministry in Berlin from the German High Command. The telegram read: "No objections to the transit of Russian revolutionaries if effected in special train with reliable escort. Organization can be worked out between representatives of IIIb [Military Passport Office] and Foreign Ministry." From the tenor of the telegram, it would seem that the German High Command was only disturbed by the possibility that the revolutionaries would escape from the train and preach revolution in Germany.

In later years Robert Grimm and Fritz Platten were to claim credit for opening the negotiations which led to the transport of the revolutionaries across Germany, but when the German Imperial archives were opened, it was seen that many other people were involved on many levels of negotiation, and even today the intricate threads are tangled. The people involved in the negotiations ranged from the Kaiser to the obscure Georg Sklarz, one of the minions of Dr. Alexander Helphand, who made a special journey to Switzerland to discuss the project with Lenin. An element of farce surrounds the negotiations, for in fact the Germans were only too eager to arrange the transport of the revolutionaries, and if they sometimes went to some pains to conceal their eagerness, there were also moments when they were horribly frightened by the possibility that the revolutionaries would not rise to the bait.

The Germans understood very well what the revolutionaries were about. They were fully informed about the lives, the love affairs, and the political ideas of the exiles in Switzerland and they were equally well informed about conditions in Petrograd. It was their aim to bring the war on the eastern front to an end in the shortest possible time, and for their purposes none of the revolutionaries possessed better credentials than Lenin, who had sworn to bring the fighting to an end, if he obtained power, and to plunge Russia into a class struggle which would inevitably weaken the military posture of Russia still further. Grimm and Platten went through the motions of conducting negotiations, while Diego Bergen in his office in the Wilhelmstrasse cynically waited for the appropriate moment when it would serve the German interests best to hurl the revolutionaries like a bomb upon Petrograd.

Of all men Diego Bergen was probably the man most responsible for arranging the journey. He was a devout Roman Catholic, trained in Jesuit schools, and he seems to have possessed an instinctive understanding of the revolutionary mind. One of his special functions in the Foreign Office was to study the possibilities of sabotage and subversion, and vast sums of money were made available to him for this purpose. He knew everything that was to be known about Lenin, and was only waiting to spring the trap.

Lenin, however, was wary. He made no overt move to contact the Germans, and he forbade members of his party to contact them. He was still pondering the possibilities of returning to Russia through France and England, and though he was conscious of a desperate need to reach Petrograd, most of his mind seemed to be occupied with the developing pattern of the revolution and the theoretical basis for the second revolution that he hoped to lead, and the practical affair of somehow crossing the frontiers took second place after the first blaze of excitement.

At this juncture Diego Bergen made the first of a series of moves by sending Georg Sklarz as his emissary to Zurich. He arrived in Zurich on March 27 and immediately sought out Lenin. He came with full authority: Bergen had notified the German legation in Berne and the consulate at Zurich to give him every assistance. The plan seems to have been to smuggle Lenin and Zinoviev through Germany in disguise without informing the Swiss authorities. From the German point of view the plan had great advantages. There would be no publicity. Quietly, stealthily, provided with false papers of remarkable authenticity by IIIb, Lenin and Zinoviev would vanish from Switzerland and they would not come to the surface again until they reached Petrograd.

No record of Sklarz's meeting with Lenin has survived, and perhaps no record was ever made. Sklarz may simply have reported on the failure of his mission to Bergen, who thereupon set about devising better and more intricate traps. There was no question that Lenin wanted to leave Switzerland at once, but to be hurried across Germany in disguise, at the mercy of the German Foreign Office, was a prospect which left a good deal to be desired. There were, after all, advantages in publicity, especially in publicity which could be controlled and directed toward specific aims. He rejected Sklarz's offer for many reasons—chiefly, it seems, because of the secrecy involved. If he followed this plan, there was nothing to prevent the Germans from murdering him casually en route, nor was there anything to prevent the Provisional Government from learning of these private negotiations and then arresting him and sentencing him to death as a traitor; for he was still a Russian, and Russia was still at war with Germany.

On the same day as the conference with Sklarz, Lenin sent a telegram to his old follower Ganetsky in Stockholm. The telegram was written on the back of a letter to Karpinsky in Berne, who had instructions to send it off from the Berne telegraph office. It read: "Berlin permit inadmissible for me. Either Swiss Government accepts railway carriage to Copenhagen, or will reach agreement on exchange of all Russian *émigrés* for interned Germans." The words "to Copenhagen" were added in Krupskaya's handwriting. The reference to "the Berlin permit" probably reflects the negotiations with Sklarz. What is clear is that the official negotiations were still far from arriving at any useful conclusions.

March 27 was a busy day for Lenin. There were letters to write, important conferences to attend, and a speech to be given to a group of Swiss workmen on "The Russian Revolution, Its Significance and Aims." The speech had been arranged some days previously, and handbills with a brief summary of the ground to be covered had been prepared by Lenin in the careful handwriting he employed whenever his words were to be printed. At the bottom of the handbill was the statement that fifty per cent of the proceeds would be set aside for the support of *émigrés* suffering from tuberculosis.

The speech was delivered at 5:15 P.M. in a small dark hall at the People's House in Zurich. Only a brief summary of the speech appeared in newspapers, but Lenin's notes have survived. Where the *Letters from Afar* are often turgid, the essential ideas vanishing under the weight of theory, these notes have a quite extraordinary freshness and fervor. Here we find him thinking out the problems afresh, setting them briefly and pungently in their proper order. These notes should be quoted in full, because they provide the background for the far more famous "April Theses," which were to follow. The speech was delivered in German, and the four opening sentences of the notes were written in German, the rest in Russian:

1. The first stage of the first revolution.
2. Not the last revolution, but the last stage.
3. In three days overthrow of the monarchist government, which had lasted for hundreds of years and in the battles of 1905–1907 . . . [*words illegible*]
4. Miracle.

First Part

1. "The world has changed in three days."
2. "Miracle."
3. How could it be overthrown in 8 days?
   F o u r principal conditions:
4. — — (1) — The revolution in 1905–1907.
   (((It broke up the ground; revealed *all* the classes and parties; unmasked and isolated *Nicholas II* and *Co* (Rasputin).
5. — — (II) — — *Three* forces contributed to this revolution:
   — — ( )   Anglo-French finance capital
6. — — ( )   The entire bourgeoisie and the landowning-capitalist class of Russia
   (and the heads of the army)
7. — — —   ( ) The revolutionary proletariat and the revolutionary part of the army, the soldier.
8.   The three forces now:
   —   ( ) Tsarist monarchy; remnants of dynasty (counterrevolution in the south)
9.   —   ( ) The new government and the bourgeoisie
10.   —   ( ) *The Soviet of Workers' and Soldiers' Deputies.*
11. *Bread, peace, freedom* =
  =   Three basic demands.
12.   The new government *cannot* grant them . . .
13.

14.   *Three courses* in the Soviet of Workers' Deputies:
15.   Resolution on *Kerensky* etc.
16.   Vacillations of Chkheidze.
17.   Course of the C.C. PSDRP. Manifesto of C.C.

SECOND PART

18.   What to do? Where and how to proceed?
       To the Commune? Explain this.
19.   Analysis of the *situation*. Rapid change of situation *day
       before yesterday*—the greatest *illegality*. Appeal to revolu-
       tionary war. War against social-chauvinism.
       yesterday—maximum revolutionary heroism in the struggle.
       today—transition, organization
       tomorrow—new struggle.
20.   *Organization*—watchword of the day.
            What organization? Party? Syndicates? etc.
21.   *Soviet of Workers' Deputies*. Quid est Thesis No. 4.
22.   Our *"government."*
23.   The Paris Commune . . . Its essence.
24.   The teaching of Marx and Engels concerning government of
       a transitional type.
25.   The proletarian *militia*. What kind . . .
26.   — *they* need   "Not to let them
27.   — — and we, too.   reestablish the police"
28.   The revolutionary-democratic dictatorship of the proletariat
       and the peasantry . . .
29.   Peace? *How* (Gorky?)
30.   — Our conditions for peace.
31.   The step (passage) to socialism.
32.   Long live the Russian Revolution, long live the beginning of
       the world proletarian revolution.

As we read these notes, we seem to see Lenin pulling the revolution into shape, giving it order and purpose, building it step by step,
throwing over it the quick mantle of theory. It will be an amalgam of
the Petersburg Soviets and the Paris Commune: the essential bricks
are 1871 and 1905. He envisages a revolutionary war, and has no fear
of it. When he says "the greatest illegality," he means "the maximum
freedom" to operate within the Provisional Government regime; and
indeed the words "the maximum freedom" appear in his draft of the
"April Theses." "Bread, peace, freedom" are to become the slogans of
the hour, and he states categorically that the Provisional Government

cannot offer them, but he does not promise that his own government will offer them. Angelica Balabanoff, who heard the speech, was particularly struck with one sentence: "Unless the Russian Revolution develops into a second and successful Paris Commune, reaction and war will suffocate it."

This blueprint for a revolution was written at a time when he was still not completely sure whether he would be able to return to Russia.

The slow negotiations continued in an atmosphere of mounting tension. The Germans were willing, and the *émigrés* were willing; but both sides took pains to avoid appearing to be too willing. The German Minister in Berne grew alarmed. He wrote to the Wilhelmstrasse saying that although he had demonstrated his willingness to co-operate, not a single representative of the *émigrés* had come to call on him. It was not until April 3 that Fritz Platten, the secretary of the Swiss Social Democratic Party, contacted him, and suggested the formula that was finally adopted. Platten himself would take charge of the *émigrés;* the train must be assured extraterritorial rights; in return they would promise to make efforts in Russia to secure the release of a number of German prisoners. The *quid pro quo* had no binding effect and was never taken seriously. The essential elements of the formula were the sealed train and Platten acting as a neutral observer and guide. Platten raised with the Minister the question of how deeply the Russians would be compromised by traveling on a German train. It was a question which haunted Lenin, who in his curiously legalistic fashion arranged that a statement approving the journey should be drawn up and signed by leading French, German and Swiss socialists. Platten was instructed to see that all the *émigrés* signed a statement testifying that they understood the conditions under which they made the journey:

> I confirm
> 1)   that the conditions agreed upon in the negotiations between Platten and the German Legation have been made known to me;
> 2)   that I shall obey the orders of travel leader Platten;
> 3)   that I have been informed of a dispatch in the "Petit Parisien," stating that the Russian Provisional Government threatens to bring travelers through Germany to trial on charges of high treason;
> 4)   that I exclusively assume the entire political responsibility for the journey;
> 5)   that Platten has guaranteed my journey only as far as Stockholm. Berne-Zurich.   9 April 1917

Ich bestätige,

1) dass die eingegangenen Bedingungen, die von Platten mit der deutschen Gesandtschaft getroffen wurden, mir bekannt gemacht worden sind;

2) dass ich mich den Anordnungen des Reiseführers Platten unterwerfe;

3) dass mir eine Mitteilung des "Petit Parisien" bekanntgegeben worden ist, wonach die russische provisorische Regierung die durch Deutschland Reisenden als Hochverräter zu behandeln drohe,

4) dass ich die ganze politische Verantwortlichkeit für diese Reise ausschliesslich auf mich nehme;

5) dass mir von Platten die Reise nur bis Stockholm garantiert worden ist.

Bern - Zürich, 9. April 1917.

1	Lenin		G. Brillant
2	Frau Lenin	13	M. Kharitonov
3	Georg Safaroff		D. Rosenblum
4	Valentina Safaroff-Mostitchkine	14	A. Abramovitch
5	Gregor Ussijevitch		S. Scheinessohn
6	Helene Kon		Tskhakaya
7	Inès Armand		M. Gobermann
	Nikolai Boitzow	15	A. Linde
	F. Grebelsky		M. Aisenbud
8	A. Konstantinowitsch		Pripevsky
	E. Mirinhoff		Soulechvili
	M. Mirinhoff	16	Ravitsch
9	A. Skowno		
10	G. Zinoviev		*Charitonoff*
11	Z. Radomyslski (und Sohn)		
	D. Slussareff		
12	B. Eltchaninoff		

Such was the list of the Bolsheviks in the sealed train, which Fritz Platten published in facsimile in his short account of the journey. It is an intriguing list and deserves some study, for much has been said about this mysterious journey and a good deal of it is erroneous. There is no doubt about the authenticity of the list, but with few exceptions the names are not signatures. Most of the left-hand column is in Zinoviev's handwriting with his characteristic curlicues and spandrels; he always wrote *ff* in this way, and they are his florid capital letters. He has made only a cursory effort to make the names look like signatures.

Most of the names are readily identifiable. Georgy Safarov, Abraham Skovno, David Souliachvili, Helene Kon, and many others, present no difficulty. Brillant was the real name of Sokolnikov. Z. Radomyslsky is Zena Radomyslskaya, the wife of Zinoviev, who took the name of Radomyslsky. Ravitsch is Olga Ravich, while the Charitonoff who appears isolated at the bottom is simply the transliteration of the Russian name near the top of the column. Some Bundists may be included in the list. It is thought, for example, that D. Rosenblum and M. Aisenbud are Bundists, but there is little doubt that the rest are Bolsheviks. Of these Zinoviev, Sokolnikov, Safarov, and Slussarev went on to high positions, while others like Nikolay Boitsov, who served in the Central Political Education Department, played minor roles. Some like Grigory Ussievich, who played an outstanding role in the Moscow uprising in November, were killed later in the civil war, and others vanished into obscurity.

One name—the odd-looking Pripevsky, which appears in an uncertain handwriting toward the end of the list—at first sight presents an insoluble problem. No one has ever heard of a revolutionary named Pripevsky; one looks in vain through all the published catalogues of Bolshevik pseudonyms for anyone with a name which is so obviously invented. The clue however is to be found in Krupskaya's memoirs, where she gives a list of twenty-three of her fellow travelers and adds the useful information that Radek traveled under an assumed Russian name. Now *pripev* means "refrain of a song," and since Radek sang well and in addition was remarkably loquacious, Pripevsky is just the kind of name which Lenin in a caustic moment would give to him. He had no high opinion of Radek's talents; only a few months before in a letter to Inessa Armand he had described Radek as "an insufferable fool." But a good servant may be a fool and still be valuable to his master. So he was given a name which satisfied Lenin's sense of humor. In his own articles Radek gave himself a sterner pseudonym: he called himself "Parabellum."

Though the majority of the names are in the hand of Zinoviev, the numbers and the curious little scratchings are in Lenin's characteristic style. It is not clear what they signify. Some, like Mikha Tskhakaya, the Georgian revolutionary, were particularly close to Lenin, but the numbers before their names have been scratched out. These numbers may relate to a seating plan which was later abandoned.

When Lenin reached Russia he felt called upon to explain the circumstances which led him to cross Germany in the sealed train. In this brief account, which appeared in *Pravda*, he mentioned that, altogether, thirty-two political exiles were on the train, and of these, nineteen were Bolsheviks, six were Bundists, and three others belonged to the Menshevik paper *Nashe Slovo*, published in Paris. Presumably the remaining four were children, for the veteran revolutionary Mikha Tskhakaya remembered that there were a number of children on the train. Lenin's figures are evidently wrong, for at least twenty-five active Bolsheviks can be identified on the list which he helped to draw up. It would appear that he scaled down the number of Bolsheviks and added to the number of non-Bolsheviks to conceal the fact that the passengers were predominantly people he had chosen. At most only two or three non-Bolsheviks traveled with him.

The list gives every appearance of having been hurriedly put together while the exiles met for lunch at the Hotel Zahringer Hof at midday on April 9. The train was to leave at 3:10 P.M., and there was time only for last-minute arrangements and the reading of the rather lengthy letter which Lenin had composed the previous day. The letter was addressed to the Swiss workers. It paid tribute to the Swiss Social Democrats and announced the aims of his party, repeating words he had said many times before, but now he spoke them with a greater urgency. Once again he proclaimed that his revolutionary aim was "to turn the imperialist war into a civil war of the oppressed against the oppressors for the attainment of socialism," and once again he cursed the socialists who had thrown in their lot with the governments conducting the war. He prophesied that the Russian revolution was merely the beginning of a wave of revolutions which would reach far beyond the borders of Russia, and he paid a curious compliment to the German proletariat, describing them as "the most trustworthy and the most reliable ally of the Russian and the world proletarian revolution." But the meat of the letter lay in two paragraphs in the middle, in which he announced that the proletarian revolution in Russia was the herald of the world-wide revolution to come:

> To the Russian proletariat there has fallen the great honor of *beginning* the series of revolutions which have been caused, with objective inevitability, by the imperialist war. But the idea that the Russian proletariat is the chosen revolutionary proletariat in all other countries is absolutely alien to us. We know only too well that the Russian proletariat is *less* organized, prepared, and class conscious than the proletariat of other countries. No special qualities, but rather the special coincidence of historical circumstances have made the Russian proletariat *for a definite and perhaps very short period* the vanguard of the revolutionary proletariat of the whole world.
>
> Russia is a peasant country, and one of the most backward of European countries. Socialism cannot triumph there immediately. But the peasant character of the country with its tremendous acreage of lands still in the keeping of the aristocratic landowners *may very well*, if we judge from the experience of 1905, give tremendous scope to the bourgeois-democratic revolution in Russia and make our revolution the *prologue* to the world socialist revolution, bringing it *a step nearer*.

Such was his farewell letter to the Swiss workers, which was addressed to them only in the most perfunctory way, for in fact it was addressed to the whole world. In a German translation the letter appeared in the Swiss socialist paper *Jugend Internationale*, and later in the year, in September, Plekhanov published it for the first time in Russian, in *Yedinstvo* (Unity), as a warning of the mischief of which

Lenin was capable. Lenin was perfectly aware that he was up to mischief, for throughout the letter he gives the impression of a man already basking in the fires of revolution and warming his hands over the flames. "The revolution will not be limited to Russia," he said ominously, and he looked forward to the time when the European and the American socialist proletariat would drown the bourgeoisie in blood.

The letter was read at the lunch table chiefly for the benefit of the few Swiss Social Democrats who were present. Then Platten gave Lenin three thousand Swiss francs, explaining that the money, to be used for expenses on the journey, had come from the co-operatives. Lenin had raised another thousand francs, and with this four thousand it was thought that he would be able to meet any eventualities which might arise on the long journey to Petrograd. One oddly unpleasant event occurred at the lunch table. A certain Dr. Oscar Blum, a member of the Social Democratic Party, wanted to come on the train. Lenin was against it, suspecting rightly or wrongly that he was a police spy. It was one of the rare occasions when Lenin offered to settle a matter by democratic vote. Accordingly, a vote was taken; eleven voted for Dr. Blum, and fourteen against. He was told that on no account would he be allowed to accompany them on the sealed train. At 2:30 P.M. they set out for the station, a small motley crowd, looking as if they were going to a picnic, with their baskets, string bags and hastily improvised parcels. Platten had arranged a ten-day supply of food, but this had already been sent to the station.*

For some reason Platten had thought it would be a perfectly simple matter for the exiles to board the train, but their leave-taking was turbulent. Already the rumor was being spread that Lenin was being paid by the Germans. A group of about fifty Russian exiles was waving banners protesting against the journey. Lenin saw the banners and smiled grimly. He wore a derby hat, the heavy coat which served

---

* There is still some doubt about the exact number of people who made the journey in the sealed train. Mikha Tskhakaya in his reminiscences says there were thirty-six, Lenin gives thirty-two, and Brockdorff-Rantzau, the German Minister in Copenhagen, telegraphed that thirty-three arrived in Malmö in a dispatch to the Wilhelmstrasse. Fritz Platten gives thirty names. Krupskaya lists: Lenin, Krupskaya, the Zinovievs, the Ussieviches, Inessa Armand, the Safarovs, Olga Ravich, Abramovich from La Chaux-de-Fonds, Grebelsky, Kharitonov, Linde, Rosenblum, Boitsov, Mikha Tskhakaya, the Marienhoffs, Sokolnikov, Radek under an assumed name, Robert (son of a Bundist woman) and Fritz Platten. David Shub in his biography of Lenin says, "The party included some twenty non-Bolsheviks. Lenin had insisted on their traveling with him in order to offset the unfavorable impression produced by his trip under German auspices." But no authority for this statement can be found.

for winter and summer, and the famous thick-soled hobnailed boots which the shoemaker Kammerer had made for him; and he carried an umbrella, which proved to be a useful weapon when a near-riot broke out on the platform. The Bolsheviks sang the "Internationale," but there were so many cries of "German spies!" and "The Kaiser is paying for the journey!" that they had to break off. Platten, small and slender, was fighting a man twice his size, but he was able to slip on the train without serious damage. There were a few well-wishers. Siegfried Bloch, the Swiss socialist, ran up to Lenin, grasped his hand, and said, "I hope to see you soon back again among us, comrade." Lenin answered, "H'm, if we come back soon it won't be a good sign for the revolution." He settled down in a second-class compartment with Krupskaya, and he was about to take out his note pad when someone told him that Dr. Oscar Blum had calmly taken a seat in the same carriage. Lenin was incensed. He jumped up, hurled himself out of the compartment, found the doctor, and pushed him off the train. At the last moment Ryazanov, a close friend of Trotsky, came running onto the platform, and seeing Zinoviev at the window he shouted, "Lenin is out of his mind! He doesn't realize what a dangerous situation it is! You're more sensible! Tell him to stop this mad journey through Germany!" Zinoviev smiled. He had carefully considered the dangers, and he had absolute faith in Lenin's star. There were no speeches, and no photographs were taken. The train pulled out of the station at exactly 3:10 P.M. The disconsolate group of exiles on the platform folded up the banners and drifted away.

Although the Swiss and German governments were both involved in organizing the journey in the sealed train, and the necessary decisions had been made on the highest levels, they were both obscurely aware that the consequences were unforseeable, and perhaps dangerous. All that day government telegrams were flying across Europe concerning the fate of those strange wayfarers. Early in the morning the German Minister at Berne dispatched a telegram to the Foreign Ministry in Berlin, saying that all preparations had been made, but it was absolutely necessary that the Russian exiles have no communication with Germans during the journey, otherwise they would be in grave danger of arrest by the Provisional Government when they reached Russia. He urged that the German press say nothing of the affair "unless it becomes known abroad," and it was especially necessary to keep silent about Swiss participation, no doubt because the Entente would not look favorably on a maneuver which owed much to a close working agreement between the Swiss and German govern-ments.

While the train was steaming toward the frontier, another tele-gram was sent to the Wilhelmstrasse by the Minister in Berne, em-phasizing that the exiles had taken no steps to procure permission to travel in Sweden. "They therefore rely absolutely on the action we have requested." This can only mean that the Germans were to use their good offices with the Swedish government to allow passage through Sweden, and had not yet done so. It was a perplexing matter, of sufficient importance to warrant the attention of the Kaiser, who had been kept informed about the various *démarches* made on behalf of Lenin. Characteristically he had a very simple solution for the prob-lem. He suggested that if the Swedes refused to co-operate it would be a comparatively simple matter to send the Russian exiles, and the others who had remained in Switzerland, through the German lines. Even more characteristically, he suggested that the Russians travel-ing through Germany should be presented with his own Easter Mes-sage to the German People, the German Chancellor's latest speech, and assorted White Papers, "so that they may be able to enlighten others in their own country." Nothing came of the Kaiser's suggestions, which were made over breakfast on the morning of April 12, for by that time the Swedish government had officially granted its permis-sion. We shall never know Lenin's reaction to the Kaiser's Easter Mes-sage, for it was never shown to him. Diego Bergen, or one of the other officials who were in charge of the journey, may have hinted tactfully that Lenin was in no mood to digest the official pronouncements of the German Reich.

It was a strange journey, and though Krupskaya described it as uneventful, strange things were continually happening. At the fron-tier the Swiss customs officers commandeered most of the food sup-plies, mainly sugar and chocolate, which had been given to them by Platten. No explanations were offered. The Germans behaved even more capriciously. They herded all the exiles into the customs shed, separated the men from the women, and kept them waiting for about half an hour. They all thought they would be arrested, and Radek, who was an Austrian subject and a deserter, expected to be stood up against a wall and shot. They thought Lenin would be the first to be arrested, and for this reason he was kept as much as possible out of sight. He stood near a wall with his friends forming a hedge round him, hiding him. No one ever discovered the cause of this curious action. No doubt telegrams were being exchanged between Schaff-hausen and Berlin; messages had failed to arrive on time; and Lenin was confronted with one more example of the inefficiency of the Germans, whom he had always regarded as models of efficiency. Suddenly they were ordered into the train, and the journey through Germany began.

It was agreed that Lenin and Krupskaya should have a compartment to themselves; in this way Lenin would be able to work quietly. At first he objected, but later he accepted with good grace. In the compartment next to him sat Safarov and his wife, Inessa Armand, Olga Ravich and Radek, who sang and told jokes and exchanged banter with Olga Ravich. He was an amusing companion, with a prodigious gift for small talk. With his side whiskers and curly hair and horn-rimmed spectacles he resembled a monkey; and his delicate nervous hands were continually weaving gestures. Olga Ravich laughed so loud at his jokes that Lenin, who could never work amid noise, decided that he could put up with it no longer. He marched into the compartment, took her hand, and led her without a word into another compartment. Characteristically, Lenin was punishing the wrong person. For the rest of the journey Radek spoke in whispers.

The Bolsheviks generally smoked incessantly; Lenin felt suffocated amid the fumes of tobacco. When the carriage became thick with cigarette smoke, Lenin decided that he had had enough of it, and he ordered that there should be no smoking except in the lavatory. Then it became obvious that there would be a rush for the lavatory, and to prevent this he wrote out tickets permitting the bearer one visit to the lavatory. The legality of his action was discussed, and someone suggested that it was a pity that Bukharin was absent, for he possessed a masterly sense of the limits of the permissible and impermissible. The discussion was brief, and Lenin's law prevailed. No one suspected at the time that the tickets to the lavatory were a strange forewarning of the system he would impose upon Russia.

While Lenin wrote, Krupskaya gazed out of the window, and when they came to villages and towns she was shocked to see how few grown-up men there were; there were only old men and old women in the fields. All the youth of Germany had vanished. They seemed to be crossing a desert, a land drained of its wealth by the war. To impress them, they were fed excellent meals, but they had only to look out of the window to know that Germany was starving. The train was a kind of Potemkin village on wheels, deliberately designed to give an impression of a victorious nation; but the exiles knew poverty when they saw it. Meanwhile Lenin shrank deeper and deeper into himself, living only for the moment when he reached Russia. Sometimes he would discuss with his companions how many days they expected to live, for while part of his brain told him he would lead the proletariat of the world in a successful revolution, another part told him he would be hanged when he stepped off the train in Petrograd.

The Germans kept their bargain; the Russians were effectively sealed off from the Germans, and they were able to boast afterward that there had been not one word of conversation between them. Platten alone talked with them; he alone was permitted to leave the train to buy the newspapers, which the travelers consumed in large quantities, and the beer, which Lenin and Zinoviev delighted in. It was a slow journey, with inexplicable pauses and shuntings; they were delayed at Karlsruhe, and again at Frankfurt, where they were told they had missed a connection. Here Platten made his purchases and incautiously went off to visit a woman in the town, telling two German soldiers to carry the beer and the newspapers into the train. The soldiers boarded the train, met Radek, and were at once greeted with a vehement call to revolution, which was interrupted only by the appearance of some German officers. The incident might have had severe consequences, but Radek fled to the compartment next to Lenin's, and nothing more was heard of it.

At Berlin they were again shunted into a siding, and these mysterious delays, which seemed to be growing longer, found their explanation only when the archives of the German Foreign Ministry were opened. Then it became clear that German efficiency had once more broken down, for the German Minister in Stockholm had received from the Swedish government the permission for the exiles to cross Sweden on the afternoon of the tenth, while on the morning of the twelfth high officials were still discussing when permission would be granted. The telegram was evidently mislaid and not discovered until late in the morning. By midday the exiles were on their way to the coastal port of Sassnitz, which they reached late in the evening. The Germans expected them to spend the night at Sassnitz. According to an ominous Foreign Ministry telegram, "Good accommodation has been assured for them there, in a locked room."

The German attitude toward the exiles was one of total expediency. The High Command favored the journey only because they looked forward to the collapse of the Russian front as a result of the propaganda of the revolutionaries. They did not care how the collapse was brought about, and they made no calculation of the consequences if Lenin came to power. They were cynically detached from the whole affair; they were prepared to make agreements and break them. They had promised the revolutionaries that there would be no contact with Germans during the journey, and they broke the promise twice: first in Karlsruhe, and then in Berlin, when they permitted German Social Democrats to board the train. In this way they hoped to find out more about Lenin's intentions. In this they failed. Lenin resolutely refused to see them, saying, "They can go to the devil!" The boy, Robert, the "son of a Bundist woman," was the only one who spoke to them. He went up to the Germans in Berlin and said in French, "Who is the conductor of the train?" They are the only words known to have been exchanged between the Russians and the Germans during the journey in the sealed train.

After Berlin, the Germans made no more effort to influence the exiles. On the whole they had behaved with propriety; they had sent special supplies of milk to the train for the children; they had cared for their comfort and had religiously kept to their own compartments in the carriage, never stepping over the chalk line drawn across the corridor which effectively separated Russia from Germany. With the journey nearly over, they were already congratulating themselves on their success and preparing to send more revolutionaries across Germany.

In the locked room at Sassnitz the exiles spent their last night on German soil, and in the morning they took the ferryboat to Sweden.

The long journey in the sealed train was over.

THE FINLAND STATION

Y AKOV GANETSKY was a man of considerable resourcefulness, who could always be relied upon to send accurate reports and press an advantage. Born in Austrian Galicia in 1879, he had
joined the Social Democratic Party at the age of seventeen. Later he
attended the early Stockholm and London conferences as a delegate
from the Polish and Lithuanian section of the party, and Lenin had
been impressed by his flair for revolutionary and conspiratorial activities ever since they met in Cracow in 1903. Lenin had appointed him
to the post of foreign correspondent of the party with his base in
Stockholm. From there he directed Bolshevik propaganda in Sweden and acted as the intermediary between Lenin and Russia; for
though no messages could be sent directly from Switzerland to Russia,
there was nothing to prevent Lenin from sending messages to neutral
Sweden with the knowledge that they would be forwarded to Petrograd.

When the February revolution broke out, Lenin largely relied on
Ganetsky to accomplish the miracle of getting him out of Switzerland.
To Ganetsky went a long series of messages, culminating in the tri-
umphant telegram of April 7:

> TWENTY OF US ARE LEAVING TOMORROW. LINDHAGEN
> AND STRÖM MUST MEET US WITHOUT FAIL AT TRELLEBORG—
> ULYANOV.

This telegram, with its imperious command that the two most important Social Democratic members of the Swedish parliament should

meet the exiles at a small port on the tip of Sweden, was a false alarm. Too busy in Berne and Zurich, Lenin completely forgot to send a following telegram, and Ganetsky was left pondering what action to take, and especially whether the two members of parliament could be induced to spend one or two days at Trelleborg waiting for the ferryboat. He calculated that if the exiles left on the eighth, they would arrive at Trelleborg on the evening of the eleventh. On that day he left his office in Stockholm in charge of his wife and took the train for Malmö, an hour's journey from Trelleborg. The ferryboat arrived and tied up at the wharf, but there was no sign of Lenin or the exiles. He returned to Malmö and spent another day and a night waiting for a message that never came. By this time he was very nearly convinced that Lenin had been taken off the train and shot by the Germans. He was already losing all hope of seeing Lenin again when on the afternoon of the thirteen he decided upon a ruse. Pretending to be a delegate of the Red Cross, he convinced the chief officer of the port that he was in charge of the arrangements for welcoming the exiles and in need of information about their numbers so that hotel accommodation could be provided for them. The port officer sent a radio message to the captain of the ferryboat: "Mr. Ganetsky would like to know whether Mr. Ulyanov is on board, and how many men, women, and children there are."

Twenty minutes later the ferryboat signaled to shore: "Mr. Ulyanov greets Mr. Ganetsky, and begs him to buy railroad tickets for x men, women, and children." Ganetsky forgot the number when he came to write his reminiscences.

He ran to the telephone, called friends in Malmö and his wife in Stockholm, bought the train tickets and set about finding a suitable place for them to eat. His wife had just received a telegram reading TODAY 6 P.M. TRELLEBORG—ULYANOV. This was the telegram which was later to become famous as the first indication that Lenin had safely crossed Germany, but it was not the first message received from him.

Ganetsky went down to the wharf at Trelleborg to wait for them. The ferryboat was delayed. There were high seas, many of the exiles were seasick, but Lenin, Zinoviev, Radek and Mikha Tskhakaya sensibly avoided the small stateroom of the Swedish ferryboat and stood on the bridge with the captain. Their real names were not included on the ship's manifest, and the captain was puzzled when Ganetsky's telegram arrived. He asked whether there was a Mr. Ulyanov on board. Lenin, who had feared arrest from the moment he crossed the German border and continued to fear arrest until he reached Petrograd, was alarmed. It occurred to him that a message must have been received from the Swedish police, and he went down to his cabin to stave off for a little while longer the inevitable moment when he would have to declare himself. As Ganetsky tells the story, "He realized there was nothing to be gained by hiding any longer, and he could hardly escape by jumping into the sea. So he admitted that he was Mr. Ulyanov." It was dusk when the ferryboat pulled into the wharf. One by one they came down the gangplank, gray with fatigue and green with seasickness, carrying their baskets and string parcels, while the children wept and their mothers tried to comfort them; and no one seeing that straggling crowd on the wharf in the gray light of a Baltic evening would have guessed they were conquerors who would soon take Russia by storm.

There was no time to lose. The train for Malmö was due to leave in fifteen minutes. Ganetsky, with his customary resourcefulness, had brought with him a copy of the issue of *Politiken* which bore Lenin's photograph with the inscription that he was the leader of the Russian revolution, and he had taken care to show this to the customs officers. They were suitably impressed. They asked him to point Lenin out to them and waived the examination of the Russians' luggage. Then they were all gathered into the train for the short ride to Malmö, where Swedish Social Democrats had prepared a feast of *smörgåsbord* for them. Worn out by more than four days of travel, they ate ravenously. But there was little time for eating, and soon they were leaving the little restaurant near the railroad station and climbing back on the train which would take them to Stockholm.

It was a long journey, and Lenin was mortally tired, but in no mood for sleeping. Half the night he talked and asked questions, read newspapers, discussed the revolutionary situation in Russia, and outlined his plans for a proletarian revolution which would follow the bourgeois revolution of February as the night follows the day. Ganetsky remembered that he pointed particularly to Kerensky as a man to be watched because he could do most harm to the party; and Ganetsky was a little puzzled, for Kerensky had not yet achieved a position of great prominence. Lenin spoke too of the need to establish "at all costs" a strong bureau in Stockholm, so that the Leninist section of the

Social Democratic Party would be able to maintain contact with the outside world. At four o'clock in the morning he was at last prevailed upon to sleep.

He slept little. At eight o'clock a small army of newspaper correspondents boarded the train. Lenin was awakened, but he refused to see them. They were told that a press release would be issued when they reached Stockholm.

At nine o'clock the train steamed into the railroad station at Stockholm. A red flag hung in the waiting room, there were brief speeches by Karl Lindhagen and Ture Nerman, whom Lenin had last seen at the Zimmerwald Conference, and then they were all taken to the Hotel Regina. Lenin's first task was to draw up an account of the journey, signed by all the members of the party; once again he wanted it especially to be known that there had been no contact with the Germans. There was a series of hurried conferences. A message had been sent to Chkheidze, asking about the attitude of the Provisional Government toward Lenin's return: the reply had just come in that all Social Democrats would be welcomed except those who were not Russian citizens. Radek and Fritz Platten by this time regarded themselves as Russians and decided to continue the journey with Lenin; they reached Tornio, and were then turned back.

All that day Lenin was on the move. He went into bookshops and came out with arms full of books. He attended a meeting of Russian exiles including Mensheviks, Socialist Revolutionaries, Bundists and anarchists. Dr. Helphand asked for a private meeting, but was rebuffed. Lenin knew he was a German agent, and in fact immediately after this rebuff Helphand left Stockholm for Berlin, where he reported to the Foreign Ministry. Lenin was so anxious to give the appearance that he had had no contact with the Germans that he asked Ganetsky and the Swedish members of parliament to sign a statement that he had refused to see Dr. Helphand. This was done, and the statement was duly signed and placed in the archives of the Swedish Social Democratic Party.

The exiles looked so drab in their well-worn clothes that it was decided to furnish them with new outfits. Characteristically Lenin rebelled; he refused to buy new clothes, claiming that nothing was to be gained by dressing up like a dandy, and his own clothes served him well enough. Radek insisted that he should at least buy a new pair of boots, since the old ones were calculated to destroy the streets of Petrograd. Lenin relented, and bought a pair of boots. Working upward, Radek pointed to his worn trousers, his coat, his tie, his shirt, and the much-loved derby hat which was carefully cleaned every spring. Lenin argued, though he knew he was defending a lost cause. He refused to buy a new coat, but he did buy a new hat of soft black felt with a ribbon round it.

The film cameramen were waiting for the Bolsheviks in one of the main streets, and there exists a short film strip showing Lenin and Karl Lindhagen leading a small procession of exiles. Lenin carries his rolled-up umbrella and is walking with great strides to keep up with the six-foot-tall Lindhagen. Krupskaya follows, looking a little like a sack of potatoes crowned with one of the wheel-shaped hats fashionable at the time. They give the impression of people who have very little time to spare.

Lenin decided to take the evening train to Finland. There was not a moment to lose, for he had been reading the Russian newspapers, and especially *Pravda*, and he was convinced that the time was ripe for a more vigorous propaganda than the Social Democrats were conducting in Russia. He was incensed by their moderation. It was time to act forcefully; he was especially enraged by an article by Kamenev which showed not the slightest indication that he understood the urgency of the times. He was in such a hurry to go that he scarcely listened to the speeches of the Swedish party members at a feast in his honor.

They had been on the move continually; for three more days they were to be cooped up in trains before reaching Petrograd. The slow journey around the Gulf of Bothnia was pure misery for Lenin who read, took notes, and gazed helplessly out of the window. The biggest shock came at Tornio, on the frontier between Sweden and Finland. There were British as well as Russian soldiers guarding the frontier post. According to Mikha Tskhakaya, the British were in no mood to let them through. They were led off one by one to be interrogated, their luggage was examined, and they were compelled to fill out a questionnaire. Lenin's questionnaire has been found. Asked to state his religion, he replied diplomatically that he belonged to the Orthodox faith. The questionnaire reads:

Name, patronymic, surname, rank: Vladimir Ilyich Ulyanov
Last residence: Stockholm (Sweden) (Hotel Regina, Stockholm)
Age, nationality, religion: Born April 10, 1870 in Simbirsk; Russian; Orthodox

For what purpose did you go abroad?: Political refugee. Left Russia
    illegally.
Give address and purpose of visit if stopping in Finland: No intention
    of stopping in Finland.
To what city are you going? Give address: Petrograd. Sister's address:
    Maria Ilyinichna Ulyanova, Shirokaya St. 48/9, Apt. 24.
Profession: Journalist
Signature: Vladimir Ulyanov

His replies were considered satisfactory, and on the back of the
questionnaire it was noted that he had received a travel permit from
the Russian Consul General in Stockholm. It remained only to send a
telegram to Maria Ilyinichna:

ARRIVING MONDAY EVENING ELEVEN O'CLOCK. TELL PRAVDA

ULYANOV.

Now at last after many delays they were free to enter Russia.
Lenin, who had been calm throughout the interrogations, was now
visibly excited, and he burst out laughing. There was a note of triumph
in his laughter. He turned to Mikha Tskhakaya, embraced him and
said, "Our trials are over, Comrade Mikha! We are in our own country
now, and we'll show them we are the worthy masters of the future!"
As he said these words, he shook his fist.

They were in Finland, but in those days Finland still belonged to
Russia, and the evidence of Russian domination was all around them.
"Everything was already familiar and dear to us," Krupskaya wrote.
"There were the rickety third-class compartments and the Russian
soldiers. It made you feel so good to see them." The Russian soldiers
were gregarious; they wandered up and down the train and invaded
Lenin's compartment. The boy Robert was with them—he had been
the apple of Krupskaya's eye throughout the journey—and now he
was throwing his arms round the neck of a bearded soldier, chatter-
ing away in French and eating the sweet *kulitch* cake which the
soldier had given him to celebrate Easter, for this day was Easter Sunday according to the Russian calendar. And whenever they came to
a station Grigory Ussievich would put his head out of the window and
shout, "Long live the world revolution!" to the bemused soldiers standing on the platform.

Lenin held his first political rally on Russian soil while the train
was taking them to Petrograd. Mikha Tskhakaya was deputed to explain to the soldiers in the compartment the purpose of their return

to Russia, and what they intended to do. The soldiers argued among themselves, and some spoke bitterly about the sufferings caused by the war. A pale lieutenant watched silently, and when Krupskaya and Lenin took refuge in an empty compartment he sat down beside them; he wanted to know why they were against the Provisional Government and why they were in favor of peace, when as good Russians they should know that they must make war against the detestable Germans. If the lieutenant was pale, Lenin was equally pale: he was exhausted by the journey, and from time to time he would remember that the officer might arrest him and hand him over for trial to a military court. Soon soldiers began to flock into the compartment, all crowding round him, some standing on the benches in order to see him better as he denounced the "predatory war of the imperialists" and demanded an end to it. So the day passed in argument and counter-argument, and by nightfall Lenin felt safe in the knowledge that he had won over the soldiers, though he had failed to convince the lieutenant.

It was nearly eleven o'clock at night when the train steamed into Belo-Ostrov on the frontier of Finland and Russia, where the train was usually held up for half an hour for customs inspection. Lenin peered out of the window at the dimly lighted platform, surprised to see a milling crowd of workmen. There were about a hundred of them, and they were shouting his name. Then he saw Kamenev, Shlyapnikov, Alexandra Kollontay and Maria Ilyinichna, and wondered what they were doing there, until Shlyapnikov came into the compartment and said he had received a telegram from Ganetsky the previous day; all the Bolsheviks in Petrograd had been warned of his coming, and the factory workers of Sestroretsk had decided to welcome him at the frontier. Lenin was still nervous and asked whether he would be arrested when he reached Petrograd. They smiled. They had reason to smile, for they had arranged such a reception for him that it was unthinkable that the police would dare to arrest him. More and more Bolsheviks entered the compartment. In later years Stalin liked to imagine he was one of them and he commissioned a whole series of paintings showing Lenin descending from the train at Belo-Ostrov, with himself standing a little above him. All official accounts of the revolution thereafter included the statement that Stalin was the first to greet Lenin when he returned from abroad. In time Stalin even came to believe that he was present, and speaking of himself in the third person he would mention that Stalin had welcomed Lenin to

Russia. He was not there, or if he was, no one saw him, for there is no reference to his being there until he began to rewrite the history books.

The workers insisted that Lenin should come out on the platform. Reluctantly, he permitted himself to be carried on their shoulders into the waiting room. In all his life he had never received such treatment before, and he was a little annoyed. "Be careful, comrades," he kept saying. "Gently there, comrades!" They set him down and demanded that he make a speech. It was a very short speech, in which he said there must be an end to the imperialist butchery and he called upon the workmen to unite against the Provisional Government. The workers made a close ring round him, to hide him from the police. This was the same maneuver which had been employed when he was crossing the frontier of Germany at Schaffhausen, and it was strange that it was being employed again now that he was twenty miles from Petrograd. Alexander Afanasiev, a middle-aged munitions worker from Sestroretsk, was present at this meeting in the waiting room. "While we were surrounding him we were as happy as children," he wrote later. But they could not surround him for long. The passport officers ordered all the passengers into the passport office. It was the last hurdle to be crossed, and Lenin was keenly aware of the dangers which lurked there, among those uniformed bureaucrats who were also agents of the secret police. However his visa, stamped by the Russian Consul General in Stockholm, was in order, and he was told to return to the train. The workers were still milling about the platform, and when Lenin appeared at the window they shouted and waved their caps. The train steamed out of the station, while the exiles sang the "Internationale" at the top of their voices. They were still not sure what fate awaited them in Petrograd.

There is a sense in which Lenin's triumphant reception at Belo-Ostrov was the beginning of his conquest of Russia. It was a strange beginning, because although the workers knew his name they had no idea what he looked like and did not recognize him until he was pointed out to them. They had read one of his *Letters from Afar* in *Pravda;* they had heard rumors about a man of iron will who had lived in exile and dedicated his life to the Russian revolution; but there was scarcely one of them who could claim to know more about him. Other Bolsheviks in Petrograd, even those who occupied high positions in the party, knew him only as a legendary figure whose occasional articles offered astonishingly simple solutions to complex problems. He had been absent from Russia for more than ten years, and he had only a small following. Yet from the moment he entered Russia he was recognized as a potential leader. Why?

The clue perhaps lies in the words he addressed to Kamenev when they met in the railroad car at Belo-Ostrov. Three weeks before Kamenev had arrived in Petrograd from his Siberian exile to take up the editorship of *Pravda*. He was normally a calm and gentle person, hating and perhaps despising all extremists, and he represented the middle road within the party. There was no warmth in Lenin's greeting to him. In a rage he shouted, "What is this you have been writing in *Pravda?* We read a few numbers and gave you a thorough cursing!" Lenin was the "one who cursed," the avenger, the judge who discovers the guilty and punishes them. He had come from his mysterious exile to exact vengeance on the criminals who prolonged the war for their own profit; and his rasping voice announcing the coming of the socialist revolution was a voice of protest and condemnation. Everyone was searching for a scapegoat; only Lenin had found it. The scapegoat was the entire state, and he had come to destroy the state.

It is only in this way that we can understand the extraordinary reception he received at Belo-Ostrov and Petrograd. The party workers had of course staged these receptions, and they commanded powerful resources, but there was no doubt of the genuine excitement and enthusiasm caused by his coming. He represented in his person an attitude toward the war and toward society which found powerful echoes among the workers who were dissatisfied by the small successes of the February revolution and wanted a clean break with the past. To them his coming was providential, and he could not have timed it better, for the Easter holiday left the workers free to spend the day preparing for his arrival.

Shlyapnikov had done his work well. He sent out couriers to the Baltic fleet, urging them to send an honor guard to the station. Trucks went out to the workers' quarters, summoning the workers, for no newspapers were being published that day. Workmen took over the Finland Station, mounting red banners. There were triumphal arches, and these too were adorned with red and gold ribbons inscribed with revolutionary slogans. Some armored cars, based on the Kshesinskaya Palace, where the Bolsheviks had installed their headquarters, were ordered to the station square, and the men in charge of the searchlights on the spire of the Peter and Paul Fortress were given instructions to throw the searchlights on the square at a given signal. It was arranged that a band should be standing at the end of the platform exactly at the place where Lenin would descend from the train. Co-ordinating committees were set up. For more than twenty-four hours the Bolsheviks were busy preparing for the arrival of the obscure theoretician who had been traveling across Europe for seven days, haunted by the thought that he would be arrested the moment he stepped off the train at the Finland Station.

When the train at last steamed into the station, Lenin was dumfounded to see the platform filled with soldiers and sailors standing rigidly at attention under the command of their officers. The Moscow and Preobrazhensky regiments, the Red Guards, and the Baltic sailors were all represented. Behind them surged a crowd of workers with banners, and in the square outside and in the streets leading to the square there were columns of workers holding up banners and torches. Most of them had been waiting for hours. They were exhausted and impatient, in that mood of expectancy and excitement which can precede a riot. They were very close to a riot. If Lenin had said "Burn down the Winter Palace" when he stepped onto the platform, the palace would have been burned.

At 11:10 P.M. Lenin stepped onto the platform, and whatever he said was drowned out by the sudden blare of the band playing the "Marseillaise." An elegant young ensign named Maximov, in charge of the detachment of Baltic sailors, was the first to welcome him to Petrograd. Maximov saluted smartly, and to his own surprise Lenin found himself returning the salute. Accompanied by Maximov he walked down the line of Baltic sailors; he seemed not to see them, and he made no reply when the young ensign expressed the polite hope that he, Lenin, would join the Provisional Government. The ensign chattered away; the band played; people shouted greetings; and as he walked under the triumphal arches Lenin seemed oddly stiff and numb, as though he could not understand what was happening and did not want to understand, for he detested ceremonies. There was worse to come when he was taken into the former imperial waiting room where Chkheidze, Skobolev and Sukhanov, representing the Petrograd Soviet, were waiting for him. Sukhanov, one of the most brilliant journalists of his time, described the meeting in his diary:

> We had to wait for a long time because the train was very late, but at long last it arrived. There came the thunderous roar of the "Marseillaise" from the platform, and people shouting their welcome. We could hear them marching along the platform under the triumphal arches, be-

tween the rows of workers and soldiers and sailors, and the band kept playing. Chkheidze, looking very gloomy, got up, and we all followed him to the middle of the room, where we waited to receive Lenin. And what a reception it was—worthy of a better pen than mine.

Shlyapnikov, the acting master of ceremonies, appeared at the doorway, hurrying portentously, looking for all the world like a well-trusted police chief announcing the arrival of the governor. Without any apparent necessity, he was continually shouting pompously, "Please, comrades, please! Make way there, comrades! Please make way!"

Following Shlyapnikov there was a small group of people with Lenin at the head, and the door slammed behind them. Lenin came, or rather ran, into the Tsar's waiting room, wearing a round hat, his face frozen with cold, and carrying a magnificent bouquet of flowers. Dashing to the center of the room, he came to an abrupt halt in front of Chkheidze as though he had encountered an entirely unexpected obstacle. Thereupon Chkheidze, still looking very gloomy, pronounced the following "welcoming speech," consistently maintaining not only the letter and the spirit but also the tone of a moralizing sermon:

"Comrade Lenin, in the name of the Petrograd Soviet of Workers' and Soldiers' Deputies and the whole revolution we welcome you to Russia . . . but we believe that the principal task of the revolutionary democracy at present is to defend our revolution from every kind of attack both from within and from without. We believe that what is needed is not disunity but the closing of the ranks of the entire democracy. We hope you will pursue these aims together with us."

Chkheidze paused. I was overcome by the unexpectedness of the thing. What attitude could Lenin possibly adopt toward that "welcome" and the magnificent "but"? Lenin apparently knew very well what attitude to adopt. He stood there with the expression of a man who is watching events which do not concern him in the least, kept looking from one side to the other, peered into the faces of the onlookers and even at the ceiling of the imperial waiting room while rearranging his bouquet (which harmonized rather badly with his whole appearance), and then turning completely away from the delegates of the Executive Committee, he "replied" as follows:

"Dear comrades, soldiers, sailors and workers! I am happy to greet in your persons the victorious Russian revolution! I greet you as the vanguard of the world proletarian army. The predatory imperialist war is the beginning of a civil war all over Europe. The hour is not far off when at the call of our comrade Karl Liebknecht the people will turn their weapons against the capitalist exploiters. The sun of the world socialist revolution has already risen. In Germany there is a seething ferment. Any day now we shall see the collapse of European imperialism. The Russian revolution you have made has prepared the way and opened a new epoch. Long live the world socialist revolution!"

Of course this was not really a reply to Chkheidze's "welcoming speech," and it was completely removed from the "context" of the Russian revolution as it was accepted by everyone who had seen or taken part in it. And how extraordinary it was! Suddenly, before the eyes of all of us, completely overwhelmed by the vulgar routines of revolutionary work, there was presented a bright, dazzling, and exotic light which obliterated everything we lived by. Lenin's voice, coming straight from the train, was "a voice from the outside." Upon us—in the midst of the revolution—there broke a music which was not at all dissonant, but was *new* and brusque and rather deafening.

This is not, of course, the whole story, for many things not mentioned by Sukhanov were happening in the imperial waiting room, as Lenin arranged the bouquet of red roses given to him by Alexandra Kollontay and stared at the ceiling. Many griefs and many triumphs were present in that room. Chkheidze, not at all the unsympathetic figure who is here depicted, had reason for his melancholy: that afternoon he had risen from a sickbed to bury his son. Originally the Georgian Tseretelli had been invited to make the welcoming speech. He flatly refused. Nor was Chkheidze's speech the work of a moralizing preacher in a Sunday school. He knew perfectly well that Lenin had come to destroy the February revolution, and when he spoke of defending the revolution "both from within and from without" he meant exactly what he said, and the words were at once a warning and a desperate appeal. In his *History of the Russian Revolution* Trotsky commenting on this scene says, "Chkheidze was better than his speech of welcome. He was a little afraid of Lenin." But this is to underestimate his fears. He had taken Lenin's measure and was mortally afraid.

A few moments later he had even more reason to be afraid, for a crowd of soldiers and sailors threw open the glass doors of the imperial waiting room, and hurled themselves on Lenin to lift him on their shoulders and carry him to the station square. Searchlights weaved across the square, lighting up the forest of red banners with gold letters. Everyone seemed to be shouting Lenin's name. Bands were playing. For a while Lenin vanished from sight. Suddenly he was being lifted up on the turret of an armored car, and it was observed that he kept stamping his feet, either because he was cold or because he was testing the strength of the armored plating. The searchlights converged on him, and everyone could see the lean, small, bareheaded man standing above them, shining brilliantly in the silver flames of the searchlights like an apparition which had descended from the skies. His coat was open, his black felt hat had been rolled up and stuffed into his pocket, and his fists were clenched.

He waited for almost a minute before the crowds were silent, and then he threw back his head and in a rasping voice greeted first the revolutionary proletariat and then the revolutionary soldiers and sailors who not only had freed Russia from tsarist despotism, but were preparing the way for the socialist revolution which, beginning in Russia, would spread throughout the world. "Long live the world-wide socialist revolution!" he shouted, and those who could hear him answered with the same cry.

For a few moments more he stood there, blinded by the searchlights, stamping his feet in a strange dance, rocking a little from side to side, smiling, all the weariness gone from him in the warmth of the welcome.

All his life had been a waiting for this moment.

THE
CONQUEST
OF POWER

We shall destroy everything, and on its ruins we shall build our temple. . . .

THE APRIL THESES

IN THE PAST when a conqueror returned from abroad, he would ride in procession in broad daylight, leading his prisoners in chains, pausing at the sacred shrines to offer sacrifices and saying little, for it was the habit of conquerors to be remote from the people, who pelted him with flowers. But Lenin's processional triumph was unlike any that had ever taken place in history. It took place in the darkest hours of a war, when the armies were crumbling and there were no victories in sight, and the conqueror himself had never held a sword in his hand or ridden over a battlefield. His prisoners were the workers of Petrograd, and the shrines where he paused were the street crossings. On that Easter Monday night, as he rode through Petrograd in triumph, all the ordinary laws of behavior seemed to be held in abeyance; it was as though history had come to a stop and an entirely new dispensation of time was beginning.

Everything about that strange triumph seemed to acquire an obscure symbolism. The darkness, the sudden flares of the searchlights, the Red Guards grimly lining the streets, the funereal pace of the armored cars as they rumbled over the cobblestones and paused at the street crossings long enough for Lenin to emerge on the turret and announce that one world order had ended and another was beginning —all these things spoke of mysteries which could be only dimly apprehended. A solemn rite was being performed, but even the workmen who followed the procession in their thousands were scarcely aware of what was happening.

From the Finland Station the procession moved across the Sampsonievsky Bridge and so to the Kshesinskaya Palace, that sumptuous and elegant palace which had been occupied only two months before by the *prima donna assoluta* who had been the mistress of the Grand Duke Andrew Vladimirovich. They had chosen this palace because it was strategically situated on the north bank of the Neva close to the Peter and Paul Fortress and the Trinity Bridge which led directly into the heart of Petrograd. Here among crystal lusters and candelabra, Chinese vases, exquisite frescoed ceilings, and wide stairways, the Bolsheviks were planning their revolution. They had removed the delicate furniture and replaced it with plain kitchen chairs, tables and benches.

The procession had taken an hour to traverse the short distance between the railroad station and the palace, and it was now nearly 12:30 P.M. Upstairs, preparations had been made for a small tea party. There were to be formal welcoming speeches by party members, while young women poured out tea from the steaming samovars, but Lenin was in no mood for empty ceremonies. He wanted to talk about tactics. The crowds were clamoring for him, and from time to time he would step out on the narrow balcony below the red banners. Sukhanov, who had followed the procession, came up just in time to hear Lenin making one of those short speeches which were to continue at intervals for another hour.

"Capitalist robbers," he shouted hoarsely. "The destruction of the peoples of Europe for the sake of the profits of a handful of exploiters . . . The defense of the fatherland means the defense of one gang of capitalists from another gang!"

A soldier down below leaned on his rifle and shouted back, "You ought to stick a bayonet into a fellow like that! What's that? What's he saying? If he'd come down here, we'd show him! We'd show him all right! He's a German for sure. He ought to be—"

The soldier, however, made no attempt to "show him"; he did not raise his rifle; like the rest of the people in the crowd he was bemused, horrified and fascinated by this man who spoke in the simplest possible terms in words of unheard-of violence, always with a compelling authority.

Inevitably there was a tea party; inevitably there were welcoming speeches. When Lenin appeared there was frenzied applause, but only polite handclapping greeted the appearance of Zinoviev. At last the welcoming speeches came to an end, and Lenin rose to reply not with the conventional salute to party members and gratitude for their kind words, but with a speech like thunder, which made them sit up in their chairs. They were like startled rabbits caught in the beams of an intense light. He did not praise them for their work; he accused them of being laggards and temporizers, little better than their bourgeois enemies, and he implied that they were traitors to the revolutionary cause.

This speech was given in the dancer's reception room. There was no platform, no table. They made a half circle of chairs around him as he stood against the wall. He said there was not a moment to lose; the first stage of the revolution had been accomplished, and the next must begin immediately; the existing republic must be destroyed, and all power must pass to the Soviets, the only possible form of revolutionary government; the land and the banks must be nationalized, and the possessions of the landed aristocracy confiscated; and it was time they rid themselves of the outworn name of the Social Democratic Party, and called themselves Communists. There were moments when he broke out into rough humor. "While I was making this journey with my comrades, I kept thinking we would be taken straight from the station to the Peter and Paul Fortress. It seems we are far from that. But let us not lose hope that we shall not escape that experience."

Sukhanov's wife was a Bolshevik in good standing, and since he was close to Gorky and knew many of the Bolsheviks, he was permitted to attend the meeting. Like all the others he was astounded by the vehemence of the speech and the appalling prospects it offered for the future. "He kept hammering, hammering, hammering, and at last he made them his captives," Sukhanov reports. There were only about thirty men in the audience, all of them except Sukhanov senior members of the party; they listened in trembling silence like school children. Soon from trembling disbelief to wide-eyed certainty they moved at the master's bidding. He showed them how power should be taken, how it could be invested in the Soviets of Workers', Soldiers' and Peasants' Deputies, and how the new leaders could bring about a "democratic" peace. Sukhanov wondered how these Soviets could be made to operate together, and he saw clearly that Lenin was advocating the *absence* of the state, a complex of free communes, such as the anarchists had advocated for fifty years. No Soviets of Peasants had been created, and Sukhanov doubted whether they would ever be formed, and if formed, whether they could exercise power. He noted that Lenin demonstrated a remarkable disinterest in the economy of Russia. "He still felt abroad." He was improvising, but it was clear that "each individual part of the speech, each element, each idea was excellently worked out, and all these thoughts had occupied his entire attention for a long time and had been defended more than once." Yet the speech was full of irreconcilable contradictions, and there was a strange imbalance between the theory and the projected application. He seemed to favor the Constituent Assembly, while at the same time denouncing all parliamentary authority. "We don't need any parliamentary republic! We don't need any bourgeois democracy!" For two hours Lenin talked, and the dawn was coming up when they finally went to their homes. Sukhanov made his way to his apartment on the Karpovka. "I felt," he said, "as though I had been beaten about the head with flails. Only one thing was clear: there was no way for me, a free person, to have Lenin as my traveling companion. With delight I drank in the air, freshening now with spring. The light was coming up; a new day was beginning."

Lenin and Krupskaya spent the night in the apartment of Mark Elizarov, the husband of Lenin's sister Anna. The apartment was halfway across the island, on Shirokaya Street. Anna and Maria were both there to welcome them, and Anna's foster son had hung over the beds the words from *The Communist Manifesto:* "Workers of the World, Unite!" When they went to bed they scarcely spoke to one another; nor was there any need to speak. "Everything was so very clear that there was no need for words," Krupskaya wrote.

What was clear was that Lenin held the party in the hollow of his hands.

It had been decided to hold a meeting of the Bolshevik delegates to the All-Russian Conference of Soviets of Workers' and Soldiers' Deputies at the Tauride Palace the next morning. In the excitement they had forgotten to tell Lenin about the meeting. When they remembered, they wondered whether they should let him sleep or whether they should send a deputation to awaken him; and reminding themselves how he spoke about the urgency of the tasks ahead, they thought it best to send the delegation. He was the head of the party, and none of the other delegates had the authority to speak in his name. Also, the All-Russian Conference of Soviets was meeting later in the day to discuss the union of all the revolutionary factions into a single party. Lenin's views were known to the thirty party members who had attended the early morning meeting, but it was necessary that the rank and file should become acquainted with them.

Lenin woke about ten o'clock, and a few minutes later the deputation arrived. Earlier he had spoken extemporaneously, improvising as he went along, now talking about the nature of the revolutionary state, now theorizing about the next stage in the struggle for power. It was necessary to give form and substance to his revolutionary beliefs and to demonstrate step by step the various objectives he had in view. What was necessary, at very short order, was to construct a revolutionary program based upon the unrehearsed theses he had pronounced earlier. There and then he wrote down in ink the headings of the new program. There was no time to write out the program in full, and it was arranged that two comrades should take down the speech as he delivered it. Meanwhile to jog his memory there was this small square of paper with a few spidery lines of handwriting written with a scratchy pen. On this scrap of paper he announced the stages which would, he hoped, bring about the coming of a new world order.

This scrap of paper may be compared with the Magna Charta or the American Declaration of Independence, for its consequences were so vast that they were beyond all human calculation. Like the ripples when a stone is flung into a pool, the influence of this document spread out in endless rings. In all his life Lenin never wrote a more potent page.

THESES

1) Attitude to war.

No concessions to "revolutionary defensism."

2) "Demand that the Provisional Government" "renounce annexations."

2 bis) Critique of Soviets of workers deputies	(α) attitude to Provisional Government (β) attitude to the Soviets of workers deputies

3) Not a parliamentary republic, but a republic of Soviets of workers, agricultural laborers, peasants and soldiers deputies.

> (α) abolition of the army, bureaucracy, police.
> (β) salaries of officials

4) Specific nature of the tasks of propaganda, agitation and organization in the period of transition from first stage of revolution to second.

Maximum legality.

Supporters *only* of "a war of necessity," "a war not for the sake of annexations"—honest, but deceived by the bourgeoisie; how deceived by the bourgeoisie.

5) Agrarian program.

(α) Nationalization. (Confiscation of all landed estates).

(β) "Model farms" on each large estate under the control of the Soviets of agricultural laborers' deputies.

$+$ (γ) Center of gravity in S. of agric. laborers D.

6) One bank under the control of Soviets of workers deputies.

6 bis) *Not* the introduction of socialism *at once,* but the speedy, systematic, progressive transition of the Soviets of Workers' Deputies to *control* of social production and the distribution of goods.

7)   Congress.

Change of program and name.

Restoration of the International. Creation of the revolutionary International . . .

Such were the theses which Lenin wrote out hurriedly on the morning after his arrival in Petrograd, the words often so abbreviated that one can read them only with the greatest difficulty, the ideas running pell-mell across the page with the effect of hammer blows raining down from all directions. Here he announced a program deliberately calculated to antagonize all the other revolutionary parties; to cut adrift from them and to destroy them; to channel the revolution into the path he had ordained for it. Almost as an afterthought in this sweeping program he proclaimed the "abolition of the army, bureaucracy, police."

Today this single sheet of paper, enclosed within a heavy red velvet frame, is given a place of honor in the Central Lenin Museum in Moscow, and well it might be. It is not only that of all the documents written in our age none has had such a pervasive effect on the lives of the people living on this planet, but there exists no other work from his pen which is so revealing of his strengths and his weak-

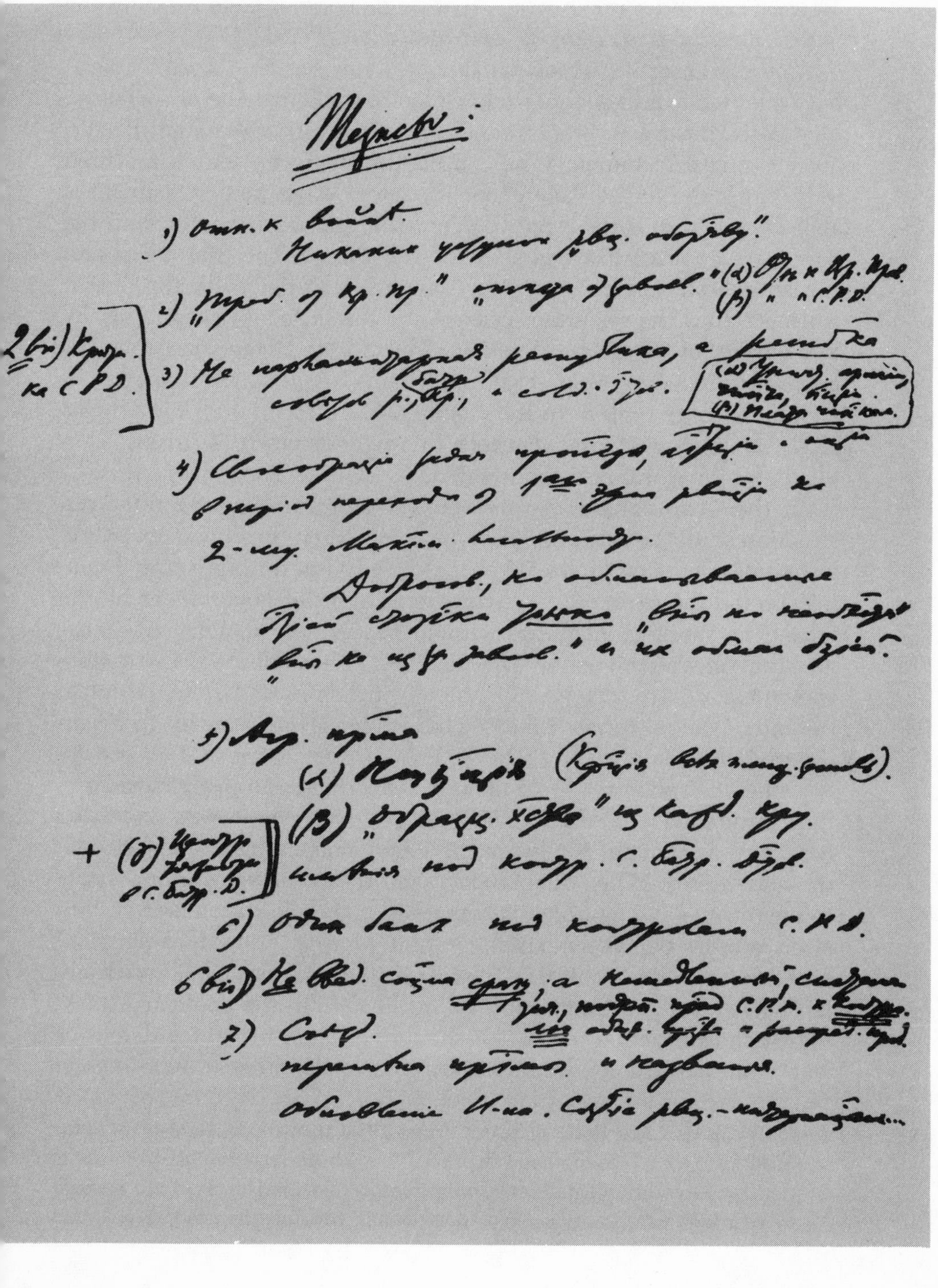
Тезисы:

nesses. There is a sense in which that single nervous page provides the perfect abstract portrait of the man.

These arguments, which came to be known as the "April Theses," have a knifelike edge. Here for once the formal language of socialism, blunted by misuse and repetition, suddenly acquires real and dangerous meanings. In one page he cancels the Russian state as it existed in his time: the theme throughout is one of destruction. Parliament is abolished, and so is the republic. The army, the bureaucracy, and the police are abolished in one short stroke; there follow the banks and the landed estates. Socialism, too, is abolished or put aside, for all that is necessary is the seizure of power over the means of production by the Soviets of Workers' Deputies. The Social Democratic Party is abolished—"Change of program and name"—and finally the state is abolished, to give place to the Communist International. The phrase at the beginning, "No concessions to 'revolutionary defensism,'" implied that the war is also abolished.

If the "April Theses" were merely a summary order for the destruction of all the existing pillars of society, then the document would have only a passing interest. What is chiefly interesting is that Lenin interpreted the revolutionary struggle in terms of government by the Soviets of Workers' Deputies without in any way showing how that government would operate. The state was to be abolished, a new state was to come into existence, but he never defines that state except in the most general terms. Like Nechayev, he seems scarcely to be interested in it.

When he spoke at the midmorning meeting in an upstairs room in the Tauride Palace, he elaborated the original seven theses under ten headings, as though they were the new commandments and he was the new Moses. When announcing each thesis, he spoke very slowly to enable the stenographer to take down the words accurately, but afterward he would sometimes permit himself hurried explanatory passages, with the result that the text is sometimes garbled, words are left out, and the meaning must be inferred from the context. Attacking the idea that the revolution should continue to fight a defensive war against Germany, he said according to the stenographic report:

> Revolution is a difficult thing. Impossible not to make mistakes. Our mistake is that (we have not exposed?) revolutionary defensism in all its depths. Revolutionary defensism is treason to socialism. It is not enough to restrict ourselves . . . We must admit the mistake. What is to be

done?—We must clarify. How to give . . . who do not know what socialism is . . . We are not charlatans.

In such broken passages we sometimes have an impression of im-
mediacy lacking in the more sustained passages. For some reason he
kept repeating, "We are not charlatans." He attacks continually, but
the thrusts seem sometimes to be desperate measures undertaken
blindly, without knowing in what direction he is going. He accuses
the Bolsheviks of having faith in the government, and he suggests
that the time has come for a parting of the ways; he would prefer to
be one man fighting a hundred rather than to capitulate before the
government. They use high-sounding phrases. Why? All revolutionary failures have come about because the revolutionaries were seduced by their own pomposity. "We must talk to the people without
using Latin words," he cries, and all his theses are saturated with
Latin words. Of the peasants he speaks simply, with the usual contempt: "What is the peasantry? We do not know; there are no statistics; but we know that it is a force." It was odd that he should say
this, for there were abundant statistics, and in the past he had studied
them at great length. There was no question of giving the land to the
peasants. He spoke of the model farms which would be carved out
of the large estates; they would be placed in charge of the Soviet of
Peasants' Deputies. The police, too, would be placed in the charge of
the Soviet of Workers' and Peasants' Deputies. He was more convincing when he said, "Learn how to rule. There is nothing to stop us!"

Sometimes in this speech he spoke as though the revolution had
been won. Once he said revealingly, "There is a proletarian dictatorship but one does not know what to do with it. Capitalism has become
state capitalism." But in April 1917 Russia was very far from the proletarian dictatorship, and state capitalism belonged to another year
or another age. "The art of government cannot be gotten out of
books," he declared. They were to rule by trial and error; Russia was
to become an experiment in chemistry.

His final thesis was at once an accusation and a vindication of his
own position. "In my own name I propose that the name of the party
be changed to the Communist Party," he said; and it was odd that he
should go out of his way to speak so personally. "The majority of the
Social Democrats all over the world have betrayed socialism and
gone over to the side of their governments." For him the old names
no longer had any meaning. They were like "dirty linen," and it was

time they were thrown away. This, too, was odd, for he had spent more than half his life fighting for Social Democracy. He was afraid the party comrades were not strong enough to break with their memories. So he flung at them a breath-taking challenge: "Have the will to build a new party!"

The "April Theses" follow closely the outline he had written hurriedly on a scrap of paper. They can be summarized as follows:

1. No concessions to be made to revolutionary defensism. The proletariat may give its consent to a revolutionary war only on condition that all power is transferred to the proletariat and the poor peasantry and the war is not undertaken for the sake of conquest. Fraternization.

2. The present situation in Russia represents the transition from the bourgeois revolution to the revolution of the proletariat and the poor peasants. This transition is characterized by the maximum of legality, Russia being the freest of all the belligerent countries in the world. Vast masses of the proletariat have only recently been awakened to political life, and the Bolsheviks are therefore in an advantageous position to adapt themselves to the changing circumstances.

3. The Provisional Government to be unmasked and exposed for the falsity of its promises, especially those relating to the renunciation of annexations.

4. Recognition of the fact that within the Soviets of Workers' Deputies the Bolsheviks are in a minority. The work of the party therefore must consist in patient, systematic and persistent criticism.

5. Not a parliamentary republic, but a Soviet of Workers' and Peasants' Deputies "throughout the land from top to bottom." Abolition of the police, army and bureaucracy. The universal arming of the people to be substituted for the standing army. All officers to receive salaries which do not exceed the average wage of a competent worker.

6. Nationalization of all lands in private possession. Creation of model agricultural settlements.

7. Immediate merger of all banks into a single general national bank controlled by the Soviet of Workers' Deputies.

8. Not the introduction of socialism as an immediate task. The Soviet of Workers' Deputies to control social production and the distribution of goods.

9. Party tasks: Immediate calling of a party convention, the party program to be changed to include the demand for a "Commune" state modeled on the Paris Commune. Change of name.

10. Restoration of the International. Taking the initiative in the creation

of a revolutionary International to fight against the social-chauvin-
ists and the "center."

In the discussion that followed the reading of the "April Theses"
some Bolsheviks protested, saying it was too early yet to speak of a
socialist revolution; and even if the time were ripe, they doubted
whether it would assume the form that Lenin declared so often to be
"the only possible form." The enthusiasm of the early morning when
he spoke extemporaneously had vanished. He spoke in a more studied
manner; they had had time to reflect, and they were no longer overwhelmed by the processional march from the Finland Station. The
debate was still going on when the Mensheviks, who were holding a
meeting in a downstairs room, decided that they had waited long
enough for the expected meeting with the Bolsheviks planned to bring
about the union of the two factions. They sent an urgent message
calling upon the Bolsheviks to come down, and they invited Lenin
to speak. Lenin saw his opportunity. He had no desire to see the
union of Bolsheviks and Mensheviks, and indeed he regarded the
Mensheviks with scorn. He spoke, and there was uproar.

From the beginning Lenin insisted that he was speaking for himself alone. He was one man against all, for though the Bolsheviks applauded him he was aware of the growing dissatisfaction among them.
The Mensheviks were outraged, seeing clearly that if his theses were
accepted, they could lead to only one form of government—the dictatorship of Lenin. His theses were his own, with no foundation in
Marxism. By some circuitous route they derived from Nechayev and
Bakunin; and Joseph Goldenberg, who had been a member of the
Bolshevik Central Committee and for many years Lenin's comrade
in arms, was so outraged that he deliberately accused Lenin of wearing the mantle of Bakunin.

"The place left vacant by the great anarchist Bakunin for many
years found no worthy successor, but now it is occupied by Lenin.
Everything we have just heard is the negation of Social Democratic
doctrine and scientific Marxism. What we have listened to is a clear
and unequivocal declaration of anarchism. Lenin has become the heir
of Bakunin. Lenin, the Marxist, the leader of our fighting Social Democratic Party, is dead. Lenin, the anarchist Lenin, is born."

Goldenberg's bitter attack did not end there; he went on to accuse
Lenin of plotting civil war within the revolution, and he spoke with
horror of "these enemies from abroad who come in the guise of

friends." Tseretelli denounced Lenin with less bitterness; he still hoped for unity within the Social Democratic Party, and he asked Lenin to remember the Marxist axiom that individuals can always make mistakes, but the classes never make mistakes. He said he was not afraid of Lenin's aberrations and extended the hand of welcome to him. Alexandra Kollontay alone ran to the defense of Lenin, but her speech in his defense was inspired by affection and not by logic, and it trailed off into incoherence. Angered by the taunts of the Mensheviks, some of the Bolsheviks left the room in despair; and Lenin, who could never endure the weapons with which he attacked others, left with them. Krupskaya was in tears. She had seen her husband raised to the pinnacle of glory, only to be cast down. Chkheidze, who presided over the meeting, watched Lenin go and commented, "Let him live outside the revolution, while we—the rest of us—continue along the revolutionary road."

Sukhanov, who was present, came to the conclusion that Lenin had committed a major error in announcing his theoretical theses, which seemed to be so palpably remote from the real revolutionary situation. He imagined that in time Lenin would reverse his stand, abandon theory, and work closely with the Bolsheviks. "It never occurred to us that Lenin would not depart by an inch from these abstractions," he wrote. "Still less did it occur to us that he would be able to conquer not only the revolution, not only all its active participants, not only the entire Soviet, but even his own Bolsheviks." The previous night he had Petrograd at his feet; now he was alone. He seemed to enjoy his loneliness.

Yet the wounds went deep. The party attacked him as mercilessly as his enemies. Kamenev denounced the theses as soon as they were published in *Pravda,* and it was observed that they were published under Lenin's name; no Bolshevik organization was prepared to be identified with them. A few days later in *Delo Naroda* Victor Chernov wrote a penetrating sketch of Lenin's character as it manifested itself on his return to Russia. He said:

> Lenin is a man of great capacities, but the abnormal conditions of underground life have dwarfed and stunted them most gruesomely. Lenin could say of himself, "I know not where I am going, but I am going there with determination." Lenin is certainly devoted to the revolution, but with him this devotion is embodied in his own person: "I am the State!" To him there is no difference between personal policy and the interests of the party, the interests of socialism. Lenin has an ex-

traordinary intellect, but it is one-sided. Lenin is an absolutely honest man, but a man with a one-track mind. For that reason his moral sense has been dulled. Lenin's socialism is a blunt socialism; he uses a big ax where a scalpel is needed.

It was a fair verdict, written without malice and perhaps with prescience, for in those confused days a man who wielded a big ax was likely to have more followers than one who wielded a scalpel.

People were beginning to ask themselves how he was able to come through Germany in the sealed train, and what promises he had made to the Germans in return for all the facilities placed at his disposal. The excitement of his homecoming gave way to a disturbed sense that he was, or might be, a traitor; and even among the Bolsheviks, to whom he showed the affidavits signed by prominent Swiss, German and Swedish socialists pronouncing his innocence, there was an uncomfortable feeling that his motives were concealed. The "April Theses," calling for civil war between the proletariat and the bourgeoisie, were admirably calculated to serve the German cause. The German High Command was jubilant. "Lenin's entry into Russia successful," wrote Steinwachs, the German agent in Stockholm. "He is working exactly as we would wish." So he was; but there were few Germans who were able to convince themselves that he would obey their orders.

The young ensign who was the first to greet Lenin at the Finland Station published a statement admitting his error; he was mortified by the thought that he had publicly welcomed a traitor to Russia. Far more serious was a resolution signed by all the Baltic sailors who acted as a guard of honor at the station. "Having learned that Lenin returned to Russia with the consent of His Majesty the German Emperor and King of Prussia," the sailors wrote, "we express our profound regret in participating in his triumphal welcome. If we had known by what paths he returned, there would have been no enthusiastic "hurrahs." Instead he would have heard our indignant cries: "Down with you! Go back to the country you came from!"

No longer the hero of Petrograd, Lenin became overnight a spy and *provocateur*. Crowds assembled around the Kshesinskaya Palace, demanding his arrest; once or twice Lenin appeared on the balcony and attempted to justify himself, explaining that he had been misunderstood, and then he quietly vanished. He had weathered many storms, and he was sure he would weather this one. Quietly and confidently he went to work on the Bolsheviks. One by one he was able to show them that the "April Theses," far from being the delirious arguments of a madman, as Plekhanov had described them, were in fact blueprints for the seizure of power, and no other course was possible if power was to be taken from the detested bourgeoisie. And since he was the technician of power, the one man within the party who had devoted his life to an understanding of power, he was listened to more readily. When the Seventh Conference of the Bolshevik Party opened on May 7, he had already won back most of the influence he had lost.

In the interval Petrograd had gone through several crises. It was as though all the problems confronting the country were insoluble, and from time to time the capital would sullenly become aware that nothing could be done, that all the talk of power was merely an indication of its powerlessness, and that there existed no political party which offered viable solutions; and then from sullen awareness of its impotence, the capital would turn to violence as a relief from an oppressive sense of aimlessness. On May 4 rioting erupted on the Nevsky Prospect. Processions streamed along the wide street with banners reading: "Long live the Provisional Government!" and these processions were met by others with banners reading: "Down with the Provisional Government." The processions met. The Red Guards were notably in evidence. There was some confused street fighting, but it was not until the afternoon that the situation became ugly and threatening. A battalion of soldiers from the Finland Regiment accompanied by some sailors and reservists were seen marching in the direction of the Maryinsky Palace. Asked where they were going, they answered: "We are going to arrest the Provisional Government." Chkheidze, who still wielded great authority as the president of the Soviets, hurried to meet them and convinced them that nothing was to be gained by arresting the government; and they returned to their barracks. Lenin denied that he had anything to do with the attempt to arrest the government, but his denials were greeted with skepticism. He was testing the strength of the enemy, throwing his men on the streets. There were more riots the next day, and this time there was shooting. The revolution had received its baptism of fire.

The cause of these riots was ostensibly a declaration by the Foreign Minister Milyukov that the Russian people were determined to continue fighting side by side with their allies until a "decisive victory" over Germany had been won. The declaration aroused jubilation on the right and a storm of protest from the left. But Milyukov's declaration was little more than the catalytic agent which permitted the chemical action to take place. His government was doomed. It had dealt ineffectively with all the pressing problems of the time—hunger, war, the large estates, the need for revolutionary changes in the basis of government. The Soviets had taken over many of the powers of government; it was intolerable that there should be these two governments perpetually at loggerheads. What was needed was a coalition government representing the Provisional Government and the Soviets. Milyukov resigned, and the Prime Minister, Prince George Lvov, called upon the Soviets to join the government. Socialist Revolutionaries and Social Democrats now became members of the government for the first time. The Mensheviks were represented by Tseretelli, who became Minister of Post and Telegraph, while the important post of Minister of Agriculture went to Chernov. The Bolsheviks were not asked to join the government; nor would they have accepted. Lenin contented himself with a few acid barbs against the new government, which in his view "would never amount to anything."

The government reigned, but did not rule. Workmen came out on strike, soldiers deserted, the overcrowded cities were filled with mobs wandering aimlessly in search of mischief. Sukhanov, who had no sympathy with the propertied classes, describes at great length the state of anarchy which had settled upon Russia. Arbitrary arrests, lootings, the burning of manor houses, the defiance of authority were the commonplaces of life in Russia as spring turned into summer. Kerensky, the Minister of War in the new government, alone seemed to possess any personal authority; he dominated the government, stiffened the morale of the army, and exhausted himself in fiery speeches in which he attempted to show that the revolution could survive everything except despair. But despair was already eating into the heart of the country.

Lenin knew exactly what he wanted to do: he would fan despair until it burst into flame. He would, if he could, wipe out the entire structure of the government with an armed uprising which would put the Bolsheviks in power. When he arrived at the beginning of April there were fifteen thousand Bolsheviks in Petrograd out of a population of two million; but by the beginning of June their numbers were rapidly increasing. The Bolshevik program was clear-cut. "All power to the Soviets"; "Down with the capitalists"; "Down with the war"—such slogans permitted no argument. While the government deli-

cately walked a tightrope and attempted to satisfy the conflicting aspirations of different groups, the Bolsheviks, interested solely in the
aspirations of the workers, prepared to cut the rope. Time was on
their side, for with every passing day the situation in Russia became
more anarchic and more intolerable.

In those days little was seen of Lenin. As Sukhanov observed, he
remained aloof "like some great aristocrat." He rarely attended the
sessions of the Soviet, and his few public appearances seemed to be
designed more in order to permit him to test the feeling of the workers than in order to work on their emotions. He was continually writing short, caustic articles. In one day *Pravda* printed five of them;
they were not notable for their good humor nor for any memorable
phrases, their purpose being to exasperate rather than to argue logically from fundamental premises. His real work—the work he wrote
about rarely—was the patient exploration of the conditions which
would permit an armed uprising.

Almost from the moment he arrived in Russia, Lenin was aware
that an armed uprising presented few problems; all that was necessary was that it should be well timed and directed with absolute
ruthlessness. Both the Paris Commune and the Moscow insurrection
of 1905 had taken place when the people and the government were
exhausted by war, without effective leadership, and divided among
themselves. There were lessons to be learned from these uprisings,
and the chief lesson was the need for co-ordination and a definite battle
plan. These uprisings had failed, but the conditions in Russia in the
summer of 1917 were far more favorable than they had ever been in
the past or were likely to be again. Lenin himself in the "April
Theses" had spoken of the extraordinary freedom permitted to any
insurgent groups; he employed the phrase "maximum legality"—
meaning, in effect, that there was a minimum of law enforcement.
The February revolution had destroyed the police, *and they had
never been replaced*. What he feared most was that the Provisional
Government, in an effort to restore stability, would reintroduce the
police. More and more his thoughts turned to the popular militia who
would take over the role of the police. Once the popular militia was
under the control of the Bolsheviks, there would be little difficulty in
sweeping the government away. The Soviet, too, could be destroyed,
for supreme power would inevitably fall into the hands of the commanders of the popular militia.

He described the functions of the popular militia in an article which appeared in *Pravda* on May 18:

> The popular militia means the real education in democracy of the *mass* of the population.
>
> The popular militia means that the poor are governed *not* by the rich and by *their* police, but by the people themselves, predominantly by the poor.
>
> The popular militia means that the control (over factories, dwellings, the distribution of products etc.) becomes *effective*, and not only on paper.
>
> The popular militia means the distribution of bread without bread lines, with no privileges *of any kind* for the rich.

He was careful, however, not to add that the popular militia would become the military arm of the revolution. In public he still spoke of the Soviets as the revolutionary power, and the slogan "All power to the Soviets" remained the battle cry of the Bolsheviks until the revolution was won.

Among the more far-sighted members of the government the question was not whether the Bolsheviks would attempt to sieze power, but when the armed insurrection would take place, and whether it could be thwarted in time. All the signs pointed to massive preparations. When the first All-Russian Congress of Soviets opened on June 16, Lenin spoke as one who believed that power was almost within his grasp. Tseretelli said that no single party had any business to take over power; they could go forward only with a government which represented all shades of public opinion. His phrasing was careless, and the words could be read as a categorical statement that no political party would dare to sieze power. It was an invitation which Lenin could scarcely disregard. He leaped to his feet and shouted, "There is such a party!" A moment later he was mounting the rostrum.

"The citizen Minister of Posts and Telegraphs," he declared, "has just stated that there is no political party in Russia which is prepared to take the entire power upon itself. I say there is! No party can refuse this, and our party does not refuse it! We are prepared at any moment to take over the entire power!"

The soldiers and sailors in the galleries cheered; they enjoyed the forthrightness of the statement. Kerensky warned the Congress of the consequences which would follow the destruction of the February revolution. An armed uprising would produce a new dictator and a vast bloodletting. Undaunted, Lenin decided upon another trial of strength while the Congress was still in session. On June 22 the preparations for a *putsch* were already far advanced. Military units and Red Guards had already received orders to march on the Maryinsky Palace where the Provisional Government was sitting. Almost at the last minute Chkheidze was informed, and once again he was able to use his authority in the Soviet to prevent the march. "This is nothing but a conspiracy," Tseretelli thundered. "It failed today because we got wind of it, but they will try again tomorrow and the next day and the day after that. There is only one way to stop them. We must disarm the Bolsheviks!" But it was already too late to disarm them. About half the workers and half the troops of Petrograd were in sympathy with the Bolsheviks, having lost any hope that the Provisional Government was in any position to control events. It was now only a question of time before the Bolsheviks would make a third coup, on so massive a scale that even the authority of Chkheidze would be incapable of preventing it.

The third coup was as unsuccessful as the others, and no one has ever succeeded in explaining how such a catastrophic failure could have taken place. There is evidence that it was carefully planned over a period of three weeks. The Kronstadt sailors, a battalion of the First Machine Gun Regiment, and the Putilov workers were standing by. Bolshevik agitators had worked feverishly to bring the pro-Government regiments over to the side of the Bolshevik revolt. The factory workers had been armed. The proclamation announcing the revolt had been set in type. It remained only to give the order to march on the government and destroy it. For some reason the order was never given. For two days soldiers and sailors marched through the streets of Petrograd, shouting slogans, killing anyone who got in their way and threatening to overturn the government, but never coming close enough to the government to cause it more than a slight discomfort.

This strange uprising began on July 16, when the First Machine Gun Regiment marched on the Tauride Palace and threatened to take it by force. With them went some twenty-five thousand workers from the Putilov factory, and thousands of other workmen. Once they reached the Tauride Palace they seemed not to know what to do with their sudden power. They chanted slogans. "Down with the Provisional Government! All power to the Soviets!" They tied up traffic. Trucks laden with soldiers and Red Guards careered along the streets. "There was excitement, with a coloring of rage, but no enthusiasm," Sukhanov wrote, and it was perhaps this lack of enthusiasm which convinced the Bolsheviks at the last moment that the time was not ripe for a *putsch*. Trotsky and Lenin both claimed that they had nothing to do with this curious show of force by undisciplined mobs, but the evidence is against them. What is certain is that something went wrong with their plans. There was nothing to prevent them from taking power. They chose not to. The inference would seem to be that the overwhelming majority of the population was against them and they would be unable to hold power for more than a few days.

On the following day some twenty thousand sailors from Kronstadt sailed up the Neva, landed on the north bank and marched to the Kshesinskaya Palace, where Lenin greeted them from the balcony. It was a perfunctory greeting. Tired and listless, he made a short speech in which he spoke of the inevitable victory of the Soviets and appealed for "firmness, steadfastness and vigilance." They were not the words one addresses to revolutionary troops on the eve of battle, or even of a skirmish. As Sukhanov observed—that inveterate eyewitness was everywhere in Petrograd in those days, and he deserves to be quoted constantly—"any small group of ten or twelve men could have arrested the government," which was then sitting in the unprotected apartment of Prince George Lvov. The Bolsheviks had advantages which they were not likely to have again. The Preobrazhensky, Semyonovsky and Izmailovsky regiments had declared their "neutrality." The troops guarding Petrograd consisted of a few companies of Cossacks and the military cadets. The people were cowed and frightened by the extraordinary behavior of the Machine Gun Regiment, the armed sailors and factory workers, who were still parading through the streets, looking for trouble. Shots rang out from a bell tower; here and there confused fighting broke out; Chernov was seized by the crowd and would have been lynched on the spot but for the sudden appearance of Trotsky, who commanded silence and asked whether there was anyone in the crowd who would assume the guilt of killing such a man, and no one answered. "Citizen Chernov, you are free," Trotsky said, and Chernov hurried back into the undefended Tauride Palace. By nightfall there were four hundred dead and wounded from the savage little skirmishes which broke out all over the city. There was no *putsch*, no seizure of power. "It was something considerably more than a demonstration and less than a revolution," Lenin said, but such a description lacks firm outlines. Pushkin, writing of the Pugachev rebellion, described it better: "A real Russian revolt, wild and senseless."

This two-day revolutionary spree brought about the temporary defeat of the Bolsheviks. The rank and file were incapable of understanding what had happened; it was as though they had wandered into a nightmare only to wander out of it again into a reality colder than they had ever dreamed of. Lenin's irresolution may have been due to illness—he spoke of his illness when addressing the Kronstadt sailors, and indeed he had only just returned from a short vacation in Finland, where he had been recuperating from a heavy cold—or it may have been due to information concerning General Polovtsev, Commander of the Petrograd Military Area, who had sworn to restore order at whatever the cost. When Trotsky, writing of these July days, said, "The enemy was easily victorious, because we did not fight," he was telling the truth, but he was not offering an explanation. There were 100,000 armed sympathizers of the Bolsheviks on the streets in July. In October, when the revolution was won, there was only a quarter of that number.

During the night of July 17 most of the demonstrators returned to their homes. Some Kronstadt sailors stayed on, seized the Peter and Paul Fortress and defied the Provisional Government to remove them. Even this victory endured no more than a few hours. By the afternoon of the following day they were lamely negotiating for safe-conducts permitting them to return to their base.

Lenin was confronted with a disastrous defeat. Sometime in the morning of July 18 he met Trotsky. "Now they will shoot us down one by one," Lenin said. "This is the right time for them."

So it was, and Kerensky, returning from the front a day later, called for reports on the two-day fiasco and ordered the arrest of Lenin and the seizure of the Kshesinskaya Palace, which was taken without a shot being fired and with most of the documents lying where they had been left by the retiring Bolsheviks. Podvoisky, who had led the Kronstadt sailors into the city and who would have led the insurrectionary forces if the order for attack had ever been received, was able to remove the documents relating to military matters only just in time; the rest fell into government hands. There were enough incriminating documents to show that the Bolsheviks had been carefully planning an uprising for more than three months, but there were not enough to show why it failed.

The Bolsheviks had already suffered a major blow; another followed with the publication of documents purporting to show that Lenin was a German agent. Some of the documents were palpable forgeries; others had the ring of truth. Ganetsky had been arrested while trying to cross the frontier; the secret police was able to extract some curious information from him, relating to moneys he had given to Lenin. The moneys may have come from the Scandinavian Social Democratic parties, but Ganetsky was known to have been in touch with Dr. Helphand, the trusted agent of the German Foreign Office. Lenin denied emphatically that Ganetsky gave him any money, but his published letters include a request to him "not to spare money on communications between Peter [Petrograd] and Stockholm." The government noted that the abortive *putsch* had been timed to coincide with a German offensive. If Lenin was not a German agent, he was acting singularly like one.

In fact, he was not. German money came into possession of the Bolshevik party and was used by the Bolsheviks for their own purposes; the aims of the Bolsheviks and the German High Command coincided to an extraordinary degree, for both were determined to destroy the state power of Russia; but there is nothing in Lenin's character to suggest that he could ever have played the role of paid agent with enthusiasm. His deliberate aim was to change the structure of world society; and he was obedient to no one but himself.

Since he arrived in Petrograd he had watched his power grow until sometimes it must have seemed that it embraced the whole city. Now he was a fugitive hurrying through the streets in a borrowed raincoat, his cap pulled low over his eyes and his chin buried in the upturned collar. If the police had arrested him, they would not have recognized him. Lenin had vanished. In his place there was a middle-aged workman named Konstantin Ivanov.

EXILE IN FINLAND

THE LIFE OF A CONSPIRATOR is one of endless improvisation and resourcefulness. He must know all the hiding places, all the exits of buildings, all the windows. He must recognize shadows and the sounds of footsteps, and distinguish in the darkness between enemies and friends. He must develop a sixth sense by which he knows when the police are after him, and from what direction they are coming.

In the days following the failure of the July insurrection Lenin was in mortal danger. Five hundred army officers, infuriated by the spectacle of the mobs careering through the streets, would have willingly shot him out of hand. Krupskaya tells of walking through the streets and listening to the conversations of the bourgeois, the fat housewives and the men of affairs. Everywhere the one topic of conversation was the imminent arrest of "the traitor Lenin." But it was not only the bourgeois who were indignant. The workers, too, were bitterly disturbed by the failure of the Bolsheviks to know their own mind; at this moment, with the Germans advancing and the country in a state of anarchy, the unforgivable sin was to do nothing. Lenin had contented himself with speeches, and in this respect he was no different from all the other members of the Soviets and the Provisional Government.

"We are still in a minority—the masses do not trust us yet," he wrote when he first arrived in Russia; and he added, "We know how to wait." He was one of the very few who could afford to wait. In the prevailing anarchy there was bound to come a time when, if he survived, he would be able to assume power, for no one else was so determined.

He survived by a series of miracles. There were continual close brushes with death. On the night of July 17 he was working in the *Pravda* office. Half an hour after he left, it was raided by military cadets, who ransacked every room, smashed the type and overturned the presses. With Sverdlov he took refuge in an apartment on the Karpovka, and there he stayed throughout the following day, writing five short articles in which he denied that the Bolsheviks had made the least effort to seize power and once more bitterly attacked "the base calumniators" who had tried to prove he was a German agent. These articles are not the most impressive of his writings. They are ragged and hysterical, written by a man at the end of his strength. On this day or the next he wrote a note which clearly showed that he was aware that he might be killed at any moment. The note was written to Kamenev and concerned a small blue-bound book left behind in Stockholm:

> Strictly *entre nous*. If I am done in, please publish my notebook *Marxism and the State*.
>
> It is held up in Stockholm. A blue binding. All the quotations are taken from Marx and Engels, also from Kautsky against Pannekoek. There are a whole series of notes and comments. They must be collated. I think you could publish it with a week's work. I think it is important, because Plekhanov and Kautsky are not the only ones who have blundered. One condition: all this must remain absolutely *entre nous*.

The blue notebook was to be his last will and testament, and it was perhaps characteristic of him that this slender book filled with excerpts from the scriptures and his annotations on them should have appeared so important at this moment of his life.

The apartment on the Karpovka was only a temporary hiding place, and it was necessary to transfer him as quickly as possible to the working-class quarters. Early in the morning of the nineteenth he slipped out of the Karpovka and made his way to the Vyborg quarter. There for two days he went from one hiding place to another, rarely spending more than a few hours in the same place. One of his hiding places was a watchman's hut in the Renault factory, where a secret meeting of the Petrograd Committee of the Bolshevik party was held. Already Lenin had come to the conclusion that the Bolsheviks could no longer work through the Soviets. Instead of "All power to the Soviets," he suggested the slogan "All power to the working class led by its revolutionary party, the Bolsheviks." As he saw it, the Soviets were traitors to the revolution, and they too must be destroyed. In their place there would arise the pure Soviets, where neither Mensheviks nor Socialist Revolutionaries were permitted to exist.

While he was in hiding, the Bolsheviks were deeply concerned with a moral problem which had arisen as a result of his disappearance. Many of the Bolshevik followers were incensed because the shepherd had abandoned his sheep. At his bidding they had poured through the streets of Petrograd; they had risked their lives in an armed uprising that failed. They had stood up and were counted, and they regarded it as the duty of Lenin to stand up and face his accusers in a public trial. However unjust the trial, nothing worse could happen to him than a prison sentence.

Lenin himself was half convinced by these arguments. He was hiding in the house of a workman called Alliluyev, whose daughter was later to marry Stalin, when Krupskaya and Maria Ilyinichna came to visit with him. Zinoviev was also hiding there.

"Grigory and I have decided to appear in court," Lenin said.

Tentative arrangements had already been made to surrender the two Bolshevik leaders to the Petrograd Soviets. The Bolsheviks demanded that they should be imprisoned in the Peter and Paul Fortress, where the guards were known to be sympathetic to them, and where their safety would be guaranteed. Lenin was still vacillating when a veteran party member, Elena Stassova, said there was a rumor spreading among the Soviets that documents had been found in the police archives proving that he had been a police spy.

These words produced an extraordinary effect on Lenin. He had been listening intently, occasionally interjecting his own arguments into the debate on the morality of surrender. Suddenly his whole face was convulsed in a nervous spasm, and he announced in a loud, determined voice that in this case he had no alternative but to surrender. A few minutes later two envoys were sent to the Soviets to arrange the final terms of the surrender, and it was while they were away that Krupskaya and Maria Ilyinichna came to the apartment.

"Go and tell Kamenev about the decision," Lenin told his wife.

She rose quickly. She was accustomed to obedience, and she was about to leave the room without another word when Lenin held her back.

"We must say good-bye," he said. "We may never see each other again."

It was one of the very rare occasions when he permitted himself a moment of sentiment. He had counted the cost: if he surrendered, he could expect no mercy from the enemy. They embraced, and then Krupskaya left to convey his message to Kamenev, who was hiding in a nearby apartment.

A few days earlier Lenin had been unable to bring himself to launch the insurrection. Now he was unable to decide whether to surrender or to go into hiding. The debate continued all afternoon and into the evening. The two envoys returned. They had demanded absolute guarantees for Lenin's safety, and they had been told that it was beyond human powers to give absolute guarantees, but everything would be done to ensure that he was brought to trial. According to Ordjonikidze, who was one of the envoys, the discussion with Anissimov, the high-ranking member of the Petrograd Soviet who would be in charge of the surrender, was heated. At one point Ordjonikidze shouted. "If you let anything happen to Lenin, do you know what we shall do? We shall cut all your throats!" The envoys returned to the hiding place. They reported that Anissimov had been unable to give the absolute guarantees they demanded, and that nothing was to be gained by continuing the negotiations. Lenin decided to go into hiding. Zinoviev agreed.

The task of hiding them was given to Nikolay Emelianov, who lived with his wife and seven children in the village of Razliv near Sestroretsk. He is usually described as a peasant, but in fact he was a skilled worker with a long history of revolutionary activity and many arrests. He had known Lenin since the autumn of 1905. It was arranged that he should meet the two leaders near the Sestroretsk station to the north of Petrograd, get them onto the train at the last moment, and take them off at Razliv, where his house was only five minutes' walk from the station. Everything went according to plan. They took the late train, which left at two o'clock in the morning, jumping onto a freight car just before the third bell rang. Emelianov remembered that Lenin was in a desperate mood, for he insisted on sitting on the steps.

"You might fall," Emelianov warned him.

"I know that," Lenin replied. "If necessary, I can jump off the train."

But there was never any need to jump off the train. They reached Razliv safely and made their way to the house in the darkness. Emelianov's wife received them. She was a capable woman, and she took charge. Zinoviev's mop of black hair and Lenin's beard were cut off, while Emelianov busied himself preparing the hayloft attached to the barn, hauling chairs and a small table up a steep ladder, making the narrow loft as comfortable as possible. There were cracks in the wall of the loft, which served as an observation post permitting them to watch everyone coming along the road. If messengers came from the party, either Lenin or Zinoviev would give the signal to the Emelianovs and the messengers would then be allowed to go up the ladder.

The barn in Razliv, however, had serious disadvantages. There were country houses and camping sites in the neighborhood, and a good many people passed it every day. Some of the newspapers announced that Lenin and Zinoviev had fled to Germany, but no one had rescinded the order for their arrest and there was still a price on their heads. Police spies might succeed in following the party messengers who came nearly every day. It was decided to find a safer hiding place in the surrounding forests. Some miles from the station, on the bank of a small lake, there was a clearing nearly surrounded by forests. It was hay-making time, and only a few peasants lived nearby. No campers ever came to the clearing, and the country villas were out of sight. In a hollowed-out hayrick, converted into a kind of hut, the fugitives spent the following three weeks. This hut became the headquarters of the maturing revolution.

This hiding place served its purpose perfectly. Lenin's kitchen consisted of a tin kettle suspended on forked sticks over a small fire, where he boiled tea and cooked potatoes. By the fire, bent over a writing pad, he would write the articles which were published a day or two later in Petrograd. The messengers came by long, circuitous routes, arriving in the evening or at night, announced by the splashing of oars as they were rowed over the lake. In the hot hours Zinoviev and Lenin bathed in the nude, and at twilight they would turn fishermen, with Emilianov's children helping to pull in the nets. The children became mature conspirators, and to reward them Lenin and Zinoviev would sometimes tell them stories into the late hours of the night.

Lenin had always enjoyed privacy, and so a study was built for him. The study consisted of a little lane carved between willow shrubs; the study was dark and quiet, a green tunnel. Here he would read the newspapers brought by the perennial messengers, delighted whenever he came upon any references to his escape from Russia on a German submarine. At such times he would roar with laughter and say, "Eh, eh, what stupid jokers they are! What will they believe next?"

One day they had a narrow escape. Zinoviev, armed with a shotgun, went into the surrounding forest to hunt for game. Suddenly he was discovered by a forester. It was too late to run. The forester took out his notebook and asked questions. "Where do you live? Where do you come from?" Zinoviev was quick-witted. He pretended to be dumb, and the forester gave up cross-examining him. He took the shotgun away and let him go. Some time later Emelianov, wanting to know whether the forester had any suspicions, went to see him. He learned that the forester had taken Zinoviev for a Finnish farm hand who did not speak Russian.

One day Ordjonikidze came to visit the hayfield. After being rowed across the lake, he saw a short, thickset man appearing from behind a hayrick, and paid no attention to him. Then he heard a voice saying, "Comrade Sergo, don't you recognize me?" He had failed to recognize Lenin without his beard.

Without his beard, after weeks of living in the open air, Lenin no longer had the appearance of a revolutionary leader: he looked like a skilled workman. Toward the end of August, plans were already well advanced for smuggling him to Finland for greater safety. A forged identity card in the name of Konstantin Petrovich Ivanov was prepared for him, and a photograph was taken to be pasted on the card. It is an astonishing photograph. He wears a Russian blouse, a workman's cap, and a wig. The flesh has filled out, there is the faintest of ironic smiles on his lips, and the eyes are hooded, one of them being scarcely more than a slit; in fact he had nearly lost an eye in a street accident in Switzerland and he was troubled with his sight for the rest of his life. But what is especially remarkable about the photograph is that Lenin in disguise reveals himself more completely than at any other time. Here he shows himself stripped of his authority, possessing a common humanity. The beard, which he cultivated in twenty different ways, changing its shape and cut according to his mood, was always the badge of his professional authority as a member of the upper middle class or of the lower nobility. He was always the *dvoryanin;* and though no one ever addressed him as "Your Excellency," he always regarded himself as a man set a little apart from his fellows, living alone, refusing even in the hayfield at Razliv to share his study among the willow bushes with Zinoviev. In the photograph he resembles a good foreman who would manage his workmen good-humoredly and intelligently.

Safety was not the only reason which dictated the flight to Finland. Autumn was coming on. The days were cold, rainy and windy. One day there was a storm, they were drowned out of their small hollowed-out hayrick and compelled to take shelter in a real hayrick, where they lived until their own hayrick dried out. They were acutely uncomfortable. Finally, it was decided that the journey to Finland could be delayed no longer. Ordjonikidze was placed in charge of all arrangements.

One day, shortly before Lenin left the hayfield at Razliv, Ordjonikidze asked him for his interpretation of events. Newspapers came regularly to the field by messenger, and special reports were continually coming in from the Central Committee. Lenin knew what was going on, and he had made a close study of the structure of power in Petrograd. He said:

"The Mensheviks are now discredited in the Soviets. Two weeks ago, without too much difficulty, they might have seized power, but they are now no longer in a position to do so. Power has been taken away from them. Now we can assume power only by means of an armed insurrection, and this will come soon—probably not later than September or October. From now on we must make the factory committees the center of gravity. They should become the organs of the insurrection."

Ordjonikidze was startled by such self-assurance. Only a few weeks earlier the July insurrection had been an abject failure. Then he remembered that one of his friends had prophesied that in August or September the Bolsheviks would seize power and Lenin would become head of the government.

"Yes," said Lenin calmly. "That is how it will happen. In one or two months I shall become head of the government."

Then he gave his instructions to Ordjonikidze, explaining that it would be necessary to bring into existence a secret Central Committee which could operate illegally and also a secret printing press to publish Bolshevik tracts; and these two things were to be done immediately.

This conversation took place at night inside the hayrick. Ordjonikidze, exhausted by the long journey, fell asleep while Lenin was talking. He had hoped to wake up at dawn, but it was eleven o'clock in the morning when he finally awoke. Lenin let him sleep, and spent the morning writing articles and letters to be delivered to the Central Committee in Petrograd.

At first it was planned to send Lenin across the Finnish frontier on foot with a trusted escort, but a reconnoitering party sent to the frontier discovered that passports were being subjected to strict scrutiny all along the line, and the plan was abandoned. Then it was decided to smuggle him across the frontier in the cab of a railroad locomotive. Hugo Yalava, a Finn who had taken a leading part in the 1905 uprising, organizing the strike of railroadmen, was approached. He was the engineer of the night train which left Petrograd for Finland. Though not a Bolshevik, he readily agreed to the plan, and it was arranged that Lenin should cross the frontier on the night of August 22.

Two or three days earlier Lenin left the hayfield and made his way to the Levashovo station about eight miles away. With him went Zinoviev, Emelianov, Shotman, who was one of the secret couriers, and a Finnish party member called Eino Rahja, who was a friend of Hugo Yalava, the engineer. They decided to take a short cut through the forest. They were walking in single file along a narrow, barely discernible path, when it occurred to them that they had lost their way. Dusk set in, and then darkness. For a while they were completely lost, stumbling through the forest. To make matters worse, they were being choked by the smoke of a forest fire, and when they came out of the forest they found themselves in a burning peat bog. At last, when they had waded across a stream, they heard the distant whistle of a locomotive. They pushed on, and finally reached the station about one o'clock in the morning. A single lantern illuminated the wayside station, crowded with military cadets. Shotman and Emelianov went off to reconnoiter the station, while Lenin, Zinoviev and Eino Rahja hid in a roadside ditch. Lenin's nerves were on edge, and he was especially angry with Emelianov, who lived in the neighborhood and should have known the way. He should also have inspected the station earlier in the day to learn whether it was under heavy guard, and there were other things he should have done.

When Emelianov and Shotman were a few yards from the station, they were both arrested and interrogated. Shotman, who had long experience of clandestine activity, had taken care to acquire the proper papers and credentials. He was searched, no incriminating documents were found on him, and he was released with orders to take the train for Petrograd which was already standing in the station. He therefore took no further part in the escapade.

Emelianov was less lucky. He had not thought out a credible story.

He explained that he possessed a small farm nearby where he had spent the night, and being thirsty he had decided to come to the station to get a drink. He was searched, and a party card was found on him. The card bore the name of a worker in Petrograd, while he, Emelianov, claimed to be a worker at the Sestroretsk armaments factory. The officer grew increasingly suspicious.

"How long have you been working at the factory?" he said.

"Thirty years."

"Then name the foremen."

Emelianov did so.

"What is the name of the medical superintendent at the factory?"

"Grech. He's the stupidest doctor you ever saw."

"Is he?" snapped the officer. "I would have you know that I am his nephew."

Emelianov was playing for time. If he could hold the attention of the officer, there was the possibility that Lenin and Zinoviev would be able to board the train without having to undergo examination by the officer who was in charge of the military cadets at the station. He purposely gave provocative answers. The officer was puzzled. There was no doubt in his mind that Emelianov was a worker in the Sestroretsk factory, but he was probably a Bolshevik. He said, "What do you think of the Bolsheviks?"

"They're good people from what I have heard."

"Are you one of them?"

"No."

"Do you know what we would do if we found you were a Bolshevik? We'd shoot you out of hand!"

About this time the train from Petrograd steamed into the station. At gunpoint Emelianov was ordered to board the train for Finland, and so he too was unable to take any further part in the escapade. He had some satisfaction in learning a little later that Lenin, Zinoviev and Eino Rahja slipped onto the last car of the Petrograd train while he was being interrogated. They reached Udelnaya on the outskirts of Petrograd later in the night and were immediately taken to the apartment of a Finnish worker called Emil Kalske, who was a member of the party. No one told him the names of the fugitives until the next morning, when Eino Rahja pointed them out.

"I opened the door in the morning," Kalske later recalled, "and saw two comrades lying on the bare floor. One was clean-shaven and wore a wig, while the other was a man with a broad face, a short mustache and a recent growth of beard on his chin and cheeks, who resembled a Mohammedan. When my friend told me one was Lenin and the other was Zinoviev, I was dumfounded."

Zinoviev spent some weeks hiding in Emil Kalske's apartment, while Lenin continued his journey to Finland. Late that night the engineer Hugo Yalava brought the train to a stop near a crossing just outside Udelnaya. Not far from the track, as he had expected, he could make out a workman wearing a cap and a light coat standing beside Eino Rahja. In a few seconds Lenin had mounted the engine, and Eino Rahja climbed into one of the coaches—his papers were in order and he had nothing to fear from the border guards.

Lenin was in good spirits. There was no coal in the tender, for the trains in Finland were wood-burning. He kept himself busy feeding wood into the furnace, enjoying the role of fireman. The regular fireman did not object; it was explained to him that the stranger in the cab was a journalist intent on understanding the mechanics of railroad engines. The fireman, who spoke no Russian, was content to smoke his pipe and watch Lenin clambering over the logs, darting backward and forward between the tender and the furnace.

At Belo-Ostrov there was always the danger that the guards would demand to see the papers of the engine crew. As they drew into the station Yalava observed an unusually large number of militiamen. They went through the train, scrutinizing the passengers and examining their passports and identity cards. There was a twenty-minute wait at the station, to enable the train to take on water, and the engineer decided to uncouple the engine and drive off at once to the water tank and to return at the last possible moment. This he did, with the result that the third bell had already sounded when the engine came steaming back to the station. Yalava quickly coupled the engine, and in the hurry and excitement the frontier guards had no time to examine the crew. Lenin crossed into Finland without further incident.

His destination was a house belonging to Eino Rahja's father-in-law in the small village of Yalkala on the seacoast near Terioki. The father-in-law was told that the newcomer was a certain Konstantin Ivanov, a writer in need of rest and composure in order to finish a book.

"Yes, of course," said the father-in-law. "But don't tell me he is Ivanov. I used to work in Petrograd, and I would recognize Lenin anywhere, even with a wig."

But though the ruse was unsuccessful, no harm was done. Lenin liked the small villa, which was set a little way from the village. He went gathering mushrooms, tried not too successfully to follow the plow—"Plowing is devilish hard work," he said—and bathed in the sea. It was noted as especially curious that he did most of his writing at night.

There were, however, serious disadvantages in staying in this obscure little village. He had difficulty maintaining his contacts with Petrograd. Couriers dispatched to Yalkala risked being picked up by the police. He was more than ever impatient to get news quickly from Petrograd and decided that Helsingfors offered the best hiding place with direct communication with Petrograd. So, after a week at Yalkala he set out for Helsingfors, staying on the way at the small sawmill town of Lahti, halfway between Terioki and the Finnish capital, and then in the *dacha* of a deputy of the Finnish Diet just outside Helsingfors before finally entering the city. It was a slow and cautious progress along the coast. Shotman and a small group of dedicated Bolsheviks formed the advance party, continually probing, testing, making sure that each of these journeys was performed in perfect safety. At Helsingfors, Shotman produced his trump card. Here the secret police were less effective than in any other great city in Russia, because the chief of police, Gustav Rovio, was himself a Social Democrat, who had been elected to office following the February revolution. He was also the chief of the workers' militia. It was arranged that they should meet late at night in a deserted square near Rovio's apartment house. There were no incidents. The meeting passed off quietly and they went at once to the fifth-floor apartment. Rovio's wife was away in the country. Lenin settled in an armchair, sipped tea, and explained casually in the tones of a schoolmaster exactly what had to be done.

"Since the newspapers come from Petrograd on the evening train," he said, "it will be your duty to go down to the station every evening to get them for me. As for mail—since we cannot trust the government mails—you will arrange for me to send my letters through your agents on the mail car on the Petrograd train."

There were more instructions, and at last Rovio went to sleep. Lenin, according to his custom, cleared the table and set down to work. For a long time the scratching of the pen could be heard in the silent room. When Rovio woke up the next morning, Lenin was asleep. There was a copybook lying on the table. It bore the title *The State and Revolution*.

Of all Lenin's works *The State and Revolution* is the one which speaks most authoritatively in the tones of Nechayev. The theme is the destruction of state power and the inevitable emergence of communism, first in the limited form of a dictatorship of the proletariat, and then in the form of the completely free society in which the state has withered away. Of that final Messianic age, when there is no state and when all people live in brotherhood, he is least convincing; but of the destruction of state power he speaks with conviction and authority —the authority of a Nechayev who announces: "Everything must be destroyed, and let the future take care of itself."

In *The State and Revolution* Lenin argues that the task of the socialist proletariat is not merely to conquer the state, but to destroy it to its foundations. The working class must "shatter," "extirpate," "utterly destroy" the existing machinery of the state, until not a stone is left standing. Since the state is an instrument for the exploitation of the oppressed classes, no other course is possible. The theory that the state provides a system of checks and balances moderating the conflicts between the classes is dismissed out of hand. The state must perish. The one task remaining to the proletariat is to concentrate all its forces of destruction on a single enemy—the state, which will inevitably defend itself with all the power at its command. And while the abolition and overthrow of the state is inevitable, and the bourgeoisie are doomed to destruction, no one should imagine that the processes of destruction will be accomplished with any ease. On the contrary it will be a period of unprecedented violence; and in Lenin's manner of expressing that violence there is a strange and ugly element of compulsiveness and a total lack of logic. Speaking of the violent overthrow of the bourgeoisie and the new state that will come to birth, he says:

> In reality this period inevitably becomes a period of unprecedentedly violent class war in unprecedentedly acute forms, and therefore the state during this period must inevitably become a state that is democratic *in a new way* (for the proletariat and the poor in general) and dictatorial *in a new way* (against the bourgeoisie).

Among these simplicities Lenin moves with staggering incomprehension. The new form of society is never defined: there will be dictatorship *in a new way* and democracy *in a new way*, and there will be violent destruction, and all these are satisfying to him, as all simplicities are satisfying, but there is never any conception of the intricate machinery of the new government which will replace the old. On the contrary, the new government will be completely simple, becoming nothing more than a distribution center:

> In order to abolish the state, it is necessary to convert the functions of the public service into such simple operations of control and accounting which are well within the capacity and ability of the vast majority of the population, and ultimately of every single individual.

The Chinese philosopher Lao Tzu believed that government should become "as simple as cooking little fishes." Lenin believed it should be as simple as a post office. He was perfectly serious in this belief. He assumed that the armed proletariat would be in command, living in communes where all their needs would be provided for them from a central distributing agency, and in their brotherliness and neighborliness they would have no desire to impose upon one another. Indeed, there would be no opportunity for them to impose upon one another, for wealth and private property would be abolished, and there would be nothing that one man could acquire which would be wanted by another. Government officials would enjoy the same salaries as workers. They must be deprived of their official grandeur and all the signs of their privileged positions, and they must regard themselves as the dedicated servants of the state rather than the masters. The Bolsheviks had once discussed the salary which should be paid to a municipal councilor and arrived at the figure of 9,000 rubles. "These Bolsheviks," Lenin wrote in an angry footnote, "are acting unpardonably. *Throughout the whole state* the maximum salary should be 6,000 rubles, which is quite an adequate sum." He seems to have based this figure on an observation by Engels that the highest salary paid by the French Communards was 6,000 francs.

The State and Revolution is a work of extraordinary interest because it is so devoid of logic, existing in a kind of utopian dream. Lenin seems to have been aware that he would be accused of utopianism; and repeatedly he disclaims any utopian aspirations:

> We are not utopians, and do not in the least deny the possibility and inevitability of excesses on the part *of individual persons*, nor the need to suppress *such* excesses. But in the first place no special machinery, no special apparatus of suppression is needed for this; this will be brought about by the armed people themselves, as simply and as readily as any crowd of civilized people, even in modern society, interferes to put a stop to a street fight or to prevent a woman from being outraged. And secondly, we know that the fundamental social cause of excesses, which consist in the violation of the rules of social intercourse, lies in the exploitation of the masses, their need and their poverty. With the removal of this chief cause, excesses will inevitably begin to *"wither away."* We do not know how quickly and in what order, but we know that they will wither away. With their withering away, the state will also *wither away.*

The theory of the withering-away of the state was not, of course, original with Lenin. He had found it in a polemical work by Engels called *Eugen Dühring's Revolution in Science,* more briefly and conveniently known as *Anti-Dühring.* In this work Engels stated categorically that "when there is no longer any class to be held in subjection, then state interference in social relations becomes, in one domain after another, superfluous, and then withers away of itself, the government of persons being replaced by the administration of things and by the conduct of processes of production." The breathtaking argument comes at the end of the polemic, and not the slightest evidence is offered in order to sustain it. Nevertheless, Engels goes on to proclaim that it is precisely when the state has withered away that man's real history on earth begins, for then and only then will he be free. Paraphrasing Engels, Lenin proposes the formula: "So long as the state exists there is no freedom; when freedom exists there will be no state."

Throughout *The State and Revolution* Lenin gives the impression of a man who is perplexed by the "withering away of the state." Of the certain end of the bourgeois state he has no doubt; this will come about amid the fearful and catastrophic battles between the proletariat and the bourgeoisie. At one point he declares that the proletarian state will begin to wither away immediately after its victory, "since in a society without class distinctions the state is unnecessary and impossible." Supported by the overwhelming mass of the population, it would enforce its will "almost without any special machinery." "Communism makes the state absolutely unnecessary, because there is *nobody* to be suppressed." But as he becomes more entangled in the argument, tossing "all" words and "no" words in the air as though they were colored balloons rising and falling in beautiful patterns, it becomes increasingly clear that his original certainties give way to hesitation, to doubt, and to denial. The balloons burst; the juggler goes home. At one moment the withering-away of the state will come about immediately after the victory of the proletariat; at the next moment he is shaking his head sadly and admitting "the protracted nature of the process and its dependence upon the rapidity of development of the *higher phase* of communism. . . . We must leave quite open the question of the length of time required for the withering-away of the state, and the concrete forms it will take, since material for the solution of these questions is *not available*." Nor could they be available, for the theory rests on no ascertainable foundations.

Even when he has come to realize that the withering process will be long and protracted, and might even stretch to infinity, Lenin continually returns to it. The theory has become his talisman, all the more valuable because it seems to vanish whenever he looks upon it. It enters as a refrain into all his arguments. At every turning of the road he greets it with open arms. The state he hopes to bring about will become "one office and one factory, with equal work and equal pay." All citizens will be hired employees of the state, "which is made up of armed workers," and they will be organized by accountants and controllers. According to Lenin, accounting and controlling "have been simplified by capitalism to the utmost extent, till they have become the extraordinarily simple operations of watching, recording, and issuing receipts, and these are within the reach of anybody who can read and write and knows the first four rules of arithmetic."

Lenin was to learn later that the state, if it wants to survive, must be much more than a calculating machine.

The themes of the withering-away of the state and the violent destruction of the state go hand in hand. They are inseparable; they twine round one another and strangle one another. The more violent the conflict between them, the more does Lenin seem to adore them. Confronted with the two faces of violence—silent annihilation and frenzied combat—he is unable to choose between them.

Much of *The State and Revolution* reads like a tract written by Nechayev or Bakunin. The notebooks used by Lenin in writing this work have survived, and it is perhaps significant that in the notebooks, but not in the text, he found confirmation for his theories in Bakunin. He attached extraordinary importance to a letter written by Karl Marx at the time of the Paris Commune in which he prophesied that the Communards "would *smash* the bureaucratic-military machine, and this is the preliminary condition for every real people's revolution on the Continent." Marx's letter was dated April 1871, and Lenin found some amusement in the fact that six months earlier Bakunin had written to a French socialist in very similar terms, saying, "It is evident to me that after the complete destruction of the administrative and government machinery, France will be saved only by the spontaneous revolutionary action of the people." Lenin wrote these words on the side of the page next to the quotation from Marx, under the heading: "An amusing reference from Bakunin."

But there is nothing in the least amusing in *The State and Revolution,* with its primitive, anarchic vision of a world saved from perdition by the total destruction of all authority. Only six chapters were completed, but enough remains to show the temper of his mind on the eve of the October revolution. He worked on the book through August and September in Razliv and Helsingfors, in the hayfield and in the apartment of the police chief, and strangely it reflects the idyllic freedom of the hayfield and the compulsive terrors of the police. On the first page of the manuscript he signed the work with yet another pseudonym, "F. F. Ivanovsky," as though he intended to publish it at some later date on the illegal Bolshevik press. In fact it was published by his orders in the spring of 1918 under the curious double pseudonym, "V. Ilyin (N. Lenin)." There was a note explaining that he had intended to write a further chapter on "The Experience of the Russian Revolutions of 1905 and 1917," but had been unavoidably interrupted. He added that "it was more pleasant and useful to go through 'the experience of revolution' than to write about it."

About the time it was published, in February 1918, Bukharin raised the question of the withering-away of the state. Lenin dismissed the subject casually, as one not worthy of inquiry. "One may well wonder when the state will wither away," he replied. "To proclaim the withering-away in advance would be to violate historical perspectives." In such a way did he dismiss a problem which had absorbed his attention six months earlier.

The State and Revolution was Lenin's major theoretical work between the July uprising and the October revolution, but it was by no means his only work. A stream of letters, statements and articles came from his pen, some angry, some cajoling, some threatening. All through the summer and autumn, Kerensky was attempting to cope with problems of government which were almost beyond solution: war, inflation and the paralysis of trade were threatening to reduce the country to a state of anarchy. General Kornilov's attempted *coup d'état* in early September only added to the intolerable confusion. Riga fell to the Germans. Kerensky appointed himself as the head of a five-man directorate and emerged as a dictator over a country which could no more tolerate his dictatorship than it could tolerate the absolute rule of the Tsar. His orders were obeyed or disobeyed, according to the prevailing moods of his officers or the Soviets. With the coming of winter the Bolsheviks were in the ascendant. Trotsky had been arrested following the July uprising; he emerged from prison to become the most powerful figure in the Petrograd Soviet, rivaling Kerensky's power in the nation's capital. By the end of September Lenin was pleading for immediate action to topple the Provisional Government. He explained that the July uprising had been premature; power could not have been maintained; the army and the provinces would have marched against Petrograd. But not now—not any longer, with Kerensky, like the country, so exhausted that he was unable to bring himself to impose order or get others to impose it. There might have been

order if Kornilov's *coup d'état* had succeeded, and if in some way
Kerensky and Kornilov could have combined their forces, the government might have survived through the winter. The fate of Russia
was sealed when, in order to prevent Kornilov's threatened attack on
Petrograd, arms were given to the workers. Then it was only a question of time before those who led the armed workers would seize
power.

From Helsingfors, Lenin watched and waited. His brain was spinning with the imponderables of the coming revolution; he chafed at
his isolation, at being so far away from the centers of power. Within a
few days, or a few weeks at most, he believed the Bolsheviks would
seize power; and with their coming to power, as inevitably as night
follows the day, he believed they would conquer the world.

No world conquerer ever looked less like one. The short, beardless
man, living alone in the apartment of the chief of police at Helsingfors, living on the tea and eggs he boiled on the gas burner, regarded
the coming revolution as only the prelude to a gigantic convulsion
which would engulf the whole world. He had, he thought, found the
Archimedean point, and with his lever he proposed to throw the world
out of one orbit into another closer to his liking. He spent half the
night reading the newspapers which Rovio brought him each evening,
and every morning Rovio found on the table the letters and articles
which had to be sent to Petrograd or Stockholm. He was a man in a
state of feverish agitation, straining for certainties—and there were
no certainties. Between the twenty-fifth and the twenty-seventh of
September the storm broke. Quite suddenly he became absolutely
certain in his mind that the time had come to deliver the final blow. In
two articles which seem to have been written at white heat he declared that the time had come, there must be no further delay otherwise everything would be lost. "History will not forgive us if we do
not assume power now," he wrote. "Assume power at once in Moscow
and in Petrograd—it does not matter which, and perhaps we should
begin in Moscow. We will win *absolutely* and *unquestionably*."

Why did he choose this precise moment to demand an immediate
uprising? The reason seems to be quite clear, for it is one which he
refers to constantly in the two articles. There were rumors that the
British and the Germans were on the eve of making a separate peace.
The rumors were patently false, but for some reason Lenin believed
them. He was haunted by the nightmare that once the British and the
Germans had concluded a separate peace, they would hurl their com-

bined forces against Petrograd and stamp out the revolutionary ferment. It was necessary to act before the Germans and the British were
at the gates of Petrograd.

"The international situation *just now*, on the *eve* of a separate
peace between the English and the Germans is *in our favor*," he wrote.
"It is precisely now that to offer peace to the people means to *win*."

His argument for bringing about the uprising now depended upon
nothing more than the rumor of a separate peace. A few weeks later
he would insist again that the moment had come for an uprising, and
this time he would base his argument on rumors of widespread mutinies in the German fleet. In each case the argument was fallacious. In
fact, no arguments were necessary. *The government was so weak that
an uprising at any time between the last week of September and the
end of October would have been successful.* There was simply no
power in Russia which could oppose an armed uprising of the workers.

Lenin, following Marx, regarded insurrection as an art. In the second of the two articles written between the twenty-fifth and the
twenty-seventh of September, he outlined the plan of attack. The
workers must be immediately mobilized, the telegraph offices captured, the government and the general staff placed under arrest, and
the Peter and Paul Fortress occupied by loyal troops. It was a sketchy
outline, and he seemed to be apologizing for it when he added that
these moves were "only intended to illustrate the idea that *an uprising
must be treated as a work of art*."

His state of frustration and fury, and the vast extent of his ambitions, can be gauged from a passage in the middle of this article in
which he proposed a revolutionary war against Germany if the Germans refused to offer a truce to the victorious insurrectionaries. He
wrote:

> Finally, only our party, after winning victory in an uprising, *has the
> power* to save Petrograd, for if it should happen that our offer of peace
> is rejected and we receive not even a truce, then *we* shall become "*de-
> fensists*," and we shall place ourselves *at the head of the war parties*,
> and we shall be *the most "warlike"* party of all, and we shall carry on
> the war in a truly revolutionary fashion. We shall take from the capital-
> ists all the bread and *all* the shoes. We shall leave them crumbs, we shall
> dress them in bast shoes. We shall send all the bread and all the boots
> to the front.
> And then we shall save Petrograd.
> In Russia there are still great resources, both material and spiritual,

for a truly revolutionary war; there are 99 chances out of 100 that the Germans will at least give us a truce. And to secure a truce at present— this means already to conquer *the whole world.*

With such thoughts in his mind, believing in imminent socialist revolutions throughout the world, Lenin could no longer tolerate being so far from the center of power. He dared not yet return to Petrograd, but there was nothing to prevent him from going to Vyborg just inside the Finnish frontier. On September 30, wearing his wig, and with the faithful Eino Rahja by his side, he took the train to Vyborg.

ON THE EVE

FOR NEARLY TEN WEEKS Lenin had been living the life of a fugitive, always disguised and always in hiding, grateful for the security provided by people he had never set eyes upon before he entered their apartments. He had stayed with workers, farmers, a Finnish deputy, a police chief. In Vyborg he stayed in the apartment of a journalist called Latukk. He remained in the apartment, cooked his own meals, read all the newspapers Latukk could find for him, and all the time he chafed at his imprisonment.

As soon as Shotman learned that Lenin was in Vyborg, he took the first train and presented himself in the apartment. Lenin was in a towering rage. Shotman had scarcely opened his mouth when Lenin snapped at him. "Is it true that the Central Committee has forbidden me to come to Petrograd?" Shotman answered that they had made the order for his own safety. Lenin demanded written confirmation of the order. Shotman took a sheet of paper and wrote:

> I, the undersigned, hereby certify that the Central Committee of the Russian Social Democratic Party (Bolshevik faction) resolved at a meeting on [such-and-such a date] that Comrade Lenin shall be forbidden to enter Petrograd until further notice.

Shotman could not remember the exact date of the meeting when he wrote his *Memoirs*, but he remembered with absolute clarity how Lenin raged at his enforced idleness when, as he felt, he should be leading the revolution.

Lenin took the sheet of paper, carefully folded it twice, and with his thumbs in his vest, began to pace hurriedly up and down the room, murmuring angrily, "I won't tolerate it! I won't tolerate it!"

Later, when he had calmed down, he threw a barrage of questions at Shotman: What was happening in Petrograd? What were the workers saying? What about the morale of the army and the sailors? He showed Shotman tables of statistics carefully compiled to show the extraordinary growth of Bolshevik strength not only among the workers, but also among the bourgeoisie. In a tone of complete conviction Lenin said, "The country is for us. That is why our chief task at this moment is the immediate organization of all our forces to take over power."

Shotman argued that they could hardly take over power while lacking the experts to run the machinery of government.

"Pure absurdity!" Lenin replied. "Any workman can learn to become a minister in a few days. There is no need for any special ability. It is not even necessary that he should understand the technicalities. That side of things will be done by the functionaries who will be compelled to work for us."

Shotman was a little startled. To Lenin it was all so very simple, while to Shotman the machinery of government was profoundly complicated. He asked what Lenin proposed to do about money after the Kerensky bank notes were declared valueless.

"There's nothing simpler," Lenin replied. "We'll simply run the bank notes off on the newspaper presses. In a few days we shall have millions of bank notes."

"Yes, and any competent forger will be able to imitate them."

"Then we'll have very complicated designs on the bank notes, and in any case it is a matter for the technicians. It's no use discussing it."

And he went on to explain that these were minor matters; the important matter was to enact decrees which would convince the Russian people that the government was theirs, and then they would defend it. Everything else would follow automatically. First, he would end the war, and the army would immediately come over to him. Then he would take away the land from the aristocrats, the priests, and the rich, and give it to the peasants, and the peasants would come over to him. The factories and plants would be taken from the capitalists and given to the workers.

"Who would then oppose us?" Lenin said, and Shotman remembered afterward that Lenin stared at him fixedly, and suddenly "he winked with his left eye and there was a faint smile on his lips." "Of course," Lenin went on, "we shall have to strike at the right moment. Everything depends on that!"

Before Shotman left, Lenin ordered him to find some way of arranging his return to Petrograd.

Lenin spent nearly three weeks in Vyborg in a state of acute tension and discomfort. The Central Committee obviously was not in sympathy with his interpretation of events. "The time is fully ripe," he wrote. "We must attack now. There is not a moment to lose." Because they did nothing, he accused them of being traitors "pursuing tactics designed to protect the bourgeoisie and the landowners." He went on to call them traitors "to democracy and freedom." In a letter of October 12 he was so incensed by their behavior that he formally tendered his resignation to the Central Committee and announced his determination "to carry on propaganda *among the lower ranks* of the party and at the Party Congress." He had never in his life been in any mood for half-measures, and he was baffled by their inaction.

He was almost prepared to defy the Central Committee and to take matters in his own hands. Smilga, the leader of the Workers' and Peasants' Deputies in Finland, was given instructions to make the most careful preparations for an armed uprising in Finland. And since he might shortly be moving around the country without the protection of the Central Committee, Lenin asked Smilga to send him "an identity card on the stationery of the Regional Committee, signed by the chairman, with the proper seal, typed or *written in very clear handwriting,* in the name of Konstantin Petrovich Ivanov, to the effect that the chairman of the Regional Committee vouches for this comrade and requests *all Soviets,* the *Vyborg* Soviet of Soldiers' Deputies as well as others, to have full confidence in him and to render him assistance at all times." He explained that he needed the certificate because "*anything* might happen, since a 'conflict' or a 'meeting' was possible." By this he seems to have meant that he intended to appeal directly to the armed workers and soldiers unless he received satisfaction from the Central Committee.

In his Vyborg exile he wrote a forty-page pamphlet with the significant title "Can the Bolsheviks Retain State Power?" He had no doubt they could retain it. He dismissed one by one all the arguments which had been brought forward against their retaining it. To Shotman he had explained that nothing could be simpler than the control of the government machinery, but he was less sanguine now; he spoke of this control as "one of the most difficult tasks confronting the victorious proletariat." In *The State and Revolution* he had written a hymn in praise of the destruction of the existing order. Now he considerably modifies his concept of destruction; he speaks of adapting "the otherwise excellent banking system and making it *larger*, more democratic, more all-embracing," by the institution of the state bank. Even the rich under socialism will be protected: they will receive union cards and be set to work, and every week, or at other regular intervals, they will receive certificates from the union certifying they have done their work conscientiously, otherwise they will receive no food cards. If they refuse to co-operate, their wealth will be confiscated and they will be imprisoned. The state will enjoy a total monopoly. Everyone will have his work-book, in which his account with the state will be recorded. In the past such work-books were regarded as badges of servility; under socialism they would be regarded as badges of honor. Banks, factories, colleges, experimental stations, all the technical facilities of the modern state will simply be taken over and placed under one management. The technicians will be paid well, but they will be given nothing to eat unless they serve the interests of the revolutionary government. With such simple solutions he prepared to inaugurate the new social order.

Here and there in the course of the pamphlet he permits himself brief autobiographical remarks, which are sometimes enlightening. Here he speaks of the difficulty of a theoretician who has never known hunger, confronted by the hunger of the masses:

> As for bread, I, who had never been in need, never gave it a thought. Bread to me appeared of itself, being a sort of by-product of a writer's work. Fundamentally, my ideas upon the class struggle for bread were reached by political analysis, by an extraordinarily complicated and involved path.

It was a strange confession, which seems curiously out of place in a polemic delivered against Gorky's paper *Novaya Zhizn,* which had accused the Bolsheviks of being unable to retain state power even if they succeeded in a victorious uprising.

"Can the Bolsheviks Retain State Power?" consists of a series of notes written good-humoredly and in a mood of complacency; there is no feeling of urgency. But he had no sooner completed these notes than he wrote an urgent message to the Central Committee and to the Bolsheviks in the Petrograd and Moscow Soviets in which he demanded an immediate uprising. "The Bolsheviks must seize power at once, and thereby save the world revolution," he declared. "To delay is a crime." He suggested the slogan "Power to the Soviets, Peace to All Peoples, Bread to the Starving," and he concluded with the most pacific statement that any revolutionary leader has ever made on the eve of an uprising: "Victory is assured, and the chances are nine out of ten that it will be bloodless." The letter was written on October 14. The Central Committee was still not prepared to launch the uprising.

They were however prepared to let him enter Petrograd, and it was arranged that he should stay in a house on the Bolshoy Sampsonievsky. The fifth-story apartment of Margarita Fofanova was selected. She worked in a reputable publisher's office, and though she had been a militant member of the party since the age of nineteen, she was the last person anyone would expect to be harboring a dangerous revolutionary. Her children were sent away to the country to stay with relatives, and she was alone in the apartment to receive him when he arrived, wearing spectacles and a wig, looking for all the world like an elderly music teacher. She says he arrived "on a Friday"; the official Soviet biographies insist that he arrived on Saturday, October 20. It is perhaps not a matter of great moment whether he arrived on a Friday or a Saturday, but Fofanova was not a woman who was likely to mistake a day which was so important in her life. Lenin reminded her to address him always as Ivanov, and he begged her to bring him newspapers every morning around eleven o'clock when he was having his breakfast. She had strict orders to see that he always wore his wig when he was in her presence. He spent the days indoors, keeping away from the windows except on the second day when he inspected the balcony of one of the rooms, to see whether he could swing over it and escape if necessary by making his way along the gutter pipes. Whenever he entered a new house, he liked to have the ground plan firmly fixed in his mind. The apartment on Shirokaya Street had been raided three times, and he was still being hunted.

Since arriving in Petrograd, he had not changed in the least. He still demanded immediate insurrection and continually repeated in his letters the maxim of Peter the Great: "To delay is death." The separate peace between Britain and Germany faded into the background, and so too did the mutinies in the German fleet. There had been a strike in Turin; it was reported briefly in the newspapers; and in Lenin's feverish mind the strike became a *levée en masse* which threatened to engulf the whole of Italy. It was one more of the many demonstrable signs of the socialist revolution which was about to spread over the whole world. Then why this intolerable delay when the time to act was now, before the enemy could regroup his forces?

On October 21 he wrote a short essay on the art of insurrection, giving it the title "Advice from an Outsider"—an ironical description of himself as a man no longer playing an active revolutionary role. Following Marx, he formulated five rules for a successful uprising:

1. Never *play* with an uprising, but once it has begun, be firm in the knowledge that you have *to carry it through to the end*.
2. It is necessary to accumulate a *great preponderance of forces* in a decisive place at a decisive moment, otherwise the enemy, being better prepared and organized, will annihilate the insurrectionaries.
3. Once the uprising has begun, one must act with the utmost *decisiveness,* and one must absolutely and without fail go over *to the offensive.* "The defensive is the death of an armed uprising."
4. One must strive to take the enemy by surprise, to take advantage of the moment when his forces are scattered.
5. One must strive *daily* for at least small victories (one might say even hourly victories, if it is a question of a single city), in order to maintain at all costs *"moral superiority."*

As Lenin saw it, all that was necessary was for the fleet, the army and the workers to surround Petrograd and to cut it off from the rest of Russia; the victory would be won. He still held to the belief that the Russian revolution would be the herald of the world revolution. "The success of both the Russian and the world revolution," he wrote, "depends upon two or three days of struggle."

On the night of October 23, in a well-furnished apartment on the Karpovka, the final decision was taken to launch the revolution which was to shake the world. The meeting place was the apartment of Nikolay Sukhanov, who spent the night in another part of town and knew nothing about the meeting until many days later. "History," he wrote, "played a merry jest on me. That meeting, where the final decisions were made, took place in my apartment (32 Karpovka, Apartment 31) without my knowing it."

The secret meeting was called by Lenin, and had been arranged by Sverdlov on twenty-four hours' notice. It began in the evening and did not break up until ten hours later. Twelve of the twenty-one members of the Central Committee were present. They were Lenin, Trotsky, Zinoviev, Kamenev, Sverdlov, Dzerzhinsky, Stalin, Uritsky, Bubnov, Sokolnikov, Lomov and Alexandra Kollontay. Varvara Yak-

ovlieva took down the minutes of the meeting, and the wife of Sukhanov served tea and sandwiches. Lenin was the last to arrive. He
came wearing his wig and with heavy spectacles, and without his
customary beard. Yakovlieva thought he resembled a Lutheran minister. Most of the others were disguised. Zinoviev had shaved off his
luxuriant hair and wore a luxuriant beard. Because of the conspiratorial nature of the meeting, the secretary was told to make only the
briefest notes, and very early in the proceedings she seems to have
abandoned her notes altogether.

Sverdlov, who was chairman, opened with reports from various
Bolshevik groups in the provinces and on the military fronts. He
seems to have been primed by Lenin, for he said exactly what Lenin
wanted him to say. He spoke of mysterious counterrevolutionary
moves taking place in Minsk, "where a new Kornilov affair is being
prepared." A Cossack detachment had been thrown around Minsk to
bottle up and later to destroy the Bolsheviks in the city, and there
were suspicious negotiations going on between the staff and the headquarters in Petrograd. Someone must have asked whether there was
any documentary evidence of the events taking place in Minsk, for
Yakovlieva's notes go on to say, "There are no documents at all. They
can be obtained by seizing the staff, which is technically quite possible in Minsk: in this case the local garrison can disarm all the troops
around. All the artillery has been driven into the Pinsk marshes." It
was a strange report, and except for the ominous underscoring of a
new Kornilov affair, it had very little to do with the main matter to be
discussed: whether the insurrection should be brought about immediately or delayed indefinitely.

Then Lenin took the floor, and what he had to say was urgent, demanding, crushing in its terrible simplicity. What he demanded was
nothing less than an immediate uprising, now, tomorrow, or the next
day, but not later. He was once more the prosecutor. Without the
least subterfuge he was implying that the Central Committee was
notably lacking in elementary courage and foresight. There had been a
decided slackening of the revolutionary impulse since the beginning
of September, and much time had been lost—all this was absolutely
inadmissible. It was time to work out the practical details of revolution and put them into operation, because the masses were tired of
words and resolutions and they wanted action under the slogan "All
power to the Soviets." These delays were incomprehensible, because
the international situation was working to the advantage of the Bol-

sheviks. In the July days the Bolsheviks could have seized power, but they could not have held it: now the majority was for the Bolsheviks, and the situation was ripe for the transfer of power.

He wanted the revolution to take place before the meeting of the Constituent Assembly, and he admitted that the Assembly "would not be for us." He admitted, too, that the masses were becoming increasingly indifferent. But he insisted that the mood of the soldiers was one of revolutionary fervor, and he seemed to be suggesting that the revolution might break out in Minsk, the headquarters of the western front, and then roll back across the country in a tide which could not be controlled.

He was in a mood of anger, almost of despair. Coldly he attacked those who had failed to recognize the dangers of postponing the revolution; and in this attack he included all the members of the Central Committee. Trotsky had set the provisional date for the uprising at "not later than the twenty-fifth of October," the day proposed for the Second Congress of Soviets. Lenin asked pointedly what the Second Congress of Soviets had to do with the matter, and in any case it was likely enough that there would be no congress at all unless they were able to seize power in the meantime. He was in no mood to minimize the strength of the enemy: there was nothing to prevent Kerensky from bringing up counterrevolutionary divisions and then throwing them around Petrograd, stifling the revolution at birth. "We dare not wait, we dare not delay," he kept repeating; and the members of the Central Committee were aware of a stern, stubborn, utterly impatient force welling out of him.

Uritsky pointed out mildly that it was useless to talk about the technique of revolt when the technical weapons were lacking. The Petrograd workers had forty thousand rifles among them, but that would not decide the issue. There had been a mass of resolutions, and no action. There had been few meetings of the Petrograd Soviets, and in any case they were disorganized. What was needed was the deliberate determination to revolt. At this point Yakovlieva's note on Uritsky's speech comes to an end, and we do not know Lenin's withering answer.

Dzerzhinsky spoke later, suggesting the formation of a Political Bureau to offer the party day-to-day guidance. This proposal was carried, and the Politburo, consisting of seven members, Lenin, Zinoviev, Kamenev, Trotsky, Stalin, Sokolnikov, and Bubnov, was elected.

All through the long night Lenin kept returning to the date of the uprising. He was in a state of ice-cold exaltation, and he wanted general agreement on a fixed date, or at least a date which could be varied only a little according to changing events and the uncertainties of the political situation. To his surprise he discovered that the two members of the Central Committee who were closest to him, Zinoviev and Kamenev, were wavering; they were not even sure that the uprising was desirable. Lenin attacked them brutally. They were never completely forgiven, and to the end of their lives they remembered Lenin's stinging reproaches and lived under the shadow of having been "traitors to the revolution."

Finally a vote was taken. By ten votes to two it was agreed that the time was ripe for an immediate uprising. With the gnawed end of a pencil, on a squared sheet torn out of a child's copybook, Lenin wrote out the resolution agreed on by a majority of the Central Committee. By this time he was too weary, or too sickened by the defection of his closest friends, to give architectural shape to the resolution, which is oddly blunted and colorless. The first paragraph enumerates in no discernible order the reasons for bringing about the uprising, and includes at least one demonstrable untruth—"the undoubted decision of the Russian bourgeoisie and of Kerensky & Co to surrender Petrograd to the Germans"—while the second paragraph states cumbrously that the uprising is inevitable and the time is fully ripe.

This document, written in a child's copybook, ranks with the "April Theses" as among the most potent and far-reaching documents written in our age. With this scrap of paper he launched the revolution.

> The C.C. recognizes that the international situation of the Russian Revolution (the mutiny of the fleet in Germany being an extreme manifestation of the growth *throughout Europe** of the world socialist revolution, the threat of a peace between the imperialists with the aim of strangling the revolution in Russia)—also the military situation (the undoubted decision of the Russian bourgeoisie and of Kerensky & Co to surrender Petrograd to the Germans),—also the fact that the proletarian parties have gained a majority in the Soviets—all this taken in conjunction with the peasant insurrection and the swing of popular confidence to our party (the elections in Moscow), finally the obvious preparations for a second Kornilov affair (withdrawal of troops from Petrograd, dispatch of Cossacks to Petrograd, encirclement of Minsk by Cossacks, etc.)—all this places the armed uprising on the order of the day.

* The words *"throughout Europe"* were added later.

①

Ц. К. признает, что как междунородное положение русской революции (возстание во флотѣ в Германіи, как крайнее проявленіе нарастанія всемірной соціалистической революціи, затѣм угроза мира империалистов с цѣлью удушенія революціи в Россіи), — так и военное положеніе (несомнѣнное рѣшеніе русской буржуазіи и Керенскаго сдать Питер нѣмцам), — так и пріобрѣтеніе большинства пролетарской партіей в Совѣтах, — все это в связи с крестьянским возстаніем и с поворотом народнаго

⌣ во всей Европѣ

2/ довѣрія к нашей партіи (выбо-
ры в Москвѣ), наконецъ явное
подготовленіе второй кор-
ниловщины (вывод войск
из Питера, подвоз к Питеру
казаков, окруженіе Минска
казаками и пр.), — все
это ставя на очередь дня
вооруженное возстаніе.

        Признавая такъ обр.,
что воооруж. возстаніе неизбѣж-
но и вполнѣ назрѣло, Ц. К.
предлагает всѣм организа-
ціям партіи руководиться
этим и съ этой точки зрѣ-
нія обсуждать и разсматр
всѣ практическіе вопросы
(съѣзда совѣтов сѣв. области,
вывода войск из Питера, вы-
ступленія москвичей и
минчан и т. д.).

Recognizing, therefore, that an armed uprising is inevitable and that the time is fully ripe, the C.C. proposes to all the party organizations to be guided accordingly, and to consider and decide all the practical questions (Congress of Soviets of the Northern region, withdrawal of troops from Petrograd, action in Moscow and Minsk, etc.) from this point of view.

Such was the secret proclamation which Lenin addressed to his associates early in the morning of October 24, 1917, after ten hours of exhausting argument, and it is worth examining in some detail, not only because it was to have such far-reaching consequences, but because it opens up some surprising clues to the state of Lenin's mind on the eve of the October revolution.

In the opening paragraph Lenin offers his reasons for believing that the international situation was working in favor of the revolution. Significantly, he attached great importance to "the mutiny of the fleet in Germany," placing it first on the list and describing it as "the extreme manifestation of the growth throughout Europe of the world socialist revolution." There had in fact been a mutiny at the German naval base at Wilhelmshaven in September. It affected only two or three ships and was immediately quelled, the mutineers being executed on the spot. The second reason for believing that the international situation was working in favor of the Bolsheviks was a still more extraordinary one. Lenin still believed, or affected to believe, that there was a danger of the Allies making peace with Germany in order to strangle the revolution in Russia, by which he clearly means a proletarian revolution organized by the Soviets, not the revolution which had been proclaimed in February. He was saying that the German and Allied governments were about to stop the war in order to crush the Petrograd Soviets. If Lenin really believed this, he was showing an extraordinary contempt for historical processes; at that moment in the death struggle, the existence or nonexistence of the Petrograd Soviets was the last thing on the minds of the German and Allied political leaders, who had no conception of the power which would later be exerted by these Soviets under the Bolsheviks.

Furthermore, there was no evidence that Kerensky intended to surrender Petrograd to the Germans: he was in fact dedicated to continuing the war as long as it was humanly possible, and it was precisely because he was determined to continue the war in the face of mutinies in the Russian army that the Bolsheviks were able to accuse him of being a warmonger. Lenin knew very well that there had been no "undoubted decision of the Russian bourgeoisie and of Kerensky & Co to surrender Petrograd to the Germans." As the Germans moved closer to Petrograd, there had been rumors that the capital would be moved to Moscow, and the Bolsheviks, especially Trotsky, had seized upon these rumors as though they were evidence of a counterrevolutionary conspiracy, and they accused Kerensky of being the head of a government "of national treachery." For propaganda purposes, Kerensky was being simultaneously accused of wanting to fight the Germans to the last Russian and of wanting to surrender to the Germans. It was curiously effective propaganda, but it had no relation to historical truth.

Lenin's fourth reason for believing that the international situation favored the Bolsheviks was "the fact that the proletarian parties have gained a majority in the Soviets." This was true, for in September the Bolsheviks had obtained the majority in the Petrograd Soviet and a few days later they acquired a majority in the Moscow Soviet. Lenin was perfectly correct in saying that there was a swing of popular confidence to the Bolsheviks and in stressing the importance of the peasant insurrections sweeping across the country. The possibility of a second Kornilov affair was also to be reckoned with.

The strange document mingled fact and fancy, probability and improbability, vast hope and illimitable despair; it was written in a state of exhaustion by a man who had spent his entire life dreaming of bringing about a world revolution according to principles he had found in Nechayev, Bakunin and Marx. Only one sentence in the secret proclamation had any real relevance to the situation. It was the sentence which Lenin had repeated constantly through the summer and autumn: "An armed uprising is inevitable, and the time is fully ripe."

By this proclamation Lenin had committed the Bolsheviks to the uprising in the very near future. The exact date had still to be determined.

Yet even at this last moment there was powerful opposition to the plan by men who were haunted by the thought of a repetition of the July days. It was not only Kamenev and Zinoviev who disputed the logic of an uprising which had no real roots among the population. Kerensky and the members of his government might be removed from the scene and the Petrograd Soviet might take power in its hands, but for how long? And for what purpose? Would there be a dictatorship of the proletariat, or a dictatorship of one man? These questions, left unanswered by the Bolsheviks, only added to the despair of the workers in that tragic winter.

Kamenev and Zinoviev wrote a closely argued attack on the position of Lenin the same day. They could see no basis for an immediate uprising, no hope of its success. It was true that the Bolsheviks were gaining in numbers, but they were still outnumbered by the peasants, who nearly all belonged to the Socialist Revolutionary Party. Lenin claimed that the majority of the people in Russia and the majority of the international proletariat were clamoring for the uprising, and both these claims were patently false. Nor was there any enthusiasm among the workers for street fighting. They did not welcome it, did not hope for it. The two dissenters wrote:

> The forces of the proletarian party are, of course, very substantial, but the decisive question is: Is the sentiment among the workers and soldiers of the capital really such that they see salvation only in street fighting, that they are impatient to go into the streets? No. There is no such sentiment. Even those in favor of the uprising state that the sentiment of the masses of the workers and soldiers is not at all like their sentiments on the eve of July 16. If among the great masses of the poor of the capital there were a militant sentiment burning to go into the streets, it might have served as a guarantee that an uprising initiated by them would draw in the biggest organizations (railroad unions, unions of post office and telegraph workers, etc.), where the influence of our party is weak. But since there is no such sentiment even in the factories and barracks, it would be self-deception to build any plans on it.

Both Zinoviev and Kamenev were revolutionaries of long experience, and for many years Zinoviev had been Lenin's closest friend. In writing their long and reasoned plea to postpone the uprising they were not going over to the enemy; they were hoping to save the revolution for a better day. Unable to bring their plea to the attention of the Bolsheviks, they decided upon a desperate gamble: they gave it to Gorky's newspaper *Novaya Zhizn*, which printed it on the morning of October 31. Lenin had no knowledge of the document until it was read to him on the telephone later that morning. When he heard what they had written, he was furious. He threatened to sever all comradely relations with them and to expel them from the party. He was particularly offended because they had criticized an *unpublished* decision of the Central Committee in a nonparty newspaper. They claimed there was no need for an uprising; in time power would come to them from the Constituent Assembly. "Then let them form their own party from candidates for the Constituent Assembly," Lenin said contemptuously. They were traitors or worse, and it hurt him to the core that they had repudiated his leadership. With a heavy heart he wrote:

> Hard times. A grave problem. A grave betrayal.
> And just the same the problem will be solved, the workers will unite, the peasant uprising and the extreme impatience of the soldiers at the front will do their work! Let us close the ranks tighter—the proletariat must win!

But the decision was no longer in his hands. For many days the Military Revolutionary Committee, with Trotsky presiding, had been in permanent session. Six days later they decided to strike.

THE CONQUEST OF PETROGRAD

THE MORNING BROKE gray and somber over a city which had long been preparing for its death. Cold winds blew the rains in from the Baltic, but there were no heavy showers—only the thin rain and the puddles in the streets. By midmorning the rain had ceased, and through the heavy clouds a few patches of pale sky could be seen. Winter was coming down, and soon there would be the first snows.

It was a morning like every other morning in late autumn. The streetcars were running, the streets were full of traffic, the newspapers with one or two notable exceptions appeared. There was no unusual activity: the bureaucrats went to their offices and the workers to their factories. Those who could afford to buy tickets were looking forward to seeing the new ballet, with Karsavina in the leading role, at the Maryinsky Theater. Chaliapin was singing, and Meyerhold was reviving Count Alexey Tolstoy's *Death of Ivan the Terrible,* the poetic drama in which Dostoyevsky had occasionally performed in aristocratic drawing rooms in the last weeks of his life. The ordinary, familiar life of the city was about to come to a stop, but no one walking through the gray streets and seeing the fashionable crowds on the Nevsky Prospect would have guessed that under the blue-and-gold cupola of the Smolny Convent overlooking the Neva where it takes a sharp turn to the south a handful of desperate men, calling themselves the Military Revolutionary Committee, were preparing a revolution which would one day extend over the whole of Russia and nearly a quarter of the world.

373

The Smolny had been taken over by the parties of the Left during the February revolution. For more than a hundred years this long gray three-story building had been a school for the daughters of the nobility. Deportment, French, and Russian history had been taught in the classrooms which had now become the offices of revolutionaries. Bolsheviks, Mensheviks, Socialist Revolutionaries and anarchists had taken possession, the names of the parties and the various splinter groups being written on sheets of paper and tacked onto the doors over the enamel tablets giving the name and number of the classroom. The rooms were spacious and seemed more spacious still for being painted white. Gradually all the revolutionary parties except the Mensheviks and Bolsheviks had drifted away, establishing their own headquarters elsewhere. By the beginning of November the Bolsheviks were coming to regard the Smolny as their own property, permitting the Mensheviks to enter only on sufferance.

Here for about two weeks Trotsky and his staff had been drawing up the battle plans for the coming insurrection. There were no guards at the gates. In the peculiarly permissive atmosphere of Petrograd no one had ever bothered to suggest that the headquarters of the revolution should be guarded. Similarly all the government buildings were left unguarded.

On the night of November 5 Kerensky, who had received many warnings of an imminent Bolshevik uprising, decided to act. He ordered a battalion of shock troops to march on the capital from Tsarskoye Selo; artillery was summoned from Pavlovsk; the cruiser *Aurora* was ordered to put out to sea; engineers were instructed to cut the telephone service to the Smolny; and the Bolshevik newspaper *Rabochy Put* was ordered to suspend publication. At five-thirty in the morning troops under the command of an officer bearing a warrant signed by the chief of the Petrograd military area broke into the offices of *Rabochy Put*, smashed the matrices, burned about eight thousand copies of the paper, removed all the documents they could find, sealed the doors, and posted a guard round the building. At about the same time the telephone lines to the Smolny were cut.

These were the first overt acts in the revolutionary war which was not to end until the whole of Russia came under the domination of the Bolsheviks.

When Trotsky woke up on the morning of November 6 he was confronted with the news that the Bolsheviks had lost their newspaper and their telephones. A motorcycle courier service was immediately organized to maintain contact with the factories and the regiments which favored the Bolsheviks. The problem of the printing press was solved by a young woman who had escaped from the building. She told how the guards had sealed the doors with sealing wax.

"Why don't we break the seals?" she asked.

"Why not?" Trotsky replied, and for years to come he would muse ironically on how the Russian Revolution began with the breaking of a few inches of official sealing wax at the suggestion of a young woman whose name he could never remember.

There remained the question of the military guards posted outside the building.

"The printers will go on working if they are given armed guards," the young woman suggested.

This was exactly the opportunity Trotsky had been waiting for. He ordered a company of the Lithuanian Regiment and a party of engineers to surround the *Rabochy Put* offices and ensure that the paper was printed. The Military Revolutionary Committee then issued a decree ordering that the printing presses of the revolutionary newspapers be kept open. This was the first of an endless series of decrees produced by the revolution. The second decree, also written by Trotsky, followed hard on the first. It was sent to all units of the Petrograd garrison and announced: "The enemy of the people took the offensive during the night. The Military Revolutionary Committee is leading the resistance to the assault of the conspirators."

In this way Trotsky could represent the uprising as an act of self-defense against a predatory government. This was especially important because it enabled the Bolsheviks to claim a revolutionary morality for their actions. Overnight the government had become "a counterrevolutionary conspiracy."

With the decision to send troops to safeguard the printing office, the Military Revolutionary Committee moved into high gear. Up to this moment no one had ever thought of posting guards outside the Smolny. Now it was transformed into a fortress, bristling with guns and cannon. Patrols were sent out to guard the main entrance; others were posted at the adjacent street corners. Cartloads of potatoes, vegetables and fruit were brought in to victual the Smolny for a siege; and in the courtyard piles of cordwood were set up like barricades to provide cover for riflemen and machine gunners. Field guns were mounted before the high stone columns in front of the building, and there were Maxim guns on the steps leading to the main floors.

Passwords were introduced. Outside, in the cold winter air, soldiers were making bonfires out of cordwood and warming themselves in the blaze.

Early in the morning there was a meeting of the Bolshevik Central Committee. Three of the members were absent: Lenin, Zinoviev and Stalin. Zinoviev may have remained away because he had no faith in the insurrection: he was probably not invited to attend. Stalin's absence may have been due to the fact that he was the editor of *Rabochy Put*. Lenin, of course, was still in hiding in Vyborg. Sverdlov acted as chairman of the meeting, but it was Trotsky who made the decisions and set out the duties of the committee members. Dzerzhinsky was placed in charge of posts and telegraphs; Bubnov of railroads; Nogin and Lomov of liaison with Moscow; Sverdlov with intelligence on the Provisional Government; Milyutin with food supplies; Kamenev and Berzin with liaison with the Left Socialist Revolutionaries who were moving closer to the Bolsheviks. None of these were strictly military duties, for Trotsky was determined to keep control of the *coup d'état* in his hands. At his suggestion it was agreed that if the Bolsheviks were forced out of the Smolny, they would make their headquarters at the Peter and Paul Fortress, where the garrison had just come over to their side. Kamenev, who rarely showed knowledge or interest in military matters, surprised everyone by suggesting that if the worst happened, the insurgent leaders would still be able to direct the uprising from the cruiser *Aurora*, which was equipped with radio. It was perhaps the most brilliant single suggestion made during the meeting.

The small corner room on the third floor of the Smolny was now the headquarters of the revolution. Here came the constant stream of messengers in sheepskin coats and muddy boots who reported on the preparations of the revolt which could not be delayed by more than a few hours, and from this small office there issued orders to the regiments, battleships and factories which had come over to the Bolsheviks. The government of Petrograd was already in their hands.

Meanwhile the Provisional Government still went through the motions of governing. At ten o'clock in the morning Kerensky summoned a meeting of his ministers at the Winter Palace to discuss the situation and to report on the measures he had taken during the night. The meeting lasted two hours, and he then left for the Maryinsky Palace, where the Pre-Parliament held its sessions. In a long and carefully reasoned speech he attacked the Bolsheviks for planning an uprising only three weeks before the election of the Constituent Assembly, which would have the authority to speak in the name of the whole of Russia. He pointed out that the Bolsheviks did not speak in the name of Russia, and their actions showed that they were consciously or unconsciously following exactly the path desired by the German militarists. They had spoken openly of an uprising, but the leaders of the conspiracy, "with their wonderful capacity for hiding themselves, will not suffer any of the consequences, which will have to be shouldered by the masses of the people." He read from *Rabochy Put* an article by Lenin deriding the Constituent Assembly and calling for an immediate uprising to support the German Social Democrats who were also attempting an uprising. In the article Lenin had asked why the proletariat of Russia was doing nothing to support the Germans "at a time when we have so many newspapers, and freedom of assembly, and are better situated than any other international proletariat." Ruefully, Kerensky noted that Lenin was asking the Russian people to come out in support of revolutionaries they knew nothing about. True, the army was demoralized. True, there was every reason to bring the war to an end, and he was sending delegates to Paris to discuss the immediate ending of the war. True, the question of the land reforms had not yet been settled, but it was clearly very close to settlement. He accused the Bolsheviks of treachery toward the Russian state. He ended his speech by saying that entire areas of Petrograd were already in a state of insurrection, and that he had ordered the arrest of the insurgent leaders.

He had scarcely completed his address when Konovalov, the Deputy Prime Minister, handed him a note. He studied it for a few moments. A strange silence descended on the palace. Then Kerensky said, "I have just been handed a document which is now being sent to all the regiments. It says: 'The Petrograd Soviet is in danger. I order your regiment to be fully prepared for action and to await further orders. All procrastination or failure to obey this order will be regarded as treason by the revolution. Podvoisky. Acting Chairman.'"

Pandemonium broke loose after the reading of the letter. Above the uproar Kerensky could be heard demanding complete powers to suppress the uprising. These powers were given to him. But by this time it was too late to put out the flames.

In the Smolny the flames were being busily fanned. The *Aurora*, ordered to put out to sea, asked the Military Revolutionary Committee what to do, and received the reply that it was to refuse all orders issued by Kerensky and place itself at the disposition of the committee. The Provisional Government kept issuing orders; as soon as they became known, the Military Revolutionary Committee countermanded them, and substituted new orders. The cat-and-mouse game was played by Trotsky with consummate daring and impertinence. When a deputation arrived from the city Duma to inquire whether the Soviets intended to begin an insurrection, he answered that there was some evidence that the government was about to rise against the people; and he invited the city councilors to join the Military Revolutionary Committee to help to preserve order. When the deputation spoke about the inevitable looting which would accompany an uprising, he presented them with one of the many orders he had written that day: "At the first attempt of criminal elements to bring about disturbances, looting, knifing or shooting in the streets of Petrograd, the criminals will be wiped off the face of the earth." The councilors left the Smolny with the obscure feeling that something had gone wrong, which would never be put right again.

Lenin too was living in uncertainty and despair. Fofanova had brought him the newspapers in the morning, and then left for her job in the publisher's office on Vasilyevsky Island. At four o'clock in the afternoon she heard that orders had been given for raising the bridges; it was the sign that Kerensky recognized the danger to his government and was determined to prevent the armed workers from entering the city. Leaving the publisher's office, she took the streetcar to the Nikolayevsky Bridge. The bridge was raised, and so was the Sampsonievsky Bridge, which she reached about fifteen minutes later. It was now half-past four, and night was falling. For some reason the Grenadersky Bridge was still open to traffic. She hurried across it and made her way to the Bolshoy Sampsonievsky, intent on reaching her apartment as soon as possible. Not far from the Grenadersky Bridge, on the same boulevard, was the headquarters of the local Bolshevik party. She went there and found they knew no more than she did. They had received no orders. Her own apartment was more than a mile to the north, and she took the streetcar. Lenin was alone in the apartment, fuming with impatience. She told him that most of the bridges had been raised. He wanted to know how many were raised and how many were still in operation, and he sent her back to the local committee. For Lenin the question of the bridges was a pressing one. If Kerensky could raise all the bridges, he could hold the inner city of Petrograd. In effect, the insurrection might become a battle for the bridges with all the advantages on the side of the government: everything depended upon capturing the inner city. He did not know that during the evening all ten bridges leading from the working class quarters to Petrograd had been quietly captured.

While Fofanova was away, he began to write the last of the long series of letters in which he urged immediate insurrection. Unknown to him, the insurrection had already begun. At nine o'clock Fofanova returned to the apartment with the news that all the bridges were in the hands of the revolutionaries, but there was still no word from the Military Revolutionary Committee. Lenin's letter said:

COMRADES!

I am writing these lines on the evening of the 24th* at a time when the situation is critical to the utmost degree. It is as clear as can be that it is death to delay the uprising now.

With all my strength I want to persuade the comrades that everything now hangs on a thread, that on the order of the day are questions which are not solved by conferences, by congresses (even by congresses of Soviets), but only and exclusively by the people, by the masses, by the struggle of the armed masses.

The bourgeois onslaught of the Kornilovists and the removal of Verkhovsky† show that we cannot afford to wait. We must at all costs, this very evening, this very night, arrest the government, after first disarming the Junkers (defeating them if they offer resistance), etc.

We must not wait! We may lose everything!

The advantage of seizing power now: the defense of *the people* (not the congress, but the people, the army, and the peasants in the first place) from the Kornilovist government, which has driven out Verkhovsky and has hatched a second Kornilov plot.

Who should take power?

This is not important at the moment. Let the Military Revolutionary Committee take it, "or some other body" which declares that it will relinquish the power only to the true representatives of the interests of the people, the interests of the Army (immediate offer of peace), the interests of the peasants (immediate seizure of the land, private property abolished), the interests of the hungry.

It is necessary that all districts, all regiments, all forces should be mobilized and should immediately send delegations to the Military Revolutionary Committee, to the Central Committee of the Bolsheviks,

---

* I.e., October 24, Old Style, corresponding to November 6, New Style.
† General Alexander Verkhovsky, the Minister of War, declared on November 3 that the Russian Army could no longer fight and that there must be an immediate peace with Germany.

insistently demanding that under no circumstances should power be left in the hands of Kerensky and company until the 25th. By no means! The matter must definitely be decided this evening or tonight.

History will not forgive revolutionaries for delays, when they could be victorious today (and will certainly be victorious today), while they risk losing much tomorrow, while they risk losing everything.

If we seize power today, we seize it not against the Soviets but for them.

Seizure of power is the basis of the uprising; its political purposes will be made clear after the seizure.

It would be a disaster or a sheer formality to await the uncertain voting of October 25. The people have a right and duty to decide such questions not by voting but by force; the people have a right and a duty at critical moments of revolution to give directions to their representatives, even their best representatives, and not to wait for them.

This has been proved by the history of all revolutions, and revolutionaries would be committing an immeasurable crime if they let this moment pass, knowing that upon them all depends *the saving of the revolution,* the offer of peace, the saving of Petrograd, the prevention of hunger, the transfer of land to the peasants.

The government is tottering. It must be given the *final push* at all costs!

Delay in starting is death.*

Having written the letter, Lenin was impatient to reach the Smolny, where decisions of the utmost importance were being taken. All the preparations for the insurrection had been made, and the Military Revolutionary Committee had already decided to strike at 2 A.M. Lenin had been kept informed of some of their plans, but not all of them, and he had been warned that the time was not ripe for him to leave his hiding place. In later years Stalin would claim that he sent a message during the late afternoon "summoning" Lenin to the Smolny, and that Lenin received the summons at the very moment that he was writing the letter, but such a happy coincidence seems unlikely. At 9:30 P.M. Lenin sent Margarita Fofanova to the Smolny,

* There is some mystery about this letter, which has survived only in a typewritten copy first printed in 1924. The official biography published by the Marx-Engels-Lenin Institute says that Krupskaya handed the Central Committee the letter the same evening, but Krupskaya, as she herself relates, reached the Smolny on a truck after Lenin had arrived. She does not mention the letter; she says she only went there to see whether Lenin had arrived safely. The official two-volume *History of the Civil War,* compiled by Stalin, Molotov, Gorky, and others says that around 9:30 P.M. Lenin wrote "a message of no particular importance and sent Fofanova off with it to the Smolny." Fofanova says she was sent off with a message, not to the Smolny but to Krupskaya. So the confusion continues, and it is not even certain that the letter was ever delivered.

presumably with an urgent request for the latest details of the uprising and almost certainly with a copy of the letter he had just written, and he told her that he would wait for her until eleven o'clock, and if she did not return by that time he would consider himself at liberty to do as he pleased. His dispatch rider, Eino Rahja, was with him.

Everything he had learned during the day pointed to the fact that the uprising was imminent. For nearly a month he had been urging the Central Committee and the Military Revolutionary Committee to strike—to strike now, at once, everywhere, before the Provisional Government could regroup its forces, and while the factory committees and the soldiers were still hot for action. Now at last he decided the time had come when he must do everything in his power "to give history a push." It was not enough to remain in hiding, to be produced triumphantly when Petrograd had fallen into the hands of the revolutionaries. At whatever the risk, he would have to reach the Smolny.

The risks were considerable. He would have to walk the whole way, because the streetcars were no longer running. There was always the danger of falling into the hands of a Cadet patrol. The bridges might be up, and then he would have to hire a boat to cross the Neva, and probably the Cadets had their searchlights playing on the river. Recognized, he would be shot out of hand.

A half hour passed while he paced up and down the room, revolving the issues in his mind. Then abruptly he decided there was nothing to be gained by remaining in the apartment and everything to be gained by reaching the Smolny. He clamped the wig on his head, and tied a large and crumpled handkerchief round his face; and Eino Rahja was instructed to tell anyone who stopped them that he was speechless with pain from toothache. Then he scribbled a note for Fofanova, who had been his diligent guardian—"I have gone where you did not want me to go. Au revoir. Ilyich"—and slipped out of the house. It was a dark, cold, windy night, but there was no snow on the ground. Thinking it might rain later in the evening, he had put on his galoshes.

The streetcars had already stopped running, or so they thought, and they were faced with a long walk down the Sampsonievsky Prospect, across the Liteiny Bridge, and so to the Smolny. The Vyborg district was already in the hands of the Red Guards, and they expected no difficulty until they came to the bridge. By good luck the last streetcar was on its way to the depot, and they jumped on it. The car was nearly empty. No one paid any attention to the man with the bandaged face and his young Finnish companion. In later years pious historians invented a strange conversation between Lenin and the conductress. Lenin is supposed to have asked where the streetcar was going, and the conductress is supposed to have replied, "Where have you come from? Don't you know what is going on in town? What sort of a workingman do you think you are if you don't know there is going to be a revolution? We're going to kick the bosses out!" Whereupon Lenin is supposed to have laughed and explained to the delighted conductress exactly how a revolution is brought about, while Eino Rahja trembled in his boots, afraid that Lenin might be recognized and betrayed. But though the official history of the civil war preserves this fragment of conversation, it is only one more of the many fictions invented to give color to events which were already so charged with color that they needed no adventitious decoration.

Lenin made his way to the Smolny in loneliness and misery, and in complete silence. He could not understand why the revolt was being launched without him. There had been no effort to contact him. An armored car could have been sent for him; Red Guards could have been ordered to take him to the Smolny; nothing was done. He had the distinct feeling that important information was being withheld from him. He made the journey to the Smolny knowing that he had little more than a one-to-three chance of getting there alive.

There were Red Guards at the Vyborg end of the bridge; they asked no questions, for these two travelers in their workmen's caps and shabby coats were obviously proletarian. A solitary cadet stood guard on the other side of the bridge, and he might have proved more troublesome if some Red Guards had not suddenly appeared from nowhere. The cadet's attention was diverted. While the Red Guards and the cadet exchanged insults Lenin and Eino Rahja slipped across the last few feet of the bridge. More than half of the journey had been accomplished in safety: the most dangerous part remained.

They were making their way down the Shpalernaya when two mounted cadets suddenly appeared in the mists, and ordered them to stop and show their passes. Eino Rahja whispered to Lenin, "Go ahead! I'll deal with them!" At that moment he had no clear idea how he would deal with them, though he had two revolvers in his pockets, and if necessary he could fight it out. Then he had an inspiration. He decided to play the role of a drunken rowdy. One of the cadets beat him across the head with a *nagaika*. To all questions about a pass, he simply answered that he did not know what they were talking about. The cadets decided to arrest him, and then thought better of it. Because there was nothing to be gained by arresting a drunken man, they let him go. He caught up with Lenin, and there were no further adventures until they reached the Smolny, where they were refused admittance. It was the oddest moment of all. The leader of the revolution, the man who had been earnestly demanding an insurrection for weeks, was refused admittance at the headquarters of the revolution. He had a white pass, which was no longer valid. The new passes were red. So, for nearly ten minutes Lenin and Eino Rahja argued with the guards, and it was only when the crowd behind him began to object to the delay that he was carried into the building on a wave of people struggling, pushing and shouting. He turned to Eino Rahja and said, "You see, our side always wins."

He had never been to the Smolny. He was like a stranger there, and he had no idea where to turn. Still in disguise, with the bandage covering half his face, he went upstairs; through an open door he saw some empty chairs by a window and he sat down, while Eino Rahja went in search of Trotsky. He had been there only a few minutes when some Mensheviks entered and sat down at a table nearby. Dan, the Menshevik leader, saw him and thought there was something strangely familiar about his appearance.

"Are you hungry?" he said. "I have a roll and some sausage."

Saying this, he began to untie a small bundle, but before he had opened it out, he took a second look at the man hiding in the shadow of a bandage. Then he whispered to his companions, hastily tied up the bundle, and left the room. Lenin laughed, and soon Trotsky sent a message that the Military Revolutionary Committee was waiting for him in Room 100. Lenin left the window seat and hurried down the corridor. He was in good humor, still laughing about the amazed look on Dan's face when he entered the room. He immediately doffed his cap. The wig came off with the cap, and there was a roar of laughter, which was completely incomprehensible to him. He stood there blinking and smiling, part of his face still covered with the bandage, and then he slapped the top of his head in a familiar gesture. He never wore the wig again.

He threw the bandage away and sat down to an eager discussion with Trotsky. He had read a report in the newspapers that the Military Revolutionary Committee had been negotiating with the commander of the Petrograd garrison. In his eyes such negotiations were intolerable; it infuriated him that they should commit this act of treachery.

"Is it true you are agreeing to a compromise?" he asked angrily.

Trotsky explained patiently that there had been no negotiations, but a statement about the nonexistent negotiations had been given to the press.

"Well, that is go-o-o-d," Lenin said, drawling the words, while the anger went out of his eyes. He enjoyed ruses of this kind, and rubbed his hands together with pleasure. He began to pace up and down the room. "That is v-e-r-y good!" he said, and for a while he went on talking about the beauty of the stratagem.

He knew nothing about the preparations for the revolt. It puzzled him that the streets were so calm and there was no sound of shooting. Trotsky explained that the military operations were already under way, and most of the bridges were in the hands of the insurrectionaries and most of the important strongpoints would be in their hands by the morning. He hoped, he said, to capture the city without firing a shot. When the subject of the order commanding that looters be shot at sight was raised, Lenin seemed to have misgivings. Then he said, "Yes, of course!" and dismissed the matter from his mind.

He was shown the battle plans, the maps with the enemy positions clearly marked, the routes to be followed by the revolutionary forces. In fact there were very few enemy positions, and there were perhaps fifty places on the maps showing concentrations of revolutionary troops. He asked a hundred questions, for he was still angry, still unsure of himself, still not quite convinced that there would be a bloodless revolution. By this time it was one o'clock in the morning, and the first detachments of Red Guards had already left the Smolny to capture the enemy strongholds. At last he grew quiet, composed himself, and in Trotsky's words, "gave his sanction to the course that events had already taken." "Yes," he said, "I suppose it can be done this way —just take the power." But a moment later there was another barrage of questions, more explanations were demanded, and the old anger returned. Even in his wildest dreams he had never hoped that success could be obtained so easily.

During the night the Bolsheviks captured the post office, the telephone exchange, the telegraph agency, the power stations, the state bank, and the Dvortsovy Bridge, the last to remain in government hands. All the railroad stations except the Finland Station were captured. Two ministers of the Provisional Government were arrested as they were driving down the empty streets. They were the Minister of Public Worship and the Director of the Chancery, and though they were immediately taken to the Smolny and cross-questioned, they could throw very little light on the intentions of the government. At daybreak the streetcars were running back and forth across the bridges as though nothing had happened, and Petrograd showed no sign that it had already fallen into the hands of the Military Revolutionary Committee. "Everything happened," wrote Sukhanov, "with fabulous ease."

Here and there during the night there were brief skirmishes. One of the first buildings to be occupied was the Tauride Palace. On their way to it the Red Guards encountered a Cossack patrol, and shots were exchanged. More shots were exchanged an hour later when Red Guards from among the railroadmen seized the telegraph office at the Nikolayevsky Station, but there seem to have been no casualties. When a combined patrol of marines and soldiers from the Kexholm Regiment drove up to the state bank, they found it guarded by men of the Semyonovsky Regiment, who immediately proclaimed they were on the side of the Military Revolutionary Committee and asked to be allowed to remain on guard duty. They were permitted to remain, but some sailors were left behind to keep an eye on them.

In this way, quietly and stealthily, the key places were occupied; and the terror of it was all the greater because scarcely a shot had been fired.

Lenin had very little sleep that night. He took no part in the mapping of strategy, for everything had been worked out to the last detail by Trotsky and his assistants. In this small and select group of assistants was an eighteen-year-old towheaded boy called Lazimir. For once, Lenin found himself in the position of a friendly adviser, depending upon others to make the final decisions.

By eight o'clock in the morning there was no longer any doubt that Petrograd had been conquered. The only remaining buildings left in enemy hands were the huge Winter Palace facing the river and the small Maryinsky Palace nearby: these could be taken at leisure. About this time Lenin wrote a proclamation addressed to the Russian people, announcing the victory of the revolution. Originally it was addressed "To the whole population"; but realizing the solemnity of the occasion he scratched out these words and substituted "To the Citizens of Russia."

In thin spidery handwriting which conveys the excitement and tension of the moment, with many erasures and sudden changes of direction, the words following one another at furious speed, he composed the epitaph of the old regime. He wrote:

To the Citizens of Russia

The Provisional Government has been overthrown. State power has passed into the hands of the organ of the Petrograd Soviet, the Military Revolutionary Committee, which stands at the head of the Petrograd proletariat and garrison.

The cause for which the people have been fighting—the immediate proposal of a democratic peace, the abolition of the landlords' ownership of land, workers' control over industry and the formation of a Soviet Government—this cause is assured.

Long live the workers', soldiers' and peasants' revolution!

The proclamation is as interesting for what it deliberately omits to say as for what it says. Originally Lenin wrote that the Military Revolutionary Committee stands at the head of "the people's fight against the government," but these words were scratched out, since there had been no uprising by the people. All reference to the people was therefore canceled, and the place of honor was given to the Petrograd proletariat and the garrison.

In the second paragraph he spoke of a meeting of the Petrograd Soviet at noon to discuss the immediate formation of a Soviet government. The whole paragraph was canceled, perhaps on the ground that such a government was still premature. Finally, in the last line, he scratched out "Long live socialism," not because of any lack of faith in socialism, but because such a declaration of faith sounded

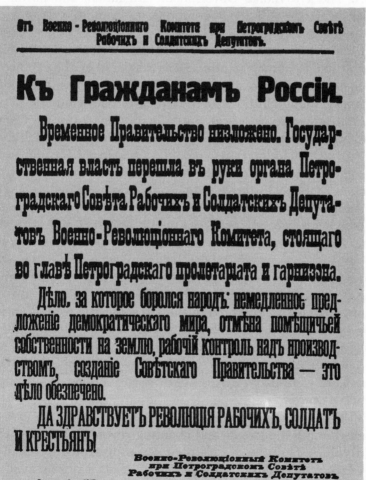

Отъ Военно - Революціоннаго Комитета при Петроградскомъ Совѣтѣ Рабочихъ и Солдатскихъ Депутатовъ.

Къ Гражданамъ Россіи.

Временное Правительство низложено. Государственная власть перешла въ руки органа Петроградскаго Совѣта Рабочихъ и Солдатскихъ Депутатовъ Военно-Революціоннаго Комитета, стоящаго во главѣ Петроградскаго пролетаріата и гарнизона.

Дѣло, за которое боролся народъ: немедленное предложеніе демократическаго мира, отмѣна помѣщичьей собственности на землю, рабочій контроль надъ производствомъ, созданіе Совѣтскаго Правительства — это дѣло обезпечено.

ДА ЗДРАВСТВУЕТЪ РЕВОЛЮЦІЯ РАБОЧИХЪ, СОЛДАТЪ И КРЕСТЬЯНЪ!

Военно-Революціонный Комитетъ при Петроградскомъ Совѣтѣ Рабочихъ и Солдатскихъ Депутатовъ.

25 октября 1917 г. 10 ч. утра.

oddly bleak at the end of the paragraph. "Long live the workers', soldiers' and peasants' revolution" appealed to concrete forces, and not to theory.

These hesitancies and sudden cancellations are revealing, because they show that Lenin was still unsure of himself, still uncertain in which direction the revolution would go. The most revealing change came with the insertion of the words "the organ of the Petrograd Soviet," at a later stage of the composition. These words were almost certainly added at the insistence of Trotsky, the leader of the Petrograd Soviet, which included members from all the revolutionary parties. The Provisional Government had fallen, and power was in the hands of the Military Revolutionary Committee. It was not yet in the hands of Lenin.

At ten o'clock in the morning the Military Revolutionary Committee published the proclamation; it was delivered on the captured radio station, telegraphed to all the provincial Soviets, and scattered in thousands of handbills through the streets of Petrograd.

About the same time that the Military Revolutionary Committee published the proclamation "to the Citizens of Russia," Kerensky came to the conclusion that it would be disastrous for him to remain any longer in Petrograd, and in an automobile borrowed from the American Embassy he drove to the front, hoping to make contact with loyal troops and to lead them back to the capital. He had no doubt that he would succeed, for it was one of his articles of faith that the Petrograd Soviet, which had raised him to power, was torn with so many inner dissensions that it was incapable of assuming power.

And in fact the Soviets had not yet assumed power, the Provisional Government had not been overthrown, and the head of the government had passed freely through the streets of the capital on his way to the front without encountering a single patrol. Petrograd had not visibly changed, except that the banks had closed down and it was a little colder than on the previous day. Two obscure ministers of the government were under arrest; Red Guards and garrison troops were occupying various strong points in the city; and on the surface this was all the revolution had accomplished. There were no vast crowds milling through the streets and chanting revolutionary slogans, as in the July days. The armed proletariat was represented by small groups of Red Guards, rarely numbering more than a dozen men. A vast indifference seemed to have seized the city, and the revolution was almost invisible.

But all this was on the surface; underground the revolution was succeeding beyond the expectations of its leaders. There was no need to destroy the government, for like the revolution the government was invisible, a mere ghost, without substance. The ministers sat in the Winter Palace as though they were about to dissolve into the fabric of the ornamental chambers of the tsars; they had long ago lost touch with the people. Trotsky was in no hurry to arrest them; all that was necessary to put them out of their misery was to send a few trucks full of troops into the palace and then sweep them into the dustbin of history.

The morning passed with no outward sign of revolutionary activity except the capture of the Maryinsky Palace. At about two o'clock in the afternoon the Petrograd Soviet met in the great hall of the Smolny, and Trotsky stepped onto the platform. Once more he declared that the Provisional Government had been overthrown. He spoke scornfully of those who prophesied that the revolution would be drowned in torrents of blood. "So far," he declared, "there has not been a single casualty, and there cannot be another example in history of a revolutionary movement embracing enormous masses of the population which has taken power so bloodlessly." This was not quite true; the enormous masses were singularly absent. But it was true that there had been little bloodshed. Then he announced that in a few minutes he expected the Winter Palace to fall.

Trotsky was greeted with a storm of applause, and when he had finished his speech he stepped back and introduced Lenin, who spoke dryly, in a hoarse voice, which lacked the sonorous bell-like quality of Trotsky's voice, so that after the first outbreak of applause there was only a polite response. There are no stenographic records of this speech, and only the brief summary which was given to the press has survived of the first public speech he made after his months of exile. He proclaimed the revolution of the workers and peasants, "of which the Bolsheviks have never ceased to urge the necessity," and went on to speak of how "the oppressed masses will themselves assume power and shatter the old state apparatus to its foundations." He was like a professor earnestly quoting from *The State and Revolution,* while forgetting the later pamphlets in which he explained the necessity for keeping that admirable machinery in operation while placing it under new auspices. He concluded the speech with the words, "Today in Russia we must set about constructing the proletarian socialist state! Long live the world socialist revolution!" There followed speeches by

Zinoviev and Lunacharsky, but it was Trotsky's hour, and their speeches were received with only perfunctory applause.

Trotsky had said the Winter Palace would fall in a few minutes, but twelve hours passed before it finally fell into the hands of the Military Revolutionary Committee.

At noon the great square outside the Winter Palace was still deserted. Gradually during the afternoon the Military Revolutionary Committee sent up troops from the garrison to form a half-circle around the building. It was a motley army, comprising detachments from the Izmailovsky, Pavlovsky and Preobrazhensky regiments and some squads from the Kexholm regiment. There were a few Red Guards, but these were mostly concentrated in Vasilyevsky Island, where they took no part in the desultory fighting which broke out later in the evening. The Soviets had armored cars, antiaircraft guns, and field artillery. The cruiser *Aurora* was anchored in the Neva. By midafternoon the attacking forces were reinforced by a thousand sailors from Kronstadt. The plan, sketched out roughly during the morning, was to ring the palace with such overwhelming forces that it would be compelled to surrender without firing a shot. At an appointed moment the Provisional Government would be presented with an ultimatum, a flag would be raised over the Peter and Paul Fortress, and fifteen minutes later, unless the ultimatum was accepted, the *Aurora* and the fortress would open fire, and the army would then pour into the crumbled ruins of the palace and take it by storm.

The defenders consisted of military cadets from the army schools around Petrograd, a detachment of Cossacks from the Urals, and the Women's Battalion consisting of 170 young women in uniform, who had no experience of fighting. A battery of field artillery from the Mikhailovsky School was also based on the palace, but took no part in the fighting. At four o'clock in the afternoon the horse teams with the gun carriages rode out to surrender to the encircling forces. In all there were fewer than two thousand troops guarding the palace, of which perhaps a quarter could be depended upon to fight. Against them were about fifty thousand soldiers, sailors and Red Guards.

The wonder is that the Winter Palace took so long to fall. Podvoisky had announced that it would fall by noon; and thereafter from hour to hour reports came to the Smolny about its imminent capture. But the attacking forces were ill-organized and suffered from divided authority, quarrels broke out among the commanders, some soldiers simply disappeared from their posts, and there were continual breakdowns in the chain of command. And if the attackers seemed to be sleepwalking, the defenders seemed to be incapable of anything so energetic as sleepwalking. They had piled up loads of cordwood to form a breastwork, and behind these, for all the Soviets knew, they had fallen soundly asleep. Within the palace the old court servants in their blue uniforms with red collars and gold braid went about their accustomed duties as though nothing was happening. General Bagratuni, in command of the defense of the palace, simply walked out and abandoned the hopeless task, apparently without regret and certainly with no intention of returning; he was arrested by a patrol, and Podvoisky, who was on a tour of inspection, took him in charge. By nightfall the defenders had dwindled to about a thousand men and women with about twenty machine guns between them. Most of these were later found to be mysteriously without breechblocks.

By six o'clock in the evening the investment of the palace was completed, and it was decided to send emissaries to demand surrender within twenty minutes. The Provisional Government was assembled in the great Malachite Hall; from the windows they could see the *Aurora* anchored off the bridge, with its guns trained on the palace. All telephone communication with the palace was thought to be cut off, but there was in fact a secret line connecting the palace with the front. The Provisional Government had been promised help from the front and lived in expectation of seeing the siege lifted. They therefore rejected the ultimatum and sat down to dinner.

Meanwhile at the Smolny, Lenin was becoming increasingly disturbed by the delay. Hourly he had been told that the palace was about to fall; hourly he heard that it was still standing. He was more than ever determined to have the Winter Palace in Soviet hands before the opening of the Second Congress of Soviets later in the evening, remembering perhaps the dictum of Bakunin that no revolution can be counted successful until the revolutionaries have taken possession of the town hall. In weariness and despair he was stretched out on the bare floor of one of the rooms next to the great hall of the Smolny, waiting for news and sometimes taking a cat nap. Trotsky lay beside him. A messenger hurried in, shook Trotsky by the shoulder, and told him that the Winter Palace was still holding out. Trotsky suggested that the *Aurora* should fire a volley of blanks. It would be a pity to destroy the palace for the sake of a few ministers, and in any event he had long ago lost any interest in the capture of the palace. Unlike Lenin, he regarded the palace as a mere backdrop of the revolutionary drama.

At nine o'clock the *Aurora* fired a volley of blanks, and these were followed by more blanks from the Peter and Paul Fortress. This was the signal for a burst of machine-gun fire from the palace. For an hour there was an exchange of shots between the attackers and the defenders. Some thousands of rounds of ammunition were expended, but in the darkness most of the bullets went wild. Nine palace guards and six sailors were killed. These were the only casualties during that long and exhausting siege.

The lights of the palace went out. The ministers, still hoping that reinforcements would arrive before morning, retired to a small dining room next to the Malachite Hall, to ponder the inexorable march of events, while the gunners in the Peter and Paul Fortress amused themselves by firing real shells which dislodged some cornices and broke some windows; and the sound of splintering glass came eerily over the Neva. So the hours passed, to the slow solemn booming of cannon and the occasional bursts of machine-gun fire, while the Red Guards warmed themselves over the watchfires in the palace square. Toward midnight the members of the Petrograd city Duma, feeling that the comedy had gone on too long, decided to march to the palace and die with the government. The mayor of Petrograd, carrying a lantern and an umbrella, walked at their head. When they reached the palace they were turned back by Red Guards.

At one o'clock Red Guards and sailors began to infiltrate the corridors, creeping quietly over the parqueted floors and under the crystal chandeliers. It was so dark that they were soon lost. More followed them. Shots were fired in the dark, and there were brief engagements with the military cadets, who alone remained to guard the palace, for the Cossacks and the Women's Battalion had already vanished from the scene. At 2:10 A.M., Antonov-Ovseyenko, one of the three men placed in charge of the attack on the palace, burst into the small dining room where the ministers were sitting and placed them under arrest in the name of the Military Revolutionary Committee. He had fallen into a puddle earlier in the evening, and the mud had dried on him. The ministers had expected to be arrested by someone who looked the part of a revolutionary, but Antonov-Ovseyenko, with his delicate chalk-white face, his long red hair and goatee, his spectacles, his wide-brimmed felt hat pushed back over his forehead, resembled a poet or a fallen angel. He threw his hat on the table and, while interrogating the ministers, absent-mindedly drew a comb through his hair. He had not slept for thirty-six hours and was at the end of his strength.

An hour later all the ministers were marched under guard to the Peter and Paul Fortress. The siege was over.

While the guns from the *Aurora* and the Peter and Paul Fortress were booming, the Second Congress of Soviets had opened in the great hall of the Smolny. Kamenev was elected chairman. On the presidium were fourteen Bolsheviks, seven Socialist Revolutionaries, three Mensheviks and one representative of Gorky's group. The hall was in an uproar. Everyone seemed to be shouting at once. All the moderate socialists were seething with indignation at the *coup* which the Bolsheviks had staged in the name of the Petrograd Soviet. Even while they protested, they were aware that they no longer had any power to change events, for the Bolsheviks were ruthless and determined to keep the gains they had won in twenty-four hours of quiet maneuvers. The meeting opened at 10:40 P.M. and was still going on in the early morning.

Trotsky and Lenin were still lying on the floor in their cheerless room, where there were no chairs or tables, or any furniture at all. Someone had laid a blanket on the floor, and one of Lenin's sisters found some pillows. So they lay there, exhausted by the day's events and too excited to sleep any more. From one of the windows, Lenin had seen the Red Guards and soldiers clustering round the street fires. Once he said, "It's a wonderful sight to see an armed worker standing side by side with a soldier round a street fire," then he relapsed into silence. Some time later he said, "Hasn't the Winter Palace fallen yet? It's dangerous if it hasn't fallen." Then Trotsky would send for a messenger and try to discover the latest news about the grotesque operations against a palace which was undefended and yet refused to fall.

Dan was speaking in the great hall, denouncing the Bolsheviks. Lenin's sister ran into the room and said the Bolsheviks were calling for Trotsky to lead the opposition against Dan. Pale, in a black silk coat and a flowing tie, Trotsky went out to deliver the *coup de grâce*.

He told the moderate socialists that they no longer had any place in the revolution, their usefulness was over, for they were divided among themselves, and incapable of holding power. "*Our* uprising has won," he declared, "and why should we give it away for the sake of coming to an agreement?" He was like a director telling the actors what roles they were permitted to play. In this play there were no roles for the moderate. And then, once more using one of his favorite phrases, he said, "Go to the place where you belong from now on—the dustbin of history!"

Strangely, they obeyed. Except for the Left Socialist Revolutionaries they left the hall, determined to have nothing to do with the Bolsheviks, whom they despised and feared; they would carry on the fight elsewhere; they would choose their own time and their own weapons. But time was running out and they had no weapons. The victory of the Bolsheviks in the streets was followed by victory in the Petrograd Soviet. Once more it was victory by default.

Lenin spoke like a man in a trance, dazed by victory. He declared that the Congress, now reduced so that it contained only deputies favorable to the Bolsheviks, possessed full powers and assumed the sovereign rule over Russia. Sukhanov, who was present that night, tells how the Bolsheviks celebrated their victory with long-drawn-out ovations alternating with the singing of the "Internationale." "Then Lenin was hailed again, hurrahs were shouted, caps flung into the air. They sang a funeral march in memory of the martyrs of the war. Then they applauded again, shouted, flung up their caps. The whole presidium, headed by Lenin, was standing up and singing, with excited, exalted faces and blazing eyes."

THE FIRST DAY OF THE REVOLUTION

WITH THE WINTER PALACE TAKEN, the ministers arrested, and the last speeches made from the floor of the White Chamber in the Smolny, the revolutionary leaders could now go to their beds with the knowledge that nothing more could be done that night and the revolution would have to follow its appointed course. It was now a little past 3:30 A.M., and the whole day had been given over to an almost uncontrollable excitement. Lenin was exhausted, for he had slept little the previous night, and indeed he had slept very little during the previous week. For some reason he decided not to spend the night at the Smolny. Instead he decided to spend the night with his friend Bonch-Bruyevich in his apartment in Peski, not far from the Smolny.

Probably what he wanted most of all was to get away from the incessant uproar at the Smolny and to go somewhere where he could be completely quiet. Bonch-Bruyevich was one of those heavy-set powerful men who radiate confidence and who speak very little. There was nothing in the least flamboyant in him, and he was far from resembling the typical revolutionary. He looked like a country doctor.

When Lenin arrived at the apartment, he resembled a man in the last stages of exhaustion. He could not remember when he had last eaten. They had a simple meal, and then Bonch-Bruyevich led him off to his own bedroom. At first Lenin refused to sleep in the bed, saying something about the absurdity of taking the only good bed in the apartment, but finally he was prevailed upon to sleep there. The bedroom was in an isolated corner of the apartment, far from the living room; there was paper, ink, a desk, a collection of books; he would not be disturbed. Krupskaya slept on a sofa in another room, while Bonch-Bruyevich slept in the room adjoining Lenin's, having first made sure that his pistol was loaded and that on a piece of paper within reach there was a list of telephone numbers of local committees and friends who could be called if anyone tried to break into the apartment.

Bonch-Bruyevich was dozing off when he suddenly became aware that there was a light under Lenin's door. He heard Lenin moving about the room, making as little noise as possible, and then the door opened and Lenin peered out to see whether his friend was sleeping. Bonch-Bruyevich pretended to be asleep. The door remained open. Tiptoeing back to the bedroom, Lenin settled down at the table, opened the inkwell, set some papers in order, and began writing. At intervals during the night Bonch-Bruyevich dozed off and then he would awake again. All through the night Lenin, with a strange absorbed look on his face, wrote, revised, copied out what he had written, consulted his notes and recopied them until it seemed that a mountain of notes was growing up on the table. Bonch-Bruyevich remembered that there was a good deal of scratching out, and the revisions seemed endless. Finally Lenin made a fair copy of what he had written, turned out the light, and went to bed. It was already dawn, with a clear autumnal light coming through the windows.

Two hours later Bonch-Bruyevich went about the apartment on tiptoe, whispering to everyone to be as quiet as possible because Lenin had spent the night working and needed a long sleep. Suddenly, when no one was expecting him, Lenin swept into the room. He was in high spirits, and all the lines of fatigue had been smoothed out.

"Let me congratulate you on the occasion of the first day of the socialist revolution," he said.

A little while later when Krupskaya came out of her room and sat down at the table, Lenin read out his Decree on the Land.

"What we have to do now," he declared, "is to proclaim and publish the decree everywhere. After this they will never get their land back again! No power on earth will be able to take back this decree from the peasants or give the land back to the landowners. This achievement is essential for our revolution. The agrarian revolution will be accomplished and put into force today!"

So he spoke, sitting beside the samovar, with the neatly written pages in front of him; and he may have known that agrarian revolutions are never accomplished overnight. Someone, probably Bonch-

Bruyevich, had the temerity to suggest that in the provinces the simple proclamation of a decree might not be enough. In the provinces especially trouble could be expected, and much bloodshed. Lenin waved the objections away. "The decree," he said, "contains the essential basis of the agrarian revolution, and they will come round to it soon enough." He went on to explain that the decree answered the demands the peasants themselves had made through the Peasants' Deputies, and was therefore entirely in their favor.

"Yes, but the Peasants' Deputies are all Socialist Revolutionaries," someone suggested. "They'll say we simply borrowed from them."

Lenin smiled.

"Let them say what they like! The peasants know we support their lawful demands. We should get closer to the peasants, to their lives and their aspirations. If there are some poor fools who laugh at us, let them! It was never our intentions to give the Socialist Revolutionaries a monopoly over the peasants! We are the ruling party, and after the dictatorship of the proletariat there is no problem more important than the agrarian revolution."

He was unusually gay and good-humored as he spoke about the effect the decree would have among the peasants; they would see the rightness of the decree and give their full support to the party in power. He would have fifty thousand copies printed immediately and given to soldiers returning to their villages; through these soldiers it would be read and discussed in the villages. The newspapers would print it. Eventually millions of copies of the decree would appear throughout Russia, and the land once taken from the landlords would never revert to them. He went on happily explaining how the decree would reach the remotest villages.

"When it is given to demobilized soldiers," he said, "the full meaning and significance must be explained to them carefully. You mustn't forget to tell them that if the landlords, merchants and kulaks are still in illegal possession of the land, they must be turned out absolutely and the land placed at the disposal of the peasant committees. We should arrange for an intelligent sailor to see where the soldier puts the decree. It should be put right down at the bottom of his bag so that he doesn't lose it, and then let him have a dozen copies close at hand to read and distribute in the train."

It was odd that he should have so much faith in the sailors that he saw them standing over the soldiers even when they were putting documents into their duffel bags. He had admired their trim neatness and revolutionary fervor the previous day, and he had forgiven them for coming so late on the scene that they held up the attack on the Winter Palace.

But if the Decree on the Land seemed the most important problem to Lenin that morning, it was not the most important problem that confronted him when he reached the Smolny. The Bolsheviks had publicly declared they had seized power, but they were uncomfortably aware that Kerensky was only a few miles away and that overnight there had come into existence a Committee for the Salvation of the Fatherland and the Revolution, which was determined to oust them from power. The railroadmen threatened to come out on strike unless a coalition government of all socialist parties was formed. It was necessary to ensure grain supplies for Petrograd, since stocks were running dangerously low. Above all, there was the problem of rallying the army to the Bolshevik cause. Lenin's first speech that day was not about the land, but about the peace. He therefore urged a "just and democratic peace," an immediate armistice, an end to the war which had plagued the working classes for so long, and he went out of his way to pay tribute to the British working classes who had played an important historical role in the socialist movement through the Chartists, and to the working classes of France and Germany "who had fought so heroically in their revolutions." He was talking to the Russian soldiers at the front, but he was also talking to the militant labor movement in Europe over the heads of their governments. Once more the theme was *brataniye*, the "brotherhood" which would put an end to national rivalries, and once again he pointed to the strikes in Germany and Italy as the signs of the imminent socialist revolution which would embrace the whole world.

John Reed was present at the Smolny while he made this address, and described him as "a short stocky figure, with a big head set down on his shoulders, bald and bulging, little eyes, a snubbish nose, wide, generous mouth, and heavy chin; clean-shaven now, but already beginning to bristle with the well-known beard of his past and future." He was still dressed shabbily in trousers which seemed too long for him. John Reed remembered him gripping the edge of the reading stand and letting his little winking eyes travel over the crowd as though he were oblivious of the ovation that greeted him. He remembered, too, that before beginning the speech on the peace, he said, "We shall now proceed to construct the socialist order." But this lapidary phrase, in this context, does not appear in the minutes of the

meeting. Later that evening he read the Decree on the Land, proclaiming the end of private ownership of land except for land belonging to "simple peasants and simple Cossacks." Sukhanov, the ever
present, describes how Lenin tried to read the decree from his own
badly written manuscript, stumbled, became confused, and finally
stopped altogether. "Whereupon," says Sukhanov, "one of those who
had squeezed onto the platform came to his rescue, and Lenin gladly
gave up his place and the illegible piece of paper." He leaves us to
understand that Safarov, the man who squeezed onto the platform,
was able to read the manuscript. It is one of the few stories told by
Sukhanov which defy credibility. Anyone who has worked on Lenin's
manuscripts knows only too well that one does not read them aloud
at a pace tolerable to any listener. One explores them patiently with a
magnifying glass, slowly, with a bemused sense of wonder that sentences that look like strings of barbed wire are finally decipherable.

While Peace and Land were the most important items on the
agenda, there were a hundred other problems to be attended to. In
discussing the peace, Lenin spoke of "the government that your Congress will elect," and he may have been too busy to give any thought
to the composition of the cabinet. Lunacharsky told Sukhanov that at
first Lenin resolutely refused to become a member of it, saying he
would take up work in the Central Committee, but his resolution
weakened when he was told that it was easy to criticize and difficult
to assume responsibility. Then he bowed to the inevitable.

There was some discussion about the form the new government
would take, and what its members would be called.

"We mustn't call them ministers," Lenin said. "It's a repulsive,
hackneyed word!"

"We might call them commissars," Trotsky suggested, "only there
are too many commissars already. Perhaps supreme commissar. No,
'supreme' is bad. What about People's Commissars?"

"People's Commissars? I like that. And what shall we call the government?"

"The Soviet of People's Commissars."

"The Soviet of People's Commissars? That's splendid. It smells of
revolution!"

Later that night the new government was constituted as a body
authorized to rule until the convocation of the Constituent Assembly.
Lenin gave himself the title of President of the Soviet of People's
Commissars (*Predsedatel Sovieta Narodnikh Komissarov*), but such a

cumbrous title demanded abbreviation, with the result that the new word *Predsovnarkom* entered the Russian vocabulary. The new government was composed of:

President of the Soviet of People's Commissars: Vladimir Ulyanov (Lenin)

People's Commissar for Internal Affairs: A. I. Rykov

Agriculture: V. P. Milyutin

Labor: A. G. Shlyapnikov

Military and Naval Affairs: Committee composed of V. A. Antonov-Ovseyenko, N. V. Krylenko, and P. E. Dybenko

Commerce and Industry: V. P. Nogin

Education: A. V. Lunacharsky

Finance: I. I. Skvortsov (Stepanov)

Foreign Affairs: L. D. Bronstein (Trotsky)

Justice: G. I. Oppokov (Lomov)

Supplies: I. A. Teodorovich

Post and Telegraph: N. P. Avilov (Glebov)

Nationalities: I. V. Dzhugashvili (Stalin)

Such was the government which in theory assumed power late in the night of November 8, but none of the commissars were under any illusions about the scope of their powers. It was a duumvirate, with Lenin and Trotsky as the supreme rulers. The least important member of the government was Stalin.

It was a government which ruled by decree, without as yet possessing the means to enforce its decrees. The commissars believed, or pretended to believe, that their decrees represented the aspirations of the entire Russian people, or at least of the proletariat, the soldiers, the sailors, and the peasants. But even in Petrograd the mood of the soldiers was angry, hesitant, not yet convinced that the revolution was pursuing the right path. John Reed visited the Mikhailovsky Riding School and found two thousand *bronoviki*, troops of the armored car regiment, listening to political speeches in the vast hall with only a single ghostly arc light burning dimly near the roof. Speakers were addressing them from the turret of an armored car. The Duma delegate pleaded for neutrality, a soldier from the Rumanian front pleaded for peace, another for war, another for a united democracy. "Never," Reed wrote, "have I seen men trying so hard to understand, to decide. They never moved, stood staring with a sort of terrible intentness at the speaker, their brows wrinkled with the effort of thought, sweat standing out on their foreheads." Krylenko, who had been sent by the Soviet government, won them over by hammering away at the theme of the revolutionary triumph of the workingmen and the poor peasants, forgetting that the Bolsheviks had no roots among the poor peasants, who continued to vote solidly for the Socialist Revolutionaries.

The railroadmen were on strike; so were the postal employees; so were the telegraph operators; so were the civil servants. The life of Petrograd had come to a standstill; the Bolsheviks had not yet won the battle for men's minds. There were decrees ordering the railroadmen and postal employees back to work, and the shops to open, and a moratorium on rents, and the suppression of the "bourgeois" newspapers, meaning any newspaper which was in opposition to the Bolsheviks; but the people of Petrograd were still waiting to see which side would win. Kerensky had joined forces with General Krasnov and was advancing on Petrograd with a force of Cossacks. They were nervous days for the Bolsheviks, and Trotsky made no effort to conceal the dangers that threatened them; nor did Lenin, as we know from his recorded telephone conversations. On November 9, Lenin was calling for aid from the Russian troops in Finland and from the sailors of the Baltic fleet. He called Sheinman, the chairman of the Helsingfors Soviet of Soldiers', Sailors' and Workers' Deputies.

LENIN: Are you authorized to speak in the name of the regional committee of the army and the fleet?

SHEINMAN: Yes, I am.

LENIN: Can you send at once to Petrograd a great number of torpedo boats and other armed vessels?

SHEINMAN: We'll get the chairman of the Tsentrobalt on the wire directly, since this is a naval question. What's the news in Petrograd?

LENIN: The news is that Kerensky's forces are approaching and have taken Gatchina, and as some of the Petrograd troops are exhausted we are in urgent need of strong reinforcements.

SHEINMAN: What else is new?

LENIN: Instead of your question "What else is new?" I expected you to say you were ready to come and fight.

SHEINMAN: It seems to me useless to repeat that. We have made our decision, and consequently everything will be done.

LENIN: Have you got stocks of rifles and machine guns, and how many?

SHEINMAN: I am handing you over to the chairman of the regional committee of the military department, Mikhailov. He can talk
              to you about the army in Finland.
MIKHAILOV: How many bayonets do you need?
LENIN: We need the maximum number available, but the men
              must be reliable and ready to fight. How many men have
              you got?
MIKHAILOV: Up to five thousand. They can be sent at once, and they'll
              fight.
LENIN: In how many hours can you guarantee they will be in Petrograd if sent with the utmost dispatch?
MIKHAILOV: Twenty-four hours at the very latest.
LENIN: By land?
MIKHAILOV: By rail.
LENIN: Can you provide food for them?
MIKHAILOV: Yes, we have plenty of provisions. We also have thirty-five
              machine guns. We can send these with their gun crews
              without detriment to our position here, and a few field
              guns.
LENIN: On behalf of the government of the Republic, I urgently
              request you to begin sending these forces immediately.
              Please inform me also whether you are aware that a new
              government has been formed, and what is the attitude of
              your Soviets to it?
MIKHAILOV: All we know about the government comes from the newspapers. The transfer of power to the Soviets has been welcomed here with enthusiasm.
LENIN: I take it the land forces will start off immediately?
MIKHAILOV: Yes, we'll start sending them off immediately and we'll
              supply provisions.

From this telephone conversation it is clear that Lenin was playing an unfamiliar role and was still uncertain of himself. He had not
announced his name. He had simply called on the direct wire, having
no idea how he would be received, nor how the soldiers would travel,
nor how they would be supplied. His purpose was twofold: he needed
troops to stop Kerensky from advancing on the capital, and he also
needed them to help put down any uprising which might take place
against his government. When he spoke "on behalf of the government
of the Republic," he was being deliberately disingenuous, for this is
precisely the phrase that Kerensky would have used. Throughout the
conversation Lenin gives the impression of a man breathing a long
sigh of relief.

The next days were as dangerous as any he lived through. It was not true that the proletariat had won a resounding victory. What had happened was that Trotsky and then Lenin had imposed themselves by sheer force of character and by their determination upon the local garrison, and with very little help from the Red Guards they had taken physical possession of Petrograd. They were like generals who have staged a *coup d'état* by throwing their armies against the government, but such armies are notably unstable. They are especially unstable if the leaders only make speeches.

From Gatchina, less than twenty miles southwest of Petrograd, Kerensky was announcing his imminent return at the head of Krasnov's Cossacks. If he had swept into Petrograd at night, he might have turned the tide. But while his proclamations became more and more confident, he was coming to realize that Krasnov's Cossacks had very little will to fight. At the same time Lenin was coming to realize that his garrison troops were equally undependable; and though his knowledge of military strategy and tactics derived from an excited reading of Clausewitz during his exile in Switzerland, and he knew nothing about problems of supply and had never fired a gun in anger, he threw himself into the military struggle as eagerly and ferociously as he threw himself into the political struggle.

The garrison troops refused to leave Petrograd. One by one Podvoisky, Antonov-Ovseyenko, Krylenko, and all the others who led the uprising appealed to them to march to the front. They claimed they were needed to guard the city. In despair, Podvoisky hurried to explain the position to Lenin at the Smolny. Let Podvoisky tell the story:

> Hurriedly I told Lenin about our failure to get the soldiers to move. I told him that the Volhynian and other trustworthy regiments had simply refused to leave, and it was beyond hope that we would be able to get a single army unit out of the city.
>
> "Then you must get them out," Lenin said calmly. "They must go out this very moment, at whatever the cost!"
>
> "Krylenko has already tried and failed," I replied, "and they wouldn't listen to me. There's absolutely nothing you can do with the regiments."
>
> Lenin went into a terrible rage, his features became unrecognizable, he fixed his sharp eyes on mine, and without raising his voice, though he seemed to be shouting, he said: "You will answer to the Central Committee if the regiments do not leave the city immediately. Do you hear me, at this very moment!"

I shot out of the room like a bullet and in a few minutes I was again at the barracks of the Volhynian Regiment. I mustered the soldiers and said very few words to them. The soldiers must have seen something extraordinary in my face. Silently, they rose to their feet, and began to prepare for the campaign. And then other regiments followed them.

Lenin's name, the threat of his name, was alone sufficient to send a regiment to the front; his presence was even more effective.

That evening he drove through the rain to the headquarters of his army. Antonov-Ovseyenko, Podvoisky and Mekhonoshin were poring over their battle maps when Lenin came into their office, soaked through, the water streaming out of his workman's cap. Podvoisky asked him why he had come. Didn't he trust his commissars?

"It's not that I don't trust them," Lenin said, "but the workers' and peasants' government is entitled to know how its military officers are conducting themselves, and how they are preparing the defense of Petrograd."

"At this moment," says Podvoisky, relating the incident, "I felt the full power of the dictatorship of the proletariat."

Lenin was, in fact, in a towering rage. He sat down at the table in front of the map and demanded a briefing. Antonov-Ovseyenko explained the battle positions as well as he could after a week without sleep. He had been an officer in the regular army, and he knew, or should have known, what he was talking about. Lenin glared at the map, sultry, withdrawn, scarcely listening. Then he began to ask questions—a torrent of questions. Why was this position not guarded? Had they taken into account the strategic importance of this railroad station? Had they called for support from Kronstadt and Helsingfors? What about the railroad line? Was it defended? Did they have enough supplies for the Red Guards? What were they doing to prevent Kerensky from cutting the Petrograd–Moscow railroad? What about artillery? And most important of all: Who was in command? Apparently they were all in command, although Antonov-Ovseyenko bore the title Commander in Chief of the Petrograd Military District. Antonov-Ovseyenko was demoted on the spot, Podvoisky was placed in command, and Lenin ordered the entire military organization transferred to the Smolny, where he could keep a sharp eye on them.

Early in the morning of November 13 the sailors arrived from Helsingfors and moved up to the front. Factory workers were given arms and sent up the line, while others were given spades and ordered to dig trenches behind the front. Slyansky, a young medical student attached to military headquarters—he later became Vice-Commissar for War—drove out his teams of horses with their gun carriages. At midday, realizing that the decisive battle might soon take place, Lenin left his own office and installed himself in the military operations room. He had a table brought in. Every five or ten minutes Podvoisky would be confronted with someone sent by Lenin "to help him." Doctors, pilots, agitators, artillery experts, came bearing urgent messages signed by Lenin, which had to be attended to immediately, at once, without a moment to lose. Lenin was constitutionally incapable of writing any messages without including the word "immediately." In later years he would usually include the word "unmercifully."

Gradually Lenin took over control of the military operations room. He gave orders over the telephone on his own responsibility. He summoned factory delegates and cross-examined them on the number of men they could throw into the battle. He ordered the workmen in the Putilov factory to mount armor plate on the railroad engines and cars, and to put guns on them and send them to the front. There were forty field guns standing uselessly in a factory. He ordered the cab drivers to take their horses to the factory and haul the guns to the front.

Podvoisky found his orders countermanded, his dispositions altered, his plans changed. Lenin was mobilizing everybody and everything for the front. He could not be argued with. When Podvoisky asked to be relieved of his command, Lenin "lost his temper completely," and shouted, "I'll have you placed on trial before the party court, and shot! Now do your work and don't get in the way of mine!"

Trotsky too threw himself into the defense of the city with the fury of an aroused lion. He visited the front, made speeches in the factories, and with ferocious determination went about the task of converting Petrograd into a fortress. In the midst of the confusion the military cadets attempted an uprising in the hope of putting an end to the duumvirate and joining forces with Kerensky, but they were already too late, the uprising was defeated, and with this defeat vanished the last hope of effective opposition within Petrograd. Trotsky was addressing the Petrograd Soviet, urging everyone to march to the front, when a rough voice called out, "Why aren't you out there with the Red Guards?" John Reed, who was present at the meeting, describes how Trotsky answered, "I'm going now!" and left the platform. It was exactly the right revolutionary gesture. Within four days Lenin and Trotsky found themselves moving at such a violent speed that they projected themselves outside of history altogether; they were entering the world of legends.

Petrograd was saved for the Bolsheviks on the heights of Pulkovo just outside the city. There were no pitched battles, only a series of skirmishes in the rain. Krasnov's Cossacks had been infiltrated by agitators. Promised safe-conducts permitting them to return safely to the Don, they saw no reason to fight for Kerensky and obligingly surrendered to Dybenko, who drew up the surrender terms on his own responsibility. Trotsky, arriving on the scene late at night, hurriedly scribbled a manifesto to be sent back to the Smolny by special courier:

> PULKOVO. STAFF, 2:10 A.M.
>
> The night of November 12 to 13 will go down in history. The attempt of Kerensky to move counterrevolutionary troops against the capital of the Revolution has been decisively repulsed. Kerensky is retreating, we are advancing. . . .
>
> The grand idea of the domination of the worker and peasant democracy closed the ranks of the army and hardened its will. All the country from now on will be convinced that the power of the Soviets is no ephemeral thing, but an invincible fact. . . .
>
> There is no return to the past. Before us are struggles, obstacles and sacrifices. But the road is clear and victory is certain.

But the road was not certain, nor even now were the Bolsheviks assured of victory. They were still a minority, still ruling by improvisation, the prisoners of their own rhetoric. There were few revolutionaries who were skilled in management. With remarkable speed Lenin could produce pronunciamentos affecting every department of civilian life, but unless they could be enforced by armies of bureaucrats, they were almost meaningless. He was learning that "control," which had once seemed so mechanical and easy, was in fact intolerably difficult and almost impossible without the use of terror; and so, at first hesitantly and then with increasing momentum, he sanctioned terror as the chief instrument of his government.

In those days he was so certain of the rightness of his cause that the least opposition would send him into fits of uncontrolled fury. Anyone who disagreed with him was a deserter or a traitor. He rejected all compromise, with the result that civil war, which might have been avoided, became inevitable.

Gorky was among those who fearlessly protested against the revolution, which seemed to have no purpose except to lead to a blood bath in which the whole of Russia would be engulfed. On November 21, two weeks after the revolt had broken out, he wrote in *Novaya Zhizn:*

> Blind fanatics and unscrupulous adventurers are rushing headlong toward "social revolution"—that is to say the road to anarchy, the ruin of the proletariat and of the revolution.
>
> Following this road, Lenin and his cohorts think it is permissible to commit all crimes: massacres in Petrograd, devastation in Moscow, suppression of free speech, senseless arrests—the same monstrous acts that were committed by Plehve and Stolypin.
>
> It is true that Stolypin and Plehve acted against the democracy, against all that was honest and sound in Russia, while Lenin has the backing of a large proportion of the working classes. I hope the common sense of the workers and the realization of their historical mission will open their eyes to the impossibility of fulfilling the promises made by Lenin and to the extent of his madness and anarchistic tendencies, which follow the line of Bakunin and Nechayev.
>
> The working classes cannot fail to realize that Lenin is experimenting with their blood and trying to strain the revolutionary mood of the proletariat to the limit to see what the outcome will be. Of course, under the existing circumstances, he does not believe in the possibility of a victory for the proletariat of Russia, but perhaps he hopes that a miracle will save the proletariat.
>
> The workingman must know that there really are no miracles, and that he will have to confront hunger, complete disorganization of industry and transportation, prolonged and bloody anarchy followed by a reaction no less sanguinary and dark. That is where the proletariat is being led by its present leaders, and one must imagine that Lenin is not an all-powerful magician, but a deliberate juggler, who has no feeling either for the lives or for the honor of the proletariat.
>
> The working classes must not allow adventurers and madmen to thrust upon the proletariat the responsibility for the disgraceful, senseless and bloody crimes for which not Lenin, but the proletariat will have to give a rendering.

In those days Gorky was still acting as the universal conscience of Russia, belonging to no party, standing in splendid isolation between the warring groups, and possessing so great an authority that no one, not even the Bolsheviks, dared to silence him. With pitiless lucidity he saw that Lenin's revolution was one of destruction—that "terrible, total, universal and merciless destruction" which had been announced by Nechayev in *The Revolutionary Catechism.* Gorky had read the

"April Theses," and he came to the conclusion that if they were ever put into practice the genuine revolutionaries would be sacrificed in the interests of the poor peasants; they would be thrown, he said, "like a handful of salt into the vapid quagmire of village life, and would dissolve without leaving any trace, vanishing without any opportunity to affect the mind, life or history of the Russian people." So he wrote many years later in his *Days with Lenin*, and he never publicly or privately retracted his early attacks against the Bolshevik revolution. On November 23 he wrote in *Novaya Zhizn* a proclamation to the workers, once more emphasizing that the revolution was being betrayed:

TO THE WORKING CLASS

Lenin has brought to Russia the socialist regime according to the methods of Nechayev "at full speed through the filth."

Lenin, Trotsky, and all the rest who are following them into the cess-pool of reality obviously agree with Nechayev that "we can drag any Russian into our affairs by dishonoring him"; and so we find the revolution and the working class coldly dishonored, and the workers made to organize bloody massacres and pogroms, and completely innocent people like Kartashev, Bernatsky, Konovalov and others are arrested.

Having led the proletariat to agree to the suppression of the freedom of the press, Lenin and his cohorts have provided the enemies of democracy with the occasion to shut its mouth; and with threats of famine and massacre against all those who disapprove of the Lenin-Trotsky form of despotism, these "leaders" justify their tyranny—such a tyranny as the best men in the country have struggled against for so many years.

These Leninists imagine they are the Napoleons of socialism, and as they go about the country, they are bringing about the downfall of Russia. And the Russian people will pay for this in a sea of blood.

Lenin is one of those men who possess a quite exceptional strength of character. For twenty-five years he has been in the front rank of those who fought for the triumph of socialism. He is one of the most energetic figures in international Social Democracy, and being a man of many gifts he has all the qualities of a "leader"—especially the complete lack of morality essential for such a role, and the aristocrat's contempt for the masses.

Lenin is a "leader" and a Russian aristocrat. He has many of the moral traits of that decayed class, and it is for this reason that he believes he has the right to saddle the Russian people with a cruel experiment which is doomed to failure from the beginning.

Exhausted and ruined by the war, our people has already sacrificed thousands of lives, and now we shall have to sacrifice tens of thousands more, and so for a long time we shall be brought low.

It does not worry Lenin in the least that Russia must suffer this tragedy: he is the slave of dogma, and his followers are his slaves. He has no knowledge of life in all its complex variety; he does not know the masses; he has not lived with them. But he has learned from books how they can be made to revolt, and—what is much easier—how their instincts can be aroused. For the Leninist the working class is like a mineral in the hands of the metallurgist. Can one, under the proper conditions, transform this mineral into a state of socialism? From all objective appearances it would seem to be impossible. Well, why not try it? And what does Lenin risk if the experiment fails?

He spends his time like a chemist in the laboratory, but with this difference—the chemist works on inert matter and produces results which are helpful to life, while Lenin works on living flesh and drags the revolution to its doom. Honest workers who follow in the path of Lenin should understand that he is performing a terrible experiment on them, and this experiment will lead to the destruction of the best forces among the workmen, and as a result the normal development of the revolution will be arrested for a very long time.

Gorky has been quoted at considerable length because he knew Lenin well and had no illusions about the destructive forces unleashed by the revolution. Trotsky was to say of Gorky that "he welcomed the revolution with the misgivings of a museum director. Stampeding soldiers and unemployed laborers terrified him." This was clever, but it was not true. Gorky was never terrified. *Novaya Zhizn* continued to attack Lenin with a desperate and unavailing courage until it was forced to suspend publication.

Very early in the revolution Gorky had seen that Lenin was unreservedly committed to terrorism in the manner of Nechayev, and that in no other way could he retain power. He was not alone. Some of the members of the government appointed by Lenin and Trotsky were so shocked by the use of arbitrary state power that they resigned within ten days of assuming office in protest against "the exploitation of political terrorism, by which alone the Soviet of People's Commissars can maintain itself in office." It was a striking defeat, but both Lenin and Trotsky were inclined to regard their resignations with satisfaction. They spoke of the "purification" of the regime, and of the "weaklings" who were lacking in revolutionary audacity—meaning that they had shown themselves incapable of making arbitrary arrests and shooting people without trial. Strong men were wanted; and since the strongest and cruelest were to be found among the Baltic sailors and the Lettish sharpshooters, these inevitably assumed positions of power and importance in the punitive squads attached to the government.

Meanwhile the revolution had been won. Unstable, inefficient, deriving its strength from ceaseless improvisation and the iron will of the two leaders who by their towering energy saved it from extinction, the revolution had become a fact which could not be written off the history books. The events of a single week in Petrograd were to change the entire course of world history.

THE EXALTATIONS OF REVOLUTION

IN THOSE EARLY DAYS, while Lenin was still new to the art of government, he gave the impression of a man who had elevated improvisation into a science. There was no problem which could not be solved by a decree, by a gesture, by a phrase, by the turning of a key in a lock. He had never given much thought to the limits of the possible—this was a province which he relinquished willingly to Bukharin—and in fact he rarely entertained the possibility of any limit to the changes he would bring about in Russia and the world. He had no false estimate of his abilities. He saw that he had judged rightly: the conquest of Petrograd was the first step to the conquest of the world.

No one entering the Smolny would have thought it possible that this small man with the piercing brown eyes, the bull-like neck, and the fringe of red hair was already planning the conquest of the world. It was not only that he did not look like a conqueror, but the setting was incongruous. The convent for the ladies of the nobility still resembled a convent. It was cold and cheerless. Icy wind from the Neva rattled the windowpanes, and electric lights burned dimly over the tables where the commissars worked. The endless gray corridors were muddy from the boots of the Red Guards; only the great hall with its Ionic columns and blazing chandeliers, which shone brightly whenever important statements were delivered, suggested a place where power was being generated.

Here in one of the upstairs rooms at the end of a long corridor he worked tirelessly to produce orders, *his* order, out of the chaos for which he was largely responsible. Trotsky worked in an office at the other end of the corridor, and it was characteristic of Lenin to suggest they would save time by learning to use roller skates. Such simple solutions delighted him. So it is with many of his decrees, written hurriedly, in handwriting which betrays the excitement of sudden discovery. He regarded himself as a man guided by Marxist logic, but in fact he was very often the creature of impulse, improvising on the spur of the moment, never at a loss for an appropriate answer, even when he misunderstood the question.

In the early days the entire government was given over to improvisation. Stanislav Pestkovsky tells the story of how he went to the Smolny in search of a job, was received by Lenin and Trotsky, and was told to apply to the Commissar of Finance, who was understaffed. The Commissar was Menzhinsky, later to become the redoubtable vice-president of the secret police. He had no staff. He was sitting on a sofa, exhausted by long hours of work. Above the sofa a strip of paper was tacked on the wall. It read: PEOPLE'S COMMISSARIAT OF FINANCE. Menzhinsky questioned his visitor about his career, learned that he had studied economics at the University of London, and then ran to Lenin's room, which was opposite his own, and returned a few minutes later with a decree signed by Lenin appointing Pestkovsky director of the State Bank.

Such improvisations were the order of the day. He enjoyed writing decrees on subjects in which he was learned and on subjects on which he knew nothing at all. As a habitual user of libraries, he sketched out a decree ordering immediate changes in the Petrograd Public Library "following the practice in the free states of the West, especially Switzerland and the United States of North America." It was an odd tribute to freedom, but the tone of the decree was inevitably dictatorial. He wrote:

1. The Public Library (formerly the Imperial Library) must immediately arrange *the exchange* of books with *all* the public libraries of Petrograd and the provinces, and also with *foreign* libraries (Finland, Sweden etc.).
2. *No charge* must be made for sending books *from one library to another* according to law.
3. The reading room in the library must be open every day, not excluding Sundays and holidays, from 8 o'clock in the morning to 11 o'clock in the evening. This is the procedure in the *private* libraries and reading rooms used by the *rich* in civilized countries.

4. An appropriate number of employees must be immediately transferred to the Public Library from the Ministry of Public Instruction (employing the services of women more widely, since the men are being drafted into the army), nine tenths of the present personnel in the Ministry being engaged in work which is not only useless but harmful.

This decree is illuminating for many reasons, for it deals with a subject very close to his heart and tells us a good deal about his attitude to education. The third paragraph was particularly reprehensible: there were almost no private libraries reserved for the rich, and he never had any difficulty in borrowing books from the specialized libraries. He was, however, an expert on libraries and could speak with authority. He liked the British Museum library most of all, detested the Bibliothèque Nationale in Paris, found the library at Cracow "detestable and the acme of inconvenience," and he had a special fondness for the Société de Lecture in Geneva where all the latest French, German and English newspapers were displayed on the racks and where he was sometimes given a room of his own, so that he could write without any interruptions, pace up and down the floor, take books from the shelves, and generally conduct himself as though he were in his own study. The Swiss library system was affiliated with the German system, with the result that during the war he was able to borrow books from German libraries. Hence the statement in the decree that the Petrograd Public Library must immediately arrange to borrow books from Finland and Sweden. It seems never to have occurred to him that the Finns and the Swedes might not have felt bound by a decree issued from the Smolny.

The decree was written in November 1917, presumably during one of his rare moments of leisure.

Not all the decrees were written in the expectation of immediate action. As Trotsky observed, a good many of them were exercises in propaganda designed to give an air of authority to his government. Power might be snatched from his hands, his government might fall, the counterrevolution might succeed, but the evidence of the decrees would remain to remind people in future ages what they had attempted to do.

The more revolutionary the decrees, the more improbable, and the more destructive of the old order, the more he delighted in them. In December came the decree abolishing all ranks in the army:

In fulfillment of the will of the revolutionary people which is concerned with the immediate and effective eradication of every inequality
in the army, the Sovnarkom hereby decrees:

1. To do away with all ranks and titles from the rank of corporal to
that of general inclusive. The army of the Russian Republic is henceforth to be composed of free and equal citizens bearing the honorable
title of "soldier of the revolutionary army";

2. To do away with all privileges and the external marks formerly
connected with the different ranks and titles;

3. To do away with saluting;

4. To do away with all decorations and other signs of distinction;

5. To do away with all officers' organizations;

6. To abolish the institution of orderlies in the army.

Such decrees were pleasant exercises in propaganda, and were not
intended to have any lasting effect. They could be reversed at will or
modified to any extent according to the demands of the moment. The
words "abolish," "do away with," "immediate," "categorically imperative" were their customary decorations, but it did not follow automatically that the words meant what they said. A new language was evolving, and this characteristic Leninist language, charged with words of
instant doom and frantic haste, lent itself to imitation and parody.
Radek and Zinoviev in particular proved to be apt imitators and paro-
dists, and Lenin was not above parodying himself. "We categorically
demand," he wrote on November 27, "that the Bolshevik deputies
imperatively demand a *voice* vote on the *immediate* invitation of representatives of the government." Sometimes he will go further, piling
demand upon demand, urgency upon urgency, until the mind reels
and the eyes close in weariness. Sometimes, too, one has the curious
feeling that one is not listening to Russian, but to some Germanic-
Russian hybrid. At his rare best he writes with amazing vigor and
clarity, but an anthology of such passages would cover only a few
pages.

Lenin's linguistic contribution to the Russian Revolution was not
among his more sober accomplishments. It is not only that he never
learned to write Russian well, but to the end of his life he wrote as he
wrote in his boyhood, from notes carefully numbered and compiled in
order, with the result that every statement appears to be contrived
and calculated according to some logical pattern. He dealt with words
as he dealt with men: they must all go into the strait jackets he has
devised for them. Nothing comes free. There is never a moment when

he is not watching the words, to see that they obey him. Characteristically, he was the first to employ the harsh abbreviations for government departments and attitudes which became the common currency of Soviet prose, and he especially liked "Sovnarkom."

In those days Lenin was in a state of extraordinary elation. To some visitors he gave an impression of being drunk with power and success. The world revolution was at hand, the downfall of the hated bourgeoisie was imminent, the new world order proclaimed in Petrograd was about to begin. His tone was messianic: nearly every sentence had its "everywhere" and "immediately."

One day shortly after the October revolution Colonel Raymond Robins went to call on him at the Smolny. Robins had been a coal miner in Kentucky and he had mined for gold in the Klondike; he had been a social worker in Chicago, and he knew his way around American politics; he was not a man to be swept easily off his feet. He admired the daring of the Bolsheviks without in any way sharing their convictions, and as head of the American Red Cross Mission to Russia he saw more of their leaders than any other American. His report, given in the third person, should be quoted at some length because it conveys better than anything else the messianic hopes of Lenin:

> When Colonel Robins called on Lenin in that famous room with the velvet hangings, Lenin said to him: "We may be overthrown in Russia by the backwardness of the Russian people, or by a foreign power, but the *idea* in the Russian Revolution will break and wreck every political social control in the world. Our method of social control must dominate the future. Political social control will die. The Russian Revolution will kill it—everywhere."
>
> "But," said Robins, "my government is a democratic government. Do you really mean that the idea in the Russian Revolution will destroy the democratic idea in the government of the United States?"
>
> "The American government," answered Lenin, "is corrupt."
>
> "That is not so," answered Robins. "Our national government and local governments are elected by the people. Most of the elections are honest and fair, and the men elected are the true choice of the voters. You cannot call the American government a bought government."
>
> "Ah, Colonel Robins," replied Lenin, "you do not understand. It is my fault. I should not have used the word corrupt. I do not mean that your government is corrupt through money. I mean that it is corrupt in that it is decayed in thought. It is living in the political thought of a bygone political age. It is living in the age of Thomas Jefferson. It is not living in the present economic age. It is, therefore, lacking in intellec-

tual integrity. . . . You refuse to recognize the fact that the real control is no longer *political*. That is why I say that your system is lacking in integrity. That is why our system is superior to yours. That is why it will destroy yours."

"Frankly, Mr. Commissioner," said Robins, "I don't believe it will."

"It will," said Lenin. "Do you know what our system is?"

"Not very well as yet," said Robins. "You've just started."

"I'll tell you," said Lenin. "Our system will destroy yours because it will consist of a social control which recognizes the basic fact of modern life. It recognizes the fact that real power today is *economic,* and that the social control of today must therefore be economic also. So what do we do? Who will be our representatives in our national legislature, in our national Soviet, from the district of Baku, for instance?

"The district of Baku is an oil country. Oil makes Baku. Oil rules Baku. Our representatives from Baku will be elected by the oil industry. They will be elected by the workers of the oil industry. You say, Who are the workers? I say, The men who manage and the men who obey the orders of managers, the superintendents, the engineers, the artisans, the manual laborers—all the persons who are actually engaged in the actual work of production, by brain and hand—they are the workers. Persons not so engaged—persons who are not at labor in the oil industry but who try to live off it without labor, by speculation, by royalties, by investment unaccompanied by any work of daily toil—they are not workers. They may know something about oil, or they may not. Usually they do not. In any case they are not engaged in the actual producing of oil. Our republic is a *producers'* republic.

"You will say that your republic is a *citizens'* republic. Very well. I say that the man as producer is more important than the man as citizen. The most important citizens in your oil districts—who are they? Are they not oil men? We will represent Baku as oil.

"Similarly we will represent the Donetz coal basin as coal. The representatives from the Donetz basin will be representatives of the coal industry. Again, from the country districts, our representatives will be representatives chosen by peasants who grow crops. What is the real interest of the country districts? It is not store-keeping. It is not money-lending. It is agriculture. From our country districts our Soviets of peasants will send representatives chosen by agriculture to speak for agriculture.

"This system is stronger than yours because it fits in with reality. It seeks out the sources of daily human work-value and, out of those sources, directly, it creates the social control of the State. Our Government will be an *economic* social control for an *economic* age. It will triumph because it speaks the spirit, and releases and uses the spirit, of the age that now is.

"Therefore, Colonel Robins, we look with confidence to the future. You may destroy us in Russia. You may destroy the Russian Revolution in Russia. You may overthrow me. It will make no difference. A hundred years ago the monarchies of Britain, Prussia, Austria, Russia overthrew the government of Revolutionary France. They restored a monarch, who was called a legitimate monarch, to power in Paris. But they could not stop, and they did not stop, the middle-class *political* revolution, the revolution of middle-class *democracy*, which had been started in Paris by the men of the French Revolution of 1789. They could not save feudalism.

"Every system of *feudal aristocratic* social control in Europe was destined to be destroyed by the *political democratic* social control worked out by the French Revolution. Every system of *political democratic* social control in the world today is destined now to be destroyed by the *economic producers'* social control worked out by the Russian Revolution.

"Colonel Robins, you do not believe it. I have to wait for events to convince you. You may see foreign bayonets parading across Russia. You may see the Soviets, and all the leaders of the Soviets, killed. You may see Russia dark again as it was dark before. But the lightning out of that darkness has destroyed political democracy everywhere. It has destroyed it not by physically striking it but simply by one flash of revealment of the future."

Raymond Robins' account of his meeting with Lenin breathes authenticity. Here is Lenin speaking like a schoolmaster to a perceptive pupil, revealing the flavor of his mind, his romanticism, his furious determination to see himself in historical perspective as the hammer which will strike at the heart of a society that is "decayed in thought." In the characteristically Russian way everything is reduced to ultimate simplicities. Lenin is not concerned to defend his thesis that the political must give way to the economic: it is too obvious to need explanation. He envisages a kind of corporate state in which the elected representatives will be selected from the various industries. He insists that the political citizen must give place to the producer, as though it were not possible for the producer to be a political citizen. Again and again we hear the characteristic nihilist vocabulary echoing raucously through the short, sharp sentences. *The idea in the Russian Revolution will break and wreck every political social control in the world. . . . Political social control will die. The Russian Revo-lution will kill it—everywhere. . . . Our system . . . will destroy yours. . . . You may destroy the Russian Revolution in Russia. You may overthrow me. It will make no difference. . . . The lightning out of that darkness has destroyed political democracy everywhere. . . .* So he goes on, seeing the world falling about his ears and all mankind obeying his destructive purposes, while the images of dark-ness gather strength until the final lightning flash.

Robins spoke to Lenin before he became wary of foreigners, in the days when the Revolution was still fresh and its machinery still unclogged. He had a genuine fondness for Lenin, and made no effort to hide it. When Lenin said, "I will cause a sufficient number of men to work a sufficient number of hours at a sufficient rate of speed to produce what Russia requires," he commented mildly, "It was a suffi-ciently Russian remark." He could sometimes banter with Lenin, and they were always friendly to each other.

Another visitor in those early days was Georgy Solomon, a man who had known Lenin since he was a student in Samara in 1892. Solomon was old enough to have been a friend of Genyeralov, who was executed with Alexander Ulyanov in 1887. At various times he had quarreled with Lenin's dogmatic approach to life, but they had remained on familiar terms. Shortly after the October revolution, Solo-mon paid a visit to Lenin at the Smolny and asked what was going on:

> "Tell me, Vladimir Ilyich, as an old comrade," I said, "what is going on? Are you really gambling on socialism on the island of 'Utopia' on a colossal scale? I cannot understand what is going on."
> "There is no island of 'Utopia' now," he said sharply in powerful tones. "We are creating a socialist state. From now on Russia will be the first state in which a socialist regime has been established. Ah, you are shrugging your shoulders. Well, you have still more surprises coming! It isn't a question of Russia. No, gentlemen, I spit on Russia! That's only one stage we have to pass through on our way to world revolution!"
> Involuntarily I found myself smiling. He squinted his small and rather narrow eyes which were Mongoloid, and burning with a little flame of ironical mischief, and said, "You are smiling! You are saying to yourself that all this is nothing more than a perfectly useless fantasy. I know what you are going to say. I know the entire arsenal of those stereotyped and hackneyed Marxist phrases which in reality are nothing more than bourgeois-Menshevik futilities—you haven't the strength to

draw away from them even by the length of a pig's snout. Well, we are and we will be turning more and more to the Left!"

Here I took the opportunity of interrupting him while he was regaining his breath. "Very well," I said, "Let us assume you succeed in making a perfect left turn; but you are forgetting the simple mechanical law of reaction and recoil. You will find yourself being thrown back by this law, and God knows where it will all end!"

"Excellent!" he exclaimed. "That's exactly right. Even if there is such a reaction, it means we must turn still more to the Left. This argument also favors me! . . ."

"What I don't understand," I said, "is what is going to happen in the future. You are only destroying things. All these requisitions and confiscations, what do they amount to unless it is destruction?"

"Quite right! Absolutely right!" he snapped back with a sudden mischievous gleam in his eyes. "What you say is absolutely true. We are destroying, but remember what Pisarev said: 'Destroy everything, smash everything! Smash, and bring everything low! The whole temple will go—everything in it that is not true to life—but the good will remain.' We are the true followers of Pisarev, the real revolutionaries—yes, we are going to tear the whole thing down! We shall destroy and smash everything, ha-ha-ha, with the result that everything will be smashed to smithereens and fly off in all directions, and nothing will remain standing!

"Yes, we are going to destroy everything, and on the ruins we will build our temple! It will be a temple for the happiness of all! But we shall destroy the entire bourgeoisie, and grind them to powder—ha-ha-ha—to powder. Remember that, you and your friend Krassin. We shall not stand on ceremony!"

"I don't understand what you are saying, Vladimir Ilyich," I said. "I really don't understand how you can speak of such things with such melancholy exaltation—this apology of destruction which leads us far beyond the scope of Pisarev's teachings in which after all there are some healthy grains. . . . In the first place, let us set aside the dubious teachings of Pisarev which can lead us very far indeed. . . . Listen . . . We, the old revolutionaries, we have never taught destruction for the sake of destruction. We have always stood, especially in Marxist times, for the destruction only of those things which have already been condemned by life—those things which are already falling away—"

"And I say that all these things have outlived their purpose and they are in a state of putrefaction. Yes, my dear sir, they are putrefied and deserve only to be destroyed. Take, for example, the bourgeoisie, or if you prefer it, democracy. They are doomed, and by destroying them we are doing no more than completing the inevitable historical process. We are advancing into life, into the very forefront of life with socialism, or more accurately, communism. . . .

"And remember that the Lenin who talked to you ten years ago no longer has any existence. He died a long time ago. In his place there speaks the new Lenin, who has learned that the ultimate truth lies in communism, which must now be brought into existence. It may not please you, and you may think it is nothing but utopian adventurism, but I assure you it isn't. . . .

"And don't talk to me. It will be better for you if you don't talk, for I shall attack mercilessly anyone who smells of counterrevolution. Against the counterrevolutionaries, whoever they are, I shall employ Comrade Uritsky, ha-ha-ha. Do you know him? It will be better for you, I think, if you don't make his acquaintance."

Such conversations would be unbelievable if others very much like them had not been recorded, if Lenin's public statements did not tally with them. That Lenin could say such things and believe them is extraordinary enough; what is still more extraordinary is that a man in such a state of exaltation was able to continue the day-to-day work of government without going mad.

It was as though a volcano had suddenly erupted, spewing out smoke and lava and the most brilliant flames, setting fire to all the woods around, while the earth trembled and the cities burned. For those who looked on, suffocating in the smoke and dying in the heat, it was as though they were living through an inferno. But there seemed to be salamanders living in the flames.

A wild hope and a furious exaltation uplifted the hearts of the Communists. It was not only Lenin who lived in expectations of a miraculous change in the nature of society. Bukharin spoke of new voyagers making more dangerous and more fruitful explorations than were ever made by Columbus. And not only dedicated Communists were roused to wonder. "In city, village, and Army, people rejoiced in the fullness of their liberation, in the limitless freedom that now summoned their creative efforts," wrote Isaac Steinberg, the Left Socialist Revolutionary who became Commissar of Justice under the Communists until he learned that there was no justice under Communism and fled into exile. The poet Alexander Blok greeted the revolution with joy, uplifted with "a new faith in the purifying power of revolution," and his most famous poem *The Twelve* describes twelve Red Guards marching through the snow with Christ at their head. He, too, was aware that new and terrible emotions had been kindled by the revolution, and he spoke in his poem *The Scythians*, written shortly after *The Twelve*, of a new destructive race coming out of the East possessing "a love like fire that burns and destroys everything in its path." In the savagery of these new Scythians there was a pure and perfect purpose, for they would sweep away all the accumulated rubbish of the past.

Exaltation, violence, dizziness, the extremes of compassion and of hate, were mingled in those early days of revolution. Deep within the Russian consciousness, engrained upon their flesh from ancient times, was the desire to do away with government, with every form of government which did not spring from the individual or from small groups of individuals. In an address to the people of Russia, printed in *Pravda* on November 19, Lenin appealed to this instinctive force in them, saying that they were all members of the government, were themselves the government:

> Comrade Workers! Remember that *you yourselves* now govern the state. No one will help you unless you unite and take *all the affairs* of the state into *your* hands. *Your* Soviets are organs of governmental power, organs with deciding voices and full powers to act.

At the time he seems to have meant what he said. He, too, was living in a state of utopian excitement. In the following January, he declared that the triumph of socialism throughout Russia would be assured "within a few months." At one of the meetings in the Smolny he told Trotsky that within six months socialism would have been achieved and Russia would become the greatest state in the world. The entrancing prospect fortified him, but there were moments when the excitement was almost too great to be borne. Just after the conquest of power in Petrograd, he turned with a kind of awkward shyness toward Trotsky and said, "You know, from persecution and living illegally to come suddenly into power, it's too rough altogether." Then he paused, searching for the right word, and said, *"Es schwindelt!—* It makes one dizzy!"* It was oddly characteristic of him that he should have spoken the words in German.

He was still dizzy three months later, when he wrote some private notes on the subject of the revolution, using the delirious words of Thucydides who spoke of his own history as "a possession for all time," valid for all eternity. So he wrote:

Revolutions are the locomotives of history.
Drive them at full speed ahead and keep them on the rails . . .

Κτῆμα ἐς ἀεί

Already conquered:
(a) Maximum of democracy
(β) Concretization of the first
     steps to socialism
(γ) Peace and the land

And if it was strange that he regarded "the maximum of democracy" as the first of his conquests, it was no stranger than that he should regard revolutions as the locomotives of history driven at full speed and always in danger of running off the rails.

The revolution was to run off the rails many times before he had finished with it. Then the wrecking crews would come along, the rails would be torn up, new rails would be laid, the locomotive would be reassembled and set once more on its course "at full speed ahead." On that dangerous and foolhardy journey, the locomotive was always coming to grief.

But in those early days, before disenchantment and cynicism set in, the exaltations of revolution seemed in themselves to be sufficient to solve all problems confronting the new state in which the people were summoned to govern themselves. They did not know, and could not have guessed, that they would not be permitted to govern themselves at all.

THE ICE
IS BROKEN

The ice is broken. The Soviets have
conquered throughout the whole world.

THE DESTRUCTION OF THE
CONSTITUENT ASSEMBLY

FOR NEARLY A CENTURY the Russians had dreamed of the day when the Constituent Assembly would become the ruling power, when a freely elected parliament would take over the functions and powers of the hated autocracy. Nechayev, standing in the witness box, had proclaimed the need to convoke the Zemsky Sobor, the medieval forerunner of the Constituent Assembly. Hundreds of revolutionaries and terrorists had sacrificed their lives in the belief that the Russian parliament was worth dying for. All over Russia there was the firmly held belief that the path of progress could only be opened by a parliament speaking responsibly on behalf of the whole people, and that anything less than a parliament would be an unendurable insult. The Bolsheviks themselves were continually clamoring for the Constituent Assembly, and one of their graver charges against the Provisional Government was that it had failed to bring the Assembly into existence.

Lenin never had the least intention of permitting the Constituent Assembly to rule as the sovereign power in the land, or even to rule in some minor capacity within the dictatorship of the proletariat. His charges against the Provisional Government were made for their propaganda effect. Once in power he was confronted with the knowledge that everyone, including those whom he liked to call "the great mass of the people," were determined that elections should be held. While the people clamored for free elections, the machinery of the Bolshevik party went into high gear to root out all the freedoms which the people wanted.

The Constituent Assembly was a nightmare which haunted the Bolsheviks. At all costs it was necessary to repudiate, compromise and destroy it. At first, according to Trotsky, Lenin attempted to banish the nightmare by indefinitely postponing it. The people must be made to submit to a fairly long tutelage, and in four or five years' time, or at some even more remote date, they would be permitted to hold elections; in the interval the Cadets, the supporters of Kornilov, and any other party which the Bolsheviks found objectionable would be proscribed. The electoral lists would be revised in such a way that only Bolsheviks would be permitted to vote. Meanwhile, there would be constant propaganda designed to show the people the true counter-revolutionary nature of freely elected parliaments.

Lenin exercised considerable thought on how to cope with a problem which was very nearly insoluble. He was caught on the horns of a dilemma. If there was a parliament, there was no guarantee that the Bolsheviks would have the majority; if there was no parliament, his enemies would point out that there was no popular basis for his government. And once the Constituent Assembly came into existence, where would its powers end and those of the Soviet Republic begin? He could say, as he had said many times before, that parliaments were merely the contrivances by which the bourgeois kept themselves in power, but now it was the peasants and workers who wanted to stand for parliament. To defy them was to defy his main supporters. He had no alternative but to permit elections to be held, and on November 9 he signed a decree ordering that the elections be held on November 25. "Every effort must be made," he wrote, "to ensure that the elections are legal and free." The Electoral Commission set up its headquarters in the Maryinsky Palace, and there began the long tussle between the electoral commissioners who wanted legal and free elections, and the Bolsheviks who wanted to stuff all the ballot boxes and to reduce the Electoral Commission to an instrument of their will.

There was, of course, no freedom of assembly, and no political meetings could be held except those authorized by the Bolsheviks. On November 11, two days after Lenin signed the decree, Podvoisky, as Chairman of the Military Revolutionary Committee, which controlled all that part of life which was not under the control of the Central Committee, issued a decree to all the citizens of Petrograd. "Petrograd and its suburbs are declared in a state of siege," he wrote. "Until special notice all gatherings and meetings in the streets are prohibited. Streetcar service goes on without hindrance." Nevertheless opposition parties were able to hold brief meetings, and they were able to obtain limited supplies of paper for posters. The Electoral Commission, which needed paper for ballots and envelopes, was hampered at every turn and barely succeeded in keeping a small office open.

The elections took place in Petrograd over a period of three days. There were nineteen tickets, including small splinter groups, like the "Feminine League for the Salvation of the Country" and the "Socialist Universalists," which could not hope for more than a handful of votes. There were more powerful groups, like the "Orthodox Parishes," which were survivals from the distant past. It was clear that the main battle would be fought between the Cadets, the Left Socialist Revolutionaries and the Bolsheviks. The results of the election were published on November 30 and gave the Cadets 245,006 votes, the Left Socialist Revolutionaries 152,230, and the Bolsheviks 424,027. The Bolsheviks therefore had only a bare majority over their combined opponents.

In Moscow and some other cities the Bolsheviks also obtained a majority. It was a different story in the provinces, where the Bolsheviks had not yet taken deep root. When all the returns were in, the Left Socialist Revolutionaries were seen to be the victors. Out of a total of 41.7 million votes, the Left Socialist Revolutionaries won 20.8 million, while the Bolsheviks polled only 9.8 million. The Mensheviks were out of the running, with only a few thousand votes. The Left Socialist Revolutionaries, who derived from the Narodnaya Volya, had a vast majority over the Bolsheviks, who derived from Karl Marx.

Lenin was not particularly surprised by the election results, and in any event he was determined not to let them stand in his way. Behind the scenes quick and brutal action was taken. The entire Electoral Commission was placed under arrest and removed to the Smolny, while Moses Uritsky, a confirmed Bolshevik, was appointed Commissar of Elections with full powers to examine and pass on the credentials of the elected members. House arrests and the closing-down of the small printing presses where opposition parties were still printing their one-sheet newspapers followed immediately. An even more significant and disturbing event took place on December 5, when the Military Revolutionary Committee was dissolved by decree, to give place to the Department for Combating Counterrevolution, which soon thereafter acquired the name of the Extraordinary Commission for Combating Counterrevolution and Sabotage. Known as the Cheka from the first letters of the first two words (*Chrezvychai-naya Komissiya*), it became the most dreaded of all the weapons in the arsenal of the Bolsheviks. Its powers were never defined, being included in the various decrees under the all-embracing "et cetera" which would generally appear at the end of a brief summary of its duties. The main purpose of the Cheka was to terrorize all the enemies of the regime into silence.

While the Constituent Assembly was preparing to meet, all the weapons of the Bolsheviks remained blunted. The threat of parliamentary power hung over them. There were some like Zinoviev who thought it would be possible to work out a *modus vivendi* between the Central Committee, the Soviets, and the Constituent Assembly, and who proclaimed that as long as the Assembly expressed the will of the workers, soldiers, and peasants, it should be permitted to continue its existence. Lenin however had no illusions about the threat it presented to his government. He was determined to destroy it.

By December 10 so many deputies had drifted into the capital from all over Russia that it was decided to open the Assembly the next day in the Tauride Palace. The deputies had not counted on the Bolsheviks, who seized the palace during the night, locked the gates, and posted a detachment of Lettish sharpshooters to prevent anyone from entering it. The next morning, processions formed in the streets behind banners reading, "All Power to the Constituent Assembly" and "Long Live the Constituent Assembly, the Sovereign of the Russian Land." It was a beautiful clear day, with no clouds and the snow lying crisp on the ground. By one o'clock all of Petrograd seemed to be converging on the palace. There was a dangerous moment when the crowd surged up to the gates, but the Letts held their fire. The mayor of Moscow asked the guards whether they were going to fire on the people.

"No," they said, "we are here to defend the Constituent Assembly."

"In that case," said the mayor, "unload your guns and let the people pass into the palace."

Inside the palace they found Uritsky. He ordered the deputies to show their credentials, but no one paid any attention to him. Only some fifty deputies were present—not enough to make a quorum, but enough to form a watch committee and to make preliminary plans. The deputies had taken physical possession of the palace, and some thought they had only to wait for the arrival of the other deputies for supreme power to fall into their hands. On that day Lenin ordered the arrest of the Cadet leaders. They were all deputies, and therefore immune from arrest, but this technicality did not bother him. In any event the most important of them were already under arrest, having been taken to the Peter and Paul Fortress from the Winter Palace immediately after the siege of the palace. Among them were Andrey Shingarev and Fyodor Kokoshkin, both men with large followings. They were capable and intelligent administrators, and they both had been ministers in Kerensky's government. Shingarev was a professor of constitutional law, and Kokoshkin a famous physician and expert on peasant problems. Their fates were to be strangely bound up with the fate of the Constituent Assembly.

If the Constituent Assembly had been able to meet in December, the story of the Russian Revolution might have been very different. It was not able to form a quorum in December, because the Bolsheviks did everything possible to prevent the deputies from reaching Petrograd.

Gradually, one by one, they made their way to Petrograd and then went into hiding. The city was in the hands of the Red Guards, who took orders only from Smolny. The Left Socialist Revolutionaries however had a vast popular following, and the time had not yet come for arresting them. It was decided to hold a full meeting of the Constituent Assembly on January 18. The delegates confidently expected that at this meeting the new revolutionary government would be inaugurated. No one has ever been able to make clear why they waited so long.

In the interval a spate of decrees issued from Smolny. These decrees effectively canceled whatever powers the Constituent Assembly might have possessed. Nothing was left to chance; every eventuality was prepared for.

On only one subject was Lenin incapable of legislating: his own life. He knew, as everyone knew, that he was in grave danger.

On the evening of January 14 he made a speech to a detachment of the newly formed Socialist Army at the Mikhailovsky Riding School, where in the past the Tsar was accustomed to review his troops. Into that vast hall, lighted by flaring torches, armored cars had been assembled in long columns. A great shout went up when Lenin arrived, and in the half-darkness, standing on the turret of an armored car in the same posture with which he greeted the crowds outside the Finland Station, he spoke to them about the need to fight valiantly for "our truly democratic regime" against the capitalists of the world, who were threatening to drown the revolution in blood. We know it was a fighting speech, because a brief report appeared in *Pravda* three days later, but for some reason the soldiers did not kindle to the words. There was applause at the end, but to some who were present it seemed perfunctory, unlike the customary ovation which would burst like the sound of a cannonade. The armored cars would leave in a few hours for the front. The soldiers, knowing they might soon die, had expected a better speech. Lenin stepped down from the armored car. To relieve the tension, Podvoisky took his place and announced that an American, Albert Rhys Williams, was present and he would address them on behalf of their comrades in America.

"Allow me to be your interpreter," Lenin said politely, and obeying some reckless impulse of his own the American answered, "No, I shall speak in Russian."

Lenin was amused. He was exhausted by overwork. He knew he had spoken badly and ineffectively, and he could feel the sullen mood of the soldiers. But as Rhys Williams began to talk in Russian, the first few polished phrases giving way to incongruous grammatical constructions, the mood changed. The soldiers laughed and applauded wildly. It pleased them that an American had come to address them, and that Lenin was acting as an occasional interpreter. From time to time the speaker would pause frantically and grope for a word. Lenin would look up and say, "What word do you want?" "Enlist." "It's *vstupit,*" Lenin would answer, and a moment later there would be another pause, another groping for a word, another burst of cheering. In the end it was Rhys Williams, not Lenin, who received the ovation.

Lenin walked into the courtyard, while the soldiers followed. He had brought Fritz Platten and Maria Ilyinichna with him. Fifty yards from the Riding School, as the car drove off through the mist, three bullets crashed through the windshield. Platten pushed Lenin down. The chauffeur accelerated, turned the nearest corner, and brought the car to a standstill. It was foolish to stop, for there was no knowing whether the attack would be resumed. The shots had come from behind, presumably from the direction of the Riding School, and only a miracle had saved them. The chauffeur got out, examined the tires, and saw that none of them had been hit. "If they had hit the tires we would have been done for," he commented. Then they made their way slowly through a sea of mist to Smolny. No one had been hurt except Fritz Platten, who had a small wound in his hand. He was very proud of his wound and mentioned it at every opportunity.

Four days later the Constituent Assembly opened. Lenin had not yet completely decided what he proposed to do about the Assembly. Cautiously, he ordered the Petrograd garrison to be on the alert: any demonstrations were to be mercilessly suppressed. The Tauride Palace was to be surrounded and guarded by Lettish sharpshooters. Uritsky was to issue tickets to the public galleries only to armed Bolshevik soldiers and sailors. The deputies were to be permitted to enter the building. At some undetermined time Lenin himself, or one of his deputies, would decide the subsequent fate of the Assembly. Meanwhile two thousand sailors from Vyborg and Helsingfors were summoned to the city.

The Assembly was due to open at twelve noon. Late in the morning the expected demonstrations took place, with large crowds converging on the Tauride Palace with banners reading, "All Power to the Constituent Assembly." It was a gray, murky day, with thick snow and a biting wind, and the crowds were in an angry mood. So were the Lettish sharpshooters, who ordered one procession moving along the Liteiny to stop. The crowd refused to stop, or did not hear the command. At a distance of two hundred feet the Letts fired on the Russians. There was only one volley, but it was enough to disperse the crowd. Eight or nine dead were left lying in the snow, and some twenty were seriously wounded. The Letts captured the banners and burned them, until only the blackened sticks were left lying in the snow. About an hour later another procession, which had advanced closer to the Tauride Palace, was fired on. Once again the banners were burned, and there were about the same number of dead lying in the snow.

At another time the crowds might have hurled themselves on the Letts and torn them to pieces, but the effect of these short, sharp volleys was exactly what Lenin had predicted. Cowed, the people simply scuttled back to their homes, dragging the wounded with them.

The Tauride Palace was an armed camp. All doors were closed except the main entrance. The entrance hall was crowded with armed sailors and soldiers, who examined the credentials of the deputies and amused themselves by commenting aloud on whether it was preferable to shoot, hang or bayonet the deputies. The Bolsheviks were deliberately cultivating an atmosphere of menace. They had cowed the demonstrators in the streets. Now it was necessary to cow the deputies.

Long before the opening of the Assembly, the deputies had heard rumors that the Bolsheviks intended to produce a show of force, but they had not expected it to happen in this way. They knew the session would be long, lasting well into the night, and so they brought candles in case the Bolsheviks turned out the lights. Some brought sandwiches. "In this way," wrote Trotsky, "democracy entered upon the struggle with dictatorship heavily armed with sandwiches and candles." It was one of Trotsky's more unpleasant utterances.

Most of the deputies were in their places by one o'clock. The Cadets were absent because they had been arrested or were in hiding, but the Socialist Revolutionaries had appeared in force. The Bolshevik deputies, though they were known to be in the building, were absent from the great glass-roofed hall. Diplomats crowded in the galleries, together with Bolshevik soldiers who occasionally aimed their rifles and revolvers in the direction of the deputies.

Around two o'clock in the afternoon Lenin set out from Smolny. With him were his wife, his sister Maria, and his secretary Bonch-Bruyevich. They drove to the Tauride Palace by a circuitous route which led them to one of the side streets running past the palace. Here there was an entrance guarded by soldiers; the gates were locked, but the chauffeur gave a prearranged signal on the horn, and the gates were opened, only to be locked again as soon as Lenin and his party had passed through. A room in the palace had been set apart for them. In a neighboring room the Bolshevik party members were meeting under the chairmanship of Varvara Yakovlieva, who had been the secretary at the secret meeting in Sukhanov's apartment. Apparently it was a stormy meeting, evenly divided between those who wanted to break up the Constituent Assembly before it began and those who wanted to break it up after it began. Everyone knew that the decision did not rest with the Bolshevik deputies. It rested with Lenin, who was quietly drinking tea. From time to time leading Bolsheviks would come to see him, then they would drift away again.

Shortly before four o'clock Lenin gave the signal to the Bolsheviks to enter the hall. He went with them, but on his way he remembered that he had left his pistol in his overcoat and went back to fetch it. To his surprise, it was no longer there, and the guards told him that no one had entered the room in his absence. Dybenko, the Commissar of War in the Soviet government, had been placed in charge of the military defense of the palace, and Lenin now summoned him and gave him a tongue-lashing for permitting the weapon to be stolen. Then, armed with another pistol, he made his way to the great hall.

At exactly four o'clock a Socialist Revolutionary deputy rose to his feet and said that according to an old parliamentary custom the first sitting should be presided over by the oldest member present. The oldest member was the veteran Sergey Shvetsov, who rose and made his way to the platform. Shvetsov was a Socialist Revolutionary, and his presence on the platform disturbed the Bolsheviks. Suddenly there was an uproar. Everyone was shouting at once, the guards were hammering their rifle butts on the floor, the Bolshevik deputies were pounding their fists on the desks and stamping their feet, while Bolshevik soldiers in the public galleries coolly aimed their rifles at the unfortunate Shvetsov, who was in danger of being rushed off his feet by the men surging from the floor. Shvetsov belonged to the right wing of the Socialist Revolutionaries and was therefore anathema to the Bolsheviks and the Left Socialist Revolutionaries. He had just time to say, "I declare the Constituent Assembly open," and to ring his bell, when the bell was snatched from him. In place of the towering white-haired Shvetsov there was the small, dark, black-bearded Yakov Sverdlov, who announced amid cries of "Hangman!" and "Wash the blood off your hands!" that the Bolshevik Executive Committee, of which he was the chairman, had authorized him to declare the Constituent Assembly open.

Such was the lunatic and terrifying beginning of the Assembly, which was to last for a little less than thirteen hours and then to die like a flame which is blown out.

Sverdlov made a long speech. He proclaimed that the October revolution had brought into being a Socialist revolution which would spread through the entire world. He demanded that the Constituent Assembly ratify all the decrees issued by the Soviet government. He reminded the audience that the French revolutionaries had proclaimed a Declaration of the Rights of Man and of the Citizens, and he read out a new declaration—one which superseded for all time the former declaration—in which the rights of man were never mentioned. In this Declaration of the Rights of the Toiling and Exploited Peoples, Russia was proclaimed a Republic of Soviets of Workers', Soldiers' and Peasants' Deputies, with all local and central power vested in the Soviets. All private property was to be abolished, all factories, banks, mines, railroads were to be transferred to the state power, a Socialist Red Army was to be instituted to protect the toilers from the exploiters, and universal labor duty was to come into being immediately. The Constituent Assembly was mentioned eleven times in the seventeen paragraphs, but always as a body whose sole purpose was to ratify decisions already taken; its purpose was merely to assent. "In supporting the Soviet and the decrees of the Soviet of People's Commissars, the Constituent Assembly admits that it has no power beyond working out some of the fundamental problems of reorganizing society on a socialist basis." The deputies learned in this fashion that all their powers were stripped from them.

The voice was Sverdlov's, but the words were Lenin's. He had written the declaration at least two days earlier; it had already been adopted by the Central Committee and published in *Izvestiya*. Written hurriedly, with a good deal of scratching out, it was not among Lenin's more precise and trenchant documents. He grapples with the problems of the Constituent Assembly, tries to find some reason for its existence, finds none, and then attempts to placate it by offering it "the fundamental task of suppressing all forms of exploitation of man by man and of completing the abolition of all class distinctions in society." In the original draft he proclaims that Russia shall become a socialist republic, then for some reason he scratched out the word "socialist." Later he decrees that "the entire land with all its buildings, inventories, and appurtenances contributing to peasant production" shall belong to the entire working community, then for some reason he scratched out "with all its buildings" and later reinstated the words by means of a series of dots underneath them. Characteristically, he begins the third paragraph with the words "The fundamental tasks." These, too, are scratched out, and he begins again: "In setting for themselves their fundamental tasks . . ." This document, clearly intended to have a historic significance equal to that of the Rights of Man, gives an impression of hurried improvisation, as though he were not yet convinced in his own mind what kind of state he envisaged. As in the draft of the "April Theses," he seems to be writing against time, in immense haste, hurling his ideas down on paper, scratching them out, revising and elaborating continually.

Sverdlov read the declaration to the end, declared for the third time that the Constituent Assembly was open, and then, as though he still believed the Assembly had some purpose to serve, he called for the election of a chairman. Before a chairman could be elected, a deputy proposed that the Assembly sing the "Internationale." It was a challenge which no socialist could resist, and for the first and last time at the meeting they were united on a single project.

The Bolsheviks presented no candidate for chairman from their own ranks. Instead they voted for Maria Spiridonova, a thin, pale, nervous woman who as a young revolutionary had assassinated the governor of Tambov and been sentenced to fifteen years' hard labor in Siberia. She was the acknowledged leader of the Left Socialist Revolutionaries. The Right Socialist Revolutionaries proposed the name of Victor Chernov, a darkly handsome man, famous for his powers of oratory. He had been Minister of Agriculture in the Provisional Government. Trotsky once described him as "emotional, feeble, coquettish, and above all, sickening." Exactly the same description might be applied to Trotsky, whose speeches suffered from the same thin and feverish brilliance.

To the surprise of the Bolsheviks, Chernov received 244 votes, to Maria Spiridonova's 151. To the sound of catcalls and cries of "Get down! Traitor! Counterrevolutionary!" he was able to make an inaugural address in which he proclaimed that the constitution of the Assembly was living testimony to the overwhelming desire of the people for socialism; what was at stake was how socialism should be applied; how the land should be distributed; how peace should be made. Peace and the distribution of the land were foregone conclusions. It remained for the Constituent Assembly to lead the country to socialism. He dwelt lovingly on what constitutional democratic government would do for Russia. Lenin listened for a few moments, and then ostentatiously stretched himself out on one of the red-carpeted steps leading to the platform and went to sleep, or pretended to sleep.

After the turbulent beginning the Constituent Assembly seemed to be getting into its stride. The Bolsheviks still pounded on their desks and stamped their feet at intervals, but the mood of ferocious intolerance seemed to have come to an end. Bukharin spoke for the Bolsheviks, attacking Chernov for his moderation, that moderation which seemed to be designed to avoid the issues confronting the Assembly; and he concluded his speech by calling upon the world proletariat to unite. The next speaker was Tseretelli, who spoke for less than ten minutes, but with an impact which was remembered many weeks afterward. He pleaded a lost cause, but commanded the respect of his opponents by the spell of his oratory and the vigor of his denunciations. He accused the Bolsheviks of being interlopers and wreckers, with no knowledge of the meaning of creative socialism; their peace was conquest from without and civil war from within. While he spoke a sailor in one of the galleries aimed a rifle at him and could be heard cursing under his breath, and Tseretelli might have died on the platform if a passing commissar had not ordered the sailor to put the rifle down. Uncompromisingly Tseretelli demanded that supreme power should be given to the Constituent Assembly.

Other speakers followed, but none made the impression that Tseretelli had made, for none had his daring. He went on talking even when a soldier jumped on the platform and waved a revolver about his face.

In the following days the Bolsheviks would vent their fury on him, for he alone had wounded them.

Around eleven o'clock the Bolsheviks demanded that the Constituent Assembly should vote on the declaration which Sverdlov had presented. There was more argument. The Socialist Revolutionaries presented their own program, and it was agreed to vote between the two programs. Lenin had left the stairway where he had been sleeping, and now occupied one of the front tier boxes. He sat there in an attitude of profound boredom. Seeing him so unconcerned, Albert Rhys Williams, the young American who had addressed the soldiers at the Mikhailovsky Riding Academy a few days earlier, came down from his place in the upper gallery and asked Lenin what he thought of the Constituent Assembly. Lenin shrugged his shoulders. He had nothing to say about the Assembly, and he seemed not to be interested. Then he spoke about the propaganda bureau where Rhys Williams was working, and his face brightened when the American told him that they had printed several tons of propaganda sheets to be sent to Germany, and then with sudden animation, remembering the American's speech from the top of an armored car, Lenin said: "How goes the Russian language? Can you understand all these speeches now?"

"There are so many words in Russian," the American replied.

"You must go at it systematically," Lenin said. "You must break the backbone of the language. I'll tell you my method of going at it!"

He explained how he would learn the vocabulary by heart, and then the grammar, and he would apply himself mercilessly to putting the words into the appropriate grammatical constructions. He warmed to the theme, his eyes glittering as he leaned out of the box. He spoke of how it was necessary to practice everywhere and upon everybody. He was talking about learning a language, but everything he said was like an echo of his political creed. Practice on everybody! Break the backbone! Mercilessly join the words and the grammar together.

When the votes were counted, the Bolsheviks had suffered another defeat. The votes showed 237 for the Socialist Revolutionary program, and 136 for the Bolshevik declaration. A recess was then called, while the Bolsheviks debated their next move. When they returned it was 1 A.M. They announced that they were withdrawing from the Constituent Assembly.

Before leaving for Smolny, Lenin wrote a note which was given to Anatoly Zheleznikov, a thickset young sailor who had been placed in charge. The note read: "The Constituent Assembly should not be dispersed till the end of the session. Tomorrow, from early morning, nobody should be admitted to the Tauride Palace."

It was the beginning of the end. For a few more hours the deputies attempted to make themselves heard. Soon the Left Socialist Revolutionaries left the hall. Chernov continued to preside, and the soldiers in the galleries continued to amuse themselves by aiming their rifles and revolvers at him. At 4:30 A.M. Zheleznikov climbed on the platform, tapped Chernov on the shoulder, and said, "You must finish now. Orders from the People's Commissar!"

"What People's Commissar?" Chernov asked.

"You can't stay any longer. The lights will be turned out in a minute. Besides, the guards are tired."

Chernov was not to be reduced to silence so easily. He snapped, "The deputies are also tired, but they cannot rest until they have fulfilled the tasks entrusted to them by the people. They have to decide on land reform and the future form of the government."

Then very quickly, knowing that time was running out, he read the draft of the new land reform bill, which did not differ remarkably from the Soviet decree which Lenin wrote immediately after the October revolution, for private ownership was abolished and all land was declared the property of the state. The sailors were shouting, "That's enough! Get out of here!" Chernov offered one final resolution: he proposed that the Assembly should formally declare that the monarchy be abolished and that Russia should henceforth have a republican form of government. This resolution was passed unanimously. At 4:42 A.M. Zheleznikov again tapped Chernov on the shoulder and indicated that his patience was exhausted. A moment later the lights went out. One by one the deputies made their way out of the Tauride Palace. Many expected to be shot by the guards as they emerged into the cold, clammy, fogbound street, but the time for reprisals and mass executions had not yet come, and all the deputies went safely to their homes and hiding places.

So ended the Constituent Assembly: in darkness and despair, with a few men moving fearfully by the light of guttering candles through the echoing corridors of a palace which had once belonged to Catherine the Great.

On that night or during the next morning, Lenin wrote down his impressions of the Constituent Assembly. He had seen cadavers moving in a kind of twilight, forming with their lips words which had lost all meaning. None of them seemed to realize that the main issue at stake was the survival of the revolution of the proletariat, which had fought its way to power. Chernov had proclaimed that there must be no civil war and no sabotage, but the revolution demanded a civil war —the very reason of its existence was the annihilation of the bourgeoisie—and as for sabotage, it could only be expected that the Chernovs and Tseretellis would employ all their resources to sabotage the revolution. So it had been in all the great revolutions of the past, in England in the seventeenth century, in France in the eighteenth, in Germany in the nineteenth. "We have lost a day, comrades," he wrote, quoting an old Latin tag. It was a troubled essay, and he seemed to realize that he had lost more than a day.

For thirteen hours people had spoken freely in a Russian parliament, while Lenin sat and watched. He would not permit them to speak freely again. Occasionally there would be heard a voice of protest, but it would be drowned in the angry denunciations of the Bolsheviks. The old autocracy had vanished, giving way to a new autocracy, unimaginably harder and sterner than its predecessor.

For Lenin, there remained only the formal act of dissolution, at once a death sentence and a coroner's report. Late the next morning there was a meeting of the Central Executive Committee of the All-Russian Soviet at Smolny. Not all the members were Bolsheviks. There was uproar at the beginning. Who was responsible for the shooting of the unarmed processions? Why had the Constituent Assembly been dissolved? When Lenin walked down the aisle to take his place on the rostrum a deputy called Kramarov, an old Socialist Revolutionary, rose to his full height of six feet five inches and shouted, "Long live the dictator!" Kramarov was in danger of being torn limb from limb. From the rostrum Lenin watched patiently until order was restored. His hands were deep in his pockets and there was an appraising gleam in his brown eyes.

What he said had been said many times before, but never under such circumstances of triumph. He spoke of the Soviets which sprang into existence in 1905, and how they had been reborn in the October revolution; they had seized power, and they left no place for the Constituent Assembly, which merely continued the policies of the Provisional Government. "The Russian Revolution," he declared, "could not stop at the stage of the bourgeois revolution, but as a result of the unheard-of sufferings caused by the war which sowed the ground for the social revolution, it had to go further." The revolutionary conflagration had not come about as the result of a single individual; no dictator had brought it into being. Chernov had said the Soviets would bring about civil war and sabotage. Lenin answered that these were unavoidable, and he seemed to welcome them. "We cannot present a socialist revolution to the people in a clear-cut, pristine and flawless form; inevitably there will be civil war, sabotage and opposition."

He went on to talk about the Constituent Assembly, evading the main issues. "The people desired us to convoke the Constituent Assembly, and therefore we called it," he said. "But the people soon realized what the vaunted Constituent Assembly really represents, and so once more we are fulfilling the will of the people, which declared, 'All power to the Soviets.' " It was a lame excuse, for the people were given no opportunity to realize "what the vaunted Constituent Assembly really represents," though they desired it and voted for their deputies in their millions.

A little while later Lenin signed the formal declaration depriving the Constituent Assembly of all its powers. From that day to this Russia has been ruled by a dictatorship.

From time to time Lenin would find himself troubled by the specter of the Constituent Assembly. He would speak of it as though it belonged to some antediluvian age, long past and forgotten, and in the next breath he would argue that the dictatorship was a superior form of democracy and it was necessary to abolish the Assembly because otherwise the superior form of democracy could not have been brought into existence; and when Kautsky, the German Marxist, wrote a book attacking the dictatorship of the proletariat for destroying representative government, Lenin replied by describing him as a bourgeois, a belly-crawler and a bootlicker, who could expect to be paid by the capitalists for services rendered. Had he forgotten the simple Marxist law that the more democracy is developed, the more the bourgeois parliaments fall under the control of the stock exchange and the bankers? Had he forgotten the suppression of strikes and the lynching of Negroes? Whenever Lenin defended the dissolution of the Constituent Assembly, the tone was shrill and curiously unconvincing.

To Trotsky, Lenin explained that he had made a mistake—it would have been much wiser to postpone the convocation of the Constituent Assembly indefinitely. "It was very incautious of us not to have postponed it," he said. "But in the end it turned out for the best. The dispersal of the Constituent Assembly by the Soviet government is a frank and complete liquidation of formal democracy in the name of the revolutionary dictatorship." "Thus," Trotsky commented, "theoretical generalizations went hand in hand with the use of the Lettish sharpshooters."

Lenin seems to have been perfectly aware of the weakness of his argument. He would seek out obscure texts from Marx and Engels to justify his action; he found precedents in the Commune, the French Revolution, and even in Cromwell's Republic of England. In the end, according to Krupskaya, he found his chief comfort in a Latin tag quoted by Plekhanov at the Second Congress in 1903. "Salus revolutionis suprema lex—The success of the revolution is the supreme law," said Plekhanov. "It follows therefore that if, for the sake of the triumph of the revolution, it becomes expedient to abrogate this or that principle of democracy, it would be criminal not to do so."

It was a very useful Latin tag, for there were no crimes which could not be defended in the name of the supreme law.

PEACE WITH GERMANY

OR THE PEOPLE OF PETROGRAD, January 1918 was a
month of disasters. It was one of the coldest winters on record, with
the clouds hanging low and the snow deep on the ground. In more
than half the city the electric light had been cut off. At night, trucks
raced through the streets on mysterious errands, and the sound of
sporadic gunfire could be heard. At Smolny the lights burned brightly.

From the large corner room on the third floor Lenin sent out a
stream of decrees and messages which had the effect of immediate
law. The room was sparsely furnished. There was an iron bed, a
couch, a small table for a secretary, three or four chairs, and two wall
telephones. The windows rattled in the wind coming along the Neva.
Sometimes the lights would grow dim, and sometimes, because it was
so cold, the commissars would huddle in their overcoats over braziers.
It was a long winter, and people wondered whether it would ever end.

For some it ended quickly—the Cheka was already at work, rounding up the enemies of the regime. The task of organizing the Cheka
had been entrusted to Felix Dzerzhinsky, a Pole, who like Lenin had
sprung from a family of small landowners. He was tall, well-built,
with a narrow face, high cheekbones, melting eyes, delicate bloodless
nostrils, an indulgent smile perpetually hovering on his lips. As a child
he had wanted to be a priest, and later a poet; he still wrote occasional verses in Polish. He looked vaguely aristocratic with his dark
pointed beard and his slender elegance; his manners were correct and
he spoke in a soft voice. His chief assistants were two Letts, Peters and
Latsis, cold-blooded and resourceful, worshiping Dzerzhinsky as he

in turn worshiped Lenin. The Red Terror had already begun, but it had not yet assumed the massive proportions it would assume in the late summer and autumn.

For the moment Lenin preferred a posture of legality. The Bolsheviks could and did take over the property of the bourgeoisie whenever they desired; such actions could be sanctioned by one or another of the decrees issuing from the Smolny. There were, however, no decrees specifically authorizing the execution of former ministers without trial. A few hours after Lenin dissolved the Constituent Assembly in a formal decree, two ministers of Kerensky's cabinet, the physician Andrey Shingarev and the professor of constitutional law Fyodor Kokoshkin were shot to death in the Maryinsky Hospital. Because they were ill, they had been removed to the hospital from the Peter and Paul Fortress. Two sailors had burst into the hospital during the night. They made their way straight to the room where the ministers were sleeping. Kokoshkin sat up and was shot at once. Shingarev was strangled and then shot. The sailors escaped. All the nurses could remember was that one of the sailors wore a cap with the name *Chaika* (Seagull) in gold letters. The *Chaika* was one of the ships in the Baltic fleet.

When Lenin heard of the murder of the two ministers the next morning, he affected to be deeply disturbed and summoned Isaac Steinberg, a Left Socialist Revolutionary who had been appointed Commissar of Justice, to his office. A decree ordering an immediate investigation of the crime and the arrest of the guilty sailors had already been prepared; it was signed by Lenin, and Steinberg observed that there was a space left for the signature of the Commissar of Justice. He was a little puzzled. Lenin insisted that he should sign, although he usually regarded his own signature as sufficient. Steinberg wanted to talk about methods of apprehending the murderers before signing, but Lenin was insistent. Bonch-Bruyevich, Lenin's secretary, was present, and both of them seemed to regard the murders with the utmost gravity. It was decided to summon Dybenko, who commanded the Baltic fleet. Over the telephone a message was sent to all government institutions in and around Petrograd to set the machinery in motion: reports were to be sent to the Smolny every two hours. When Dybenko arrived and was told about the murders, he replied calmly, "I shall write an appeal to the sailors not to do such things again and to bring the culprits to justice." A moment later he said, "Of course they will only regard this affair as an act of political terror." Steinberg learned for the first time that under the Bolsheviks the words "political terror" had the magic quality of sanctifying all crimes.

A committee of investigation, consisting of Dybenko, Bonch-Bruyevich, Steinberg and a representative of the sailors, was formed. Step by step they were able to reconstruct all the details of the crime. At the hospital the guards, the nurses and doctors were interrogated. When the names of the murderers were learned, Steinberg confidently expected them to be brought to justice. When he brought up the matter of their arrest at a meeting of the People's Commissars, Lenin merely showed him some telegrams received from the sailors of the Baltic fleet, saying they regarded the murder of the ministers with equanimity: it was an act of political terror, and therefore justified.

"Do you want us to go against the sailors?" Lenin asked.

"Yes," said Steinberg. "If we don't go against them now, it will be more difficult later to quench their thirst for blood. This was murder—not political terror."

It was a delicate situation. None of the other commissars spoke. As usual, they were waiting for Lenin to give his views.

"I don't think the people are interested in such matters," Lenin said at last. "Ask any worker or peasant, and you'll find he has never heard of Shingarev."

There were other commissars from the Left Socialist Revolutionaries. They argued that it was a simple matter to apprehend the sailors, who were stationed at the marine barracks. Surely the Commissar of Justice had power to arrest criminals! If murder could be committed with impunity, where would it end?

"I can only arrest them if I have full powers," Steinberg said. "I shall need a detachment of Red Guards with machine guns to surround the barracks and take the culprits by force."

The detachment was not given to him, and the culprits were never arrested. Three weeks later the Left Socialist Revolutionaries resigned from the government when the Bolsheviks signed the Brest Litovsk Treaty with Germany, and Steinberg was out of office.

Lenin's attitude toward the Germans was that of a chess player who has lost most of his pieces, but who still hopes to win by superior strategy. Knights, bishops, and pawns were lost; there were vast empty spaces on the board in which he could maneuver his queen. If necessary, his own headquarters could be moved from Petrograd to Moscow, or to the Urals or to Vladivostok; and his resilient queen, the Communist Party, could dart like lightning across the board, breaking through the enemy ranks, appearing in places where she was never expected, in disguise, unknown and unrecognizable. He had studied end games, caring little for the skirmishing in the middle. He was playing the game according to his own rules, which were not the rules of the German High Command.

Trotsky had returned from Brest Litovsk with the formula: "No peace, no war." It was a formula of limited application, for the German Army was in a position of preponderant power and the High Command could enforce the peace or insist on war at its pleasure. As the price of peace, the Germans demanded the annexation of Poland, Lithuania, and vast areas of the Ukraine and White Russia, together with an indemnity amounting to three billion rubles.

Lenin was prepared to accept the German peace terms on the grounds that his primary concern was to safeguard the socialist revolution *under any conditions*. He hoped and expected that the revolutionary flame would sweep through all of Europe. His propaganda machine was working at full blast to subvert the Germans in the trenches. The key word, which he never tired of repeating, was "brotherhood"—*brataniye*—meaning that the soldiers of all nations would cross the battle lines, embrace one another, and declare themselves for the red flag. In a few days or a few months he believed the red flag would be flying in Berlin, Vienna, Budapest, London and Paris.

On January 20, immediately after Trotsky's return from Brest Litovsk, Lenin wrote out his "Twenty-one Theses," in which he analyzed in his customary fashion the play of forces existing at the time. It is a brilliant, erratic, and uncomfortable statement, because his calculations are based largely on wish-fulfillment and many of the real forces at work were disregarded as having no relevance to the issues at stake. The core of the argument rested on the European revolution. He wrote:

> There is no doubt that the socialist revolution in Europe must and will come about. All our hopes for the *definitive** triumph of socialism rest on this certainty and this scientific predication. Our propaganda activity and the organization of fraternization especially must be strengthened and developed. Yet it would be a mistake of the Socialist Government of Russia to base its tactics on the hypothesis that within the next six months (or some comparable short period) there will be a European revolution or, to be more precise, a German revolution of a socialist

* Lenin uses the word *okonchatelniy*, which can also mean "final."

character. It is impossible to make such predictions, and every attempt to do so is simply to embark on a game of chance.

Even though it was a game of chance, it was a chance he took willingly. By concluding a separate peace, he argued, he was giving aid to those potential revolutions which would be encouraged by the existence of the dictatorship of the proletariat in Russia. The Socialist Republic of Russia would become a model for all the other nations to imitate, but this republic could not be confirmed in its powers without the few months of peace necessary to bring about the total reorganization of the country. It was not to be expected that the European revolutions would come about overnight; the German war against England and America would go on for a long time; the bourgeoisie would resist the revolutionaries with all the strength they commanded.

Janus-faced, Lenin hammered two contrary theses into one. With one pair of eyes he saw the imperialist powers fighting a prolonged war; with another pair of eyes he saw the revolutionaries triumphant everywhere. In his mind these two irreconcilable actions took place simultaneously, for the wish furthered the thought, even though he had long ago trained himself to observe only the realities of a situation. He knew that Russia could not embark on a revolutionary war. The poor peasants were in no mood to fight, the military supply machine had disintegrated, there was a shortage of horses to draw the gun carriages, and so the artillery was in a state, as he expressed it, of "hopeless chaos." Russia could not defend its shore line—from Reval to Riga there was nothing to oppose the German forces. "We have abrogated the secret treaties, we have offered all nations a just peace, and we have prolonged the peace negotiations in various ways in order to give other nations a chance to join." But the other nations had refused to accept peace on the Soviet terms.

His final conclusions were based, as one might have expected, less on the realities of the situation and even less on the immutable laws of Marxist science than on the desire to throw the problem away. He discarded the carefully constructed diagram of forces and returned to his initial theorem: he would build socialism in one country and let the imperialists grapple with their own problems to their hearts' content. He would nationalize industry and the banks and organize the natural exchange of products between the cities and the villages. By "natural" he seems to have meant that the products of the villages would be expropriated by decree. He wrote:

By concluding a separate peace we rid ourselves *as far as present circumstances admit* of both the imperialist groups which are fighting against one another. We can take advantage of their warfare and their strife—which makes it difficult for them to reach an agreement at our expense—and we can take advantage of this period while our hands are free to develop and strengthen the Socialist Revolution. We can re-organize Russia on the basis of the dictatorship of the proletariat, on the basis of the nationalization of the banks and heavy industries, and the natural *exchange of products between* the towns and the small peasant co-operatives in the villages, and all these are economically feasible provided we have the assurance of a few months of peaceful work. Such a reorganization would make socialism unconquerable not only in Russia but in the whole world, and at the same time it would lay the solid economic basis for a powerful workers' and peasants' Red Army.

So he wrote, employing his characteristic "all" language which sometimes dissolved all problems into universals; but in the entire "Twenty-one Theses" there was no mention of the very real possibility of a split between the Bolsheviks and the Left Socialist Revolutionaries if the peace treaty was signed. When Trotsky insisted that the only possible formula was "No peace, no war," Lenin answered:

"For the moment the question is the fate of the revolution. We can restore balance in the party. But before everything else we must save the revolution, and we can save it only by signing the peace terms. Better a split than the danger of a military overthrow of the revolution. The Lefts will cease raging and then—even if it comes to a split, which is not inevitable—return to the party. On the other hand, if the Germans conquer us, not one of us returns. Very well, let us admit your plan is accepted. We refuse to sign the peace treaty. And the Germans at once attack. What will you do then?"

"We will sign the peace terms under bayonets," Trotsky replied. "Then the picture will be clear to the workmen of the whole world."

Lenin was not convinced by Trotsky's argument; he had no reason to believe that the Germans would permit the Russians to sign a peace treaty later. "This beast springs suddenly," he kept repeating, and being himself an expert in sudden springs and how effective they could be, he wondered whether anything was to be gained by not signing. He was all for peace—peace at any price, even with annexations and indemnities, for he had no intention of paying the indemnities and the annexations would prove perhaps to be meaningless since the frontiers were fluid and the German revolution would put an end to them. Lenin read his theses to "about sixty of the more prominent active members of the party in Petrograd," and when the vote was taken, he suffered a complete defeat. Lenin's proposal to sign an immediate peace with Germany received 15 votes, Trotsky's formula of "No peace, no war" received 16 votes, and Bukharin's proposal, backed by Dzerzhinsky, Uritsky and others, to wage a revolutionary war against Germany received 32 votes. But a mere matter of votes rarely disconcerted Lenin, who returned to the attack the following day at a meeting of the Central Committee. At this meeting the proposal for a revolutionary war was defeated by 11 votes to 2. The proposal to continue negotiations was carried by 12 votes to 1. Trotsky's formula of "No peace, no war" was carried by 9 votes to 7. These votes could be reconciled only on the assumption that negotiations would be carried on as long as possible in an effort to delay the inevitable signing of the peace treaty. Trotsky returned to Brest Litovsk with no assurance that he would be able to carry out his mission.

Into the debates leading to this decision the Communist rulers had poured their reserves of emotion and invective. The struggle was bitter and relentless. At one point Radek rose from his seat and shouted at Lenin, "If we had five hundred courageous men in Petrograd, we would put you in prison!"

Lenin answered, "Some people, indeed, may go to prison, but if you will calculate the probabilities you will see that it is much more likely that I will send you than you me!"

With Bukharin, too, there were violent differences of opinion. Lenin's views were not popular. When his ideas were rejected at the informal meeting, it was decided to canvass the views of two hundred local Soviets. Only Petrograd voted unreservedly for peace; from Moscow, Ekaterinburg, Kharkov and Kronstadt, and all the rest, there came the full-throated cry for a revolutionary war. There was the widespread belief that the revolutionary war would spark the flame of revolution in Europe. But while Lenin believed unreservedly in the world-wide revolution as an article of faith, he put his trust in facts. "You should not put too much faith in the German proletariat," he said cautiously. "Germany is only pregnant with revolution. The second month must not be mistaken for the ninth. But here in Russia we have a healthy, lusty child. We may kill it if we start a war." To Bukharin he said, "There is nothing to prevent the Germans from taking Petrograd with their bare hands."

Yet Lenin too could clutch at straws. When the "Twenty-one Theses" were finally printed in *Pravda* in February, he added a triumphant twenty-second thesis, which read:

> The mass strikes in Austria and Germany, followed by the formation of soviets of workers' deputies in Berlin and Vienna, finally the armed clashes and streets fights which broke out in Berlin beginning 18–20 January, all these entitle us to recognize as a fact that the revolution has begun in Germany.
>
> It follows from this fact that we still have it in our power to draw out and delay for some length of time the peace negotiations.

But in fact the German revolution had not begun; there were no soviets of workers' deputies in Berlin or Vienna; all the strike meetings were broken up by the police, and the strike leaders were arrested. The German Army took over all large industries, for exactly the same reason that Lenin took over heavy industry in Russia: to use them without interference or obstruction. Whatever decisions were to be reached at Brest Litovsk, the Communists no longer could rely on the threat of armed insurrection in the rear of the German Army. On February 10, Trotsky to the stupefaction of the Germans announced that Russia was withdrawing from the war without signing a peace treaty. "We are issuing orders for the full demobilization of all troops now confronting the armies of Germany, Austria-Hungary, Turkey and Bulgaria." To justify his refusal to sign a peace treaty, he declared, "We cannot enter the signature of the Russian Revolution under conditions which carry oppression, sorrow and suffering to millions of human beings." General Hoffmann complained that the Bolshevik actions were *unerhört*—"unheard of"—and so they were. Armies, especially German armies, do not simply melt away on the battlefield and declare themselves out of the war. For six days the Germans hesitated, apparently wondering what action to take. Then they announced that the armistice would come to an end at noon on February 18, unless the Russians immediately signed the peace treaty.

The decision, so long delayed, now had to be faced. No longer were there any advantages in temporizing, while German airplanes were flying over the Russian front. The debates within the party became more acrimonious than ever, but Lenin's ascendancy was such that he felt strong enough to carry the day. Trotsky's formula had failed. "Delay is impossible," Lenin said. "We must sign at once."

Then he said, as he had said so often when speaking of the Germans, "The beast springs quickly."

But the Germans also were capable of playing a waiting game; they were in no hurry to sign. New and harsher terms for an armistice were invented, and meanwhile they took the offensive. In five days the Germans covered 150 miles. They captured vast supplies of ammunition. There seemed to be nothing to prevent them from reaching Petrograd. As Lenin well knew, the revolution was in jeopardy. "Yesterday we still sat firm in the saddle," he told Trotsky while the Germans were attacking, "and today we are only holding fast to the mane. But it is also a lesson—a very good lesson if only the Germans and the White Guards do not succeed in overthrowing us."

The deeper the Germans attacked, the greater was the enthusiasm in Petrograd for a revolutionary war. Lenin saw no advantages in a revolutionary war. He wanted to sign the treaty and get it over with, otherwise he would be compelled to take flight. He was perfectly serious when he spoke of establishing a Soviet in the Urals. "The Kuznetsk Basin is rich in coal," he said. "We will form a Ural-Kuznetsk Republic based on the industry of the Urals and the coal of the Kuznetsk Basin, on the proletariat of the Urals, and on the Moscow and Petrograd workers we can take with us. If need be, we can go further east—beyond the Urals. We can go to Kamchatka, but we will stand together!"

The beast had sprung, and as Lenin looked about in search of dangerous weapons it occurred to him that there was still a possibility of using the English and French against the Germans. French and British agents were present in Petrograd. They were approached. Could they provide military supplies to hold off the threatened German occupation of all western Russia? Bruce Lockhart, the British agent, went to Smolny to discuss whether aid could be sent from England. He had half thought he would be confronted with a superman. Instead, he found a man who resembled a provincial grocer, "with short, thick neck, broad shoulders, round, red face, high intellectual forehead, nose slightly turned up, brownish mustache, and short, stubbly beard." He had "a quizzing, half-contemptuous, half-smiling look." He was cool, unemotional, determined, and Lockhart could well understand how the other commissars looked to him before making their decisions.

Lenin spoke of the German advance, and of how the Bolsheviks were prepared to withdraw to the Volga and the Urals unless help

came to them in time or unless the Germans were halted. He was prepared to compromise with the capitalists.

"I am prepared to risk a co-operation with the Allies," he said,
"which should be temporarily advantageous to both of us. In the event
of German aggression, I am even willing to accept military support.
At the same time I am quite convinced that your government will
never see things in this light. It is a reactionary government. It will
co-operate with the Russian reactionaries."

Lockhart pointed out that if the Bolsheviks made peace with Germany, then the Germans would be able to throw all their forces
against the western front. They might crush the Allies, and then they
would turn about and destroy the Bolsheviks at their leisure; and their
own starving people would be fed on grain forcibly expropriated from
Russia. Lenin smiled. He was perfectly familiar with these arguments;
only a few days before he had written in a note, "It is obvious that all
the Germans want is our grain." But there were other arguments,
equally compelling, which Lockhart had failed to raise.

"You ignore the psychological factors," Lenin said. "This war will
be settled in the rear and not in the trenches. But even from your point
of view your argument is false. Germany has long ago withdrawn her
best troops from the eastern front. As a result of this robber peace she
will have to maintain larger and not fewer forces in the east. As for her
being able to obtain supplies in large quantities from Russia, you may
set your fears at rest. Passive resistance—and the expression comes
from your own country—is a more potent weapon than an army that
cannot fight."

Not that Lenin was in any mood to wage a war of passive resistance—such weapons were to be employed only as a last resort. The
immediate task was to stave off the German advance. Appeals for a
revolutionary war were still being heard; opposition newspapers were
still being printed; and the wildest rumors were flowing through the
city. In the workers' section, in Vyborg and the Petersburg Side, tempers were inflamed against the Bolsheviks. Someone had spread the
rumor that Lenin had absconded to Finland with thirty million rubles
from the State Bank and that the Grand Duke Nikolay Nikolayevich
was advancing with two hundred thousand troops from the Crimea
to save Russia from the Bolshevik traitors. The workers were up in
arms. Two long columns of armed workers made their way to Smolny.
Lenin was sitting in his third-floor room, receiving telephone messages
from the front. The workers had almost reached the gates of the

Smolny when the guards rushed into Lenin's office and asked for orders to fire. Lenin leaped to his feet. He had known nothing about the two converging processions of armed workers. "No, don't fire!" he said. "We will talk to them! Tell their leaders to come in!"

So they came into the office, men with bayoneted rifles in their hands and automatic pistols at their waists, sullen and angry. They were the armed proletariat and the nucleus of the future Red Army, but they were now in opposition. Colonel Raymond Robins, the American agent, was present. He told how Lenin addressed them calmly, reminding them that, far from having fled to Finland, he was still working for the revolution; he had been working for it before some of them were born, and he would be working for it when some of them were dead. "I stand always in danger," he said. "You stand in more danger." He went on to say that he did not blame them for not always trusting their leaders; it was surprising that the leaders had been trusted for so long. They wanted to fight the Germans? He had nothing against fighting the Germans in principle, but it was more important to fight for the revolution. What good would they do by dying at the hands of the Germans? The revolution would fail, the Tsar would come back, everything would be as it was before. As for the peace treaty—

"They tell you I will make a shameful peace," he said. "Yes. I will make a shameful peace. They tell you I will surrender Petrograd, the Imperial City. Yes. I will surrender Petrograd, the Imperial City. They tell you I will surrender Moscow, the Holy City. I will. I will go back to the Volga, and I will go back behind the Volga to Ekaterinburg; but I will save the soldiers of the revolution and I will save the revolution. Comrades, what is your will?"

At such moments Lenin was at his best—tough, determined, in complete command of the situation. The armed workers had it in their power to provoke an insurrection which would have put an end to Bolshevism. Dazed, they kept shouting Lenin's name, and walked out more quietly than they entered.

Lenin was perfectly serious in his threat to abandon Petrograd and Moscow, if necessary. Even at this late hour, he spoke of resisting the German terms if the Allies could guarantee their support. On this subject both Robins and Lockhart received convincing testimony, which they communicated to their governments, receiving replies which showed how little these governments understood Lenin's position. Early in March he transferred his government to Moscow. The

Treaty of Brest Litovsk was signed on March 3, but ratification was delayed until the All-Russian Congress of Soviets opened on March 14 in the Hall of the Nobles. Robins was present. He went to see Lenin, who immediately asked him whether he had heard from his government.

"No, I have not heard yet," Robins replied.

"Has Lockhart heard from London?"

"Not yet," Robins answered, and still hoping there would be a breathing space before the treaty was ratified, he said, "Couldn't you prolong the debate?"

Time was running out.

"No," said Lenin, "the debate must run its course."

It was an angry debate, lasting two days, with the Left Socialist Revolutionaries proclaiming the need for the revolutionary war against Germany to the bitter end. Bukharin and Martov implored the assembly not to take the fatal step of ratifying the treaty. Lenin rebuked them, speaking of their theories which were compounded "half of despair and half of empty words," and of their failure to look cold-bloodedly on the pressing realities. It was true that the peace was unbelievably hard and humiliating, but so too was the Treaty of Tilsit which Napoleon imposed on Alexander I. But that treaty like many others had been enforced only for a little while. "We are adopting a strategy of retreat," he declared, "and no one can deny that men can retreat as heroically as they advance. We are waiting for the international socialist proletariat to come to our aid, and then the second socialist revolution will begin, this time on a world scale."

Late in the evening of March 15 he made his final appeal to the Congress. His speech was prepared, but there was still a last minute possibility of a *rapprochement* with the Allies. Raymond Robins was sitting on the steps of the platform, and Lenin beckoned to him.

"What have you heard from your government?" he asked.

"Nothing. What has Lockhart heard from London?"

"Nothing," answered Lenin, and then after a pause, "I shall now speak for the peace. It will be ratified."

It was a long speech. He spoke for an hour and twenty minutes, castigating his enemies with unusual bitterness, speaking of them as school children who did not understand the first principles of history, taunting Martov especially, because he seemed to want to turn back the clock and expunge the October revolution from the record, and reserving his heaviest sarcasm for the Left Socialist Revolutionaries who had accused him of hauling down the flag of revolutionary war. "They do not realize," he declared, "that revolution is a difficult and complex science. For them it is merely a question of words; the histories of revolutions are full of these word-spinners, and what remains of them? Only smoke and a bad smell."

He carried the Congress. The resolution to ratify the treaty was passed by 784 votes to 261. Then it remained for him to consolidate his dictatorship over a country shorn by the treaty of a quarter of her territory and nearly a half of her population.

THE CORRUPTIONS OF POWER

WHEN LENIN LEFT PETROGRAD for Moscow, he left secretly. He was under heavy guard; the Nikolayevsky railroad station was in a blackout and surrounded by Lettish sharpshooters. He left Smolny in darkness and made his way to the station by a circuitous route. Preparations for the journey had been entrusted to Bonch-Bruyevich, who had spent whole days poring over maps and interrogating railroad officials. The entire government was being transported to Moscow; and now in the darkness, around ten o'clock at night, they were moving like shadows through the deserted station, where the only light came from their pocket flashlights, the flare of matches, or an occasional railroadman's lamp. They were like thieves slipping away in the night.

There were many reasons for secrecy. It was not only the fear of White Guards and of sympathizers of the old regime; there was also the fear of sabotage from the workers of Petrograd, who felt they were being deserted in the hour of trial when the Germans, for all they knew, were about to pounce on the city. Though all arrangements for the journey had been made in the closest secrecy, the workers came to know about it. There was talk of holding Lenin as a hostage. If Moscow was to become the capital, then what would happen to Petrograd, the city where the revolution had first broken out? The workers were angry, confused, dangerous. Bonch-Bruyevich thought it advisable to tell Lenin about the mood of the workers and especially of the Left Socialist Revolutionaries among them.

455

"There is only one question," Lenin said. "Can you guarantee that we shall reach Moscow in perfect safety?"

"Yes, I guarantee it," Bonch-Bruyevich replied, and no more questions were asked about the journey.

It was a long journey, much longer than anyone had expected. Lenin had given orders that the train should go at the maximum speed, but the line was choked with trains full of demobilized soldiers and they were continually having to halt; a journey which would normally take about twelve hours took twice as long.

There was no radio transmitter on the train, no means of sending or receiving telegrams. For nearly twenty-four hours he was out of touch with the world, alone in a first-class compartment with his wife, his sister Maria, and a few books. He used the time profitably to write a short essay, "The Principal Task of Our Time," in which he surveyed the progress of the revolution up to that moment and prophesied how it would develop into the future. The essay was composed with unusual care, in a mood which is at once contemplative and exalted. He knew—no one knew better—that history was flowing through him, with the result that the essay, which is concerned essentially with the history of humanity, becomes a statement of an intensely personal character. Significantly the last words of the essay are a paean in praise of the disciplined organization of the German mind; no one who was wholly Russian could have written them. The Germans have just inflicted on the Russians an intolerable peace, and Lenin contemplates them with admiration. There is something almost feminine in his salute to the victor.

"The Principal Task of Our Time" should be quoted at some length because it shows with astonishing clarity the springs of his mind. Here, for once, the habits of vituperation are abandoned. There are no easy jibes, no plays to the gallery. Here with a kind of quiet desperation, seeing himself as one who wears the robe of destiny, he contemplates himself in the mirror of history.

In our day the history of humanity has reached one of those immensely great and difficult turning points, of vast—and one may add without the least exaggeration of world-liberating—significance. From war to peace; from the war fought between plunderers, those plunderers who have thrown millions of the exploited and of the working class into battle in order to establish new ways of dividing the spoils among the strong, to the war of the oppressed against the oppressors as they free themselves from the yoke of capital; from the abyss of suffering and torture and hunger and barbarism to the shining future of Communist society, and the welfare of all, and enduring peace.

It is not to be wondered at that at this most abrupt moment of abrupt change, while all around us the old world crashes and falls to pieces amid frightful uproar and the new world comes to birth in indescribable torment, there are some whose heads are spinning, and others who are stricken with despair, and still others who hide in the shelter of seductive phrases to escape from a reality which has at times grown too bitter for them.

It has been given to Russia to have observed with clarity, and with extraordinary sharpness and anguish to have lived through one of the most sudden turns of history, the turn which leads away from imperialism to the communist revolution. In a few days we utterly destroyed one of the most ancient, powerful, barbaric, and ferocious monarchies. In a few months we have moved through various stages of conciliation with the bourgeoisie and seen the defeat of petty-bourgeois illusions; it has taken other countries tens of years to pass through these stages. In a few weeks, having toppled the bourgeoisie from power, we have been confronted with its open hostility in civil war, and we have conquered it. From one end of our immense country to the other we have seen the victorious and triumphal march of Bolshevism. We have raised up the lowest strata of the toiling masses, who were oppressed by Tsarism and the bourgeoisie, to freedom and independence. We have inaugurated and strengthened the Soviet Republic, a new kind of state, immeasurably superior and more democratic than the best of the bourgeois parliamentary republics.

So he boasted only a few hours before the crushing peace treaty with Germany was ratified—when all that remained of Russia was a relic of her former greatness. Not all these statements were true. It was not true, for example, that "the victorious and triumphal march of Bolshevism" had spread from one end of the country to the other, for there were vast areas where Bolshevism had not yet penetrated. Nor was it true that the Soviet Republic was "immeasurably superior and more democratic than the best of the bourgeois parliamentary republics," if only because there is nothing in the least democratic in a dictatorship. He saw himself projected against the backdrop of history, dominating the entire world "at this most abrupt moment of abrupt change," and it gave pleasure to him, and it was nearly true.

But though the picture he drew of himself and of his times was largely accurate, he was aware that Russia was still pathetically weak. He dreamed of a time when "Russia will cease being wretchedly poor and weak, and become in the fullest sense of the words powerful and abundant." And that will come about only when the Russians have cast aside their despairs:

All this will come about when Russia has set aside all her despairs and pretty phrases, when she clenches her teeth, musters all her strength and strains every nerve and tightens her muscles, and when she realizes that her *only* salvation lies along the road of the international socialist revolution, upon which we have set our feet. By marching forward along this road, never being dismayed by defeat, by laying stone by stone the firm foundations of a socialist society, by working indefatigably to build up discipline and self-discipline, and to consolidate everywhere organization, order, efficiency, the harmonious cooperation of all the forces of the people, and over-all accountancy and control of the production and distribution of products—that is the way to build up military power and socialist power.

From these visions he passes inevitably to the cliché. In the opening paragraphs we are made aware of vast historical forces moving toward known goals. Now there is only firm determination, a centralized economy, harmony, discipline and accountancy—the old dream that supply and demand could be regulated by a government bureau with a staff of trained accountants. He has no conception of the delicate complexities of a modern industrial civilization. All that is necessary is "to consolidate everywhere organization, order, efficiency." The words have a Germanic ring, and the conclusion of the essay would have given pleasure to any German sergeant major or industrialist:

"Hate for the Germans! Down with the Germans!" Such was and remains the watchword of our ordinary—i.e., bourgeois—patriotism. But we say, "Hatred for the imperialist beasts of prey, hatred for capitalism, death to capitalism!" and we also say, "Learn from the Germans! Remain faithful to the brotherly alliance with the German workers. They have delayed coming to our aid. We are playing for time, and we shall wait for them, and they *will certainly come* to our aid!"

Yes, learn from the Germans! History goes its roundabout and zigzag way. So it happens that today Germany embodies a ferocious imperialism, but it also embodies the principles of discipline, organization, harmonious cooperation on the basis of modern machine industry, and the strictest accounting and control.

Now this is exactly what we lack. This is what we have to learn. This is what our great revolution needs so that, after its victorious beginning and after experiencing difficult trials, we shall attain final victory. This is what is needed by the Russian Socialist Soviet Republic so that it shall no longer be wretchedly poor and weak, but will become forever powerful and abundant.

So he wrote on the train, and when he reached Moscow around eight o'clock on the evening of the next day the demonstrable signs of Russia's weakness were all about him in the city which was strangely quiet and still bore the traces of the savage fighting which had broken out the previous November between the Bolsheviks and those who were determined that the Bolsheviks should not rule over Russia. Lenin set up his headquarters in the National Hotel. There was little food, and he lived on English bully beef from the military stores. In theory Russia was at peace; in fact war had begun or was about to begin on eight or nine separate fronts. Lenin reflected grimly, If we eat this tinned meat, what are the soldiers going to eat on the fronts?

He stayed at the National Hotel only for a few days. The heart of the government should, he thought, be in the Kremlin, the ancient seat of authority, and accordingly with Sverdlov and Bonch-Bruyevich he made his first inspection of the great fortress which was to become his home. He had no intention of living in one of the palaces, and decided to settle in one of the buildings of the Court of Chancery in the apartment of the public prosecutor of the High Court. It was a five-room apartment on the second floor, with three bedrooms, a narrow dining room and a spacious kitchen. Beyond these, but on the same floor, were his offices, which included a study and a conference room, where the meetings of the Soviet of People's Commissars were held. Everything was in disorder when he arrived. The ceilings were cracked and the stove had broken down; and some weeks passed before he was able to take possession of the apartment. For five weeks after leaving the National Hotel he lived in a small apartment in the Kavalersky building on the other side of the Kremlin, where Peter the Great spent his childhood. Trotsky lived across the corridor, and half the members of the government found temporary lodging in this secluded rabbit warren formerly occupied by the royal servants. The past was everywhere. The great Kremlin bells no longer played "God Save the Tsar"; they played the "Internationale"; but the gilded crosses on the cathedrals still shone in the spring sunlight, and the double-headed eagles still kept watch from the gates, their crowns removed. Trotsky had suggested that instead of the crowns there should be hammers and sickles, but nothing was done. Everyone was too busy.

As Lenin was constantly repeating, the new Soviet Republic was in mortal danger. Though there was a precarious peace with Germany, it must have sometimes seemed to Lenin that there was war with the rest of the world. Early in April, British and Japanese forces landed in Vladivostok, Kharkov was occupied by the Germans, who went on to take Odessa and the Crimea, and soon the Czechoslovaks were making armed attacks on the soviets in the Volga. There were White Guards operating within a hundred miles of Moscow, and counterrevolutionary troops were poised in Esthonia and Finland for an attack on Petrograd. Lenin's task was to put order, efficiency and organization into the chaos, and characteristically he set about writing a program on "the successive tasks of the Soviet power" in which he outlined far-reaching plans of economic reconstruction with the emphasis on rigid efficiency—without however having the means to enforce them. What could be done was done. Highly paid specialists were to be employed at salaries far in excess of those enjoyed by the Communist leaders. In his speeches he amused himself by adding up these salaries until they reached astronomical proportions; and then he would say, "Even so, comrades, it is worth while." But if the bourgeois specialists were paid, the kulaks, the rich peasants, were simply expropriated, and in fact everything that could be expropriated was expropriated. The labor force was put under military discipline. "Work, discipline and order will save the Soviet Republic," pronounced Trotsky; and those who did not work were undisciplined and disorderly, were accordingly punished with penalties which would have provoked violent disorders under the tsarist regime, but were now accepted as the necessary rigors of a revolutionary age. Lenin had a judicial interest in punishments, and he was continually scribbling little notes which had the effect of massive death sentences. He wrote in May, "It is essential to introduce *immediately* and with demonstrative swiftness a bill making the penalty for bribery (perjury, bribery, collusion, etc.) *not less* than ten years' imprisonment followed by ten years of hard labor." The last seven words appear to have been an afterthought.

In that same month he suppressed all the newspapers hostile to his regime, with the result that political life as it was normally understood came to an abrupt standstill. Freedom was not yet completely destroyed. Here and there workers could be heard demanding an end to the dictatorship, the establishment of representative government, new elections, the restoration of democratic organizations; and the cry "All Power to the Constituent Assembly" was still heard, though it was growing fainter. Early in May, Red Army recruits at Saratov on the Volga came out in open rebellion; the rebellion was put down with unexampled ferocity. All over Soviet-occupied Russia there were these small uprisings, each capable of fanning a flame which, if not put out at once, might have destroyed the revolution when it was scarcely six months old. Trotsky, now Commissar of War, was chiefly responsible for breaking up these pockets of resistance to authoritarian rule, and he was ably assisted by his deputy, a twenty-six-year-old medical student called Slyansky, who took command whenever Trotsky was absent from Moscow.

With the coming of summer the tempo grew more violent. Instead of small uprisings there came the large-scale revolt in the ancient city of Yaroslavl. Boris Savinkov, a legendary terrorist responsible for the assassination of half a dozen tsarist ministers, commanded the anti-Soviet forces. Tanks, planes and heavy artillery were engaged in the struggle, which lasted for twelve days. Fighting was still going on when Count Wilhelm Mirbach, the German envoy to the Kremlin, was assassinated by a Cheka official in the German Embassy.

Exactly what prompted the assassination of Count Mirbach is still a matter of debate. The Bolsheviks claimed that it was brought about as a prelude to an uprising in Moscow by Left Socialist Revolutionaries, who deplored the peace treaty with Germany. At her trial, which took place later in the year, Spiridonova herself claimed to have organized the assassination, but she was not completely convincing. The assassin was Yakov Blumkin, twenty years old, and already occupying a high position in the Cheka in close contact with Dzerzhinsky. He was tall, thickset, dark-eyed and dark-bearded, and carried himself with the air of a young Jewish warrior. He was a man who could be relied upon to carry out a mission to its successful conclusion.

At three o'clock on the afternoon of July 6, Blumkin and his accomplice Andreyev, also from the Cheka, drove to the German Embassy in the Denezhny Pereulok, showed a pass signed by Dzerzhinsky, and asked to be taken into the presence of the Ambassador on an urgent matter. When the Ambassador came to meet them, he was a little surprised to discover that the matter they had come to discuss was not one of outstanding interest; it related in fact to a certain Count Robert Mirbach, who had been captured by the Russians and was now being used for their obscure purposes by the Cheka. Count

Robert Mirbach belonged to an Austro-Hungarian branch of the family and was only very distantly related to the Ambassador, if indeed there was any relationship. The conversation had been going on for about ten minutes when Blumkin suddenly slipped his hand into an attaché case, pulled out a pistol and shot at point-blank range at the Ambassador and two of his aides who were sitting with him round the table. He missed them all. The two aides dropped to the floor, while Mirbach fled into an adjoining room with Blumkin running after him, shooting. One bullet caught him in the back of the head, and he died instantly. With the Ambassador spread-eagled on the floor, Blumkin hurled an infernal machine at him. There was a tremendous explosion. The windows were blown out and the chandelier came crashing to the ground. In the confusion Blumkin and Andreyev escaped, jumping out of a window into a garden and then climbing an eight-foot iron fence. The engine of their automobile was running. They vanished from sight, and nothing was heard of them for many months.

It was a strange murder, for it seemed to be lacking in any motive. The Ambassador had been pouring millions of rubles into the Bolshevik treasury for the purpose of keeping the Bolsheviks out of the war, and only a month before he had written to Diego Bergen calling for a minimum payment of three million rubles a month. He had no particular faith in the Bolsheviks and regarded them as crude bunglers who remained in power only by the use of terror. "People are being quietly shot by the hundreds," wrote the Counselor of the embassy. "All this is not so bad, but there can no longer be any doubt that the physical means with which the Bolsheviks are maintaining their power are running out." At this stage the Germans were prepared to help the Bolsheviks to the limit of their ability: they wanted peace on the eastern front.

According to the Bolsheviks the murder was a deliberate and carefully contrived plot carried out by Left Socialist Revolutionaries in order to bring about war. Circumstantial stories were told of how Dzerzhinsky and Latsis were arrested by the Left Socialist Revolutionaries when they went to make inquiries about the murder, and how they providentially escaped. What is certain is that Maria Spiridonova and many other Left Socialist Revolutionaries were attending a conference at the Bolshoy Theater with the Bolsheviks while the murder was taking place, and that at a signal the Bolsheviks quietly left the theater and the building was surrounded by troops and all the Left Socialist Revolutionaries were arrested. The next morning a barracks occupied by Left Socialist guards came under artillery fire, but most of the guards escaped in the direction of the Kursk railroad station.

In spite of the confessions extracted from the Left Socialist Revolutionaries, the weight of evidence suggests that the murder of Mirbach was ordered by Lenin.

From Lenin's point of view, there were solid advantages to be gained by murdering him and throwing the blame on the Left Socialist Revolutionaries. Although Mirbach was feeding the Bolshevik government with gold, his usefulness was coming to an end. He was already wavering, already looking forward to the time when the Bolsheviks would have reached the end of their resources and another government composed of moderates from the right wing would be installed in power. "In the event of a change of orientation here," he wrote to Diego Bergen on June 25, "we would not even have to apply a great deal of force, and we could to some extent keep up appearances in our relations with the Bolsheviks right up to the last moment. The continual mismanagement here, and the equally continual violent blows being struck against our interests, could be used as a motive for a military advance at any time *we* chose." Such messages, though sent in cipher, almost certainly reached the Bolshevik high command, and even if the Bolsheviks had no agents in the German Embassy and did not tap his telephone wires—though there is considerable evidence to show that they did have their agents inside the Embassy and were continually tapping the wires—they knew from their frequent contacts with him the way his mind was working. By killing him they were ridding themselves of an enemy, and they guessed rightly that the German government would be understanding when it was pointed out to them that this unprovoked murder was committed by Left Socialist Revolutionaries, whose leaders had been immediately arrested and punished for the crime. In this way the Bolsheviks rid themselves of Mirbach and the Left Socialist Revolutionaries, and they demonstrated to the German proletariat that they were not afraid of the German aristocracy.

Trotsky tells an extraordinary story of how Lenin went to the German Embassy to offer his condolences after first discussing the murder with his associates. When Trotsky remarked, "It seems as though the Left Socialist Revolutionaries would be the cherry stone that we are destined to stumble over," Lenin replied, "I have thought that very thing. The fate of the wavering bourgeoisie lies in that very point. They come to the help of.the White Guards like a cherry stone. Now at any price we must influence the character of the German report to Berlin. The motive for military intervention is quite sufficient, particularly when you take into consideration that Mirbach has continually reported that we are weak and a single blow would suffice."

At first, according to Trotsky, news reached the Kremlin that Mirbach was wounded. Now came the news that he was dead, and it was arranged that Sverdlov and Chicherin should accompany Lenin to the German Embassy. Lenin was puzzled about what to say to the Germans. "I have already talked to Radek about it," he explained. "I wanted to say: *Mitleid* (sympathy), but apparently I must say: *Beileid* (condolence)." Then he left by car for the Embassy. Here is Trotsky's account of these last moments:

> He laughed a little, put on his coat and said firmly to Sverdlov: "Let us go." His face changed and became stone-gray. The drive to the Hohenzollern Embassy, to offer condolences over the death of Count Mirbach, was not an easy thing for Ilyich. As an inward experience it was probably one of the most difficult moments of his life.

Trotsky's account leaves a great deal unsaid, but it provides a number of clues. Lenin evidently had read Mirbach's secret dispatches to Berlin, and he was delighted by the prospect of putting the blame on the Left Socialist Revolutionaries—the cherry stone. He was in a good humor, laughing slyly, until the moment before he left the Kremlin and realized that he would have to go to the scene of the murder—"His face changed and became stone-gray." Trotsky's picture describes a band of conspirators congratulating one another on their success.

Before leaving for the German Embassy Lenin dispatched a circular telegram to all regional committees of the Communist Party and all staffs of the Red Army. It read:

> About three o'clock this afternoon two bombs were thrown in the German Embassy, seriously wounding Mirbach. This is clearly the work of Monarchists or of those *provocateurs* who want to drag Russia into a war in the interests of the Anglo-French capitalists who have also been bribing the Czechoslovaks. Do everything at once to catch the culprits. Stop *all* automobiles and detain them for triple checking.

In spite of this telegram, Blumkin was never apprehended. According to his own account he spent the following days in a Moscow hospital, being treated for the wound he suffered when he leaped over the fence.

Blumkin's subsequent career throws considerable light on the murder. He remained an officer of the Cheka, fought through the civil war, and was admitted into the Bolshevik party in 1921. He was never punished for murdering Mirbach; on the contrary he was given high positions. He was one of those who organized the Red Army in Mongolia. He claimed to have led a revolutionary expedition against Teheran, which was called off at the last moment. He went on important missions to India, Egypt and Turkey. He was so highly regarded that he was given an office next to Chicherin's in the Hotel Metropole at a time when Chicherin was Commissar for Foreign Affairs. He enjoyed all the luxuries which were reserved for important dignitaries in the Communist Party: he had a car, a well-furnished apartment in the Arbat, and a succession of mistresses. He talked openly about the murder. Once he told a friend, a young revolutionary called Victor Serge, exactly how he accomplished it. "I was talking with him and looking straight in his eyes, and all the time I was thinking: I have to kill this man. There was a Browning hidden among the papers in my attaché case . . ." Then he explained how the Ambassador's aides dropped to the ground, and how Mirbach went running in the direction of the ballroom, and how he hurled the infernal machine on the marble floor. The friend asked whether there was any reason for murdering Mirbach, and Blumkin replied, "We knew of course that Germany was disintegrating and was in no position to begin a new war with Russia. We wanted to insult Germany. We were counting upon the effect it would produce in Germany itself." Then he went on to describe how the Bolsheviks had carefully considered a plot to assassinate the Kaiser: the plot failed, because the Russians were unable to discover a single German who would assume the responsibility.

The key to the mystery may very well lie in the words "We wanted to insult Germany." Lenin knew the shattering psychological gains to be derived from well-directed insults: he had spent a lifetime beating down his enemies by the massive power of his insults. As a result of the assassination of Mirbach the Germans became strangely acquiescent to Bolshevik demands, and within a few weeks a new ambassador arrived in Moscow.

A few weeks later George Solomon discussed the assassination with Leonid Krassin in the Soviet Embassy in Berlin. At Krassin's invitation Solomon had been appointed First Secretary. They were both shaken by the recent events. Krassin had known Lenin well, and he explained the murder as an excuse for the destruction of the Left Socialist Revolutionaries. In effect there was an internal loan among the revolutionaries, who were to be "borrowed" for the occasion: the "borrowing" took the form of a liquidation of assets. "I knew Lenin very well," Krassin said, "but I never before noticed such a cruel cynicism in him. He told me about the cruel decision of the government and how it was carried out by choosing several dozen counter-revolutionaries in prison and executing them as accessories in the assassination of Mirbach—'to satisfy the Germans,' Lenin added with a smile. 'In this way,' Lenin went on, 'we are pleasing our socialist comrades, and at the same time we are proving our innocence without doing harm to our own people.'"

Such was the explanation offered by Krassin, but it is not the only explanation. Many threads were bound together; many plots and counterplots were involved. What is certain is that the assassination of Mirbach was deliberately designed to accomplish a number of complex and differing purposes, and it accomplished these purposes.

Ten days later there came the assassination of a person of far greater importance than Count Mirbach—the Tsar of all the Russias.

The decision to kill the Tsar was taken by Lenin and Sverdlov, apparently without consultation with any other members of the party. Once again the aim was to "insult" the enemy with a shattering psychological blow. The Tsar, the Tsaritsa, the Grand Duchesses Olga, Tatiana, Marie and Anastasia, the young Tsarevich, the Tsarevich's doctor, the Tsaritsa's maid, the Tsar's valet and a cook were being held under close arrest in the Ipatiev house at Ekaterinburg. On the night of July 16 the "entire responsory" was shot, clubbed and bayoneted to death together with the three servants and the doctor. Five days later White Guards and Czechoslovak troops entered Ekaterinburg. At first nothing could be discovered about the fate of the imperial family. Gradually, piece by piece, the evidence of the murder began to accumulate until it became possible to reconstruct it in minute detail. The small relics of the holocaust were discovered at the bottom of a mine shaft near the village of Koptiaki twelve miles to the northwest of Ekaterinburg. Among the documents left behind by the fleeing Bolsheviks was a coded telegram signed by Belobdorov, the chairman of the Ekaterinburg executive committee, reading: "Inform Sverdlov entire family shared fate of head. Officially family will be destroyed during evacuation."

The Bolsheviks had inherited the imperial family from the Provisional Government. Arrested immediately after the February revolution, the Tsar accepted his fate as though he had long expected it and was relieved that he no longer had to bear the burden of ruling a people with whom he had never been at ease. Mildly contemplative, cautious, incapable of anger or resolution, he gave the impression of a man who had drifted into imprisonment in the same manner that he had drifted into power. His last gesture was to throw out his arms to protect his son; then he was shot at point-blank range in the face. The Tsaritsa, the Grand Duchesses Olga, Tatiana and Marie, the doctor, the cook and the valet were all killed by bullets, but for some reason the Bolshevik guards preferred to use their bayonets and the butt ends of their rifles in dispatching the Grand Duchess Anastasia and the maidservant Anna Demidova. Their instructions were to kill, and the manner of the killing was left to their own judgment.

In his diary Trotsky describes a conversation with Sverdlov which took place after the fall of Ekaterinburg. He asked what had happened to the Tsar and learned that he had been killed together with his whole family.

"All of them?" Trotsky enquired.

"Yes, all of them," Sverdlov replied. "What about it?"

Sverdlov deliberately paused, waiting to see the effect on Trotsky. Cautiously Trotsky made no comment. He affected not to be surprised, but could not prevent himself from asking the inevitable question, "Who made the decision?"

"We decided it here," Sverdlov answered. "Ilyich believed we should not leave the Whites a live banner to rally around, especially under the present difficult circumstances."

Trotsky asked no further questions. He fully agreed with the decision, although during the previous months he had looked forward to the time when the Tsar could be brought to Moscow and placed on public trial. Lenin, more realistically, had wondered whether there was time enough for such a trial. The ultimate decision rested in his hands. Krupskaya wrote in her memoirs: "The Czechoslovaks were advancing on Ekaterinburg, where Nicholas II was being held prisoner. On July 16 we had him and his family shot." To her, and perhaps to Lenin, it was as simple as that.

In reality it was not quite so simple, and Trotsky, writing many years later, reflected the opinions of the Bolshevik leaders when he explained that two separate purposes were involved in the execution. He wrote:

The execution of the Tsar's family was needed not only in order to frighten, horrify, and dishearten the enemy, but also in order to shake up our own ranks, to show them that there was no turning back, that ahead lay either complete victory or complete ruin. In the intellectual circles of the Party there probably were misgivings and shakings of heads. But the masses of workers and soldiers had not a minute's doubt. They would not have understood and would not have accepted any other decision. *This* Lenin sensed well. The ability to think and feel for and with the masses was characteristic of him to the highest degree, especially at the great political turning points.

According to this view the destruction of the Tsar and his family was an act of terror designed to put panic fear into the hearts of the enemy, but also—and perhaps more importantly—to put panic fear into the hearts of the men fighting on the side of the Bolsheviks. By this act it was hoped to imbue them with the belief that there was no turning back, for they were accomplices in the crime, and before them lay only ruin if they failed to destroy the Whites. The motives which lay behind the murder were therefore very nearly as complex as those which lay behind the murder of Mirbach. In one respect the plan failed. All observers reported that the masses were completely indifferent to the Tsar's murder; and those who fought for the Bolsheviks fought neither better nor worse because he had been killed. He seemed to belong to ancient history.

At first the Bolsheviks reported that the Tsar alone had been killed. A few days later it was announced that the rest of the family were killed "during the evacuation," leaving it to be understood that the decision had been taken at the last moment, when the White Guards and Czechoslovaks were at the gates of the city. At no time did the Bolsheviks admit they had killed the innocent bystanders, Dr. Botkin, the cook Kharitonov, the valet Alexis Trupp, and the maid-servant Anna Demidova. For Lenin, it was enough that they had been in attendance on the imperial family: they richly deserved their fate. He did not regard them as innocent bystanders, but at the same time he did not permit their deaths to become common knowledge. Some lingering modesty prevailed upon him to announce the death of the Tsar, while keeping secret the death of a poor maidservant.

The murders of a German aristocrat and a Russian emperor would not appear to be matters of great moment at the present time. They were however of vast importance in their time, and they have left indelible traces on the march of Communism. With these murders the

Bolsheviks showed how close they were to the philosophy of Nechayev. They showed, too, that they were proficient in the arts of
terror, and that terror was complex and many-sided. It was a weapon
which could be used simultaneously against the enemy and against
waverers in their midst. They never forgot this lesson, and in the
hands of Stalin the weapon of terror was used with such devastating
effect that the entire population of Russia lived in fear of it, and Stalin
himself lived under its shadow.

During the weeks following the murder of the Tsar, Lenin faced
some of his greatest trials. The fabric was falling apart. Everywhere
he looked there were signs that the enemy was recovering from the
massive onslaughts suffered during the winter. Yet in this desperate
situation he never lost hope. Something of his mood at this time can
be gathered from a letter he wrote to Clara Zetkin:

> We are now experiencing what are perhaps the most difficult weeks
> of the whole revolution. The class struggle and the civil war have pene-
> trated into the depths of the population. Everywhere in the countryside
> there is the division—the poor are for us, the kulaks are furiously against
> us. The Allies have bribed the Czechoslovaks, the counterrevolution is
> raging, and the entire bourgeoisie is making every effort to overwhelm
> us. Nevertheless we firmly believe we shall avoid the customary fate of
> the revolutions of 1794 and 1848 and defeat the bourgeoisie.

He had completed the letter when the new state seal was brought
to him, and he decided that it would please Clara Zetkin to see it.
He had designed it himself and was proud of it. He added a postscript:

> Just this moment they have brought me the new state seal. I am
> sending you an impression. It reads: *Russian Socialist Federal Soviet
> Republic. Workers of all countries, unite!*

He was like a child playing with a new toy. He had invented a new
kind of state, for which it was necessary to invent a new name. It was
a strange name, unlike any name that any nation had borne before,
so top-heavy with descriptive adjectives that it seemed to be in danger of foundering under their weight; and it seems never to have occurred to him that it was neither socialist, nor federal, nor republican,
and since the power of the soviets had withered away, it could
scarcely be called soviet. In time some of these adjectives would be
abandoned, and even the word "Russian" was to disappear in the

anonymity of the Union of Socialist Soviet Republics. But it was the slogan "Workers of all countries, unite!" which comforted him during these hours of trial, as he waited expectantly for the world-wide revolution. All through that summer he was looking toward Germany for the revolution that never came.

A ROOM IN THE KREMLIN

ALL THROUGH HIS ACTIVE LIFE as a revolutionary Lenin was absorbed in one subject—power. The nature of power, its methods of operation, its peculiar properties, manifestations and divisions, the way it sometimes concealed itself in the guise of weakness or arrayed itself in borrowed garments, all these were subjects of absorbing interest which he studied with minute care and patient tenacity. He was not in the least concerned with the trappings of power: such things were for children. He had only a casual, historical interest in the ceremonies which were the outward and visible symbols of power in the past. He had never known the least desire to wear a colorful uniform or to take part in triumphal processions. What interested him was the precise point of application, the cutting edge of power shorn of all its decorative aspects. What he wanted and what he obtained was power in its ultimate naked majesty.

When Lenin came to power, the habits of a lifetime remained unchanged. Just as he read voluminously when he was in exile, so now, installed in the Kremlin, there was scarcely a day when he did not set aside three or four hours for reading. In exile he had usually taken his meals with Krupskaya in the kitchen, and he continued to eat his meals in the kitchen. Then, too, there were certain hours set aside for conferences, and there was always an hour a day set aside for exercise and another hour for answering his correspondence. On the surface nothing changed. His life in the Kremlin was scarcely to be distinguished from his life in London or Paris or Zurich. To the end he remained a creature of habit.

Power did not change him, because he had exercised power through the greater part of his adult life. The revolutionary exile had always exerted power over his followers and intimidated his enemies; and power over a small group can be just as satisfying as power over an empire. He had known almost from the beginning the responsibilities of power.

When visitors came to the Kremlin they were surprised to discover that the nerve center of the vast Communist empire was totally devoid of the appurtenances of power. No chamberlains ushered them into the Presence, no royal guards stood at salute, and there was no throne. They came into a small room with a potted palm tree in one corner and maps and bookcases in another. There was a rather shabby carpet, and there were no draperies. There was a desk, and next to this a small conference table with a green baize cloth, and five or six leather armchairs. There was an almost complete absence of decoration. It was such a room as might have belonged to the headmaster of an obscure provincial school. All one could tell from the first glance was that the headmaster had a taste for geography and the social sciences, and possessed an absolute abhorrence of frivolities of any kind.

A second glance however would reveal that the headmaster had once possessed a curiously romantic attitude toward life, and it would also reveal that the means of exerting power were abundantly present —they took the form of no less than five telephones. The romantic attitude was expressed in a relief which hung on the wall facing him: we shall have more to say about it later. For the moment it is necessary to look at the telephones which in his hands became the instruments of naked power.

Some twenty years before, when the telephone was coming into widespread use, nearly all Russians who could afford it greeted it as a boon. Only Tolstoy was terrified of it. "Beware," he said, "of the Genghis Khan who rules by telephone." Now at last Genghis Khan was provided with a full battery of telephones.

There were three telephones on the table, one on the wall, another on the window ledge. There were other telephones in the corridors outside, where a signal corps had set up a switchboard. Lenin's telephones did not give off a ringing sound: instead there was a low buzz. On the telephone which he used most often a light glowed whenever someone called him. They were among the few telephones in Russia in good working order. They were examined frequently and kept in good repair. He had very little feeling for mechanical things, but the intricacies of telephones delighted him. He was less interested in clocks. The wall clock rarely showed the correct time, even though the watchmaker who wound and repaired all the Kremlin clocks was continually being called in.

The telephone and the telegraph were the instruments through which he exercised his power. At this time a primitive form of teletype, called the Hughes telegraph machine, was in use, and a battery of these machines filled the corridor which led from his apartment to his office. Here messages were received from the fighting fronts and from all the towns under Bolshevik rule. These messages would be laid on Lenin's desk, and he would telephone his orders and decisions to a secretary; they would then be transmitted on the Hughes telegraph machine. The nerve center of the Communist government was a room and a corridor.

Though the greater part of the messages were sent by telegraph, Lenin had a particular fondness for making long-distance calls. He had an almost personal affection for his battery of telephones, and he was always gesticulating at them as though they were living presences; and it was observed that when he addressed the telephone he would cock his head a little to one side and screw up his eyes in the same way as when he talked to someone sitting close to him. He would say, "She is behaving very well today," or, "I heard you quite well a moment ago, but now she is fading away." If there was a fault in the line, the engineers would be hurriedly summoned and workmen would be sent out to repair the line. When the Kharkov line kept failing during the civil war, he would shout into the telephone in a fury of frustration; and he ordered the Cheka to discover whether sabotage was involved. The Commissar of Post and Telegraph was constantly receiving penciled notes on scraps of paper commanding him to take immediate action to improve the system, with little result. Lenin had the best telephone in Russia, but war and revolution and winter storms played havoc with the lines.

The telephones stood on the right-hand side of his desk; they represented the orderly transmission of commands, the visible sign that this was a command post. Over the rest of the desk a happy confusion usually reigned. Papers concerning entirely different projects would lie together, various files and newspapers would crowd up on one side of the desk and gradually gather momentum until they had invaded the whole desk, whereupon they would all be bundled together and heaped on the floor or on a chair, and the whole process would start again. He was credited with possessing a calm, orderly, logical mind; it was neither calm, nor orderly, nor logical. He was continually losing papers. Files containing reports on the agricultural system would be laid out on the table. An hour later a mysterious wind would blow through them and they would be discovered three weeks later in files relating to the Cheka. Once he told his secretary, "X has all his papers in order. Why can't I do the same?" He would apply himself very seriously to the question of reducing his paper work to logical order, and he always failed. New file systems were continually being introduced, with no discernible results. Finally it was decided to file documents in the order of their relative importance. This system too was a failure, for it was soon discovered that the file marked "most urgent and most important" occupied his entire attention, while the file marked "very urgent and very important" would remain untouched, and he never so much as glanced at the files marked "urgent and important." His lapses in orderly paper work were perhaps of no great consequence. The real work of the office was done in personal conference and over the telephone.

Even without the cumulation of newspapers and documents, the desk was crowded. There was a quite extraordinary number of pens, and pencils sharpened to a stiletto point. There were two desk calendars, two heavy pairs of scissors, a mother-of-pearl paper knife, bottles of mucilage with rubber stoppers which he called "my mucilage with a nose," an ornamental ink stand with two small hanging lamps attached, an ash tray with a lighter shaped like a sea shell, and a motley collection of souvenirs presented by admirers including a large figure, in cast iron, of an ape sitting on a pile of books and intently examining an oversize human skull. This chilling statue had a prominent place on his desk and dominated everything else.

When Lenin looked up from his desk he would see directly facing him a door, maps hanging on the wall, and a rarely used escritoire, with a large portrait of Karl Marx resting on the shelf. Just above Karl Marx, and a little to the right, was the wall clock which never kept time, and to the left stood a bronze plaque bearing the features of Stepan Khalturin. By placing Khalturin beside Marx, Lenin was demonstrating that he had a special affection for the young revolutionary who was executed in 1882 for the assassination of General Strelnikov, the military procurator of Odessa. The artist had etched the name KHALTURIN at the bottom of the plaque, but it did not stand out, and Lenin experimented with several ways of making the letters more prominent, at first rubbing chalk into them, and finally painting the letters in gold.

But it was not for the assassination of General Strelnikov that Lenin placed the portrait of Stepan Khalturin on the wall of his study. This young peasant occupied a very special place in his affections. He was a rawboned handsome man, intelligent and recklessly daring, who had sworn to assassinate the Tsar and very nearly succeeded. Under the name of Batishkov, he applied for and obtained a job as carpenter on the imperial yacht. He was regarded as an excellent workman and a loyal subject of the Tsar, and he attracted the favorable notice of the officers in charge of the upkeep of the Winter Palace, where he soon obtained employment as a joiner and polisher. The other workmen liked him. He pretended to be slow and a bit stupid, and his superiors sometimes rebuked him for his habit of gaping and scratching his neck. He was an excellent actor, and he played his role to such perfection that Petrotsky, the corporal of gendarmes in charge of the palace workmen, offered him his daughter in marriage, imagining that the honest joiner would one day become a master carpenter. All the time Khalturin was smuggling dynamite into the palace. He slept in a small bed in the palace cellars, and stored the dynamite under his pillow.

He had little difficulty in bringing the dynamite into the palace; the difficulty lay in living with it, for the fumes gave him terrible headaches and there were continual night searches. At last he was forced to put the dynamite in the box where he kept his spare shirt and a few personal belongings, and the danger of discovery became greater. The box however had one advantage. It was movable and could be placed where the dynamite would do most damage. By endlessly asking questions and maintaining an air of foolishness, he came to know a good deal about the movements of the royal family. He hoped to detonate the dynamite in such a way that it would destroy the cellar, the guard room immediately above, and the Tsar's dining room on the next floor. The Tsar usually dined between half past five and six o'clock. If it was detonated shortly after six o'clock he had a reasonable chance of killing the Tsar and the immediate members of the royal family.

While Khalturin was still bringing the dynamite into the palace, the police arrested a revolutionary and found in his possession a plan of the palace in which the dining room was marked with an ominous red cross. Thereafter the cellars were more carefully watched. A post of gendarmery was established within a few feet of the dynamite. One day the Tsar himself made an unannounced tour of inspection, passing so close to Khalturin that he was to say bitterly, "If I could have got hold of a hammer, I would have killed him." With extraordinary coolness he continued to work out the details of the final explosion. An iron pipe led along the wall, and he arranged the fuse in such a way that it was hidden by the pipe. On February 16, 1880, at about fifteen minutes past six, he calmly lit the fuse with the stump of a candle and walked out of the palace. There was a tremendous explosion. All the lights of the palace went out. There were screams in the dark, and soon the stretcher-bearers were running out with their cargo of dead and maimed. For half an hour the rumor ran through St. Petersburg that the Tsar was dead. In fact he was very much alive, for he had delayed entering the dining room until an unusually late hour because Prince Alexander of Hesse had arrived the previous day and there had been many matters to discuss in private audience. Ten soldiers and one civilian had been killed, nearly sixty more were seriously wounded. The *coup* failed, but the Executive Committee of the Narodnaya Volya remained impenitent. They had demonstrated that even in his palace there was no safety for the Tsar.

Nechayev, in his small dark cell in the Peter and Paul Fortress, was overjoyed by the news. "We have failed this time," he told the guards. "Watch out! The next time we shall succeed!" In fact, a little more than a year later the Tsar was killed by a bomb thrown by the same group of revolutionaries.

What Lenin particularly admired in Khalturin was his directness, his simplicity of approach, and his unrelenting determination to destroy the monarchy. He was a man who took upon himself the entire burden of a destructive act. For Zhelyabov, the leader of the Narodnaya Volya, he had profound respect, calling him on one occasion "the most resolute of the mechanics of revolution," but Zhelyabov was not the pure revolutionary who assumes in himself the entire responsibility of his actions, since he was the director of a group of dedicated revolutionaries who obeyed his orders. Khalturin had plotted to destroy the Tsar *and* the Winter Palace; and for Lenin there was a kind of mathematical beauty in a destruction so complete, so wanton, and so far-reaching.

Whenever he looked up, there were these two portraits to remind him of the past. There were no portraits of his father or of his elder brother. He had no false pride and was perfectly aware of his own importance on the stage of history, but portraits of himself in the newspapers filled him with horror. He had a vast and towering pride, but no vanity.

In all this he resembled his father, the stern and meticulous inspector of schools who had climbed from the lowest rung of the ladder to a place of eminence in Simbirsk. To the end Lenin retained the habits of a provincial schoolmaster. He was a ruthless teacher, for those who failed his examinations were shot.

From that desk in the Kremlin orders went out over the length and breadth of Russia to the armies in the field, to the factories, to the commissars and to foreign communists. The least suggestion from him had the force of law. Whatever he wanted was immediately given to him, whole armies appeared at his bidding, and he had only to make a speech for the entire economic current of the country to be diverted according to his wishes. He was the new Moses, whose words were the revelations of ultimate authority and truth.

It was a role which he played with astonishing adroitness. Outwardly he gave an impression of good humor, even of geniality. To friends and acquaintances he was considerate and charming. Trotsky said "he had a way of falling in love with people," and there is not the least doubt that he had a strong affection, amounting almost to love, for some of his associates. He always thanked people who rendered him some service; he would thank the charwoman who lit the stove in his office, the secretaries who took down his dictation, the guards who stood outside his office. He was especially solicitous of the health of his friends. When Tsyurupa, the Commissar for Food, fainted of starvation during the famine, he went to some pains to see that commissars should eat at least as well as factory workers and established a Kremlin kitchen for their benefit. Tsyurupa worked eighteen hours a day, and Lenin would sometimes shake a finger at him, saying, "Be careful! You are wasting government property!"

When visitors came, he gave the impression of a man who was all attention, eagerly looking forward to hearing whatever the visitor might tell him. Vyacheslav Karpinsky, who knew him well, describes how a delegation of peasants came to meet him. As soon as they entered the room, Lenin rose from his chair and shook hands with them, leaning forward a little, a smile playing on his lips, his eyes looking deep into theirs. He asked their names, where they came from, where they would like to be seated. He would fuss over their seating, and there would be no conversation until they were relaxed and comfortable. He always remembered their names, addressing them by their first names and patronymics, employing the polite form of "you," though an older man would sometimes be addressed as "thou" in familiar respect. He was a gracious host who put his visitors at ease, even when, as sometimes happened, they were unable to conceal their indignation.

Karpinsky tells of a peasant who suddenly leaped to his feet, overwhelmed by an uncontrollable emotion.

"Listen, Comrade Lenin," the peasant shouted. "What is happening in our village is absolutely intolerable! They're driving us out of our minds! That's all they do—drive us out of our minds!"

Lenin was puzzled.

"Now calm yourself, Ivan Rodionovich," he said. "Tell me clearly what it is all about! What's hurting you?"

"What's hurting me? It's the village soviet which is hurting me and the rest of us! They're always making impossible demands on us!"

"Who elected the village soviet?"

"I suppose we did—"

"Of course you did, and you can vote them out of office."

The peasant looked surprised. It had never occurred to him that there was such a simple way of ridding a village of its soviet.

"Can we really do that?" the peasant asked.

"You not only *can* do it, but you *must* do it. According to Soviet law every deputy can be voted out of office before the expiration of his term, whenever he has abused the confidence of people. So you see what has to be done, Ivan Rodionovich."

Deftly and kindly Lenin had succeeded in putting the peasant at his ease.

It was the same with distinguished visitors from abroad. When H. G. Wells visited the Kremlin in the autumn of 1920, he came expecting a struggle with a doctrinaire Marxist, and found nothing of the kind. Someone had told him that Lenin lectured people and refused to tolerate argument. Instead they argued pleasantly for an hour. Lenin spoke confidently and keenly, "as a good type of scientific man will talk," with very few gestures and never raising his voice. Wells remembered there was a disorderly heap of papers on the desk, and that even when he was sitting on the edge of his chair Lenin's short legs scarcely reached the floor. The room was well-lighted, and there was a pleasant view of palatial spaces from the window.

Wells had visited Petrograd, where life seemed to have come to a stop. The desolation had brought home to him the fact that the form and arrangement of a town is determined by shopping and marketing, and with the abolition of trading, most of the large buildings had been rendered useless. Lenin was not put out by the statement. It seemed to him a perfectly logical result of Communism that towns should "wither away."

"The towns will get very much smaller," Lenin said. "They will be different. Yes, quite different."

Wells went on to suggest that under Communism the great buildings would survive merely as relics, like the temples at Paestum. Lenin agreed cheerfully. It was a matter of indifference to him whether the towns survived. In much the same way his Chuvash ancestors, living in their remote pastoral huts, must have viewed the existence of the great cities of their time.

In the same casual, cheerful way Lenin went on to discuss how the towns would have to be rebuilt to conform to Communist usage, and the shapes and contours of farms would also follow the inevitable laws of change. He spoke of how the farms would be managed, not by peasants, but by workers: there would be enormous farms stretching over whole provinces.

"The government," he said, "is already running big estates with workers instead of the peasants, where conditions are favorable. That can spread. It can be extended first to one province, then another. The peasants in the other provinces, selfish and illiterate, will not know what is happening until their turn comes. . . ."

Wells says that when he spoke of the peasant, Lenin leaned forward and his manner became confidential, as if after all the peasants *might* overhear.

As they spoke, they were like two men signaling across an unbridgeable gulf, a little surprised whenever they were able to read each other's signals; and in their different ways they were both bewildered. Wells was bewildered because he felt Lenin had stripped off the last pretense that the Russian Revolution was anything more than the inauguration of an age of limitless experiment and limitless destruction. The towns and the peasants would "wither away"; there would be no more trade, no more state, no more people—only the mindless automata moving according to the dictates of a mechanical law. And Lenin in turn was bewildered because the Communist revolution was not reaching out to Europe. "Why doesn't the social revolution begin in England?" he asked. "Why do you not work for the social revolution? Why are you not destroying capitalism and establishing the communist state?" To the end of his life Lenin was genuinely puzzled because western Europe refused to follow in the path he had ordained for it.

As Wells tells the story, Lenin was completely at ease, lively, talkative, smiling. He was a man very conscious of his power, who knew exactly how far he could go at any given moment. While he dreamed of the vanishing towns and the vanishing peasantry, he resembled a practical, solid, sensible man of affairs.

Lenin gave this impression to all those who met him when he was in power. He was, or seemed to be, a man completely in command of himself, never assaulted by doubts, incapable of personal caprice. But the outward calm concealed an inner storm. There were times when he was on the verge of madness.

The ordinary human sins had no appeal for Lenin; his sin was pride, which devours all those who suffer from it. His pride led him to believe that he alone was in possession of an infallible dogma which had been handed down from Marx; he saw himself as the vehicle of a new social order, a new dispensation of time, a new era of destruction. Those who opposed him must be struck down *immediately, mercilessly, at whatever the cost, absolutely and irrevocably*. So he wrote in a letter to Grigory Sokolnikov in May 1919. It was not enough that they should be killed once; they must be killed over and over again, as the interminable adverbs swoop down on their prey.

Sitting quietly in his warm study, with his books around him and a litter of state documents on his desk, he would give way to sudden rages. He had been slighted; something had gone wrong; his orders were not being carried out promptly; immediately there is the flash of lightning followed by the rumbling of thunder. A workman called Bulatov complained to him about the actions of the Soviet government in Novgorod. Some days later Lenin learned that Bulatov had been arrested. Lenin regarded the arrest as an intolerable abuse of power. It was clear to him that Bulatov was in prison because he had dared to approach the President of the Soviet of People's Commissars. Without a further thought, he wrote off a telegram to the Executive Committee of the Novgorod *guberniya*:

> Apparently Bulatov has been arrested for complaining to me. I warn you that I shall have the chairmen of the *guberniya* executive committees, the Cheka and members of the executive committee arrested

for this and see that they are shot. Why did you not answer my question immediately?

In his rage Lenin was sentencing the government of Novgorod *guberniya* to be shot for having arrested one man. In her memoirs Krupskaya refers to this telegram. "It was," she wrote, "a very characteristic one."

Why did he write this telegram? Did he seriously believe that the executive committee, to whom it was addressed, would turn themselves in and arrange to be shot by the Cheka, which would then turn the weapons on itself? It is much more likely that he sent the telegram merely to inspire them with terror, to frighten them out of their wits. But there is very little difference between frightening men out of their wits and killing them, especially when you have the power to kill them.

The letters written in that quiet room sometimes reek with terror—with terror wielded as a weapon and with terror felt on the nerves and sinews. There were times when he was mortally frightened, when all his dreams seemed about to collapse, when he was alone in his cell, waiting, like the doctor in Chekhov's story "Ward No. 6," for the blow to fall, knowing that only by a desperate expedient would he be able to survive it. Engels had once described terror as "the domination of men who are themselves terrorized." Lenin may never have known what Engels thought of terror, but his eagerness to employ the weapon hints that he was himself its victim rather than its master. It was always terror "at saturation point." It was never a question of shooting one man in ten, as a warning to the remaining nine. He must shoot five, or six, or seven, and go on until there are only the shreds of a man left. He practiced terror like the Romans. When the Emperor Gallienus cried out, "Tear, kill, exterminate!—*Lacera, occide, concide!*" he was saying no more than Lenin, who spoke of destroying "immediately, mercilessly, at whatever the cost, absolutely and irrevocably."

LENIN TO ZINOVIEV: June 1918

Comrade Zinoviev, only today did we in the Central Committee learn that the Petrograd *workers* want to react to the assassination of Volodarsky by mass terror and that you—I am not talking about you personally, but about the Petrograd members of the CC and CP—have restrained them. I most emphatically protest . . . This is in-ad-missible . . . It is necessary to cultivate the mass nature of the terror against counterrevolutionaries and push it forward with even greater energy, especially in Petrograd, whose example is *decisive*. Greetings! LENIN.

LENIN TO EUGENE BOSH: August 1918

Your telegram received. It is necessary to organize an intensive guard of picked reliable men to conduct a merciless mass terror against kulaks, priests and White Guards; suspects to be held in a concentration camp outside the city. Punitive expedition to set out at once. Telegraph re mission accomplished. *Sovnarkom* LENIN.

LENIN TO THE SOVIET OF NIZHNI NOVGOROD: August 1918

An open uprising of White Guards is clearly in preparation in Nizhni Novgorod. You must mobilize all forces, establish a triumvirate of dictators, introduce immediately mass terror, shoot and deport hundreds of prostitutes who ply soldiers and officers with vodka. Do not hesitate for a moment. You must act promptly: mass searches for hidden arms; mass deportations of Mensheviks and security risks. *Sovnarkom* LENIN.

Such messages were continually being sent from the quiet room in the Kremlin. It had become a habit to write the word *shoot,* so that in the end it became almost meaningless; it was like brushing off flies. He had such a horror of the processes of death that he refused to have flowers in the room, knowing that they decayed, but death in the abstract and at some remote telegraphic distance pleased him. He would write, "Shoot and deport," without pausing to wonder whether anyone could be deported after being shot. What is chiefly remarkable about these murderous telegrams is their vulgarity.

In all wars and revolutions excesses are committed; and the most hideous barbarities are excused on the grounds of expediency. Lenin, however, made no excuses. For him mass terror was the most useful and therefore the most desirable of weapons. Single acts of terror had little appeal for him: it was only when the terror was being waged on a massive scale that he rejoiced, the pulse of the sentences demonstrating his excitement, his urgency, and his barbarity. Marx praised the Paris Commune for being innocent of the violence common in revolutions. Lenin gloried in violence: it was the drug which stimulated him to further action, the whip which goaded him, the solace of his studious temperament.

At various times in the past Lenin had claimed that terror was "not the right road," but in fact he always accepted terror gratefully. "In principle we have never renounced, and cannot renounce terrorism," he wrote in *Iskra* in 1901; and he added, "It is an act of war, indispensable at a certain point in the struggle." But these "certain points" were being continually prolonged until it seemed that Lenin was encouraging the permanent reign of terror with no end in sight. A new and entirely un-Marxist theory of the state was emerging. Terror was to become the chief instrument of state power; and Lenin discovered to his surprise that terror was so formidable an instrument that no others were necessary.

The theory of the permanent terror was not wholly of Lenin's invention. It owed much to Nechayev and Bakunin, and many of the grace notes were added by Trotsky, who went on to write an entire thesis on the subject. But although terror is a useful weapon for a dictator determined to remain in power, it suffers from certain irremediable defects. Terror has its own laws: it is not a conventional weapon which can be turned on or off at will. Terror has the special quality of breeding more terror, and there is never an end to it. It is like a cancer; it assumes monstrous and unexpected forms; it poisons all who touch it, including the man who wields it.

Lenin never watched an execution squad at work, never saw the effects of the terror he had created. He rarely traveled outside Moscow; for weeks on end he remained within the walls of the Kremlin, spending all the available time in his study, poring over documents, sending out telegrams, and sometimes raising his head to smile at his

Lenin often attached hurried, repetitive notes to the memoranda sent from his office. This characteristic note, in the author's possession, says: "Read through, grasp, follow through very quickly, and let me know the result."

hunchback secretary as she laid the state papers on his desk. It was a life of devotion and monkish solitude, interrupted late every evening by a meeting of the Council of Commissars in the adjoining room. These meetings were held ostensibly to discuss the urgent problems of the day, but in time they came to resemble briefings at which Lenin gave his orders. The commissars met, talked, argued, and debated, while Lenin scribbled notes or read a book or worked on some theoretical paper, only half listening to them. Finally someone would say, "What does Vladimir Ilyich think about it?" Then, very concisely, in a few sentences, he would give his opinion; and this was the opinion which was nearly always acted upon.

In his Kremlin office Lenin wielded absolute power such as few dictators have ever wielded. In that small, drab room with the blue wallpaper and the potted palms he ruled Russia as no Tsar had ever ruled it before. Neither Ivan the Terrible nor Peter the Great had half his effective power. From this powerhouse he continued to generate power until it seemed that nothing happened in Russia but that he was directing and controlling it, so great was the terror inspired by his name.

LENIN WOUNDED

At eleven o'clock on the morning of August 30, 1918, Moses Uritsky, the chairman of the Petrograd Cheka, was coming out of his office in the Commissariat of Internal Affairs when he saw a young intellectual standing on the sidewalk. He caught the eyes of the young man, said something to his guards, and was about to step into his car when a shot rang out. Then he fell to the ground, screaming. The young intellectual had shot him through the left eye.

There followed an extraordinary battle between Uritsky's guards and the young man, everyone firing at once, no one getting hurt except a Red Army guard who was slightly wounded in the leg. The guards, in the intervals of shooting, lifted the dying Uritsky into the car, and two of them drove him off to hospital. In the excitement the young man, whose name was Kannegiesser, mounted his bicycle and vanished. Uritsky died an hour later, never having regained consciousness.

The death of Uritsky was a matter of grave concern to the Bolsheviks. He had been a capable and ruthless organizer, a much-trusted and intimate friend of Lenin, and after Dzerzhinsky the leading figure in the Cheka. He had been one of those who attended the secret meeting in Sukhanov's apartment just before the seizure of power, and though he had been a Menshevik in the past, he was regarded as a Bolshevik of proved loyalty who would inevitably be entrusted with greater powers in the future. As soon as he heard of the assassination Dzerzhinsky hurried to Petrograd to take charge of the inevitable investigations. The assassin was arrested the same evening. He spoke very calmly under cross-examination, admitted the crime, produced a Colt automatic pistol, and astonished his examiners when he burst out laughing and said he had fired altogether eighteen shots and only one of them hit the target. Kannegiesser explained that he had three motives for killing Uritsky. He could not forgive the Bolsheviks for killing his friend Lieutenant Perlzweig, he could not forgive the peace of Brest Litovsk, and he was revolted by the fact that so many of the Bolsheviks were Jewish. He was himself a Jew, an army officer, and a poet of distinction.

Lenin was immediately informed about the assassination. Krupskaya was attending a meeting, and he lunched with Bukharin and Maria Ilyinichna. Both urged him not to go out that day. Sverdlov, who saw Lenin early in the afternoon, felt that the assassination might be the signal for a counterrevolutionary uprising, and he solemnly forbade Lenin to make any public appearance for fear that he might be the next person on the list. Lenin laughed off the dangers. He had arranged to make two speeches that day, and he had no intention of breaking his engagements. He spent the afternoon working in his office. At five o'clock, having sent a message to his chauffeur to have the car ready, he went to the apartment to say goodbye to Maria Ilyinichna. She had been unwell for some days, and to his surprise she was dressed for going out. Frightened, she insisted on coming with him. "Absolutely not," he said. "You stay at home." The tall, burly chauffeur, Stepan Gil, drove him to a workers' meeting at the Corn Exchange in the Basmannaya district northwest of the Kremlin, where he proposed to speak on the subject of Soviet power versus the power of the "capitalist conspirators" who were mounting offensives in the Caucasus, the Ukraine, along the Volga, and in Siberia. The news from the front was bad, and his purpose in making these speeches was to ensure that the Moscow workers would exert themselves to produce the greatest number of offensive weapons in the shortest possible time.

He spoke for about an hour at the Corn Exchange, deliberately painting a dark picture of current events, refusing to conceal the gravity of the situation. In recent days the White Guards and the Czechoslovak mercenaries had recaptured large areas where the Soviets had been in control. "What do we see on the ruins of the Soviets?" he asked. "What we see is the total triumph of the capitalists and the land owners, the groans and curses of the peasants and workers. The land is being given back to the nobility, the workshops and factories are returning to their former owners, the eight-hour day is being abolished, the workers' and peasants' organizations are being dissolved, and the tsarist zemstvos and the old police powers are being restored. If there is any worker or peasant who still hesitates on the question of power, let him look to the Volga, to Siberia, and to the Ukraine, and he will see clearly and finally where the power should lie!" There was the customary vociferous applause, and it was about a quarter past six when he went on to address the second workers' meeting at the Michelson factory south of the city.

As usual he sat in the back seat of the car, while Gil sat at the wheel. There were no guards, no companions in these sudden journeys across Moscow to attend these well-advertised meetings, which took place as regularly as clockwork every Friday evening. Gil was instructed to go fast, but no other precautions were taken. When they arrived at the huge Michelson factory on the Serpukhovaya, there was no reception committee waiting at the gates, because it was known that he detested these committees. He walked straight into the factory, took his place on the rostrum, and immediately launched into his speech.

It was very much the same speech he had delivered at the Corn Exchange, a bitter attack on the forces of reaction, and made notable by an unusually savage indictment of the United States. "Look at America, the freest and most civilized nation in the world," he said. "What do we find in this democratic republic? What we find is the impudent domination not of millionaires but of billionaires, a whole people reduced to servitude and slavery. From the moment the workshops, the factories, the banks, and the entire wealth of the country passes into the hands of the capitalists, from that moment the democratic republic becomes only another name for the enslavement of millions of workers and an absolutely irredeemable misery!" Then, having excoriated the United States, he went on to attack the secret treaties and the still smoldering desire of the Allies to bring Russia back into the war against Germany, a war which was being fought for the benefit of capitalists, and capitalists alone. He spoke from a platform in the machine shop where, until his arrival, the workmen had been making hand grenades.

In the deserted factory courtyard Gil sat at the wheel of the car, waiting patiently for Lenin to reappear. He had been sitting there for about a quarter of an hour when a woman in a faded black dress, clutching a handbag, seemed to appear out of nowhere. She had markedly Jewish features, but there was little to distinguish her from thousands of other women walking the streets of Moscow. She went up to Gil and asked whether Lenin had arrived.

"I don't know who has arrived," Gil answered.

"You're his chauffeur," she said. "How is it that you don't know?"

He knew exactly how to deal with her. He was under instructions never to reveal the name of his passenger, or where he was going, or where he had come from.

"Why ask me?" he said carelessly. "There are so many speakers nowadays, it is impossible to keep track of them."

Still clutching her handbag, the woman went into the factory. She soon found the machine shop and sat down at a table near the rostrum. It was remembered afterward that she smoked incessantly and there were dark rings under her eyes.

Lenin was calling upon the workers to mobilize all their strength to rout the forces of the counterrevolution. He demanded a maximum effort against the Czechoslovaks who were hypocritically using the slogans of liberty and equality in an attempt to destroy the Soviets, while shooting down hundreds and thousands of workers and peasants. He said the revolution had not been brought into being in order to let the landlords return to their properties; these parasites, who sucked the blood of the people for so long, must know that neither liberty nor equality would give them back their lost wealth, now safely in the hands of the workers. "Everything for the workmen, everything for the toilers!" he shouted, and he closed the speech with a ringing cry: "There is only one issue! Victory or death!"

An hour had passed since Lenin entered the Michelson factory. Gil knew the speech had come to an end, because he could hear the workmen singing the "Internationale." Then the first wave of workmen came pouring out of the factory, but there was no sign of Lenin. As usual he was being delayed by people with questions and petitions, and it was some little time before he finally emerged, talking rapidly and eagerly to a crowd of workers. Lenin made his way slowly to the car, pausing to talk to two women who had asked him some question about food supplies. Gil heard him saying, "Yes, it's perfectly true that the people in charge of provisioning have done many illegal things, but it will certainly be put right." Two other women were standing beside him, pressing close to him. For two or three minutes the conversation about food supplies went on. At last Lenin turned toward the car. Someone had already opened the car door. Gil was watching Lenin closely. Suddenly a shot rang out. Gil turned to see the woman who had spoken to him in the deserted courtyard standing only a few inches away with a Browning pistol in her hand. Two more shots followed. Lenin fell to the ground. Gil reached for his pistol, clambered out of the driving seat, and went running after the woman. She was bareheaded, and he aimed for her head, but he did not shoot because the courtyard was crowded with people milling about in the excitement of the moment. He knew that his duty was to be with Lenin, and so he turned toward the car. He was still walking rapidly toward the car when he realized that a strange and terrible silence had descended, like the silence of death. A moment later there came wild cries: "They've killed him! They've killed him!" Everyone in the courtyard seemed to be shouting the words. Then, to Gil's astonishment, the crowded courtyard emptied as everyone ran off panic-stricken through the main gates and out into the Serpukhovaya.

Gil bent over Lenin to see whether he was still breathing. Lenin's eyes were open, and he was still conscious.

"Did they get him?" Lenin asked, scarcely articulating the words. He thought he had been attacked by a man.

"You mustn't talk," Gil said. "It will only make you tired."

From the moment when Lenin stepped toward the car, everything that happened was strange and unpredictable, and extraordinary things continued to happen. Suddenly a man in a sailor's cap emerged from the factory, one hand deep in his pocket, the other making wild gestures. He looked like a madman, his face contorted. It occurred to Gil that the man in the sailor's cap could only be coming to deliver the *coup de grâce* to Lenin. He squatted down, covering Lenin with his body, and shouted "Halt!" but the man kept coming.

"Halt, or I'll fire!" Gil shouted, but the man paid no attention to him.

Gil covered him with his pistol. The man ran across the courtyard, veering to the left of the car and finally running out through the open gates.

Relieved by the man's disappearance, Gil turned to see how Lenin was faring. A woman who suddenly appeared in the courtyard began to shout, "Don't shoot!" She evidently thought Gil was about to shoot Lenin. About this time three men came out of the factory, and Gil whirled round once again to confront them with his pistol.

"Who are you? Halt, or I'll fire!" he shouted.

"We're from the factory committee," one of the men replied, and Gil, remembering that he had seen one of them before, decided to trust them.

"You'll have to take him to the nearest hospital," one of the men said.

"No, I'm taking him home," Gil replied, and from Lenin there came a whisper, "Home, home."

They helped Lenin up and lifted him into the car. He slumped down into a corner of the back seat. One of the factory committeemen sat beside him, and another sat beside Gil, as he raced to the Kremlin with his foot hard on the accelerator. Normally he would have to stop to show his papers at the Troitsa Gate, but this time he shouted "Lenin!" as he drove at full speed through the gate. The car did not stop until they reached his house.

They lifted him out of the car, but he refused to be carried up the stairs to his apartment. He looked deathly pale and weak. They kept begging to be allowed to carry him, but he only answered, "I'm going up alone." Still, they were able to support him and to take some of the weight off his feet. He said, "I'll be more comfortable if you remove my coat." They slipped the coat off him, and he went up the stairs in his shirt sleeves.

There were two flights of stairs, and Gil remembered afterward that he did not moan and was in full possession of his faculties. They rang the bell, a servant opened the door, and Gil half carried him into his bedroom. Blood was running down his shirt. Gil found some scissors and ripped the shirt open. At that moment Maria Ilyinichna entered the bedroom. She asked what had happened, and Lenin murmured something about a slight wound in the arm. Maria Ilyinichna ordered Gil to summon the doctors and to wait downstairs in order to tell Krupskaya as soon as she returned from work.

Lenin was attacked at seven-thirty, and it was now a few minutes past eight. One by one the doctors arrived and hurried up the stairs. A car had been sent to fetch Krupskaya, and Gil did not have long to wait. He told her haltingly about what had happened in the courtyard of the Michelson factory: a woman had shot at Lenin, and he was slightly wounded. Krupskaya had only to look at him to know that this was not the whole story.

"Tell me, is he alive or dead?" she asked.

"On my word of honor, Vladimir Ilyich is only slightly wounded," Gil replied.

Krupskaya then hurried up the stairs, to discover the apartment crowded with strangers. All the doors were wide open, and there were unfamiliar coats hanging on the coat tree. Sverdlov was standing in the hallway, looking gray and worried, his expression confirming her worst fears. She said helplessly: "What can we do now?"

Without thinking what he was saying, Sverdlov said, "We are making all the arrangements for Ilyich."

She was sure then that he was dead. By "arrangements" he could only mean that the undertakers had been summoned and they were preparing to put him in his coffin. Grief-stricken, but outwardly composed, she made her way to the bedroom, where the bed had been pulled away from the wall to allow the doctors to examine the patient more freely. Already five, and perhaps six, doctors had arrived. Lenin was still conscious. Deathly pale, he looked for a long time at Krupskaya, and then he said in a voice that seemed to come from a long way away, "You've come. You must be tired. Go and lie down." But she scarcely listened to his voice, for his eyes told her something else altogether. His eyes said, "This is the end."

She left him and stood in the doorway so that she could see him without being observed. Lunacharsky, thoroughly shaken, was standing by the bed, and she heard Lenin saying, "What is there to look at?"

The apartment had become a camp, with strangers moving in and out at will. A dressing station was being set up in a small adjoining room, inhalators, gauze, bandages, mysterious bottles were appearing in large quantities, so that the apartment began to resemble the operating theater in a hospital. All these machines and medicaments, and the strangers moving about the apartment, terrified Krupskaya as they terrified the Lettish maidservant, who could bear it no longer and simply locked herself in her room. In the kitchen someone lighted the oilstove. For some reason the doctors forgot to bring enough bandages, and bloodstained dressings had to be boiled before they could be used again. The doctors established that two bullets had struck him—the third had torn harmlessly through his coat. One bullet had passed through his neck from left to right, missing the aorta by a fraction of an inch, and after piercing the lung it lodged in the neck, above the right clavicle. The other bullet was in his left shoulder. The first wound was the more serious, because blood had filled up the pleural cavity and altered the position of the heart, with the result that he breathed with difficulty and there was almost no pulse. He had evidently been turning away from the woman who shot him, and this sudden turn had saved his life.

The doctors dared not operate, and in fact there was little they could do. Hours passed, while they watched and whispered, removed dressings, took his pulse and temperature. Sometimes Lenin groaned.

In Lenin's office, Sverdlov and other high officials waited out the long vigil. Around eleven o'clock, when the issue was still in doubt, Sverdlov signed what was tantamount to a decree ordering a merciless reign of terror in reprisal for the attempt on Lenin's life. The decree read:

ALL SOVIETS OF WORKERS, PEASANTS AND RED ARMYMEN'S DEPUTIES, ALL ARMIES, ALL, ALL, ALL

A few hours ago a villainous attempt was made on the life of Comrade Lenin. The working class will respond to attempts on the lives of its leaders by still further consolidating its forces and by a merciless mass terror against all the enemies of the revolution.

SVERDLOV

Such was the decree which was broadcast by radio and tapped out on innumerable telegraph machines, and as Sverdlov intended, there was an immediate holocaust of victims. The Petrograd Cheka immediately executed 512 people and in the course of the following month executed 300 more; the Nizhni Novgorod Cheka executed forty-six prisoners in a single day; and all over Russia, wherever the Cheka could lay its hands on Socialist Revolutionaries, former officers and members of the bourgeoisie, they were shot. People were arrested, put up against a wall, and shot out of hand. The Kronstadt sailors had some five hundred bourgeois locked up in their fortress. The next day they had no more prisoners, for all were dead.

The reign of terror which swept over Russia was more terrible than any that had gone before, for it was anarchic and mindless, selecting its victims at random. No one felt safe, the Communists least of all. They were striking out at their enemies in blind fury. All through August they had suffered a mounting feeling of frustration, seeing enemies everywhere and not knowing where to turn. The mass terror, when it came, resembled a hurricane moving aimlessly. But the mass terror had already been in preparation. All through August there had been intimations of its coming. On August 4 a chilling series of commandments called "The Catechism of the Class Conscious Prole-

tarian," evidently modeled on *The Revolutionary Catechism* of Nechayev, had appeared in *Pravda*. Two of the commandments were
more chilling than the rest. They read:

> Workers and paupers, take a gun in your hands. Learn to shoot well.
> Be prepared for uprisings by kulaks and white guards. To the wall with
> all those who agitate against the Soviet power. Ten bullets for everyone
> who raises a hand against it.
>
> The bourgeoisie is an indefatigable enemy. The rule of capital will be
> extinguished only with the death of the *last* capitalist, the *last* land-
> owner, priest, and army officer.

So now, with Lenin wounded, the first fruits of a terror prepared
many weeks in advance were being gathered, and the Chekist leaders
and political commissars at the front vied with one another in rounding up hostages and shooting them without trial, and sending messages to Sverdlov, now acting head of the Soviet government, to
proclaim their determination to destroy "the criminal conspirators"
wherever they might be found. Stalin telegraphed to Sverdlov from
Tsaritsyn that "the Military Soviet of the North Caucasus, having
learned of the wicked attempt of capitalist hirelings on the life of the
greatest revolutionary, the tested leader and teacher of the proletariat, Comrade Lenin, answer this base attack from ambush with
the organization of open and systematic mass terror against the bourgeoisie and its agents." Similar messages came from all the fronts.
They were notable not only for their venom and for their inaccuracy
—the woman who had shot at Lenin was a Socialist Revolutionary and
very far from being a capitalist hireling—but also for the effusive
epithets which were attached to the name of Lenin as though he were
already dead, already in the limbo of history. It would not have
pleased him to be called "the greatest revolutionary." He would have
said, as Thomas Mann once said, that extravagant praise belittles
both the giver and the taker.

While the mass terror swept across Russia and the hostages died,
Lenin fought his way back to recovery. Bulletins were issued three
times daily. At nine o'clock in the morning of August 31 the bulletin
read: *Temperature 38.3. Pulse 110–120. Patient feels better. Flow of
blood in pleural area is not increasing.* Three hours later the bulletin
read: *Temperature 37.2. Pulse 112.* At seven-thirty in the evening it
read: *Temperature 36.9. Pulse 102.* Altogether, some thirty-five bulletins were issued over a period of ten days, and after the first two or

three days it became evident that his strong constitution was success-fully resisting the shock and physical damage caused by the bullets.

Fanya Kaplan, the woman who shot Lenin, was one of those women who are always to be found on the margin of a revolution. She was a dedicated Socialist Revolutionary who had been imprisoned for eleven years at hard labor for attempting to kill a tsarist official in Kiev. She had been freed during the general amnesty following the February revolution, and returning to Moscow she made a living as a milliner. Small, dark, intense, with features of a commonplace ugli-ness, she had dedicated her life to the revolution, and since she be-lieved that Lenin had betrayed the revolution when he dissolved the Constituent Assembly, she had no compunction in attempting to mur-der him. The Bolsheviks believed the murder of Uritsky and the at-tempted murder of Lenin were both part of a deliberate Socialist Revolutionary plot to take over the government, but there was in fact no connection between the two incidents.

Arrested, Fanya Kaplan was taken to the Lubyanka, the head-quarters of the Moscow Cheka. There, briefly, Bruce Lockhart of the British Mission, who had been arrested the same day, caught a glimpse of her. Her face was colorless, and her eyes were set in a fixed stare. The fixed stare was probably due to her near-blindness, for she had practically lost the use of her eyes in the Malzev prison; and Lenin was alive because she was so nearly blind.

But she was too important a prisoner to be retained for long at the Lubyanka, and soon she was removed to a basement strong room under the quarters of Sverdlov in the Kremlin. Interrogated continu-ally, she refused to say where she obtained the pistol. She told them that her parents were in the United States, and that she had four brothers and two sisters, all workers. She had planned to kill Lenin long ago, and she insisted that she had no accomplices. When it be-came clear that no more information could be gotten from her, it was decided to shoot her. On September 3 a young Chekist called Pavel Malkov removed her from the strong room and shot her in the back of the head. For many years it was rumored that Krupskaya had inter-ceded for her and her punishment was lifelong imprisonment in Si-beria, but these rumors were unfounded.

Within a week Lenin was sitting up in bed, reading the mountain of telegrams which were continually arriving. On September 7, when the doctors pronounced that he was out of danger, he was able to write a penciled note in a shaky hand to Sereda, the Commissar of

Agriculture. "I am very sorry you did not come to see me," he wrote. "You should have paid no attention to those overzealous doctors of mine." He went on to ask for reports on the poor peasants of Yelets who had apparently forgotten to reply to Soviet demands about the amount of grain they had reaped. Characteristically he added, "There are simply no reports coming in from *anywhere* to show that the work is *in full swing.*" His wounds had not made him more forgiving, and on the following day, in answer to a telegram from the Fifth Army headquarters wishing him a speedy recovery, he wrote, "Thank you. Excellent progress toward recovery. Am convinced that the suppression of Kazan Czechs and White Guards together with their bloodthirsty kulak supporters will be a model of mercilessness. Hearty greetings." This telegram was sent to Trotsky, who had taken part in the battle for Kazan, which he always regarded as the turning point of the civil war. "It was the first great victory," Trotsky wrote. "In this serious and terrifying moment, we saw the young Republic being saved from a complete rout." There were more victories to come, as the Fifth Army raced on to Simbirsk, Lenin's native town. On September 12 another telegram was sent off to Trotsky: "Congratulations for taking Simbirsk. It is my opinion that we must now exert our maximum strength to speed up the take-over of Siberia. Spare no money on bounties." These successes encouraged and strengthened Lenin, and a few days later he was once again presiding over the Central Committee and holding conferences with his advisers.

About this time Maxim Gorky came to visit him. It was their first meeting since the October revolution. Lenin was still weak, scarcely able to move his neck and with difficulty moving the fingers of his left hand. Gorky's editorials in *Novaya Zhizn* still rankled, and Lenin was not in the best of tempers. When Gorky expressed his indignation at the attempted assassination, Lenin replied in the tones of a man dismissing a fact which no longer interested him: "A brawl. Nothing to be done. Everyone acts in his own way."

Though Lenin made light of the affair, there was not the least doubt that he was deeply troubled by it. He was troubled, too, by Gorky's gentle insistence that nothing was to be gained by the simplification of ideas, or of life. Long ago Gorky had spoken of Lenin as "the great simplifier." Now in hot temper Lenin repudiated the charge, and once more he found himself falling into one simplification after another.

"He who is not with us is against us!" he said heatedly. "It's pure fantasy to think of people having an existence outside of history. Even if we grant that such people once existed, at present they no longer exist and they cannot exist. They are not needed any more. Every last one of us is thrown into the whirlpool of reality, which has become more complex than ever before. You say I am simplifying life too much, and all these simplifications threaten civilization with ruin, eh? Well, according to you, millions of peasants armed with rifles—don't they threaten civilization? I suppose you think the Constituent Assembly could have coped with all this anarchy? You who talked such a lot about the anarchy in the villages should be able to understand our work better than others. We have to put before the Russian masses something essentially simple, something well within their grasp. The Soviets and communism, that's simple enough surely?"

The two titans were meeting head on, both of them impenitent, both of them incapable of changing their hard-won positions. Gorky was always complaining bitterly about the intolerable cruelties committed by the communists, and Lenin was always replying that these cruelties were forced upon him by his enemies. And while Gorky admired Lenin's extraordinary strength of will and those human qualities which occasionally made him so likable, he detested the doctrinaire who simplified all problems into utmost black and utmost white. He wrote once that Lenin's words "brought to my mind the cold glitter of steel shavings," and though he went on to say that out of these cold words the truth emerged, he was never comfortable among steel shavings. He said something about the need to put intellectuals into positions of authority. They were the servants of truth and justice and mercy. Surely they could be used in the government.

"You are talking about a union of the workers and the intelligentsia, eh?" Lenin said. "Well, I have nothing against it. Tell the intelligentsia to come and join us. According to you they are the true servants of justice. Then what is the matter with them? Of course they should come and join us. We are the ones who have undertaken the colossal task of putting the people on their feet and telling the whole world the truth about life, showing them the straight road out of slavery, misery, and degradation to a more human life!"

Then he laughed, and Gorky thought he detected no resentment in his voice when he said, "That is why I received a bullet from the intelligentsia."

The truth was of course that Lenin profoundly distrusted the intelligentsia, perhaps for the same reason that he distrusted and despised the peasants: he was not one of them. Among ideas he was never at ease. Like Nechayev, he was hagridden by a single idea: that the proletariat should inherit the earth. Beyond this idea he was incapable of entertaining any other. His greatest victories were not in the realm of ideas, but in the practical operations of power. When he said, "We are the ones who have undertaken the colossal task of putting the people on their feet and telling the whole world the truth about life," he was no longer giving expression to ideas; he was merely asserting his right to make everyone obey him.

The conversation grew heated, for Gorky was magnificently fearless, saying exactly what he wanted to say. He insisted that nothing was to be gained by killing the intellectuals: they were necessary to whatever government ruled over Russia. Lenin realized the force of the argument.

"I don't quarrel with your idea that the intellectuals are necessary to us," he said in a tone of annoyance and sadness. "What I quarrel with is their hostility toward us, how little they understand the needs of the time. Don't they realize how powerless they are without us, how incapable they are of reaching down to the masses?" Then he added, "They will be to blame if we break too many heads!"

The dialogue between Gorky and Lenin bore fruit: intellectuals and savants who would otherwise have been condemned to death were sometimes spared, and for a period Gorky himself became the mediator between the human intelligence and the stark brutality of communist practice. It was a role he played cleanly and passionately until August 1921 when Lenin, grown weary of his intransigence, ordered him to leave the country on the grounds that he needed medical attention abroad. To the end of his life, Gorky was to be haunted by the memory of the number of people he might have saved.

Lenin, wounded, was like a lion at bay. He would joke about the medical bulletins, writing for example on the last of the bulletins which appeared in *Pravda* on September 19: "I make a most earnest and personal request that no one should bother the doctors with telephone calls and questions any more now that I have recovered"—but the wound left deep scars. Always merciless, he became more merciless. "It was in those tragic days," wrote Trotsky, "that something snapped in the heart of the revolution. It began to lose its 'kindness' and forbearance." He might have added that it began to lose all meaning, because it was being betrayed.

Although Lenin insisted that he was recovering his health, the doctors knew better and ordered him to take a vacation in the country. It was decided to send him to the palace which had once belonged to the millionaire Savva Morozov at Gorki some twenty-three miles from Moscow. The word *gorki* means "little hills," and the palace stood squarely on top of one of the hills overlooking a pleasant valley. It was surrounded by woods, fir trees, silver birches, limes and oaks. There were pleasant gardens with carefully tended flower beds, and winding avenues had been carved through the woodland. The palace was furnished with every kind of luxury; and Lenin and Krupskaya, who had spent their lives in ordinary middle-class comfort, were at first dismayed by so much panoply, so many columns and chandeliers and chevalglass mirrors with ornamental frames in white and gold. Lenin came to like the comforts of the Morozov palace, particularly enjoying the enormous plate-glass windows, which offered an unrestricted view of fields and woods, but to the end he was a little uncomfortable in it.

The security guards occupied the ground floor, while Lenin and Krupskaya occupied one of the wings on the upper floor. The guards had already taken up residence in the palace when Lenin arrived toward the end of September. They snapped to attention, saluted, and offered him an immense bouquet. There was a welcoming speech, which he answered gruffly, for he had no taste for such ceremonials and was glad when he reached the upper floor, where the guards were not permitted to go. For himself he chose the smallest room with a wonderful view overlooking gardens. In addition there was a study, a library, a dining room, and a bedroom for Krupskaya. The curtains, the carpets, and the pictures on the wall were all in gay colors. Light flooded through the windows. Everything about the palace suggested the genteel traditions of its former owners.

It was as though some strange reversal of values was taking place. The harsh, embittered dictator of the proletariat, continually issuing orders for the merciless extermination of the class enemies, lived in palatial luxury. Himself a member of the nobility, he was now living for the first time in the luxury traditionally associated with his class.

When the veteran revolutionary Angelica Balabanoff arrived in Moscow early in October, she had scarcely stepped off the train when a messenger announced that Lenin wanted to see her immediately. At breakneck speed she was driven out to Gorki, where she found him sunning himself on the balcony. She embraced him silently, overcome by the thought of how closely he had escaped assassination. He was still weak, was not yet permitted to walk in the grounds, but looked well. On Krupskaya the strain of the last months was pathetically visible, for she looked old and haggard.

Lenin was in good spirits. The Great War was coming to an end with the inevitable defeat of the Central Powers, and he was looking forward to the time—which could not be far distant—when the whole of Europe would be consumed in the communist flame. He prided himself on being a man without illusions. With a kind of mathematical clairvoyance he explained how one by one all the countries of Europe would be compelled to follow the example of Russia, and when she objected hesitantly, pointing out that only in Italy was there a hard core of Bolshevik sympathizers, he dismissed her arguments with a contemptuous shrug. He had been reading Barbusse's *Le Feu* and had been especially struck by the scene of fraternization between the French and German soldiers. The frontiers would fall apart, and the war would end with the massive fraternization of soldiers. Fraternization—*brataniye*—the word was never far from his lips at this time. And after the soldiers had proclaimed their fraternal faith in one another, they would turn about, destroy their capitalist masters, and introduce the reign of socialism. Lenin was elated with his vision. It was astonishingly simple. In a month, in two months, the socialist flag would fly from Petrograd to the Pyrenees.

Halfheartedly Angelica Balabanoff raised objections, disturbed by his exaggerated estimate of communist influence in labor movements abroad. She suggested that it would be useful if she returned to Switzerland, but at first he would have none of it. He had more important plans for her—he wanted her to be secretary of the Communist International which he proposed to inaugurate as soon as Germany had come under the communist flag—but for the moment he kept his plans secret. She had the uncomfortable feeling that he was drawing further and further away from the realities of the world. They spoke briefly about Fanya Kaplan and her execution. Strangely, he confessed that the decision to shoot her would have been easier if some other Soviet commissar had been involved. For some reason her execution weighed heavily on him. It weighed more heavily on Krupskaya, who later burst into tears and showed that she was deeply affected by the thought of revolutionaries condemned to death by a revolutionary power.

When the Rolls-Royce came later in the afternoon to take the visitor back to Moscow, Lenin sent it away and insisted that she remain for dinner. He shared with her the extra rations which had been provided for his convalescence.

"Look," he said. "This bread has been sent to me from Yaroslavl, this sugar from comrades in the Ukraine. The meat, too. They want me to eat meat during my convalescence."

He spoke almost as though unreasonable demands were being made on him.

Some time later she expressed her feelings about a group of Mensheviks who had been condemned to death for counterrevolutionary propaganda.

"Don't you realize," Lenin replied, "that if we don't shoot a few of those leaders we may be placed in a position when we shall have to shoot ten thousand workers?"

It occurred to her that he was not speaking unsympathetically; he was neither cruel nor indifferent; the extermination of his enemies had become a tragic necessity. Yet she suspected that it had already become a habit, a reflex action which sprang into existence the moment he encountered an obstacle in his path.

When the Rolls-Royce drove her to Moscow, she was already aware that something had gone irremediably wrong.

THE THIRD INTERNATIONAL

THOUGH ILL AND TIRED, still suffering from pain and spending most of the day in bed, Lenin was incapable of resting. The Central Committee had agreed that no political papers should be sent to him at Gorki, but not even the Central Committee could prevent him from working. Karl Kautsky had written a short book *The Dictatorship of the Proletariat* in which he attempted to show that the dictatorship, far from being the inevitable and logical form of the state when power has been seized from the bourgeoisie, was in fact a retrograde form at variance with the principles of Marx. By selecting the appropriate quotations he was able to prove to his own satisfaction that the Russian Revolution was un-Marxist, heterodox, and outside the current of the European revolution. Lenin, however, had made his own selection from the writings of Marx. His attack on Kautsky, which he called *The Proletarian Revolution and Renegade Kautsky*, was written during his convalescence. The tone is harsh and angry, with a shrill edge to his vituperation. He makes no effort to hide his hatred of "the renegade," who is described as a traitor to the Marxist cause, a man who has sold himself to the enemy.

Kautsky's work evidently touched him on a raw nerve, and the unconcealed rage is not pleasant to look at. At the very beginning of his counterattack Lenin describes him as a windbag "who chews rags in his sleep." Kautsky's definitions are wrong, he has only a limited understanding of Marx's teaching, and what little he has understood is outweighed by his intolerable misunderstandings. Occasionally, like a blind puppy sniffing eagerly in one direction and then another, Kautsky unwittingly arrived at a correct or at least tolerable idea. Kautsky had said that Marx never envisaged the reign of a dictator unrestricted by any laws, for such a dictatorship would be no different from those of ancient Greece and Rome. He declared that these personal tyrannies should have no place in the European socialist movement. Lenin replies deftly that the question of personal tyranny has never arisen, and all these references to Greece and Rome only show that Kautsky has the equipment for teaching ancient history in a secondary school; he has no right to speak in the name of European socialism. But "dictatorship is power, based directly on force, and unrestricted by any laws." On this subject there can be no disagreement, but Kautsky must understand that the dictatorship of the proletariat is unlike all hitherto existing dictatorships and has nothing in the least to do with personal tyranny: it is the expression of an inviolable social law.

Lenin's arguments are all of the same kind. Employing his own definitions, Lenin can argue in any direction he pleases, secure in the knowledge that no one can controvert him. In his hands "dictatorship" and "democracy" are interchangeable terms, and he can say for example that "proletarian democracy, of which the Soviet government constitutes one of the forms, has given a development and expansion of democracy hitherto unprecedented in the world." When Kautsky speaks of democracy, it is pointed out to him that he is merely referring to "the stinking corpse of democracy" as it is practiced in the West, which is far removed from the "true and pure" democracy practiced by the Soviets. We are reminded that "proletarian democracy is a million times more democratic than any bourgeois democracy, and the Soviet government is a million times more democratic than the most democratic bourgeois government."

Lenin is particularly annoyed because Kautsky insists that there can be no socialism without basic freedoms, and that by denying basic freedoms the Russian Revolution is not socialist. Lenin replies that there can be no real freedom of the press as long as the newspapers are in the hands of the bourgeoisie. Only now, under the Soviets, can there be a real freedom of the press, because the power of the bourgeoisie has been extinguished. Kautsky demands freedom of assembly, and Lenin employs the strange argument that freedom of assembly is guaranteed by the Soviet government because "thousands and thousands of the best houses have been taken from the exploiters, and in this way the right of assembly, without which democracy is a fraud, becomes a million times more democratic." What the expropriation of houses has to do with freedom of assembly is not explained; and in fact Lenin is in no mood to explain. Everything is a million times better in the Socialist paradise than in any other country, and what right therefore has Kautsky to deplore the way the revolution is going?

In this way, without argument, by constantly making larger and larger claims, by distorting Marx and history, and by employing a not inconsiderable vocabulary of denunciation—the words "banal," "philistine," "hypocritical" and "dirty" occur on nearly every page—Lenin disposes of Kautsky and buries him underground. But Kautsky unaccountably refuses to lie still, and there follows another chapter in which he is buried all over again. There are eight chapters, and each chapter is clearly intended to dispose of him once and for all. There are times when *The Proletarian Revolution and Renegade Kautsky* sounds like a scream of pain.

Kautsky's short pamphlet is well-mannered, logical, only mildly reproving. He claims to be a theoretician with no practical knowledge of revolution, and he points unerringly to five fatal flaws which have appeared in the Russian Revolution. They are:

1. The Soviet government, as constituted, could survive only as the tyranny of one man or a small group of men.
2. The destruction of the Constituent Assembly was designed to increase the power of the tyrants and effectively disposed of the last vestiges of democracy.
3. Lenin was using the armed peasantry to enforce a government of intellectuals who called themselves the "dictatorship of the proletariat." In the nature of things such a government could not be either stable, or representative, or intelligible.
4. Government by expropriation is not socialist government. By "expropriating the expropriators" Lenin had brought upon himself an unnecessary civil war at a time when the country needed peace to recover from its wounds.
5. Lenin staked everything on the outbreak of a European revolution, and there was no reason to believe that such a revolution would take place either immediately or in the foreseeable future.

To the first four of these arguments Lenin replied by appealing to the purity of his intentions and the self-evident success of the Bolshevik policies. His dictatorship was the purest form of democracy, the destruction of the Constituent Assembly had no other purpose than to make the democracy more widespread, the armed peasantry were the essential element of the proletarian vanguard, and expropriation was the inevitable and necessary tool with which the government waged war against the bourgeoisie. Concerning the fifth charge he answered that he had not "staked everything" on the outbreak of a European revolution. On the contrary, he had coldly calculated the scientific inevitability of the European revolution; there was not the least doubt that it would take place; and if Kautsky, writing his pamphlet in August 1918, was unable to hear the revolutionary stirrings in Germany, then he was remarkably deaf. On the last page of his book Lenin wrote triumphantly:

> The foregoing lines were written on November 9, 1918. In the night of the ninth to tenth, news announcing the beginning of a victorious revolution was received at first in Kiel and then in other northern towns and seaports, where power has passed into the hands of Soviets of Workers' and Soldiers' Deputies, and then in Berlin, where power has also passed into the hands of the Soviet.
>
> The conclusion which I had intended to write on Kautsky's pamphlet and on the proletarian revolution is now superfluous.

For Lenin it was a moment of exquisite triumph. Not words, but the insurmountable and formidable logic of events had proved Kautsky wrong. The flame of revolution was about to spread across the whole of Europe, and his prophecies, based on a close study of Marxist principles, were being proved correct. Krupskaya relates that for four days he was in a seventh heaven, beaming and smiling, addressing meetings all over Moscow to welcome the coming of the German revolution. "These days," she says, "were the happiest of his life."

For weeks and months he had dreamed of this inevitable revolution which would be at once the safeguard and the capstone for his own. Even more than for a Russian revolution, he had prayed for a German one. In an extraordinary note written to Sverdlov in October he had promised that Russia would form a brotherly alliance with revolutionary Germany, offering vast quantities of grain and military aid. "We must sacrifice our lives to help the German workers," he declared. Two deductions could be made from the fact that Germany was on the eve of revolution. The first was that ten times more effort must be made to gather the grain crop "both for ourselves and for the German workers." The second was that ten times as many soldiers must be enrolled in the army. "We must have an army of three millions *by the spring* to help the international workers' revolution." The note to Sverdlov was written with vast excitement, with a great deal of wavy underlining of words, and it concluded with the demand that these two deductions in the form of decrees must be broadcast by telegraph "over the whole world." Accordingly, a telegram was dispatched "to all, to all," announcing the triumph of revolutionary forces in Kiel and Berlin.

The deception was a cruel one. The German High Seas Fleet mutinied, but none of the leaders knew what to do once they had disarmed the officers and run up the red flag; and the mutiny died a natural death. It was the same in Berlin, where the revolutionaries were quietly rounded up by the police. For a moment it had seemed that the sailors on the battleships *Thüringen* and *Helgoland* would light a fire that would spread through all Germany, but there was no fire, only a spark, and the spark went out. During the following weeks Lenin would scan the newspapers for a sign of the expected revolution, and when the Spartacists under Karl Liebknecht rose in Berlin in January 1919, he once more announced the coming of the European revolution. The Spartacists held out for ten days, then the revolt was quelled by German troops. Karl Liebknecht and Rosa Luxemburg, the two leaders of the revolt, were murdered while in the custody of the police. Lenin sorrowed for the death of Liebknecht, but there was little sorrow to spare for Rosa Luxemburg, who had dared to attack him for his pitiless use of terror and for a temper so authoritarian that he could never permit the slightest deviation from his wishes. She had spoken of life under Lenin as "a mere semblance of life," the people so brutalized by oppression that they were no longer able to think for themselves, surrendering their power "to a dozen party officials of inexhaustible energy and boundless experience." Like the pedantic Kautsky, she believed that the Russian Revolution suffered from fatal flaws.

In one of those gently sorrowing letters which Rosa Luxemburg wrote from prison before she helped to lead the Spartacist uprising, she said: "*Wir sind alle Tödten auf Urlaub*—We are all dead men on furlough." Throughout her long career as a revolutionary, she had held fast to the belief that brutality and oppression had no part in the revolution. No doubt men must die in all revolutions, and every revolutionary must expect to be killed. But what is important in a revolutionary is his humanity, his understanding of the human condition. He must learn through suffering to understand the sufferings of others.

Lenin and Rosa Luxemburg stood at poles apart: the one so remote from pity, so aristocratic, so much the slave of his theories; the other so warm and generous that the mere sight of people walking in the streets could bring tears of joy to her eyes. For her, people were like angels, and it was beyond belief that they could be punished by theories.

That winter Lenin was to endure more real suffering than he had endured since his youth. His body had suffered when he was wounded by Fanya Kaplan; now his spirit suffered. The bright hopes of a German revolution were dashed, famine was spreading over Russia, there was an unfamiliar note of uncertainty in his letters and speeches. Krupskaya had nursed him back to health. When he recovered, she was so exhausted that she was put to bed. She suffered from Basedow's disease, a form of goiter, and though the disease had been checked by an operation, it now began to spread more virulently; in addition the doctors found evidence of heart disease. Her face and ankles were monstrously swollen; she had become a strange parody of herself. It was decided to send her to a children's school in a forest just outside Moscow. She adored children, and it was thought that in the calm of the forest, with children around her, and with no talk of politics, she would recover. She spent December and January at the children's school in Sokolniki. They were the months when Lenin was clutching at straws.

He could not bear to be without her, and every evening he would drive out to the school. On January 19, which was the feast of the Epiphany according to the Slavonic calendar, he arrived late. Moscow was deep in snow, and it was growing dark. As usual Gil was the chauffeur. In the back seat sat Lenin, Maria Ilyinichna and Cherbanov, Lenin's bodyguard, who was holding a jug of milk on his lap, a present for Krupskaya. Just before they reached Kalanchevskaya Square, a man wearing a military cap shouted: "Halt!" Gil stepped on the accelerator and swerved to avoid him. Lenin was alarmed and asked what had happened. Gil made light of the incident, saying it was probably a drunk, but it was not a drunk, as they learned when they had crossed the square and were driving into Sokolniki. Six or seven men were standing across the road, all armed, and determined to bring the car to a halt. In his account of the incident, Gil relates that his instinct was to drive through them, but Lenin, thinking it was probably a military control, ordered him to stop. A moment later Lenin knew he was among bandits. One pulled at his sleeve and jerked him roughly out of the car. Maria Ilyinichna and Cherbanov were also ordered out, but for some reason the bandits paid no attention to Gil, who was armed and debating with himself whether to shoot it out and endanger Lenin's life or to remain quiet. Two bandits stood beside Lenin, both aiming their revolvers at his head, while a third searched him and removed the small Browning automatic which he carried habitually in his coat pocket and a wallet bearing his identity card.

Maria Ilyinichna could not contain herself and shouted, "How dare you search him? Don't you recognize Lenin? Where are your warrants?"

"We don't need any warrants!" one of the bandits answered grimly, and he added, "We have a right to do this!"

The words may have found a somber echo in Lenin's mind. He had used the same words many times in the past, and he would use them again.

Meanwhile the bandits had taken notice of the presence of Gil and they ordered him out of the car. He was six feet tall, heavily built, and an expert shot, yet he dared not shoot. He was hardly out of the car when the bandits jumped in, and drove away, leaving them stranded. Lenin turned angrily on Gil, but his anger abated when the chauffeur explained patiently that he had been perfectly prepared to shoot, but he had held his fire because Lenin would certainly have been wounded or killed before the battle was over. They had escaped with their lives, and this was the important thing. Suddenly, seeing Cherbanov standing there still nursing the milk jug, they burst out laughing.

This was not quite the end of the adventure, for when they walked up the road and presented themselves at the Sokolniki Soviet, they were refused admittance. Lenin had no identity card; the bandits had taken his wallet with them. Finally the chairman of the Soviet arrived, recognized Lenin, and received the inevitable dressing down for permitting bandits to operate in his area. A call was put in to Dzerzhinsky, who asked whether there had been any political motive for the attack.

"No, there was no political motive," Lenin answered. "Otherwise they would have finished me off!"

Krupskaya remembered that when her visitors arrived at last in the schoolhouse at Sokolniki, there was something very queer about them. At first Lenin said nothing about the bandits, for fear of distressing her. Finally he told her the whole story and went off to join the children round the fir tree. The presents he had bought for them were lost; they were in the car.

Exemplary punishment was ordered for the bandits and sweeping laws against banditry were placed on the statute book. That night the car was found near the Krymsky Bridge south of the Kremlin. A police-man and a Red Army soldier lay dead beside it in the snow. Evidently the bandits had been ordered to stop and had shot their way to free-dom. They were never arrested.

For Lenin the year 1919 was one of unrelieved calamity. The daily companions of his misery were blockade, war, famine, typhus, and exhaustion. The armies of Denikin, Kolchak and Yudenich fought over vast stretches of Russia, occupying nine tenths of its land area and leaving to the undisputed rule of the Soviet government only a circular area eight hundred miles in diameter with its center in Moscow. On the circumference of the circle three armies supported by the United States, Britain, France and Japan pressed heavily.

The Bolsheviks still lived in dreams of a European conflagration. Lenin would peruse the rare newspapers that came to Moscow from abroad and point hopefully to strikes in France or Italy as portents of the coming revolution. In March 1919 a Soviet Republic was formed in Hungary, followed in April by the proclamation of a Soviet Re-public in Bavaria by Kurt Eisner. Lenin took heart. Once more he spoke of the triumph of the socialist revolution across the world. Zinoviev proclaimed that there now existed three Soviet Republics, and he expected there would be another three before the ink was dry on the page. "Old Europe," he wrote, "is rushing toward revolution at breakneck speed." But Europe was not rushing toward revolution, and the Europeans saw little reason to arrange their lives to fit Lenin's theories.

Visitors to Moscow in early 1919 saw a city which had come to a standstill. Everyone was hungry and cold. The electric light was con-tinually failing. It was the city of a people worn out by years of suffer-ing and privation, where typhus and the terror reigned impartially. There were no medicines for typhus, and the dead were simply taken to the cemeteries and stacked up like logs; the frozen bodies presented no danger, and the ground was too hard to dig. The terror was more terrible than ever, for it had become institutionalized. Hostages were shot regularly in reply to real or imagined murders which had taken place in territory occupied by the enemy. Even among the Bolsheviks there was the feeling that time was running out.

When Arthur Ransome, the English biographer and folklorist, ar-rived in Moscow in February, he found Lenin outwardly in good heart, amused by everything, laughing easily, tilting his chair this way and that as he interrogated his visitors. His belief in the immediate revolution of Europe was undimmed; and he pointed enthusiastically to the French strikes and the obvious imminence of the revolution in England to prove his case. Patiently Ransome explained that England lacked the revolutionary temper and in the event of revolution would be immediately cut off from its food supplies. Nothing had happened, nothing was likely to happen, to bring about a violent upheaval in that country dedicated to moderation in all things. Lenin dismissed Ransome's ideas about England with incredulity. It was absurd for anyone to believe that England was not on fire with revolutionary fervor; a bitter struggle was already being waged between the English proletariat and the bourgeoisie which could only end in the triumph of the proletariat; wait a few more days, and the king would be dethroned and the red flag would be flying from the Houses of Parliament.

Lenin was one of those men who could believe at one and the same time two entirely contradictory ideas. He told Ransome that revolution in England was imminent, and a moment later he was saying that England was the stronghold of reaction and might be the last of all countries to surrender to socialism. He envisaged a war fought by the "entire world" against the English, until at last socialism was triumphant everywhere. But sometimes, descending from those cloudy regions where "all" and "the whole world" and "violent destruction" held sway, he would say simple things simply. "Russia," he said, "was the only country in which the revolution could start." Speaking of the vast distances in Russia he said, "The distances saved us. The Germans were frightened of them, at the time when they could indeed have eaten us up and won peace, which the Allies would have given them in gratitude for our destruction. A revolution in England would have nowhere whither to retire." A moment later he was back again in the cloudy country where all problems are solved by employing the words "all" or "everywhere." Speaking of the Soviets he said, "In the beginning I thought they were and would remain a purely Russian form; but it is now quite clear that under various names they must be the instruments of the revolution everywhere."

It is now quite clear . . . must be . . . everywhere . . . This useful formula was one of the legacies he bequeathed to Russia, and may in the end prove to be the most dangerous of the many dangerous legacies he bequeathed. For this formula is destructive of concrete and humane thought.

While Ransome was still in Russia, Lenin launched the Third

International, which he described in his usual categorical manner as "a great historical event of universal significance."

Ransome and others who were present were considerably less impressed by the birth pangs of the Third International. "There was a make-believe side to the whole affair," Ransome wrote, and Angelica Balabanoff, who was also present and who was to become the first general secretary, quoted these words approvingly when she wrote her own account of the meeting, which took place in a small hall in the old Courts of Justice near Lenin's apartment in the Kremlin.

There were only thirty-five delegates, all hand-picked, and very few of them represented anything at all. The Japanese Communists were represented by a Dutch-American engineer named Rutgers who had once spent a few months in Japan. England was represented by a Russian *émigré* named Feinberg, who was on Chicherin's staff; Hungary by a war prisoner who returned to Trieste as an official Comintern agent and promptly spent the money that had been entrusted to him in the brothels; France by Jacques Sadoul, who originally came to Russia as an attaché of the French military mission in 1918; the United States by Boris Reinstein, a former member of the American Socialist Labor Party. Prisoners of war, foreign radicals who happened to be in Russia at the time, various employees of the Russian Foreign Office were corralled into becoming founding members of the Third International. Only Hugo Eberlein, who represented the German Spartacus League, was a duly elected delegate possessing documents certifying his authenticity as a representative from another country.

All the important Bolsheviks were present in force. Lenin, Trotsky, Zinoviev, Kamenev, Chicherin, Bukharin, Karakhan and Litvinov made speeches of varying degrees of unreality. In his opening speech Lenin went so far as to declare that "the Soviet system has triumphed not only in backward Russia, but also in Germany, the most advanced nation in Europe, and in Britain, the oldest of the capitalist countries." It was untrue, and he knew it was untrue, but he was in no mood for comparative statements when superlatives were available. "The victory of the world communist revolution is certain!" he declared, and he must have known in his bones that it was far from certain and that the small room in the Courts of Justice hung with blood-red curtains and filled with hand-picked delegates had seen greater trials of strength in the past; for he dominated this meeting as easily as he had dominated a hundred others.

Only Eberlein, sitting next to him on the raised platform, protested vigorously when Lenin proposed that the gathering constitute itself the first Congress of the Third International. He declared that he had no right to commit himself without consulting his party. The Russians, and particularly Lenin, were horrified by this abject appeal to democratic procedure, but since the Spartacus League represented the only real Communist Party outside the borders of Russia, and the memory of Karl Liebknecht and Rosa Luxemburg was still fresh—Lenin had called for a minute of silence in their honor at the beginning of the meeting—it was decided to obey Eberlein's wishes. Accordingly, it was officially declared that this was *not* the first Congress of the Third International.

During the night the official verdict was reversed. Lenin demanded that at the next meeting there should be a clear statement that the first Congress had in fact opened, and he left to his subordinates the task of breaking down the resistance of Eberlein or of outvoting him. Angelica Balabanoff explains in her memoirs how it was done:

> In the very midst of one of the sessions an Austrian ex-war prisoner who had spent several months in Russia before returning to his native land, arrived on the scene. Breathless, full of emotion, and bearing all the marks of an adventurous journey, he asked for and was given the floor. He had just returned from Western Europe, he reported, and in every country he had visited since he left Russia, capitalism was disintegrating, the masses on the verge of revolt. In Austria and Germany, particularly, the revolution was at hand. Everywhere the masses were fascinated and inspired by the Russian Revolution, and in the approaching upheaval they were looking to Moscow to lead the way.
>
> The convention was immediately electrified by this over-optimistic—though probably sincere—report. Four delegates took the floor and proposed a resolution for the immediate launching of the Third International and the drafting of the program. Eberlein continued to protest in the name of his party, but he was overruled. The resolution was passed.

In this way the Third International was born, and Lenin could derive considerable satisfaction from the way a small hand-picked audience had permitted him to link his government with the two historic Internationals of a former age. The stage management, if not convincing, had served its purpose. Henceforward Lenin possessed a weapon which could be used against all the emerging Communist parties in the world; they could no longer serve their own national interests; all would have to be bound by the edicts of the Third International, which served the purposes of his government.

Not everyone was satisfied. Eberlein kept protesting to the end, and Trotsky, magnificent in leather coat and fur hat with five-pointed star, seemed oddly indifferent and remote. Angelica Balabanoff was caught up in the general enthusiasm when the International was finally launched, but when Lenin passed her a note which read, "Please take the floor and announce the affiliation of the Italian Socialist Party to the Third International," she wrote back on the same note, "I can't do it. I am not in touch with them. There is no question of their loyalty, but they must speak for themselves." Arthur Ransome wondered whether the "delegates" from England and America were likely to communicate with their constituents.

Lenin's maneuvers at the founding of the Third International were characteristic of the man. He believed, and openly admitted, that all subterfuges were permissible to those who are guided by the higher interests of humanity, and that it would be criminal not to employ these subterfuges. But the startling apparition of the former Austrian prisoner of war with his tale of the imminent collapse of capitalism, which he had seen with his own eyes, has a curiously medieval quality about it. In just such a way might Ivan the Terrible have convinced his nobles of the imminent collapse of the enemy.

The enemy was not collapsing. Lenin was continually repeating that the enemy was about to be strangled to death by its own inner contradictions and at the same time he would warn his followers of the long and desperate war which would have to be fought until final victory over the enemy. In a long speech to the Congress he advanced twenty-two theses in which he outlined once more the historical basis of his claim that the Soviet government represented the highest form of government known to man, yet for some reason he was concerned to defend the legitimacy of his government. The long-forgotten specter of the withering-away of the state receives its appropriate tribute. "All socialists, with Marx at their head, agree that the abolition of state power is their aim," he declared. "Until this aim is achieved, true democracy, i.e. liberty and equality, cannot be realized." Predictably, he went on to declare that Soviet democracy had this aim constantly in view and was working toward "the complete destruction of the whole state."

Lenin was so carried away by the triumph of the Third International represented by its thirty-five delegates that even before it was officially constituted, he wrote for *Pravda* an astonishing paean of victory:

The ice is broken.

The Soviets have conquered throughout the whole world.

They have conquered first and foremost in the sense that they have won the sympathy of the proletarian masses. This is the most important thing. Neither the bestiality of the imperialist bourgeoisie, nor the persecution and murder of Bolsheviks can take this conquest from the masses. The more the "democratic" bourgeois rage, the more unshakable become these conquests in the hearts of the proletarian masses, in their spirits, in their consciousnesses, and in their heroic preparations for battle.

The ice is broken.

It would have been more accurate to say there were faint cracks on the ice. Victory was far from certain. The White Armies were hoping to close the ring and take Petrograd and Moscow by storm. Denikin's army was massing for the attack which would bring him close to Tula. By the summer most of southern Russia was in his hands; the great cities fell one after another. Kharkov was captured on June 25, then followed Tsaritsyn, Poltava, Odessa and Kiev, while the Red Armies staggered back in confusion. As Lenin admitted to the Eighth Party Congress in March, "The task of building up the Red Army has in no way been prepared, even in theory." In fact Lenin knew very little about the Red Army, and he was indignant when Trotsky told him that it was being led by thirty thousand officers from the ancient tsarist regime. Nevertheless the statement was true, and from indignation Lenin moved to delighted awareness of the strength of a regime "which knew how to build communism out of the bricks left behind by the capitalists." To Trotsky went the major task of organizing the Red Army, and he pursued this task with single-minded ferocity and considerable skill. In his absence his enemies fought for positions near the throne and proved surprisingly successful.

Lenin's relationship with Trotsky was strangely ambivalent. He recognized and could not help recognizing that Trotsky was largely responsible for the success of the October revolution, while never forgiving him for his opposition in the years when they were both in exile. Lenin was suspicious, dogmatic, interested chiefly in the labyrinths of theory, while Trotsky was as free of suspicions as he was of dogma, and he had no profound belief in theory. Lenin saw the world in monochrome, Trotsky saw it in vivid colors. One saw himself as the servant of a historical process; the other saw himself as a revolutionary leader permanently in the forefront of the battle. They depended upon one another, and half despised one another, and were never completely at ease in one another's presence. Trotsky tells a revealing story of how he was visited at the front by Menzhinsky, who warned him that Stalin was plotting against him in the Kremlin. On his next visit to Moscow Trotsky sounded Lenin out. Here is Trotsky's account of the conversation:

> I told him about Menzhinsky's visit to the southern front. "Is it really possible that there is any truth in it?" I asked. I noticed that Lenin immediately became excited, and that the blood rushed to his face. "All trifles," he kept repeating, though not in a very convincing way.
>
> "I am interested in knowing only one thing," I said. "Could you possibly entertain, if only for a moment, such a horrible thought as that I was picking up men to oppose you?"
>
> "Trifles," replied Lenin, but this time with a firmness that instantly reassured me. The little cloud that had hung over us seemed to melt away, and our parting was unusually friendly. But I realized that Menzhinsky was not talking through his hat. If Lenin denied it without telling me everything, it was only because he wanted to avoid a conflict, a personal quarrel.

But in fact on Trotsky's evidence Lenin had not denied it, and it had never occurred to him to give a direct answer. The seeds of the disaster which was to overtake Trotsky were sown during the summer of 1919 when Stalin plotted in the Kremlin, and Trotsky saved the government at the front.

By the autumn the White armies were reeling back in confusion. Trotsky had hammered the Red Army into shape, making it for the first time the effective instrument of Lenin's policies. Wherever there were battles, his armored train would appear as though by magic. The train was equipped with radio, a printing press, agitators, food and clothing for the soldiers, and thousands of blank order forms already signed by Lenin which gave added force to whatever orders Trotsky wrote on them. Those order forms were among Lenin's most extraordinary inventions, for they enabled Trotsky to win a war which Lenin very nearly lost.

It was a war of maneuver fought with almost unbelievable ferocity, with constantly shifting battle fronts, with no quarter given on either side. In October Denikin was advancing deep into Central Russia while Yudenich advanced to the outskirts of Petrograd. Lenin made plans to flee with his government to the Urals. "Finish with

Yudenich *immediately*, then we can turn *everything* against Denikin," Lenin wrote in a characteristic telegram to Trotsky. Petrograd was to be defended "to the last drop of blood," every house must become a fortress, every street a battlefield. But the battle was never fought in the streets. Yudenich with his British tanks reached the outskirts of the city only to discover the tanks of the Red Army, hastily improvised at Trotsky's orders out of automobiles and ships' plating. Yudenich was hurled back, Denikin's army disintegrated, Kolchak was defeated in Siberia. By December there was no longer any doubt about the outcome of the civil war.

In a speech delivered on December 5, Lenin asked how it had come about that Soviet power had succeeded in maintaining itself for two years in a backward, impoverished and war-weary country which had become a vast battlefield; and he answered, as one might have expected, that it was wholly due to the existence of the dictatorship of the proletariat.

THE MAN OF SORROWS

WHILE LENIN effortlessly identified himself with the dictatorship of the proletariat, he was in fact the dictator of Russia. Once he was in power, no member of his government disputed his claim to rule by arbitrary edict. On important matters there would be discussions among the commissars, but more often than not these discussions were purely theoretical, and Lenin would spend his time at these meetings reading a book, with one ear cocked for the moment when someone, usually Zinoviev or Radek, would say: "What does Ilyich think?" Thereupon, with his thumb inside the book to mark the page, Lenin would launch into a statement of his own opinions on the subject. The discussions of the commissars were merely the background noises which helped him to think.

Lenin's attitude toward his commissars was one of genuine liking mingled with genial contempt. Only two of the commissars were accorded unalloyed respect: they were Trotsky and Dzerzhinsky, the one because he was so singularly endowed with revolutionary talents, the other because he was singularly dedicated. The story was told of how Dzerzhinsky, when he was a prisoner in Poland, had asked for and received the right to clean out the latrines of the other prisoners as an act of penance for all the sufferings that had been brought on them. Tall and thin, usually wearing a private's threadbare greatcoat, he seemed to have stepped straight out of a novel by Dostoyevsky. When he became head of the Cheka he was completely merciless, signing death sentences with the casual eagerness of a child defacing a book with his scribbles. It was not that he enjoyed killing people;

it was simply that he loved them so much that he was incapable of pardoning their sins. The killings were part of his sacramental devotions, like cleaning out the latrines.

Lenin, of course, publicly defended the terror, but he took care to speak of the terror only in the abstract, disassociating himself from the individual acts of terrorism, the murders in the basement of the Lubyanka and in all the other basements. He took no joy in them, while Trotsky after each killing was likely to congratulate himself for having performed a revolutionary act. Dzerzhinsky would congratulate himself for a different reason—he had removed some weeds from the garden.

Lenin's attitude toward killing is important because it lies at the heart of the mystery of the form of communism which he imposed upon Russia. From the beginning terror was the weapon which he employed with unremitting skill and with complete indifference to human values. Confronted with any difficult problem, it was the first weapon he called for; and since terror was valid at all times and solved small and large problems with exquisite impartiality, he was usually content to let terror do the work which might more efficaciously have been done by hard thinking. He despised and distrusted bourgeois intellectuals, and if they did not jump to his orders immediately, he would employ the weapon of terror against them. Sometimes he would wonder why they feared him.

Lenin kept himself so remote from the terror that the legend has grown up that he took no active part in it, leaving all decisions to Dzerzhinsky. It is an unlikely legend, for he was a man constitutionally incapable of deputing authority on important matters. In fact he often made the decisions and ordered the executions. Few accounts of Lenin's involvement in these decisions have been published, for understandable reasons. One of the most convincing has been given by Simon Liberman, a Menshevik who enjoyed a position of trust in the Central Timber Committee. He was one of the favored few who were permitted to visit Lenin at regular intervals and he was sometimes permitted to attend meetings of the Soviet of Labor and Defense.

At one of these meetings, following a Soviet decree ordering peasants living near government forests to transport cordwood to the nearest railroad stations, there was a general debate on the failure of the decree to produce the requisite wood. Dzerzhinsky listened for a while and then offered a motion which, he believed, would solve the problem. He suggested that the foresters be made responsible for the fulfillment of the peasants' quota and in addition each forester was to fulfill the same quota—a dozen cords of wood. It was a pleasant and simple solution to the problem. Simon Liberman relates the sequel:

> A few members of the council objected. They pointed out that foresters were intellectuals not used to heavy manual labor. Dzerzhinsky replied that it was high time to liquidate the age-old inequality between the peasants and the foresters.
>
> "Moreover," the Cheka head declared in conclusion, "should the peasants fail to deliver their quota of wood, the foresters responsible for them are to be shot. When a dozen or two of them are shot, the rest will tackle the job in earnest."
>
> It was generally known that the majority of these foresters were anti-Communist. Still, one could feel an embarrassed hush in the room. Suddenly I heard a brusque voice: "Who's against this motion?"
>
> This was Lenin, closing the discussion in his inimitable way. Naturally, no one dared to vote against Lenin and Dzerzhinsky. As an afterthought, Lenin suggested that the point about shooting the foresters, although adopted, be omitted from the official minutes of the session. This, too, was done as he willed.

In this way, without malice and with the utmost secrecy, some hundreds of foresters were doomed. It never seems to have occurred to Lenin that terror was a weapon which, although dreadfully effective in war, is least effective in increasing production. By ordering the deaths of hundreds of foresters he was destroying thousands of years of experience.

The solution of the problem of cordwood wears the air of a murderous improvisation. Indeed, improvisation, sometimes of the wildest kind, had become the order of the day: every short cut and every ludicrous invention were carefully examined in the hope that they would provide fuel or energy for the lagging war machine. Simon Liberman tells of a young Red Army soldier who came to him with a machine for conserving the energy of lumberjacks. The machine consisted of a small motor attached to the lumberjack's neck, accumulating the energy of the fall of each tree as it was cut down. The Red Army man had to be listened to, because Dzerzhinsky was especially impressed with the invention. Lenin himself was particularly impressed by a dentist's plan for solving the fuel problem by ordering the collection of pine cones throughout Russia. Simon Liberman protested. He pointed to the cost of gathering the cones, of transporting and storing them, and he explained that in Sweden, where there was more than a sufficiency of cones, no one had thought of employing them as fuel in large-scale industry: whereupon Lenin publicly reprimanded him for putting forward unhelpful arguments. An hour later, when Liberman had left the meeting, the telephone rang in his apartment. "Comrade Liberman," Lenin said, "I noticed that the Council's resolution made you sad. Ah, but you are a soft-skinned intellectual! The government is always right. Go on with your work as before!"

Liberman was lucky. Other men who brought forward unhelpful arguments got bullets in the back of their necks.

Lenin was continually searching for new fuels. He had long discussions with the veteran Bolshevik, Gleb Krzhizhanovsky, the Chairman of the State Planning Board, on the adventurous exploitation of existing fuels. In December 1919 Krzhizhanovsky broached the subject of peat, pointing out its self-evident use in firing the boilers of electric power stations. A few hours later a letter arrived at his house. It read:

> Gleb Maximilianovich, your statements about peat have profoundly interested me. Would you write an article on this subject for *Economic Life* and later a little pamphlet for a review.
>
> It is necessary to examine this question in the press.
>
> The value of existing deposits goes into the hundreds of thousands.
>
> I mean its value as a fuel.
>
> There are deposits in the neighborhood of Moscow. *Around Moscow, near Petrograd.* Give precise indications.
>
> The ease of extracting it compared with oil and schist.
>
> The workers and peasants *of the region* can work the deposits, *even if at the beginning they only work four hours daily.*

Characteristically, Lenin had no sooner seized upon the idea than he had calculated the precise amount of forced labor needed to implement it.

A number of similar letters to Krzhizhanovsky have survived, all with underscorings, marginal notes, exclamation marks, and sudden adventures into capital letters, testifying to his excitement. Krzhizhanovsky tells us in his reminiscences about a long discussion he had with Lenin about the vast network of power lines in the United States, where electricity had become "truly democratic," reaching down among the lowest levels of the population. Together they set about discussing how after the first desolate ten years of Soviet government they would "popularize" electricity in Russia on a scale undreamed of in the United States. Some weeks later, in a burst of extraordinary enthusiasm, Lenin remembered the conversation and drew up his own visionary program in a letter which shows his flamboyant delight in large numbers, his determination that village libraries and soviets should have two lamps each, and his curious belief that copper wire could be extracted from church bells. He wrote:

Gleb Maximilianovich, the following idea has just occurred to me.

We must make propaganda for electricity. How? Not only by words, but by example.

What does this mean? It means above all—popularizing it. Therefore a plan must be worked out at once for bringing electric light to *e v e r y house* in the RSFSR.

It will be a long business, for it will be a *long* time before we have enough for wire and the rest for 20,000,000 (—40,000,000?) lamps.

Nevertheless we need a plan *immediately*, if only for a few years ahead.

This is the first point.

The second point is that an *abridged* plan must be worked out at once, and then—this is the third and most important point—we must promptly kindle both the *emulation and initiative of the masses* so that they immediately get to work on it.

Could not a plan (approximate) be worked out at once on the following lines:

1. Electric light to be installed in all rural district centers (10–15 thousand) within 1 year.

2. In all villages (½–1 million, probably not more than ¾ million) within 2 years.

3. In the first place—village libraries and soviets (2 lamps each).

4. Poles to be prepared immediately in such and such a way.

5. Prepare insulators *at once from our own supplies* (the porcelain factories, if I am not mistaken, are local ones and small?), prepare them *in such and such a way.*

6. *Copper* for the wire? *Collect it ourselves* in each county and rural district (subtle hint at church bells, etc.)

7. Organize the teaching of electricity on such and such lines.

Could not something *along these lines* be devised, elaborated and decreed?

There was nothing in the least Olympian in Lenin's attitude toward science. He was like a child playing with a new toy, admiring it and holding it up to the light, ignorant of its workings and always in danger of breaking it. Soon he was declaring that "Communism is the Soviet government plus the electrification of the whole country" —a statement which clearly indicated the importance he attached to electrification, while demonstrating that he was perfectly prepared to define communism in any way he thought fit. At the Eighth All-Russian Congress held in December 1920 he spoke of the day when Russia would be covered with a dense network of power stations, and those who attended the Congress remembered the freezing cold of the hall and how dimly the lamps burned.

To the end Lenin's attitude toward science was curiously ambivalent. All sciences were useful which served the Communists; the rest were useless. Reminded that professors of mathematics were dying of starvation, he would throw up his hands in mock horror and launch into a speech on how the Soviets could well do without those dry-as-dust bourgeois professors. He despised the universities, perhaps because he had been expelled from the University of Kazan, and he made no effort during the dark years of starvation to keep them alive. But by 1920 his attitude was changing. Dimly, out of the ruin of the civil war, he foresaw a time when science would be placed at the service of Communism.

Yet science worried him. Like the arts, it refused to fit neatly into the dogmatic patterns of class structures and Marxian dialectics. He told a story of visiting some peasants in the Volokolamsk district in a remote corner of Moscow *guberniya*. The village street was bright with electric lamps, and one of the peasants said, "We peasants were unenlightened, and now light has appeared among us, an unnatural light, which will light up our peasant darkness." Lenin commented, "I was not astonished by these words." Thereafter one of his favorite phrases was "the electrical education of the masses."

His new-found enthusiasm for science served a useful purpose. His rough-and-ready figures, his failure to understand the basic principles of science, and the odd way in which his scientific plans always seemed to end in exacting punishment—of a new scientific planning board, he wrote characteristically that the members "must absolutely work a fourteen-hour day, not a moment less"—all these things were of little importance compared with his genuine enthusiasm. He never read a scientific textbook in his life and if a mathematical equation was presented to him he would shake his head sadly like a man confronted with intolerable mysteries, but he had an intuitive grasp of the benefits of electric power. All his life he had been a student of power, and electric power was one of its manifestations.

The abiding subject of his study however was Soviet power, that strange entity which came into existence when the workers of Petrograd and Moscow formed revolutionary councils during the uprising of 1905. He was continually examining the idea of Soviet power, fitting it into new and more complex theoretical patterns, and he was continually making the wildest claims for it. In a pamphlet called "The Infantile Malady of Communism," which he wrote in the spring of 1920, he declared: "The idea of Soviet power has now come into existence *throughout the entire world,* expanding with prodigious rapidity among the proletariat of all countries." But he was never able to make clear exactly what Soviet power was. Was it workers' councils? Was it the dictatorship of the proletariat? Was it simply another way of describing his own personal dictatorship? In his tortured articles and speeches he would attack the problem from all directions, endlessly improvising provisional definitions, balancing "Soviet," "dictatorship," "proletariat" and "communism" in various patterns. Once, at a Congress of the Soviets in 1921, he made a speech in which he admitted that the proletariat as a class in the Marxian sense did not exist in Russia. Greatly daring, Shlyapnikov, the man who had arranged his reception at the Finland Station, said, "Then permit me to congratulate you on being the vanguard of a nonexistent class." It was not a remark which commended itself to Lenin.

Again and again in his writings he goes over the familiar ground, explaining how the Soviets of 1905 developed into the Soviet government of 1917. In "The Infantile Malady of Communism" he proclaims the legitimacy of the descent. In 1905 the Soviets succeeded in bringing about a strike, which "in its amplitude and vigor was unprecedented in the world." The March 1917 revolution brought about "a bourgeois democratic republic which was more free than any other in the world." There followed the October revolution when "the workers took power for the first time anywhere in the world." But these assertions, though they were pleasing to Lenin, do not offer a theoretical basis for the emergence of the Communist state. He is on safer ground when he explains that revolutions can only be successful when the country is already shattered by a national crisis, when those "who are below" seize the opportunity to take power from "those who are above," and the task becomes all the easier because the existing government is mesmerized by its own powerlessness. Of that particular moment he speaks with authority, but he is less convincing when he speaks of the infantile malady of communism, meaning the seeming incapacity of other communist parties to take power. Their crime is that they are not "sufficiently attentive, sufficiently conscious and sufficiently thoughtful." They are afraid of victory and lose themselves in febrile arguments, disputing all the while about the nature of the communist state they intend to bring into existence, as though the triumph of Russian communism had not shown them the way. They lack subtlety and the spirit of compromise. Lenin explains that compromise is the very essence of the climb to power: one compromises with one's allies to the extent of living with them until it is necessary to destroy them. And remembering how he was once attacked by bandits and escaped alive, he puts forward the chauffeur's theory that it is better to lose an automobile than to lose one's life. The art of revolution is the art of compromise.

So he attacks the foreign communists, proclaiming the rightness of his own carefully contrived compromises while pouring scorn on theirs. He seems to be obscurely aware that the parties in Germany, Italy and France are hopelessly caught on the horns of a dilemma. The workingmen are all in favor of workers' councils, but beyond this they refuse to go. They will not tolerate the iron rule of a few self-selected intellectuals who have never done any manual work in their lives and who know labor only through the mists of theory. "In our party," Lenin writes, *"there have always been* attacks against the dictatorship of the leaders, the first of these attacks, so far as I remember, going back to 1895 before the party had come formally into existence. Even in April 1920, at the Ninth Congress of our party, there was some slight opposition against the dictatorship of the leaders, the oligarchy, etc." It was one of those rare occasions when he admitted that the problem existed.

"The Infantile Malady of Communism" is the least impressive of Lenin's pamphlets. It is oddly garrulous, branching off into disquisitions on subjects which are removed from the main subject, full of complacent tributes to the rightness of the Leninist cause, and astonishingly lacking in awareness of some of the problems which lay at the heart of the Communist mystery. Why was it necessary to have a dictatorship of the proletariat at all? And if by some divinely sanctioned law it was necessary, how could the proletariat exert its dictatorship without surrendering its power to a tyrant? And why had the long-promised European revolution never come about?

During the summer and autumn Lenin learned some hard lessons.

The Poles invaded Russia in force, occupied Kiev, and threatened to occupy the whole of the Ukraine. For a month Pilsudski held Kiev before he was forced to withdraw. Lenin was puzzled. He thought he had excellent sources of information, and he had been told that the Polish workers were busily forming themselves into Soviets. He had received messages from Poland, proclaiming his leadership in the world socialist revolution. His own works were being translated into Polish. Then how could it happen that the workers and peasants of Poland, who served in Pilsudski's army, would dare to attack the fatherland of socialism? He had no answers to these questions except the inevitable answer that the Polish landlords and capitalists were being supplied with German money, and they had hurled themselves against Russia in a mood of panic and desperation.

He decided that the time had come to teach the capitalists a lesson. Against Trotsky's advice he ordered the Red Army to march on Warsaw and to liberate the oppressed workers and peasants from their oppressors. The order to march seems to have been given lightly. Armies of agitators were sent behind the lines, leaflets were dropped by airplane, and it was expected that the well-tried methods of persuasion by terror and by propaganda would be as effective against the Poles as they were against the Russians. For Lenin, Poland was the bridge between Russia and his beloved Germany. Once across the bridge, with the German and Russian Soviets marching together, he would confront Europe with the unpleasant evidence of Soviet power. Then at last there would come about that conflagration which sustained him in his hours of trial. He firmly believed that a Communist victory over Germany meant the conquest of the world.

During those early days, while the Red Army was marching on Warsaw, he was already savoring his triumph. A Polish revolutionary government had been formed in Moscow, and was merely waiting for the signal to take over power. Lenin wrote a long series of hurried telegrams emphasizing the importance of establishing the revolutionary government as soon as possible. Vast sums of money were placed at its disposal, and treaties between the two governments were already drawn up.

Meanwhile a French military mission under General Maxime Weygand had arrived in Warsaw. Lenin possessed for the French mission the same contempt which he felt for all the other foreign military advisers who had helped Yudenich, Denikin and Kolchak on their way to defeat. He was supremely confident of the ability of his young generals, Tukhachevsky and Yegorov, to conquer Poland, and he was especially fond of Budyenny, the young and impulsive cavalry officer with the flaring mustaches, who seemed to have stepped straight out of Gogol's *Taras Bulba*. Trotsky had no faith in the adventure, insisting stubbornly that the Poles would fight tooth and nail for their own soil. Lenin regarded these scruples with a curious mingling of contempt and respect. He felt that Trotsky was incapable of understanding the mentality of the Poles, and at the same time he was continually asking Trotsky for advice, as he searched restlessly for certainties. There were no certainties. There was no carefully thought-out plan of operations. Yegorov, ordered to march on Warsaw, followed the advice of Stalin, his political commissar, and swung west toward the great industrial town of Lvov, in the belief that the workers would immediately rise and join forces with the Red Army. The vanity of Stalin demanded that he should enter Lvov in triumph at the same time that Tukhachevsky entered Warsaw. The Poles waited until the Red Army was at the gates of Warsaw, then they struck. The Russians, caught unawares, thinking they had only to enter the city to be greeted with open arms, panicked, and the headlong retreat degenerated into a wild rout which came to a halt only when the survivors reached Minsk.

Lenin's fury was unbounded. The Second Congress of the Communist International was in session while Tukhachevsky's army was approaching Warsaw. Almost delirious with joy, he briefed the delegates with details of the advance, pointing with a ruler to a large wall map. These briefings were held daily, to the accompaniment of applause and congratulations; and some of the delegates remembered his constant warnings in speeches and articles that revolution can never be imported into another country at the end of a bayonet, a theory which was in direct conflict with the experience of Napoleon. When the news came that the Red Army was in full flight, he called a meeting of the War Council, threatened Yegorov and Stalin with a court martial, and blamed everyone except himself. Yet in his heart he knew he was responsible.

In public speeches he declared that he had never wanted a war with Poland and that he had done everything possible to avoid imposing any more burdens on the sorely tried Russian peasants. At other times he would say that "we were obliged to resort to war under pressure of dire necessity, when our negotiations for an armistice ended in utter failure." To Clara Zetkin, the veteran German Communist, who was then lying ill in Moscow, he was considerably more frank. He told her there were die-hards in the Party who were determined to continue the war and beat Poland to her knees, even if it meant fighting through another long winter, but he had refused in spite of the temptation to build a bridge to Germany. As he sat by her bed, he looked worn and ill, and there were long minutes when he was sunk in reflection. He said:

"So it has happened in Poland, as perhaps it had to happen. You know, of course, all the circumstances that were at work; that our recklessly brave, confident vanguard had no reserves of troops or munitions, and never once got enough dry bread to eat. They had to requisition bread and other essentials from the Polish peasants and middle classes. And in the Red Army the Poles saw enemies, not brothers and liberators. They felt, thought and acted not in a social, revolutionary way, but as nationalists, as imperialists. The revolution in Poland on which we counted did not take place. The workers and peasants, deceived by the adherents of Pilsudski and Daszynski,* defended their class enemy, let our brave Red soldiers starve, ambushed them and beat them to death."

He was making a brave show for the honor of the Red Army, but there was no doubting the sense of bewilderment and grief. He pretended to see the war in terms of the simplicities of the class struggle, the Polish peasants and workers seduced by their reactionary leaders, but he was perfectly aware that the Red Army had committed brutal excesses in its march across Poland. The soldiers had set fire to whole villages, raped and murdered at leisure; and among the many reasons which brought about the defeat of the Red Army were those "requisitions" which Lenin mentioned only in passing.

Lenin was not completely frank with Clara Zetkin, but he was as frank as a man of his temperament could be. He told her that Radek had opposed the invasion from the beginning, and he hinted at violent disagreements between them and a complete break in their relations which ended only when "we were reconciled a short while ago by a long political conversation over the telephone in the middle of the night, or rather toward morning." There is the suggestion that Lenin's conscience troubled him so much that after a sleepless night he called Radek on the telephone, for it is inconceivable that Radek would dare to call him "toward morning." And since he normally regarded Radek as a political simpleton and took pains to make jokes at his expense, there was no satisfaction to be found in the fact that he was wrong and Radek was right.

To veteran Bolsheviks, especially women, Lenin would sometimes open out, and in the most revealing of all the passages in their long conversation he spoke of his dread of another winter of war. He rarely spoke about death. It was a subject which those who knew him carefully avoided mentioning in his presence. Now, suddenly, he found himself confronting death, employing an image which was curiously hard and impersonal, for he spoke of a winter "when millions would starve, would freeze, would die, *desperately silent*." It is the only reference to his particular way of looking at death which has come down to us.

* Daszynski was the leader of the Polish Social Democratic Party.

The conversation with Clara Zetkin seems to have taken place in early October, when Lenin was still overwhelmed by grief over the death of Inessa Armand, who had died of typhus in the Caucasus. Her body was brought back to Moscow. Like a ghost he attended her funeral, so pale and shrunken that he was almost unrecognizable. He had loved her more than he had loved any woman, with a fierce and unrelenting devotion. Krupskaya was his nurse, his companion, his confidante, the woman who saw that he ate regularly and had his hair cut, but it was Inessa Armand, the half-French, half-Scottish daughter of traveling players who gave him joy in life. Her death, following so closely on the defeat of the Red Army in Poland, was a shock from which he never recovered, and from that date he began to age rapidly. Clara Zetkin speaks of his face so lined and troubled, so haunted by grief, that it resembled the dead Christ of the Isenheim altar:

> While Lenin was speaking, his face shrunk before my eyes. Furrows, great and small, innumerable, engraved themselves deeply on it. And every furrow was drawn by a grave trouble or a gnawing pain. An expression of unspoken and unspeakable suffering was on his face. I was moved, shaken. In my mind I saw the picture of a crucified Christ of the medieval master Grünewald. I believe that the painting is known by the title "The Man of Sorrows." Grünewald's crucifixion bears no trace of resemblance to that of Guido Reni's famous, sweet, forgiving martyr, the "soul's bridegroom" of so many adoring old maids and unfortunately married women. Grünewald's Christ is the martyr, the tortured man, cruelly done to death, who "carries the sins of the world." And as such a "man of sorrows" Lenin appeared to me, burdened, pierced, oppressed with all the pain and all the suffering of the Russian working people.

Clara Zetkin's portrait of Lenin as the crucified Christ may not be to everyone's taste. Lenin himself would have been distressed by the comparison, though he sometimes spoke of bearing a cross too heavy for his shoulders. As a confirmed atheist, dedicated to the destruction of the entire priesthood and of all religious worship, he regarded Christ with undisguised hatred, saying that "during all the years of his so-called worship he has been the tool of the oppressors." But the comparison was not completely ill-founded. He was a sick and tortured man, harassed by overwork and by responsibility, suffering continually from insomnia, wracked by headaches, with a bullet in his body which may or may not have been smeared with poison. Krupskaya relates that he looked dreadfully ill at the end of 1919, and at such times he would sometimes sit completely still, doing nothing, simply staring at the wall. A photograph taken in July 1920 shows him peering at the camera with an expression of feverish intensity, heavy rings under the eyes, the lips pursed as though in pain; and breaking through the long furrows across his forehead are those other furrows, like the branches of a tree, which are sometimes found among the mad. It is the face of a man consumed by anxiety, crying out for help and knowing that it is inconceivable that help would ever reach him.

During the hard days at the end of 1919 Inessa had come to see him often, sometimes bringing her youngest daughter Varvara. They would sit in the kitchen, and he would tell stories about the great future of Communism, when there would be peace and plenty for all, the child's eyes sparkling. Those were among his rare moments of pleasure. Now Inessa was dead, and the daydreams were dead, and there was only the long, grueling journey ahead toward an implacable future. "Hard and merciless is the task of communism," he had written, and it was to prove harder and more merciless than he had ever expected.

THE MACHINE BREAKS DOWN

THE YEAR 1921 brought peace to Russia. The White armies which had marched unhindered almost to the gates of Moscow and Petrograd had dissolved and vanished at last, leaving a land in ruins. There had been no real victories during the seven years in which Russia had been continually at war; there were only defeats. Lenin was to claim that the Bolsheviks had triumphed over their enemies because they possessed a superior strategy and because "the whole world admitted to the rightness of the Soviet cause," but in fact the Soviet government came into possession of the land by default. The White generals could not, or would not, introduce the moderate social revolution demanded by the people; Lenin's extreme communism filled the vacuum. It was not what the Russian people wanted, for they were not consulted.

With the wars over, Lenin was the acknowledged master of Russia. He alone possessed the prestige and the authority to invent the rules and regulations by which Russia was to live. Within the Central Committee the commissars would go through the motions of debating on important matters and voting on them, but these nightly meetings seemed to be designed to give him some companionship. He wrote the decrees and saw that they were implemented. He held them all in the hollow of his hand.

Inevitably, with the coming of peace, there was a vast restlessness. Indeed, there was scarcely ever a time when the people were not restless under his autocratic rule. In the spring of 1919 the workers of

530

the Putilov factory had paraded through the streets of Petrograd with banners reading:

> *Doloi Lenina s koninoi.*
> *Daitye tsarya s svininoi.*

> Down with Lenin and horseflesh.
> Give us the Tsar and pork.

Now once again they were restless and discontented, demanding an end to the inhuman sacrifices imposed on them. The Cheka saw to it that the most vocal among them were arrested and shot. But the Bolsheviks were to learn that shooting workers was the least efficient way of entering their good graces. Discontent was reaching high into government circles. Most of the factories were shut down for lack of raw materials; the peasants were destroying their grain and livestock to prevent them from falling into the hands of the requisition squads; the economic life of the country was coming to a standstill. Lenin knew that the country was in desperate straits. Writing to Krzhizhanovsky in February 1921, he said, "It is quite useless to work on vast bureaucratic schemes of state economy. We are beggared. This is what we are—starving, destitute beggars."

Over his ruined kingdom Lenin was determined to rule singlehanded. He refused to admit any diminution of his powers. When friends and long acquaintances suggested that the time had come to restrict the powers of the Central Committee at least to the extent of surrendering the control of the factories to the trade unions, Lenin shot back with the announcement that such suggestions bordered on treason and consisted of "anarcho-syndicalist deviations." The two leaders of the movement, Shlyapnikov and Kollontay, were regarded as heretics. Shlyapnikov was a former metalworker, Kollontay a former journalist, and neither had the intellectual equipment to fight off Lenin's massive attacks on them, which were delivered with his customary irony and sarcasm. But the movement, which came to be known as the "Workers' Opposition," pointed to the growing dissatisfaction of the workers. Had they gone through those seven years of war only to be ruled by a small clique in the Kremlin which never listened to their justifiable demands?

For Lenin power was always one and indivisible. He could not tolerate, or even imagine, a state of affairs in which the monolithic power of the party was divided. At all costs authority must be upheld, and anyone who ventured to dispute his authority must be crushed. Ironically, the first to dispute his authority were the sailors of Kronstadt. Trotsky called them "the pride and glory of the revolution." Lenin had held them in even greater honor, for at times of danger he would say: "We can't fail because we have the sailors with us."

The Kronstadt sailors were no longer with him. They detested one-man rule and wanted to be heard. They had a new slogan: "The Soviets without Communism." If this slogan spread over Russia Lenin knew that there would be an end of the party.

On March 1, 1921, an open-air rally was held at Kronstadt attended by 16,000 sailors. The meeting had been summoned by the sailors of the *Petropavlovsk* and the *Sevastopol,* who had drawn up a lengthy resolution protesting against the excesses of the regime. The preamble of the resolution dismissed in a single sentence all the pretensions of the Soviet government. It stated:

> Whereas the present Soviets do not represent the will of the workers and peasants, new elections should be held immediately by secret ballot, and before the elections a free campaign should be conducted among all workers and peasants.

There followed fourteen clauses demanding freedom of speech, press and assembly, the right of the peasants to keep cattle, the equalization of rations, the abolition of political control by a single party, and the freeing of prisoners who had been arrested in connection with labor and peasant movements. There were clauses demanding the abolition of specifically Communist detachments in the army and the dissolution of the Communist shock brigades which kept guard over the factories. The final clause demanded the return of small-scale private enterprise.

The Kronstadt resolution was in effect an appeal to a more flexible kind of socialism, without tyranny and without the intolerable abuses of the Cheka. It appealed for the return of the rights and privileges of the workers. It stated, very clearly and authentically, that the sailors were weary of being ruled by the dogmatic machine in Moscow and wanted immediate changes. The apologists for the Kronstadt sailors were to say there was nothing in the least rebellious in the resolution. On the contrary the resolution was itself an act of rebellion against the Soviet power, and Mikhail Kalinin, who represented the government at the meeting, returned to Moscow full of foreboding, knowing that only two alternatives confronted the government—either it must submit to the demands of the Kronstadt sailors and lose its authoritarian character, or it must destroy the rebellion.

The officers at Kronstadt advised the sailors to seize Petrograd at once. They refused. They were fired by a belief in the invincibility of their cause: it was enough to proclaim the new freedom and the whole of Russia would rise against a government "which had withdrawn from the masses and proved itself incompetent to deal with the situation." They seized the local printing plant, and on March 3 published the first issue of their newspaper, the Kronstadt *Izvestiya*. On the first page of the first issue appeared an appeal for a calm and pacific temper:

> Comrades and citizens! The Revolutionary Committee is anxious that not a single drop of blood be shed. The Committee is exerting all its efforts to bring about revolutionary order in the city, the fortress and the fortifications. Do not stop work! Workers, remain at your machines. Sailors and soldiers, remain at your posts. All Soviet workers and institutions should continue at their posts. The Revolutionary Committee calls upon you, comrades and citizens, to work unceasingly in good order to bring about the conditions necessary for honest and just elections of the new Soviet.

The sailors of Kronstadt were brave men, but inept revolutionaries. They believed wholeheartedly in their pacific propaganda. It was as though they suffered from some strange disease compounded of hope and benevolence, and believed they could infect the whole of Russia with their disease. It never occurred to them until too late that Lenin was implacable and ruthless, and would sign the death warrant of the Kronstadt sailors with the same careless ease as he had signed the death warrant of the bourgeoisie.

Lenin ordered the destruction of Kronstadt unless the sailors surrendered. "Believe me," he wrote, "there can only be two kinds of government in Russia—tsarism or the Soviets." The free soviets of the sailors constituted a third, impermissible kind of government. He was particularly disturbed by the sailors' public demand for the revival of the Constituent Assembly.

Trotsky was given full powers to quell the rebellion. He arrived in Petrograd on March 5, and his first act was to issue an ultimatum in the name of the government. He declared that if they persisted in their folly they would be shot down "like partridges." The workers of Petrograd were seething with discontent; but the Cheka was watchful, and

Zinoviev, who occupied the position corresponding to lieutenant governor of Petrograd, was determined to keep a tight rein on the workers. At his orders workmen who came out on strike in sympathy with the sailors were shot. Even when it became evident that the Soviet government was prepared to throw all available forces against Kronstadt, the sailors made no effort to attack. They could have wiped out the shore batteries at Sestroretsk and Lisy Nos; they could have taken Oranienbaum with ease; they could have steamed up the Neva and stormed Petrograd; at the very least they could have used their ships to plow up the thin ice to prevent troops from making their way across the ice against them. If they had known what would happen, they would have delayed calling for a revolt against the government until the ice had melted, when Kronstadt would have been unassailable and impregnable. Instead, they invited disaster. For seven days the Kronstadt *Izvestiya* preached passive revolution. On the eighth day the army of Trotsky struck.

The shore batteries opened fire, while picked Communist troops clad in white capes made their way across the ice in the teeth of a snowstorm. Wave after wave of white-clad troops were hurled against Kronstadt only to be thrown back. On March 8 the extraordinary *Izvestiya* reported mournfully:

> Then to your misfortunes there was added a terrible snowstorm while black night shrouded everything in darkness. Nevertheless the Communist executioners, without counting the cost, drove you across the ice, threatening you in the rear with their machine guns aimed by the Communist squads.
>
> Many of you perished that night on the icy vastness of the Gulf of Finland. When day broke and the storm died down, there was only a pitiful remnant of you left, exhausted and hungry, scarcely able to move, coming to us clad in your white shrouds.

Day after day armies were sent across the ice, while the sailors fought with the fury of despair. Red military cadets, tribesmen from Central Asia, Lettish sharpshooters, Chekists and regular troops from all the garrisons within reach of Petrograd were thrown into the fighting. The sailors had not even troubled to send their own men to Oranienbaum to seize the food stored there: they believed in the justice of their cause and relied on Providence to support them. They fought magnificently, but they were hopelessly outnumbered and outmaneuvered, and Providence was in no mood to protect those who do not help themselves. The final attack came on the night of March 16 with simultaneous assaults from the north, south and east. By morning the battle was over, and there remained only the brief mopping-up campaign.

Even Tukhachevsky, who was in operational command of the final assault, was surprised by the desperate determination of these men fighting against hopeless odds. "It was not a battle, but an inferno," he wrote. "The sailors fought like wild beasts. I cannot understand where they found the strength for such furious rage. Every house had to be taken by storm."

Nearly all the sailors who survived the final assault were shot. Barely a hundred escaped over the ice to Finland. Kronstadt became a desert.

Lenin had given the order for the destruction of Kronstadt. In no mood for half-measures, he suggested that the ships of the Baltic fleet should be sunk: they were no more than useless encumbrances to his regime. He explained that the sailors served no useful purpose and consumed food and clothing of which the country was desperately short. He had convinced himself that they were reactionaries, anarchists, Mensheviks and White Guards; foreign money had been poured into Kronstadt; they were being led by a tsarist general. All these statements were untrue. In an incautious moment at the Tenth Party Congress, which was being held while Kronstadt was under fire, he admitted that "they do not want the White Guards, nor do they want our power." And he took what comfort he could from the fact that only 35,000 men died in the battle. "It was an absolutely insignificant incident," he declared in an article published in the Petrograd *Pravda*. "It was a much smaller threat to the existence of the Soviet power than the uprising of the Irish against the British Empire."

So perhaps it was; but the circumstances were very different. The sailors were Russians fighting on Russian soil on behalf of the free Soviets, a peculiarly Russian form of government; they were not ethnic enemies with a long history of bitterness behind them. The Kronstadt and Irish uprisings were not "absolutely insignificant events." They were both major catastrophes.

Lenin blamed everyone except himself. He blamed foreign interventionists, though they were notably absent. Many of the sailors came from the peasantry, and so he blamed "the dissatisfaction among the peasantry." He blamed the Socialist Revolutionaries working in co-operation with the White Guards; but except for his unsupported statement, there was no evidence that the Socialist Revolutionaries or White Guards were present. By blaming all he blamed none. He knew he was guilty, for he abruptly changed the course of Soviet history by introducing the New Economic Policy, so giving some small freedoms to the hard-pressed Russian people.

The New Economic Policy involved a radical departure from the theory of communism as Lenin described it in *The State and Revolution*. By abolishing the state monopoly of trading in grain, by abandoning the system of requisitioning grain and by substituting a fixed tax in kind or in currency, Lenin knew that he was opening the way to a modified form of capitalism. But though capitalism was being revived, it was state capitalism. All large industry and all foreign trade remained in the hands of the Soviet government. Small industries, involving no more than seventy men, were leased to private ownership. The peasants were allowed to trade their surplus grain on the open market. The idea of selling for profit, which had previously been regarded as a crime against the state, was now officially encouraged.

Outwardly these changes represented only a marginal factor in the total economy, but the psychological effects were breathtaking. The economic machine had ground to a standstill, and the government had been powerless to move it. Where the government failed, private initiative stepped in to provide the new blood which coursed through the whole economy. Under the New Economic Policy the machine began to move forward hopefully.

Lenin described the New Economic Policy as a strategic retreat, a difficult military operation calling for the utmost discipline:

> This discipline must be all the more conscious and it must be imposed a hundred times more strictly because, when a whole army retreats, it has no clear understanding and cannot see where it will stop: it sees only retreat. Sometimes a few panic voices are enough to start everyone running. At such times the dangers are immense. When such a retreat is carried out by a real army, then machine guns are brought forward and when the orderly retreat becomes a rout, the command is given: "Fire!" And rightly so . . . At such moments it is indispensable to punish strictly, severely, and mercilessly the slightest breach of discipline.

Lenin had no illusions about the difficulty of reconciling a retreat with the forward march of socialism, and when he spoke of "strictly, severely, and mercilessly" punishing the slightest breach of discipline he meant exactly what he said. The New Economic Policy was state capitalism severely rationed, and with the new economic freedom went a tightening of ideological discipline. Toward the end of November 1917 he had described free criticism as "the duty of the revolutionary." Now criticism of any kind was outlawed, and the duty of the revolutionary was only to obey.

After the Tenth Party Congress an absolute obedience to the decisions of the Central Committee was demanded. In the past, of course, Lenin's word had been law, and the decisions of the Central Committee had the effect of law. But there had always been permissible areas of discussion both before and after the passing of the law, and indeed within clear limits discussion was officially encouraged. Kronstadt taught Lenin that there must be changes in the form of socialism, but it also taught him that he was far from possessing the unalloyed allegiance of the country; and the Cheka was once more given strict orders to root out the enemies of the regime. The "free association of independent, critically thinking and courageous revolutionaries" came at last to an end, and what was left of the Menshevik and Socialist Revolutionary Parties perished during that spring before the firing squads of the Cheka or escaped into exile abroad.

Lenin's hold on the country was still tenuous. Revolts were continually breaking out. The most serious was the peasant rebellion in Tambov province under Gerasim Antonov, which was put down by Tukhachevsky with the usual merciless vigor. But massacre by Bolshevik troops was not the worst of the evils which confronted the long-suffering peasants. Already in spring there were reports of droughts, dust storms and invasions of locusts in the rich farming land of the Volga. The famine was even more widespread than the famine of 1891. The peasants abandoned their farms and sought safety in the towns, which could neither feed them adequately nor give them shelter. They came like hordes of locusts which ate up everything in their path. They died in their millions. No accurate figures were ever made available; nor could they be made available, though Sverdlov computed that some 27,000,000 were affected.

The horror of the famine exceeded anything that had happened in four years of war and three of civil war. The despised capitalist countries, which Lenin had hoped to destroy, came to the rescue. Nansen's Red Cross Relief and the American Relief Administration under Herbert Hoover were permitted under stringent regulations to save the lives of the Russian peasants. Lenin was so appalled by the thought of America contaminating the Soviets that he gave instructions that American relief could be given only to children, who were assumed to be immune from capitalist contagion; and for a whole year his ordinance was observed. Finally it was decided that it was impracticable to feed the children while letting their parents starve, and the Americans quietly disobeyed the ordinance. About half of the Russians who served under the Americans in the relief organization were later arrested on the grounds that contact with the Americans must inevitably have led them to become "counterrevolutionary elements."

Lenin's attitude toward the famine was curiously remote, cold and disinterested. He seemed to regard the famine as only one more of the obstacles that had blocked his path since he became the undisputed dictator of Russia. He kept apart from the negotiations and made only one appeal for help; characteristically the appeal, which appeared in *Pravda* on August 6, 1921, was addressed to the workmen and small farmers of the world—as though he wanted to impose severe limits on the sources of charity. The appeal took the form of a violent attack on the capitalists, blaming them for the war and the civil war, and warning of more capitalist interventions and conspiracies in the future. He wrote:

> In Russia in several *guberniya* there is a famine scarcely less extensive than the famine of 1891.
> This is the difficult legacy which has come to Russia after seven years of war, first the imperialist war and then the civil war, which landlords and capitalists of all countries imposed on the workers and peasants.
> Help is demanded. The Soviet republic of workers and peasants expects this help from the working people, those who live by their labor and the small farmers . . .
> The capitalists of all countries are taking revenge on the Soviet republic. They are making new plans for further incursions, interventions and counterrevolutionary conspiracies.
> We are convinced that the workers and small farmers from all over the world, who live by their labor, will come to our rescue with still greater energy and self-sacrifice.

There is no escaping the authoritarian tone—"Help is demanded. *Trebyuetsya pomoshch*." The Patriarch of the Russian Orthodox Church, having taken care to secure Lenin's permission, appealed in more generous terms to the Christians of the entire world to help the hungry women and children of Russia. But neither the Patriarch nor

Lenin was so effective as Maxim Gorky who sent a telegram to Herbert Hoover appealing to "all the honest men and women in Europe and America to render help to the Russian people by giving us bread and medical supplies" and received an affirmative answer the same day. Hoover's representative met Litvinov in Riga to discuss the terms under which the supplies were to be distributed. Litvinov seemed to be more concerned with drawing up an elaborate protocol than in getting immediate help. When the American objected to the length and complexity of the agreement, saying, "After all, Mr. Litvinov, you ought to remember that what we want is to get food into Russia," Litvinov, the master of socialist dialectics, answered: "Food can be a weapon."

Food was indeed a weapon, and no one was more conscious of it than Lenin, who resented as an intolerable abuse of power the army of American soup kitchens.

There were many other things he resented. The state he had brought into existence could only be managed by a vast army of bureaucrats. Now with the coming of peace the administrative officers began to replace the ideologists; on the innumerable committees sat the bureaucrats and party functionaries who had replaced the revolutionary idealists. The new bureaucracy was as incompetent and high-handed as the bureaucracy under the Tsar. Bribery, corruption, all the vices of the old capitalist order, remained to haunt the new socialist republic. The country, bureaucratized to the last degree, was being strangled in red tape. Appalled, Lenin wrote letter after letter urging the bureaucrats to behave as servants of the public, not as their masters. He ordered that every Soviet institution put up a sign giving its reception days and hours, "not just inside the building, but outside as well, so that the people can avail themselves of this information without applying for a pass." People must be permitted to enter all government buildings freely and there must be a visitors' book to record the name of the visitor and the purpose of his errand. And while the bureaucrats on the public level behaved with their habitual indifference toward the public, the bureaucrats at a much higher level were behaving in exactly the same way. Three high officials, Tsyurupa, Kursky and Avanessov, had been placed in charge of producing Fowler plows. After months of deliberation and planning, and after producing a mountain of letters, reports, and suggestions for improvement, they had finally produced five experimental plows, although two thousand had been demanded. Lenin exploded in a long letter to Bogdanov in which he pointed out that the culprits should be brought to trial even if their only punishment was to be rapped lightly on the wrists, since they were men who had occupied important positions during the revolution and extreme punishment could therefore not be demanded of them. He wrote out the text of a suggested reprimand, and added:

> Surely, if such an *exemplary* decision were handed down, you could not deny its usefulness? Its *social* importance is 1,000 times greater than a secret-inside-the-party-chekist-idiotic-suppression-without-publicity of a filthy affair of dirty red tape.
> You are in principle absolutely wrong. You don't know how to try people publicly for dirty red tape: for that we should all of us, together with the People's Commissariat of Justice, be emphatically hanged on putrid ropes. And I have not lost hope that one day we shall be deservedly hanged.

The letter was written toward the end of December after a year of endless frustrations, of growing awareness of his own guilt, and of bewilderment before the monster he had created. Kronstadt, the Antonov rebellion, the New Economic Policy, the massive famine of the summer and autumn, all these things seemed to have been invented by the devil to torment him just at the moment when he had hoped to bring about the world-wide revolution of socialism. He had hoped to see America and Europe shriveling in the revolutionary flame, and instead Americans and Europeans were giving food to his peasants.

Increasingly he felt out of touch with the mood of his own people. The Kronstadt sailors complained that life under his tyrannical rule was "dull and lifeless"; and now at last he too was complaining of the dullness and lifelessness of the regime over which he ruled. He found no sustenance in poetry or in the arts, rarely visited the theater, and saw less and less of the common people. Earlier in the year he was incensed when he discovered that 5,000 copies had been printed of a book of poems by Mayakovsky. "It's nothing but rubbish, stupidity, double-dyed silliness and pretentiousness," he wrote. "In my opinion 500 copies would have been enough." He was troubled with insomnia, nausea, and fainting spells. He had reduced the amount of his work, taken long rests, and he was beginning to recognize the need for a long vacation. On December 7, finally bowing to his doctors' orders, he left the Kremlin and retired to Gorki. On that day he wrote to Molotov:

> I am leaving today. In spite of my reduced quota of work and an increased quota of rest during these last days, insomnia has devilishly strengthened its grip on me. I am afraid I shall not be able to speak either at the party conference or at the Soviet Congress.

The machine was breaking down.

THE LONG DEATH

I am, I believe, strongly guilty before the workers of Russia. . . .

THE BITTEREST BLOW

FOR LENIN the bitterest blow of all was that he should be incapacitated at a time when he felt he was most needed. The machinery of government had ground to a standstill, and he knew that he alone could set it in motion again.

His rage and despair were boundless, and he made no effort to hide his bitterness. He who had ruled by decree and invented a hundred new administrative offices was in a mood to consign decrees and administrative offices to the dustbin of history. He wrote to Tsyurupa on February 21, 1922: "Everything among us is drowned in a filthy swamp of bureaucratic 'administrations.' Great authority and strength will be needed to overcome them. Administrative offices—madness! Decrees—lunacy! Search for the right men, ensure that the work is properly carried out—that's all that's necessary!" A week later he wrote to the chief administrative officer of the State Bank: "The truth is that the State Bank is nothing more than a series of bureaucratic paper tricks. That's the truth, if you want to know the *truth*, and not the sweet nothings of our Communist bureaucrats, which no doubt you feed on, since you are a high official." He went on to talk of the lies spread by Communist bureaucrats and the Potemkin villages they had erected in the name of bureaucracy, and in all this the State Bank was "zero, less than zero."

He was suffering from terrible headaches which drove him almost frantic with pain, and he was already a very sick man when he addressed the Eleventh Congress of the Communist Party at the end of March. He made four speeches, which were notable for their harsh and relentless tone. His original notes for the speech delivered on March 27 have survived. Here in those tightly knit sentences fired at the page like bullets he expressed his belief in the continuing supremacy of the Soviet State above all other states, though there are some occasional complaints of the appalling cultural inferiority of the Communists who rule the state. Among the notes are to be found the following ideas to be developed more fully in the speech:

State capitalism. The state is *"us."*

End of the retreat. Not in the sense: "We have already learned," but in the sense: not nervously, not inventing anything, but learning within definite limits, "regrouping and preparing our strength" = the slogan of the day.

Slogan = Prepare for an offensive *on private capital.*

Compare the conqueror and the conquered: which is the more cultured? Of 4700 responsible communists in Moscow and the Moscow bureaucracy.

We have enough strength to win the battle for the New Economic Policy, both politically and economically. The *"only"* question is *culture.*

The White Guards (including *Mensheviks* and *Socialist Revolutionaries* and Co.) see in this something they can use! How wrong they are! Survey of what has been done and what has been left undone would be useful.

The Soviet state. First in the world. A new age: worse than *the first steam engine!!*

The heart of the question does not lie in administrations, nor in reorganizations, nor in new decrees, but in *people* and ensuring that *they fulfill their tasks.*

The crucial question (the link in the chain) = the gap between the immensity of our tasks and our *poverty* not only in materials but also *in culture.*

We must be at the head of the masses, or else we are only a drop in the ocean.

The time for propaganda by decree is over. The masses understand and value *only* effective, practical work, *practical* success in economic and cultural work.

As for the Mensheviks and Socialist Revolutionaries: *they should be shot as traitors.*

When Lenin rose to speak, these single bullets were transformed into barrage after barrage of machine-gun fire. The undisguised hatred of the enemy was never so sharply expressed. He elaborates and embroiders on the original notes, but they lose none of their desolate power in the elaboration. Of the Mensheviks he says:

> They are saying now: "The revolution went too far. We have always said what you are saying here; permit us to repeat it for you." And we answer: "Permit us to put you up against the wall . . ." For the public advocacy of Menshevism our revolutionary courts must pass death sentences.

The time had come to put an end to the New Economic Policy, or at least to impose heavy restrictions upon free trading:

> For a year we have been retreating. We must now say in the name of the Party—Enough! The purpose of the retreat has been achieved. This period is coming, or has already come to a close. Now our purpose is different—to regroup our forces.

He poured scorn on the communist bureaucrats who thought that simply by calling themselves communists they were therefore better men than the capitalists:

> By your side there is the capitalist going about the business of being a robber and making profits, but he knows his job. And you—you are trying new methods; you make no profits; you have communist principles, excellent ideals—they are written large on you—you are holy men who will enter paradise alive—but do you know your business?

So he hammered away at the inadequacies, stupidities, and irrelevancies of Soviet government; the abuses of power, the stagnation in the administrative departments, and the intolerable weight of red tape. These were matters on which he could speak with authority, since he had largely brought them into being; and while paying tribute to the culture of "the old Western civilization" and taunting the Soviets for being without culture, he yet maintains that his own program is the only one, the correct and inevitable one. At intervals amid the scorn comes the threat of naked power directed not only against the Mensheviks and Socialist Revolutionaries but against any party members who disagree with him.

Decisions made at the Eleventh Congress were to affect the future of Russia for generations. The hard line, the threat of continual purges, the determination to abandon the New Economic Policy, and the ambivalent attitude toward capitalism were to remain unchanged. A tired, sick, baffled man had spoken in scorn and detestation of the bureaucracy which was to increase its powers vastly, but there were no magic potions which could make it vanish in thin air. The measure of Lenin's dissatisfaction with the Soviet state was given in the curious preliminary note: "The Soviet state. First in the world. A new age: worse than *the first steam engine!!*" As he explained in his speech, "Our machine is a bad one, but the first steam engine is said to have been a bad one. The State machinery may be execrable, but it exists; the greatest of all inventions has been accomplished; the Proletarian State has been created." He had created an iron child, and was not pleased with it.

One further decision made during the course of the Congress was to affect the lives of nearly all those who were close to Lenin during his rise to power. Stalin was appointed general secretary of the Central Committee. How this was accomplished is unknown, for he had spent the greater part of his time in the comparatively minor post of Commissar of Nationalities and his elevation to the Workers' and Peasants' Inspectorate was not thought to be a steppingstone to great authority. Lenin liked him because he got things done; he had no moral scruples against using a man who had never considered the existence of moral scruples. Stalin was hard-working, ambitious, supremely competent. He was that very rare thing—a Georgian with a Germanic talent for organization. Trotsky would say that Lenin despised Stalin long before the Eleventh Congress, but there is no evidence for it. Stalin had exceptional talents, but they were not of the highest order; and the mystery is how he maneuvered himself into Lenin's affections to the extent of being given such a high office: for there is no doubt that he was Lenin's appointee.

The decision to appoint Stalin to the post of general secretary seems to have been made on April 3, the day after the Congress closed. It was announced in *Pravda* the following day. A week later Lenin proposed that Trotsky should be made deputy chairman of the Council of People's Commissars, thus becoming heir to the throne. It was a sumptuous gift, but Trotsky rejected it for reasons which were characteristic of his subtle and nervous mind. Pride and humility were equally balanced in the rejection. He knew he was unworthy of the position; he also knew that no one else was worthy. He felt, too, that it was an honor to be fought for, not received as a gift. The majority of members of the Central Committee were Jews, and he was acutely conscious of his Jewishness and the anomaly of a small group of Jews ruling over a country where the Jews had never been completely assimilated in the population. He felt strongly that the leader of the country should not be a Jew; he was equally convinced that he should not be a Georgian. He prized his own talents highly, but they were no more than talents. In Lenin he recognized the quality of genius, and for all the affection between them, and for all Trotsky's highhanded manner and natural haughtiness, he recognized his inferiority in the presence of genius. At the moment when he rejected the succession, he seems to have known dimly that he was signing his own death warrant.

Exhausted by conferences and speechmaking, Lenin returned to Gorki. The headaches were growing worse: a German doctor gave it as his opinion that they were due to lead poisoning from the two bullets still embedded in his body. Dr. Rozanov was consulted; he said he had never heard of headaches due to lead poisoning from bullets, and he strenuously objected to removing the bullets at all. If necessary, the bullet in the neck could be removed without too much difficulty. "Very well," said Lenin, "remove the one in the neck. Then I won't be bothered, and people won't be expressing their fears all the time."

X rays were taken; and on the following day, April 23, the operation took place. Only a local anesthetic was given. Lenin took the operation calmly and seems to have suffered no pain. According to Maria Ilyinichna the bullet was found to have a crosswise incision like a dumdum bullet and to have been smeared with curare. "He was saved for us by an infinitely rare chance," she wrote. "The explosive bullet did not explode, and for unknown reasons the poison lost its virulence." But Dr. Rozanov, who provides a lengthy account of the operation, says nothing about curare or about a dumdum bullet. It was so slight an operation that he thought it likely that Lenin would return to the Kremlin within half an hour. The actual operation was for obvious reasons performed by Dr. Burkhardt, a German specialist, with Rozanov acting as his assistant. Burkhardt had brought a great array of instruments with him. Lenin refused to be intimidated by them; a day or two later he explained how he would himself have performed the operation: "I would have pinched the flesh and cut. The bullet would have jumped out. All the rest is merely decoration." The doctors laughed; they were aware that in his own way he was a master surgeon.

He was kept under observation for a day and a night. Krupskaya and Maria Ilyinichna came to the hospital, to see that he was well cared for. He occupied a room in the female ward and made no objection when the doctors gave him a physical examination. There were no alarming symptoms except that he was suffering from nervous exhaustion due to overwork; he complained of headaches, sleeplessness and lassitude, but gave an impression of healthy vigor. He laughed and joked, and went to some pains to put the doctors at their ease. When Rozanov was asked whether he had any desire which Lenin could fulfill, he answered that he would like to take a holiday in Riga.

"Why not a holiday in Germany?" Lenin asked.

"If I went to Germany I would be running to see all the clinics and hospitals," Rozanov said.

"Very well, you shall go to Riga."

In spite of the inexplicable headaches, he was more concerned with the health of Krupskaya, who was being treated by Dr. Guetier, and he therefore asked Dr. Rozanov to make sure that Krupskaya would pay more attention to her doctor.

"Even when she is ill," Lenin complained, "she says she is feeling well."

"Well, you do the same," Rozanov said.

Lenin laughed and said, "What else can I do? I have to get on with my work."

He spent about a week in the Kremlin and then returned to Gorki.

His most important work was concerned with punishment. He enjoyed drawing up codes of law, and the time had come for a comprehensive law which would finally dispose by death sentences of the Mensheviks and the Socialist Revolutionaries. The full weight of the terror must be brought against them. As he explained in a letter to Kursky, the Commissar of Justice, the time for half-measures had passed, and the need to change the existing laws was overdue. He therefore drew up in legal form a statement of the crime and the resulting punishment as he would like it to appear in the law books. It read:

> Propaganda or agitation or participation in an organization or cooperation with organizations having the effect (propaganda and agitation) of assisting in the slightest way that part of the international bourgeoisie that does not recognize the equal rights of the communist system which is coming to take its place, and which is endeavoring to overthrow it by force, whether by intervention or by blockade or by espionage or by financing of the press, or by any other means whatsoever—

is punishable by death, or in mitigating circumstances by imprisonment or exile beyond the frontiers of the country.

It was a strange law, and it was put to strange uses, for Stalin appealed to this law when he decided to bring about the downfall of all the associates of Lenin who might become his rivals for power. Stalin rarely invoked the clause relating to "mitigating circumstances."

The savage letter to Kursky was written on May 17. Nine days later the telephone rang in Dr. Rozanov's office at ten o'clock in the morning. It was Maria Ilyinichna speaking from Gorki: "Please come at once. Volodya has pains in the stomach and he is vomiting."

In such circumstances a doctor never goes alone to attend his patient. He calls in other doctors, so that he will not be accused of counterrevolutionary behavior if anything goes wrong. In the automobile taking him to Gorki were seven or eight other doctors including Dr. Dmitry Ulyanov, Lenin's brother, Semashko, Belenky, and Levin, who was later executed for giving poison to Maxim Gorky. The manor house where Lenin was living was being repaired and he was now living in a much smaller house in the grounds. He had eaten fish the previous day, and there was some doubt whether it was fresh: perhaps that was the explanation of the vomiting. He had slept badly, walked in the garden during the night, and in the morning he had suffered acute stomach pains and headaches. But more troubling to the doctors was the slurring of his speech and traces of partial paralysis on the right side. "It is one thing to establish a diagnosis and to confirm the cause of a man's sufferings," wrote Dr. Rozanov, "but it is quite another thing to recognize suddenly that a man is suffering from an irremediable disease." For the first time the doctors were aware that Lenin's brain was damaged. He could still talk; he could still invent laws; he could still govern; but they knew that he had had his first stroke.

Maria Ilyinichna went on talking hopefully about the fish, until they asked her whether anyone else had vomited after eating it. No one had.

He was ordered to rest, to restrict his work to a minimum, and to see no visitors. He must spend most of the day in bed. The doctors prepared for a long tussle with a difficult patient.

Three weeks after the first stroke he was loudly protesting that he was perfectly well and should be allowed to read and write letters and see visitors. The doctors were pitiless, insisting that he must do no work at all; and when he asked what he was suffering from they were deliberately evasive. He had some trouble with his eyes, and when Dr. Mikhail Auerbach called to examine them, Lenin took him aside and said, "They say you are a brave man. Tell me the truth. Is it paralysis, and is it getting worse?" Then the voice changed, and he said, "If it is paralysis, what use would I be, and who would have need of me?" It was the only time in his life he ever begged for mercy.

Dr. Auerbach was lucky, for at that moment a nurse came in, and the questions were left unanswered.

By mid-July he had intimidated the doctors to the extent that he was permitted to read, to order books from his library in the Kremlin, and to see a few visitors. He was forbidden however to read newspapers. Victor Ulyanov, the five-year-old son of his brother Dmitry, came to stay at Gorki, and they would wander out in the afternoon to pick berries. Anna Elizarova also came. Mostly the visitors were relatives. Once Stalin came, and he reported later that Lenin had the air of a front-line soldier who "after strenuous battles has been removed to a rest camp far behind the battle lines." To Stalin he looked well, and his illness had not affected the ironical glint in his eye.

"They won't let me read the newspapers," Lenin told Stalin. "I'm not allowed to talk politics. So I carefully avoid even the smallest piece of paper lying on the table for fear it might be a newspaper. I must obey the doctors' orders."

Thereupon they laughed and disobeyed the doctors' orders by talking politics.

A month later Stalin came again. He found Lenin changed for the better, with no traces of nervousness, quietly content. There had been a good harvest for the first time since the Soviets came to power.

"The hardest days are behind us," Lenin said. "The good harvest makes everything easier. Industry and the financial situation will improve. Now the task is to rid the state of everything that is redundant and useless. We shall have to decrease the number of administrative departments and improve the work of those that remain. If we do this, and if we insist firmly on good work being done, then we shall come out of it with flying colors."

Of the capitalist powers he said, "They are greedy and detest each other, and will end by tearing each other apart. Useless to put pressure on us. Our road is certain: we are for peace and general harmony, but we will not be enslaved by them. We must keep a firm hand on the wheel, and follow our own road, whatever they do to us. Menaces and flattery won't help them."

According to Stalin, who published an account of their conversation in September, he was as merciless as ever to the Mensheviks and Socialist Revolutionaries.

"They have given themselves the aim of defaming the Russia of the Soviets, making it easier for the imperialists to fight against us. Drowned in the mud of capitalism, they are plunging into the abyss."

Stalin spoke about the many legends of his death circulating in foreign newspapers. Lenin laughed and said, "Let them lie and console one another. One should not remove the last consolations from those who are in agony."

Though he was ill, it was clear that he had not become gentler. The All-Russian Central Executive Committee, the Soviet parliament of delegates from municipal and village soviets, had always had a Russian in the chair. The parliament met irregularly, and its purpose was to rubber-stamp the decisions of the Central Committee. Lenin decided that the time had come to attack Great Russian chauvinism, which he had long detested. He wrote:

> I declare war to the death on Great Russian chauvinism. As soon as I get rid of this damned tooth, I'll set all my good teeth into it and devour it.
>
> We must *absolutely insist* that the Union All-Russian Central Executive Committee should be presided over in turn by (a) a Russian, (b) a Ukrainian, (c) a Georgian.

The letter was dated September 6. About this time a photographer took a series of photographs of him in Gorki. Some twenty photographs were taken. We see Lenin reclining in his study or walking among the pines, wearing the familiar workman's cap, a military jacket buttoned at the neck, and the laced-up boots with the heavy heels which permitted him to add an inch to his stature. He seems to enjoy being photographed, and looks gentle enough. His cheeks are plump, he has developed a paunch, the mustache and thick stub of beard have been trimmed, and he smiles faintly. One of these photographs shows him sitting alone on a white bench, wearing a greatcoat, with his hands folded on his lap, and there is about that face a look of extraordinary pride and self-assurance, but it is not the face of the

"I declare war to the death on Great Russian chauvinism. . . ." On the bottom-left-hand corner of the second sheet Stalin added the word "Correct" and his initials "J. St."

Lenin we have known. It is as though he had borrowed the mask of someone else, as though another face lay beneath it. The eyes are more Mongoloid than ever, the lips more pursed. The calm is illusory. For the first and last time we are permitted to watch the progress of his disease.

Toward the end of September the doctors relented. There was still a faint slurring of the speech and fleeting traces of paralysis on the right side, but after four months of rest it was thought that he had recovered sufficiently to resume work in the Kremlin on a reduced scale. The doctors ordered him to work no more than five hours a day on five days a week: instead he worked ten hours a day, and on the two days he was not permitted to work he held conferences in his apartment.

He arrived in Moscow on October 2. On the previous day he had sent a message to his office: "I am coming tomorrow, prepare everything, minutes of meetings, books." He was in high spirits. His staff became his willing accomplices in the conspiracy against the doctors. When one of the doctors found him hard at work, he answered, "I'm not working—just reading." He attended the evening meetings of the Central Committee as before, permitting himself the luxury of holding them a little earlier: it pleased the doctors to know that he was going to bed earlier. A stream of orders and letters poured from his desk. He was in harness again.

His first public appearance took place at the meeting of the All-Russian Central Executive Committee on October 31, 1922. The meeting was held in the vast seventy-foot-high Throne Room of St. Andrew in the Great Kremlin Palace, with its painted ceiling and immense gilded columns. The throne was still in its accustomed place, but invisible behind a huge red sounding board mounted on the platform. Some three hundred delegates were present, wrapped in their fur coats, for the ice was already beginning to form on the Moskva river. He arrived while Krylenko was drearily announcing the new laws. He made his way quietly along the side of the hall, passed the press table, and was still some steps away from the platform before he was recognized, then a great cheer went up. George Seldes, who was present, wrote that he wore a cheap gray semimilitary uniform and gray-black trousers with the crease already giving because there was so much shoddy in the wool. His tunic was open at the neck, and there was a glimpse of a flannel shirt and a bright-blue necktie loosely tied. He looked oddly small and unimpressive; there was no magnetism in him. Krylenko rounded off his speech, and then there was another ovation for Lenin, which lasted forty-five seconds. When Lenin raised his hand, the clapping stopped.

He said the doctors had permitted him to speak for fifteen minutes, and he spoke for exactly fifteen minutes. Seldes from his observation post a few yards away says he spoke with "a thick, throaty, wet voice," his eyes twinkling with laughter. He had a clever gesture of swinging his arm across his chest, thus permitting him to steal a glance at his wrist watch. Sometimes he would point both index fingers upward on a level with his shoulders, like the conventional picture of a Chinese dancer. He spoke rapidly and informally. He announced that Vladivostok had finally been wrested from the Japanese, and said with the tone of a convinced imperialist, "We shall never give up a single conquest we have won." He seemed surprised by the sudden burst of nationalist applause. He was giving a general report on victories abroad and defeats on the home front. "We have pruned and pruned our bureaucracy," he said, "and after four years we have taken a census of the government staff, and we have an increase of twelve thousand." He concluded by calling on them to follow "the inevitable and necessary road" marked out for them.

Afterward in an adjoining room there was the inevitable picture-taking. The American correspondents gathered around him, and he spoke of his interest in Pettigrew's *Plutocratic Democracy* and the speeches of Senator Borah. When an artist from a New York newspaper made a quick sketch of him, saying: "The world says you are a great man," he answered: "I am not a great man. Just look at me."

In the same vast hall he spoke again two weeks later, addressing the Congress of the Third International. Three days earlier he had carefully composed his speech, which he delivered in German. This time he was permitted to speak for an hour. His subject was "Five Years of the Russian Revolution and the Prospects of the World Revolution." He said very little about the world revolution, and he was curiously apologetic about the Russian revolution. For the first time, he admitted that the Soviets had not come into power as a result of the overwhelming popular enthusiasm for Bolshevism; they had come into power because the enemy lost its head. "Moments always occur in times of revolution when the enemy loses his head," he said, "and if we attack at precisely these moments, then we achieve an easy victory." He spoke of the introduction of state capitalism, admitting that it had no fundamental basis in socialism. He went on to discuss the progress of the Russian ruble, saying that the amount in circulation exceeded a quadrillion. He added that "the zeros can always be crossed out." There was huge laughter at this, but the audience grew silent when he turned to the objectives of the socialist government among the peasantry. He noted that there had been no uprisings since 1921, but said nothing about the famine which had decimated them or the Antonov rebellion in Tambov province which resulted in the massacre of 200,000 peasants. He paid a rare tribute to the peasants:

> The peasantry were for us. It would have been difficult for anyone to be more for us than the peasantry. They knew that behind the Whites were the landlords, whom they hated more than anything in the world. That is why the peasantry gave us all their enthusiasm and loyalty. It was not difficult to get the peasantry to fight for us against the Whites. The peasantry, who hated war before, did everything possible in the war against the Whites, in the civil war against the landlords. And yet this was not all, for in fact the only issue here was whether power was

to remain in the hands of the landlords or of the peasants. For us this was not enough. The peasants know that we seized power for the workers and that we had before us a definite aim—to establish the socialist order with the help of this power.

He was admitting that the peasants had been inveigled into defending a system they had not wanted. They had been promised the land, but the land now belonged to the state. "We hold the land in our hands, it belongs to the state," he declared. A new and more implacable landlord had come into existence; and there was scarcely a single peasant in all Russia who had wanted it this way or who would have fought for the Bolsheviks if he had known that the annihilation of the peasantry was to be the reward of their self-sacrifice.

He returned again and again to the subject of the peasants, as though there was some wound which had to be explored, some guilt to be exorcised. With one breath he says, "The peasants were for us." With another breath he says, "For the first and last time the peasants in 1921 were against us not consciously but instinctively, and the reason for this was that the transition to a purely socialist form of economy was beyond our strength." He would say two opposite things and believe them both, for he had never had any difficulty believing what he wanted to believe.

In a mood of irony he declared, "We have made a colossal number of blunders—nobody can see that better than I." In his manner of saying these words he resembled an old man looking back approvingly on the errors of his misspent youth. He took some comfort from the fact that the enemy—he included among "the enemy" all the capitalists and all the socialists of the Second International who disagreed with him—had also committed blunders, and he pointed especially to the United States, Britain, France and Japan, who supported Kolchak "without calculation, without reflection, and without circumspection, and this is a blunder which defies all understanding." When the Bolsheviks miscalculated, it was to say: "Two plus two equals five." When the capitalists and the Second International miscalculated, it was to say: "Two plus two equals a tallow candle." But these were easy debating points, and he spoke more wisely toward the end of the speech when he deplored the language of the reports of the Third International, "which are entirely unintelligible to foreigners who cannot be expected to hang them in the corner like icons." These reports were written in the Russian manner, about purely Russian problems. It was as though he was at last aware that other countries were not necessarily or inevitably bound to follow the Russian pattern. Lenin spoke for an hour. He was followed by Trotsky, who spoke for seven and a half hours in Russian, German, and French until it seemed that the entire revolution was to be drowned in a flood of words.

A week later at a plenary session of the Moscow Soviet Lenin spoke publicly for the last time in his life.

Here he announced the succession, saying that Tsyurupa, Rykov and Kamenev would in future do the work he had performed. He announced the names very early in the speech, with an air of conviction, pointing out that his own time, "owing to my reduced work-capacity, to use the professional term," was necessarily restricted to "affairs"— meaning perhaps only the most urgent and important affairs. It was a very short speech, with no fire in it. The Second International was never mentioned, and the hated capitalists were not once reviled. On the contrary Lenin praised them for their business acumen and their determination to get things done. He seemed to be proclaiming that the old romantic days were over, and it was time the Communists abandoned their hatred and sought for a *modus vivendi* with the enemy. He said:

> In the past the Communist said: "I am giving my life," and it seemed very simple to him, though it was not always so simple. Now however we Communists are faced with quite a different task. We must now take all things into account, and each of you must learn to make your calculations. We must calculate how in a capitalist environment we may best ensure our existence, how we can gain advantage from our opponents who will certainly bargain, having never forgotten how to bargain, and they will continue to bargain at our expense. We won't forget that, and least of all shall we imagine that these merchants will become lambs, and then, being transformed into lambs, showering us with all kinds of blessings free of charge. This won't happen, and we do not expect it to happen: we count on the fact that we are accustomed to putting up a fight and we shall find a way out and prove ourselves capable of trading and accumulating wealth and emerging from difficult economic situations. And this is a very difficult task.

Lenin told the story of Leonid Krassin, the Soviet trade envoy in London, sitting down to discuss trade with the British millionaire Leslie Urquhart, "the man who was the head and backbone of the entire intervention." There were no theoretical discussions. Instead

Urquhart said simply: "What's the price? How many? For how many years?" The stenographic report of the meeting reveals that applause broke out at this point. It was as though the audience was only too willing to abandon theory and to get down to business.

Lenin's last speech was a plea for coexistence with the capitalist powers, but there was not the least suggestion that the hard socialist line would be modified. "Socialism," he said, "is no longer a matter of the distant future, nor is it an abstract painting, nor is it an icon. We still have our old opinion about icons—they are very bad." It was a rather tame ending to the speech, and the stormy, prolonged applause at the end was more a tribute to the man than to anything he had said.

Often as he spoke the words were slurred, and he paused several times like a man who has lost the thread of his argument. He looked gaunt and frail. On November 25, five days after delivering the speech, he was ordered to take a week's rest with absolutely no work. For a few days he obeyed the doctors, remaining in his apartment and reading quietly. Thereafter he divided his time between Gorki and the Kremlin, working a little, fuming at his inactivity and occasionally writing the familiar notes in which he warned of dire punishment unless "accurate figures are sent to me immediately." The question of the state monopoly of foreign trade had arisen, with Bukharin and others opposing it. Predictably Lenin insisted that there could be no Soviet state without a complete monopoly of foreign trade, and his view was accepted. He was appalled when he heard that a certain Professor Rozhkov, a Menshevik, was being permitted to live openly in Moscow. He wrote that the Mensheviks have their own slogan: "Lie, resign from the party, and stay in Russia." On December 13, 1922, he had the satisfaction of learning that the Central Committee had banished the professor from Moscow.

On that day he had two attacks of nausea and vomiting. The doctors were summoned. When they announced categorically that all work must cease, he replied that he thoroughly agreed with them and would need only a few days to put his papers in order. He spent the next two days dictating letter after letter, working at extraordinary speed, "in case my illness should take me unawares." Insomnia and the headaches had returned. On the sixteenth he suffered another attack which lasted thirty-five minutes. This time the doctors decided that they could play the cat-and-mouse game no longer, and ordered him to bed. Ever since the first stroke, they had been expecting a second. There had been three vomitings in a period of three days, and now at last there were the visible signs of paralysis on the right side. Now, with the doctors standing around the bed, he knew he was doomed, but he would go on fighting to the end.

LAST TESTAMENT

ON THAT DAY IN DECEMBER when he was struck down, power, which he had fought for so bitterly, finally left him. Never again would he have any effective control over the destiny of Russia. The small men, who always flock around the heels of dictators, seized the power and divided it among themselves; and during the period of the *interregnum* they seemed scarcely to know what to do with it.

Lenin knew he was seriously ill and perhaps dying, but while he accepted it, he also fought against it with every ounce of his remaining strength. His restless mind was constantly engaged in outwitting the doctors. "If it is paralysis," he had said to Dr. Auerbach, "what use would I be, and who would have need of me?" He was determined not to be useless. From being absolute dictator he was to become nothing, and the thought was too terrible to be borne. Because the habits of power were deeply ingrained in him, he fought on relentlessly from his sickbed.

Krupskaya read to him, the secretaries came to take dictation, he wrote articles and letters, but no longer presided over the government. The aching awareness of powerlessness is evident in all the writings of his last months. Anger, horror, rage were his bedside companions; sometimes they would give way to momentary acquiescence; then the rage would return. He had, after all, been a dictator for a very long time. Indeed he had been dictating the policies of the party for twenty years of unremitting toil and mind-breaking concentration, and never for a moment had he been unconscious of his gifts. A dictator, suddenly confronted with his own powerlessness, is likely to go mad.

There is at the heart of dictatorship an unresolved mystery. No one has ever adequately explained why men should want total power over others, or what satisfactions they derive from it. To rule absolutely is to abandon the dialogue with one's fellow men: to hear oneself babbling in an interminable monologue until at last the words become meaningless, devoid of all human context. So Hitler would talk to his secretaries, until even the most worshipful were exhausted by the torrential flow; and in the same way there must have been times when the most worshipful admirers of Lenin were sickened by the interminable hammer blows, the words "all," "destruction," "unmercifully," "dictatorship" always falling in their accustomed place, appearing with unfailing regularity, like parodies of a speech delivered long ago. He had spent his life devising simple solutions for terribly complex problems; now he was confronted with a problem which admitted no simple solution—his own death.

He was a bad patient. If the doctors said he could read for an hour a day, he would read for two hours. He employed considerable conspiratorial skill in outwitting them. It was observed that he was kinder than ever to his friends. When they came in threadbare coats he would warn them of the dangers of influenza and lend them his own overcoat hanging uselessly on the wall. Previously, he seemed never to listen to people, or rather he would use only a tenth part of his mind in listening to them, while reserving nine tenths for formulating his replies: now the full force of his attention was concentrated on those who came to see him. There were however very few visitors in the early days after his stroke.

He was mortally tired, and his conscience troubled him. For the whole of the past year he had been aware of a sense of guilt before the workers of Russia. The state which he had built on so much blood, hoping to bring about a paradise for the working classes, had failed to live up to his expectations. "Powerful forces have diverted the Soviet state from its proper road," he had declared at the party congress in April; and in the summer and autumn those powerful forces had only gathered in strength, becoming more and more oppressive, more and more dangerous. For a long time he had brooded on the reasons for this, and now at last he was aware that there existed a solution for the evils which had fallen on the state. The Central Committee, the driving force of the state, consisted of a small hand-picked group of intellectuals and policemen; there were no workers in it. What would happen if the Central Committee was broadened to include fifty or even a hundred working-class members? It was a suggestion he would never perhaps have tolerated when he held power in his hands, but as he saw it there was no other safeguard for the continuing existence of the state.

There were other problems which absorbed him while he lay on his sickbed. He feared that the country would fall into the hands of a more rapacious and self-seeking dictator than he had ever been. Corruption among the Communist party officials, the senseless brutalities committed in Georgia, the need for overseers who would examine the actions of party officials, and long-overdue changes in the State Planning Commission weighed heavily upon him. On December 23 he begged the doctor to let him dictate for five minutes that evening. At first the doctor refused, but he relented when it became evident that Lenin would refuse to obey him. He was in a state of great excitement, and the doctor hoped the few minutes of dictation would relieve his mind.

"If I do not do it now, I may never be able to do it," Lenin said.

To his wife he said he hoped the notes he intended to dictate would be submitted to the next party congress after his death.

That evening, around eight o'clock, Maria Volodicheva, one of his secretaries, came into the bedroom. A small table had been set up for her by the sickbed. He was looking gaunt and weak, and Volodicheva was terrified by his appearance. He must have memorized the statement, for he delivered it rapidly in four minutes, one minute less than the time stipulated. The statement read:

> I would very much like to advise that a number of changes in our political organization be undertaken at this Congress.
>
> I would like to share with you those considerations to which I attach the greatest importance.
>
> I suggest, as of primary importance, that the size of the C.C. membership be enlarged to several score or even a hundred. It is my belief that our Central Committee would be exposed to grave danger in case future developments should not be altogether favorable to us, and this is something we cannot count on.
>
> Then I intend to propose that the Congress consider giving legislative force under certain conditions to the resolutions of the State Planning Commission, thus meeting to some extent and under certain conditions the desires expressed by Comrade Trotsky.

Referring to the first point, the enlargement of the C.C. membership, I believe it is necessary for the raising of the authority of the C.C. and for serious work aimed at raising the efficiency of our apparatus, and also to prevent conflicts between small sections of the C.C. which might gravely affect the destiny of the party.

I believe that our party has the right to demand fifty to a hundred members of the working class, and they could be acquired without undue strain on its resources.

Such a reform would lay the foundation for a greater stability of our party, and would help it in its struggle under the conditions of encircle-ment by hostile states, a struggle which in my opinion is bound to be-come more acute in the immediate future. I believe that the stability of our party would gain a thousandfold by such a measure.

When Maria Volodicheva had read the statement back to him, he asked what date of the month it was, and went on to ask about her health, for she too looked pale and weak. He wagged a finger at her and said: "Well, you'd better be careful, or else—" He did not com-plete the sentence, but she guessed what the threatened punishment would be: she would not be allowed to take dictation any more.

On the following day he dictated the continuation of the state-ment for ten minutes during the evening. The doctors had insisted that he should rest, but he explained to them that he would refuse treatment altogether unless he was allowed to dictate his "diary"— the word was cunningly chosen and was meant to put the doctors off the scent. He slept little during the night and suffered from excru-ciating headaches. That evening he dictated the most impressive of the many brief documents he was able to dictate before he lost the power of speech. This document, together with two postscripts writ-ten on subsequent days, has come to be known as "Lenin's Testa-ment." He began by referring to the split in the Central Committee, largely brought about by the divergent personalities of Stalin and Trotsky, and once more he emphasized the urgency of flooding the committee with new members from the working class to give a broader basis to the government and to prevent a head-on collision between the two rivals for power. He said:

Comrade Stalin, having become General Secretary, has concentrated immeasurable power in his hands, and I am not sure that he always knows how to use that power with sufficient caution. On the other hand Comrade Trotsky, as was proved by his struggle against the C.C. in connection with the question of the People's Commissariat of Railroads, is distinguished not only by his exceptional abilities—personally, to be sure, he is perhaps the most able man on the present C.C.—but also by his excessive self-assurance and excessive enthusiasm for the purely administrative aspect of his work.

These two qualities of the two most eminent leaders of the present C.C. might, quite innocently, lead to a split, and if our party does not take steps to prevent it, a split might arise unexpectedly.

I will not further characterize the other members of the C.C. as to their personal qualities. I will only remind you that the October episode of Zinoviev and Kamenev was not, of course, accidental, but neither can it be used against them any more than the non-Bolshevism of Trotsky.

Of the younger members of the C.C. I want to say a few words about Bukharin and Pyatakov. They are, in my opinion, among the most outstanding among the younger members, and in regard to them the following should be borne in mind: Bukharin is not only the most valuable and most important theoretician of the party, but he also may be considered legitimately as the favorite of the entire party; but his theoretical views can only with the very greatest reserve be regarded as fully Marxist, for there is something scholastic about him—he has never studied dialectics, and I think he has never fully understood them.

At this point Lenin paused—there was no more strength in him. He had said the most important things: in one statement he had formed a simple plan for the liquidation of the dictatorship, and in the second he had given his precise evaluation of the party leaders, clearly showing that he preferred Trotsky and Bukharin above the rest, and that he had finally forgiven Zinoviev and Kamenev for their "treachery" in 1917. On the following evening Maria Volodicheva was summoned to add a brief postscript on Pyatakov, "a man undoubtedly distinguished in will and ability, but too much given over to administrative methods and the administrative side of affairs to be relied upon in a serious political question." There was a final paragraph in which he gave a general benediction to Bukharin and Pyatakov, "those outstanding and loyal workers," who might, if they supplemented their knowledge and corrected their one-sidedness, be of even greater service to the party.

He was well aware of the explosive nature of these statements. Several times he warned Maria Volodicheva that on no account must their existence be made known. As soon as she had taken them down in shorthand and they had been read back to him, they were typed in five copies. One copy remained with him, three were given to Krup-

skaya, and the fifth went into the secret file in his office. The secretary
remembered that he paused between sentences, but never paused for
a word. He had spent many long hours revising and polishing them
in his mind, and he was word-perfect.

On the sealed envelope enclosing the statements he ordered the
secretary to write: "To be opened only by V. I. Lenin, or in the event
of his death by Nadezhda Konstantinovna." For some reason Maria
Volodicheva could not bring herself to write the last words.

So the days passed, while Lenin lay in bed, and in the evenings at
eight o'clock, as regularly as clockwork, there would come one of the
secretaries to take down the "diary," those political notes which were
intended to act as high explosives to be set off at the appropriate
moment. Once more, though half-paralyzed, he was the political agitator, strenuously making war against his enemies. He was perfectly
aware of the drama in the dimly lighted bedroom: the fate of Russia
and the Communist International was at stake. He did not know, and
perhaps could not have guessed, that all these statements were hostages which would fall into the hands of his enemies.

On December 24 the Politburo held a conference with the doctors
attending Lenin. Stalin was among those who took part. Strict rules
were established, and it was agreed that no visitors should be allowed,
and he must expect no reply to any letters he wrote. Except for the
doctors and his immediate family, he was permitted to see only his
secretaries, who would be admitted for a few minutes every evening.
He was to be isolated almost as completely as a prisoner in the Peter
and Paul Fortress.

Among the more stringent regulations was one stating that no
political information was to be given to him either by the secretaries
or by the family. This was agreed upon by both Krupskaya and Maria
Ilyinichna, both of them experienced revolutionaries, who showed
not the slightest intention of carrying out the orders of the doctors
and the Politburo; and so small scraps of information were fed to
Lenin. In particular Krupskaya kept a watchful eye on Stalin, employing all the resources of Lenin's efficient secretariat. While he lay
ill, she was his ears and eyes, his sole powerful contact with the outside world.

Every evening the "diary" was continued for five minutes, ten
minutes, then for fifteen minutes. Before the new year Lenin had
somehow convinced the doctors that to safeguard his health and
sanity he needed twenty minutes of dictation in the morning and

another twenty in the evening. He was adamant. He promised that at the end of twenty minutes, even if he was in the middle of the sentence, he would stop, and of course he broke his promise. There followed a long statement, dictated over three days, on the subject of attributing legislative functions to the State Planning Commission. Originally it was Trotsky's idea, and Lenin rejected it on the grounds that the scientific and technological experts who largely controlled the Commission were infected with bourgeois ideas, and few of them were active members of the Communist Party. As matters stood, the decisions of the experts had to be reviewed and approved by members of the party who were overworked and in no position to understand complex scientific problems. The chairman of the Commission was Krzhizhanovsky, the vice-chairman was Pyatakov, and both were under attack, the first for being too lenient to non-Communists and the second for being too harsh to the scientists and completely ignorant of scientific matters. Lenin proposed that the Commission be headed by a scientist of broad experience, whether he was a Communist or not, and that within the Commission there should be a small nucleus of dedicated Communists to keep the bourgeois scientists in line. In effect he was suggesting that extraordinary powers could be safely given to the Commission headed by a bourgeois provided there was adequate supervision.

More and more his mind was turning to the need to supervise the supervisers. Political control was breaking down because orders were not being properly carried out. "Our *apparat* is no use to anyone," he said in a statement dictated to Maria Volodicheva on December 29. It was an admission of defeat, for he had spent a very large part of his life since coming to power in building up a governmental system of controls which would ensure that orders would be carried out in the shortest possible time. Now he saw the whole pack of cards, erected with so much care, falling to the ground. The government was neither efficient nor capable of exerting power; it had no head and its limbs were suffering from gangrene. He demanded once again that the Central Committee be broadened to include a hundred members, adding that some five hundred inspectors should be attached to the Committee to see that its orders were carried out.

These statements, written in the curiously dull and lifeless style of Communist polemics, reflected an intense drama. He was confronted with a moral crisis, from which there was no issue except the radical alteration of the state. For years he had spoken of the dictatorship of the proletariat, knowing full well that it was in fact a dictator-ship of armed Marxist intellectuals. Now in these last days he saw that the only salvation of the state lay in giving the government back to the workers and peasants. He wanted a Central Committee to include a majority of workers and peasants assisted by five hundred members of a Workers' and Peasants' Inspectorate, and he must have known it was too late. By the very nature of the Communist revolution it would remain, and have to remain, the dictatorship of one man, and there-fore an intolerable tyranny.

As he faced these problems, he became more and more convinced that for all the sacrifices made by the people to bring about a Com-munist state, little had changed since the days when the tsars ruled Russia with the help of the *nagaika* and the secret police. With dismay and horror, and also with a strange latter-day honesty, he was com-pelled to admit that the Soviet state had committed so many errors that it was almost past praying for.

On December 30 he denounced Stalin, Ordjonikidze and Dzer-zhinsky by name, and by implication the entire ruling body of the Soviet government was included in the denunciation. They were "typ-ical Russian bureaucrats, rascals and lovers of violence." The immedi-ate cause of the tirade was a report that Ordjonikidze had led Soviet troops against the autonomous Georgian Soviet. Some hundreds of Georgians were executed, thousands were thrown into prison. Dzer-zhinsky, sent to Georgia to report on the situation, had returned with the news that there had been "some excesses," but Georgia was now calm. Gradually, through Krupskaya and others, Lenin learned that there had been a blood bath. On whose orders? On what grounds? The orders clearly came from Stalin, the grounds were to force the Georgian Soviet Republic into union with the U.S.S.R., although the law of the land demanded a voluntary association of states. Like a man who was finally convinced of his own guilt, he wrote:

> I am, I believe, strongly guilty before the workers of Russia for not having intervened energetically or drastically enough in the notorious question of "autonomization," which, it appears, is officially called the question of the Union of Soviet Socialist Republics.
>
> In the summer, when the question arose, I was ill, and then in the autumn I had great hopes I would recover and be able to press the matter at the October and December plenary meetings. However, I was unable to attend the October plenary meeting (when the question came

up) or the December meeting, and so the question was discussed with almost no intervention by me.

I had only time for a talk with Comrade Dzerzhinsky, who came from the Caucasus and told me how matters stood in Georgia. I also had time to exchange a few words with Comrade Zinoviev and expressed my apprehensions concerning the question. From what I was told by Comrade Dzerzhinsky, who headed the commission sent by the Central Committee to "investigate" the Georgian incident, I could only derive the greatest apprehensions. If matters had come to such a pass that Ordjonikidze could go to the extreme of applying physical violence, as Comrade Dzerzhinsky informed me, then you can imagine what a swamp we have gotten into. Obviously the whole business of "autonomization" was radically wrong and badly timed.

They say that unity was needed in the apparatus. But where do these assertions come from? Is it not from the same Russian apparatus which, as I observed in one of the previous sections of my diary, we have taken over from Tsarism, only tarring it a little with the Soviet brush?

He went on to attack Great Russian chauvinism, "the scoundrels and lovers of violence" who have immemorially ruled over Russia as bureaucrats and chiefs of police. There were only a small number of Communists ruling over a vast population, and he foresaw that the Communists would be drowned in "the Great Russian sea of chauvinist riffraff like a fly in milk." Then he invoked the spirit of Derzhimorda, the police chief in Gogol's *The Inspector General,* the traditional symbol of stupid oppression, and immediately afterward he denounced the haste, impulsiveness and spitefulness of Stalin, as though he wanted to establish the equation: Derzhimorda = Stalin.

This unhappy letter was continued on the following day, December 31. Once again he raged against Great Russian chauvinism, the contempt of the Great Russians for the Poles, the Ukrainians and the Georgians. He demanded exemplary punishment for Ordjonikidze, and he laid the blame for the Great Russian nationalistic campaign on Dzerzhinsky and Stalin, without however suggesting that they should be punished. He demanded that the national languages should have equality with Russian, and he saw danger in the railroad administration, which would inevitably attempt to bring uniformity into all its works: he seemed to be suggesting that all time tables must be made available in the national languages. It was odd that the Great Russian chauvinists should be, for once, not Great Russians at all; Dzerzhinsky was a Pole, and Stalin was a Georgian. Lenin was especially disheartened by the emergence of Soviet imperialism, because he foresaw that vast changes would soon come about among the hundreds of millions of people in Asia. "It would be unpardonable opportunism on our part," he wrote, "if we, on the eve of the emergence of the East and at the dawn of its awakening, permit our authority to be undermined by our own coarseness and injustice toward our nationalities." He had no qualms about speaking of Soviet imperialism. It was one more unpalatable fact of existence.

The solution, if there was one, seemed to lie in education; and on the following day he wrote a short article on literacy and the appalling cultural standards under the dictatorship of the proletariat. As usual he spoke in superlatives. "Nowhere else are the masses so interested in culture as they are in our country; nowhere else are the problems of culture approached so profoundly, so consistently as they are in our country; and nowhere else is state power in the hands of the working class." And having stated that culture in Russia had reached heights unapproached in any other country, he is compelled to admit that "our proletarian culture is in a parlous state even when compared with bourgeois culture."

He complained that culture had developed far too slowly in Russia, public education was too limited, elementary education was at a standstill; and while the state publishing house was producing mountains of books, the government had forgotten the primary need to teach children how to read. In the rural districts especially there was a terrifying lack of culture. He suggested that factory workers under their own auspices, or under the auspices of the party or the trade unions, should go to the villages and teach the peasants. It was as though finally he had decided that the Narodniki who went out among the peasants in the Seventies and Eighties of the last century were right after all, though previously he had despised them. As he lay ill, the past was continually coming to confront him.

The following day there were more pages for his diary. This time it occurred to him that "the entire people must go through an entire period of cultural development." Everyone must be taught to be efficient, literate, and to acquire a talent for trading in a cultured manner. "Our people are far from being cultured merchants," he wrote. "They are trading in an Asiatic manner, but to be a merchant one must be able to trade in a European manner. A whole epoch separates them from that." Since he had almost abolished trade by giving the state a complete monopoly, while permitting the people only marginal possibilities of trade through the New Economic Policy, his dream of "cultured co-operators working within the social ownership of the means of production" was strangely remote from reality. He never defined what he meant by culture. It was another totem word and could mean whatever he wanted it to mean. "The cultural revolution would now be sufficient to transform our country into a completely socialist country," he wrote; and he seemed to be looking forward to a time when all Russians would love books and acquire good manners.

These pages of his diary, which were published in *Pravda*, are curiously unlike his other writings. The bite, the toughness, are missing. Suddenly, on January 4, 1923, he dictated to one of his secretaries, Lydia Fotieva, a postscript to the letter written in December in which he described the characters of the leading Bolsheviks, and the authentic thunder is heard again.

This postscript is justifiably famous. Though marked by an extreme bitterness and disenchantment, it was strangely prophetical. When he wrote, "I am, I believe, strongly guilty before the workers of Russia," he was speaking of events which had already happened and could no longer be completely rectified, for the murders had already taken place. Now he was speaking of events which could still be rectified if men acted in time. With extraordinary clairvoyance he saw that of all the errors he had committed the most dangerous and the most destructive was to have given high position to Stalin. He wrote:

> Stalin is too coarse, and this fault, though tolerable in dealings among us Communists, becomes unbearable in a General Secretary. Therefore I propose to the comrades to find some way of removing Stalin from his position and appointing somebody else who differs in all respects from Comrade Stalin in one characteristic—namely, someone more tolerant, more loyal, more polite and considerate to his comrades, less capricious, etc. This circumstance may seem to be a mere trifle, but I think that from the point of view of preventing a split and from the point of view of what I wrote above about the relations between Stalin and Trotsky, it is not a trifle, or else it is a trifle which may acquire a decisive importance.

It was as though some sixth sense told him that the succession would go to Stalin, and in these remaining hours of sanity he quailed before the possibility of surrendering Russia to a man who was so coarse, so uncultured, and so unprincipled. The word he used to describe Stalin was *grub*, which is more than "rude." It suggests coarse buffoonery at one end of its spectrum of meanings and the working of intolerable hardship on people at the other end. *Grubkiy khokhot* means a "horse laugh." It was an unpleasant word for an unpleasant thing.

Lenin's attitude toward Stalin went beyond a recognition of his general unpleasantness. Ever since his return from Gorki, he was aware that Stalin was acting as a law unto himself, accumulating more and more power and interfering in the work of all the other government departments. There was not the least doubt of his violent ambitions, his determination to seize power once Lenin was out of the way. But Lenin stubbornly refused to die. He was back in harness at the Kremlin, and keeping a sharp eye on Stalin's extraordinary maneuvers when he had his second stroke. The news of the stroke was kept secret and Stalin was not informed until the evening. From that moment he seems to have realized that his task, in order to gain power, was to bring about the death of Lenin in the shortest possible time.

It was not, of course, an easy matter to kill Lenin. He was well guarded, the doctors could not be bribed, his secretaries were loyal to him. There was however one weak link in the chain. This was Krupskaya, who suffered from heart disease. Any sudden shock was likely to reduce her to hysterics, or worse. Lenin's heart attack on December 16 had made great inroads in her reserves of strength, and she was in no condition to withstand any further shocks. The effect on Lenin, if she collapsed, would have been disastrous.

On December 22 Lenin felt the need to dictate a short message to Stalin. He was very ill; the doctors had forbidden him to dictate that day, but had relented only because the matter clearly preyed on his mind and he was likely to be in better spirits afterward. Also he promised that the message would be very short. He was so ill that even on the following day he was permitted to dictate for only five minutes.

The exact contents of the message are unknown, but they can easily be imagined. The message was a reproof and a warning, and Krupskaya's name appeared on it, for Lenin always insisted that the name of the person taking down his words should be recorded.

As soon as he received the message Stalin called Krupskaya to the telephone. He was outraged, or pretended to be outraged. He may have been drunk, but it is more likely that he was coldly calculating. He heaped coarse insults on her and told her she had no right to feed Lenin with information or discuss with him party matters about which she was ignorant. His tone was threatening, well calculated to reduce her to hysterics. In her misery she turned to Kamenev, to whom on the following day she wrote an urgent plea for help:

LEV BORISOVICH!

Because I took down a short message by dictation from Vladimir Ilyich by permission of the doctors, Stalin permitted himself yesterday an unusually coarse outburst directed at me. This is not my first day in the party. During all these thirty years no comrade has ever addressed me with such coarse words.

The business of the party and of Ilyich are not less dear to me than to Stalin. I have to have the greatest self-control. I know better than any doctor what can and what cannot be discussed with Ilyich, because I know what makes him nervous and what does not, and in any case I know better than Stalin. I am turning to you and to Grigory [Zinoviev], as being much closer comrades of V.I., and I am begging you to protect me from rude interference in my private life and from these invectives and threats. I have no doubt what will be the unanimous decision of the Control Commission, with which Stalin sees fit to threaten me. However I have neither the strength nor the time to waste on this stupid quarrel. I am a human being and my nerves are strained to the utmost.

N. KRUPSKAYA

Krupskaya did what she had to do: she waged war against Stalin without telling Lenin, who was too ill to be told. She kept the secret for two and a half months. Neither Kamenev nor Zinoviev were strong men; and when Kamenev took the letter to Stalin, presumably to demand an explanation, he found himself enmeshed in a conspiracy to form a triumvirate consisting of Stalin, Zinoviev and Kamenev, which would seize power once Lenin was dead; and his death, according to Stalin, would not be long delayed.

There is no evidence that Krupskaya sent any message for help to Trotsky, who would no doubt have mentioned it. She seems to have relied implicitly on the political strength of Kamenev, who held power in Moscow, and Zinoviev, who held power in Petrograd; she did not know that outside these two areas Stalin's influence was rapidly increasing so that he would be able to pack the next Congress of the Soviets, which would open in the late spring, with his own men.

On January 25, *Pravda* published Lenin's article, "How We Should Reorganize the Workers' and Peasants' Inspectorate," with the subtitle "A Proposal to the Twelfth Party Congress." Lenin was aware of the importance of the forthcoming Congress, and he was hoping to head off disaster with a plan for increasing the Central Control Commission with seventy-five to a hundred workers and peasants, while reducing the staff of the Workers' and Peasants' Inspectorate to three or four hundred persons with purely secretarial duties. These arid additions and subtractions may not seem very exciting. They were however matters of important concern to the future of Russia, for the Inspectorate was under the direct control of Stalin and by reducing the number of officials serving under him, Lenin hoped to destroy some portion of his power. Lenin described the existing form of government in scathing terms—it was "absolutely unworkable and indecently prerevolutionary." It was merely the survival of the former bureaucracy "with a superficial new coat of paint." Stalin was not mentioned in the article, but it was clearly designed to injure him. He intended to broaden the attack against Stalin with an article on the troubles in Georgia, and he called for all the documents in the case. When Stalin arrived in Moscow a few days later and was approached for the documents, he refused to surrender them without the sanction of the Politburo and he told Fotieva that he was dissatisfied with her behavior. He had read the article on the reorganization of the Inspectorate, and it was clear that Lenin knew a good deal more than he was supposed to know. He had obviously been reading the newspapers, or they were being read to him in defiance of doctors' orders. Fotieva said she had told Lenin nothing, merely acting as his secretary; and Stalin may have realized that Krupskaya, far from being intimidated, was actively helping Lenin to plan his strategy.

The Georgian affair was a complicated one, and Lenin gave it to his secretaries to study. The Politburo had agreed to let him see the documents, but the question of the Inspectorate was still uppermost in his mind, and over a period of several days he dictated a lengthy article under the title "Better Fewer but Better." His health seemed to be coming back, and he was in good spirits. His opinion of the machinery of government had not improved. "The condition of our state machinery is so deplorable, not to say disgusting," that it needed a complete overhaul. There were reasons for this deplorable condition: everything had been happening at such speed that the state institutions had not kept pace with the changing circumstances. But of all the institutions introduced by the Soviets, the Inspectorate was the most inefficient, the most stupid, and the most intolerable. "Let us speak plainly. The People's Commissariat for the Workers' and Peasants' Inspectorate enjoys not the slightest prestige. Everyone knows that there is no more badly organized institution than our Workers' and Peasants' Inspectorate, and that under present conditions nothing can be expected from the People's Commissariat." With these words he flung down the gauntlet. The attack on Stalin was undisguised. There could only be war to the death between them.

Toward the end of the article Lenin wrote one of his best pages. In forcing himself to come to terms with the massive inner contradictions of communism, he saw the vast disparity between the revolutionary idea and the art of government. Theory and practice were continually at odds, and why this should be had always escaped him. Now in the very last article he ever wrote, he found the answer to a question which had tormented him ever since he assumed power. He wrote:

> In all spheres of social, economic and political relationships we are "terribly" revolutionary. But as regards precedence, the observation of the forms and ceremonies of office routine, our "revolutionism" often gives way to the mustiest routine. Here, more than once, we have witnessed the very interesting phenomenon of a great leap forward in social life being accompanied by an amazing timidity whenever the slightest changes are proposed.
>
> This is understandable, for the boldest steps forward were taken in a field which had long been reserved for theoretical study, which had been cultivated mainly and almost exclusively in theory. The Russian found solace from the bleak bureaucratic realities at home in unusually bold theoretical constructions, and that is why these unusually bold theoretical constructions assumed among us an unusually lopsided character. Among us theoretical audacity in general constructions went hand in hand with amazing timidity with regard to certain very minor reforms in office routine. A great universal agrarian revolution was worked out with an audacity unheard of in any other country, and at the same time the imagination was lacking to work out a tenth-rate reform in office routine. The imagination or the patience was lacking to apply to this reform the general propositions which produced such "splendid" results when applied to general problems.
>
> So it happens that in our social life an astonishing degree of desperate audacity goes hand in hand with timidity in making very minor changes.
>
> I believe this is what happened in all truly great revolutions, for truly great revolutions grow out of the contradictions between the old, between the trends which work to exploit the old and the abstract striving for the new, which must be so new that not the tiniest grain of the old remains.
>
> And the more abrupt the revolutions, the longer will be the time we are confronted with an entire series of these contradictions.

Such was his final verdict on the abrupt revolution he had brought into being, and there was no comfort to be derived from that last bleak paragraph.

These reflections however were only incidental to the main purpose of the article, which was to remove Stalin from his position of power and influence. At a meeting of the Politburo, where the article was discussed, Stalin suggested that it should not be printed, and Kuibyshev went so far as to suggest a stratagem: a special, single copy of *Pravda* containing the article should be published. This would be given to Lenin, and no other copy with the article would appear. Trotsky and others intervened, and the article appeared on the front page of *Pravda* on March 4.

On the following day, about noon, Lenin called his secretary Volodicheva into his bedroom and dictated two letters to her. When the doctor asked him about the letters, fearing their effect on his health, he answered that they were merely business letters. They were not business letters. In one he threatened to break off all comradely relations with Stalin, and in the other he asked Trotsky to carry on the fight for Georgia in the Central Committee. The letters read:

To Comrade Stalin:
Copies for Kamenev and Zinoviev
DEAR COMRADE STALIN!
You permitted yourself a rude summons of my wife to the telephone and you went on to reprimand her rudely. Despite the fact that she told you she agreed to forget what was said, nevertheless Zinoviev and Kamenev heard about it from her. I have no intention of forgetting so easily something which has been done against me, and I do not have to stress that I consider anything done against my wife as done against me. I am therefore asking you to weigh carefully whether you agree to retract your words and apologize, or whether you prefer the severance of relations between us.
Sincerely: LENIN

To Comrade Trotsky:
DEAR COMRADE TROTSKY!
I wish very much to ask you to take upon yourself the defense of the Georgian case in the Central Committee of the Party. At present the case is under the "judgment" of Stalin and Dzerzhinsky, and I cannot trust their judgment. Quite the opposite. If you were to agree to undertake the defense, my mind would be at rest. If for some reason, you can-

not agree to do so, please return the entire dossier to me; I shall consider that a sign of refusal from you.

With best comradely greetings: LENIN

These letters were dictated over a period of about fifteen minutes. Volodicheva was instructed to have them typed in the usual five copies, and they were to be brought to him the following day. The task of dictating the letters had depleted his strength, and he was now feverish.

Later in the day Fotieva was summoned. She wrote in her diary that Lenin gave her "a number of commissions," but says nothing more about them. Among these commissions was probably a telephone call to Trotsky, giving him the substance of the letter and preparing him for the tasks ahead. Trotsky at this time was living in the Kavalersky Building, a stone's throw from Lenin's apartment; he was suffering from lumbago, bed-ridden, and under doctor's orders not to leave the apartment. Kamenev was preparing to leave on a mission of inquiry to Georgia. Stalin was living in his country estate outside Moscow. The battle was being waged by people who never saw each other, who communicated by silences, by sudden explosions of temper, and by brief letters which were to affect the destiny of Russia for generations to come.

Fotieva's diary entry for March 6 reads:

> In the morning Vladimir Ilyich summoned me and M. A. Volodicheva, and dictated to her a line and a half in all.
> He read over the letter to J. V. Stalin, which he had dictated on the previous day. He commissioned me to hand the letter personally to J. V. Stalin and bring back the answer.
> Vladimir Ilyich was unable to read J. V. Stalin's answer, for on the day he received the answer his illness grew worse. From this day the health of Vladimir Ilyich took a sharp turn for the worse.

The last paragraph must have been added later, for Stalin refused to reply immediately to the letter. By this time at least one of the doctors attending Lenin was in his pay, and he hoped that Lenin would be dead before it became necessary to write an abject apology, which could later be used against him. He delayed as long as possible, but by the seventh or eighth of March, when Kamenev visited him, the letter of apology was written, and Krupskaya had the small satisfaction of reading it.

Fotieva mentions a letter dictated to Volodicheva on the morning of the sixth. This letter, which was among the documents given to Trotsky the following day, read:

To Comrades Mdivani and Makharadze
Copies for Trotsky and Kamenev
ESTEEMED COMRADES!
    I am heart and soul behind you in this matter. Ordjonikidze's brutalities and the connivance of Stalin and Dzerzhinsky have outraged me. On your behalf I am now preparing notes and a speech.
                                                    With esteem: LENIN

This was the last letter he ever dictated. It was a little longer than "a line and a half in all," but not much longer. It was his final protest against three men he had raised to positions of power and eminence, and if he did not add that he was guilty before the workers of Russia, it was because guilt was implicit in every word of the letter.

For one more day he was able to wage his ineffectual war against Stalin. On March 7 Fotieva and Maria Gliasser, a secretary attached to the Soviet of People's Commissars, were instructed to see Trotsky. They put the entire file of the Georgian atrocities into his hands together with all the relevant correspondence. Lenin was staking everything on getting Trotsky's help. "Vladimir Ilyich is preparing a bomb for Stalin at the Congress," Fotieva said excitedly, and now for the first time Trotsky realized that the matter was desperately serious. He asked the secretaries whether he had Lenin's permission to discuss the matter with Kamenev, who as acting chairman of the Central Committee in Lenin's absence was in theory the most powerful man in Russia. Fotieva was dubious. Her instructions were to place the matter wholly in Trotsky's hands; no one else must be allowed to deal with it. She decided to run back to Lenin's apartment and get final confirmation. A quarter of an hour later she returned, out of breath. She had spoken to Lenin and he had told her it was a matter for Trotsky alone.

    "Kamenev will immediately show everything to Stalin," he said, "and then Stalin will make a rotten compromise and deceive everyone."

    They talked for another hour. Trotsky still felt unsure of himself. As he explained later, he had no desire to remove Stalin and Dzerzhinsky from their posts, nor to expel Ordjonikidze from the party. Lenin wanted Ordjonikidze expelled "for at least two years," according to Fotieva. What Trotsky wanted was a kind of gentlemen's agreement, "an honest co-operation among the higher spheres of the party." They were to set their house in order and commit no further excesses. It would be a simple house cleaning, with nothing accomplished, and Fotieva left Trotsky's apartment in a mood of despair, to report to Lenin that Trotsky was unwilling to undertake the task singlehanded. This time Fotieva returned with the letter to Mdivani and Makhara-dze. She pointed to the words "Copies for Trotsky and Kamenev." Trotsky was surprised when he was shown the letter.

"So Vladimir Ilyich has changed his mind?" he asked.

"Yes," replied Fotieva, and with this single word she seemed to be conveying Lenin's hopeless realization that Trotsky would never fight Stalin singlehanded.

She went on to speak about Lenin's health.

"His condition is getting worse every hour," she said. "You must not believe the reassuring statements of the doctors. He can speak now only with difficulty. . . . The Georgian question worries him terribly. He is afraid he will collapse before he can undertake anything. When he handed me this note he said: 'Before it is too late. . . . I am obliged to come out openly before the proper time!' "

"This means I can talk to Kamenev?" Trotsky interrupted.

"Obviously."

"Ask him to come and see me."

Kamenev arrived an hour later. He was pale and agitated. He had come from Lenin's apartment, where he had talked with Krupskaya, who was still waiting for Stalin's letter of apology. She had spoken of Lenin's determination to crush Stalin politically. Kamenev was on his way to see Stalin to extract the letter from him. Apart from this, he had little to say, except that he was not looking forward to his meeting with Stalin.

And there the matter ended: for the vast confused battle between giants was never fought to a conclusion. Ironically at the very moment that Stalin was writing his letter of apology, Lenin began to sink rapidly.

Two days later, on March 9, exhausted by his struggle with Stalin, Lenin suffered his third stroke, which deprived him of the power of speech, completely paralyzed his right side, and partially affected his left. In addition, he was running a dangerously high temperature. The first bulletin, issued on March 12, spoke of "the marked deterioration in his health" and "a weakening of the movement of the right arm and the right leg." But this bulletin was deliberately evasive. Though Dr.

Guetier hopefully predicted he would recover, there were few doctors who agreed with him. They thought that in a few weeks, or at most a few months, he would be dead. Instead he lived on for ten more months.

In those days, just before the last attack, he sometimes spoke cryptically to the intimates who somehow evaded the guard which Krupskaya put round her husband. Once he said, with sadness and tenderness, "They say Martov is dying, too." To his friend Krzhizhanovsky he said, "Yes, it seems that I took too heavy a load upon myself." And to his friend Vladimirov he said, "I am still not dead, but they, with Stalin at their head, are burying me."

On March 11 Dr. Rozanov came to see him. Lenin was still conscious, and he could still understand, however dimly, what was going on around him. With his good left hand he shook the doctor's hand, and then he did something which was childish and pathetic—he began to caress the doctor's hand.

Some years before, when Bukharin and Sverdlov were disagreeing with his policies, Lenin took Trotsky aside and said, "What if they kill you and me, can Bukharin and Sverdlov get away with it?"

"Perhaps they won't kill us," Trotsky suggested.

"The devil knows what they will do," Lenin said, and laughed.

THE LIVING DEATH

THE DAYS PASSED QUIETLY. He lay in bed at Gorki, speechless and paralyzed, never sleeping, his eyes open all night as he fought the disease relentlessly. For two months he was desperately ill. Gradually the strength returned, and by the end of July he could walk a little and he was sleeping regularly. He seemed indestructible.

In September he surprised the doctors by making his way downstairs, holding onto the banisters. He understood what was said to him, but he could not answer. There was no trace of paralysis on his left side; the color came back to his face; Krupskaya was teaching him to speak. He walked with a cane, dragging his right foot. He went out gathering mushrooms and was taken for drives through the forest. There was a special alleyway on the estate, which he liked, and he would sit there on a bench, gazing quietly into space. He could read newspapers, but preferred being read to. He was even learning to write again, with his left hand. So the days passed, while he struggled back to life with a strange half-smile on his lips.

By the beginning of October he seemed to be well on the road to recovery. On October 9 Molotov announced that during the summer the doctors had hesitated to render a verdict, but they were now convinced that he was improving rapidly; only his speech left much to be desired. In fact, he could enunciate only a few simple words, but even this was more than the doctors had hoped for. Sometimes with great difficulty he was able to form short sentences, and he would help out his short vocabulary with gestures and inclinations. And every day the vocabulary increased. He worked at learning to speak with extraordinary assiduity, spending long hours at it, and sometimes exhausting himself so that, as Maria Ilyinichna wrote to one of the doctors, "he has to be held in check."

He still laughed with that sharp whipcrack laugh of his, and he would still gaze at people intently, his head cocked to one side, his attention concentrated upon the visitor as though there was no one else in the world. He understood perfectly what people were saying. Only one thing was missing: the power to express himself freely.

One day he went out gathering mushrooms with Dr. Rozanov, who like most town people found the greatest difficulty in finding any mushrooms at all. Lenin could recognize a mushroom twenty yards away, and he would pounce on it eagerly, shouting with laughter because the doctor had failed to see it.

According to Dr. Rozanov, he was an unusually gentle and obedient patient. He gave an impression of calm kindliness, but as the autumn progressed there was a quickening of the will, occasional flurries of anger. He made it clear that he wanted to eat with everyone else. He took a dislike to Dr. Foerster, whom he had previously held in high regard, and accordingly the German doctor was banished from his sight, though he remained nearby and the other doctors continued to consult with him. The continual processions of nurses annoyed him, and they too were kept out of sight as much as possible. His leg had improved so much that orthopedic boots were ordered for him. He tried them on and wore them without complaint, but he refused to take any medicines except quinine. Dr. Rozanov remembered how he would point to the quinine bottle and say "poison," and then he would drink the quinine without making a grimace. The Russian word for "poison" is *yad*. It was a word he could pronounce easily.

He was so far improved in the autumn that his doctors were talking of sending him to the Crimea. Every day he gained in strength and understanding. Zinoviev spoke of the time which could not be far distant when state documents would be sent to him and the government would be taking his advice. "It is not the doctors who are directing the treatment, but Lenin himself," Zinoviev declared, and it was true, though the doctors continued to give advice secretly to Krupskaya. He could now convey quite complicated ideas. On October 19[*]

---

[*] There is some mystery about the exact date of the journey. Alexander Belmas, one of the guards who accompanied the party in another car, says it took place "one day in October." Fotieva, who is usually accurate about dates, says it took place on the nine-

he said he wanted to visit the agricultural exhibition which was being held in Moscow.

Krupskaya and Maria Ilyinichna did everything they could to dissuade him, but he was insistent. He laughed at their fears and indicated that he was determined to go and nothing would stop him. Wrapped in a heavy coat, with Krupskaya and Maria Ilyinichna beside him, and with his chauffeur at the wheel, he drove off. He was in high spirits. When he came within sight of Moscow he began to point out the sights with his good hand, and he saluted passers-by by removing his cap and waving to them. The journey resembled a processional triumph. Everywhere he was recognized. He saw the exhibition and then ordered the chauffeur to take him to his old apartment in the Kremlin. Outside the Kremlin gate the astonished guards snapped to attention, and he smiled and waved back at them. He spent the night in the apartment; in the morning he looked into his office and the conference hall, and went out for a walk in the Kremlin grounds. There is a story that on one of his visits to his office he discovered that a secret drawer in his desk had been opened, and he was so appalled by the knowledge that his private papers had been rifled that he broke down. He returned to Gorki that evening, and during the following days it was noted that he was unusually sad and thoughtful. He never saw Moscow again.

A few days later, toward the end of October, an old friend Ossip Piatnitsky, veteran of many early struggles, went to visit him, with a small group which included the old Bolshevik Dr. Boris Weissbrod, one of Lenin's doctors, and Ivan Skvortsov, the theoretician. Piatnitsky had read in the foreign newspapers that Lenin was now no more than a shadow of himself:

> Imagine my surprise therefore when I saw he was exactly the same as I remembered him. There was the same face, the same wonderfully intelligent eyes, the same expression, the same smile which I had seen hundreds of times before when over a period of twenty years I went to visit him on party matters.
>
> At first you were not aware that he had any difficulty in speaking, for he usually spoke very little when he was receiving you. He would get you to speak, listen quietly, reacting in a normal way to what you said. Those who knew him well watched his expression and weighed

---

teenth. The authoritative *Lenin v Kremle* gives the eighteenth, and the official chronology in the *Sochineniya* gives the tenth. All available accounts of the journey seem to have been severely edited.

the amount of attention he gave them; in this way they knew what he was thinking. And that was how he behaved now to Skvortsov and me.

Skvortsov began to tell Vladimir Ilyich about the elections to the Moscow Soviet. He was only half listening, one eye on Skvortsov, the other ranging over the titles of the books on the table around which we were sitting. When Skvortsov enumerated the amendments brought forward by the workers in the factories and workshops and tabled at the Moscow Committee, amendments relating to the lighting in the streets where the workers and the poorer classes lived, and about the prolonging of the streetcar lines into the suburbs, and the closing of the cabarets, and so on, Vladimir Ilyich listened intently, and sometimes he would interrupt the other's discourse with the only word he could utter well. "There! There!" he would say. But he would say this word with so many different intonations that we understood him perfectly, as in the days before he became ill, and it was clear to us that he approved these amendments, that he regarded them as sensible and just, and that he felt it necessary to put them into operation.

Then it was my turn, and not without emotion I told Vladimir Ilyich about my work on the executive committee of the Communist International, and about what was happening among the various groups, about the trial of Comrade Bordiga in Italy and about the Italian Communist Party generally, and how in Great Britain the Communists were supporting the Labor Party except in a few places where they were offering their own candidates.

He paid very little attention to what I was saying, until I went on to speak of the breakdown of social democracy in Germany, the disastrous economic situation of the German workmen, the appalling unemployment figures and the misery which has fallen on millions of working men and women, and when I told him how the workmen were leaving the trade unions en masse, and about the role played by the factory committees, and the continually growing influence of the German Communist Party, he became animated and gave me his full attention and never took his eyes away from me. And there would come a shaking of his head, or a "There! There!" to emphasize his interest in affairs taking place in Germany. I forgot that I was in the presence of a sick man who must on no account be fatigued. It seemed to me I was in his office and he was listening to a report on the situation of the German working class, and from the expression of his face, his remarks, and his total absorption in the subject, he was showing a lively interest in the subject.

This may have been the very last political discussion in which Lenin took part. From time to time Krupskaya would ask the kind of question which Lenin would have asked, and then once again Lenin would shake his head or say "There! There!" with intonations that somehow suggested whole sentences. And when Piatnitsky and Skvortsov took leave of him, they were so impressed by his awakening intelligence that they discussed the time when he would be returning to the office. "Only of course, he must not work as hard as before," they said.

A few days later, on November 2, he met for the last time with a delegation of workers. They came with a gift of eighteen cherry trees to be planted in the conservatory attached to the house. Kholodova, one of the women workers, remembered Maria Ilyinichna saying behind closed doors: "Volodya, some friends have come to see you." The door opened, and Lenin came out of his room smiling, removing his cap with his left hand and putting it into his right; and then with his left hand he shook hands with all of them. They presented him with a written address, and there was a brief speech, and soon they were all in tears. A sixty-year-old workman threw his arms round Lenin. His name was Kuznetsov, which means "blacksmith." "I'm an old blacksmith," the old man kept saying through his tears. "Yes, Vladimir Ilyich, I'm a toiling blacksmith. I'll forge all you want . . ." They had difficulty in separating the old blacksmith and Lenin, who clung to one another. Maria Ilyinichna had said they could only stay for five minutes, and so they left him a little while later, each one kissing him in turn. There were only five members in the delegation, they had traveled a long way, and they were invited to spend the night at Gorki. During the dinner Maria Ilyinichna questioned them at length about the conditions at the textile mill, evidently with the purpose of informing Lenin. The next morning she told them he had sat up late reading the address they had given him over and over again.

Kholodova struck one curious note in her account of the meeting. She says that when Lenin came through the door, he said clearly and distinctly: "How glad I am that you have come." (*Kak ya rad chto vy priekhali.*) She was quite certain she heard him say these words, but as Krupskaya said later, workmen who came to visit him during his illness were always hearing entire sentences and reporting them to the newspapers, when he had merely smiled and said at most a few disconnected words.

So the days passed, while winter storms blew over Gorki, and health and intelligence came back to him. Krupskaya continued to read to him the articles he would point out to her, and because he had always liked Gorky she began reading his autobiography, *My Uni-*

versities. He had always had a weakness for the crude jingles of Demyan Bedny, and these too she read to him. Then there were the usual arduous exercises in speech formation, and every day he would learn three or four new words.

January 7, 1924, was Christmas Day according to the calendar of the Greek Orthodox Church. Krupskaya decided to set up a Christmas tree for the children of the neighboring village of Gorki. A fir tree was cut down and erected in the palatial living room. Candles were stuck on the tree, presents were gathered around it, workers' and peasants' children came trooping in. They danced round the fir tree, and when Lenin entered the room, they gathered round him and sat on his knees. Krupskaya and Maria Ilyinichna tried to shoo them away, but with no success. He wanted to have them round him.

About a week later Zinoviev, Kamenev and Bukharin paid a short visit to Gorki. They found him walking in the snow-covered park. He smiled when he saw them, and Zinoviev was particularly struck by the sweetness of his smile. He took off his cap, and shook hands with them, but apparently no words were exchanged. They returned to the house for a short talk with Krupskaya. "Everything is going well with us," Krupskaya told them. "He went out hunting, but he wouldn't take me along—he said he didn't want a nurse. His studies, and the reading, go on well. He is in a good mood, cracks jokes, and laughs uproariously. The doctors are all agreed that he will be able to talk by the summer. . . ."

On January 19 Krupskaya read to him Jack London's powerful story *Love of Life*. It is a strange story to read to a sick man, and why she chose this story to read to him out of the three thousand volumes of the library is something of a mystery; perhaps he asked for it, for he had a great affection for Jack London.

The story is one of unremitting gloom. It is an account of a journey into nightmare, the last extremities of a dying man as he wanders through the pitiless desolation of the Arctic wastes after being deserted by his comrade. The snow falls, and he does not know where he is going. Day after day he walks mechanically through the wilderness, numbed by hunger, his feet bleeding, his heart troubling him. He has a rifle, but no bullets. He goes stalking after ptarmigan, but they rise as soon as he approaches. One day he feeds on a small stringy onion sprout, another day on four ptarmigan chicks which he finds in a nest, on another day he finds the bones of a caribou calf picked clean by the wolves, and he crushes the bones and eats them. He sees a minnow in a pool and goes after it, but the minnow eludes him even after he has drained the pool with a bucket—it has vanished into a crack in the pool wall. The days pass; sometimes the mist closes in, but there are days when he can see for miles in the weak Arctic sunlight. What he sees brings him no comfort: there are only the wolves, the caribou, and sometimes a bear. One day he finds the bones of the companion who has deserted him shining pink in the sun; they too have been picked clean by the wolves.

In its relentless description of the endless frustrations confronting a dying man, the story is painfully effective. Nothing is spared the reader. The anonymous hero is seen at close quarters, hugely magnified so that he seems in some curious way to dominate the wilderness, becoming larger and more terrible as the last shreds of his human dignity are torn from him. He loses his hunting knife and his rifle; he walks empty-handed except for his watch, which he winds every day. Soon he can no longer walk, but crawls on hands and knees, leaving a bloodstained trail behind him; a sick wolf, following him, licks up the blood. His nights are haunted by the presence of the wolf waiting for him to die, its yellow tongue lolling. The coughing of the wolf, its way of staring at him drives him almost to madness. One day, gathering nearly all his remaining strength, the man hurls himself on the wolf and suffocates it. Then he drinks its blood.

All this time he has been making his way blindly toward the coast. Members of a scientific expedition on a whaling ship see a strange creeping thing moving along the coast. They lower a whaleboat and go in search of it. "They saw something which was alive but which could hardly be called a man. It was blind, unconscious. It squirmed along the ground like some monstrous worm. Most of its efforts were ineffectual, but it was persistent, and it writhed and twisted and went ahead perhaps a score of feet an hour."

According to Krupskaya, Lenin was "extraordinarily pleased" with the story, and the next day he asked her to read another. This time she read Jack London's story of a ship's captain who promises the owner he will sell his cargo of grain at a good price, and loses his life in order to keep his word. In Krupskaya's view Jack London was a magnificent writer who was sometimes seduced by bourgeois morality, and Lenin evidently agreed with her, for he burst out laughing and waved his good hand in mockery. It was the last story she ever read to him.

That morning, when he woke up, he felt listless and drowsy, complained of a headache and took no breakfast. Toward evening he told Krupskaya that his eyes were hurting him. The doctors who lived on the estate and others were summoned, but with his horror of doctors it was clear that he would refuse to see any of them. Suddenly Krupskaya remembered the famous eye specialist, Dr. Mikhail Auerbach. When she asked him whether he would consent to see the specialist, he readily agreed. Dr. Auerbach received an urgent telephone call from Maria Ilyinichna about eight o'clock in the evening, and he was in the house in Gorki by ten. A crowd of doctors had already assembled, and he recognized Foerster, Guetier, Rozanov, Kramer and Osipov, and there were others. None of them had been able to examine the patient. Krupskaya would tell them about his condition, they would then hold a consultation and tell her what they thought should be done.

For nearly two years Lenin had been wearing spectacles for reading, but he possessed a normal human vanity about being seen wearing them. Auerbach had advised on the spectacles, and Lenin had been struck by the casual brilliance of the young doctor, who was famous all over Europe.

The doctor was taken at once to Lenin's study and was surprised to find the patient in high spirits. As usual, Lenin showed solicitude for the doctor, who examined his eyes and found nothing wrong. The doctor thought Lenin must have touched the eyeball with one of the awkward movements he made with his hands. The doctor spent three quarters of an hour with the patient, and then went to an adjoining room, where Krupskaya and Maria Ilyinichna were waiting for him. He said he could find nothing wrong, and drank tea with them.

Suddenly the door opened, and Lenin walked in. He stayed for a few minutes, talked, and went away, only to return half an hour later to ask whether the doctor had been given anything to eat and to make sure he would be well covered during his journey back to Moscow. The doctor had the impression that Lenin deliberately came in and out of the room to show that he was feeling well and was no longer troubled by the pain in his eyes. He suggested that the doctor should spend the night at Gorki, but this was impossible: the doctor had patients to see in Moscow the next morning.

Earlier in the evening there had been a curious demonstration of Lenin's power to throw people into a panic. After examining the patient, Dr. Auerbach went down to the living room to tell the other doctors the results of his examination. One of the medical students who kept silent watch outside Lenin's door suddenly ran into the living room with the news that Lenin was on his way down. As it happened, he was not on his way down, but all the doctors except Dr. Auerbach scuttled away like rabbits.

Of all the available reports on Lenin's illness those of Dr. Auerbach and Dr. Rozanov ring truest; they are also the reports which show the greatest human sympathy for the patient. There is no mistaking the tone of affectionate understanding. Speaking of Lenin's condition, Dr. Auerbach repeatedly uses the purely human rather than the purely medical words. He uses words like *bodro* (vigorously) and *razdushno* (warmly) to describe Lenin's behavior. In telling about Lenin sitting down to talk, he uses the word *pobyesedoval*, which can only mean that they engaged in a friendly exchange of ideas. He was describing a patient who was well on the road to recovery.

At last, shortly before midnight, Dr. Auerbach accompanied Lenin to the door of his study. He said, "You must be tired, Vladimir Ilyich. You should go to bed." Then he took leave of the patient. He remembered afterward that there was a firm strength in Lenin's handshake. It was already January 21 when the doctor drove through the stormy night to Moscow.

Lenin had only a few more hours to live.

On January 16 the Thirteenth Party Conference opened in Moscow. The purpose of the conference was to lay the groundwork for the Thirteenth Party Congress which would be held later in the spring. To say that the conference "laid the groundwork" is to employ a euphemism. What happened at these conferences was that decisions were made by a small group of party members, and these would be rammed through the congress: anyone who disagreed with these decisions would be pilloried as a traitor to the revolution. Lenin had always stage-managed these conferences. In his absence they continued to be stage-managed.

The Thirteenth Party Conference differed from all those that had gone before by the absence of Lenin and of Trotsky, who had been ordered by the Kremlin doctors to take a rest cure only a few days before. With the absence of the two men who were chiefly responsible for bringing about the revolution, the way was open for the battle of the succession.

In fact the battle of the succession had already been won by Stalin. Most of the party members attending the conference were his hand-picked nominees. Kamenev and Zinoviev were sidetracked into occupying decorative positions. Kamenev was president, his role being limited to the formal opening and closing speeches. Zinoviev was permitted to speak on the international situation. The colorless Rykov, who had lived so long in Lenin's shadow that he appeared to have no independent existence of his own, was permitted the task of introducing the resolutions on economic policy. Stalin reserved for himself the right to make the major speeches on government policy. The battle lines were cleared, and one man was defiantly advancing to occupy the position of supreme power.

No one reading the stenographic report of the conference can avoid the sense of a pitiless drama being unfolded before his eyes. Stalin emerges as a figure of astonishing audacity and determination. He taunts his enemies, smiles at them good-naturedly, warns them gently of their errors, and then clubs them into insensibility. There is something strangely mechanical in his arguments, which are buttressed by appeals to earlier and long-forgotten works by Lenin. It is as though a powerful primitive engine of destruction had suddenly irrupted upon the stage to subdue and pulverize everyone within sight. The future Stalin was already contained in the two speeches he delivered at the Thirteenth Party Conference.

Stalin calculated well: only two men now stood between him and a position of supreme power. He could attack Lenin only obliquely. He could attack Trotsky, whose weaknesses he had studied with exquisite care, with all the energy at his command.

Against Trotsky he wielded a sledge hammer, raining down blow after blow on a man who was making his way in a slow train to the Caucasus and who could therefore not defend himself. Stalin accused him of "six major errors": one would have been enough to hang him. He was presumptuous, he had refused to accept the discipline of the Central Committee, he was continually demanding that the voice of the students should be heard, and he placed them on a higher footing than the old guard, he was encouraging the intellectuals against the party. He had opposed the apparatus to the party, as if party work could be carried on without the apparatus. "Trotsky's error," declared Stalin, "lies in the fact that he has elevated himself into a superman standing above the Central Committee, above its laws, and above its decisions, and in this way he has provided certain groups within the party with a pretext for undermining confidence in the Central Committee." In Stalin's view these were more than "errors"; they formed the basis for a charge of high treason.

But this was only the beginning. The trap was sprung when Stalin read to the conference the secret clause which had been proposed by Lenin and adopted by the Tenth Congress, which decreed that a member of the Central Committee could be expelled from the party "by a two-thirds majority of the most responsible leaders of the party in general assembly." Up to this time the secret clause had remained in abeyance. Stalin had found the weapon for destroying opposition, and was busily sharpening it.

When Vrachev, one of the opposition speakers, said, "It seems to me we have only a few more hours of full democracy left, and let us use these hours," he was saying no more than the truth. The time when delegates at the conferences would still be permitted to debate was fast running out. A little while later, when Vrachev was wondering aloud what the secretary general would report at the next meeting, Lominadze, one of Stalin's supporters, replied, "You won't be there to hear!" And when Evgeniy Preobrazhensky accused Stalin of intimidating the party and baiting Trotsky, both of these statements being demonstrably true, Stalin answered with some rambling stories of Trotsky's insulting behavior designed to show that he deserved whatever baiting he got. "It is not true that I am intimidating the party," Stalin declared. "But I hope I am intimidating the factionalists." A Communist student called Kazaryan had the courage to ask a question which was in the minds of hundreds of thousands of people living under the Soviet government. He said, "Are we living under a dictatorship of the proletariat or under a dictatorship of the Communist Party over the proletariat?" "The only difference between Trotsky and Kazaryan," Stalin observed, "is that Trotsky merely thinks we have become corrupt, while Kazaryan thinks we deserve to be driven out, because all we have done is to saddle ourselves on the proletariat."

Preobrazhensky led the opposition against Stalin with extraordinary boldness, but from the beginning it was a losing battle. Even Radek joined in the debate with the accusation that a Directory had been set up inside the Central Committee. Stalin did not reply to the accusation directly. He simply bludgeoned Radek into silence by saying he was a slave of his tongue, the servant of whatever sounds came blurting from his mouth: only fools would listen to him.

Of Lenin, Stalin spoke respectfully, but with a curious undertone of bitterness. "The opposition is always extolling Lenin and proclaiming him to be the greatest of geniuses," Stalin said. "So he is, but I am afraid the praise is insincere and conceals some clever stratagems. When they clamor about his genius, they are merely covering up the distance that separates them from Lenin, and at the same time they are emphasizing the weakness of Lenin's disciples. But it is not for us, who are his disciples, to fail to appreciate him as the greatest of geniuses; men of his caliber come only once in many centuries." This praise perhaps conceals many clever stratagems.

So for three days, from January 16 to January 18, 1924, the Thirteenth Party Conference met in an atmosphere of threats, menaces and intimidation. Over the entire conference brooded the implacable figure of the Georgian conspirator, "the man of steel," unbending in his demand that the party apparatus should continue in the path he had chosen for it. For the first time he was imposing his absolute will upon Russia; and having wrested power, he was to remain in authority for thirty blood-drenched years. Only with his death was he to lose that authority; and even then for many years he was to continue to speak from the grave.

Neither Krupskaya nor Maria Ilyinichna tell us whether Lenin was informed about the sudden rise to power of the man with whom he had broken off all comradely relations, but since the newspapers were regularly read to him, he could hardly have failed to realize what was happening. It could have been no comfort to him that Stalin was now the undisputed master of the Communist empire.

Lenin hated, despised and feared Stalin. Stalin in turn hated, despised and feared Lenin. Stalin had taken the measure of Trotsky, who could be disposed of at his leisure, but there could be no question of disposing so easily with Lenin if he recovered his health. The visit of Zinoviev, Kamenev and Bukharin to Gorki had confirmed his worst fears. All the doctors prophesied that Lenin would be back at work by the summer.

It was to Stalin's advantage that at this moment Lenin should die.

THE MURDER OF LENIN

I**N THE MORNING** of January 21 the maidservant Evdokia Smirnova brought Lenin his breakfast, putting it down on the table in his study. She knocked at the door of his bedroom, and when he emerged there was nothing to suggest any change from the previous day: he greeted her in exactly the same kindly manner. Normally he would sit down at the table facing the windows which looked out over the park. It was the custom of the maidservant to remain in the room with him, helping him with the breakfast; she would pour the coffee, pick up a fallen spoon or plate, and provide company. He went to the table, but instead of taking breakfast he abruptly returned to the bedroom and lay down on the bed.

The maidservant was a sensible woman, thirty-three years old, a former garment worker in Moscow, and she had been in his employ since the previous March. She had no knowledge of nursing. She was selected because she was sensible, straightforward and capable. She may have been a distant relative of Lenin.

She waited all morning, keeping the coffee warm. From time to time Krupskaya or Maria Ilyinichna came to peer into the bedroom. Lenin told Maria Ilyinichna that he was not feeling well, but they were not unduly perturbed; it was expected that he would suffer from occasional indispositions, especially in winter. The trouble, whatever it was, seemed to have nothing to do with his eyes. Because he was resting, the servants were ordered to walk about as quietly as possible, and some of them removed their boots and went about in their stocking feet. The telephone kept ringing. It was the Central Committee, the Sovnarkom, the Cheka, all inquiring about the health of Lenin. Maria Ilyinichna complained about the incessant ringing of the telephone, but there was nothing she could do about it.

Vladimir Sorin, a leading member of the Communist Party in Moscow and an infrequent visitor to Gorki happened to be visiting his old friend Alexey Preobrazhensky, who lived in the small house nearby. When Lenin wearied of the large house, he sometimes spent a few days with Preobrazhensky, whom he had known since they worked together in Samara in the 1890s. He was the director of the local sovkhoz and an old family friend. When Sorin wanted news about Lenin, he had only to go to the small house.

Sorin arrived at the house about noon. He learned that Maria Ilyinichna had come to see Preobrazhensky earlier in the morning, and had brought the news that Lenin was not feeling well, but there was no real change in his condition. Then, shortly after Sorin's arrival, one of the doctors dropped in. Maria Ilyinichna's news was faintly disturbing, and he was therefore asked about Lenin's health. "Well, he's sleeping now," the doctor said. "There's one thing quite certain—he is going to be completely cured by the summer."

Except for the incessant ringing of the telephone, the afternoon passed quietly. Lenin slept or dozed. At some time during the morning he drank a little tea, but he took no food except for a few small morsels at lunch. Immediately after lunch he went back to bed. Sometimes he would awake and recognize his wife or his sister, and then he would fall asleep again. It was the dead of winter, and darkness came down early.

Around six o'clock some servants keeping watch in the bedroom observed that he was breathing with difficulty. Dr. Foerster, who was on duty, was immediately summoned. Krupskaya and Maria Ilyinichna hurried to the bedroom. Because the patient detested the sight of doctors, and because they were afraid of the adverse effect on him if he saw the doctor in the room, a simple stratagem was devised. A screen was set up near the bed, and Dr. Foerster stationed himself behind it. Here, without being seen, he could listen to the patient's breathing and suggest measures which could be taken. As it happened, the breathing improved, and soon the patient was breathing peacefully. The doctor left the room. It was agreed that there had been nothing more than a slight scare.

The doctor had scarcely left the room when the breathing became irregular again. This time the slow, heavy, labored breathing assumed an entirely different character: it was the breathing of a man fighting for his life. Soon the patient was in convulsions, his temperature soared, and it became clear that he had not long to live.

Vladimir Sorin was spending a quiet evening at the small house. Suddenly the door burst open, and a servant sent by Maria Ilyinichna was loudly asking whether there was any camphor available. "Why camphor?" Sorin asked, and he was told that camphor was a heart stimulant. He went outside, and observed that all the upstairs lights in the large house were on, and this was something he had never seen before. He fell into conversation with one of the guards. "Comrade Pakaln is up there!" the guard said, and then Sorin knew the worst, for it was well known that Pakaln was forbidden to enter Lenin's rooms except in an emergency.

The doctor did what he could, but from the beginning of the convulsions he knew there was little hope. Soon he was joined by Dr. Elistratov and Dr. Osipov, and they remained at the bedside. The breathing became more labored, the convulsions more intense, as Lenin's small body was lifted up and hurled from one side of the bed to the other by the force of the convulsions which were almost continuous. At last the breathing became intermittent, and Lenin was pronounced dead at 6:50 P.M.

Not long afterward the body was taken downstairs to the large living room, where it was laid, according to the Russian custom, on a table. Everyone who had heard of the death came hurrying to the house to gaze at the man who had once been the acknowledged leader of world Communism and the dictator of Russia. Krupskaya sat beside him, holding his hand. She showed no emotion except for the occasional quivering of her lips.

Vladimir Sorin had been watching the house from a distance, not daring to go in. Then for the second time that evening he saw a door burst open. It was the door of the large house, and a woman was standing there, screaming at the top of her lungs.

As he lay on the table, Lenin looked very much as he looked in life. Death had not disfigured him; he seemed vigorous; there was color in his cheeks. His arms were stretched along his sides, and his fists were clenched. "He's looking well today," a peasant said, and then fell silent. Vladimir Sorin, who had finally steeled himself to enter the large house, was struck by the power which still seemed to radiate from the dead man. "I had the feeling," he wrote later, "that in a moment or two Lenin would concentrate all the strength of his muscles and rise from the table."

Because she could not endure her grief, Maria Ilyinichna paced nervously up and down the room, sobbing helplessly. The doctors, too, were sobbing. Only Krupskaya, whose grief was greatest, remained calm.

The news of Lenin's death reached the Kremlin. Zinoviev was perfectly aware of the solemnity of the moment, and in his oddly insensitive way he reached out immediately for a sheet of paper to record his feelings. These impressions, which he recorded at intervals during the next six days, are not perhaps of any great value, for they demonstrate only too convincingly the shallowness of his mind, but he was in a position of great power and among the few who could have reached out for the succession. Here he tells of the visit of six members of the Central Committee to Gorki shortly after Lenin's death:

Just a moment ago they telephoned that Lenin is dead.

In an hour we shall go to Gorki to the dead Ilyich. Bukharin, Tomsky, Kalinin, Stalin, Kamenev and I. (Rykov is ill.) We shall go by auto-sleigh. And just as in the past, when he was alive, we always hurried to Gorki at Lenin's summons, so now we shall fly on wings. But now . . .

We gaze at the stars and try to talk to one another. Ilyich is dead. We wonder what will happen. The journey takes so long, all of two hours. Gorki. We enter the house. Lenin lies on the table. Already they have put a new double-breasted coat on him. Flowers. Pine branches. He lies in the large room. It opens out on a veranda. Frost. On this veranda in the summer of 1920 we drank tea and made our decisions on the attack on Warsaw. He lies there as though he were still alive. He is at rest, and still breathes. Surely there is the rising and falling of his chest. His face is quiet and peaceful. He looks better than when we saw him. The wrinkles are smoothed out. The leathery folds on the lower part of the face near the cheek remain. His hair has been recently cut. He looks young. He looks so well, so fresh. Only the "old man" seems to be discontented, and that is why we gaze at him for such a long time and the tears fill our eyes. Kiss his forehead, his incomparable forehead. The forehead is as cold as marble. Our hearts are transpierced by the thought that this is an event for the ages, for eternity.

We had arranged to hold a meeting of the plenum of the Central Committee at two o'clock in the morning. We returned by train. An hour late. None of us will ever forget the moment when we arrived at the meeting. Fifty men were sitting there, and all were plunged in silence. Silence of the grave. Evidently they had been sitting there in silence for a long time, in fact from the time they arrived. They were all fearless Leninists, fighters chosen from the ranks of the whole party, who had looked often in the face of death. They sat there with their lips tightly compressed. No words came. At last they began to talk. They sat there till morning. Orphaned. During those hours they were closer to one another than ever before.

In Zinoviev's account there is no grief: only the impassive journalist's interest in death. All the clichés—"cold as marble," "an event for the ages"—are dragged out and introduced into a document which is clearly intended to have historical significance. All he can remember is that on the veranda, drinking tea, he once helped to make important decisions.

The six members of the Central Committee returned to Moscow, and during the evening the sculptor Merkulov made the death mask. The autopsy was begun the next morning at 11:10 A.M. and not completed until nearly six hours later. Ten doctors were present. They opened the body and found no signs of disease: the heart, the lungs, and other vital organs were such as were to be expected in a healthy man of his age. They found the bullet lodged in the left shoulder; they noted that the bullet was "deformed," but it was apparently not a dumdum bullet nor did it bear any traces of curare. They found, as they had expected, the bullet scar in the lung. They noted that the stomach was empty, its walls collapsed, and the intestines were normal. The stomachs of the dead are very rarely empty, and they were evidently using the term in a relative sense. No chemical analysis of the contents of the stomach was made, perhaps because they were not looking for poison or were afraid to look for it.

They opened the skull case and found evidence of a recent stroke. Dr. Semashko, the Commissar of Health, who was present, spoke later of how the doctors were thunderstruck when they discovered that the blood vessels of the brain had calcified, and metal instruments touching the brain gave off a ringing sound. But the autopsy only indicates that the middle cerebral artery was "very thin, hardened, but upon section still showing a thin small slit." Legends appeared after Lenin's death saying that the brain had shriveled to the size of an apple, but the autopsy describes a brain of the normal weight and size. The doctors found sufficient damage to the brain to conclude that he had died of arteriosclerosis. A long and carefully drawn-up report was made (see Appendix) and a brief bulletin was issued. The bulletin read:

On January 21 the condition of Vladimir Ilyich suddenly underwent sharp aggravation. At 5:30 P.M. his breathing was interrupted and he lost consciousness. Convulsions followed. At 6:50 P.M. Vladimir Ilyich died from paralysis of the respiratory organs. An autopsy, performed at 2 P.M. on January 22, revealed grave changes in the blood vessels of the brain and a recent hemorrhage into the arachnoid pia mater in the area of the corpora quadrigemina: these were the immediate causes of death.

The bulletin was signed by Abrikosov, Foerster, Osipov, Bunak, Deshin, Weissbrod, Obukh, Elistratov, Rozanov, Semashko, and Guetier. For some reason the last-named, who was the personal physician of both Lenin and Trotsky, did not sign the autopsy.

One puzzling aspect of the autopsy has been left unexplained: the delay of sixteen hours and twenty minutes before it was performed. The only possible explanation seems to be that the doctors were waiting for approval from the Kremlin, which was not given until corruption had set in. An autopsy performed shortly after a death is, in the very nature of things, more valid than one performed many hours later. If there had been poison, all traces of it could have been removed in sixteen hours. For reasons unknown, the short official bulletin says the autopsy was performed at 2 P.M. on the day after the death, while the detailed report of the findings of the doctors says that it was begun shortly after 11 A.M. and ended shortly before 4 P.M. Such discrepancies may not be very important, but they suggest a certain carelessness toward elementary facts, and we are entitled to wonder whether any other discrepancies exist.

The death when it came was unexpected; and the timing of it served the purposes of Stalin so well that even among Communists there were rumors that he had poisoned Lenin "to put an end to his agony." But there is no evidence to show that he was in any agony until shortly before his death.

Of the unexpectedness of his death all testimonies except one agree. The official communiqué broadcast on January 22 spoke of his continuing good health. "There was nothing," says the official communiqué, "to suggest the proximity of death. During these last days the health of Vladimir Ilyich had been sensibly improving, and there was every reason to believe that this improvement would continue.

But yesterday evening the state of his health suddenly became worse." The testimony of the doctors agrees with the official communiqué. "On the day of his death," wrote Dr. Elistratov, "Vladimir Ilyich was a little weaker and more apathetic than usual, and he lay down more than usual, but there was not the slightest indication of the possibility of a serious attack." Dr. Foerster wrote that "on that fatal Monday, January 21, there was nothing to suggest an attack was imminent until it came. Suddenly and unexpectedly at six o'clock he suffered an attack which continued for fifty minutes and ended with his death." Both doctors were present at the deathbed, and they spoke with authority.

When great men die sudden deaths, the manner of their dying is rarely taken for granted. Legends spring up, and stories are whispered about the strange portents which accompanied their passing. Very few of Russia's rulers have died natural deaths: dynamite, poison, the gun, the rope, the knife, and the suffocating pillow have killed more often than disease. And the death of Lenin was a very sudden one.

Now it happens that we have many accounts of Lenin's last days written by many observers over a long period of time. Some have revised their accounts, adding and subtracting from the first original impressions, but there are a large number of accounts written and published shortly after Lenin's death. The doctors' accounts were printed in *Pravda* on January 31. In an amazingly short time Boris Volin and Mikhail Koltzov compiled and edited a brochure called *Kak Lenin Umer* (How Lenin Died), which was published on January 26. The brochure contains statements by doctors and others, and prints the full text of the autopsy. In March a comprehensive study of the known facts of Lenin's death appeared in *Proletarskaya Revolutsiya*. Other accounts have appeared in the various volumes of reminiscences of Lenin published at intervals over the last forty years. We have the testimonies of his wife, his sister, the doctors who attended him, the guards who patrolled the grounds, and the maid-servant who brought him coffee on the morning of the day he died, together with the reminiscences of high government officials and Communist Party members. With rare exceptions the information they have to offer fits into a general pattern. Minor discrepancies can be found; there are also major discrepancies, and these are sometimes alarming.

Without exception, the doctors report on his continued improvement. Dr. Rozanov, Dr. Foerster and Dr. Auerbach all spoke of full recovery by the summer. They speak of his "glow of health," and of how he walked and made efforts to talk with increasing assurance. Krupskaya and Maria Ilyinichna, who were continually at his side, noted a consistent improvement. He was gaining ground every day. His vocabulary was increasing, he was more alert, and they believed he understood everything they said to him.

The doctors were also in agreement that during these last days and all through the summer and autumn, the patient had shown what appeared to be an unreasoning fear of doctors, and of some doctors more than others. He could not abide them, refused to have any contact with them, and accepted the advice only of his wife and sister; he had the same intolerance of the guards stationed in the grounds of the estate, who had orders to remain out of sight whenever he appeared. Chekist guards like Pakaln and Belmas were continually reporting his activities to Moscow, but in fact they rarely saw him, and derived their information from Krupskaya, Maria Ilyinichna, or the house servants who were ordered to report to them. Throughout his stay in Gorki daily reports on him were sent to the Kremlin.

If we assume that Lenin's mind was clear and that his actions were motivated by prudence rather than unreasoning fear, then it follows that he had good cause to avoid the doctors and the guards. Dr. Rozanov more than hints that Lenin was afraid of poison, for he tells how Lenin wanted to eat with everyone else, and then immediately relates the story of Lenin holding up a bottle of quinine and saying "Poison," and then laughing. A good deal depends on how he said the word and how he laughed. One imagines it was mirthless laughter.

By itself, Trotsky's testimony that Lenin asked Stalin to give him poison in February 1923 could be discounted. Trotsky himself could scarcely bring himself to believe that it happened; it was a nightmare which only with great difficulty could be hammered into words. As he relates the story Trotsky seems to be bemused by its irrelevance, by its curiously unanchored quality, and by the fact that it puts Stalin in an unaccustomed light as a merciful protector. Here is Trotsky's entry in the diary he wrote in exile in 1935, eleven years after the death of Lenin:

> When Lenin felt worse again, in February or the very first days of March 1923, he summoned Stalin and addressed to him an insistent request to bring him some poison. Afraid lest he lose the power of speech again and become a toy in the hands of the doctors, Lenin wanted to remain the master of his fate. It was no accident that at one time he had

expressed his approval of Lafargue, who preferred by his own act to "join the majority" rather than to live an invalid.

According to Trotsky, Stalin refused to bring the poison after taking up the matter with the Politburo, and he may have guessed that Lenin had no intention of taking poison, but was simply testing Stalin's loyalty, or perhaps—for Trotsky was inclined to think that many motives were involved—Lenin did want the poison, and there was a kind of irony in accepting it from the hands of his greatest enemy. It was, after all, such a request as could only be directed to a stanch revolutionary, and "it is beyond dispute," says Trotsky, "that Lenin regarded Stalin as a stanch revolutionary." Trotsky tells the story and goes on to relate how in 1926 Krupskaya told him that Stalin "lacks the most elementary human honesty," saying that these words had been spoken by Lenin.

Trotsky's diary entry was unknown until the diary came into the possession of Harvard University. It was published in full in 1958, nearly twenty years after his death. It was not the only time he spoke of Stalin giving Lenin poison; ten days before he was assassinated in Mexico there appeared in the magazine *Liberty* an article written by him in which he suggested a little diffidently that Lenin had been poisoned, but he brought up no supporting evidence and went into no details.

The story, as Trotsky tells it, is curiously unconvincing: it is thrown off too casually—even for a diary entry—to suggest that he had given it much thought. Krupskaya or Fotieva may have told him that they feared that Stalin was about to poison Lenin, and on that slender basis Trotsky may have imagined the entire incident of Lenin demanding poison from the man he regarded as his enemy. But if Stalin did not poison Lenin in February 1923, did he poison him eleven months later?

In 1955, more than thirty years after Lenin's death, there appeared for the first time a circumstantial account of Lenin's death by poison. This account appears in *Face of a Victim*, Elizabeth Lermolo's autobiographical narrative of her arrest and imprisonment following the murder of Sergey Kirov in 1934. She had a brief acquaintance with Leonid Nikolayev, who killed Kirov, and she was immediately arrested as a material witness. For the following eight years she was a prisoner in various "isolators." These were the prisons which effectively isolated important political prisoners from the outside world.

Occasionally in these isolators political prisoners were allowed to take exercise in small groups, and so they would meet and talk. One day, about a year after her imprisonment, Elizabeth Lermolo encountered an Old Bolshevik called Gavril Volkov, who had taken part in the uprising in 1917. He told her that until 1923 he had been employed in the Kremlin as manager of a dining room maintained for high party officials, and that he was then sent to Gorki to become Lenin's personal chef. Krupskaya had known him and found him thoroughly dependable. For nearly a year he prepared all Lenin's meals.

Volkov told her that at various times during the winter Krupskaya was called on urgent business to Moscow, remaining there for one or two days. The first time, when she returned, she found that Lenin's health had taken a sudden turn for the worse. Special treatment was prescribed, and he soon recovered. No harm had been done, and he returned to normal life.

About ten days later Krupskaya was again called to the Kremlin, and this time she stayed longer. Once again Lenin's condition took a turn for the worse, and he apparently went through a crisis of fear. Volkov, bringing him his morning tea, had some difficulty understanding why he was so agitated. Finally it transpired that Lenin wanted Volkov to reach Krupskaya, to tell her he was feeling worse, to drop everything, and to return immediately to Gorki. Volkov was told not to telephone; at all costs he must give the message to Krupskaya in person. But that day a severe snowstorm sprang up, and he was unable to go to Moscow. Also, a message had arrived from Stalin ordering the entire staff and all the physicians at Gorki to remain at their posts until the health of "our dearly beloved Comrade Lenin" had improved, with the result that Lenin grew worse and it was some time before Krupskaya returned from Moscow.

Volkov also told her about the last day of Lenin's life. Here she tells his story:

> And then on January 21, 1924 . . . At eleven in the morning, as usual, Volkov took Lenin his second breakfast. There was no one in his room. As soon as Volkov appeared, Lenin made an effort to rise and extended both his hands, uttering unintelligible sounds. Volkov rushed over to him and Lenin slipped a note into his hands.
>
> As Volkov turned, having hidden the note, Dr. Elistratov, Lenin's personal physician, ran into the room, apparently having been attracted by the commotion. The two of them got Lenin back to bed and gave

THE MURDER OF LENIN

him an injection to calm him. Lenin quieted down, his eyes half closed. He never opened them again.

The note scratched in a nervous scrawl, read: "Gavrilushka, I've been poisoned . . . go fetch Nadya at once . . . tell Trotsky . . . tell everyone you can."

"Two questions," Volkov said, "have troubled me all these years. Did Elistratov see Lenin give me that note? And if he did, did he inform Stalin? These questions have ruined my peace, poisoned my existence. I have felt every minute that my life is hanging on a thread."

"How frightful!" I exclaimed.

"Later on, I ran into Dr. Elistratov a few times, but we never exchanged a word. We merely looked at each other, that was all. I thought I detected in his eyes the same torment of a deeply hidden secret. I may be wrong, but he seemed a slave of his secret like myself. What became of him, I don't know—he soon disappeared from Gorki."

Elizabeth Lermolo describes her meeting with Gavril Volkov without embroidery. She never raises her voice. She tells of her experiences in the isolators in the same quiet tones with which one might describe a visit to a friendly place. Reading her book, one has the predisposition to believe everything she says, if only because she writes with such quiet authenticity. But it is another question whether we can believe Volkov. His unsupported testimony alone would convince no jury.

When crimes are committed, it is the custom of the police to interview all those who are in any way connected with the crime and to collect and examine their signed affidavits. To rumors they will attach only such weight as rumors can bear. What interests them particularly are the curious discrepancies which will sometimes appear in the accounts of witnesses, pointing in the direction of the criminal. Among the many accounts of the last days of Lenin, there is one which differs markedly from all the rest, and there is perhaps some significance in the fact that it was written by a member of the secret police at Gorki.

Alexander Belmas was a Latvian, appointed by Dzerzhinsky himself the previous autumn to be one of Lenin's guards. He had fought in the civil war and was a trusted member of the OGPU. He wrote a brief account of Lenin's last days:

19th January 1924. I kept the night watch over Vladimir Ilyich. In the morning, when my period of watching was over, Ilyich did not come out for breakfast. Then Pyotr Petrovich [Pakaln] came up to me sadly and said, "Ilyich is not feeling well today and won't be going out for his walk." Some time later Maria Ilyinichna sent me to the telephone to call Dr. Foerster at the Botkinsky hospital. Once more grief filled the house. Everyone was immersed in gloom. Nadezhda Konstantinovna and Maria Ilyinichna took up an uninterrupted vigil by the bedside of Ilyich. The telephone kept ringing. Calls were coming in from the Central Committee, the Sovnarkom and the OGPU, all asking about the health of Lenin. We were all anxious and silent. Only Maria Ilyinichna went about reproving anyone who made a noise: she complained about the telephone and the noise we made with our feet. I took off my felt boots, so that they would make no noise.

20th January. About one o'clock at night Lenin became unconscious. Everyone was stricken with grief. People came from the Central Committee, and with them came all Lenin's doctors. Kramer, Foerster, Rozanov, Obukh, Guetier, Semashko were all there. While they were discussing what to do, the attack came to an end, but Lenin remained weak. He had eaten nothing since the previous day.

21st January. Telephone ringing, everyone fearfully calling up about Lenin's health. The doctors have not left him, and there are two others, his wife and his sister, who have maintained the vigil for the third day.

Suddenly Maria Ilyinichna ran to the telephone and in a voice of terror she said: "Lenin is dead." She flung down the receiver and went running back to Lenin's room. I quietly picked up the receiver and put it back on the hook. It was beyond belief. It could not have happened. Lenin was alive. It must have been some mistake of the doctors. The telephone kept ringing: "How is Lenin?" I replied, "Lenin is alive." Then again and again the telephone kept ringing. It was as though the whole of Moscow was afflicted with our sorrow, and they were all saying, "How is Lenin?" And to them all I replied, "Lenin is alive."

A little while later Comrade Pakaln, in command of the bodyguard, came up to me and said, "Go tell the boys that Lenin is dead." So I went to fulfill this last errand. I went to the people waiting about the house. They all said, "Tell us . . . Tell us quickly . . ." And I said, "Lenin is dead."

As a member of the OGPU, Belmas was trained to report accurately and fully about everything he saw. He was a former peasant, but he clearly knew how to express himself. And what is remarkable about this report is that it is at variance with all the others. We have only Belmas's word for the attack which took place at one o'clock at night on January 20. He says Rozanov was present; but Rozanov, according to his own account, had already left the house. He says that Lenin was already ill on the morning of January 19, and that Lenin's wife and sister kept a three-day vigil by the bedside. He mentions

endless calls coming in from the Central Committee, the Sovnarkom
and the OGPU, all inquiring about Lenin's health on a day when, according to all other witnesses, Lenin showed not the slightest sign of
being ill. There is something ominous about those reiterated calls
demanding news of the health of a man who was well. Belmas may
have confused times and places, he may have thought he observed
things he did not see. From his own account, he was never in the
bedroom; he kept watch outside the door. His story of Maria Ilyinichna coming from the bedroom and saying into the telephone, "Lenin is dead," and then leaving the receiver dangling, rings true: it is
exactly what one might expect from her. No doubt Pakaln, the commander of the bodyguard, did come out and say: "Go tell the boys
that Lenin is dead," and the word "boys" (*rebyata*) is exactly what
we might expect from an officer of the OGPU. The words in their
context mean: "Go and tell the rest of the gang." But everything else
in Belmas's report has the ring of falsity. It is as though he were not
in fact present in the house until shortly before Lenin's death, or as
though he were describing another death altogether.

It is not only that his report is irreconcilable with all the others
and is particularly at variance with the accounts of Krupskaya and
Rozanov, but it is possible to detect a deliberate design in the falsi-
fication. He wishes us to understand that for three days Lenin lay
mortally ill, that there was an uninterrupted vigil by the bedside, and
that Lenin ate nothing after the nineteenth, when his health suddenly
took a turn for the worse. We are also asked to believe that late on
the night of the twentieth he suffered an attack, which is otherwise
unrecorded.

Now if we assume that there was an attempt to poison Lenin by
administering larger and larger doses over a period of three days, we
would arrive at a general pattern close to the pattern depicted by
Belmas. There was nothing to be gained by a quick death. A decline
of health over a period of three days would have admirably suited
Stalin's purpose. This would give him time to prepare warning bulletins and to prepare the Russians for the explosion of grief which
would inevitably follow the announcement of Lenin's death; he would
then be able to channel the grief along whatever political lines he
pleased. The death would be all the more credible if it were prolonged.

Belmas's report reads as though he incorporated the original plan
of the crime, which miscarried. There seems to be no other way to

explain how a trained OGPU agent could get so many facts wrong. We can explain his report only on the grounds that he was not present at Gorki on the nineteenth and twentieth of January, but arrived there on the twenty-first in time to become the messenger of death. "Go tell the boys that Lenin is dead."

Stalin had ample means to commit the crime. Some twenty OGPU guards were in residence at Gorki. The gardeners, the chauffeurs, the woodcutters, even the launderers and the cooks on the Gorki estate were all agents of the OGPU. Only the serving maid Evdokia Smirnova seems to have had no connection with them, having been privately brought into the household by Krupskaya. She may have been a distant relative, for Smirnova was the name of Lenin's grandmother. Dzerzhinsky, who might conceivably have remained loyal to Lenin, though he was bitterly attacked in Lenin's last letters, had been replaced as chief of the OGPU by Menzhinsky, whose loyalty was to Stalin. Stalin was in a position to exert his will on every aspect of life at Gorki. If he had wanted to poison Lenin, there was nothing to prevent him.

Most of those who were present at the white house in Gorki are now dead. Maria Ilyinichna and Krupskaya died long ago, and none of the doctors who attended Lenin are among the living. Vladimir Sorin, whose graphic account of the last days is among the best that have survived, was executed by Stalin in 1944. He has since been posthumously rehabilitated, and his execution is now ascribed to "the calumnies of his enemies." Volkov, Pakaln and Belmas have passed out of sight. In the course of forty years many secrets have been taken to many graves.

But if there is no evidence to permit us to point directly to the murderer, there is such an abundance of clues that it is no longer possible to believe he died a natural death. The small clues amount to a large clue. The unsupported testimony of Volkov or Trotsky, who wrote shortly before his own murder about his growing suspicions that Lenin had been murdered, scarcely amount to a bill of accusation, but when supported by the testimony of the doctors, who innocently or ingenuously added their share of incriminating evidence, we are compelled to take them seriously. When Rozanov mentions casually that Lenin wanted to eat with everyone else and spoke of the quinine, which he took without grimacing, as "poison," we are entitled to believe that Lenin himself was perfectly aware that poison might be administered and was mortally afraid of it. When Auerbach speaks of Lenin's radiant good humor on the night before his death, while an officer of the OGPU speaks of the house being plunged in gloom because Lenin had suffered a heart attack, are we to believe the officer of the OGPU? Belmas has provided damaging evidence that the OGPU saw things which no one else saw. He speaks of visitors from the Central Committee arriving on January 20. No one else saw them. If they had come, it would be highly suspicious: it is all the more suspicious that Belmas should report their coming, when in fact they did not appear.

The decision to murder Lenin seems to have been taken about January 15, when it was known that Trotsky was about to leave Moscow. He did in fact leave Moscow the next day. At one time Krupskaya or Maria Ilyinichna had remained with Lenin whenever he was taking food, but gradually as the months passed they had become less strict, and the serving maid or one of the other attendants were permitted to bring him his meals. Since according to Belmas the first relapse took place on the nineteenth, we may assume that an effort was made to administer the first dose of poison that day. Lenin did not however take the poison, or if he took it, it had no effect on his strong constitution. Nevertheless the OGPU agent believed that Lenin was worse, and the information was sent to his superiors. Similarly on the next day the attempt failed, producing no effect except sharp pain in the eyes. We have it on the authority of Dr. Semashko that Lenin drank some tea on the morning of the twenty-first, shortly before lunch, and that he took a little lunch. The massive dose may have been in the tea or in the lunch. From this dose he never recovered.

Something of this kind must have happened. We rarely know the precise details of a murder, and there is nearly always some element of doubt about the exact way poison is administered. When a man is shot, we know exactly how his death came about. When he is poisoned, there must be some element of surmise. There are clues in abundance, and each one taken singly is of no very great value, but in the mass they must be taken seriously. The most damaging clue was left by Alexander Belmas, whose strange account of Lenin's death was first published in 1960. Of Belmas nothing more is known except that in the course of time he retired from the OGPU and received a pension from Stalin.

THE APOTHEOSIS OF A GOD

THE NEWS OF LENIN'S DEATH was kept secret for sixteen hours. The rumors began to spread around Moscow late the following morning, but some especially favored ones heard it a little earlier. So it happened that Wilhelm Pieck, who had come to Moscow as a member of the German delegation to the All-Union Soviet Congress, heard the news by telephone from the Kremlin at exactly half-past ten, and a few minutes later from the telephone booth in the Lux Hotel he was able to convey it to Clara Zetkin. At first neither believed that Lenin was dead. For weeks the doctors had been spreading encouraging bulletins of his imminent recovery. Visitors to Gorki returned with accounts of how he talked and smiled and went hunting, and would soon be returning to take over the reins of government.

When President Kalinin opened the session of the Congress at 11:50 A.M., he requested everyone to stand. Tears were streaming down his face. He faced the audience, unable to say another word. The silence was broken by the Soviet funeral march played on a phonograph, but the music came to an abrupt end when Kalinin, mastering his emotions, murmured brokenly: "I bring you terrible news about our beloved comrade, Vladimir Ilyich—"

He said no more for a little while. Somewhere high up in the gallery a woman gasped out her grief, and the sound of moaning and sobbing broke out in different places in the vast hall.

"Yesterday," Kalinin went on in a faltering voice, "yesterday he suffered a further paralytic stroke and—" He could not go on. For some seconds he peered at the audience—like a man hovering at the

edge of a precipice, unable to nerve himself to move backward or forward—until at last his whole body seemed to say the words, "And
died."

There came then a gradual ground swell of grief, with sobbing and
moaning spreading pitifully around the hall, gathering strength and
echoing from wall to wall, so that an outbreak of mass hysteria
seemed inevitable. The name of Lenin was heard in many different
tones, as though people thought that by calling upon him he would
return to life. Kalinin could do nothing to quell the mounting hysteria.
On the contrary, by his mere presence there on the platform, a slight
bearded shivering man whose face was silver with tears, he seemed
in some curious manner to augment it. Suddenly the heavy voice of
Abel Yenukidze, Secretary of the Russian Federal Union, could be
heard demanding silence. Kalinin with difficulty read out the official
bulletin.

It was a strange bulletin, for after announcing that Lenin had
died unexpectedly the previous evening after a period when he
seemed to be well on the road to recovery, it went on to declare that
the Eleventh All-Union Soviet Congress "would make all the necessary decisions to ensure the uninterrupted march in the affairs of the
Soviet government," as though power had fallen from the hands of
Lenin into the hands of the members of the Congress, although everyone knew that power was being wielded in a disorganized manner by
a triumvirate composed of Stalin, Zinoviev and Kamenev. There followed a few phrases in the official bureaucratic jargon, claiming that
the Soviet government, "which interprets the will of the toiling
masses," would continue along the road that Lenin had marked out
for it.

Later in the day a longer and even more prolix proclamation was
issued in the unmistakable style of Zinoviev. "Death has taken from
us the founder of the Communist International, the leader of world
Communism, the pride and glory of the international proletariat, the
banner of the oppressed Orient, the chief of the dictatorship of the
proletariat of Russia." There had been no figure to equal him since
Marx; he alone had the vision and the clear-sightedness to penetrate
through the mists of history and create the state of the future. Boundless and superhuman were his gifts of intelligence and his application
to work. Prodigiously had he increased the treasures of Marxism; and
no other man had ever borne on his shoulders so profound a responsibility to the workers and the international proletariat. With his death,

the party will go forward all the more firmly and ardently along the road that Lenin had marked out for it, "bearing in its hands the testament which he left to us."

There may have been here a half-ironical reference to Lenin's three-page testament, in which Zinoviev had been pardoned and Stalin excoriated; but it is more likely that he was using the word in a conventional meaning. The testament was to be read aloud at a party conference the following June, but there is some reason to believe that the triumvirs already had their agents in Lenin's secretariat and knew of its existence long before Krupskaya officially presented it to the party.

Zinoviev was the least gifted and the most ineffectual of the small men who had once surrounded Lenin, but he could sometimes strike off a memorable phrase; and in that long and turgid exordium there was one passage of four lines which rose above the rest in its simplicity and concentrated passion:

> Lenin lives on in the heart of every good workman.
> Lenin lives on in the heart of every poor peasant.
> Lenin lives on in the millions of colonial slaves.
> Lenin lives on in the camp of our enemies, in the hate they have for Leninism, Communism, and Bolshevism.

All over Russia men knew the stupor of grief. The death of Lenin, so long expected and so long feared, brought about a strange numbing of the senses. While Lenin was alive, there was always the hope that the revolution could be channeled and contained in ways which would prove ultimately fruitful. He was the merciless taskmaster, the hammer which had broken the mold, and the creator of the new. Almost singlehandedly he had brought the revolution into existence: all the rest had simply moved like chessmen at his bidding. Instinctively they were aware that he possessed a fund of conscience, although many years were to pass before they learned how deeply troubled he had been in the last year of his life. Now that he was gone, they saw the future in hopelessness and despair; and from all over snow-covered Russia in that bitter winter there came messages of grief mingled with harsh hysteria. In the provinces *Pravda* and *Izvestiya* came out with their local tributes sometimes couched in terms of ineffectual rage. For example, under the heading "Damnation to Traitors," the Smolensk *Pravda* published a statement by the workers of the Romodovana co-operative: "The entire assembly of the laborers and white collar workers of the Romodovana co-operative curse the people who betray the interests of the working classes, at whose hand Lenin was killed. Let the swine know that they killed the body of Lenin, but not his holy legacy [*svyati zaveti*]." Many believed, or pretended to believe that Lenin's death was brought about by foreign agents. They did not know, and could not have guessed, that it was brought about by Stalin.

Trotsky was one of those who had reasons for believing that Stalin had some hand in Lenin's death. A decoded telegram was handed to him on the train at Tiflis, while he was on his way to the seaside town of Sukhum to recover from a long and mysterious illness. Even before he looked at the telegram he knew from the expression on the face of his secretary that the news would be terrifying. He read the telegram and then passed it to his wife; she had already guessed the contents. The telegram was very brief; it said only that Lenin had died. It was from Stalin.

When great grief comes to men, they normally behave in one of two ways. Either they give way to a flood of tears, to passionate anger and remonstrance like the workers of the Romodovana co-operative, or they absorb their grief into themselves, letting it sink deeper and deeper within them in silence. Trotsky had no feeling of anger. He was numbed, broken, deprived of the power to think logically. He reached the Kremlin on the direct line and was told that the funeral would take place the next day, he would not be able to return in time, and he should continue his treatment. He accepted this advice unthinkingly, and he seems to have been dimly aware that by not attending the funeral he would be accomplishing his own ruin.

When Trotsky came to write his autobiography, he mentioned that he had composed at the urging of his comrades in Tiflis a brief article on the death of Lenin for the local newspapers. The train was held up for half an hour to allow him to complete the article, which was later reprinted all over Russia. He had no desire to write it. "I could not stretch my hand to lift my pen," he wrote. And what he wrote was confused, repetitive, and strangely inert. It was as though he could not come to grips with the fact of Lenin's death. Images occurred to him—gigantic rocks crashing into the sea, the blood suddenly stilled in human veins, the prick of a needle. But he could do very little with these images. He was searching for words, not finding them, and sometimes saying the wrong ones—and not caring so long as he got something down on paper. What finally emerges is the portrait of one great revolutionary leader looking at the dead body of another great revolutionary leader, too blinded by suffering and tears to make any intelligible statement. He wrote:

There is no Lenin. Lenin is no more. The dark laws which govern the working of the arteries have destroyed his life. Medicine has proved powerless to accomplish what was so passionately hoped for, what millions of human hearts have desired.

How many there are who would have unhesitatingly sacrificed their own blood to the last drop to revive and renew the work of the arteries of the greater leader Lenin—Ilyich, the unique, the irreplaceable. But there was no miracle, and science was powerless.

Now there is no Lenin. Like gigantic rocks crashing into the sea, the words fall upon our consciousness. Beyond belief, beyond thinking.

The consciousness of the toilers of the entire world cannot grasp the fact: for the enemy is still very strong, the road is long, and the great work, the greatest in history, remains unfinished; for the working classes of the world needed Lenin as perhaps no one in the history of the world has yet been needed.

His second attack, more severe than the first, lasted for more than ten months. The arteries were constantly "playing with him," as the doctors said with bitterness in their voices. They played a terrible game with the life of Lenin. We could expect improvement, but also catastrophe; we could expect full recovery, but instead we have been given catastrophe. The breathing center of the brain refused to function, and the mind of great genius was snuffed out.

There is no Vladimir Ilyich. The party is orphaned. The working class is orphaned. Such was the feeling aroused by the news of the death of our teacher and leader.

How shall we go forward, how shall we find the road, shall we not lose our way? For Lenin, comrades, is no more.

There is no Lenin, but Leninism remains. The immortal in Lenin—his doctrine, his work, his method, his example—all these live on in us, in the party which he founded, in the first workers' state, whose head he was and which he guided.

Our hearts are now so overwhelmed with grief, because we were the contemporaries of Lenin, because we worked with him and learned from him, and all this was given to us as a grace by history. Our party is active Leninism, our party is itself the collective leader of the working classes. In each of us lives a small part of Lenin, which is the best part of each of us.

How shall we go forward? With the lamp of Lenin in our hands. Shall we find the way? With the collective mind, with the collective will of the party we shall find it.

Tomorrow and the day after, and in weeks and months to come we shall find ourselves asking whether Lenin is really dead. For a long time his death will seem to us improbable and impossible, a terrible arbitrariness of nature.

May the sting of the needle which we shall feel in our hearts every time we remember that Lenin is no more be for each of us an admonition, a warning, an appeal.

Your responsibility is now increased. Be worthy of the training given to you by your leader. In grief, sorrow and affliction we bind our ranks and hearts together, uniting for the new battles ahead.

Comrades, brothers, Lenin is no longer with us.

Farewell, Ilyich! Farewell, our leader!

TIFLIS STATION, *January 22, 1924.*

Trotsky does not quote the article in his autobiography, and it is possible that he was ashamed of it, for this litany is too much like the slow babbling of an orphaned child. Only once does he seem to come to grips with his grief, and that is when he speaks of the sting of the needle (*ukol igly*). Was he thinking of the hypodermic needle loaded with poison?

He finished the article and ordered the train to go on. While the battle for power was being fought in Moscow, he spent the next months at Sukhum in the sunshine.

There was no sunshine in Moscow. Under leaden skies, the snow falling and bitter winds driving through the streets in one of the coldest winters on record, the body of Lenin was brought to Moscow in a crimson coffin. The lid was provided with three windows on the top and sides to permit his face to be seen. For four miles men had carried it on their shoulders in the early morning of December 23 through the snow-covered woods which lay between Gorki and the nearest railroad station; then in Moscow, while a storm came up, it was again carried on men's shoulders from the Paveletsky railroad station south of the city to the House of Trade Unions, the former Nobles' Club, north of the Red Square.

By order of Dzerzhinsky red flags trimmed with black mourning bands hung from every window, and soldiers stood shoulder to shoulder along the whole length of the procession. At first the soldiers of the Kremlin barracks had claimed the right to carry the coffin of Lenin on a gun caisson drawn by six white horses, but they were ordered back. For nearly five miles of snowbound streets the small procession moved at a snail's pace, pausing at intervals while the leaders took turns to act as coffin-bearers. No guns fired in salute: that would come later, when the body was placed in the small crypt dug out of the Red Square.

From the crowded windows the people of Moscow watched in silence. The wind whipped the red flags at gale force; flurries of snow sometimes hid the cortege from sight. An embroidered and tasseled curtain protected the coffin from the snow.

At last the body of Lenin was placed on a platform hastily erected in the Hall of Columns in the House of Trade Unions. A banner proclaimed: "Lenin is dead, his work lives on." In that same building most of Lenin's former associates were later put on trial by Stalin and heard themselves sentenced to death.

Framed by four columns, which somehow suggested that he was lying on an old-fashioned four-poster bed, Lenin lay under a dark-red blanket, only his head showing. Those who saw him say that the face was yellow-white like wax, without the slightest wrinkle. The eyes were closed, but there was a suggestion of someone merely resting, still possessed of an astonishing vitality. At the four corners stood members of the Central Committee and the Council of Commissars on guard. They were replaced at intervals of ten minutes. For four days the body was to remain on view.

From all over Russia the people came in their uncounted thousands to see the body, forming lines six deep in the snow, with the temperature at 20° below zero. Huge bonfires were lit at the street corners, in the hope of warming a few bones, but during all those days a snowstorm played over Moscow. So many people fainted of cold in those long, shuffling processions that doctors and ambulances were sent out. Sometimes the waiting multitude would break out into revolutionary songs.

At first it was decided to close the gates of the House of Trade Unions each night, but they were not closed until the evening of the twenty-sixth. The people who entered the House of Trade Unions seemed hypnotized. They would keep looking at the body quietly and expressionlessly long after they had passed beyond it, their heads turned toward a yellow face and a snow-white pillow. They walked like automatons, grateful for the warmth of the hall, their white breaths forming a cloud that sometimes hid Lenin from sight. A red carpet was stretched on the floor to guide them, and many observers recorded how they paid no attention to the carpet and sometimes blundered against the wall.

Most of those who came to see Lenin lying in state had never seen him before. They came in silence and went in silence. The poet Mayakovsky remembered that the people who formed the long procession did not wave their arms to keep off the cold, and they had the look of "Chinese whipped into surrender," meaning that they were unnaturally calm, polite, and respectful. In his poem *Vladimir Ilyich Lenin* Mayakovsky described his feelings as he walked through the Hall of Columns:

We are burying
                    the most earthy
Of all the men
                    who ever walked
                    the earth.
He was of the earth
                    but not of those
Whose eyes
See no further
                    than their troughs.
For he embraced
                    in a single glance
All the earth,
                    seeing
                    all that time
                    has hidden from us.
He was like you
                    and like me.
Who today
                    would have wept
                    for my little death
In the grief
                    for this death
                    which is without end?
They hold high the battle flags
                    and all of Russia
                    seems now
                    to have become
                    a country of nomads.
And the Hall of Columns

> trembles under the feet
> > of those who pass by his body.
> And there are no words
> > in the telegraph,
> > only the sounds of grief.
> The tears of snow
> > are falling
> From the eyelids of flags red with weeping.
> > What did he ever do?
> > Who is he?
> > Where did he come from?
> > This man who is
> > more human than any of us.

So they passed, hour after hour, day after day, and they would have come continually for many months if it had been permitted. A deeply felt religious emotion was being expressed. It was as though there had been a sacramental need for his death, and he had answered the need, and therefore they were grateful to him. They honored him more in death than they ever honored him in life; and long afterward they continued to honor him by visiting his tomb.

The sudden outpouring of religious emotion surprised the Bolshevik leaders, who had apparently intended originally to bury the body on the twenty-fifth, for in the provincial newspapers there were announcements that he would be buried at four o'clock in the afternoon of that day. But the mourners kept coming on every train, and they refused to have the doors closed on them. Mongols, Uzbeks, Kalmucks, Chinese, Ukrainians, they came from all the regions of Russia to look upon him for the last time. Whole factories closed to permit the workers to pay tribute. It was as though time had come to a stop on those dark, windy days when the huge fires burned and the snow whipped through the streets. There seemed to be some significance in the fact that he died in winter, in the darkest time of the year.

Krupskaya kept watch by the body. She was like a graven image, silent, motionless, lost in her dreams. The others who stood guard were also silent, as though they too were caught up in the silence of death. To many it seemed that a new religion with all its attendant ritual was gradually coming into existence around the body of Lenin. Faintly through the palatial Hall of Columns there echoed the revolutionary songs sung by the thousands waiting outside.

On January 26, the day when the last mourners streamed through the House of Trade Unions, the Second All-Union Congress of Soviets met to render official homage to the dead leader. Kalinin, Krupskaya, Zinoviev and Stalin paid their final tributes. After Kalinin spoke, Chopin's "Funeral March" was played, and then Krupskaya spoke in a low, clear voice. Her speech was short and moving in its simplicity:

> Comrades, during those days when I stood beside the coffin of Vladimir Ilyich, I passed his whole life in review in my mind, and this is what I want to say to you. His heart beat with a burning love for all workers, for all those who are oppressed. He never said this himself, and probably I would not have said it at any less solemn moment. If I say it now, it is because this sentiment was something he inherited from the heroic Russian revolutionary movement. It was this sentiment which led him to search passionately and ardently for the answer to the question, What roads should we follow to bring about the liberation of the workers? He found the replies to his questions in Marx. He did not come to Marx as a man in love with books. He came as a man searching for answers to the pressing problems that tormented him. And he found the answers. And he took them to the workers.
>
> It was in the Nineties. In those days he could not speak at meetings. He went to Petrograd in the workingmen's circles. He went to tell them what he had learned from Marx, to give them the answers he had found in Marx. He did not come to the workers as an arrogant professor, but as a comrade. He did not only speak and explain matters to them, but he listened attentively to what the workers told him. The Petrograd workers did not only speak to him of what was happening in the factories, and of the oppressions they suffered; they spoke to him too about their villages. . . .
>
> We speak a good deal today about the alliance between the workers and the peasants. This alliance, comrades, history herself has created. The Russian workman is on one side a workman, on the other a peasant. This work among the Petrograd workmen, these conversations with them, the great attention he paid to their words, all these gave him an understanding of the great thought of Marx—the thought that the working class stood in the vanguard of all the toilers, and that all the toiling masses and all who were oppressed would follow behind them, and this was the strength and the pledge of his victory. . . .

The eulogies of Zinoviev and Kalinin were couched in the traditional, mechanical language of Bolshevism, saying nothing at considerable length. Stalin's speech was of another kind altogether, for he had observed the religious significance which was being attached to Lenin's death, and he was concerned to depict himself as a humble follower of a saint who in departing this life remained all the more living and all the more powerful. With almost Biblical phrasing, derived from his early ecclesiastical training, he invented a liturgical and devotional series of holy commandments followed by responses; and when this speech was later published in his collected works he ordered that these commandments and responses, which appear at intervals in an otherwise turgid commentary on the greatness of Lenin, be printed in capital letters:

In departing from us, Comrade Lenin enjoined on us to hold high and keep pure the great calling of member of the party.

We vow to thee, Comrade Lenin, that we will honorably fulfill this thy commandment.

In departing from us, Comrade Lenin enjoined on us to guard the unity of our party as the apple of our eye.

We vow to thee, Comrade Lenin, that we will honorably fulfill this thy commandment.

In departing from us, Comrade Lenin enjoined on us to guard and strengthen the dictatorship of the proletariat.

We vow to thee, Comrade Lenin, that we will not spare our strength to fulfill honorably this thy commandment.

In departing from us, Comrade Lenin enjoined on us to strengthen with all our might the union of workers and peasants.

We vow to thee, Comrade Lenin, that we will honorably fulfill this thy commandment.

In departing from us, Comrade Lenin enjoined on us to strengthen and extend the union of republics.

We vow to thee, Comrade Lenin, that we will honorably fulfill this thy commandment.

In departing from us, Comrade Lenin enjoined on us to remain faithful to the principles of the Communist International.

We vow to thee, Comrade Lenin, that we will not spare our lives to strengthen and extend the union of the working people of the whole world—the Communist International.

With these words, Stalin announced himself as the high priest of the cult of Lenin, and the commander of the faithful. Not for many years was it to become generally known that "in departing from us" Lenin had vowed eternal enmity to Stalin. Yet this fact weighed lightly on Stalin's conscience; and the arrogance, duplicity and cynicism of this strange antiphonal chant was a fit prelude to his assumption of power.

At this Second All-Union Congress of Soviets the decision was taken to elevate Lenin to the status of a god. Every conceivable honor, and in particular all those honors which he would have detested during his life, were accorded to him by acclamation. Petrograd, the city of the revolution, once named after Saint Peter, was henceforth to be known as Leningrad, and the anniversary of his death was to become a day of national mourning. In all the chief cities of the Soviet Union his statue was to be erected, and all the words he ever wrote were to be solemnly collected and edited in a complete edition of his writings. His body was to be embalmed and placed in a gigantic mausoleum so that all could see him, as powerful in death as he was in life. The elements which went into the celebration of his divinity derived from the Pharaohs, the Caesars, and the great tribal chieftains who once roamed the steppes of Russia. The funeral ceremonies of the tsars, who were quietly buried in the Peter and Paul Fortress in St. Petersburg, were humble by comparison.

Of all the delegates to the Congress, only one spoke up against the deification of Lenin: this was Krupskaya, who was faithfully following Lenin's wishes when she protested against all the honors heaped upon him and the reverence paid to his person. But her protests went unheard. Several days later a small paragraph appeared in the top-right-hand corner of *Pravda*, addressed to the workers and peasants who had expressed their sorrow. She wrote:

> Great is my prayer to you: do not allow your grief for Ilyich to assume the form of external reverence for his person. Do not raise memorials for him, do not name palaces after him, do not hold splendid celebrations in his honor. To all these things he attached so little importance in his life, they were so burdensome to him. Remember how much poverty and disorganization there still remains in our country. If you want to honor the name of Vladimir Ilyich, build crêches, kindergartens, houses, schools, libraries, dispensaries, hospitals, homes for invalids, etc., and above all, follow his principles in your lives.

She pleaded, but to no avail, for Lenin was no longer in her keeping. Quietly and determinedly she protested against the renaming of Petrograd, the mummification of his body, and the erection of a mausoleum in the Red Square. Almost overnight she had lost her usefulness to the party.

On Sunday, January 27, the storm which had hovered over Moscow for a week suddenly abated. The skies shone clear and frosty, and smoke hung in the air from the bonfires at the street corners. During the night Lenin's body had been placed in a red-draped coffin, and once again in the morning from eight o'clock onward the honor guards stood at attention, the names of the guards being preserved for posterity so that men should know the progress of the desperate battle for power now being waged among members of the Central Committee. The first honor guard was composed of Zinoviev, Stalin, Kalinin and Kamenev, who evidently regarded themselves as the rightful heirs. When the guard changed ten minutes later there appeared the heirs of the second rank: Bukharin, Rykov, Molotov and Tomsky. Then came the heirs of the third rank: Dzerzhinsky, Chicherin, Petrovsky and Sokolnikov; then came Kuibyshev, Ordjonikidze, Pyatakov and Yenukidze. The niceties of protocol were elaborated with punctilious care, and the exact degrees of power and influence were minutely indicated in the program. It was observed that there were subdivisions within the ranks, for when at nine o'clock the body was carried out of the house of Trade Unions, it was borne on the shoulders of Zinoviev, Stalin, and six symbolic workers, and was later taken over by Kalinin, Kamenev, Kursky, four workers and a peasant. The minor position accorded to the symbolic peasant was calculated with momentous care by Zinoviev and Stalin, who constituted themselves masters of the ceremony.

All morning and all afternoon the red-draped coffin lay on a kind of tribune in the Red Square, close to the hastily dug vault beneath the Kremlin wall. The Red Square was a sea of red flags. Everyone wore black arm bands edged with scarlet. The bands played funeral marches, and the red-ribboned wreaths gathered around the red coffin. Then for hour after hour speeches were made by obscure trade union officials, railroadmen, factory workers and foreign Communists, all praising Lenin and extolling his virtues. Few of these speeches were recorded, for the leaders had already spoken, and these public ceremonies were designed to permit the underlings to offer their tributes.

Exactly at four o'clock, the machines too offered their tributes. For three minutes, all over Russia, everything that could make a noise was turned on. The sirens of thousands of factories, the steam whistles of hundreds of locomotives, the foghorns and sirens of all Russian ships were sounded, and all the shore batteries and all the heavy guns pounded out an ear-splitting salute. Salvo after salvo resounded from the garrisons, the naval stations and the artillery parks. Never before, and perhaps never afterward, was there such an explosion of noise coming from so many different sources in a single country. The machines, too, must be enlisted to render their roar of anguish at the death of the leader.

In those three minutes, eight men walked the four steps down to the shallow vault: Kamenev, Zinoviev, Stalin, Molotov, Bukharin, Tomsky, Dzerzhinsky and Rudzutak, the last being a trade-union official who was being groomed by Stalin for high position. They carried the red coffin into the vault. When they emerged a car drove them to the Kremlin. A half-moon rose in the mist over the white frozen city. All night in the freezing cold the crowds remained on the snow-covered square, and toward morning they began to disperse. Then at sunrise the crowds gathered again. Guards with naked bayonets stood around the vault. Then the snow fell and hid the vault from sight.

Strangely the site of the vault was not far from the stone mound known as the Lobnoye Mesto, the Place of the Skull. On this mound in the days of Ivan the Terrible and Peter the Great state criminals were executed, while the Tsar watched from a high tower. Here Stenka Razin, the Cossack chieftain who had raised the peasants of the Volga in revolt, was beheaded. From that mound the heralds read the laws, and the medieval Muscovites believed that when Moscow became the Third Rome and inherited the earth, then the laws pertaining to the whole earth would be read from the mound. For them the mound was the center of the earth, a place eternally radiating secret power.

The directive of the Second All-Union Congress announced that a "suitable mausoleum" was to be raised over the tomb, but gave no indication of its size or shape or of what other purposes it would serve: all this was left to the future. It was generally assumed that the mausoleum would take the form of granite columns supporting a gigantic statue of Lenin in bronze or hammered iron. Only gradually over the years, after discarding thousands of architects' and artists' drawings, did the present mausoleum made of massive porphyry and granite blocks acquire its shape.

At first there was only the wooden vault, twenty feet high. Then a wooden hut was built over it, and for four and a half months only the doctors who were embalming the body and the security police were allowed to enter the hut. The body was packed in ice to delay the processes of putrefaction. The doctors claimed they had discovered an embalming process which would preserve it for a thousand years. At rare intervals they would report that the work was almost completed, but it was not until the summer that the vault was officially opened to the public. Whatever method the doctors had used to embalm the body, it was a failure. Like Father Zossima in *The Brothers Karamazov*, Lenin proved to be mortal, all too mortal.

In the course of those four and a half months the vault had been enlarged, painted, provided with wooden floors, hangings and carpets, but it was still primitive. The coffin lay on a balk of timber swathed in red silk, and both the coffin and the coffin lid, which stood upright against the wall, were also swathed in red silk. Two banners, said to be the banners of the Paris Commune, stood against the wall, one scarlet and black, the other scarlet and gold. On the black ceiling a hammer and sickle were worked out in red. Powerful electric lamps blazed, and the scarlet hangings were blinding.

He lay in the red coffin with a red blanket covering him up to the waist, and the face was enclosed in a kind of glass sheet. In those four and a half months remarkable changes had taken place: he was waxen gray, wrinkled, horribly shrunken. Beeswax and mortician's fluid had worked a change in him. Yet there was no doubt that this was his mortal body. The viscera had been removed, and the brain was in the keeping of the Soviet Brain Institute, where it was cut up into twenty thousand microscopic sections for purposes of study, but no one doubted that this face, so wrinkled and waxen, and so worked upon by the doctors, was his authentic face. In the first hours of death he looked strangely calm. Now he looked angry and sullen, tormented by guilt.

In those days special permits had to be obtained to view the body, and it was thought dangerous to allow too many people to enter the death chamber at once. Two thermometers hung prominently on the wall. Visitors were permitted only a quick glance before they were hurried out. It was feared that their hot breaths and their body heat would cause a rise in the room temperature.

Then gradually the restrictions were lifted, and the familiar snake-like processions winding across the Red Square appeared for the first time. Most of those who came to see the body were peasants, and of these the greater part were women who would invariable cross themselves before they entered the vault to the discomfiture of the Red Army guards who would remind them that it was not a church and they were not praying at the grave of a saint. When the peasants left the vault they invariably looked bewildered, as though they were not sure what they had seen.

From time to time the vault was closed, and no secret was made that the embalming process had proved unsatisfactory. Deterioration set in rapidly; nor could it be avoided since the doctors worked in inadequate conditions, without air conditioning or weatherproofing. More doctors were summoned, but the processes of decay were now irreversible. For the next two years doctors worked at intervals to mold the face back into its original shape.

Suddenly in the spring of 1926 the wrinkles vanished, and there was no more discoloration. From being a very old man he acquired the look of middle age, with a keen ascetic profile: the alteration was ascribed to a new embalming process discovered by Dr. Ilya Zbarsky, who claimed to have learned the exact nature of the fluids employed by the Egyptians and to have improved upon them. It was rumored that all efforts to embalm the body had failed, and that far from having rediscovered the processes employed by the Egyptians, Dr. Zbarsky had simply abandoned the struggle. It was said that the body had been cremated and the ashes placed in an urn which was dropped into the Volga at Simbirsk, now renamed Ulyanovsk. So widespread was the belief that the mausoleum contained only a wax effigy that an official investigation was opened, and a German doctor traveling in the Soviet Union was invited to participate in the inquiry and render a report. He was not however permitted to make more than a cursory examination. He reported that he had observed frostbites on the skin, felt the cheeks, and lifted one of Lenin's arms. He gained the impression that Lenin had been wonderfully preserved and seemed not to be dead but sleeping. He inquired about the techniques of embalming and was told they were secret but would be fully revealed in three or four years' time when they had been proved effective; and nothing more was ever heard about the secret formula.

When finally in 1930 a huge mausoleum of red Ukrainian granite and Karelian porphyry was erected in the Red Square, Lenin's body vanished from sight for many months. A few months previously the flooded Kremlin sewers had overflowed into the tomb, and careful measures were undertaken to repair the damage. From being middle-aged, Lenin began to wear the look of youthfulness. Not only had the last remaining wrinkles been smoothed away, but the flesh looked firmer and was more vividly colored. The fine-drawn ascetic features, with the high cheekbones, the domed forehead, the thin beard, suggested an early icon. Gone was the roughhewn Mongoloid face which habitually wore an expression of determination; the new image was gentle and remote, almost abstract. The left hand rested on the breast of a khaki jacket tightly buttoned at the neck; it was no longer clenched. It was observed that the tapering fingers were delicate and well-shaped, rosy pink. He lay now beneath a glass sarcophagus, with a formidable orange-red light pouring down on his face; the rest of the death chamber was enveloped in darkness.

The huge mausoleum now resembled the burial place of a king. Some thirty steps led down to the vault, cavernlike in the somber lighting. The ruthless revolutionary had at last acquired the trappings of majesty; and if, as many suspected, there was no more than the authentic skull covered with alternate layers of wax and paint, still, within the tomb, there was the suggestion of a living presence. In more than one interview Dr. Zbarsky congratulated himself on having "restored" the original features, producing the effect of a man "who is not dead, but sleeping." In no other country in the world was any dead man worshiped in this way, but this worship seemed to answer to the needs of the uncounted millions who came to see him lying there in a crystal case, like some ancient king or saint who permits himself to be seen briefly by all his subjects.

The ritual attending on his burial did not end with the ceremonial visits of the devout. The vast mausoleum, which resembled a bomb shelter, was adaptable to many uses. It could be indefinitely expanded to include other revolutionary leaders, so that in time it would come to resemble the Pantheon in Paris. It could be used, like the nearby Place of the Skull, as a platform where the new laws could be announced to the people. Instead, it became the reviewing stand for the great processions which from time to time made their way across the Red Square, and the precise order in which the Soviet officials presented themselves on the stand was regarded as an indication of their relative power. The positions would change; new faces would appear; and the exact gradations were minutely studied by foreigners and Russians alike as they sought to penetrate the secret and mysterious logic of the new ruling class. In this way the mausoleum served the uses of power.

During the war years the embalmed body was evacuated to Kuibyshev, and later to Kazan, to prevent it from being captured by the Germans. In 1945 it was returned to Moscow.

For nearly thirty years Lenin rested alone in the Red Square, except for the period during World War II. After the war the processions were resumed with even more devotion than before, for it was believed that Lenin was in some mysterious way responsible for the victory of Russian arms; and strange stories were told of how Stalin would drive to the mausoleum in the dead of night to commune with the spirit of the man he had murdered.

When Stalin died at last, having misruled Russia in the manner of a medieval tsar, it was decided that he should be laid beside Lenin since he was thought to be deserving of equal honor. Once again there was a lying-in-state in the Hall of Columns. Once again there was a ceremonial procession across the Red Square with the carefully chosen pallbearers taking up their position in order of rank. Just as many of Lenin's pallbearers were to die subsequently in the purges, so among the pallbearers of Stalin there was at least one who died violently shortly afterward. Only one man acted as a pallbearer to both Lenin and Stalin: this was Molotov. Among the pallbearers of Stalin there were many whom Lenin had never known.

Even at this time voices were raised against placing Stalin in the mausoleum. They protested that the thirty years in which he had ruled over Russia were not equal to Lenin's five years. Nevertheless the heavy marble slab which bore the name LENIN in large letters was removed; in its place, in smaller letters, were substituted the names of Lenin and Stalin with the first superimposed on the second. To that extent was Lenin reduced by his adversary.

Eight years passed before the decision was reached to reduce Stalin from his eminence. In January 1962 the mausoleum was closed and a seven-foot fence was put up to keep out the curious, while workmen busied themselves removing the marble slab for the second time. The place where the slab had been was covered with a tarpaulin. When at last the tarpaulin was removed, Lenin was alone in his tomb and only his name shone over the gateway.

We know what Lenin would have thought of the mausoleum and the cult associated with his name, for he wrote at the beginning of *The State and Revolution:*

> During the lifetimes of great revolutionaries, the oppressive classes constantly hounded them and received their teaching with the most savage hostility, the most furious hatred, the most unscrupulous campaign of lies and slander. After their deaths attempts are made to convert them into harmless icons, as it were to canonize them, and surround their *names* with a certain halo for the consolation of the oppressed classes with the object of duping them, while at the same time emasculating and blunting the *real essence* of their revolutionary teachings, reducing them to vulgarity.

THE APE AND THE SKULL

*The Russian intelligentsia produced a faith
based upon a strange syllogism:
Man is descended from the apes,
therefore we must love one another.*
                                —VLADIMIR SOLOVYEV

O
N LENIN'S DESK in the Kremlin there stood,
for most of the years he worked there, a strange bronze statue of an
ape gazing with an expression of profound bewilderment and dismay
at an oversize human skull. It stood about ten inches high, and occupied a dominating position on the desk behind the inkwell. The ape
was sitting, or rather squatting, on a heap of books in a posture which
is a grotesque parody of Rodin's *Le Penseur*. There is nothing in the
least amusing about the appearance of the ape, which is sordidly
bestial, with its small head and great curving shoulders and long
dangling arms; and the human skull, with gaping mouth and empty
eye sockets, is even less amusing. The ape gazes ponderously at the
skull, and the skull gazes back at the ape. We can only guess at the nature of the interminable dialogue which is being maintained between
them.

Lenin made no secret of his affection for the ape, which was displayed in such a prominent position for all to see. It was the only piece
of sculpture on the desk, the first thing that met the eye; and whenever Lenin looked up from his desk to gaze at the very large photograph
of Karl Marx and the plaque bearing the name of Stepan Khalturin in

gold letters, he would inevitably see the ape. There is a sense in which its vivid presence dominated the room.

Long after Lenin's death, when his study in the Kremlin was converted into a museum and when all the objects originally on the desk —the telephone, the scissors, the paper knives, the cigarette lighter he used for burning papers—were placed in the exact positions they had occupied in his lifetime, then the ape was not forgotten. This, too, was placed in its proper position, and so it appears, usually half hidden but nevertheless clearly discernible, in the photographs taken of the study. His devout followers were concerned to maintain the room exactly as he left it. Not even the ape must be removed.

This ugly and vulgar statue was not designed especially for Lenin. It was mass-produced toward the end of the nineteenth century. As a dubious ornament or conversation piece, it could be seen in countless homes in France, Germany, Scandinavia and Russia, where it appealed to bourgeois taste, its very ugliness and vulgarity contributing to its popularity. It represented, if it represented anything at all, a mocking commentary on the Darwinian theory and showed the ape, having long outlived the human race, interrogating in its bemused fashion the existence of man.

Lenin was one of those men who knew exactly what he liked and disliked. There was no object in the room which did not have a precise meaning for him. There was, for example, a strip of felt on the floor under his desk, to prevent his feet from becoming chilled in winter. His secretaries decided to replace it with a white bearskin rug. Immediately there was an uproar. He wanted to know why he was expected to live in capitalist comfort, and who exactly was responsible for this attempt to smother him in luxury. His secretaries pointed out gently that even minor officials permitted themselves the luxury of a small bearskin rug, but he was never completely reconciled to its presence: it did not fit into the orderly image he had conceived for the room in which he spent most of the day.

Then there was the tall potted palm with glossy green leaves which stood near the window. This, too, had a special and intricate meaning for him. Every day he would wash down the leaves, examining them to see that no blight had touched them. It was the only other living thing in the room, and for some reason he wanted it to flourish. He could not stand having cut flowers in the room; he hated the dropping of the petals, the visible evidence of decay. The palm however was permanent; it resisted decay, and was always glossy. People were puzzled that he paid so much attention to the palm, but there was a very simple explanation. In Simbirsk and Kazan, and later in Moscow and St. Petersburg, his mother had always possessed a collection of potted plants, and as a child and as a young man it was one of his duties to wash down the leaves. The potted palm was therefore not an irrelevant decoration in an otherwise utilitarian office. The palm was the outward and visible sign of his affection and attachment to his family.

Since all the other objects in the room had a definite meaning for him, it is necessary to discover the meaning he attached to the ape, which occupied such a commanding position in the room. In just such a position a deeply religious man would have placed a crucifix, a statue of Buddha, or some other symbol representing his faith. Lenin placed an ape. Why?

The explanation would seem to lie in the idolatrous attitude of the nineteenth-century Russian intelligentsia toward science. An absurd autocratic state had come into existence, which completely failed to answer the needs of the people. It was transparently out of date, inefficient, corrupt, and sterile. Men turned their backs on the state and the Orthodox Church, which was also becoming increasingly remote from the people, and pinned their faith on science. Science alone provided the key to the future. For a Russian intellectual to dispute Darwinism or any other acceptable scientific theory was to commit a heresy. Science, however mechanical, however dangerous and arbitrary, was itself an article of faith. When the great philosopher Vladimir Solovyev wrote, "The Russian intelligentsia produced a faith based upon a strange syllogism: man is descended from the apes, therefore we must love one another," he was saying in effect that the Russian intelligentsia firmly believed that science would produce the reign of love among men; and Lenin, who never tired of insisting against all the evidence that Marxism was purely scientific in character, firmly believed that once the Marxist state had been established, then and only then would men be able to live together in peace and concord.

But it is in the nature of science to be inhuman. It cannot legislate for men in their infinite variety; it can only legislate for them as statistics, as trends, or as obstacles to the carrying out of scientific laws. Lenin was perfectly prepared to regard men as statistics or as trends; he was equally prepared to regard them as obstacles standing in the path of his scientific dictatorship, and he had no compunction in destroying whole classes in order to vindicate the laws of science. The aristocracy, the bourgeois, the peasantry, and the Orthodox priests, all

these must be destroyed in order that the dictatorship of the proletariat might be established. It was a breath-taking enterprise, for it
meant destroying or forcing into new molds considerably more than
nine tenths of the population of Russia.

In spite of the fact that the enterprise was essentially absurd, and
the scientific theories lacked any basis in science, he persisted in it.
Inevitably he came to regard men simply as statistics, as ciphers, to be
moved about according to his will. It was not that he despised men or
wanted to humiliate them in any way—one cannot despise or humiliate statistics—it was simply that they no longer had any existence for
him, as men. They were figures printed on a page, having no existence
outside the page. They were nullities, possessing only the value which
he chose to place on them. There was nothing to prevent him tearing
out whole pages of statistics, to make the book smaller, more compact
and more manageable.

The character that emerges from his actions and his writings is that
of the pure nihilist, utterly remote from normal human preoccupations,
possessed of an unyielding belief in the validity of science, adept in
all the arts of destruction. Like Nechayev, he was dedicated to "terrible, total, merciless and universal destruction." He was a man whose
conviction of the worthlessness of existence was such that he could
make life interesting for himself only by projecting his personality on a
thousand years of history. He was utterly without fear, because nothing mattered to him except that the laws of his pretended science
should be vindicated, whatever the cost in life or suffering. He demanded absolute loyalty, yet he himself had no loyalty to any individual, not even to his most devoted followers, whom he could discard
without a pang, or manipulate as though they too were a portion of
the statistics of power. His temperament was aristocratic, remote,
ironical, faintly contemptuous. In the end all Russia had to become
his private estate, which he ruled from the Kremlin and his palatial
house at Gorki.

In the light of Lenin's character and beliefs, the ape and the skull
acquire a terrible significance. They are the emblems of the nullity
and degradation of the human spirit. They represent the anarchic
forces on which he was determined to impose scientific order: all men
are apes, and they must move about at his bidding, or else they will
become skulls. They must be trained and herded into schools, to receive the instructions of the schoolmaster. They must not dispute with
him or with any of his successors, for freedom to dispute is not granted

to them. He demands mindless obedience because, being apes, they are mindless and deserve no better fate.

Lenin had many sins, but the gravest was a supreme contempt for the human race. Like Marx he possessed an overwhelming contempt for the peasants. In a famous passage Marx spoke of "the idiocy of rural life" and described the peasantry of France as nothing more than a lifeless sack of potatoes which could never be stirred into activity: it was like a corpse thrown down to rot. But Lenin went beyond Marx. Not only the peasants, but all classes of society were anathema to him—except the proletariat, with which he had almost no contact. He surrounded himself with intellectuals and theoreticians, and he despised them as much as he despised the peasants, for he never found one who was his intellectual equal. His tragedy was that he was never able to sharpen his mind against one morally and intellectually more powerful than his own. The little men clustered at his heels. Zinoviev, Radek, Kamenev, Bukharin, and all the rest fade into shadows beside him. They, too, were his servants, who aped their master without possessing either his intellectual acumen or his remorseless power to carry his theories to their logical conclusion.

Those conclusions were among the hardest which have been visited on the human race. They involved slavery to a theory which demanded the absolute submission of the individual to the brooding genius of the state, the Grand Inquisitor, the relentless power which alone possesses the key to the mystery. So in *The Brothers Karamazov* Dostoyevsky puts into the mouth of the Grand Inquisitor as he addresses Christ, the words: "We shall convince them that they can never be free until they renounce their freedom in our favor and submit wholly to us, and they will all be happy, all the millions, except the hundred thousand who rule over them. We have corrected your great work, and we have based it on Miracle, Mystery and Authority." But the Grand Inquisitor was not appealing to the Miracle, Mystery and Authority of Christ; he was appealing to his own theory that men deserved only to be enslaved.

Lenin was the great simplifier, but there are no simple solutions. He wanted to bring about the ideal state—and there is no doubt about the genuineness of his passion for the ideal state—but the ideal eluded him, as it has eluded everyone else. Toward the end of his life he realized that after the Russian people had suffered and submitted to intolerable sacrifices under his dictatorship, he had led them along the wrong path. "I am, it seems, strongly guilty before the workers of

Russia," he declared; and those words were his genuine epitaph. There are few rulers in history who have uttered so clear a *mea culpa*.

That Stalin should have been his successor was a fearful irony. That coarse, brutal and paranoid dictator possessed none of Lenin's intellectual gifts and could scarcely write a sentence which was not a mockery of the Russian language. Under him Communism became a tyranny of such vast proportions that it exceeded all the tyrannies the world had known up to his time. Lenin, with his harsh intellect, his egotism, his phenomenal vigor, his always flawed yet ever impressive achievement, remained oddly human; Stalin was a monster. Yet it is important to observe that there could have been no Stalin without Lenin. Stalin was Lenin's child; and Lenin, who hated and despised and feared him, must bear sole responsibility for bringing Stalin to power.

Once Lenin had decided that all means were permissible to bring about the dictatorship of the proletariat, with himself ruling in the name of the proletariat, he had committed Russia to intolerable deprivations of human freedom. His power was naked power; his weapon was extermination; his aim the prolongation of his own dictatorship. He would write, "Put Europe to the flames"—and think nothing of it. He could decree the deaths of thousands upon thousands of men, and their deaths were immaterial, because they were only statistics impeding the progress of his theory. The butchery in the cellars of the Lubyanka did not concern him. He captured the Russian Revolution and then betrayed it, and at that moment he made Stalin inevitable.

The lawlessness of Communist rule was of Lenin's own making. Ordinary human morality never concerned him; from the beginning he was using words like "extermination" and "merciless" as though they were counters in a game. Whatever he decreed was law, and whoever opposed his decree was outside the law, and therfore possessing no rights, not even the right to breathe. Yet he had, on occasions, the intellectual detachment which permitted him to see that some of his decrees were senseless, and with the New Economic Policy he admitted the error of his ways. Stalin, possessing no intellectual detachment, never admitted the error of his ways, and he went on murdering mercilessly and exalting his own cult as though "scientific Marxism" had come into existence for no other purpose than to satisfy his lust for power. Lenin, too, lusted for power, but he had sufficient common humanity to regard the cult that grew up around him with detestation.

"Lenin is not in the least ambitious," wrote Lunacharsky. "I believe he never looks at himself, never glances in the mirror of history, never even thinks about what posterity will say about him—he simply does his work." Lunacharsky was writing while Lenin was still alive and before his papers were published; and there is more than enough evidence in his papers to show that from a very early period he regarded himself as a figure of history. He believed, quite simply, that he was ushering in a new age. He had no false modesty. He saw himself as the heroic defender of a new faith and as one come to avenge the injustices and miseries of the past.

We who come after him do not have to take him at his own valuation. The state he brought into being proved to be more unjust and incomparably more tyrannical than the state he overthrew. He announced that everything would be new, but in fact there was nothing new except the names; for all tyrannies are alike, differing only in their degree of tyranny. The Cheka was only the tsarist Okhrana under another name: more unpitying, more terrifying, and effective only when it exterminated opposing groups to the last man. Under Stalin, the Cheka, more murderous than ever, became the real ruler of the country; and one by one its leaders died in the same manner as the victims.

When the rule of a country is given over to the secret police, then by the very nature of things it loses its humanity, places itself outside the frontiers of civilization, and possesses no history; for the repetition of crimes is not history. The government which Lenin introduced, believing it to be new, was as old as man, for there is nothing new about tyranny. Such a government is only "government by the ape and the skull."

He was one of those who knew that human misery is rooted not in the laws of nature but in those institutions which man must learn to change. So he changed them, and the tragedy was that the change was only superficial. The autocracy remained autocratic, and the continuing public debate, which since the time of Cleisthenes had been the characteristic of a civilized community, was never permitted. The autocrat told the philosophers what to think, the poets what to write, the artists what to paint, and the workmen when and how to work; and all obeyed him, because he had the power to enforce obedience. That the autocrat should then believe that he was conferring benefits on the human race is the final irony.

In *The 18th Brumaire of Louis Napoleon* Karl Marx explained in a pregnant paragraph what happens when revolutions take place and how they are imprisoned by the dead weight of the past. He said:

> Men make their own history, but they do not make it just as they please; they do not make it under circumstances chosen by themselves, but under circumstances directly found, and given and transmitted from the past. The tradition of all the dead generations weighs like a nightmare on the living. And just when they seem engaged in revolutionizing themselves and things, in creating something entirely new, precisely in such epochs of revolutionary crisis they conjure up the spirits of the past to their service and borrow from them names, battle slogans and costumes in order to present the new scene of world history in time-honored disguise and this borrowed language.

So it was with Lenin, who never realized that he was conjuring up the dead spirits of the past when he was sketching those vast plans for the reorganization of every aspect of life in Russia. "We shall destroy everything," he said, "and on the ruins we shall build our temple." He destroyed everything he could destroy, and built a new temple which was only the old temple with a new façade. In our own age such temples have become anachronisms. It is not by virtue of savage doctrinaire minds that the world's purpose will be assured, but by open debate and by gentle persuasion. We no longer need to watch the ape playing with the skull. We have learned that doctrines are poison, and that dictatorship of any kind is an affront to human dignity. We have also learned that the state which becomes a prison camp ultimately includes the rulers within the barbed-wire walls.

For a little while longer the specter of Lenin will continue to haunt the earth, the implacable doctrinaire still ordering millions of people from the grave. Soon he will sink into the shadows to join the ghosts of all the ancient, anachronistic kings and conquerors who proclaimed themselves to be the sole guardians of the truth, the God-given leaders of mankind. He was a man utterly without fear, his spirits rising in adversity, humble and proud by turns, human and inhuman, half Chuvash tribesman and half dry-as-dust German professor dedicated to a theory of destruction, and by one of the strangest accidents of history he conquered Russia and came to dominate the world's stage. He belongs to the company of Sennacherib, Nebuchadnezzar, Genghis Khan and Tamerlane—and therefore to ancient legend.

APPENDIXES

1. LENIN'S AUTOPSY

REPORT

ON THE PATHOLOGICAL-ANATOMICAL EXAMINATION OF THE BODY OF VLADIMIR ILYICH ULYANOV (LENIN), CARRIED OUT ON JANUARY 22, 1924, STARTED AT 11 HOURS 10 MINUTES IN THE MORNING AND COMPLETED AT 3 HOURS 50 MINUTES.

The examination was carried out by Prof. A. I. Abrikosov in the presence of Prof. O. Foerster, Prof. V. N. Osipov, Prof. A. A. Deshin, Prof. B. S. Weissbrod, Prof. V. V. Bunak, Dr. F. A. Guetier, Dr. N. I. Elistratov, Dr. V. N. Rozanov, Dr. V. A. Obukh and the Commissar of Health of the R.S.F.S.R., N. A. Semashko.

EXTERNAL EXAMINATION

Body of an elderly man of normal build, adequately nourished. Small pigmented spots are noted on the interior aspect of the chest (acne). Obvious signs of cadaveric hypostasis are noticeable on the posterior aspect of the trunk and the extremities. A linear cicatrice 2 c.m. in length is noted on the skin in the area of the anterior end of the clavicle. Another cicatrice having an irregular outline and measuring 2 x 1 cm. is located on the external surface of the left shoulder area. A round cicatrice about 1 cm. in diameter is found on the skin of the spine above the ridge of the scapula.

The outlines of the skeletal muscles are quite prominent.

In the left clavicle at the border of the lower and middle third there is a slight thickening of the bone (bone callus). Above this area in the posterior part of the deltoid muscle, a solid roundish body can be palpated. Upon incision of this area, a deformed bullet is found, enclosed in a capsule of connective tissue at the border between the subcutaneous fatty tissue and the deltoid muscle.

INTERNAL EXAMINATION

The cranial bones are unchanged. Upon removing the skull cover, a solid fusion of the dura mater with the inner surface of the cranium is noted, primarily along the course of the longitudinal sinus. The outer surface of the dura is dull, pale; pigmentation of a yellowish hue is noted in its left temporal and partly frontal area. The anterior part of the left hemisphere seems slightly collapsed in comparison with the corresponding part of the right hemisphere. The longitudinal sinus contains a small quantity of liquid blood. The internal surface of the dura mater is smooth, shiny-moist, easily separating from the underlying arachnoid membrane except in areas bordering the saggital suture where there are areas of fusion in the region of the Pacchionian granulations. The dura of the base of the brain is normal; the basal sinuses contain liquid blood.

Brain. Weight immediately after removal, freed of the dura mater, is 1,340 Gm. In the left hemisphere: 1. in the anterior central gyrus; 2. in the area of the temporal and occipital pole; 3. in the area of the fissura paracentralis, and 4. in the area of the high gyri, there are noticeable signs of pronounced collapse of the cerebral surface. In the right hemisphere at the border between the temporal and occipital poles there are also two adjacent spots of collapse of the brain surface.

Above the described areas of collapse, the arachnoid membrane is dull, whitish, in places yellowish.

In some areas overlying the fissures, including even some parts where there is no collapse, whitish regions are noted in which the arachnoid is hard and appears thickened upon section.

Vessels of the base of the brain. Both arteriae vertibrales, and also the arteria basilaris are thickened, do not collapse; their walls are hard, irregularly thickened, of a whitish and in places yellowish color. Upon section, their lumen is seen to be extremely narrowed in places down to the dimensions of a tiny slit. Identical changes are also found in branches of the arteries in question (aa. cerebri posteriores). The internal carotid arteries, and also the anterior cerebral arteries are similarly hardened, with an irregularly thickened wall and in spots greatly narrowed lumen. The left internal carotid artery in its intracranial course has a completely obliterated lumen and upon section appears merely as a homogeneous solid whitish band. The left Sylvian (i.e. middle cerebral) artery is very thin, hardened, but upon section still shows a thin small slit.

Incision into the vermiform process of the cerebellar convolutions reveals no change of the brain tissue.

The fourth ventricle is free of any pathological contents.

Resection of the brain according to Flessing shows the brain ventricles, particularly on the left side, to be widened and containing a transparent fluid.

In the above noted areas of collapse of the brain there are areas of softening of the tissue, having a yellowish color and accompanied by formation of cyst-like structures filled with a turbid liquid. The areas of malacia involve the white as well as the gray brain matter. In other parts of the brain the tissue is moist, pale. The vascular plexus overlying the corpora quadrigemina is well irrigated with blood and there are signs of fresh hemorrhage in this area.

Upon removing the skin of the trunk the good development of the subcutaneous and fatty tissue is noted. The muscular system is adequately developed. The muscular tissue is of the usual maroon color.

The positions of the organs of the abdominal cavity are regular with the exception of the cecum which lies somewhat higher than is the norm. The omentum and the mesentery are rich in fat. The diaphragm runs from the level of the fourth rib on the right hand side to the fourth intercostal space on the left. At the region of the pulmonary apex, fibrous synechiae are visible in the right pleura. The left pleura also forms synechiae with the diaphragm in its lower part. No pathological conditions are noted in the region of the heart sac; the mediastinum shows no particular changes.

Heart. Dimensions: transverse 11 cm.; longitudinal 9 cm.; thickness 7 cm. The epicardial surface is smooth and shiny; under the epicardium, mainly in the area of the left ventricle, spotty accumulations of fat are noted. The semilunar valves of the aorta are somewhat thickened at their bases. The mitral valve shows some thickenings at its margins and whitish opaque spots of the anterior cusp. The valves of the right half of the heart are without special changes. The interior of the ascending aorta shows a small number of convex yellowish plaques. The wall thickness of the left ventricle is 1¾ cm. and of the right one ½ cm. The coronary arteries gape upon section; their walls are very hard and thickened; their lumen definitely constricted.

The inner surface of the descending aorta and also the inner surfaces of the large arteries in general show numerous very prominent yellowish plaques, partly undergoing ulceration and calcification.

Lungs. The right lung is of the normal size and configuration; soft throughout, feels spongy. Resection of pulmonary tissue reveals it full of blood, a foamy liquid appears. The pulmonary apex shows a small retracted scar. The left lung is of the usual size and shape, its consistency being soft throughout. The posterior inferior part of the upper lobe has a scar reaching from the surface to a depth of 1 cm. into the pulmonary tissue. At the apex of the lung there is a small fibrous thickening of the pleura.

The spleen is slightly enlarged and moderately filled with blood upon section. The form and size of the liver are normal. The border of the left lobe is somewhat sharp. The surface is smooth. Section reveals a moderate degree of so-called grapiness. The gall bladder and the bile ducts reveal no special changes.

The stomach is empty. Its walls are collapsed. The mucosa shows clearly visible and normally arranged creases. No special conditions to be noted regarding the intestines.

The kidneys are of normal size. Their tissues are clearly identifiable and the substance of the cortex can be easily distinguished from the medullary part. The capsule comes off easily. The surface of the kidney is smooth with exception of some small areas where small depressions of the surface are present. The lumina of the renal arteries gape upon section.

The pancreas is of normal size. No special changes are noted following its section.

GLANDS OF INTERNAL SECRETION

No special changes are noted in the pituitary gland.

The adrenals are somewhat smaller than the norm, especially the left one; the cortical substance is rich in stipples; the medulla is pigmented and brownish in color.

ANATOMICAL DIAGNOSIS

Generalized arteriosclerosis with pronounced degree of affection of the cerebral arteries.

Arteriosclerosis of the descending aorta.

Hypertrophy of the right ventricle of the heart.

Multiple foci of yellow cerebromalacia (based on vascular sclerosis) of the left cerebral hemisphere in a stage of resolution and of cystic change.

Fresh hemorrhage into the vascular plexus overlying the corpora quadrigemina.

Bone callus of the left clavicle.

Incapsulated bullet in the soft tissue of the left shoulder.

CONCLUSION

The basic disease of the deceased was disseminated vascular arteriosclerosis based on premature wearing out of the vessels (*Abnutzungssklerose*). The narrowing of the lumen of the cerebral arteries and the disturbances of the cerebral blood supply brought about focal softening of the brain tissue which can obtain all symptoms of the disease (paralysis, disturbance of speech). The immediate cause of death was: 1. The aggravation of the circulatory disturbance of the brain, and 2. Hemorrhage into the arachnoid pia mater in the area of the corpora quadrigemina.

Gorki, 22 January 1924

PROF. A. I. ABRIKOSOV
PROF. FOERSTER
PROF. V. OSIPOV
PROF. V. BUNAK
PROF. A. DESHIN
PROF. B. WEISSBROD
DR. V. OBUKH
DR. ELISTRATOV
DR. V. ROZANOV
N. SEMASHKO

2. BIBLIOGRAPHY

SELECTED BIBLIOGRAPHY

My chief debt is to the massive three-volume *Reminiscences of Vladimir Ilyich Lenin* (*Vospominaniya o Vladimire Ilyiche Lenine*) published in Moscow between 1956 and 1960, and to the fifth edition of the *Complete Works* (*V. I. Lenin: Polnoe Sobraniye Sochinenii*) which at the time of writing had reached its thirty-ninth volume, bringing the story down to December 1919. For the missing years I have largely used the thirty-volume edition which appeared between 1935 and 1937. I have also used the collection of supplementary material known as *The Lenin Collection* (*Leninskiy Sbornik*) in twenty volumes, which began to appear in 1924 under the editorship of Kamenev, but a good deal of this material is now incorporated in the complete works.

These collections seem to me to be reliable. I have found little evidence of deliberate tampering. The sin is in the omission and deliberate concealment of documents known to exist, especially of Lenin's private letters and diaries. A few documents addressed to Stalin are obvious forgeries, and no doubt they will eventually be removed from the canon. But though there are occasional forgeries and the concealment of important documents on such a ruthless scale is scarcely forgivable, such a wealth of documentation exists that a full and rounded portrait of Lenin can be drawn around the existing material. My obligation is therefore to the Marx-Lenin Institute in Moscow, where scholarship of a high order goes hand in hand with cautious suppression.

WORKS IN ENGLISH

Abramovitch, Raphael R. *The Soviet Revolution.* New York, International Universities Press, 1962.

Balabanoff, Angelica. *My Life as a Rebel.* New York, Harper and Brothers, 1938.

Beatty, Bessie. *The Red Heart of Russia.* New York, The Century Co., 1918.

Bryant, Louise. *Mirrors of Moscow*. New York, Thomas Seltzer, 1923.

Bunyan, James and Fisher, H. H. *The Bolshevik Revolution 1917–1918*. London, Oxford University Press, 1934.

Carr, E. H. *A History of Soviet Russia*. New York, The Macmillan Company, 1951.

Carr, E. H. *Studies in Revolution*. London, Macmillan and Co., 1950.

Deutscher, Isaac. *The Prophet Armed: Trotsky 1879–1921*. New York, Oxford University Press, 1954.

Deutscher, Isaac. *The Prophet Unarmed*. New York, Oxford University Press, 1959.

Duranty, Walter. *I Write as I Please*. New York, Simon and Schuster, 1935.

Eudin, Xenia Joukoff, and Fisher, Harold H. *Soviet Russia and the West*. Stanford University Press, 1957.

Fischer, Louis. *The Soviets and World Affairs*. Princeton University Press, 1951.

Footman, David. *Civil War in Russia*. London, Faber and Faber, 1961.

Footman, David, editor. *Soviet Affairs*. London, Chatto and Windus, 1962.

Fotieva, Lydia. *Pages from Lenin's Life*. Moscow, Foreign Languages Publishing House, 1960.

Fox, Ralph. *Lenin, A Biography*. New York, Harcourt, Brace and Co., 1934.

Gorky, Maxim. *Days with Lenin*. London, Martin Lawrence, n.d.

Hart, B. H. Liddell, editor. *The Red Army*. New York, Harcourt, Brace and Co., 1956.

Hill, Christopher. *Lenin and the Russian Revolution*. London, English Universities Press, 1957.

Hill, Elizabeth, and Mudie, Doris, editors. *The Letters of Lenin*. New York, Harcourt, Brace and Co., 1937.

Hobson, J. A. *Imperialism, A Study*. London, George Allen and Unwin, 1948.

Kerensky, A. F. *The Crucifixion of Liberty*. New York, John Day, 1934.

Kerzhentsev, P. *Life of Lenin*. New York, International Publishers, 1939.

Lawton, Lancelot. *The Russian Revolution (1917–1926)*. London, Macmillan and Co., 1927.

Lermolo, Elizabeth. *Face of a Victim*. New York, Harper and Brothers, 1955.

Levine, Isaac Don. *The Man Lenin*. New York, Thomas Seltzer, 1924.

Liberman, Simon. *Building Lenin's Russia*. Chicago University Press, 1945.

Lockhart, B. H. Bruce. *British Agent*. New York, G. P. Putnam's Sons, 1933.

Luxemburg, Rosa. *The Russian Revolution*. Ann Arbor, University of Michigan Press, 1961.

Marcu, Valeriu. *Lenin*. London, Victor Gollancz, 1928.

Maxton, James. *Lenin*. London, Peter Davies, 1932.

Maynard, Sir John. *Russia in Flux before October*. London, Victor Gollancz, 1946.

Moorehead, Alan. *The Russian Revolution*. New York, Harper and Brothers, 1958.

Nicolaevsky, Boris I., editor. *The Crimes of the Stalin Era*. New York, *The New Leader*, 1962.

Pares, Sir Bernard. *The Fall of the Russian Monarchy*. New York, Alfred Knopf, 1939.

Piatnitsky, O. *Memoirs of a Bolshevik*. New York, International Publishers, n.d.

Pollack, Emanuel. *The Kronstadt Rebellion.* New York, Philosophical Publishers Library, 1959.

Radkey, Oliver Henry. *The Sickle under the Hammer.* New York, Columbia University Press, 1963.

———— *The History of the Russian Revolution.* Ann Arbor, University of Michigan Press, 1957.

Ransome, Arthur. *Russia in 1919.* New York, B. W. Huebsch, 1919.

Rauch, Georg von. *A History of Soviet Russia.* New York, Frederick A. Praeger, 1957.

Reed, John. *Ten Days that Shook the World.* New York, Random House, 1960.

Sack, A. J. *The Birth of the Russian Democracy.* New York, Russian Information Bureau, 1918.

Schuman, Frederick L. *Russia since 1917.* New York, Alfred Knopf, 1957.

Seldes, George. *You Can't Print That.* New York, Payson and Clarke, 1929.

Shub, David. *Lenin.* New York, Doubleday and Co., 1950.

Solomon, George. *Among the Red Autocrats.* New York, Arno C. Gaebelein, 1935.

Sorokim, Pitirim. *Leaves from a Russian Diary.* New York, E. P. Dutton, 1924.

Stalin, J. V., and others. *The History of the Civil War in the U.S.S.R.* Moscow, Foreign Languages Publishing House, 1946.

Steinberg, I. N. *In the Workshop of the Revolution.* New York, Rinehart and Co., 1953.

Sukhanov, N. N. *The Russian Revolution, 1917* (trans. Joel Carmichael). New York, Oxford University Press, 1955.

Treadgold, Donald W. *Lenin and His Rivals.* New York, Frederick A. Praeger, 1955.

Trotsky, Leon. *Lenin.* New York, Grosset & Dunlap, 1960.

———— *My Life.* New York, Charles Scribner's Sons, 1930.

———— *Stalin.* New York, Harper and Brothers, 1941.

———— *Terrorism and Communism.* Ann Arbor, University of Michigan Press, 1961.

Venturi, Franco. *Roots of Revolution.* New York, Alfred Knopf, 1960.

Wells, H. G. *Russia in the Shadows.* London, Hodder and Stoughton, n.d.

White, William C. *Lenin.* New York, Harrison Smith, 1936.

Williams, Albert Rhys. *Lenin: The Man and His Work.* New York, Scott and Seltzer, 1919.

———— *Through the Russian Revolution.* New York, Boni and Liveright, 1921.

Wilson, Edmund. *To the Finland Station.* New York, Doubleday and Co., 1953.

Wolfe, Bertram D. *Khrushchev and Stalin's Ghost.* New York, Frederick A. Praeger, 1957.

———— *Three Who Made a Revolution.* New York, Dial Press, 1948.

Zarudnaya, Elena, editor. *Trotsky's Diary in Exile.* Cambridge, Harvard University Press.

Zeman, Z. A. B. *Germany and the Revolution in Russia, 1915–1918.* London, Oxford University Press, 1958.

WORKS IN FRENCH

Aline. *Lénine à Paris: Souvenirs inédits.* Paris, Les Revues, n.d.

Beucler, André, and Alexinsky, G. *Les amours secrètes de Lénine.* Paris, Editions Baudinière, 1937.

Fréville, Jean. *Inessa Armand.* Paris, Editions Sociales, 1957.

Serge, Victor. *Mémoires d'un Revolutionnaire.* Paris, Editions de Seuil, 1951.

Walter, Gerard. *Lénine.* Paris, Julliard, 1950.

WORKS IN RUSSIAN

Andreyev, A. *Lenin v Kremle.* Moscow, Politicheskoi Literaturi, 1960.

Gaponenko, L. S. *Velikiy Oktyabr: Sbornik dokumentov.* Moscow, Izdatelstvo Akademii Nauk S.S.S.R., 1961.

Genkina, E. B. *Lenin: Predsedatel Sovnarkoma.* Moscow, Izdatelstvo Akademii Nauk S.S.S.R., 1960.

Gililov, C. V. *I. Lenin, Organizator.* Moscow, Gosudarstvennoe Izdatelstvo, 1960.

Ivansky, A. I. *Molodiye godi V. I. Lenina.* Moscow, Molodaya Gvardiya, 1960.

Krupskaya, N. K. *Izbrannie Pedagogicheskie Proizvedeniya.* Moscow, Izdatelstvo, Akademii Pedagogicheskikh Nauk, 1955.

———— *O Lenine: Sbornik Statei.* Moscow, Gosudarstvennoe Izdatelstvo, 1960.

———— *Vospominaniya o Lenine.* Moscow, Partizdat, 1933–4.

Lenin, V. I. *Pisma k rodnim (1894–1917).* Moscow, Gosizdat, 1930.

Moskalev, M. *V. I. Lenin v Sibiri.* Moscow, Gospolitizdat, 1957.

Pospelov, P. N., editor. *Vladimir Ilyich Lenin: Biographiya.* Moscow, Institut Marksizma-Lenina, 1960.

Shaginyan, Mariette. *Semya Ulyanovikh.* Moscow, Molodaya Gvardiya, 1958.

Solomon, G. A. *Lenin i evo semya.* Paris, Travailleurs Intellectuels, 1931.

Suliashvili, David. *Vstrechi s V. I. Leninim v emigratsii.* Tiflis, Izdatelstvo Zarya Vostoka, 1957.

Ulyanova-Elizarova, Anna Ilyinichna. *Aleksandr Ilyich Ulyanov i delo l Marta 1887 g.* Moscow, Gosizdat, 1927.

———— *Vospominaniya ob Ilyiche.* Moscow, Partinoe Izdatelstvo, 1934.

Valentinov, N. *Vstrechi s Leninim.* New York, Izdatelstvo imeni Chekhova, 1953.

Veretennikov, Nikolay. *Vospominaniya o detskokh godakh V. I. Lenina v Kokushkine.* Moscow, Izdatdetlit, 1941.

Yarovslavsky, E. *Biographiya Lenina.* Moscow, Partiinoe Izdatelstvo, 1934.

Zinoviev, G. *Vladimir Ilyich Ulyanov: Ocherk zhizni i deyatelstvo.* Petrograd, 1918.

3. CHAPTER NOTES

THE FORERUNNER

A lengthy account of Nechayev is given in Robert Payne, *The Terrorists* (New York, Funk and Wagnalls Company, 1957, pp. 3–130). There is a useful summary in Franco Venturi, *The Roots of Revolution* (New York, Alfred Knopf, 1960, pp. 354–388).

The quotation on pp. 29–30 comes from an article by Vladimir Bonch-Bruyevich, "Lenin o khudozhestvennoi literature"—Lenin on artistic literature—which appeared in the Moscow magazine *Tridsat Dnei* (January 1934, p. 18). *Tridsat Dnei* was a popular monthly with serious as well as satirical articles. The article by Bonch-Bruyevich was written to commemorate the tenth anniversary of Lenin's death.

FAMILY TREE

The first serious attempt to inquire into the origins of Lenin was made by the novelist and poetess Mariette Shaginyan in an article entitled "Predki Lenina s otsovskoi storoni"—Ancestors of Lenin on his Father's Side—which appeared in *Novy Mir* (No. 11, 1937, pp. 262–285), and in her biographical novel *Semya Ulyanovikh*—The Family of the Ulyanovs—(Moscow, Goslitizdat, 1938), being subsequently reprinted in her collected works in 1959. The article in *Novy Mir* has photographs of tombstones and documents from the Astrakhan archives. I have relied heavily on her evidence, while sometimes differing from her interpretations.

Mariette Shaginyan was the first to give the main outlines of the family tree, without however drawing up the tree in the formal manner which appears here for the first time.

Some mysteries remain. Little is known about the origins of the Blank family. The name Groshopf is probably Flemish. Mariette Shaginyan states explicitly that Alexander Blank was entered in the register of nobility in Kazan, and more about his origins may become known when a copy of the register becomes available.

A NEST OF GENTLE FOLK

The stories about Lenin's childhood are taken from the reminiscences of his brother and sisters, Dmitry, Anna, and Maria. Anna is by far the most reliable and informative. There is some useful background material in the reminiscences of Lenin's cousin, Nikolay Veretennikov, and in Ivansky's *Molodiye godi.*

DEATH OF A HERO

P. 71   Anna Ulyanova-Elizarova, *Alexandr Ilyich Ulyanov i delo l Marta 1887 g.,* p. 340.

P. 73   Alexander Kerensky, *The Crucifixion of Liberty,* p. 13.

THE YOUNG LAWYER

The story of Arefeyev is told by Dmitry, but the account of Lenin's life in Samara is largely based on Anna, who was much closer to Lenin.

There is a useful edition of Chernyshevsky's *What Is To Be Done?* in the translation by Benjamin R. Tucker and Ludmilla B. Turkevich published by Vintage Books, 1961.

Lenin's letters of appeal and complaint to the educational authorities are given in the appendix to *Sochineniya,* I, pp. 549–562. There are thirteen letters altogether.

THE CONSPIRATOR

Krupskaya's account of Lenin's early revolutionary career becomes invaluable. She writes of these days with clarity and energy; there is a notable falling-off as the story proceeds, and the last volume shows signs of considerable editing and censorship by Stalin.

The reminiscences of Kniazev are given in *Vospominaniya I.*

P. 102   *Sochineniya* I, 312.

SHUSHENSKOYE

P. 118   *Sochineniya* II, 285.

P. 120   *Sochineniya* II, 461.

THE ENCHANTED KINGDOM

P. 131   *Pisma k rodnim,* 113 R.

The full text of Ekaterina Kuskova's *Credo* was reprinted by Lenin in *The Protest of the Russian Social Democrats,* printed in *Sochineniya* IV, 165–169.

WHAT IS TO BE DONE?

P. 144   *Sochineniya* IV, 343–344.

P. 146   *Sochineniya* IV, 352.

P. 146   Dmitry Pisarev, *Selected Philosophical, Social and Political Essays* (Moscow, Foreign Languages Publishing House, 1958, p. 147).

P. 146   Karl Marx, *Capital, I* (Moscow, Foreign Languages Publishing House, 1961, p. 760).

P. 148   *Sochineniya* VI, 9–10.

P. 149   *Sochineniya* VI, 28.

P. 151   *Sochineniya* VI, 130.
P. 152   *Sochineniya* VI, 127.
P. 153   *Sochineniya* VI, 172–173.
P. 154   *Sochineniya* VI, 183.

THE LONDON YEAR

P. 161   *Sochineniya* (4), XXVIII, 274.

THE BANGING OF THE DOOR

P. 172   *Sochineniya* VII, 428–430.
P. 175   *Sochineniya* VIII, 265.
P. 176   *Sochineniya* VIII, 333.
P. 182   *Sochineniya* IX, 136.

THE YEAR NINETEEN FIVE

P. 184   The full text of Father Gapon's petition is given in A. J. Sack, *The Birth of the Russian Democracy* (New York, Russian Information Bureau, 1918, pp. 99–104).
P. 185   *Sochineniya* IX, 136.
P. 187   *Sochineniya* X, 359–360.
P. 189   *Sochineniya* (4), IX, 315–316.
P. 194   The reminiscences of Nikolay Vilenkin are quoted from Isaac Don Levine, *The Man Lenin*, p. 19.
P. 196   *Sochineniya* XII, 292.
P. 199   *Sochineniya* (4) XI, 221.

ELIZABETH DE K.

The description of Apollinaria Yakubova comes from Sophia Nezvorova-Chesternina's reminiscences in *Vospominaniya I*, and from Krupskaya, together with information kindly given to me by Boris Nicolaevsky.

The chief source of the love affair between Lenin and Elizabeth de K. is André Beucler and Grigory Alexinsky, *Les Amours secrètes de Lénine.* Inevitably the authenticity of these letters had been questioned. Boris Nicolaevsky tells me that he has seen the originals and is satisfied that they are in Lenin's handwriting. Final proof of their authenticity will come about only when the letters are published in holograph copies, but it should be pointed out that a forger would be hardly likely to produce letters so lacking in political cunning. The letters are not in Lenin's customary style, and the opinions he expresses, notably concerning the suicide of Lafargue, contradict opinions he expressed elsewhere, but a man writing to a cultivated and beautiful lady would not write in the style of political polemics.

THE LONDON CONFERENCE

P. 216   *Sochineniya* XV, 341.
P. 217   *Vospominaniya o V. I. Lenine* (Moscow, Molodaya Gvardiya, 1955, pp. 21–22).
P. 221   *ibid.,* p. 29.

PARIS

P. 228   *Sochineniya* XVIII, 239–240.
P. 229   *Sochineniya* XVIII, 212–213.

Jean Fréville's *Inessa Armand* remains the only available study of her. Some fragmentary recollections were published in Russia in 1926 under the title *Pamyati Inessi Armand*, edited by Krupskaya, who refers to her continually in her three-volume recollections of Lenin. Gérard Walter was the first to give her real name and to examine her background at any length.

WANDERINGS

P. 252   *Sochineniya* XXX, 327–328.

LETTERS FROM AFAR

P. 278   *Sochineniya* (4) XXIX, 337.
P. 279   *Sochineniya* (4) XXIX, 339.
P. 282   *Sochineniya* XXXI, 37.
P. 283   *Sochineniya* XXXI, 48–49.

THE SEALED TRAIN

P. 288   *Sochineniya* XXXI, 480–482.
P. 291   The most easily accessible holograph of the document is given in Lenin, *The Revolution of 1917*, Book II (New York, International Publishers, 1929, p. 312).
P. 294   *Sochineniya* XXXI, 91–92.

THE FINLAND STATION

The reminiscences of Tskhakaya and Ganetsky are given in *Vospominaniya I*. Raskolnikov has an important eye-witness account of the arrival at the Finland Station in *Proletarskaya Revolutsiya* (No. 13, 1923, pp. 220–236), which has the advantage of having been written while Lenin was still alive. The photograph of the *émigrés* in Stockholm is given in Helmut and Alison Geinsheim, *The Recording Eye* (New York, G. P. Putnam's Sons, 1960, p. 161).

P. 305   Warren B. Walsh, *Readings in Russian History* (Syracuse University Press, 1950, p. 578). The original is in the Central Lenin Museum, Moscow.
P. 310   N. N. Sukhanov, *The Russian Revolution 1917*, edited by Joel Carmichael (New York, Harper and Brothers, 1962, Part I, p. 272).

THE APRIL THESES

P. 323   The holograph of the outline of the "April Theses" has been reproduced from *Sochineniya* XXXI, 101.
P. 324   *Sochineniya* XXXI, 105.
P. 326   *Sochineniya* XXX, 113–116.
P. 328   Lenin, *The Revolution of 1917*, Book I, p. 373.
P. 333   *Sochineniya* XXXII, 26.

EXILE IN FINLAND

P. 339   *Sochineniya* (4) XXIX, No. 177.
P. 350   *Sochineniya* XXXIII, 35.
P. 350   *Sochineniya* XXXIII, 78.
P. 351   *Sochineniya* XXXIII, 91.
P. 358   *Sochineniya* XXXIV, 245.

ON THE EVE

P. 361   *Sochineniya* XXXIV, 332
P. 363   *Sochineniya* XXXIV, 383.
P. 366   *Sochineniya* XXXIV, 393.
P. 371   Lenin, *Towards the Seizure of Power*, Book II, p. 331.
P. 372   *Sochineniya* XXXIV, 422.

THE CONQUEST OF PETROGRAD

P. 379   *Sochineniya* XXXIV, 435.
P. 386   *Sochineniya* XXXV, 1.

THE FIRST DAY OF THE REVOLUTION

P. 400   *Sochineniya* XXXV, 28–29.
P. 401   *Sochineniya* XXXV, 32–33.
P. 403   *Petrograd, October 1917* (Moscow, Foreign Languages Publishing House, 1957, pp. 42–43).

THE EXALTATIONS OF REVOLUTION

P. 412   *Sochineniya* XXXV, 133.
P. 414   James Bunyan and H. Fisher, *The Bolshevik Revolution 1917–1918: Documents and Materials* (Stanford University Press, 1934, p. 299).
P. 415   Albert Rhys Williams, *Lenin: The Man and His Work* (New York, Scott and Seltzer, 1919, pp. 139–146).
P. 418   G. A. Solomon, *Lenin i evo semya* (Paris, Travailleurs Intellectuels, 1931, pp. 45–46, 86–90). See also George Solomon, *Among the Red Autocrats* (New York, Arno C. Gaebelein, 1935, pp. 10–11).
P. 421   *Sochineniya* XXXV, 66.
P. 422   *Sochineniya* XXXV, 189.

PEACE WITH GERMANY

P. 445   *Sochineniya* XXXV, 245.
P. 447   *Sochineniya* XXXV, 250–251.
P. 449   *Sochineniya* XXXV, 251–252.
P. 451   R. H. Bruce Lockhart, *British Agent* (New York, G. P. Putnam's Sons, 1933, p. 237).

THE CORRUPTIONS OF POWER

P. 456   *Sochineniya* XXXVI, 78–79.
P. 458   *Sochineniya* XXXVI, 80.

P. 458 *Sochineniya* XXXVI, 82.

P. 463 Count Mirbach's letter to Diego Bergen is given in Z. A. B. Zeman, *Germany and the Revolution in Russia 1915–1918* (London, Oxford University Press, 1958, p. 139).

P. 464 Leon Trotsky, *Lenin* (New York, Garden City Books, 1959, pp. 156–157).

P. 464 *Sochineniya* XXIX (4), 485.

P. 465 Lenin's explanation to Krassin concerning the execution of the Socialist Revolutionaries is given in George Solomon, *Among the Red Autocrats*, p. 37.

P. 468 *Trotsky's Diary in Exile: 1935*, translated by Elena Zarudnaya (Cambridge, Harvard University Press, 1958, p. 81).

A ROOM IN THE KREMLIN

P. 480 *Sbornik Lenina* XXIV, 179.

P. 482 (a) *Iz Istorii Vserossiiskoi Chrezvychainoi Komissii* (Moscow, Sbornik Dokumentov, 1959).
(b) *Sochineniya* (4) XXIX, 489.
(c) I. Steinberg, *In the Workshop of the Revolution* (New York, Rinehart and Company, 1953, p. 149).

THE THIRD INTERNATIONAL

P. 504 *Sochineniya* XXXVII, 331.

P. 511 Angelica Balabanoff, *My Life as a Rebel* (New York, Harper and Brothers, 1938, pp. 215–216).

P. 513 *Sochineniya* XXXVII, 513.

P. 514 Leon Trotsky, *My Life* (New York, Grosset and Dunlap, 1960, pp. 449–450).

THE MAN OF SORROWS

P. 518 Simon Liberman, *Building Lenin's Russia* (Chicago, Chicago University Press, 1945, p. 14).

P. 519 *Sochineniya* (4) XXIX, 430.

P. 520 *Sochineniya* (4) XXIX, 465.

P. 526 Clara Zetkin, *Reminiscences of Lenin* (New York, International Publishers, 1934, p. 18).

P. 528 *ibid.*, p. 20.

THE MACHINE BREAKS DOWN

P. 533 Emanuel Pollack, *The Kronstadt Rebellion* (New York, The Philosophical Library, 1959, p. 29).

P. 534 *ibid.*, p. 46.

P. 536 *Sochineniya* (4) XXVII, 339.

P. 538 *Sochineniya* (4) XXVII, 477.

P. 540 *Sochineniya* (4) XXIX, 45.

P. 541 Trotsky Archive T-715.

THE BITTEREST BLOW

P. 546   *Sochineniya* (4) XXVII, 213–217.
P. 547   (a) *Sochineniya* (4) XXVII, 240.
          (b) *Sochineniya* (4) XXVII, 238.
          (c) *Sochineniya* (4) XXVII, 232.
P. 550   *Sochineniya* (4) XXVII, 296.
P. 556   *Sochineniya* (4) XXVII, 349–350.
P. 558   *Sochineniya* (4) XXVII, 364.

LAST TESTAMENT

P. 563   *Letter to the Congress* (Moscow, Foreign Languages Publishing House, n.d., p. 9).
P. 564   *ibid.*, p. 11.
P. 568   *ibid.*, p. 22.
P. 571   *ibid.*, p. 12.
P. 573   Quoted by Nikita Khrushchev at 20th Congress of the Communist Party of the Soviet Union. See *The Crimes of the Stalin Era*, annotated by Boris I. Nicolaevsky (New York, the New Leader, 1962, pp. 10–11).
P. 575   *Sochineniya* XXVII (4), 414.
P. 576   *The Crimes of the Stalin Era*, pp. 11–12.
P. 576   Leon Trotsky, *Stalin*, New York, Grosset and Dunlap, 1941, p. 361.
P. 577   *Vospominaniya*, III, 366.
P. 578   Leon Trotsky, *Stalin*, p. 361.

THE MURDER OF LENIN

P. 596   *Proletarskaya Literatura*, No. 3 (26), March 1924, pp. 19–21.
P. 600   *Trotsky's Diary in Exile*, p. 34.
P. 602   Elizabeth Lermolo, *Face of a Victim* (New York, Harper and Brothers, 1955, pp. 156–157).
P. 603   *Vospominaniya* III, 340–341.

THE APOTHEOSIS OF A GOD

P. 625   *Sochineniya*, XXXIII 5.

4. CHRONOLOGICAL TABLE

All dates are given in the New Style. Up to February 1918 the Russians customarily employed an archaic system which differed by about thirteen days from the system employed in the West. Hence the occasional references to the February and October revolutions which occurred according to the Western calendar in March and November.

1870	April 22	Birth of Vladimir Ilyich Ulyanov (Lenin).
1871	March 18–May 28	Paris Commune.
1873	January 20	Nechayev condemned by Moscow District Court to 20 years' hard labor in Siberia.
1879	November 7	Birth of Lev Davydovich Bronstein (Trotsky).
1879	December 21	Birth of Yosif Visarionovich Djugashvili (Stalin).
1880	February 16	Stepan Khalturin blows up part of the Winter Palace.
1881	March 13	Alexander II assassinated.
1882	December 3	Nechayev dies in Peter and Paul Fortress.
1886	January 24	Death of Ilya Ulyanov.
1887	May 20	Alexander Ulyanov hanged.
1887	August 25	Lenin enters Kazan University.
1887	December 17	Lenin arrested for participation in student protest.
1890	September	Lenin visits St. Petersburg for examinations.
1894	March	Lenin writes *What the "Friends of the People" Are and How They Fight Against the Social Democrats*
1895	May–September	Lenin goes abroad.
1895	December 21	Lenin arrested.

1897	February 10	Lenin exiled to Siberia.
1897	May 20	Lenin reaches Shushenskoye.
1898	March 13–15	First Congress of the Russian Social Democratic Party in Minsk.
1898	July 22	Lenin marries Nadezhda Krupskaya.
1899	April	Publishes *The Development of Capitalism in Russia.*
1900	February 10	Leaves Shushenskoye for European Russia.
1900	March	Meets Vera Zasulich in St. Petersburg.
1900	June 3	Arrested, and released ten days later.
1900	June 20	Visits Krupskaya at Ufa.
1900	July 29	Goes abroad.
1901	May	Works on *What Is to Be Done?*
1902	April 12	Settles in London.
1903	May	Abandons London for Geneva.
1903	July 30–August 23	Second Congress of the Russian Social Democratic Party in London.
1903	December	Resigns from *Iskra.*
1904	March 14	Resigns from Central Committee of Party.
1905	January 4	Publishes first number of *Vperyod.*
1905	January 22	Father Gapon leads procession to the Winter Palace.
1905	April 25–May 10	Third Congress of the Russian Social Democratic Party.
1905	June 27	Mutiny on cruiser *Potemkin.*
1905	November 21	Lenin arrives in St. Petersburg.
1905	December 16	St. Petersburg Soviet arrested.
1906	May 22	Lenin addresses meeting at house of Countess Panina.
1907	January–April	Lenin living in Kokkala (Finland).
1907	January	Lenin is arraigned before Party tribunal.
1907	April 13–June 1	Fifth Congress of the Russian Social Democratic Party opens in London.
1907	December	Settles in Switzerland.

1908	April	Visits Gorky in Capri.
1908	October	Completes *Materialism and Empirio-Criticism*.
1908	December	Abandons Geneva for Paris.
1910	November	Founds *Rabochaya Gazeta*.
1911	Summer	Holds revolutionary school at Longjumeau near Paris.
1912	January	Prague Conference.
1912	June	Settles in Cracow.
1913	May	Moves to Poronino.
1913	June–August	Visits Switzerland and Austria.
1914	August 8	Arrested at Novy Targ.
1914	August 19	Released.
1914	September 5	Leaves for Switzerland.
1915	September 18–21	Zimmerwald Conference.
1916	May 6–12	Kienthal Conference.
1917	March 8	February Revolution begins.
1917	March 15	Nicholas II abdicates.
1917	April 16	Lenin arrives at the Finland Station.
1917	April 17	He delivers "April Theses."
1917	July 17–18	"July Days."
1917	July 24	He hides in Sestroretsk.
1917	Summer and autumn	Lenin hides in Finland and writes *The State and Revolution*.
1917	October 23	Secret meeting in Sukhanov's apartment.
1917	November 6	Lenin leaves his hiding place and comes to Smolny late in the evening.
1917	November 8	Winter Palace falls. Decree on Land.
1917	December 20	Cheka established.
1918	January 18–19	Constituent Assembly meets, and is destroyed.
1918	January 20	Lenin writes "Twenty-one Theses."
1918	February 8	Gregorian calendar adopted.
1918	March 10	Lenin leaves Petrograd and establishes his government in Moscow.

1918	July 17	Royal family executed at Ekaterinburg.
1918	August 30	Uritsky assassinated; Lenin wounded.
1918	September	Red and White Terror.
1918	September 11	Kazan occupied by Red Army.
1918	September 16	Lenin returns to work.
1918	November 10	He completes *The Proletarian Revolution and the Renegade Kautsky*.
1919	March 2–6	First Congress of Communist International.
1919	March 16	Death of Sverdlov.
1919	July	Red Army captures Ekaterinburg and Chelyabinsk.
1919	October	Denikin's army close to Orel and Yudenich close to Petrograd.
1920	Spring	Lenin writes *Infantile Malady of Communism*.
1920	July 21–August 6	Second Congress of the Communist International.
1920	August 17	Red Army begins retreat from Poland.
1920	November 10	Red Army recaptures Crimea.
1921	March 1–18	Kronstadt uprising.
1921	August 11	Official publication of decree announcing New Economic Policy.
1922	February 6	Cheka reorganized as G.P.U.
1922	March	Lenin's health failing.
1922	May 26	Lenin suffers first stroke.
1922	Summer	Spends most of his time at Gorki.
1922	December 16	Lenin has second stroke.
1922	December 25	He dictates his Testament.
1923	March 9	Lenin has third stroke: end of his public career.
1923	April 17–25	Twelfth Party Congress: the first without Lenin.
1923	October 19	He visits Moscow.
1924	January 16–18	Thirteenth Party Conference condemns Trotsky.
1924	January 18	Trotsky leaves Moscow for Sukhum.
1924	January 21	Death of Lenin.
1924	January 27	Funeral.

ACKNOWLEDGMENTS

So many people have helped in the writing of this book that a list of their names would cover many pages. I note here only a very few; though gratitude can be expressed in many ways, it is least served by lists that resemble telephone directories. Also, it is in the nature of things that some of the names would have to be clothed in anonymity. I am especially grateful to Prince X and to Comrade Y, who are accustomed to anonymity and will recognize themselves in these disguises.

I was surprised by the kindness of the keepers of archives. Among them were:

Mr. Sherrod East, Director, World War II Records, National Archives and Records Service, Alexandria, Virginia for permission to examine the documents known as the Smolensk Archives.

Dr. W. H. Bond, Curator of Manuscripts of the Houghton Library, Harvard University for permission to examine the open section of the Trotsky Archive.

Dr. Philip E. Moseley and Mr. Leo Magerovsky of Columbia University for permission to examine the manuscripts in the possession of the Russian Institute.

Mrs. Lydia N. Sienitsky of the American Committee for Liberation, Inc., who placed the resources of the Committee's research library at my disposal.

The directors of the Slavonic Section of the New York Public Library, who tolerated with good humor my requests for mountains of books.

Not the least of my debts are to Mr. Samuel L. M. Barlow, who came to my rescue with a mint copy of Baedeker's *Russia*, when my own had fallen into tatters, and to Mr. Michael V. Korda, my editor, who gently suggested a few minor cuts but otherwise made no effort to invade the privacy of my text. Editors are rarely so reticent. When they are, authors are immeasurably grateful.

INDEX

Abramovich, Rafael, 198, 214, 215, 216

Abramovitch, A., 277, 292, 295n

Abrikosov, Dr., 598

Adler, Victor, 248

"Advice from an Outsider," 363

Afanasiev, Alexander Mikhailovich: quoted, 308

"Agrarian Program of Russian Social Democracy, The," 160

Aisenbud, M., 292

Alexander I, 453

Alexander II: 66, 67, 97; assassination of, 33, 93

Alexander III, 70

Alexander of Hesse, Prince, 476

Alexander the Great, 13

Alexeyev, Nikolay A., 156, 160

Alexis, Prince, 31, 32

All-Russian Congress of Soviets, 333, 453

Allies, the, 369, 451-3, 469, 487, 509

Alliluyev, Sergey Yakovlevich, 340

America, 446, 538-40

American Declaration of Independence, 321

American Relief Administration, 537

Anastasia, Grand Duchess, 466, 467

Andreyev, Andrey Andreyevich, 461, 463

Andreyev, Leonid, 193

Andreyeva, Maria Fyodorovna, 193, 194

Andreyushkin, 66-68

Anissimov, 341

Antonov, Gerasim, 537, 540, 556

Antonov-Ovseyenko, Vladimir Alexeyevich, 392, 400, 403, 404

"April Theses": 288, 289, 324, 329, 330, 332; outline of, 321, 322;

read by Gorky, 407, 408; summarized, 326, 327

Ardashevs, the, 108

Arefyev, 89, 90

Arkady (fictional), 59, 60

Armand, Inessa: 211, 233-6, 239-41, 246, 249, 252, 292-5n, 298; death of, 528, 529

Aristotle, 153

Asia, 570

Auerbach, Dr. Mikhail Yosifovich, 552, 561, 588, 589, 599, 606

Augier, Marie, 146

Aurora, 374, 376, 377, 390-3

Austria, 244, 247, 248, 417, 449, 511

Austria-Hungary, 449

Avanessov, Varlaam Alexandrovich, 539

Avilov, N. P. (Glebov), 400

Axelrod, Paul Borisovich: 105, 108, 116, 143, 144, 154, 171, 174, 213, 243, 251; described, 106

Azis-Rozin, 215

Babushkin, Ivan Vasilyevich, 100, 101

Bagratuni, General, 391

Baku, 416

Bakunin, Mikhail Alexandrovich, 31, 32, 327, 353, 370, 391, 407, 483

Balabanoff, Angelica: 216, 290, 498-500, 510; quoted, 511, 512

Balmont, Konstantin Dmitryevich, 194

Baltic fleet, 443, 444

Barbusse, Henri, 499

Bavaria, 508

Bazarov (fictional), 35, 59, 60, 229

Bebel, August, 209

Bedny, Demyan (real name: Pridvorov, Yefim Alexeyich), 586

Beethoven's *Appassionata*, 249
Belenky, 551
Beletsky, 241-3
Belmas, Alexander Vasilyevich, 582n,
    600, 605-7;
    describes Lenin's last days, 603, 604
Belobdorov, 466
Belo-Ostrov, 307-9, 347
Bergen, Diego, 286, 287, 297, 462,
    463
Berkeley, George, 228
Berlin, 107, 279, 299, 300, 449, 504,
    505
Bernatsky, 408
Berne, 248, 249
Bernstein, Eduard, 112, 131, 132, 134,
    164
Berzin, Jan Antonovich, 376
"Better Fewer but Better": 574;
    quoted, 575
Bismarck, Otto, Fürst von, 131
Blank, Alexander Dmitrievich, 43, 44,
    59
Bloch, Siegfried, 296
Blok, Alexander:
    The Twelve, 420
    The Scythians, 421
"Bloody Sunday," 183, 186, 189
Blanquists, the, 120
Blum, Dr. Oscar, 295, 296
Blumenfeld, I. S., 147
Blumkin, Yakov Grigorievich, 461,
    462, 464, 465
Böcklin, Arnold, 245
Bogdanov, Alexander Alexandrovich:
    164, 180, 181, 239, 540;
    attacked by Lenin, 228-30
Boitsov, Nikolay, 292, 295n
Bolsheviks: 177, 178, 193-7, 213-6,
    326-8, 331-40, 369-71, 374-7,
    425-7, 431-3, 444, 450, 451, 530;
    founding fathers of, 130;
    split with Mensheviks, 169;
    on sealed train, 292, 293;
    await Lenin's return, 310;
    Seventh Conference of, 330;
    defeated, 336, 337;
    accuse Socialist Revolutionaries,
    461-5

Bonapartism, 175, 178
Bonch-Bruyevich, Vladimir Dmitrie-
    vich, 34, 220, 395-7, 432, 443,
    444, 455, 456, 459
Borah, Senator William Edgar, 556
Bordiga, 584
Bosh, Evgeniya Bogdanovna, 482
Botkin, Dr., 468
Brailsford, H. N., 212
Brest Litovsk, 445, 448, 449
Brest Litovsk Treaty, 444, 453, 486
Britain, *see* England
British Empire, 535
Brockdorff-Rantzau, Count, 295n
Brussels, 169
Bubnov, Andrey Sergeyevich, 213,
    363, 365, 376
Budyenny, Semyon Mikhailovich, 525
Bukharin, Nikolay Ivanovich, 245,
    298, 354, 411, 436, 448, 453,
    486, 510, 559, 565, 580, 586,
    592, 598, 620, 621, 630
Bulatov, 480
Bulgaria, 449
Bunak, Dr., 598
Bundists, 213, 214
Burkhardt, Dr., 549
Byron, George Gordon, 180

Cadets (Constitutional Democrats),
    194-9, 427, 429, 432
"Can the Bolsheviks Retain State
    Power?," 360, 361
Capri, 221
"Catechism of the Class Conscious
    Proletarian, The," 492, 493
Catherine the Great, 39, 43, 46, 438
Caucasus, The, 486
Central Powers, 499
Central Committee: 358-66, 428, 501,
    530, 531, 537, 548, 562, 563,
    567, 590, 591, 596;
    split in, 564, 565;
    battle for power, 620
Central Control Commission, 573, 574
Chaliapin, Fyodor Ivanovich, 373
Chapovalov, Alexander, 126, 127
Chartists, 398

Cheka (Extraordinary Commission for Combating Counterrevolution and Sabotage), 427, 428, 442, 461, 492, 531-3, 537, 632

Chekhov, Anton Pavlovich: 90-2, 153, 218;
"Ward No. 6," 90-1, 481

Cherbanov, 506, 507

Chernov, Viktor Mikhailovich: 95, 331, 335, 435, 436, 438-40;
describes Lenin, 328, 329

Chernyshevsky, Nikolay Gavrilovich: 19, 69, 94;
What Is To Be Done?, 75-77, 147, 235

Chicherin, Georgy Vasilyevich, 464, 465, 510, 620

Chirikov, Evgeniy, 193, 208n

Chkheidze, Nikolay Semyonovich, 242, 243, 289, 304, 310-2, 328, 330, 334

Christ, 528, 630

Chuvash, 38, 39

Clausewitz, Karl von, 186, 403

Cleisthenes, 153, 632

Cluseret, Gustave-Paul, 186

Collapse of the Second International, The, 250, 251

Columbus, Christopher, 420

Committee for the Salvation of the Fatherland and the Revolution, 398

Communards, 180

Communist Manifesto, The, 90, 127, 132, 320

Communist Party: 324, 325;
First Congress of, 129;
Eleventh Congress of, 545-8;
All-Russian Central Executive Committee, 553;
Lenin addresses, 555

Constantinople, 280

Constituent Assembly: 276, 320, 365, 371, 372, 377, 434, 440, 503, 533;
destruction of, 425-40

Copenhagen, 212

Cossacks, 184, 206, 273

Cracow, 244-6

Credo of the Young, 132-134

Crimea, the, 451, 460

Cromwell's Republic of England, 441

Czechoslovaks, the, 460, 464, 466-9, 486, 488

Dan, Fyodor (real name: Fyodor Ilych Gurvich), 213, 215, 216, 383, 393

Danishevsky, Hermann, 214

d'Annunzio, Gabriele, 210

Darwinian theory, 627, 628

Das Kapital, 82, 90, 121, 146, 164

Daszynski, 527

David, 165

Demidova, Anna, 467, 468

Denikin, General Anton Ivanovich, 508, 513-5, 525

Derzhimorda (fictional), 569

Descartes, René, 229

Deshin, Dr., 598

Deutsch, Lev G., 213

Development of Capitalism in Russia, The, 164

Dobrolyubov, Nikolay Alexandrovich, 60

Donetz coal basin, 416

Dostoyevsky, Fyodor Mikhailovich: 155, 373, 516;
The Possessed, 14, 29, 33, 34;
quoted, 66;
House of the Dead, The, 111;
Brothers Karamazov, The, 622, quoted, 630

Duma, 242

Dybenko, Pavel Efimovich: 400, 406, 432, 444;
quoted, 443

Dzerzhinsky, Felix Edmundovich, 214, 363, 365, 376, 443, 448, 461, 462, 485, 507, 516-8, 568, 569, 576, 578, 603, 606, 613, 620, 621

Eberlein, Hugo, 510-2

Echo, 198

Egypt, 465

Egyptians, 623

Ehrenburg, Ilya Grigorievich, 227

Eidelman, Boris, 130n

Eighth All-Russian Congress, 521

Eighth Party Congress, 513
Eisner, Kurt, 508
Ekaterinburg, 452, 466, 467
Electoral Commission, 426, 427
Elistratov, Dr.: 595, 598, 602, 603;
  quoted, 599
Elizabeth de K., 201-11
Elizarov, Mark T., 83-86, 89, 122,
  272, 320
Eltchaninoff, B., 292
Emelianov, Nikolay Alexandrovich,
  341-3, 345, 346
Engberg, Oscar, 122, 123, 125, 126,
  128, 135
Engels, Friedrich: 131, 188n, 228,
  229, 289, 339, 441;
  Eugen Dühring's Revolution in Science, 351;
  paraphrased by Lenin, 352;
  quoted, 481
England, 119, 120, 163-6, 212, 280,
  286, 305, 355, 356, 362, 398,
  417, 439, 446, 450, 460, 479,
  508-10, 557, 584
Esperanto, 210
Essen, Maria Moisseyevna (Zver),
  179, 180, 193
Esthonia, 460

Fabianism, 131
February revolution, 301, 309, 312,
  332-4, 374
Fedoseyev, N. Y., 82, 83, 114, 128,
  129
Feinberg, 510
Finland, 193, 197, 219, 305-7, 343-7,
  357, 360, 402
Finland Station, 309, 310, 327, 329
Foerster, Dr. Otfried: 582, 588, 594,
  598, 604;
  quoted, 599
Fofanova, Margarita Vasilyevna, 362,
  378-81
Fotieva, Lydia Alexandrovna: 571,
  574, 578, 579, 582n, 601;
  diary quoted, 577
France, 161, 162, 223, 280, 286, 398,
  417, 439, 450, 508, 509, 525, 557
French Revolution, 417, 441

Gallienus, Emperor, 481
Ganchin, Alexey, 103
Ganetsky, Yakov Stanislavovich (Furstenburg): 211, 244, 245, 247,
  277, 287, 301, 302, 304, 307,
  337;
  quoted, 303
Gapon, Father George, 183, 185-7,
  192
Gatchina, 401, 403
Geneva, 167-9, 178-81, 185-91, 279
Genghis Khan, 472, 633
Genyeralov, 72, 418
Georgia, 563, 568, 569, 574, 576-9
German Spartacus League, 510, 511
Germany: 107, 131, 147, 211, 236,
  275-80, 285-7, 290, 296-302, 304,
  308, 311, 324, 329, 330, 337-9,
  354-7, 362, 366, 369, 370, 377,
  398, 437, 439, 455-66, 470, 487,
  504-6, 509-11, 525, 526, 584,
  624;
  peace with, 444-54
Gil, Stepan Kasimirovich, 486-91, 506,
  507
Gliasser, Maria Ignatievna, 578
Gobermann, M., 292
Goethe's Mephistopheles, 60
Gogol, Nikolay Vasilyevich:
  Taras Bulba, 525;
  Inspector General, The, 569
Goldenberg, Joseph, 327
Goloshchekin, F. I., 242
Golubeva, Maria, 96
Goncharov, Ivan, 47
Gorki, 498, 541, 549, 550, 551, 581-8,
  596-606
Gorky, Maxim (Alexey Maximovich
  Peshkov): 142, 193, 194, 228,
  232, 239, 244, 246, 249, 289,
  319, 361, 371, 380n, 406, 551;
  quoted, 212-5, 221, 407-9, 539;
  describes Lenin, 217, 218;
  attacked by Lenin, 282, 283n;
  Days with Lenin, 408;
  visits Lenin, 495-7;
  My Universities, 585, 586
Great Britain, *see* England
Grebelsky, F., 292, 295n

Greece, 502

Grimm, Robert, 251, 272, 273, 279, 285, 286

Grinevitsky, Ignaty Ioachimovich, 66

Gromov, Ivan, 91

Groshopf, Anna Ivanovna, 43

"Group for the Emancipation of Labor," 105

Grünewald (Mathis Nithart), 528

Guchkov, Alexander Ivanovich, 274, 280, 283

"Guerrilla Warfare," 220

Guetier, Dr. Fyodor Konstantinovich, 550, 580, 588, 598, 604

Hamsun, Knut:
    Hunger, read by Lenin, 205

Hauptmann, Gerhart, 107

Heine, Heinrich, 86

Helphand, Dr. Alexander, 285, 304, 337

Helsingfors, 348, 355, 401, 404

History of the Civil War, 380n. .

Hitler, Adolf, 562

Hobson, J. A.:
    quoted, 180, 181;
    Imperialism, 251

Hume, David, 228, 229

Hungary, 508

Hoffmann, Major-General Max von, 449

Homer, 164

Hoover, Herbert, 537, 539

"How The Spark Was Nearly Extinguished," 143, 145, 146

"How We Should Reorganize the Workers' and Peasants' Inspectorate," 573

Imperialism, The Highest Stage of Capitalism, 251

India, 465

"Infantile Malady of Communism, The," 522-4

Irish, 535

Isaiah, 165

Iskra, 144, 147, 154, 159-66, 170-8, 181

Italy, 362, 398, 499, 508, 584

Ivan the Terrible, 39, 97, 484, 512, 621

Ivanov, Ivan Ivanovich, 20-3

Japan, 460, 508, 555, 557

Jefferson, Thomas, 415

Jewish Socialist Bund, 170, 177

John Grafton, 186

July insurrection, 334, 338

Kalinin, Mikhail Ivanovich: 532, 596, 617, 620;
    announces death of Lenin, 608, 609

Kalmykova, Alexandra, 104, 177

Kalske, Emil:
    quoted, 346, 347

Kamchatka, 450

Kamenev, Lev Borisovich (Rosenfeld): 213, 225, 240, 305, 307, 328, 339-41, 363, 365, 376, 393, 510, 558, 576-9, 586, 590, 592, 596, 609, 620, 621, 630;
    editor of Pravda, 309;
    attacks Lenin, 370, 371;
    Lenin forgives, 565;
    plea for help from Krupskaya, 573

Kammerer, Adolph, 251, 296

Kamo (real name: Semyon Arshakovich Ter-Petrossian), 220

Kannegiesser, Leonid, 485, 486

Kant, Immanuel, 228-30

Kaplan-Roid, Fanya, 494, 499, 506

Karakhan, Lev Mikhailovich, 510

Karamazov, Alyosha (fictional), 66

Karamzin, Nikolay Mikhailovich, 47

Karpinsky, Vyacheslav Alexeyevich: 278, 279, 287;
    describes Lenin, 477, 478

Karpov, 196, 197

Karsavina, Tamara, 373

Kartashev, 408

Kashkadamova, Vera, 69

Katz, S., 130n

Kautsky, Karl: 164, 188, 236, 339, 440, 505;
    supports war, 248;
    attacked by Lenin, 249, 250, 274;
    Dictatorship of the Proletariat, The, 501-4;

quoted, 503
Kazan, 495, 624
Kazan University, 75-83
Kazaryan, 591
Kerensky, Alexander Fyodorovich, 273, 274, 289, 303, 331, 333, 336, 354, 355, 359, 366, 369, 370, 374-80, 388, 398, 401-6, 429
Kerensky, Fyodor:
  describes Lenin as student, 73, 74
Key, Ellen, 234
Khalturin, Stepan Nikolayevich: 626;
  portrait of, 474;
  plots assassination of Tsar, 475, 476
Khardin, Andrey, 85
Kharitonov, M., (Charitonoff), 292, 295n
Kharkov, 460, 513
Kholodova, Pelagaya Ananyevna, 585
Khrustalyov-Nosar, Georgy, 192
Kiel, 504, 505
Kiev, 513, 524
Kirov, Sergey Mironovich, 601
Kniazev, Vladimir Alexandrovich: 98;
  describes Lenin, 99, 100
Kokoshkin, Fyodor Fyodorovich: 429;
  shot to death, 443
Kokushkino, 56, 57, 59
Kolchak, Admiral Alexander Vasilyevich, 508, 515, 525, 557
Kollontay, Alexandra Mikhailovna: 274-6, 307, 312, 363, 531;
  defends Lenin, 328
Koltzov, Mikhail, 599
Kon, Helene, 292
Konovalov, Alexander Ivanovich, 377, 408
Konstantinowitsch, A., 292
Kornilov, General Lavr Georgievich, 354, 355, 426
Kostroma, 20
Kramarov, 439
Kramer, A., 130n
Kramer, Dr., 588, 604
Krasnov, General Petr Nikolayevich, 401, 403, 406
Krasnoyarsk, 112-117

Krassin, Leonid Borisovich: 419, 465, 558;
  quoted, 466
Kremlin, 459, 471-84
Kronstadt, 404, 534, 535, 537, 540
Kronstadt sailors, 334-6, 390, 492, 532, 533, 540
Kropotkin, Prince Peter, 155
Krupskaya, Elizaveta Vasilyevna, 125-8, 135, 177, 178
Krupskaya, Nadezhda Konstantinovna: 94, 104, 108, 165-7, 224, 248, 250, 274, 320, 340, 380n, 490, 491, 583, 595, 596, 600-7, 616;
  meets Lenin, 98;
  described, 96, 97, 202;
  announces plan to marry Lenin, 124;
  exiled to Siberia, 124-9;
  describes What Is To Be Done?, 148;
  quoted, 170, 174, 176, 180, 181, 194, 219, 220, 231, 244, 306, 467, 481, 586, 619;
  attitude toward husband's female friends, 179, 235;
  ill health, 245, 246, 506, 550;
  wages war against Stalin, 573;
  speaks after Lenin's death (quoted), 617
Krutovsky, V., 113
Krylenko, Nikolay Vasilyevich, 400, 401, 403, 555
Krzhizhanovsky, Gleb Maximilianovich, 114, 117, 121, 122, 135, 519, 531, 567, 580
Kuibyshev, Valerian, 576, 620
Kurbsky, Prince Andrey, 97
Kursky, D. I., 539, 550, 551, 620
Kuskova, Ekaterina, 132-4, 144
Kuznetsk Basin, 450
Kuznetsov, Alexey Kirilovich, 22, 23, 585

La Chaux-de-Fonds, 277, 295n
Lafargue, Paul, 107, 209, 229, 230, 601

Lansbury, George, 212

Lao Tzu, 350

Latsis, Martyn Ivanovich, 442

Latukk, 358

Latvian Social Democrats, 213, 215

League for the Emancipation of Labor, 152

Left Socialist Revolutionaries: 394, 427, 429, 433, 435, 438, 447, 453;

   resign from government, 444;

   accused of murder by Bolsheviks, 461-5

Lenin (Ulyanov, Vladimir Ilyich):

   legend of, 13-15;

   reads *Revolutionary Catechism*, 29;

   student of Nechayev, 33, 34;

   family tree of, 37-46;

   birth of, 48;

   childhood of, 48-59;

   taste in literature, 59, 60;

   sees his father die, 62;

   takes father's place, 63;

   brother Alexander hanged, 72;

   enters law school, 75;

   influenced by Chernyshevsky's *What Is To Be Done?*, 77;

   arrested in student revolt, 78;

   requests readmission to university, 81;

   reads Marx's *Das Kapital*, 82;

   receives permission to take law examination, 87;

   passes final law examination, 88;

   as lawyer, 89, 90;

   reads Chekhov, 90, 91;

   nihilism of, 92;

   arrives in St. Petersburg, 93;

   known as Nikolay Petrovich, 93;

   attacks Narodnaya Volya, 95;

   debates with Vorontsov, 96;

   meets Nadezhda Krupskaya, 98;

   described by dockworker, 99, 100;

   writes pamphlet against bourgeois, 101;

   contracts pneumonia, 104;

   plans revolutionary newspaper, *Rabocheye Dyelo*, 108;

   in prison, 109;

   assumes the name of Lenin; 110;

   exiled to Siberia, 111, 112;

   delivers attack on the law, 118;

   writes *The Tasks of the Russian Social Democrats*, 119-21;

   marriage plans announced, 124;

   attacks *Credo of the Young*, 132, 133;

   attacks Plekhanov, 143-7;

   writes *What Is To Be Done?* 147;

   expounds revolutionary philosophy, 148, 149;

   Nechayev's influence on, 150;

   German influence on, 151;

   quotes Pisarev, 153;

   arrives in London, 155;

   fights Plekhanov once more, 161;

   meets Trotsky, 162;

   compared with Trotsky, 163;

   prefers Germans to English, 165;

   lust for power, 170, 171;

   attacks Martov, 174-9;

   attitude toward forthcoming revolution, 188, 189;

   returns to Russia, 192;

   shadowed by secret police, 193;

   described, 194;

   explains tactics to Lunacharsky, 195;

   stand against Mensheviks, 195;

   attacks Cadets, 197;

   tried by party court, 198;

   known as William Frey, 203;

   meets Elizabeth de K., 203;

   writes to Elizabeth de K., 207-10;

   on liberty, 211;

   duels Martov again, 214;

   speaks at London conference, 217;

   visits Gorky, 221;

   Materialism and Empirio-Criticism published, 227;

   attacks Bogdanov, 228-30;

   attached to Inessa Armand, 235;

   dominates Prague conference, 243;

   rages against Mensheviks, 247;

   jailed in Austria, 248;

   attacks Kautsky, 249, 250;

   mother dies, 252;

   addresses Swiss workers, 252;

exiled in Switzerland, 271;

hears of revolution in Russia, 274;

fears Tsarist counterrevolution, 275;

plans return to Russia, 277;

writes to Vyacheslav Karpinsky, 278;

writes *Letters from Afar*, 280, 281;

attacks Gorky, 282, 283;

addresses Swiss workmen on revolution, 288, 289;

farewell letters on revolution to Swiss workers, 294;

boards sealed train through Germany, 296;

takes ferryboat to Sweden, 300;

crosses to Finland, 306;

returns to Russia in triumph, 308;

hails the revolution, 311, 312;

writes "April Theses," 321;

writes article for *Pravda*, 333;

defeated, 336, 337;

in danger, 338, 339;

crosses into Finland, 347;

writes *The State and Revolution*, 348;

writes of overthrowing bourgeoisie, 350;

describes withering away of state, 351;

describes successful uprising, 363;

attacks Zinoviev and Kamenev, 366;

writes proclamation on eve of October revolution, 366;

attacked by Kamenev and Zinoviev, 370, 371;

writes letter urging insurrection, 379, 380;

announces overthrow of Provisional Government, 386;

reads Decree on the Land, 396-9;

President of Soviet of People's Commissars, 399, 400;

takes control of military operations, 405;

orders library reforms, 412, 413;

addresses people of Russia, 421;

describes revolutions, 422;

orders arrest of Cadet leaders, 428, 429;

grapples with Constituent Assembly problem, 434;

signs decree voiding Constituent Assembly, 440;

writes "Twenty-one Theses," 445-7;

debates with Trotsky, 447;

answers besieging workers, 452;

writes "The Principal Task of Our Time," 456-9;

arranges assassination of Tsar and family, 466-8;

writes to Clara Zetkin, 469;

absorbed with power, 471, 472;

writes on terror tactics, 481, 482;

shot, 489;

visited by Gorky, 495;

distrusts intelligentsia, 496; 497;

writes *The Proletarian Revolution and Renegade Kautsky*, 501;

escapes from bandits, 506, 507;

launches Third International, 509-13;

attitude toward killing, 517;

writes to Krzhizhanovsky on science, 519, 520;

writes "Infantile Malady of Communism, The," 522-4;

defends Red Army, 526, 527;

describes New Economic Policy, 536;

warns against capitalists, 538;

suffers from ill health, 540, 541;

speaks at Eleventh Congress, 546, 547;

in hospital, 549;

writes savage letter to Kursky, 550, 557;

suffers first stroke, 551;

pays tribute to peasants, 556;

last public speech, 558;

seriously ill, 560;

suggests changes in political organization, 563, 564;

warns of split in Central Committee, 564, 565;

denounces Stalin, 568, 569, 571, 574, 575;

writes to Stalin and Trotsky, 576, 577;

last letter, 578;
suffers third stroke, 579;
enjoys Jack London story, 587;
last hours of, 588, 589;
death of, 595;
rumors about his death, 598-601;
his last days described, 602-7;
announcement of his death, 608, 609;
public mourns, 613-6;
cult of, 618-20;
tomb of, 621-4;
place in history, 630-3
Leningrad, 619
"Lenin's Testament," 564, 565
Lepechinsky, Panteleimon Nikolaye-vich, 114, 169
Lermolo, Elizabeth:
  Face of a Victim, 600-2
"Letters to a Comrade on Our Or-ganizational Tasks," 162
Letters from Afar, 281, 282, 284, 285, 288
Levin, Dr. Lev Grigorievich, 551
Levine, Isaac Don, 250
Liberman, Simon: 517, 519;
  quoted, 518
Lieber, M. I., 216
Liebknecht, Karl, 311, 505, 511
Linde, A., 292, 295n
Lindhagen, Karl, 301, 304, 305
Lisy Nos, 534
Lithuania, 445
Litvinov, Maxim Maximovich (Meyer Wallach), 213, 510, 539
Lobachevsky, Nikolay Ivanovich, 40, 41
Lockhart, Robert Hamilton Bruce:
  451-3, 494;
  describes Lenin, 450
Loguivy, 161
Lominadze, V., 591
Lomov, see Oppokov, Georgy
London, 155-167
London, Jack:
  Love of Life, 586, 587
London conference, 212-8; 220
Lukashevich, 70
Lunacharsky, Anatoly Vasilyevich:

180, 181, 185, 194, 195, 239, 240, 390, 399, 400, 491;
  quoted 192, 632
Luxemburg, Rosa, 214, 217, 505, 511
Lvov, Prince George Evgenyevich, 331, 335
Lyadov, M. N., 213
Lvov, 526

Mach, 230
Magna Charta, 321
Makharadze, Phillip Iyesevich, 578, 579
Malinovsky, Andrey, 240
Malinovsky, Roman Vatslavovich, 241-4, 246, 247
Malkov, Pavel, 494
Malmo, 302, 3
Mann, Thomas, 493
Marat, Jean Paul, 273
Marie, Grand Duchess, 466, 467
Marienhoff, E., 292, 295n
Marienhoff, M., 292, 295n
Martov, see Tsederbaum, Yury Osipo-vich
Martynov, 216
Marx, Karl: 13, 69, 95, 121, 134, 135, 147, 150, 188n, 200, 228, 271, 282, 289, 339, 356, 363, 370, 427, 441, 474, 482, 501-4, 512, 609, 617, 626-31;
  studied by Lenin, 82, 83, 85;
  understanding of, 107;
  interpreted by Lenin, 101, 127;
  redefining of, 131;
  attacks capital, 146;
  Civil War in France, 187;
  negation of, 327;
  quoted, 353;
  18th Brumaire of Louis Napoleon, The, quoted, 633
Marxists, 94, 95, 96, 98, 105, 132
Materialism and Empirio-Criticism, 225-30
Maximov, 310
Mayakovsky, Vladimir Vladimirovich: 540;
  poem Vladimir Ilyich Lenin, quoted, 615, 616

Mdivani, Budu, 578, 579
Medem, Vladimir, 214, 215
Mekhonoshin, 404
Mensheviks: 176-80, 195-200, 213-7,
    247, 248, 327, 328, 331, 374,
    393, 482, 500, 537, 559;
  split with Bolsheviks, 169;
  attacked by Lenin, 546, 547;
  death sentences for, 550
Menzhinsky, Vyacheslav Rudolfovich,
    412, 514, 606
Merkulov, 597
Mesopotamia, 280
Mehring, Franz, 236
Meyerhold, Vsevolod, 230, 373
Michelet, Jules, 29
Michelson factory, 487, 488, 490
Mikhailov, Alexander Dmitrievich, 66,
    104, 402
Mikhailovsky School, 390, 400, 429,
    437
Military Revolutionary Committee:
    372-5, 377-81, 383, 385, 390,
    392;
  gains power, 386, 388;
  dissolved, 427
Milyukov, Pavel Nikolayevich, 274,
    280, 283, 330, 331
Milyutin, Vladimir Pavlovich, 376,
    400
Minsk, 364, 365, 366, 369, 526
Minsk Congress, 129, 130, 133, 169
Minusinsk, 114, 135
Mirbach, Count Robert, 461, 462
Mirbach-Harff, Count Wilhelm von:
  assassinated, 461-6, 468
Mitchell, Isaac, 156
Molotov, Vyacheslav Mikhailovich
    (Scriabin), 380n, 541, 581, 620,
    621, 625
Mona Lisa, 210
Mongolia, 465
Morozov, Savva, 220, 498
Moscow, 355, 366-70, 407, 427, 452-
    61, 471-84, 513, 530, 613, 614
Moscow uprising, 192, 193, 292, 332
Munich, 147
Mutnik, M., 130n

Nansen, Fridtjof, 537
Napoleon, Emperor, 13, 453, 526
Narodnaya Volya, 32, 33, 94, 95, 133,
    149, 427, 476
Nebuchadnezzar, 633
Nechayev, Sergey Genadievich: 19,
    59, 60, 71, 90, 99, 110, 140, 174,
    189, 199, 200, 277, 281, 324,
    327, 353, 370, 425, 497, 629;
  aliases of, 21;
  murder of Ivanov, 22, 23;
  writes *Revolutionary Catechism*, 24-
    29;
  flees Russia, 30;
  arrest and trial of, 31;
  death of, 33;
  Revolutionary Catechism, 92, 149,
    157, 407, 493;
  quoted, 476;
  influence of, 120, 121, 147, 150,
    349, 408, 409, 469, 483
Nerman, Ture, 304
New Economic Policy, 536, 537, 540,
    547, 571, 631
Nicholas II: 197, 288;
  assassinated with family, 466-8
Nikolayev, Leonid, 601
Nikolayev, Nikolay, 22, 23
Nikolayevich, Grand Duke Nikolay,
    451
Nizhni Novgorod, 482, 492
Nogin, Victor Pavlovich, 213, 376, 400
Novaya Zhizn, 193, 194, 197, 203,
    204, 208
Novgorod *guberniya*, 480, 481
Nowy Targ, 248

Oblomov (fictional), 47
Obolensky, Prince, 140, 141
Obukh, Dr., 598, 604
October revolution, 433, 439
Odessa, 190, 191, 460, 513
Okhotnikov, 56
Okhrana, 240, 632
Olga, Grand Duchess, 466, 467
Olminsky, Mikhail Stepanovich, 180,
    181
One Step Forward, Two Steps Back,
    174-6

Oppokov, Georgy Ippolotovich (Lomov), 363, 376, 400

Oranienbaum, 534

Ordjonikidze, Grigory Konstantinovich, 242, 341, 343, 344, 568, 569, 578, 620

Osipanov, 68, 72

Osipov, Dr., 588, 595, 598

Paestum, 479

Pakaln, Pyotr Petrovich, 595, 600, 603-6

Panina, Countess, 196, 197

Pannekoek, 339

Paris, 106, 107, 161, 180, 206, 207, 222-37, 377, 417, 624

Paris Commune, 223, 277, 289, 290, 326, 332, 482

Pavlovsk, 374

Pavlosky Regiment, 273

Perlzweig, 486

Perovskaya, Sophie, 66

Pestkovsky, Stanislav, 412

Peter the Great, 31, 32, 39, 164, 362, 459, 484, 621

Peters, Yakov Christophorovich, 442

Petrograd: 272n, 273, 280-2, 286, 287, 309, 310, 317, 318, 322, 330-7, 340, 341, 354-66, 369, 370, 374-94, 398, 400-7, 410, 411, 421, 426-31, 448, 450, 452, 455, 460, 481, 492, 513-5, 530-4, 617;

renamed Leningrad, 619

Petrotsky, 475

Petrovich, Nikolay (fictional) 35, 60

Petrovich, Pavel (fictional), 60

Petrovsky, 620

Petrusevich, K., 129n, 130

Pettigrew's Plutocratic Democracy, 556

Philistines, 165

Piatnitsky, see Pyatnitsky

Pieck, Wilhelm, 608

Pilsudski, Bronislav, 67, 70, 72

Pilsudski, Joseph, 67, 70, 72, 524, 527

Pisarev, Dmitry Ivanovich: 419;

On the Shedo-Ferrotti Pamphlet, 146;

influence on Lenin, 147;

quoted by Lenin, 153

Plato, 230

Platten, Fritz, 251, 272, 273, 285, 286, 290, 292, 295n, 279, 299, 304, 430

Plehve, Vyacheslav Konstantinovich von, 182, 407

Plekhanov, Georgy Valentinovich: 108, 116, 133, 154, 160, 164, 170, 178-80, 213-5, 243, 295, 330, 339;

described, 105, 106, 142, 143;

editor of illegal newspaper, 139-41;

attacked by Lenin, 143-7;

fights with Lenin, 161, 165, 166;

and Mensheviks, 177;

studied, 186;

supports war, 248, 249;

quoted, 174, 242, 441

Podolsk, 141

Podvoisky, Nikolay Ilyich: 336, 377, 390, 391, 403, 404, 426, 430;

quoted, 403, 404

Pokrovsky, Mikhail Nikolayevich, 93, 213

Poland: 245, 445, 527;

invades Russia, 524;

invaded by Russia, 525, 526

Polish Social Democrats, 213, 215

Politburo, 365, 574, 576

Polovtsev, General, 336

Poltava, 513

Popova, Claudia G., 113

Poronino, 211, 246, 247

Port, Monsieur, 55, 56, 215

Potresov, A. N., 144, 176

Prague conference, 242-4

Pravda, 280, 281

Preobrazhensky, Alexey, 594

Preobrazhensky, Evgeniy Alexeyevich, 591

Prince Potemkin, 190, 191

"Principal Task of Our Time, The":

quoted, 456-9

Prizhov, Ivan Gavrilovich, 22, 23

Proletarian Revolution and Renegade Kautsky, The: 501, 503;

quoted, 504

Proletary, 220, 225
Prominsky, 122, 123, 126, 128
Protopopov, Alexander Dmitrievich, 47
Proust, Marcel, 169
Provisional Government: 273-6, 280-2, 287-90, 296, 307, 326, 330, 336, 354, 376, 386, 425, 439;
 awaits Lenin's return, 304;
 Lenin attacks, 308;
 falls, 386-9
Prussia, 417
Pskov, 139, 140
Pugachev, Emelyan Ivanovich, 39, 58
Pugachev rebellion, 336
Pushkin, Alexander Sergeyevich: 59, 60;
 quoted, 336
Putilov workers, 334, 405
Pyatakov, Grigory Leonidovich, 565, 567, 620
Pyatnitsky, Yosif Aaronovich [cf. Piatnitsky, Ossip Aaronovich]: 585;
 describes Lenin, 583, 584
Pyrrho, 229

Quelch, Harry, 156

Rabocheye Dyelo, 108
Rabochy Put, 374-7
Radchenko, S., 129n
Radek, Karl (Karl Berngardovich Sobelsohn), 251, 255, 292, 293, 295n, 297-9, 302, 304, 305, 414, 448, 464, 516, 591, 630
Radomyslskaya, Zena, 292
Rahja, Eino Abramovich, 346, 347, 357, 381-3
Raichin, 117, 122, 128
Rakhmetev (fictional), 76, 77, 235
Ransome, Arthur: 508, 509, 512;
 quoted, 510
Rappoport, Charles, 240
Rasputin, Grigory Efimovich, 288
Ravich, Olga (Ravitsch), 272, 292, 295n, 298
Raymond, 158, 159
Razin, Stenka, 39, 621
Razliv, 341-4

Red Army, 461, 513-5, 525-7
Red Cross Relief, 537
Red Guards, 382-5, 392, 429
Red Terror, 443
Reed, John:
 describes Lenin, 398;
 quoted, 400, 401;
 describes Trotsky, 405
Reinstein, Boris, 510
Reni, Guido, 528
Rennenkampf, General, 100
Reval, 446
Riga, 354, 446
Right Socialist Revolutionaries, 435
Rilke, Rainer Maria, 234
Robespierre, Maximilien, 174, 201
Robins, Colonel Raymond:
 reports conversation with Lenin, 415-8;
 describes Lenin, 452, 453
Rodin's *Le Penseur*, 626
Romans, 481
Rome, 502
Romodovana workers, 610, 611
Rosenblum, D., 292, 295n
Rovio, Gustav, 348, 355
Rozanov, Dr. Vladimir Nikolayevich, 549-51, 580, 582, 588, 589, 598, 600, 604-6
Rozhkov, 559
Rudzutak, Ianis Ernestovich, 621
Rumania, 191
Rumyantsev, Mikhail, 203, 204, 206
Russian Orthodox Church, 538, 628
Russo-Japanese War, 182, 184
Rutgers, 510
Ryazanov, D. B. (real name Goldendach), 296
Rykov, Alexey Ivanovich, 213, 231, 400, 558, 590, 596, 620

Sadoul, Jacques, 510
Safarov, George, 251, 292, 295n, 298, 399
Safarov-Mostitchkine, Valentina, 292, 295
Saint Peter, 619
St. Petersburg: 66-9, 88, 93-104, 108, 139-42, 182-94, 198, 206;

renamed Petrograd, 272n

Samara, 90

Saratov, 461

Sassnitz, 299, 300

Savinkov, Boris Victorovich, 461

Sazonov, Yegor Sergeyevich, 182, 271

Scheinessohn, S., 292

Schmidt, Nikolay, 220

Schmidt legacy, 224, 225, 236, 243

Schwabing, 147

Schwartzman, 242

Second All-Union Congress of Soviets, 617, 618, 621

Second Congress of the Communist International, 526

Second Congress of Soviets, 365, 391, 393

Second International, 557

Seldes, George, 555

Semashko, Dr. Nikolay Yosifovich, 551, 597, 598, 604, 607

Semyonovsky Regiment, 193, 385

Sennacherib, 633

Sereda, 494

Serge, Victor (real name: Victor Lvovich Kibalchik), 465

Sestroretsk, 341, 534

Shakespeare, William, 180, 229

Shaumyan, Stepan Grigorievich, 213

Sheinman, 401, 402

Shevyrev, Pyotr Yakovlevich, 66-68, 70, 72

Shigalov (fictional), 14

Shingarev, Andrey Ivanovich: 429, 444;
    shot to death, 443

Shlyapnikov, Alexander Gavrilovich, 249, 307, 309, 311, 400, 523, 531

Shotman, Alexander Vasilyevich, 348, 358-60

Shub, David, 295n

Shulyatikov, 231

Shushenskoye, 111-35

Shvetsov, Sergey, 433

Siberia, 111-23, 486, 487, 495, 515

Sibiryakov, 83, 84

Simbirsk, 47, 48, 495

Sklarz, Georg, 285-7

Skobolev, N., 310

Skovno, Abraham, 292

Skvortsov, Ivan, 400, 583-5

Slussarev, D., 292

Slyansky, Efraim Markovich, 404, 461

Smilga, Ivan Tenisovich, 360

Smirnov, Alexey, 37, 38

Smirnova, Evdokia Ivanovna, 593, 606

Smolny Convent, 373-7, 380-5, 389-93

Social Democrat, 225, 230, 232

Social Democratic Party: 119, 120, 133, 162, 187-91, 194, 199, 238, 331;
    First Congress of, 169;
    Second Congress of, 169-77;
    Fifth Conference of, 224, 225;
    Lenin attacks, 324-7

Socialist Revolutionaries: 161, 162, 194, 198, 393, 397, 401, 432, 433, 437, 492-4, 535-7;
    attacked by Lenin, 546, 547;
    death sentences for, 550

Sokolnikov, Grigory Yakovlevich (Brillant), 292, 295n, 363, 365, 480, 620

Solomon, Georgy Alexandrovich: 465;
    describes conversation with Lenin, 418-20

Solovyev, Vladimir Sergeyevich:
    quoted, 626, 628

Sorin, Vladimir Gordeevich, 594, 595, 606

Sosipatych, 123

Souliachvili, David Sokratovich, 292

Soviet Brain Institute, 622

Soviet of People's Commissars, 399, 459

Soviet of Workers' and Peasants' Deputies, 325, 326

Soviets of Workers' and Soldiers' Deputies, 288, 504

Soviets of Workers' Deputies, 275, 283, 284, 289

Spandaryan, Suren, 242

Spartacists, 505

Spiridonova, Maria Alexandrovna, 435, 436, 462

Stalin, Yosif Vissarionovich (Dzhugashvili): 14, 15, 307, 340, 363,

376, 380n, 400, 469, 493, 514, 525, 526, 551-4, 564, 566, 572, 573, 576-80, 596, 598, 614, 617, 620, 621, 631, 632;
described, 213;
appointed general secretary of Central Committee, 548;
denounced by Lenin, 568, 569, 571, 574, 575;
dominates Thirteenth Party Conference, 589-92;
and Lenin's death, 600-7, 609-11;
pays tribute to Lenin (quoted), 618;
death of, 625
Starkov, V. V., 114, 121
Stassova, Elena Dmitrievna, 340
State and Revolution, The, 277 348-54, 361, 389, 536, 625
State Planning Commission, 567
Steinberg, Isaac Zakharovich, 420, 443, 444
Steinwachs, 329
Stevenson, Robert Louis, 29
Stockholm, 304
Stolypin, Pyotr Arkadevich, 407
Strelnikov, General, 474, 475
Ström, 301
Struve, Peter Berngardovich, 129n, 130, 131, 169
Sukhanov, Nikolay Nikolayevich (Himmer): 318-20, 331, 332, 394, 432, 485;
quoted, 310-2, 328, 335, 363, 385, 399
Sverdlov, Yakov Mikhailovich: 339, 363, 364, 376, 433, 434, 437, 459, 464, 466, 486, 491, 494, 504, 531, 580;
launches terror, 492, 493
Svyatopolk-Mirsky, Prince, 182
Swan, Reverend F. R., 212
Sweden, 205, 297, 299-305, 519
Switzerland, 105, 107, 142, 166, 167, 248, 271-87, 296-301
Syria, 280

Takhtareva, Apollinaria, 159

Takhterev, K. M., 202
Tambov province, 537, 556
Tamerlane, 13, 39, 633
Taratuta, V. K., 220, 231
Tartars, 38, 39
Tasks of the Russian Social Democrats, The, 119-21
Tatiana, Grand Duchess, 466, 467
Tchaikovsky, Nikolay, 155
Teheran, 465
Tenth Party Congress, 535, 537
Teodorovich, Ivan Adolfovich, 400
"The Agrarian Question and the 'Critics of Marx,'" 147
Third International:
founded, 509-13;
Lenin, speaks at, 556, 557
Thirteenth Party Conference:
dominated by Stalin, 589-92
Thucydides, 421
Tilsit, Treaty of, 453
Tkachev, Pyotr, 151
Tolstoy, Count Alexey:
Death of Ivan the Terrible, 373
Tolstoy, Count Leo: 40, 60, 90, 218;
death of, 208, 209;
quoted, 472
Tomsky, Mikhail P., 215, 231, 596, 620, 621
Tornio, 304, 305
Trelleborg, 301, 302
Trepov, General, D. F., 30, 140
Trotsky, Lev Davidovich (Bronstein):
14, 164, 165, 171, 174, 201, 213, 243, 335, 365, 370-6, 383-5, 389, 390, 391, 399-401, 403-6, 412, 421, 448-50, 459, 510, 512, 515-7, 532-4, 548, 558, 563-5, 576-80, 589-92, 601, 603, 606, 607, 611;
meets Lenin, 162;
described, 163, 172;
quoted, 176, 245, 336, 409, 432, 436, 441, 460, 463, 464, 467, 468, 495, 497, 514;
rise of, 191-4;
attacks Lenin, 216;
History of the Russian Revolution, 312;

debates with Lenin, 447;
organizes Red Army, 513;
diary of, quoted, 600, 601;
pays tribute to Lenin, 612, 613
Trupp, Alexis, 468
Tsarskoye Selo, 140, 141, 374
Tsaritsyn, 513
Tsederbaum, Yury Osipovich (Yulius
    Martov): 114, 129, 139-42, 144,
    147, 159, 160, 163, 171, 193,
    213, 225, 232, 243, 251, 279,
    453, 580;
    attacked by Lenin, 174-9;
    duels with Lenin, 214, 216
Tseretelli, Irakly Georgevich, 216,
    312, 328, 331, 333, 334, 436, 439
Tskhakaya, Mikha Grigorievich, 213,
    271, 274, 292, 293, 295n, 302,
    305, 306
Tsyurupa, Alexander Dmitrievich,
    477, 539, 545, 558
Tuchapsky, P., 130n
Tukhachevsky, Mikhail Nikolayevich,
    525, 526, 535, 537
Tula, 513
Turgenev, Ivan Sergeyevich: 58;
    Fathers and Sons (quoted), 35, 60;
    59, 229;
    Nest of Gentlefolk, A, 59
Turin, 362
Turkey, 449, 465
"Twenty-one Theses":
    quoted, 445-7, 449
Tyszka-Yogiches, Jan, 214-16

Ufa, 142
Ukraine, 445, 486, 487, 524
Ulyanov v. Arefyev, 89
Ulyanov, Alexander Ilyich (brother):
    61-4, 75-9, 98;
    described, 49, 50;
    influence on Lenin, 52;
    plans assassination of Tsar, 65-7;
    arrest of, 68;
    defends terrorism, 71;
    hanged, 72
Ulyanov, Dmitry Ilyich (brother), 51,
    54, 64, 85, 115, 116, 142, 551

Ulyanov, Ilya Nikolayevich (father):
    49, 53, 56, 58, 60, 61;
    birth of, 38;
    marries Maria Blank, 41, 42;
    children of, 42;
    death of, 62
Ulyanov, Nikolay Vasilyevich, 38, 39
Ulyanov, Vasily, 38-40, 44, 46
Ulyanov, Vladimir Ilyich, see Lenin
Ulyanova, Alexandra, 37, 39
Ulyanova, Maria Alexandrovna
    (mother): 48, 49, 64, 65, 70, 72,
    79, 87-9, 94, 108, 142;
    described, 41, 42;
    family of, 43-45;
    tries to save Alexander's life, 69;
    Germanic leaning of, 86;
    death of, 252
Ulyanova, Maria Ilyinichna (sister),
    142, 150, 231, 340, 430, 486, 549,
    582-5, 493-6, 600, 604-7
Ulyanova, Olga (sister), 51, 64, 87,
    88
Ulyanova-Elizarova, Anna Ilyinichna
    (sister): 50-6, 60-5, 68, 70, 72,
    79-83, 124, 142, 552;
    writes poem about family (quoted),
    85, 86
Ulyanovsk, 623
United States, 415, 487, 508, 519,
    520, 557
Urals, the, 450, 514
Uritsky, Moses Solomonovich: 363,
    365, 420, 427, 428, 431, 448;
    shot to death, 485, 486, 494
Urquhart, Leslie, 558, 559
Uspensky, Gleb, 84
Uspensky, Pyotr, 22, 23
Ussievich, Grigory A., 292, 295n, 306

Vaneyev, Anatoly Alexeyevich, 108,
    109, 114, 133
Vannovsky, A., 129n
Vasilyev, Mikhail Ivanovich:
    quoted 190, 191
Venets, the, 47
Veretennikov, Nikolay, 41, 44, 79
Verkhovsky, General Alexander, 379n
Victory of the Cadets, The 195, 196

Vienna, 449
Vigdorchik, I., 130n
Vilenkin, Nikolay Mikhailovich (Minsky): 193;
    quoted, 194
Vladimir, Grand Duke, 185
Vladimirov, 580
Vladivostok, 460, 555
Volga, the, 450, 452, 460, 461, 486, 487, 537
Volhynian Regiment, 403, 404
Volin, Boris, 599
Volkov, Gavril: 606;
    describes Lenin's last day to Lermolo, 602, 603
Volodarsky, V. (M. M. Goldstein), 481
Volodicheva, Maria Akimovna, 563-7, 576-8
Vorontsov, Vasily, 94-6, 101
Voroshilov, Klementy Yefremovich, 213
Vorovsky, Vatslav Vatslavovich, 181
Vperyod, 181, 182, 185
Vrachev, 591
Vyborg, 357, 358, 360, 376

Warsaw, 525, 526
Webb, Sidney and Beatrice, 127, 131
Weissbrod, Dr. Boris Solomonovich, 583, 598
Wells, H. G.:
    describes Lenin, 478-80
Weygand, General Maxime, 525
What Is To Be Done? 147-54, 162, 166, 187, 234
White Armies, 513, 514, 530
White Guards, 455, 460, 463, 466, 468, 482, 486, 495, 535, 536
White Russia, 445
Wilhelmshaven, 369
Williams, Albert Rhys, 430, 437
"Working Class and Revolution, The," 187
World War I:
    breaks out, 247

Yakovlev (a Chuvash), 56
Yakovlieva, Varvara Nikolayevna, 363-5, 432

Yakubova, Apollinaria Alexandrovna, 201, 202
Yalava, Hugo Erikovich, 347
Yalkala, 347, 348
Yaroslavl, 461
Yegorov, A. I., 525, 526
Yelets, 495
Yenukidze, Abel Safronovich, 609, 620
Yeo, Mrs., 156, 159, 202
Yudenich, General N. N., 508, 514, 515, 525
Yukhotsky, 128

Zarya, 144, 147
Zasulich, Vera Ivanovna, 30, 105, 139, 140, 143, 144, 147, 159, 160, 163, 165, 177, 178
Zbarsky, Dr. Ilya, 623, 624
Zelikson-Bobrovskaya, Celia Samoilovna: 77, 178, 179;
    describes Lenin, 177
Zemsky Sobor, 425
Zetkin, Clara: 236, 469, 526, 527, 608;
    quoted, 528
Zheleznikov, Anatoly Grigorievich, 437, 438
Zhelyabov, Andrey Ivanovich, 66, 67, 71, 104, 476
Zhordania, Noah, 216
Zhukovsky, Vasily Andreyevich, 209, 211
Zimmerwald Conference, 250
Zinoviev, Grigory Evseyevich (Evsey Aaronovich Radomyslsky, Hirsch Apfelbaum): 213, 223, 225, 232, 240-8, 274-7, 286, 292-4, 295n, 340-3, 345-7, 363-6, 390, 414, 428, 510, 534, 573, 586, 592, 609, 617, 620, 621, 630;
    attacks Lenin, 370, 371;
    quoted, 508, 582;
    Lenin forgives, 565;
    account of Lenin's death, 596, 597;
    pays tribute to Lenin, 610
Zossima, Father (fictional), 622
Zurich, 106, 251, 252, 272-87
Zyrianov, Apollon, 117, 123, 125

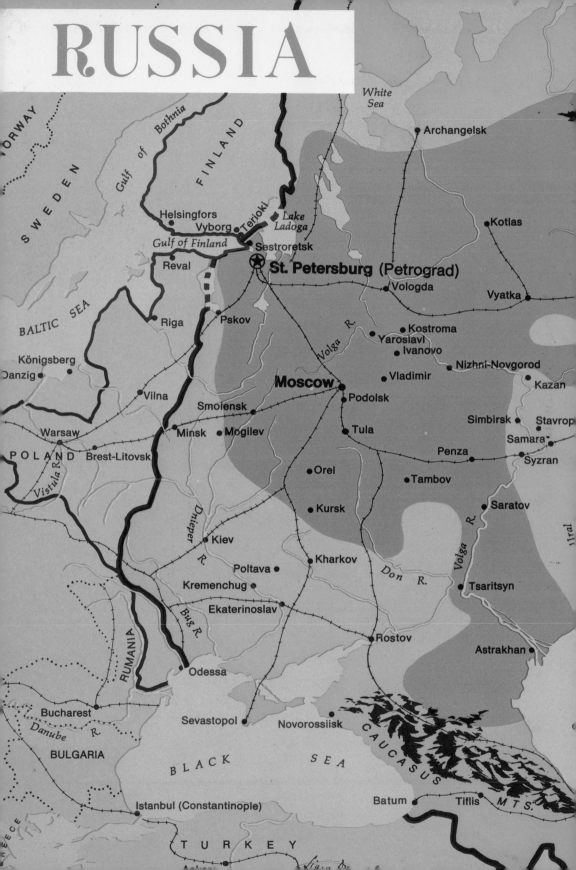

RUSSIA